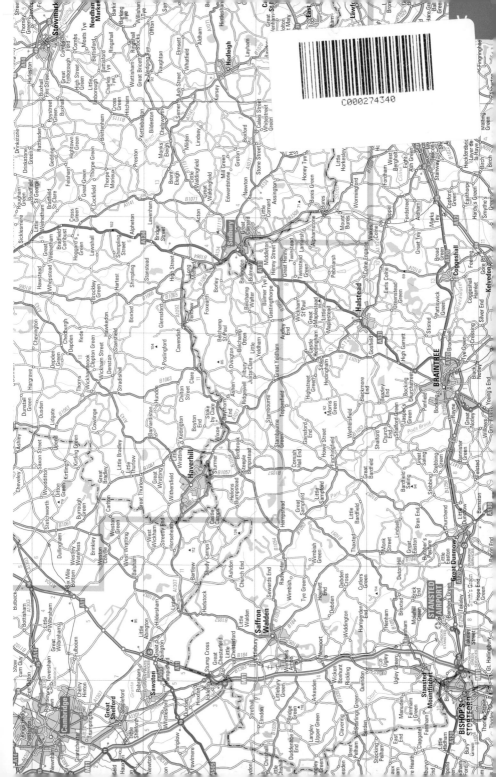

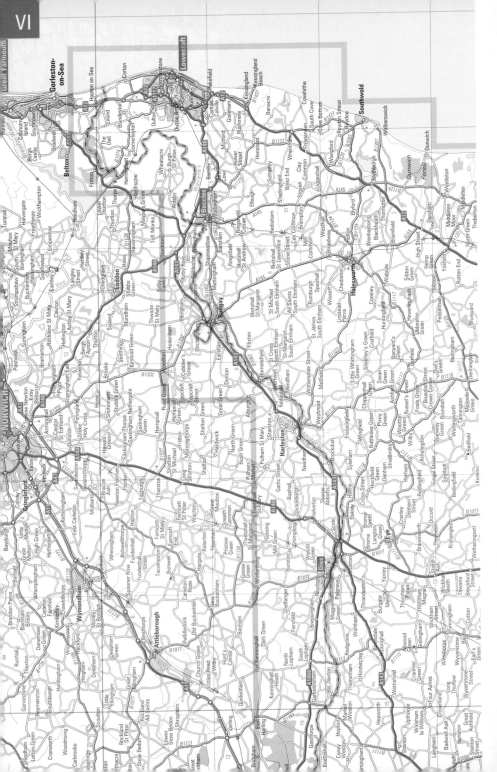

PHILIP'S

STREET ATLAS

Suffolk

Bury St Edmunds, Felixstowe, Ipswich, Lowestoft, Newmarket

First published in 2003 by

Philip's, a division of
Octopus Publishing Group Ltd
2-4 Heron Quays, London E14 4JP

Second edition 2007
First impression 2007
ŚUFBA

ISBN-10   0-540-08997-4 (pocket)
ISBN-13   978-0-540-08997-0 (pocket)

© Philip's 2007

Ordnance Survey

This product includes mapping data licensed from
Ordnance Survey® with the permission of the
Controller of Her Majesty's Stationery Office.
© Crown copyright 2007. All rights reserved.
Licence number 100011710.

Contents

II	**Key to map pages**
IV	**Route planning**
VIII	**Administrative and Postcode boundaries**
1	**Key to map symbols**
2	**Street maps** at 1⅓ inches to 1 mile
109	**Street maps** at 2⅔ inches to 1 mile
154	**Street maps of centres of Bury St Edmunds and Ipswich** at 5⅓ inches to 1 mile
156	**Index** of towns and villages
159	**Index** of streets, hospitals, industrial estates, railway stations, schools, shopping centres, universities and places of interest

Digital Data

The exceptionally high-quality mapping found in this atlas is available as digital data in TIFF format, which is easily convertible to other bitmapped (raster) image formats.

The index is also available in digital form as a standard database table. It contains all the details found in the printed index together with the National Grid reference for the map square in which each entry is named.

For further information and to discuss your requirements, please contact Philip's on 020 7644 6932 or james.mann@philips-maps.co.uk

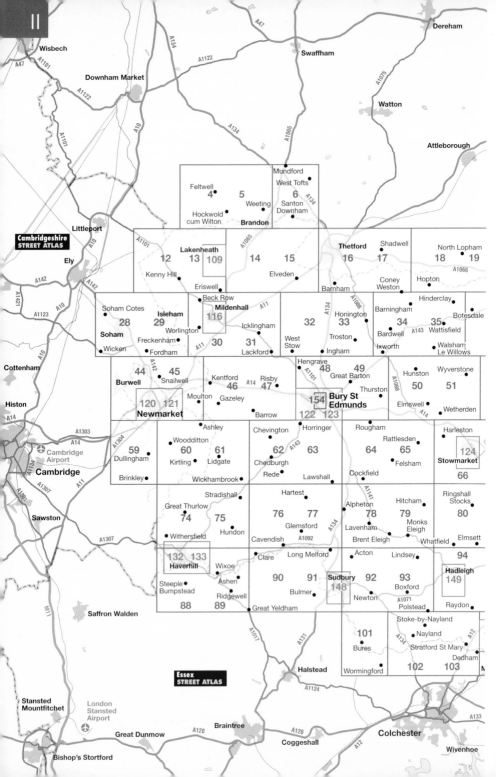

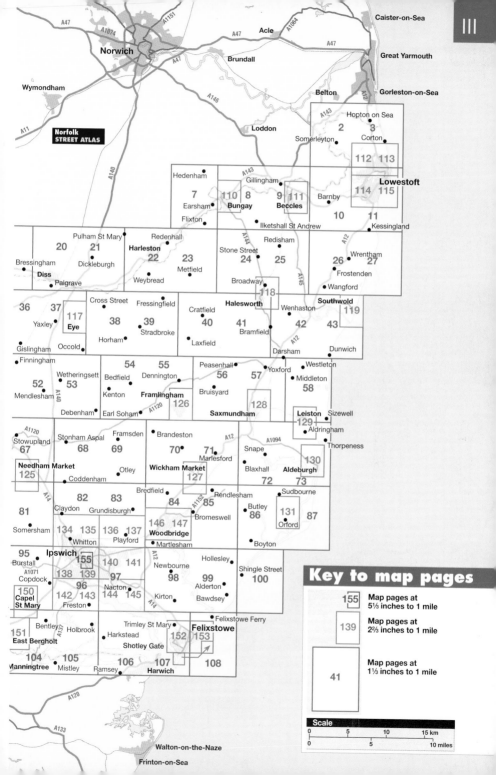

III

Caister-on-Sea

Great Yarmouth

Gorleston-on-Sea

A47 Acle

Norwich

Brundall

Wymondham

Belton

A11

Norfolk
STREET ATLAS

Loddon

Somerleyton

Hopton on Sea

2   **3**
Corton

112 **113**

Lowestoft

Hedenham

Gillingham

7   **110** **8**   **9** **111**
Earsham   **Bungay**   **Beccles**   Barnby

Flixton

Ilketshall St Andrew

114 **115**

10   **11**
Kessingland

Pulham St Mary   Redenhall   Redisham

20   **21**   **Harleston**   Stone Street   **24**   **25**   **26** Wrentham **27**
Bressingham   Dicklebugh   **22**   **23**   Frostenden

Diss   Weybread   Metfield   Broadway   Wangford   Southwold

Palgrave   **118**   **119**

Cross Street   Fressingfield   Cratfield   Wenhaston

36   **37**   **117**   **38**   **39**   **40**   **41**   **42**   **43**
Yaxley   **Eye**   Stradbroke   **Bramfield**

Gislingham   Occold   Horham   Laxfield   Darsham   Dunwich

Finningham   **54**   **55**   Peasenhall   Westleton

Wetheringsett   Bedfield   Dennington   **56**   **57** Yoxford   Middleton

52   **53**   Kenton   **Framlingham**   Bruisyard   **58**

Mendlesham   **126**   **128**   **Leiston** Sizewell

Debenham   Earl Soham   **Saxmundham**   **129**   Aldringham

Stowupland   Framsden   Brandeston   Snape   Thorpeness

67   **68**   **69**   **70**   **71**   **130**
Needham Market   Marlesford   Blaxhall   **Aldeburgh**

125   Otley   **Wickham Market**   **72**   **73**
Coddenham   **127**

Bredfield   Rendlesham   Sudbourne

82   **83**   **84**   **85**   Butley   **86**   **87**
81   Claydon   Grundisburgh   Bromeswell   Orford   **131**

Somersham   **134** **135** **136** **137**   **146** **147**   Boyton
Whitton   Playford   **Woodbridge**   Martlesham

95   **Ipswich**   **155**   **140** **141**   Hollesley

Burstall   **138** **139**   **97**   Newbourne   **98**   **99**   Shingle Street
Copdock   **96**   Nacton   Alderton   **100**
150   **142** **143** **144** **145**   Kirton   Bawdsey
Capel   Freston
St Mary

151   Bentley   Holbrook   Trimley St Mary   **Felixstowe**
East Bergholt   Harkstead   **152** **153**

104   **105**   Shotley Gate   **108**
Manningtree   Mistley   Ramsey   **Harwich**

Key to map pages

155	Map pages at 5⅓ inches to 1 mile
139	Map pages at 2⅔ inches to 1 mile
41	Map pages at 1⅓ inches to 1 mile

Scale
0   5   10   15 km
0   5   10 miles

Walton-on-the-Naze

Frinton-on-Sea

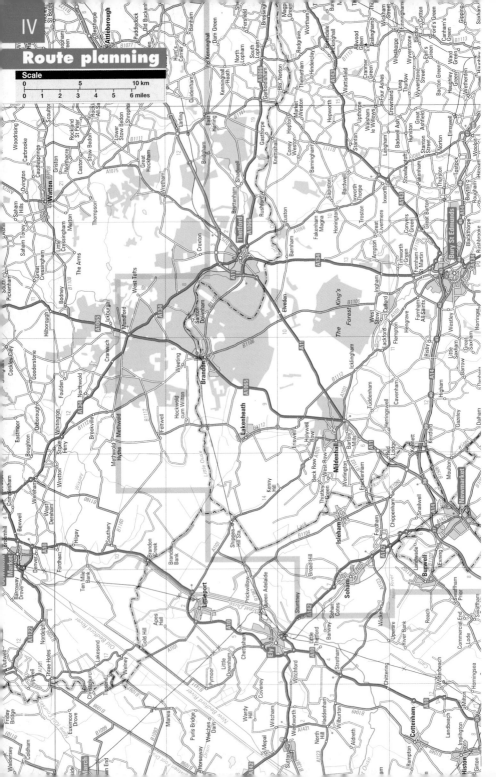

IV

Route planning

Scale

0   5   10 km

0   1   2   3   4   5   6 miles

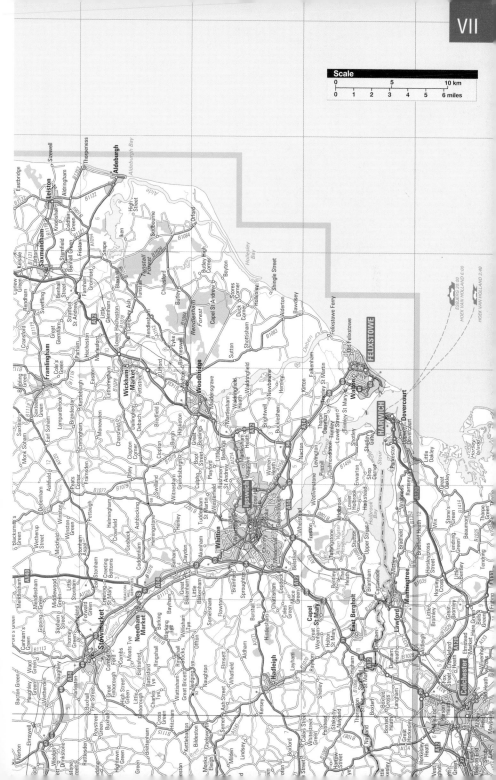

Administrative and Postcode boundaries

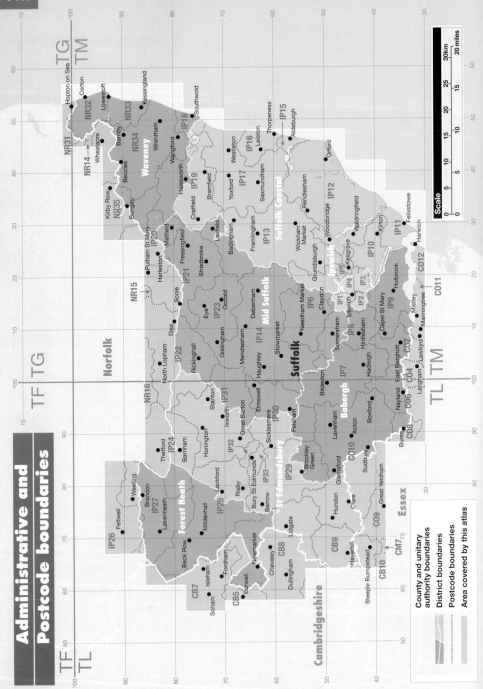

Scale

0 5 10 15 20 25 30km
0   5   10   15   20 miles

County and unitary authority boundaries

District boundaries

Postcode boundaries

Area covered by this atlas

Motorway with junction number (22a)	
Primary route – dual/single carriageway	
A road – dual/single carriageway	
B road – dual/single carriageway	
Minor road – dual/single carriageway	
Other minor road – dual/single carriageway	
Road under construction	
Tunnel, covered road	
Rural track, private road or narrow road in urban area	
Gate or obstruction to traffic (restrictions may not apply at all times or to all vehicles)	
Path, bridleway, byway open to all traffic, road used as a public path	
Pedestrianised area	
DY7 Postcode boundaries	
County and unitary authority boundaries	
Railway, tunnel, railway under construction	
Tramway, tramway under construction	
Miniature railway	
Railway station	
Private railway station	
Metro station (South Shields)	
Tram stop, tram stop under construction	
Bus, coach station	

♦	Ambulance station
♦	Coastguard station
♦	Fire station
♦	Police station
✚	Accident and Emergency entrance to hospital
H	Hospital
+	Place of worship
i	Information Centre (open all year)
	Shopping Centre
P P&R	Parking, Park and Ride
PO	Post Office
Ⓧ ⌂	Camping site, caravan site
✕	Picnic site
▶	Golf course
Prim Sch	Important buildings, schools, colleges, universities and hospitals
	Built up area
	Woods
River Ouse	Tidal water, water name
	Non-tidal water – lake, river, canal or stream
	Lock, weir, tunnel
Church	Non-Roman antiquity
ROMAN FORT	Roman antiquity
87	Adjoining page indicators and overlap bands The colour of the arrow and the band indicates the scale of the adjoining or overlapping page (see scales below)
237	

Enlarged mapping only

	Railway or bus station building
	Place of interest
	Parkland

Acad	Academy	Inst	Institute	Recn Gd	Recreation Ground
Allot Gdns	Allotments	Ct	Law Court	Resr	Reservoir
Cemy	Cemetery	L Ctr	Leisure Centre	Ret Pk	Retail Park
C Ctr	Civic Centre	LC	Level Crossing	Sch	School
CH	Club House	Liby	Library	Sh Ctr	Shopping Centre
Coll	College	Mkt	Market	TH	Town Hall/House
Crem	Crematorium	Meml	Memorial	Trad Est	Trading Estate
Ent	Enterprise	Mon	Monument	Univ	University
Ex H	Exhibition Hall	Mus	Museum	W Twr	Water Tower
Ind Est	Industrial Estate	Obsy	Observatory	Wks	Works
IRB Sta	Inshore Rescue Boat Station	Pal	Royal Palace	YH	Youth Hostel
		PH	Public House		

■ The small numbers around the edges of the maps identify the 1 kilometre National Grid lines ■ The dark grey border on the inside edge of some pages indicates that the mapping does not continue onto the adjacent page

The scale of the maps on the pages numbered in blue is 4.2 cm to 1 km • 2⅔ inches to 1 mile • 1: 23810

| 0 | ¼ | ½ | ¾ | 1 mile |
| 0 | 250m | 500m | 750m | 1 kilometre |

The scale of the maps on pages numbered in green is 1.96 cm to 1 km • 1⅓ inches to 1 mile • 1: 50688

| 0 | ¼ | ½ | ¾ | 1 mile |
| 0 | 250m | 500m | 750m | 1 kilometre |

The scale of the maps on pages numbered in red is 8.4 cm to 1 km • 5⅓ inches to 1 mile • 1: 11900

| 0 | 220 yards | 440 yards | 660 yards | ½ mile |
| 0 | 125m | 250m | 375m | ½ kilometre |

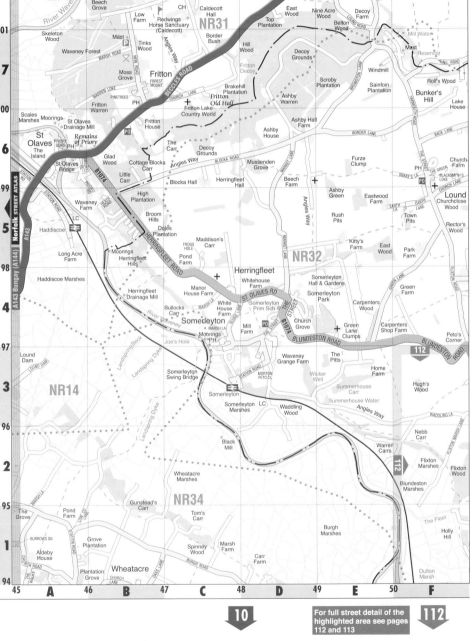

Scale: 1⅓ inches to 1 mile

0   ¼   ½ mile
0   250m 500m 750m 1 km

Norfolk STREET ATLAS

A143 Great Yarmouth (A12)

SHORT RD

CHERRY LANE

Mill Hill
(Tumulus)

Cherry
Lane Farm   CH
L Ctr   Browston Hall
                              Golf Course

Pettingell's
Drainage Mill

Green
Hills

Round
Hills

Mill
Hill   Crossways
                        Farm   Browston
                                             Green

Bell Hill

Foxburrow
Hang

HOBLAND ROAD

Seven Mile
House

Bell Hill
(Battery)

P   P

East
Wood   Nine Acre
                    Wood

Decoy
Farm

Beech
Grove

CH

Caldecott
Hall

Low
Farm

Redwings
Horse Sanctuary
(Caldecott)

NR31

Top
Plantation

Belton
Wood

Mill Water

Skeleton
Wood

Mast

P
Tinks
Wood

Border
Bush

Hill
Wood

Decoy
Grounds

Windmill

Mast

Reservoir

HALL ROAD

Waveney Forest

MARSH ROAD

NEW ROAD

Moss
Grove

Fritton

FOREST
MOUNT

Fritton
Decoy

Scroby
Plantation

Sainfoin
Plantation

Rolf's Wood

Bunker's
Hill

Lake
House

Scales
Marshes Moorings

St Olaves
Drainage Mill

PINETREES

PH

Fritton
Warren

WARREN LOKE

CHURCH LANE

Brakehill
Plantation
Fritton
Old Hall

Fritton Lake
Country World

Ashby
Warren

Ashby Hall
Farm

BORDER LANE

BACK LANE

THE GREEN

BRANCASTER ROAD

**St
Olaves**

The
Island

PRIORY
GDNS

Remains
of Priory

PH

St Olaves
Bridge

Glad
Wood

Cottage

Little
Carr

Blocka
Carr

PO

Fritton
House

The
Carr

Decoy
Grounds

Angles Way

BLOCKA ROAD

Ashby
House

Mussenden
Grove

Furze
Clump

Church
Farm

PH

THE GREEN

BLACKSMITH'S
LOKE

CHURCH LANE

Lound

Haddiscoe

B1074

HRINGFLET ROAD

High
Plantation

Blocka Hall

Herringfleet
Hall

Beech
Farm

Angles Way

Ashby
Green

Eastwood
Farm

EARTH
LA

EARTH
LANE

Churchclose
Wood

Waveney
Farm

LC

Broom
Hills

Doles
Plantation

Maddison's
Carr

FROGS
HOLE

Rush
Pits

Town
Pits

Rector's
Wood

Long Acre
Farm

Moorings
Herringfleet
Hills

Pond
Farm

NR32

Kitty's
Farm

East
Wood

Park
Farm

FLIXTON ROAD

Haddiscoe Marshes

Herringfleet
Drainage Mill

River Waveney

Bullocks
Carr

Manor
House Farm

Herringfleet

MARSH LA

Whitehouse
Farm

ST OLAVES RD

Somerleyton
Hall & Gardens

Somerleyton
Park

Carpenters
Wood

GREEN LANE

Green
Farm

Somerleyton

White
House
Farm

Somerleyton
Prim Sch

B1074

Church
Grove

Green
Lane
Clumps

Carpenters
Shop Farm

Joe's Hole

MARSH LA

Moorings
PH

Mill
Farm

PO

THE STREET

BLUNDESTON ROAD

Peto's
Corner

BLUNDESTON ROAD

112

Lound
Dam

LOUND DAM

Landspring Beck

Landspring Dyke

Somerleyton
Swing Bridge

Waveney
Grange Farm

MORTON
PETO CL

The
Pitts

Wicker
Well

Home
Farm

Hugh's
Wood

NR14

Somerleyton

STATION ROAD

Somerleyton
Marshes

LC

Waddling
Wood

Summerhouse
Carr

Summerhouse Water

Angles Way

WADDLING LA

Landspring Dyke

Black
Mill

Nebb
Carr

Warren
Carrs

112

Flixton
Marshes

FLIXTON MARSH LANE

Flixton
Wood

Wheatacre
Marshes

Blundeston
Marshes

NR34

Gunstead's
Carr

Tom's
Carr

MARSH LA

The
Grove

Pond
Farm

LOW RD

Grove
Plantation

Spinney
Wood

Marsh
Farm

Burgh
Marshes

The Fleet

Holly
Hill

BURROWS GN

STATION ROAD

Aldeby
House

CHURCH ROAD

Wheatacre

Plantation
Grove

CHURCH
LANE

BURGH ROAD

OAKS RD

Carr
Farm

Oulton
Marsh

**For full street detail of the
highlighted area see pages
112 and 113**

112

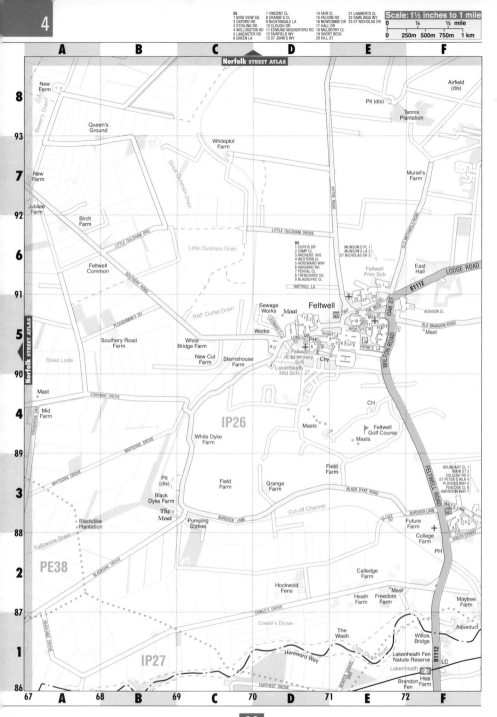

Scale: 1½ inches to 1 mile

0   ¼   ½   mile
0 250m 500m 750m 1 km

E5
1 BIRD VIEW SQ
2 OXFORD RD
3 STIRLING RD
4 WELLINGTON RD
5 LANCASTER RD
6 GREEN LA

7 VINCENT CL
8 CRABBE'S CL
9 NIGHTINGALE LA
10 CLOUGH DR
11 EDMUND MOUNDFORD RD
12 FAIRFIELD WY
13 ST JOHN'S WY

14 FAIR CL
15 FALCON RD
16 NEWCOMBE DR
17 HALL DR
18 MULBERRY CL
19 SHORT BECK
20 HILL ST

21 LAMBERTS CL
22 RAWLINGS WY
23 ST NICHOLAS DR

D5
1 CURTIS DR
2 CAMP CL
3 ARCHERS' AVE
4 WESTERN CL
5 HEREWARD WAY
6 HARVARD RD
7 PORTAL CL
8 TRENCHARD SQ
9 BLACKDYKE CL

New Farm
Queen's Ground
Whiteplot Farm
Airfield (dis)
Pit (dis)
Tennis Plantation
New Farm
Muriel's Farm
Jubilee Farm
Birch Farm
LITTLE OULSHAM DRO
LITTLE OULSHAM DROVE
Great Oulsham Drain
KYTHE ROAD
OLD METHWOLD ROAD
Feltwell Common
Little Oulsham Drain
MUNSON'S PL 1
MUNSON'S LA 2
ST NICHOLAS DR 3
Feltwell Prim Sch
East Hall
LODGE ROAD
B1112
SOUTHERY ROAD
HAYHILL LA
ADDISON CL
Sewage Works
Moat
Feltwell
THE BECK
OLD BRANDON ROAD
PLOUGHMAN'S DV
RAF Outfall Drain
Works
LEGRICE'S LA
SHORT LA
HIGH ST
OAK ST
Mast
Southery Road Farm
White Bridge Farm
New Cut Farm
Sternshouse Farm
LONG LANE
PH
PAYNE'S LA
WILTON ROAD
Feltwell Elementary Sch
Chy
Lakenheath Mid Sch
Mast
CORKWAY DROVE
CH
Mid Farm
FODDERFEN DRO
IP26
White Dyke Farm
Masts
Feltwell Golf Course
Masts
WHITDIKE DROVE
WHITDIKE DROVE
Field Farm
Field Farm
Pit (dis)
Field Farm
Grange Farm
BLACK DYKE ROAD
BOUNDARY CL 1
MAIN ST 2
COLLEGE RD 3
ST PETER'S WLK 4
PLOVERS WAY 5
PEACOCK CL 6
HARRISON WAY 7
Black Dyke Farm
Cut-off Channel
BURDOCK LANE
FELTWELL ROAD
'The Moat
Blackdike Plantation
Pumping Station
BURDOCK LANE
SLUICE DV
Future Farm
College Farm
MAIN'S LANE
Sallowrow Drain
BLACKDIKE DROVE
SOUTH STREET
PH
PE38
Calledge Farm
Maytree Farm
Hockwold Fens
Heath Farm
Freedom Farm
Mast
HEADLAND DROVE
COWLES DROVE
The Wash
Wilton Bridge
Aqueduct
Cowle's Drove
B1112
IP27
Hereward Way
Lakenheath Fen Nature Reserve
Little Ouse River
LC
Lakenheath
FURTHEST DROVE
HISS
Brandon Fen
Hiss Farm
MERCERS DRAIN

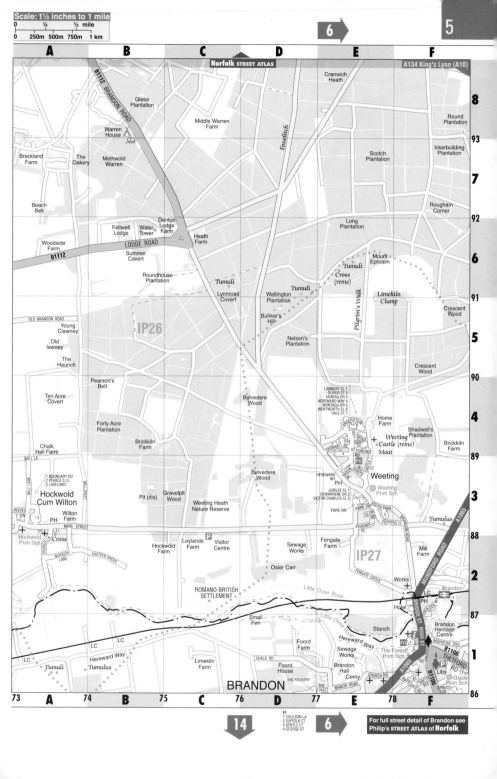

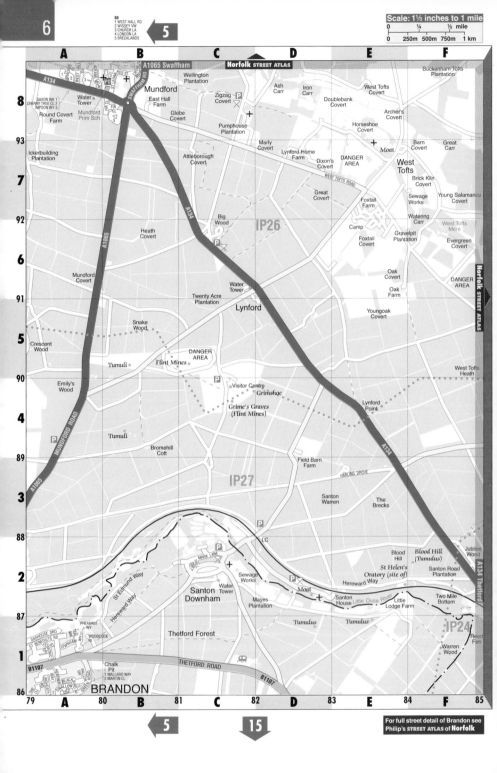

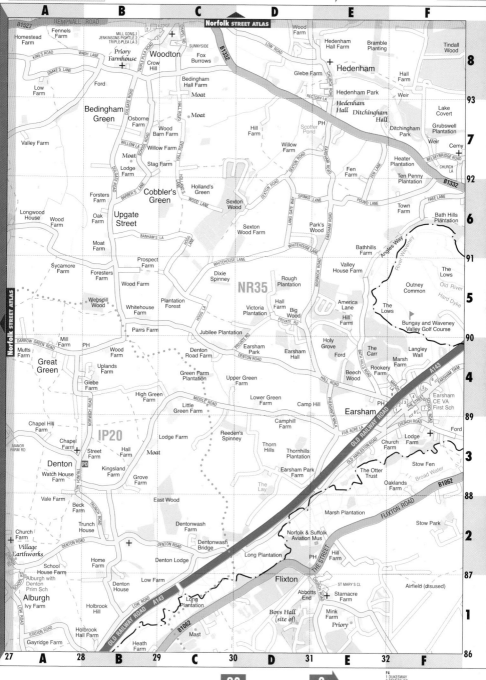

Norfolk STREET ATLAS

F4
1 DUKESWAY
2 STATION RD
3 MARSH LA
4 KINGSWAY
5 PRINCESS WAY
6 ELMS CL
7 QUEENSWAY
8 THE GREEN
9 BEECH TREE WAY

Norfolk STREET ATLAS

A B C D E F

8

Wood Farm
Moat Tindall Hall
Belsey Bridge
Spink's Hill
The Shrub
Brick Kiln Road
Hungry Hill
Bunjay Road
Old Bungay Road
Rayner's Lane
School Road
Kirby Cane
The Hall
Bungay Road
Bungay Road
Pewter Hill
Sheepwalk Farm
Manor Farm
Wardly Hill
A143
Kirby Hill
Gravel Pit
Léet Hill

93

Broome Fruit Farm
Rectory Road
Ellingham Hall
Old Hall Farm
Lodge Plantation
YARMOUTH RD 1
LOCKHART RD 2
CRISP RD 3
OLD POST OFFICE LA 4
CHAPEL LA 5
WOODLAND DR 6
PH
Kirby Row
NEWGATE LA
Leet Hill Farm
Geldeston
West End
KELL'S ACRES

7

Cemy
BELSEYBRIDGE ROAD
New Covert
Ivy House Farm
HOME FARM RD
Ellingham
WILLOW LANE
Broome Place
Ellingham VC Florence Way Prim Sch
MILL ROAD
MILL
Henry's Plantation
BRAGES
Main Run
KELL'S WY

92

DRAPERS LANE
Hollybush Farm
Sewage Works
BAKERS LANE
110
Longford Bridge
Stonewall Plantation
STATION ROAD
Osier Carr
STATION ROAD
Church Farm
GELDESTON ROAD
Boon's Plantation
PH
PO
All Hallows Farm
TUNNEY'S LANE
LODDON ROAD
Street Farm
OLD STATION ROAD
Station Farm
MILL POOL LA
Sewage Works
Dockeney
BIG ROW

6

Home Farm
NORWICH ROAD
WILDFLOWER W.
WAVENEY RD
Sch
Tumuli
Enclosure
GREEN LA
Broome Common
River Waveney
New Dyke
Benstead Marshes
Ellingham Marshes
Willow Farm
Geldeston Marshes

Ditchingham
B1332
PH
Broome
Broome Marshes
LOW ROAD
Prospect Farm
Bensteads Farm
Alder Farm
White House Farm
Geldeston Lock
Geldeston Marshes

91

Old River
A144
P
Sports Gd
NR35
THOROW STREET
Valley Farm
DEER ROW
MILL HILL LA
By Road Farm
Cherry Tree Farm
Shipmeadow Marshes
GREEN LA E

5

Wainford
Low Fell
PH
Manor Farm
Sewage Farm
Nunnery Farm

90

110
BROAD ST
NETHERGATE S.
FALCON LA
River Waveney
Sch
Liby
PH
WATCH HO HL
110
Mettingham
Top Farm
The Hall
Moat
Angles Way
Church Farm
THE HILL
B1062
Shipmeadow

4

Castle (rems)
CASTLE LA
BECCLES ROAD
Sch
GARDEN DR.
Grove Farm
VICARAGE LANE
Angles Way
NR34
Laurels Farm
High Common

BUNGAY
B1435
UPPER OLLAND STREET
HILLSIDE RD E
Annis Hill
Trinity Farm
Castle Farm
NEW RD
Crow's Nest Wood
Highfields Farm
Shipmeadow Common
Boundary Farm
CLARKE'S LANE

89

ST JOHN'S ROAD
PO
HILLSIDE RD W
KINGS ROAD
Sch
Moats
Round Wood
CASTLE ROAD
Mettingham Wood
The Mount
MANOR FARM ROAD
Orchard Farm
HALL RD
Low Farm

3

FLIXTON ROAD
B1062
MARGARET'S RD
Sch
110
ST JOHN'S ROAD
The Firs
St Johns Lodge Farm
LODGE ROAD
Manor Farm
LOW ROAD
Birchams Farm
MILL LANE
BARTERS LANE

88

St Margaret's Plantation
Manor Farm
Three Ash Farm
St Johns Hall
Tithe Farm
Ilketshall St Andrew
SCHOOL RD
Moat Farm

2

Uplandhall Farm
ST MARGARET'S ROAD
Angles Way
Hill Farm
St John's Hall
Great Common
Green Farm
Glebe Farm
GREAT COMMON LANE
St Andrew's Hall

87

Shadowbarn Farm
Hill Farm
Hill Farm
Grove Farm
Church Farm
A144
Willow Farm
Water Tower
Willow Tree Farm

1

The Elms
MILLS LANE
TOP ROAD
Hanna Barn Farm

33 A 34 B 35 C 36 D 37 E 38 F
86

For full street detail of the highlighted area see page 110

7

24

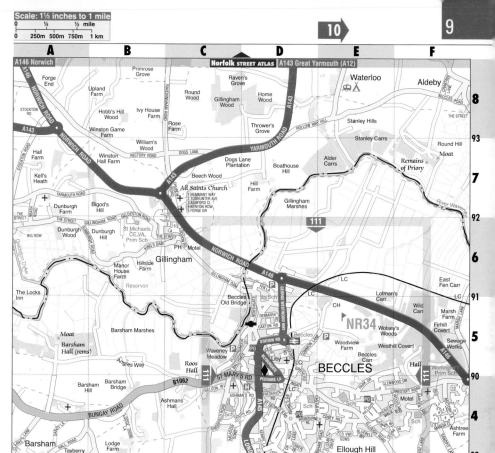

A146 Norwich   **Norfolk** STREET ATLAS   **A143 Great Yarmouth (A12)**

A   B   C   D   E   F

Forge End
Upland Farm
Primrose Grove
Raven's Grove
Waterloo
Aldeby

NORWICH ROAD
STOCKTON RD
Hobb's Hill Wood
Ivy House Farm
Round Wood
Gillingham Wood
Home Wood
Stanley Hills
THE STREET

Hall Farm
Winston Game Farm
Rose Farm
Thrower's Grove
Stanley Carrs
Round Hill Moat

Kell's Heath
Winston Hall Farm
William's Wood
RECTORY ROAD
DOGS LANE
Dogs Lane Plantation
Boathouse Hill
Alder Carrs
Remains of Priory

YARMOUTH ROAD
Dunburgh Farm
Bigod's Hill
Beech Wood
Hill Farm
Gillingham Marshes
River Waveney

THE STREET
HEAD LANE
Dunburgh Wood
Dunburgh Hill
St Michaels C.E.VA. Prim School
All Saints Church
1 HEMMANT WAY
2 TODHUNTER AVE
3 ASHFORD CL
4 KENYON ROW
5 FORGE GR

BIG ROW
Manor House Farm
Hillside Farm
PH Motel
THE STREET
KING'S DAM
Gillingham
NORWICH ROAD
A146

Gladston Dyke
Reservoir
GILLINGHAM DAM
FEN LA
GEORGE WESTWOOD WAY
111

The Locks Inn
Beccles Old Bridge
DENMARK RD
CAXTON RD
LC
East Fen Carr
Lotman's Carr
LC

Moat
Barsham Marshes
Angles Way
STATION RD
Beccles
Woodview Farm
Wolsey's Woods
Westhill Covert
Firhill Covert
Marsh Farm
Wild Carr
Sewage Works

Barsham Hall (rems)
Roos Hall
ST MARY'S RD
PO
Liby
COMMON LANE
NR34
Beccles Carr
Hall
Worlingham Prim Sch
111

Barsham Hill
Barsham Bridge
B1062
NELSON WY
PEDDARS LA
INGATE
GROVE RD
PARK DR
GLENWOOD DR
LOWESTOFT RD
90

BUNGAY ROAD
Ashmans Hall
ASHMAN'S RD
ST FREDERICK
ST GEORGE'S
CONEY HILL
Sch
Motel
MANOR RD

Barsham
Tayberry Farm
Lodge Farm
Barnaby Farm
Ellough Hill
Ashtree Farm

Field End
City Farm
White House Farm
Orchard Farm
LC
Cucumber Lane Farm
BENACRE ROAD

Grange Farm
Gables Farm
Granary Farm
Cromwell Road Crossing
111
Chenery's Farm
Ellough Moor

Furze Common
Old Hall Farm
Ringsfield
Grove Farm
Marlborough Farm
Playters New Farm

Church Farm
POLLS LANE
Hall Farm
Church Farm
CHURCH LANE
Playters Old Farm
Ellough Wood

Ringsfield Hall
Kiln Covert
RUSSELL'S GN PH
Woodland Farm
CROMWELL ROAD
Church Lane Farm
HULVER ROAD

Ringsfield Corner
Homestead Farm
Cottage Walpole Farm
Weston Hall
Weston
Church Lane
Ellough
Jakie's Wood

Lemans Farm
SCHOOL RD
Ringsfield CE VCP Sch
Pound Farm
Sewage Works
Old Hall Farm
KING'S LANE
Glebe Farm

Low Farm
Ringsfield Common
Brick Kiln Farm
Grove Farm
Hill Farm
New House Farm

Bottle & Glass Wood
St James's Church
Home Park
Park Farm
A145
St Marys Farm

Redisham Hall Farm
Farm Wood
Eight Acre Covert
LC

39   A   40   B   41   C   42   D   43   E   44   F   86

F4
1 PEPYS AVE
2 PAINS CL
3 ALL SAINTS GN
4 HOLM CL
5 WAINFORD CL
6 MIRBECK'S CL
7 BROOKWOOD CL
8 ASH TREE CL
9 MANOR CL
10 SUTTONS RD
11 JANET HADENHAM CL
12 COPPLESTONE CL

25   10   For full street detail of the highlighted area see page 111

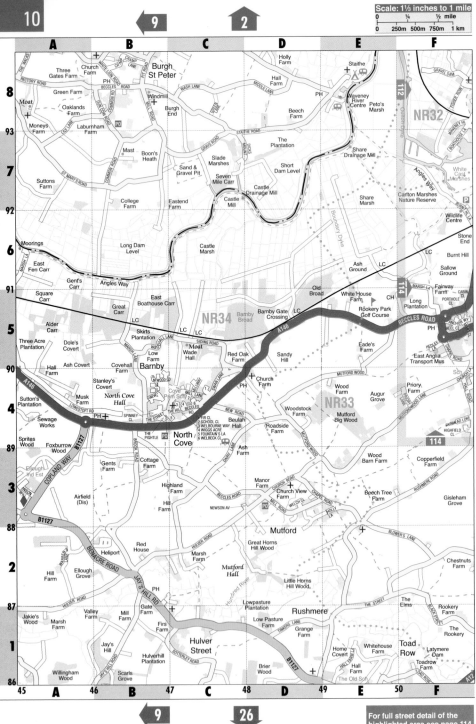

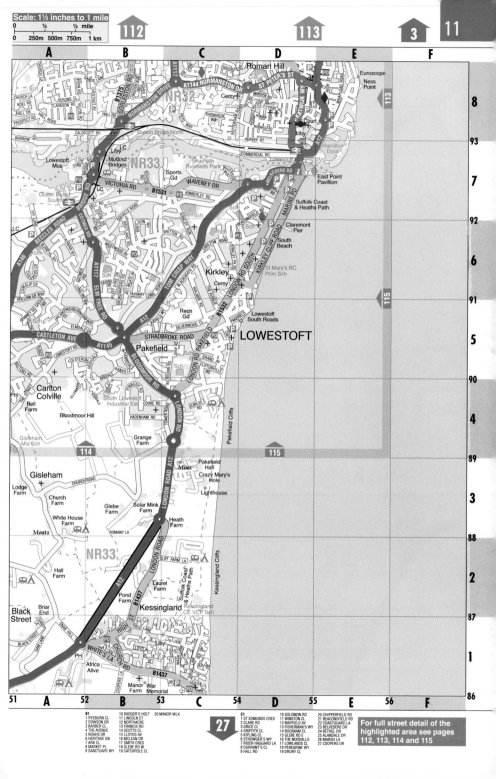

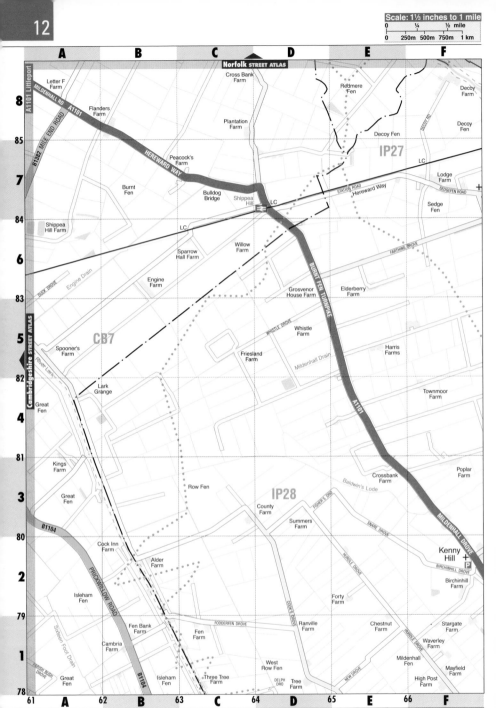

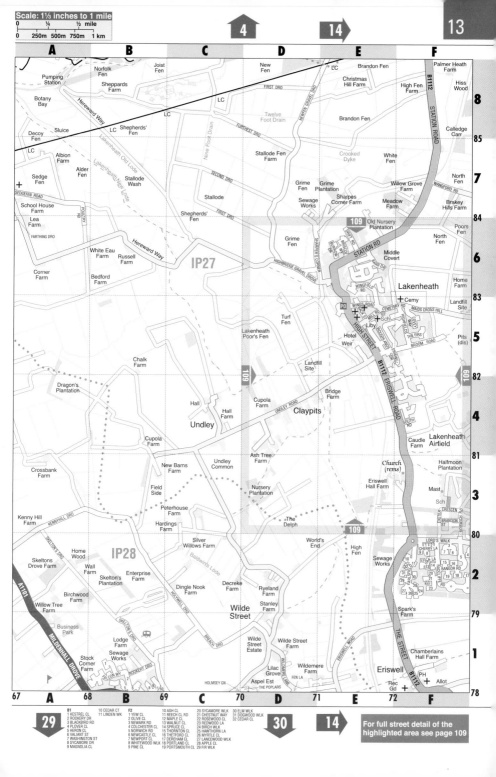

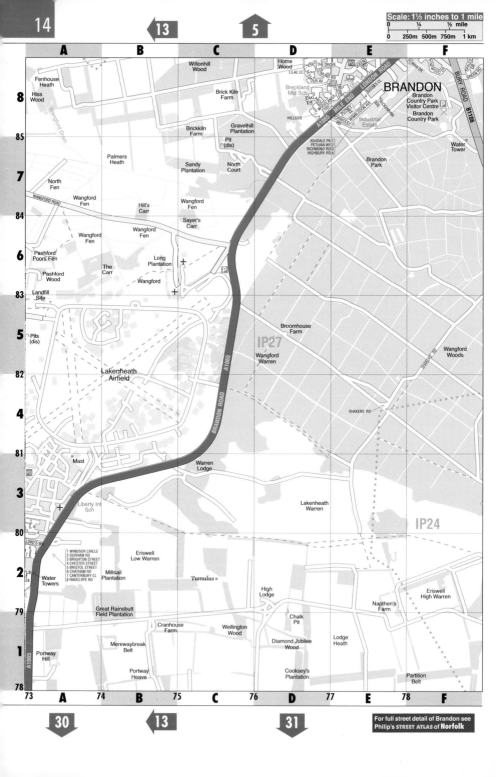

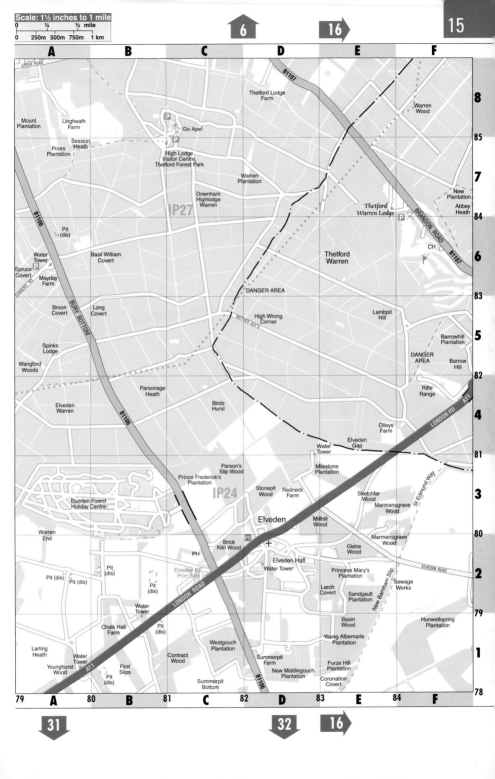

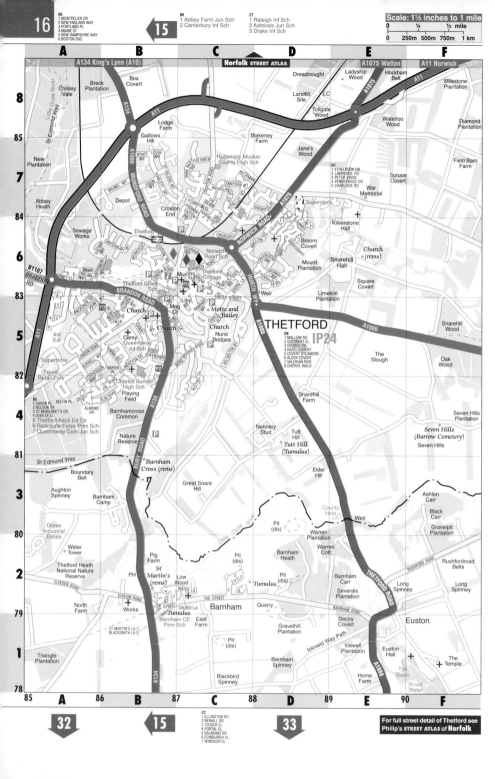

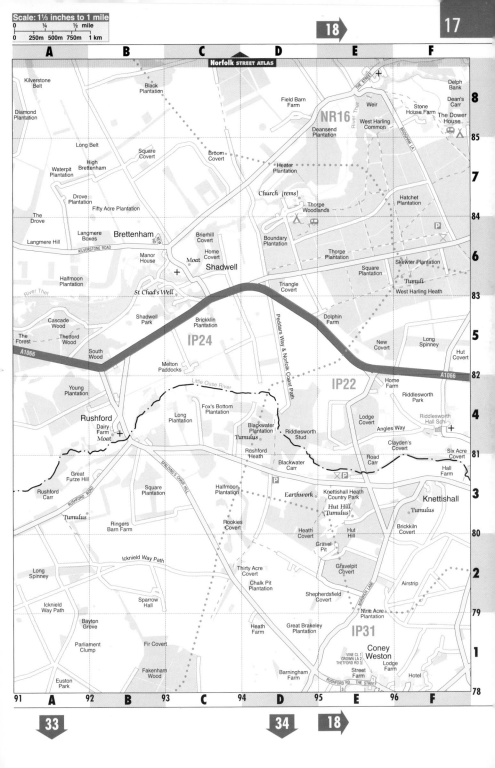

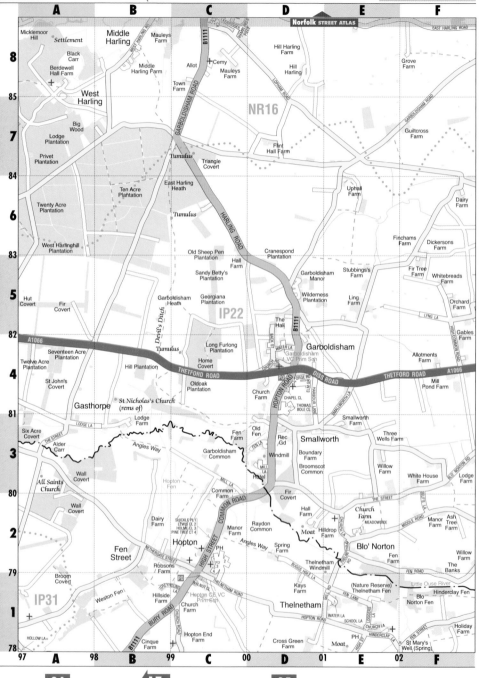

8

85

7

84

6

83

5

82

4

81

3

80

2

79

1

78

A   B   C   D   E   F

Micklemoor Hill *Settlement* Middle Harling Mauleys Farm
Black Carr Middle Harling Farm Allot Cemy Mauleys Farm Hill Harling Farm Hill Harling
Berdewell Hall Farm Town Farm Grove Farm
West Harling NR16
Big Wood Guiltcross Farm
Lodge Plantation
Privet Plantation *Tumulus* Triangle Covert Flint Hall Farm
HARLING ROAD Uphall Farm Dairy Farm
Ten Acre Plantation East Harling Heath
Twenty Acre Plantation *Tumulus* Finchams Farm Dickersons Farm
West Harlinghill Plantation Old Sheep Pen Plantation Cranespond Plantation Fir Tree Farm Whitebreads Farm
Hall Farm Garboldisham Manor Stubbings's Farm Orchard Farm
Hut Covert Fir Covert Sandy Betty's Plantation Wilderness Plantation Ling Farm LYNG LA
Garboldisham Heath Georgiana Plantation IP22
Devil's Ditch The Hall B1111 Gables Farm
Seventeen Acre Plantation *Tumulus* Long Furlong Plantation WATER LA Garboldisham Allotments Farm
Twelve Acre Plantation Hill Plantation Home Covert Garboldisham VC Prim Sch THETFORD ROAD A1066
St John's Covert Oldoak Plantation DISS ROAD Mill Pond Farm
Gasthorpe St Nicholas's Church (rems of) Church Farm FORGE LA CHAPEL CL THOMAS BOLE CL
LODGE LA Lodge Farm HOPTON ROAD Smallworth Farm
Six Acre Covert THE STREET Fen Farm Old Fen Rec Gd Smallworth Three Wells Farm
Alder Carr Angles Way Garboldisham Common TEN LA Windmill Boundary Farm Willow Farm White House Farm Lodge Farm
Wall Covert MILL LA Broomscot Common
All Saints Church Hopton Fen Common Road Fir Covert THE STREET
Wall Covert Dairy Farm SHICKLE PL 1 LEWIS CL 2 HOLM CL 3 PINE TREE CT 4 Manor Farm Raydon Common Hall Farm Hilldrop Farm Church Farm MEADOWRIDE Manor Farm Ash Tree Farm
Fen Street Hopton HIGH STREET Moat Blo' Norton Willow Farm
Broom Covert Robsons Farm PH Angles Way Spring Farm Thelnetham Windmill Fen Farm The Banks
IP31 GREYHOUND LA Hillside Farm BURY ROAD Church Farm Kays Farm Thelnetham (Nature Reserve) Thelnetham Fen Little Ouse River Blo Norton Fen Hinderclay Fen
Weston Fen Hopton CE VC Prim Sch Thelnetham WATER LA SCHOOL LA CHURCH LA Holiday Farm
HOLLOW LA Cinque Farm Hopton End Farm Cross Green Farm Moat PH St Mary's Well (Spring)

97   A   98   B   99   C   00   D   01   E   02   F

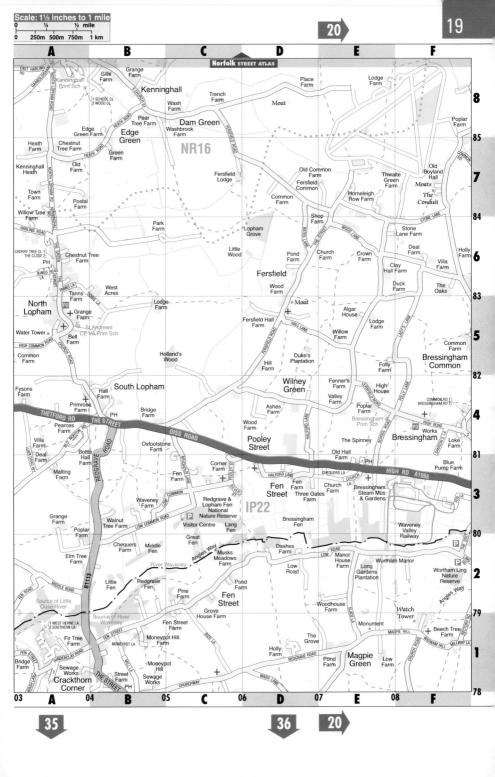

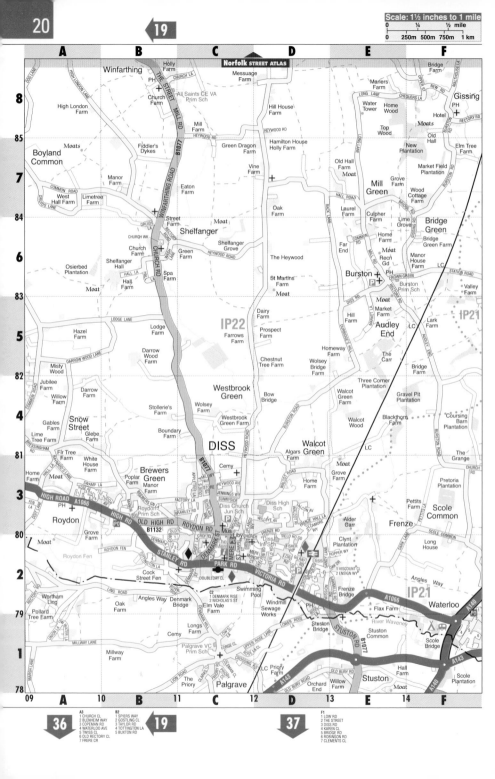

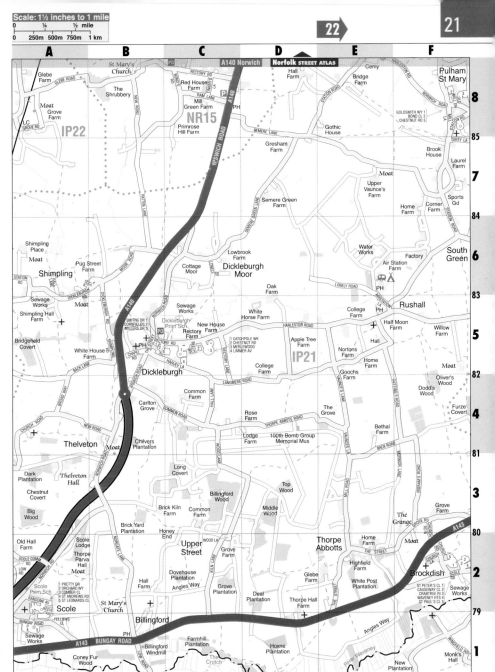

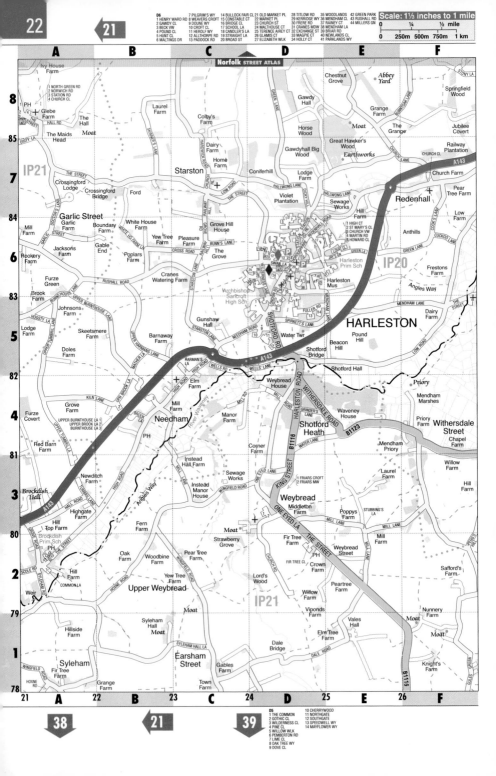

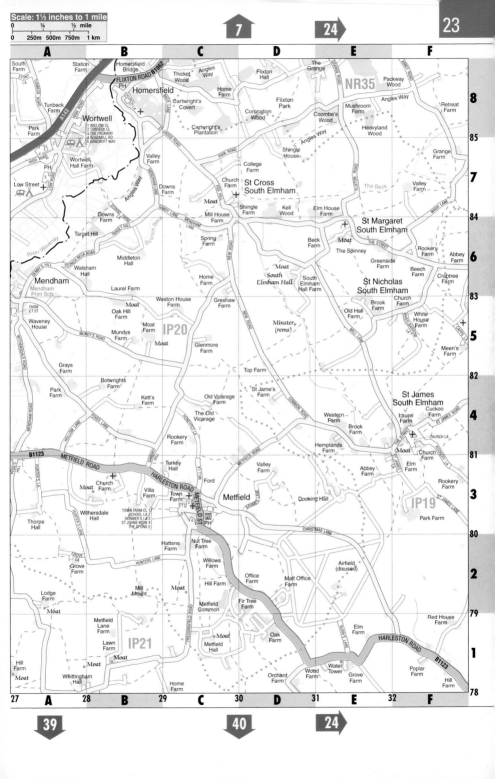

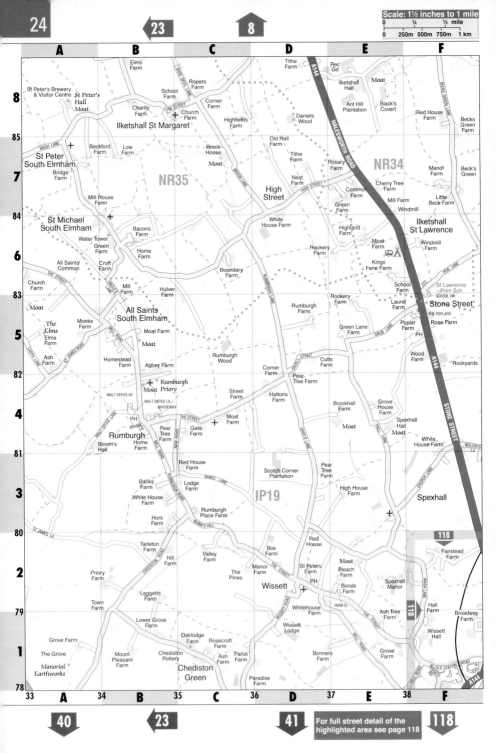

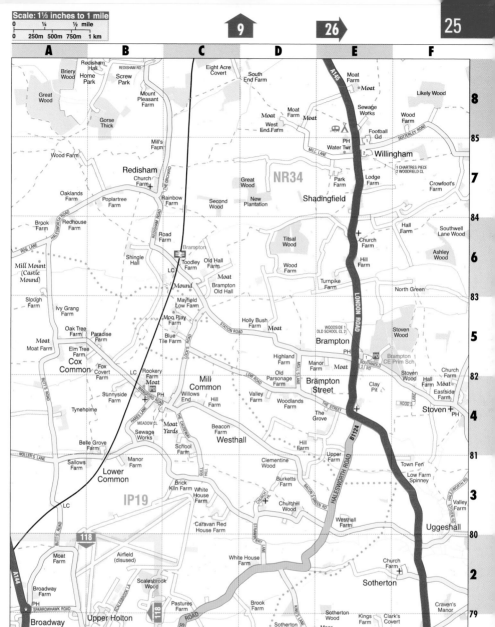

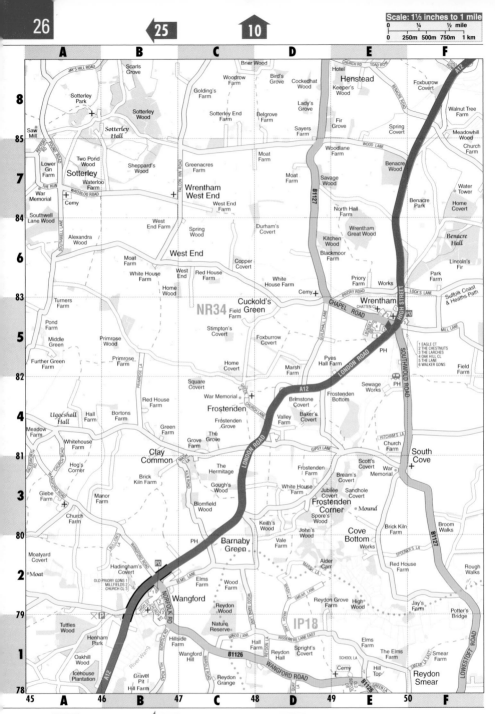

Scale: 1⅓ inches to 1 mile

0 ¼ ½ mile
0 250m 500m 750m 1 km

NR33
Kessingland Beach
PH
CHURCH RD
Blackcap Wood
Sewage Works
Churchfarm Marshes
Holly Grange Road
Kessingland Level
Suffolk Coast & Heaths Path
Benacre
War Memorial
Church Covert
Beachfarm Marshes
Pumping Station
The Denes
Northwalk Plantation
Beach Farm
THE STREET
Hall Farm
Blackwater Covert
Alder Carr
Wood Farm
Coney Hill
Boathouse Covert
Craft Plantation
Benacre National Nature Reserve
Holly Hang
NR34
Benacre Broad
Holly Grove
North Common Wood
Chancel Covert
Long Covert
Ausgates
St Andrew's Church
Church Farm
Covehithe
Covehithe Cliffs
Porter's Farm
Green Heath
Covehithe Broad
Warren House
Suffolk Coast & Heaths Path
The Warren
Easton Wood
Benacre National Nature Reserve
Easton Home Covert
Easton Broad
Pottersbridge Marshes
Easton Marshes
IP18
Easton Bavents
Easton Cliffs
EASTON LA.

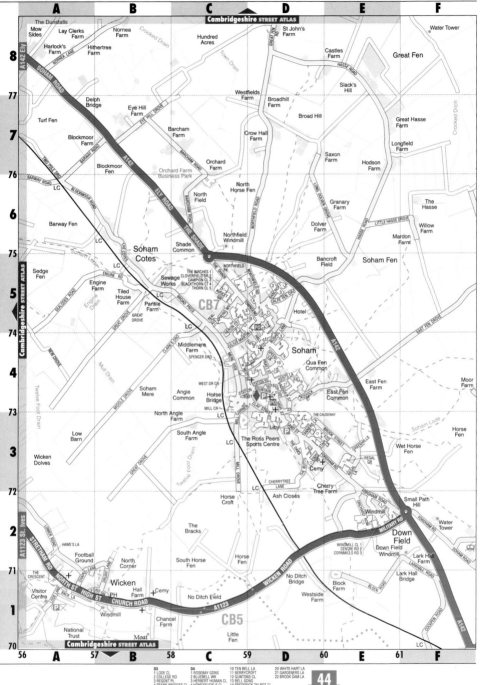

Cambridgeshire STREET ATLAS

Scale: 1⅓ inches to 1 mile

0	¼	½ mile
0	250m 500m 750m	1 km

D5
1 NORTH DR
2 ST FELIX CL
3 CALFE FEN CL
4 OLD SCHOOL CL
5 HOLMES LA
6 SNOWBERRY WY

7 FOX WOOD N
8 MARTIN CL
9 POPPY FIELDS
10 PRIMROSE LA
11 FOX WOOD S

Great Fen

Water Tower

The Dunstalls
Mow Sides
Lay Clerks Farm
Harlock's Farm
Hithertree Farm
Nornea Farm
Crooked Drain
Hundred Acres
Town Drain
St John's Farm
Castles Farm
Slack's Hill

Turf Fen
Delph Bridge
Eye Hill Farm
Barcham Farm
Westfields Farm
Broadhill Farm
Broad Hill
Great Hasse Farm

Blockmoor Farm
Orchard Farm
Crow Hall Farm
Saxon Farm
Longfield Farm

Barway Fen
Blockmoor Fen
Orchard Farm Business Park
North Field
North Horse Fen
Dolver Farm
Hodson Farm
Granary Farm
The Hasse

Sedge Fen
Soham Cotes
Shade Common
Northfield Windmill
Bancroft Field
Willow Farm
Mardon Farm
Soham Fen

Engine Farm
Tiled House Farm
Sewage Works
Partile Farm
THE BIRCHES 1
CLOVERFIELD DR 2
CAMPION CL 3
BLACKTHORN CT 4
THORN CL 5
Northfield
CB7
Hotel

Middlemere Farm
Spencer Drd
Soham
Qua Fen Common
East Fen Farm
Moor Farm

Soham Mere
Angle Common
Horse Bridge
East Fen Common

North Angle Farm
South Angle Farm
Liby
Horse Fen

Low Barn
Wicken Dolves
The Ross Peers Sports Centre
Cemy
Wet Horse Fen

Cherrytree Lane
Cherry Tree Farm
Small Path Hill
Water Tower

Horse Croft
Ash Closes
Windmill
Down Field
Lark Hall Farm

The Bracks
WINDMILL CL 1
CENTRE RD 2
CORNMILLS RD 3
Down Field Windmill
Lark Hall Bridge

Football Ground
North Corner
South Horse Fen
Horse Fen
No Ditch Bridge
Block Farm
Westside Farm

The Crescent
Visitor Centre
Wicken
Hall Farm
Cemy
No Ditch Field
CB5

National Trust
Windmill
Chancel Farm
Moat
Little Fen

D3
1 LODE CL
2 COLLEGE RD
3 REGENT PL
4 FRANK BRIDGES CL
5 REDHOUSE GDNS
6 THE CRESCENT
7 FORDHAM RD
8 MEADOW CL
9 MILL CFT

D4
1 ROSEBAY GDNS
2 BLUEBELL WK
3 HERBERT HUMAN CL
4 HONEYSUCKLE CL
5 NIGHTALL RD
6 CHESTNUT DR
7 GIMBERT RD
8 QUEENSWAY
9 WEATHERALLS CL

10 TEN BELL LA
11 BERRYCROFT
12 GUNTONS CL
13 BELL GDNS
14 FREDERICK TALBOT CL
15 CHURCHGATE ST
16 MARKET ST
17 ADELAIDE CL
18 EASTERN AV
19 BREWHOUSE LA

20 WHITE HART LA
21 GARDENERS LA
22 BROOK DAM LA

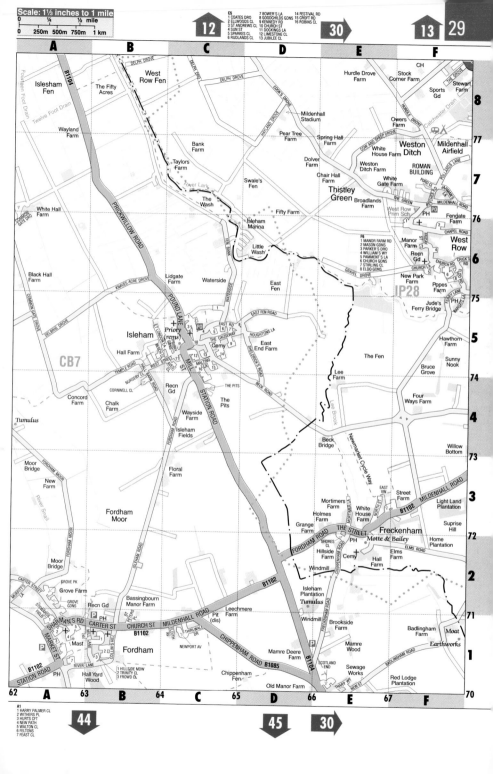

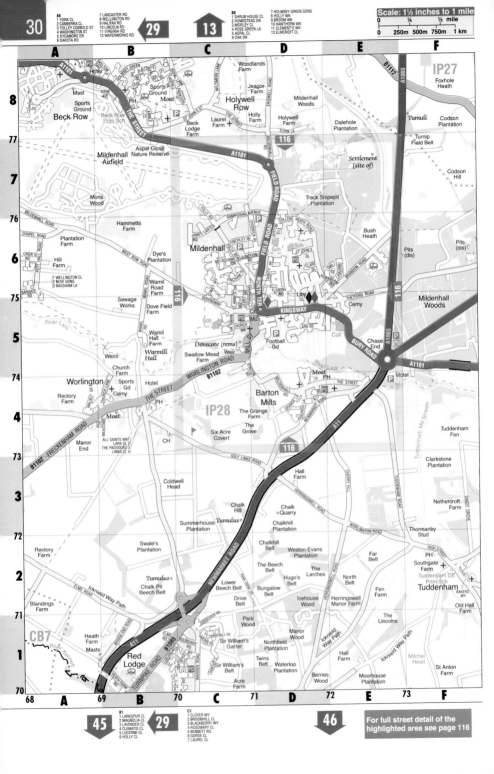

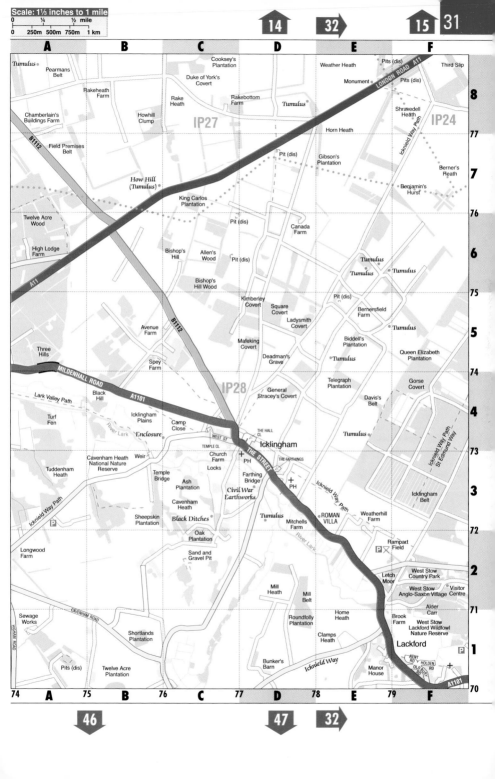

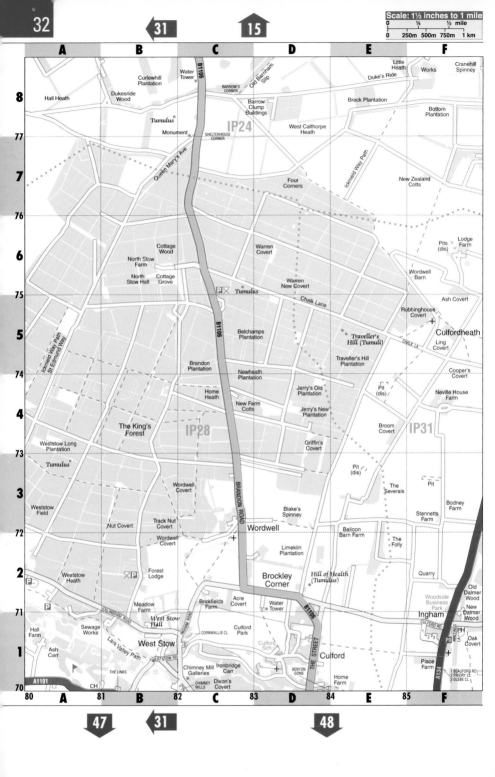

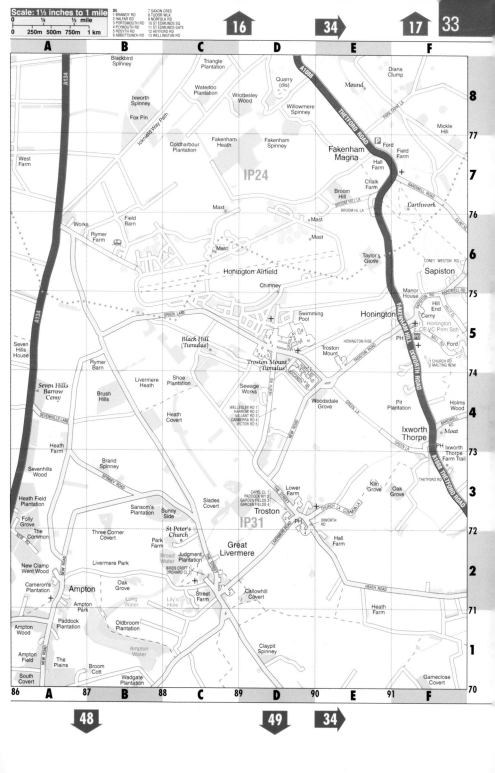

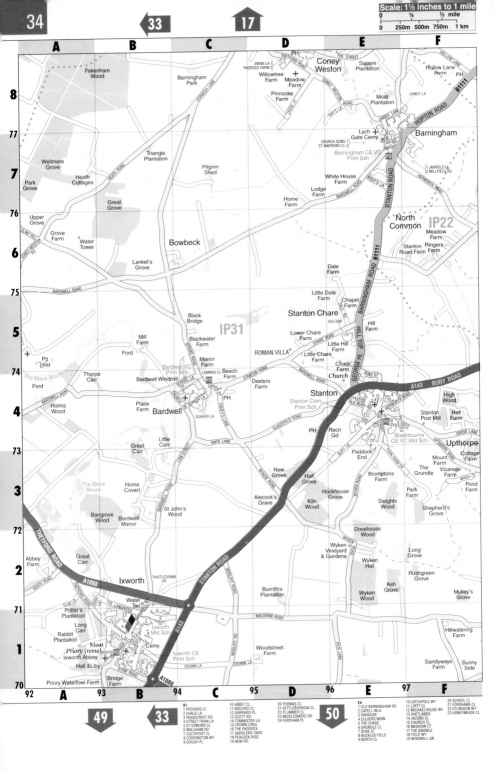

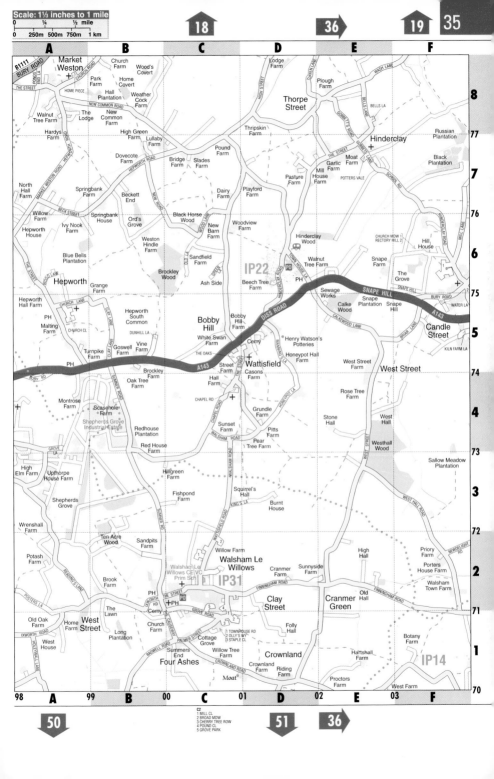

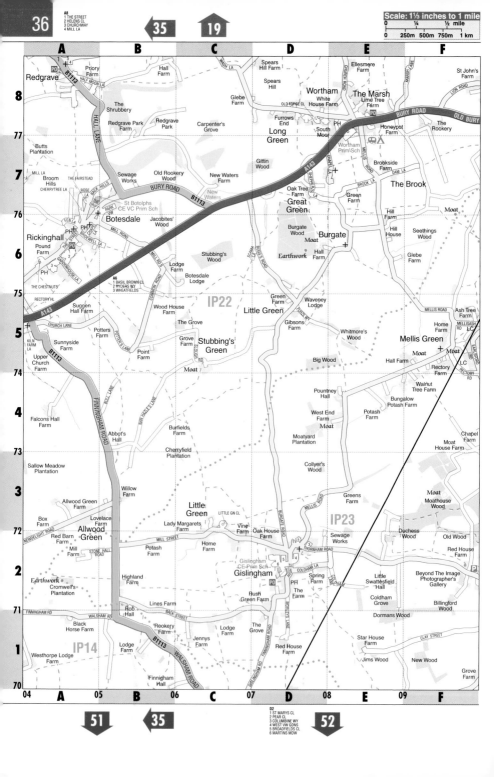

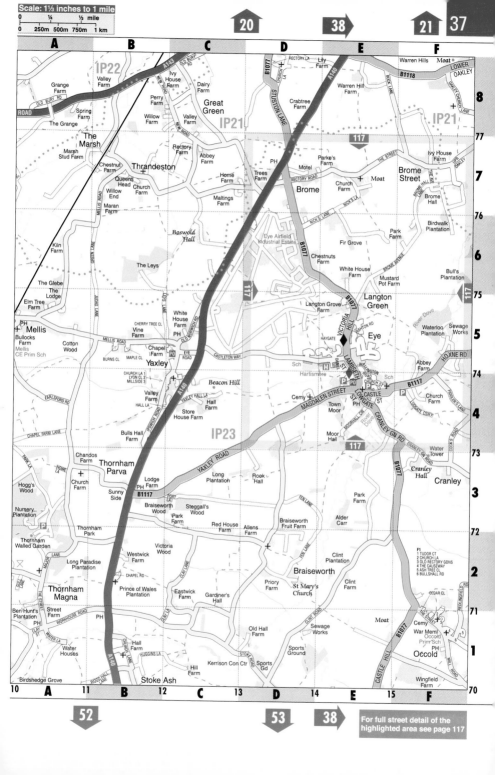

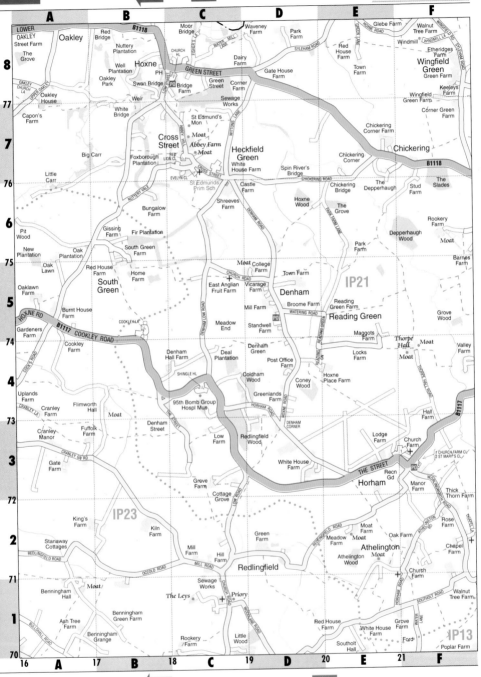

A   B   C   D   E   F

LOWER OAKLEY
Oakley Street Farm
Oakley
The Grove
Red Bridge
Nuttery Plantation
B1118
Moor Bridge
CHURCH HL
WHITE LANE
TISSE'S LA
Waveney Farm
Park Farm
SYLEHAM ROAD
Glebe Farm
HOXNE ROAD
GREEN LANE
Windmill
Walnut Tree Farm
WINGFIELD RD
WINDMILL LA
SYLEHAM ROAD
Etherides Farm
Wingfield Green
Green Farm

8

Capon's Farm
CHURCH LA
UPPER OAKLEY
OAKLEY LA
Oakley House
Well Plantation
Hoxne
PH
Oakley Park
Swan Bridge
Green Street
GREEN STREET
Dairy Farm
Corner Farm
Bridge Farm
Gate House Farm
Red House Farm
Town Farm
Wingfield Green Farm
Keeleys Farm
Corner Green Farm

77

White Bridge
Weir
Sewage Works
Chickering Corner Farm
Chickering
B1118

7

Big Carr
Little Carr
Foxborough Plantation
St Edmund's Mon
Moat
Abbey Farm
Moat
RED LION CL
BERRY HILL
Cross Street
Heckfield Green
White House Farm
Spin River's Bridge
CHICKERING ROAD
Chickering Corner
Chickering Bridge
The Depperhaugh
Stud Farm
The Slades

76

Pit Wood
New Plantation
Gissing Farm
Fir Plantation
NUTTERY VALE
EVELYN CL
St Edmunds Prim Sch
CROSS STREET
Castle Farm
Shreeves Farm
DENHAM ROAD
Hoxne Wood
The Grove
PACK FARM LANE
Depperhaugh Wood
Rookery Farm
Moat
Barnes Farm

6

Oak Plantation
South Green Farm
Bungalow Farm
College Farm
Park Farm

75

Oaklawn Farm
Oak Lawn
Red House Farm
South Green
Home Farm
Moat
East Anglian Fruit Farm
CHURCH ROAD
Vicarage Farm
Town Farm
Denham
Reading Green Farm
IP21
Grove Wood

5

HOXNE RD
Gardeners Farm
B1117
Burnt House Farm
COOKLEY ROAD
COOKLEY LA
Cookley Farm
Mill Farm
Broome Farm
WATERING ROAD
Reading Green
Maggots Farm
Thorpe Hall
Moat
Valley Farm

74

COCKS ROAD
Uplands Farm
CRANLEY LA
Flimworth Hall
Moat
DENHAM LOW ROAD
Denham Hall Farm
Meadow End
Deal Plantation
SHINGLE HL
Denham Green
Standwell Farm
Post Office Farm
READING GREEN
Locks Farm
Hoxne Place Farm
THORPE HALL ROAD
Hall Farm
B1117

4

Cranley Farm
Cranley Manor
Suffolk Farm
LOW STREET
Denham Street
95th Bomb Group Hospl Mus
HORHAM ROAD
Coldham Wood
Greenlands Farm
Coney Wood
HOXNE ROAD
DENHAM CORNER
Lodge Farm
Church Farm
 ST MARY'S CL
CHURCH FARM CL

3

CRANLEY GN RD
Gate Farm
IP23
Grove Farm
LOW ROAD
Cottage Grove
Low Farm
Redlingfield Wood
White House Farm
THE STREET
Horham
Recn Gd
PO
Manor Farm
ROSE GROVE ROAD
Thick Thorn CL

72

King's Farm
Stanaway Cottages
REDLINGFIELD ROAD
Kiln Farm
Mill Farm
Green Farm
REDLINGFIELD ROAD
Meadow Farm
Moat Farm
ATHELINGTON ROAD
Oak Farm
Athelington
Moat
Rose Farm
Chapel Farm

2

Benningham Hall
Moat
OCCOLD ROAD
Mill Farm
Hill Farm
MILL ROAD
Redlingfield
Athelington Wood
Church Farm

71

BULL SMALL ROAD
Ash Tree Farm
Benningham Grange
Benningham Green Farm
The Leys
Sewage Works
Priory
CHURCH ROAD
Rookery Farm
Little Wood
WOODLANE ROAD
Red House Farm
Southolt Hall
White House Farm
Ford
Grove Farm
WATER LANE
SOUTHOLT ROAD
Walnut Tree Farm
IP13
Poplar Farm

1

16   A   17   B   18   C   19   D   20   E   21   F

70

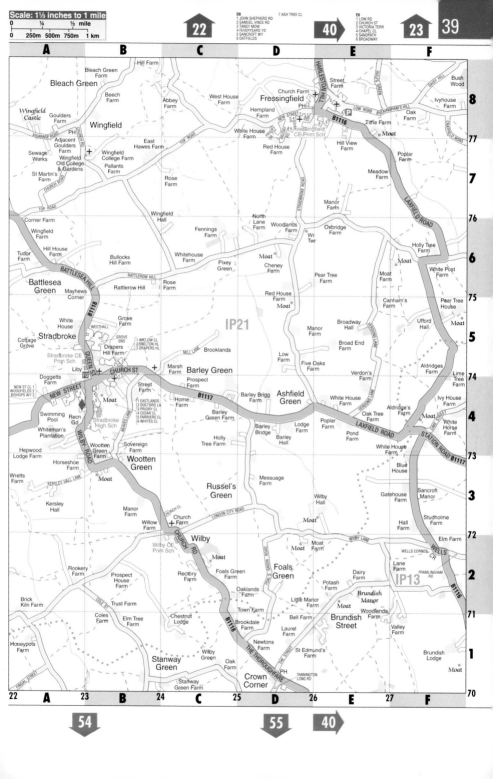

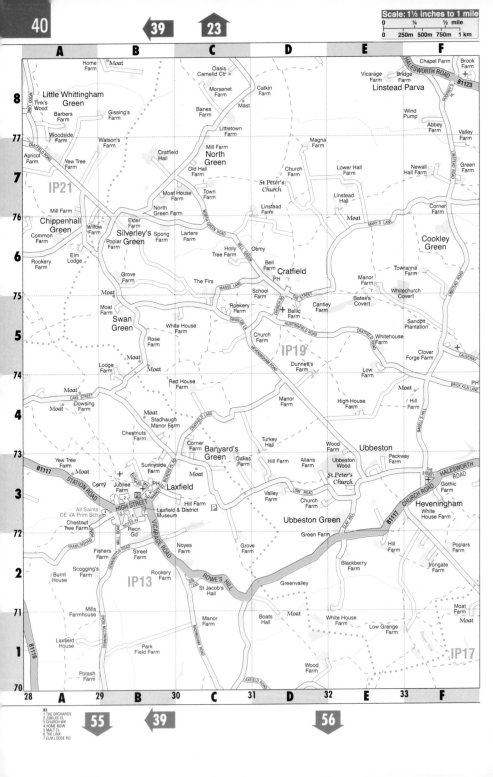

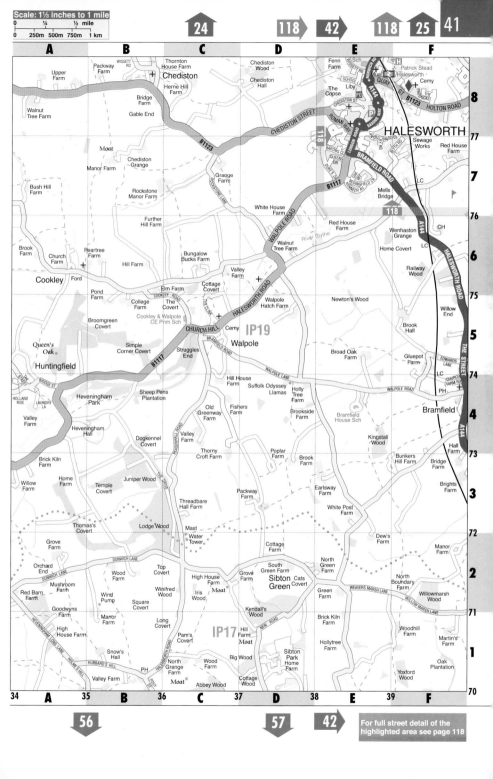

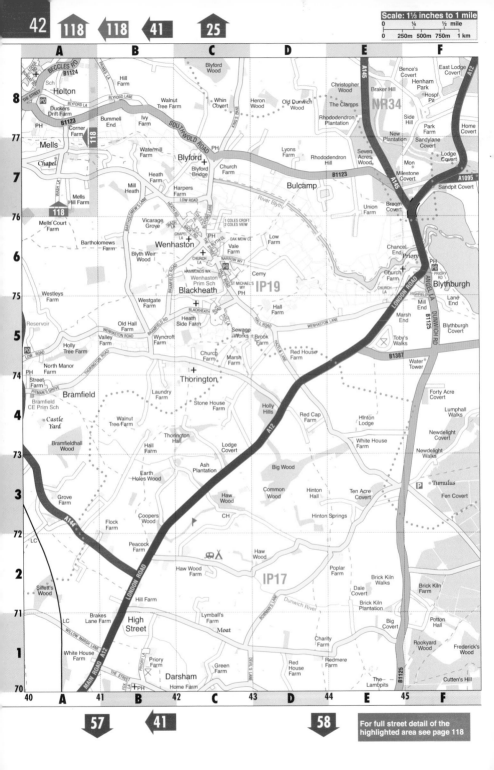

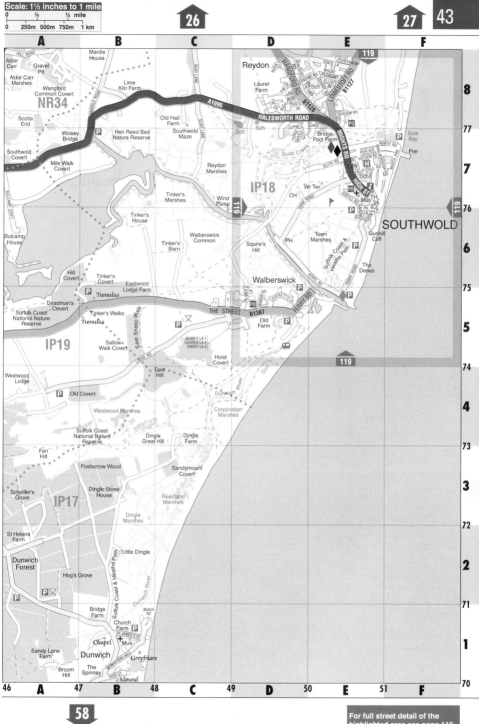

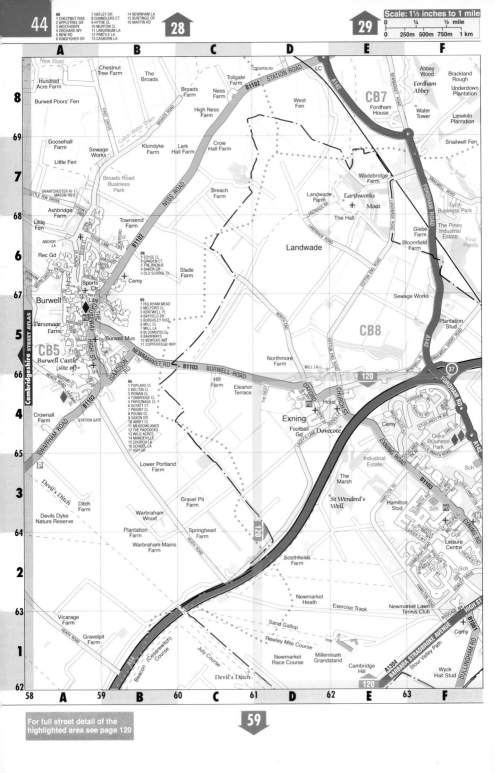

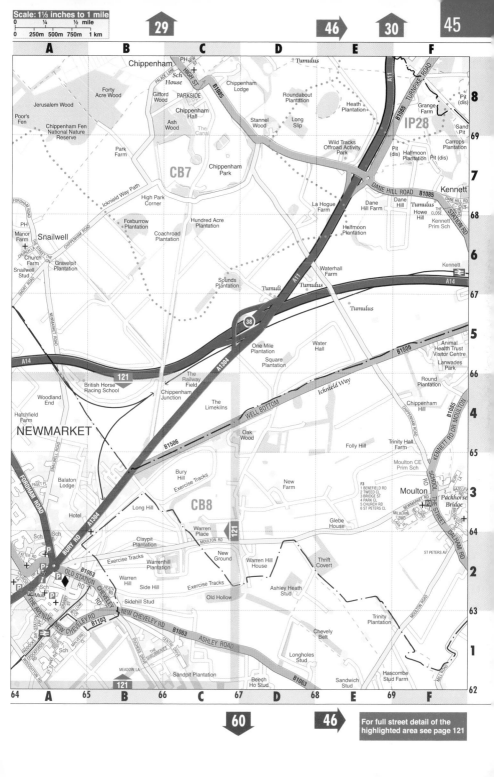

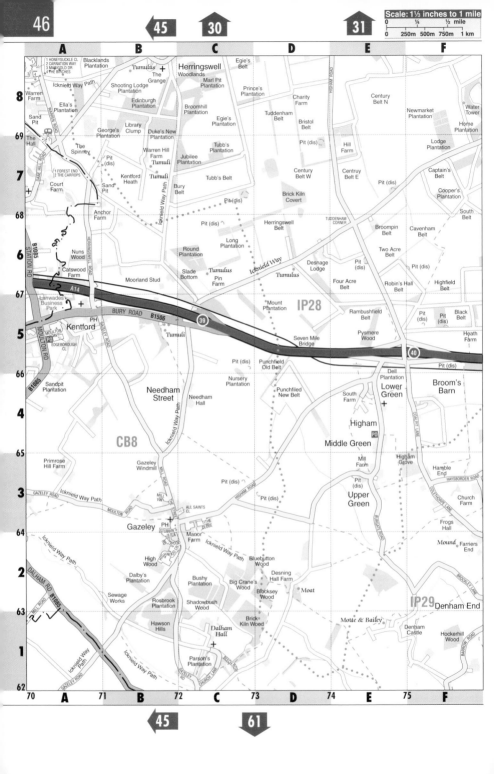

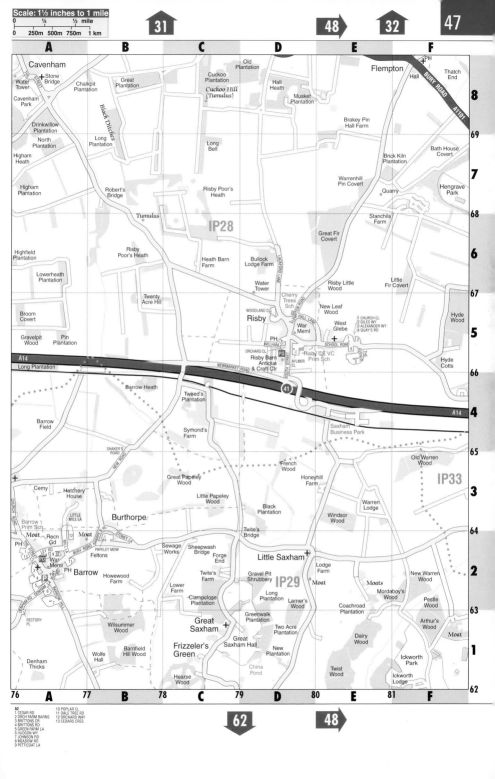

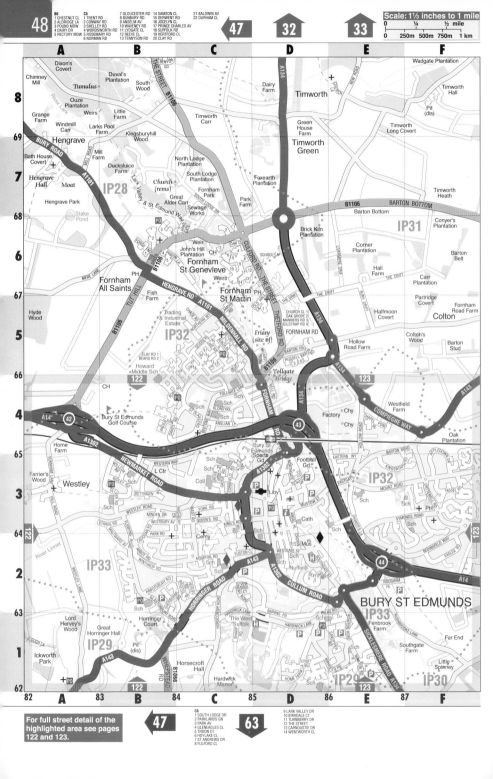

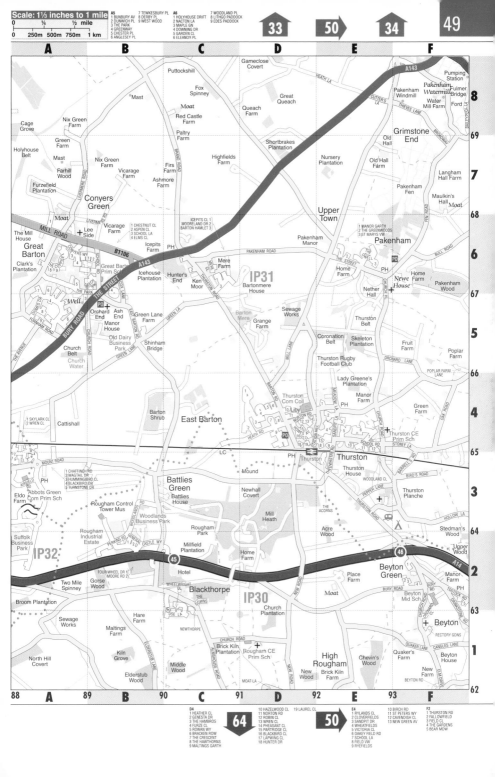

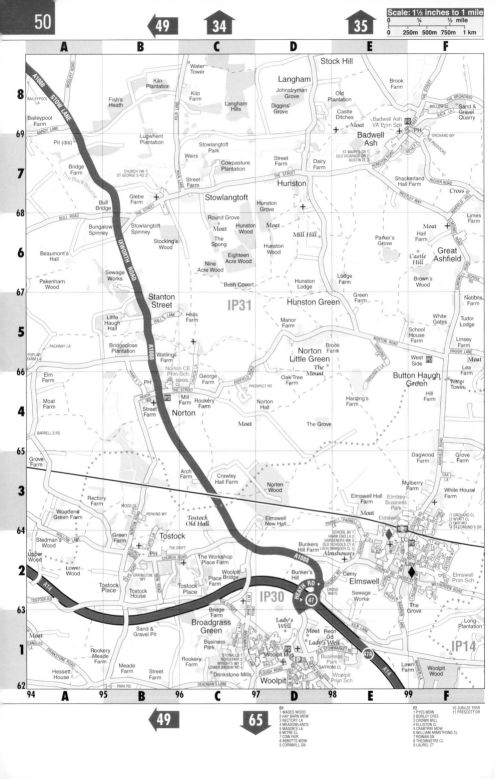

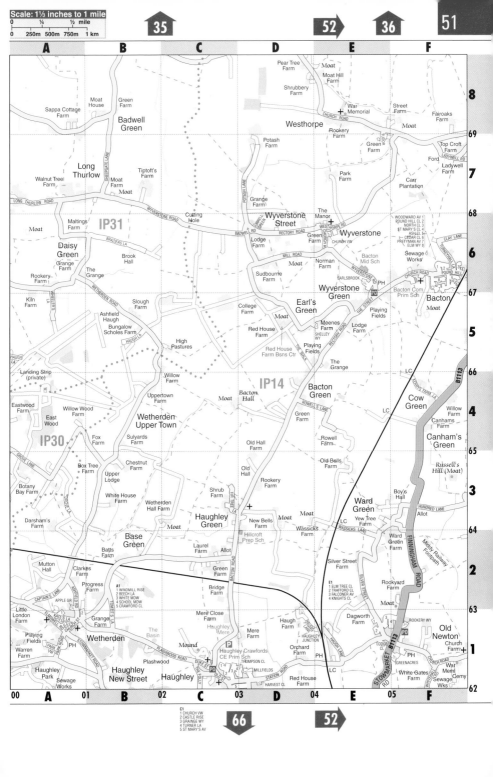

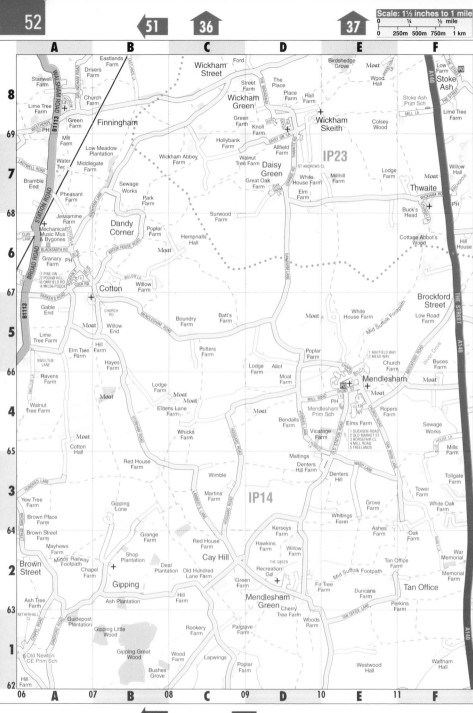

Scale: 1½ inches to 1 mile

0   ¼   ½ mile
0   250m 500m 750m 1 km

A **B** **C** **D** **E** **F**

8

Stanwell Farm

Lime Tree Farm

Green Farm

Finningham

WALSHAM ROAD B1113

CHURCH

PH

WESTHORPE RD

Eastlands Farm

Drivers Farm

Church Farm

EASTGATE LA

Ford

Wickham Street

Street Farm

Wickham Green

THE BROADWAY

Green Farm

Knoll Farm

The Place

Place Farm

Hall Farm

Birdshedge Grove

Moat

Wood Hall

Wickham Skeith

Colsey Wood

Stoke Ash Prim Sch

A140

Stoke Ash

Low Farm

THE STREET

Lime Tree Farm

69

Mill Farm

Low Meadow Plantation

Water Twr

Middlegate Farm

Bramble End

7

LADYWELL ROAD

STATION ROAD

BROAD ROAD

Hollybank Farm

Wickham Abbey Farm

Walnut Tree Farm

Daisy Green

Great Oak Farm

St Andrews Cl

White House Farm

Elm Farm

Millhill Farm

IP23

Lodge Farm

Moat

Thwaite

Willow Hall

Buck's Head

PH

68

Pheasant Farm

Jessamine Farm

Mechanical Music Mus & Bygones

CLAY LANE

BLACKSMITH RD

Granary Farm

PH

Sewage Works

Park Farm

Dandy Corner

Poplar Farm

Surwood Farm

Hempnalls Hall

Moat

DANNAH LANE

Cottage

Abbot's Wood

Hill House

6

1 PINE VW
2 POUND HILL
3 OAKFIELD RD
4 MILE6 PDDCK

COCK RD

PARKER'S ROAD

Cotton

Willow Farm

WILLOW LA

Moat

Brockford Street

Low Road Farm

67

Gable End

CHURCH RD

MENDLESHAM ROAD

Boundry Farm

Batt's Farm

Moat

White House Farm

Mid Suffolk Footpath

5

Lime Tree Farm

Elm Tree Farm

Hill Farm

Willow End

Hayes Farm

Potters Farm

Lodge Farm

Allot

Poplar Farm

1 MAYFIELD WAY
2 MEAD WAY

Church Farm

CHAPEL

River Dove

Buces Farm

66

SWILLTUB LANE

Ravens Farm

Moat

Lodge Farm

Moat

Moat

Eldens Lane Farm

Moat

Mendlesham

Moat

Mendlesham Prim Sch

PH

GLEBE WY

Ropers Farm

Sewage Works

A140

4

Walnut Tree Farm

Moat

Whicks Farm

Bendalls Farm

Vicarage Farm

Elms Farm

OLD STATION ROAD

1 DUCKSEN ROAD
2 OLD MARKET ST
3 HORSEFAIR CL
4 MILL ROAD
5 FREELANDS

HOUSE LA

Mills Farm

65

Cotton Hall

Red House Farm

Wimble

Maltings

Denters Hill Farm

Denters Hill

WASH LANE

Tollgate Farm

3

Yew Tree Farm

Brown Place Farm

Brown Street Farm

Gipping Lone

Martins Farm

IP14

Whitings Farm

Grove Farm

Tower Farm

White Oak Farm

64

Mayhews Farm

Middy Railway Footpath

Grange Farm

Red House Farm

Kerseys Farm

Hawkins Farm

Willow Farm

Ashes Farm

Oak Farm

War Memorial

2

Brown Street

Chapel Farm

Shop Plantation

Deal Plantation

Old Hundred Lane Farm

Cay Hill

THE GREEN

Recreation Gd

Green Farm

Fir Tree Farm

Tan Office Farm

Duncans Farm

Tan Office

Memorial Farm

Mid Suffolk Footpath

63

Ash Tree Farm

NETHERHALL CL

Guidepost Plantation

Ash Plantation

Hill Farm

Mendlesham Green

Cherry Tree Farm

Woods Farm

TAN OFFICE LANE

Perkins Farm

1

Old Newton CE Prim Sch

Gipping Little Wood

Gipping Great Wood

Rookery Farm

Wood Farm

Palgrave Farm

Lapwings

Poplar Farm

Westwood Hall

Waltham Hall

62

Hill Farm

Bushes Grove

A 06 **A** 07 **B** 08 **C** 09 **D** 10 **E** 11 **F**

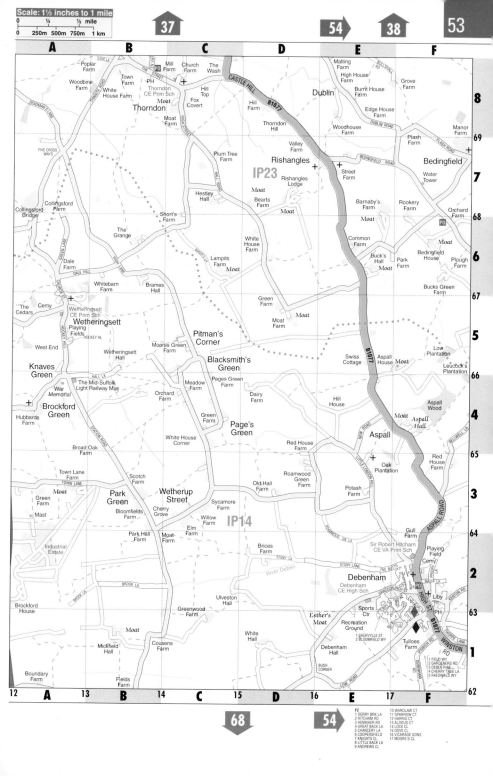

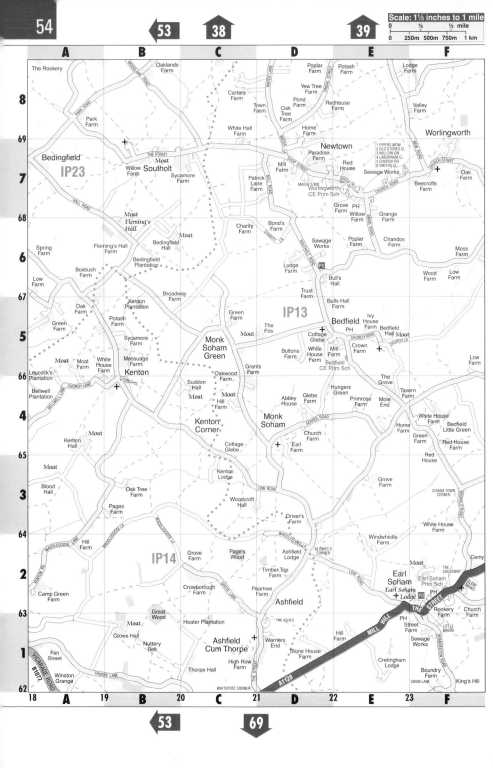

Scale: 1⅓ inches to 1 mile

0   ¼   ½ mile
0   250m 500m 750m 1 km

A   B   C   D   E   F

8

The Rookery

Oaklands Farm

Carters Farm

Poplar Farm

Potash Farm

Lodge Farm

Town Farm

Yew Tree Farm

Pond Farm

Redhouse Farm

Valley Farm

Park Farm

White Hall Farm

Oak Tree Farm

Home Farm

Worlingworth

69

Bedingfield

IP23

THE STREET

Moat

Southolt

Newtown

Paradise Farm

Red House

1 PIPERS MDW
2 OLD STORES CL
3 WILLOW GN
4 LABURNUM CL
5 CHURCH RD
6 SMITHS CL

Sewage Works

Oak Farm

Willow Farm

Sycamore Farm

Patrick Lane Farm

Mill Farm

MAISIE'S MD
Worlingworth
CE Prim Sch

Grove Farm

PH
Willow Farm

Beecrofts Farm

7

HALL ROAD

Moat
Fleming's Hall

Charity Farm

Bond's Farm

CHARITY LA

Grange Farm

68

Fleming's Hall Farm

Bedingfield Hall

Moat

Sewage Works

Poplar Farm

Chandos Farm

Moss Farm

Spring Farm

Boxbush Farm

Bedingfield Plantation

Lodge Farm

P

Wood Farm

Low Farm

6

Low Farm

Broadway Farm

Kenton Plantation

Green Farm

Bull's Hall

Trust Farm

67

Oak Farm

Potash Farm

The Firs

Bulls Hall Farm

IP13

Bedfield

Ivy House Farm

Green Farm

Sycamore Farm

Monk Soham Green

Moat

Cottage Glebe

PH
CHURCH ROAD

Bedfield Hall

Moat
CHURCH LA

Low Farm

5

Moat
Messuage Farm

White House Farm

Boltons Farm

White House Farm

Mill Farm

Crown Farm

Leucock's Plantation

Kenton

Oakwood Farm

Grants Farm

Bedfield CE Prim Sch

The Grove

66

Bellwell Plantation

CHURCH LANE

CHURCH CL

Suddon Hall

Moat
Hill Farm

Abbey House

Glebe Farm

Hungers Green

Primrose Farm

Tavern Farm

Mole End

Moat

BELLWELL LANE

Kenton Corner

Monk Soham

SCHOOL ROAD

White House Farm

Bedfield Little Green

4

Moat

Kenton Hall

Cottage Glebe

Earl Farm

Church Farm

Home Farm

Green Farm

Red House Farm

65

Moat

Blood Hall

Pages Farm

Kenton Lodge

LOW ROAD

Grove Farm

Red House

3

Oak Tree Farm

Woodcroft Hall

Driver's Farm

SOHAM TOWN CORNER

WADDLEGOOSE LANE

WADDLEGOOSE LA

WADDLEGOOSE LA

White House Farm

64

Hill Farm

Grove Farm

Page's Wood

Ashfield Lodge

CLOWES'S CORNER

Windwhistle Farm

Cemy

2

KENTON RD

IP14

Crowborough Farm

GROVE LANE

Timber Top Farm

LOW ROAD

Moat

THE CAUSEWAY

Earl Soham

Earl Soham Prim Sch

GLEBE MEWS

Camp Green Farm

Peartree Farm

Ashfield

Earl Soham Lodge

P

PH

Rookery Farm

Church Farm

63

Great Wood

Heater Plantation

THE ASHES

MILL HILL

THE STREET

PH

Street Farm

LITTLE GREEN

Grows Hall

Moat

Warners End

Hill Farm

Cretingham Lodge

Sewage Works

1

Fen Street

VICARAGE ROAD

Nuttery Belt

Ashfield Cum Thorpe

High Row Farm

Stone House Farm

Boundry Farm

SWAN LANE

King's Hill

Winston Grange

B1077

THORPE LANE

Thorpe Hall

WHITEPOST CORNER

A1120

BRANDESTON ROAD

REDFIELD ROAD

62

18   A   19   B   20   C   21   D   22   E   23   F

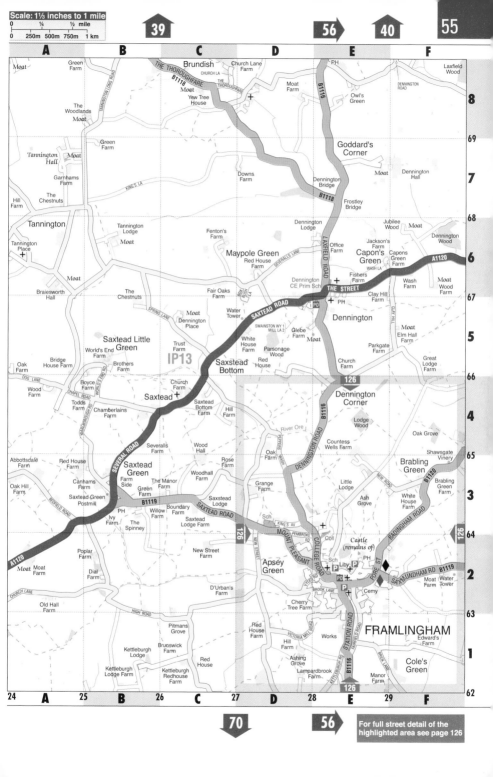

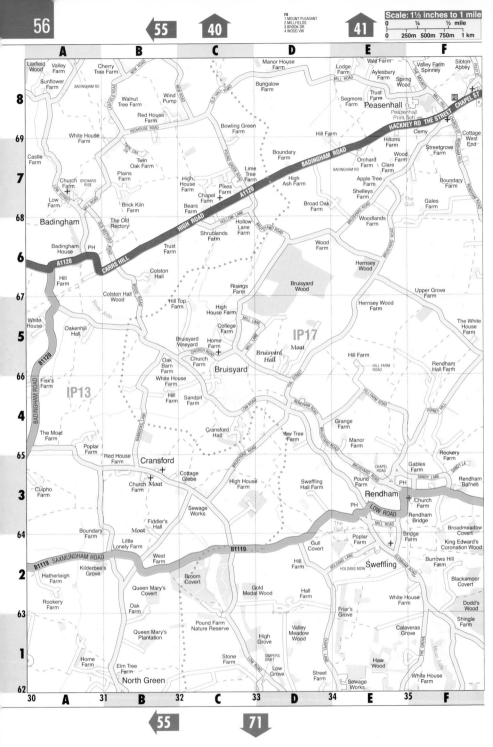

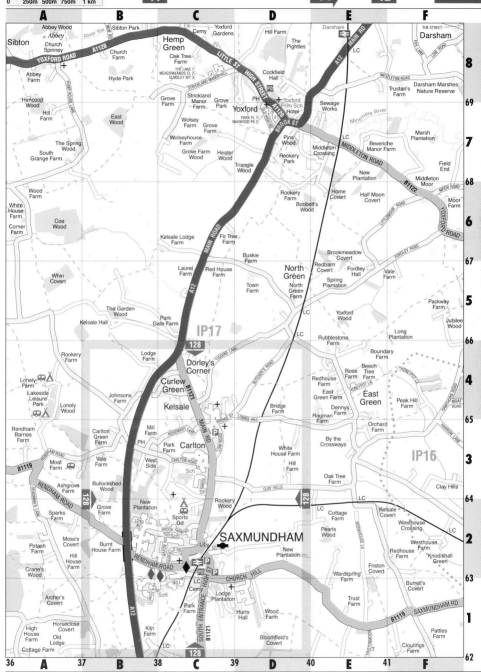

A   **B**   **C**   **D**   **E**   **F**

Abbey Wood
Sibton Park
River Yox
THE STREET
Darsham
Sibton
Abbey
Church
Spinney
YOXFORD ROAD
A1120
Hemp
Green
Church
Farm
Cemy
Yoxford
Gardens
Hill Farm
The
Pightles
Darsham
LC
LOW ROAD
LONG LA
8

Abbey
Farm
+
Hyde Park
Oak Tree
Farm
THE LANE 1
MEADOWLANDS CL 2
ELMSLEY WY 3
WESTLETON ROAD
Trustan's
Farm
Darsham Marshes
Nature Reserve

Hencoop
Wood
Grove
Farm
Strickland Manor Hill
Grove
Park
Yoxford
PH
PARK PL 1
OAKWOOD PK 2
+ Yoxford
Prim Sch
Yoxford
Hotel
Sewage
Works
Minsmere River
Marsh
Plantation
69

Hill
Farm
East
Wood
Strickland
Manor
Farm
Wolsey
Farm
Grove
Farm
PO
Cockfield
Hall
Middleton
Crossing
MIDDLETON ROAD
Beveriche
Manor Farm
Field
End
7

The Spring
Wood
Wolseyhouse
Farm
Grove Farm
Wood
Heater
Wood
Pins
Wood
Rookery
Park
New
Plantation
Half Moon
Covert
Middleton
Moor
B1122
MOOR ROAD
Moor
Farm
68

South
Grange Farm
Triangle
Wood
Rookery
Farm
Bobbett's
Wood
Home
Covert
Half Moon
Covert
LITTLEMOOR ROAD
YOXFORD ROAD
6

Wood
Farm
White
House
Farm
Coe
Wood
Kelsale Lodge
Farm
Fir Tree
Farm
Brookmeadow
Covert
FORDLEY ROAD
67

Corner
Farm
Laurel
Farm
Red House
Farm
Buskie
Farm
North
Green
Redbarn
Covert
Fordley
Hall
Vale
Farm
5

Whin
Covert
The Garden
Wood
Town
Farm
North
Green
Farm
Spring
Plantation
Yoxford
Wood
Packway
Farm
Jubilee
Wood

Rookery
Farm
Kelsale Hall
Park Gate Farm
IP17
MAIN ROAD
A12
LC
Rubblestone
Farm
Long
Plantation
66

Lonely
Farm
Lakeside
Leisure
Park
Lonely
Wood
Lodge
Farm
128
Dorley's
Corner
TIGGINS LANE
BUTCHER'S ROAD
LC
Boundary
Farm
Rose
Tree
Farm
Beech
Tree
Farm
HONEYPOT LA
Peak Hill
Farm
HARROW LANE
MOAT ROAD
4

Rendham
Barnes
Farm
RENDHAM ROAD
Johnsons
Farm
Curlew
Green
B1121
Kelsale
BRIDGE ST
LOWES HILL
Bridge
Farm
Redhouse
Farm
East
Green Farm
Dennys
Farm
East
Green
Orchard
Farm
Clay Hills
65

Moat
Farm
Ashgrove
Farm
Carlton
Green
Farm
Mill
Farm
ROSEMARY LANE
PH
Park
Farm
Carlton
White
House Farm
Rogman
Farm
By the
Crossways
IP16
3

B1119
Sparks
Farm
Vale
Farm
West
Side
CARLTON ROAD
Sch
Hill
Farm
Oak Tree
Farm
LC
Kelsale
Covert
Westhouse
Crossing
LC
64

Grove
Farm
Bullockshed
Wood
128
New
Plantation
P
Rookery
Wood
CLAY HILLS
Cottage
Farm
WORKHOUSE LA
Westhouse
Farm
128
Redhouse
Farm
2

Moss's
Covert
Burnt
House Farm
LONG AV
Sports
Gd
BROOK
SAXFIELD
Pearls
Wood
Friston
Covert
Knodishall
Green

Potash
Farm
Hill House
Farm
RENDHAM ROAD
SOUTH RD
SAXMUNDHAM
Liby
New
Plantation
Wardspring
Farm
Burrell's
Covert
63

Crane's
Wood
MILL
Sch
PO
P
CHURCH HILL
Wood
Farm
Trust
Farm
B1119
SAXMUNDHAM RD
Pattles
Farm

High
House
Farm
Horseclose
Covert
Old
Lodge
A12
Kiln
Farm
LC
Cemy
Park
Farm
Lodge
Plantation
B1121
Hurts
Hall
Bloomfield's
Covert
FRISTON
Cloutings
Farm
1

Cottage
Farm
128
SOUTH ENTRANCE
62

36   **37**   **38**   **39**   **40**   **41**

A   **B**   **C**   **D**   **E**   **F**

72   **58**

For full street detail of the
highlighted area see page 128

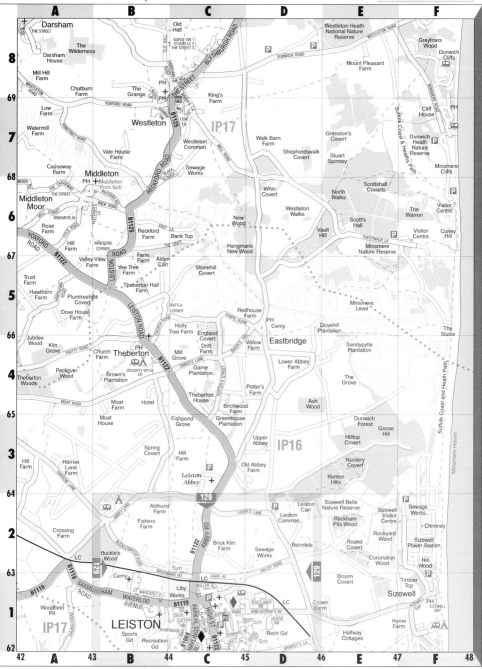

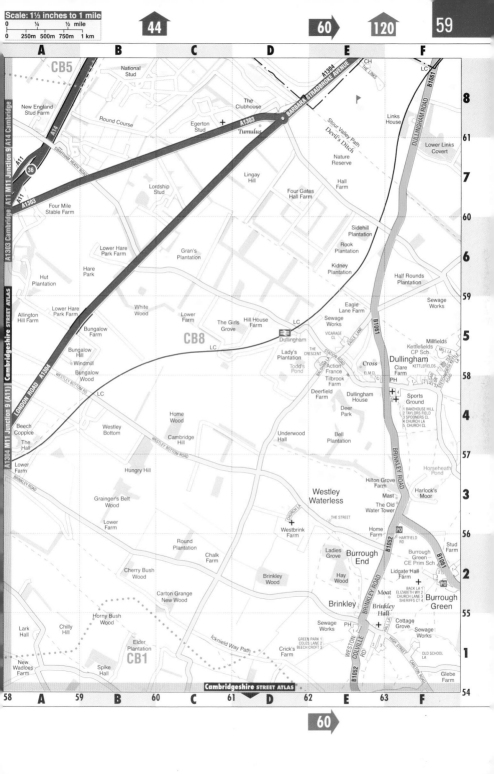

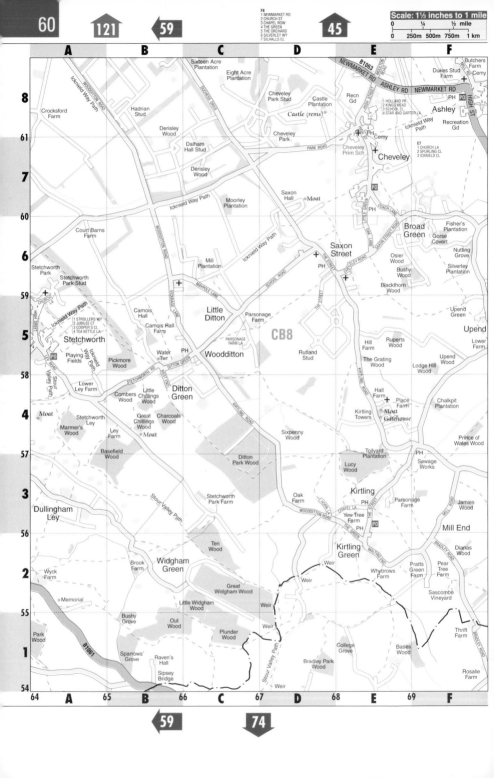

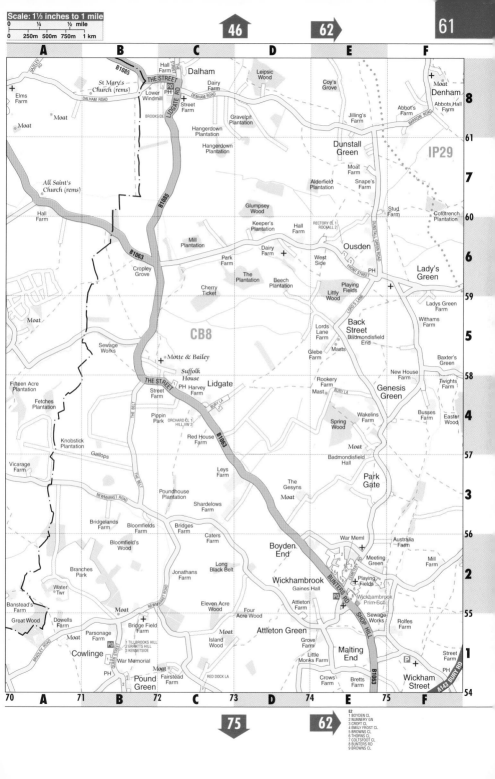

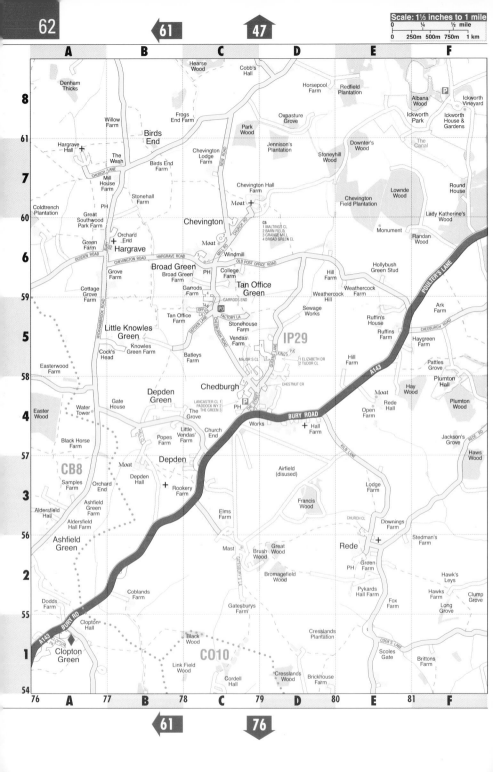

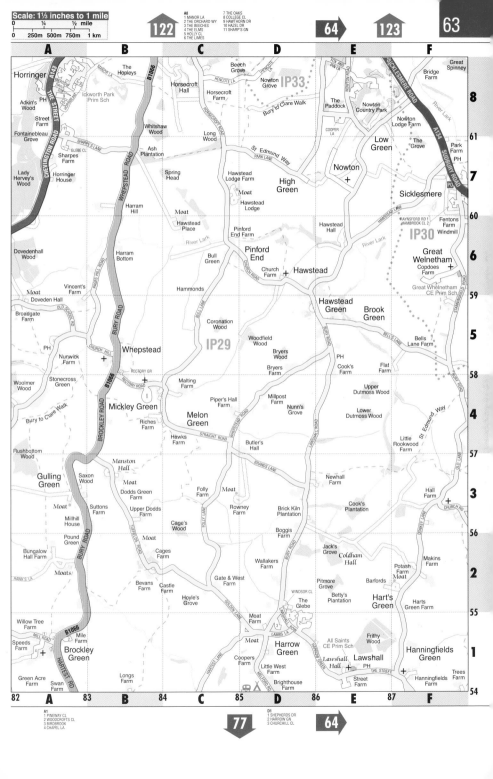

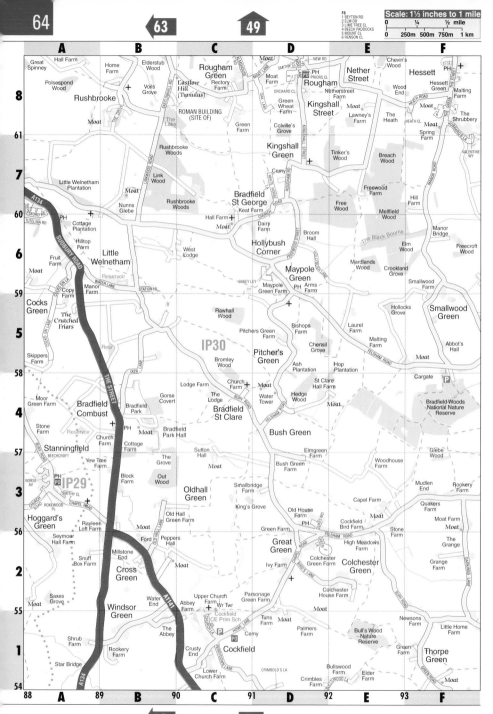

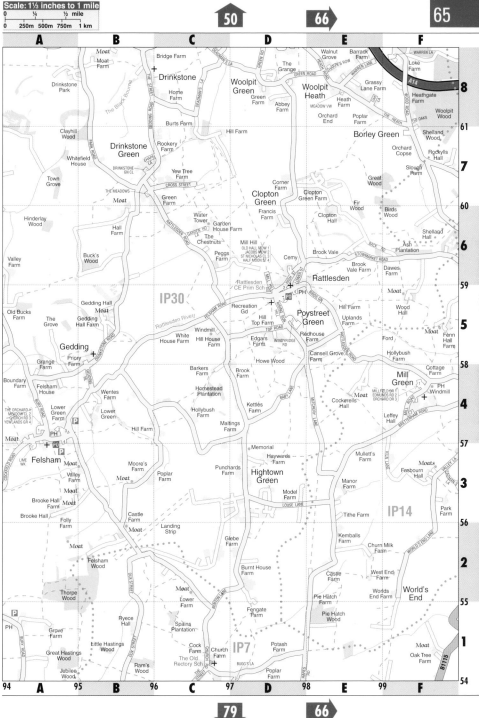

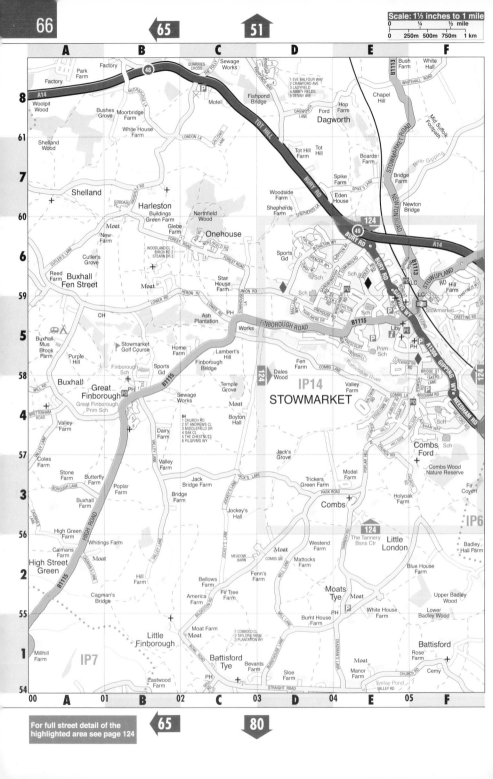

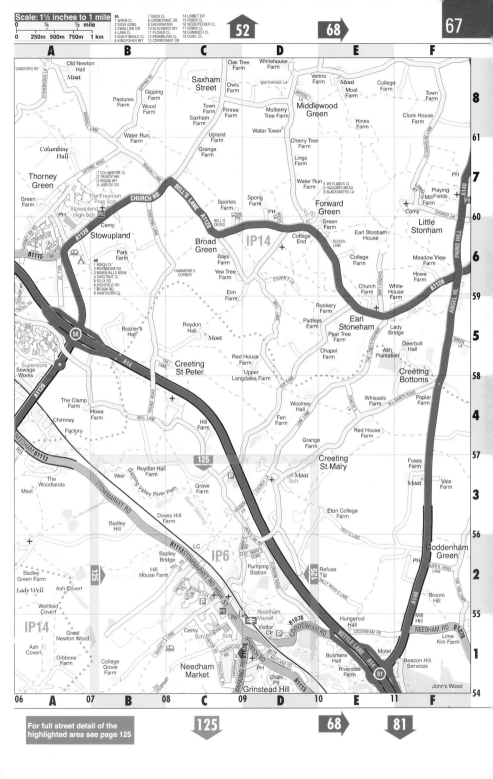

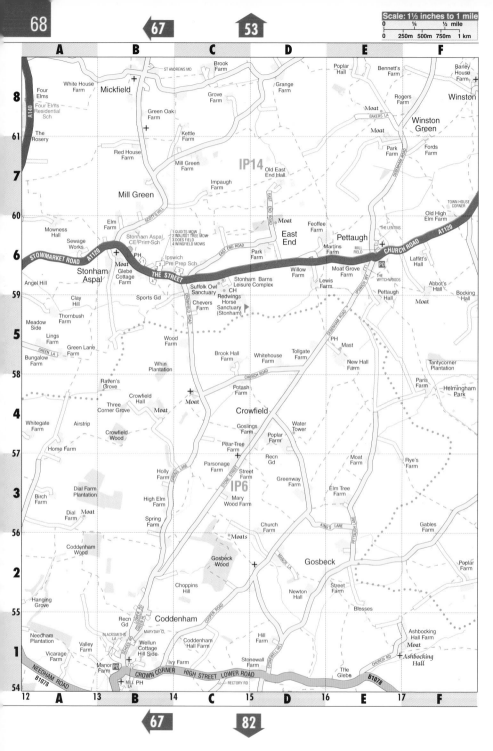

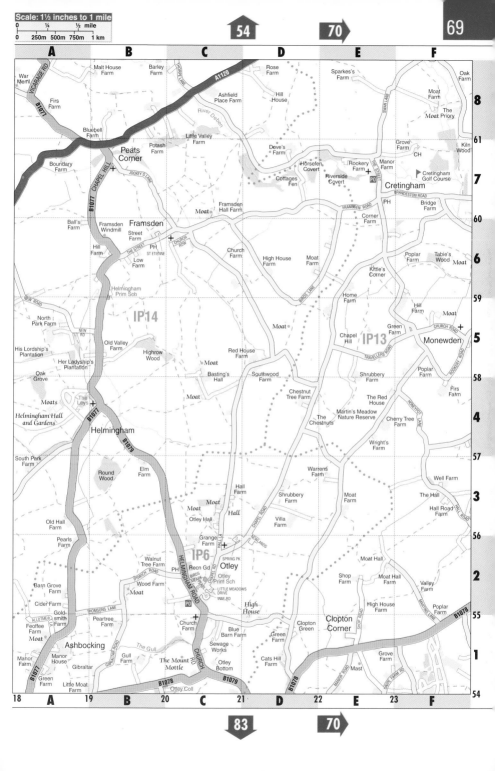

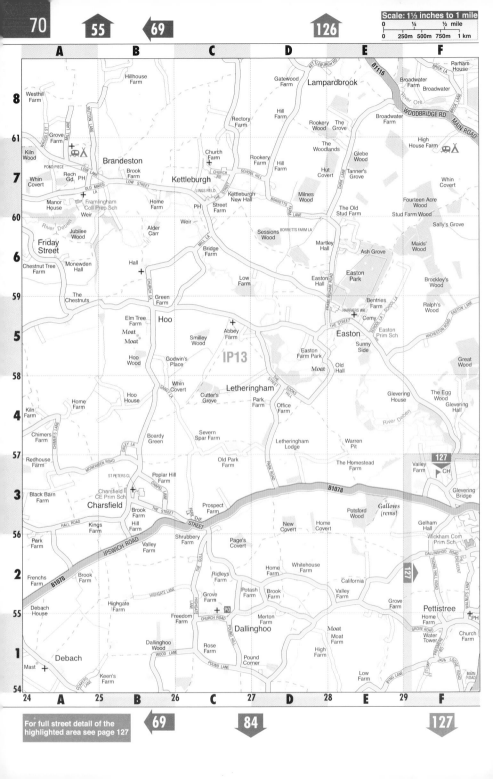

A **B** **C** **D** **E** **F**

Parham House

Brick LA

8

Westhill Farm

Hillhouse Farm

Gatewood Farm

Lampardbrook

KETTLEBURGH RD

B1116

River Ore.

Broadwater Farm

Broadwater

WOODBRIDGE RD

MAIN ROAD

61

Grove Farm

Kiln Wood

BRIDGE ST

MUTTON LANE

MILL LANE

Rectory Farm

Rookery Wood

The Grove

Broadwater Farm

High House Farm

POND PIECE

Brandeston

LOW ST

Church Farm

Hill Farm

The Woodlands

Glebe Wood

7

Rech Gd. PH

Brook Farm

Kettleburgh

CHURCH RD

SCHOOL HILL

Rookery Farm

Hill Farm

Hut Covert

Tanner's Grove

DARK LANE

Whin Covert

Whin Covert

OLD MAIDS LA

LOW STREET

LINGS FIELD

THE STREET

Kettleburgh New Hall

BORRETTS FARM

Milnes Wood

The Old Stud Farm

Fourteen Acre Wood

Framlingham Coll Prep Sch

60

Manor House

Home Farm

PH

Street Farm

Weir

LANE

Stud Farm Wood

Weir

Friday Street

River Deben

Jubilee Wood

Alder Carr

Sessions Wood

BORRETTS FARM LA

Martley Hall

Ash Grove

Sally's Grove

Maids' Wood

6

Chestnut Tree Farm

Monewden Hall

Hall

CHURCH LA

Bridge Farm

MILL LA

Low Farm

Easton Hall

Easton Park

Brockley's Wood

59

The Chestnuts

Green Farm

Hoo

Smiley Wood

Abbey Farm

FRAM UPLAND ROAD

Bentries Farm

HARRIERS WK

Cemy

SCHOOL SCHOOL LA

Ralph's Wood

EASTON LANE

5

Elm Tree Farm

Moat

Moat

Godwin's Place

IP13

Easton Farm Park

THE STREET

Easton

Easton Prim Sch

Sunny Side

NACHESTON ROAD

Great Wood

58

Hoo Wood

Whin Covert

SAND LA

Cutter's Grove

Letheringham

Moat

Old Hall

Glevering House

The Egg Wood

Glevering Hall

4

Kiln Farm

Home Farm

Hoo House

CHIMPS LANE

Boardy Green

Severn Spar Farm

Park Farm

COCKS HILL

Office Farm

River Deben

Warren Pit

The Homestead Farm

127

Valley Farm

CH

Glevering Bridge

57

Chimers Farm

Redhouse Farm

DAISY LA

MONEWDEN ROAD

ST PETERS CL

Poplar Hill Farm

Old Park Farm

Letheringham Lodge

PARK ROAD

B1078

127

3

Black Barn Farm

Charsfield CE Prim Sch

Charsfield

CHAPEL LANE

THE STREET

Prospect Farm

Potsford Wood

Gallows (rems)

Gelham Hall

Wickham Com Prim Sch

56

Park Farm

Kings Farm

Brook Farm

Hill Farm

IPSWICH ROAD

Valley Farm

Shrubbery Farm

THE BULL

Page's Covert

New Covert

Home Covert

DALLINGHOO ROAD

THORPE HALL LANE

DALLINGHOO FOREST

CRESCENT

2

Frenchs Farm

Brook Farm

B1078

HIGHGATE LANE

Ridleys Farm

Whitehouse Farm

Home Farm

California

Valley Farm

Grove Farm

127

Pettistree

Home Farm

JAVA LANE

Debach House

Highgate Farm

Grove Farm

HIGHGATE LANE

CHURCH ROAD

PO

Freedom Farm

Potash Farm

Brook Farm

Merton Farm

GROVE ROAD

Church Farm

PH

55

Mast

OGDENS LANE

Keen's Farm

Dallinghoo Wood

WOOD LANE

Rose Farm

POUND HILL

Dallinghoo

Moat

Moat Farm

High Farm

Water Tower

PRESSINGS

STUMP LANE

MAIN ROAD

1

Debach

Pound Corner

POUND LANE

BYING ROAD

Low Farm

54

A 24 25 **B** 26 **C** 27 **D** 28 **E** 29 **F**

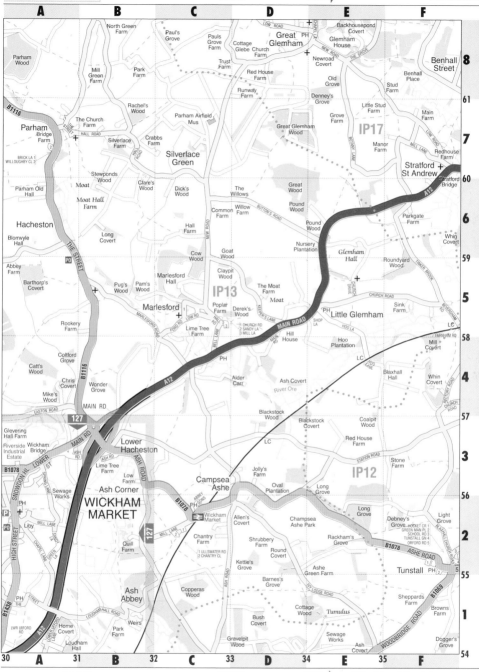

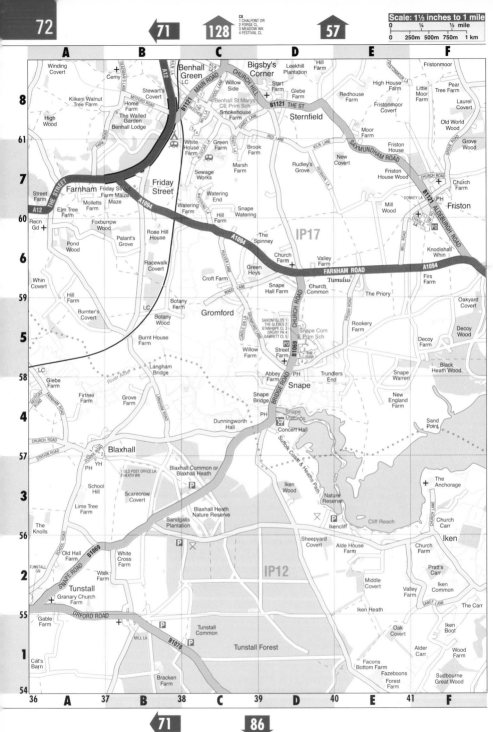

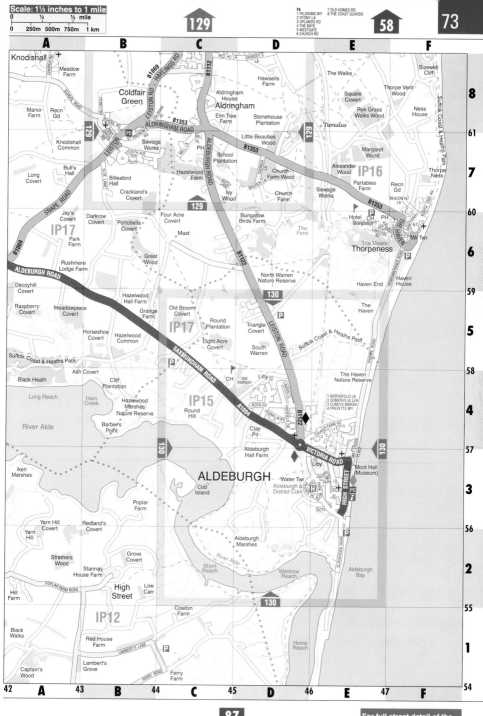

60

Cambridgeshire STREET ATLAS

A B C D E F

River Stour
Ford
B1061
Weir

Carlton
Hall Farm
Moat
ASH ROAD
BRUNKLEY RD
CHURCH RD
CARLTON GREEN RD

Waterfield Barn Farm
Mill Farm
WATER LA
THE STREET
FOX GN

8

Handy Bar Grove

Matthews Farm
EVERGREEN LA

CB8

53

Church Farm

Carlton Wood

Great Bradley

Moat

MATTHEWS LA

Fox Farm
CLARENDALE EST

Doley Wood

7

Ever Green

THURLOW ROAD

Stour Valley Path

52

Lopham's Hall Farm

Hart Wood

Little Bradley

BROAD ROAD

6

Carlton Green

Lopham's Wood

Moat

Mill Mound

Almshouses

Little Thurlow Green

Wadgell's Wood

Finchley Farm

CHURCH ROAD
Thurlow CE Prim Sch

51

Gover's Grove

Girton Farm

Sewage Works

Little Thurlow

Grove Wood

Temple End Plantation

Temple End

School House

Great Thurlow

Bury Road

5

Temple End Stream

PH

Manor Farm

Drift Side

Foxburrow Wood

Temple End Farm

Wasteland Plantation

THE STREET

Goldings Farm

Great Thurlow Hall

CB1

The New Plantation

Dowsett Wood

Windmill

PH

Playing Fields

Trundley Wood

50

Cadge's Wood

Smoothies Plantation

Moat

Glebe Plantation

WEST END LANE

CB9

Willow Hall Plantation

Ganwick Wood

4

North Wood

Tuffill's Plantation

Hunts Park Farm

WITHERSFIELD ROAD

WRATLOW RD

Gravel Pit Plantation

Stour Valley Path

49

Exhibition Farm

Littley Wood

The Spinney

High Noon Plantation

High Noon Plantation

Hungry Hill Plantation

Nursery Plantation

Hill Wood

Pelican House Farm

Greenfields Farm

THE STREET

Maltings Farm

3

Lawn Farm

Lawn Wood

SOPHER LANE

Stour Brook

Charity Farm

Moat

Bittons Farm

Abbacy Wood

Moor Pasture Plantation

Jarvis Hill

Moor Pasture Farm

Paradise Farm

WITHERSFIELD ROAD

Rook Tree Farm

Hall Farm

THURLOW RD

Ford

PH

Wash Farm

48

Sports Ground

PH

Withersfield

Recreation Gd

Lilley Farm

CHURCH ST

TURNPIKE HL

PH

Great Wratting

Church End

SCHOOL RD

P

Chimney Factory

2

HOLLOW HL

SILVER ST

HORSEHEATH RD

Church Farm

Hall Farm

GREENS RD

HOMESTALL CR

Burton Ley Plantation

Water Twr

Little Wratting

OLD HAVERHILL RD

Sports Gd

B1061 HAVERHILL RD

Silver Street Farm

Sewage Works

Howe Wood

Norney Plantation

Reservoir

A143

Hilltop Farm

47

Spring Grove Farm

A1307 Cambridge

132

Hanchet End

Bridge End

BELLINGS RD

WITHERSFIELD RD

133

Boyton Hall

Boyton Hall Farm

PH

WRATTING RD HAVERHILL RD

Great Wilsey Farm

Kedington

1

A1307

Hanchet Hall Farm

132

HANCHET END

CHISWELL

BAINE'S DONE?

HAWTHORN

WITHERSFIELD RD

A1307

ABBOTS RD
CHAPEL DR

Samuel Ward Upper Sch & Tech Coll

Great Field Plantation

Moat

46

MELLIS CL 1
LANGHAM WY 2
NOTLEY DR 3
HOPTON RI 4

64 A 65 B 66 C 67 D 68 E 69 F

88
For full street detail of the highlighted area see pages 132 and 133

132

133

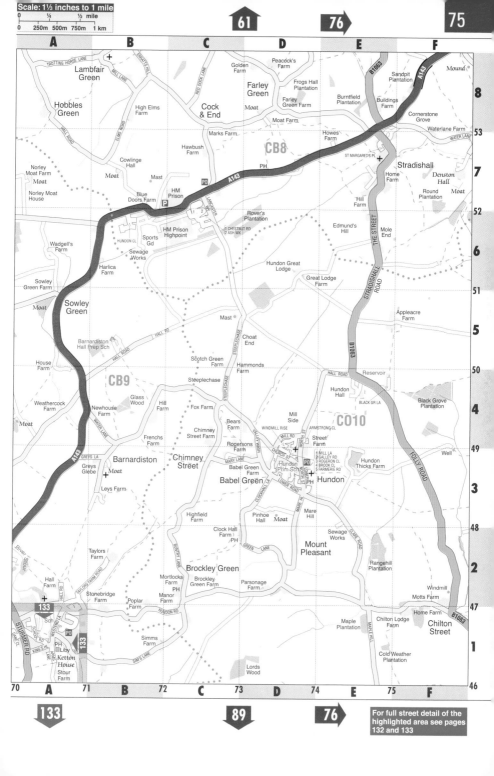

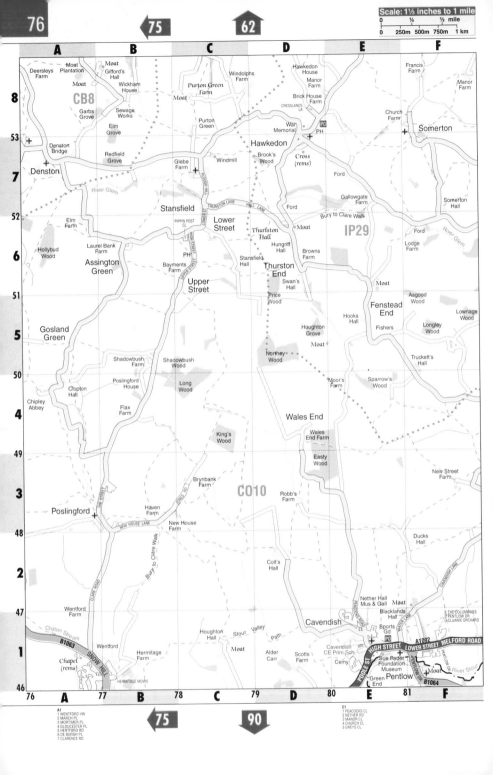

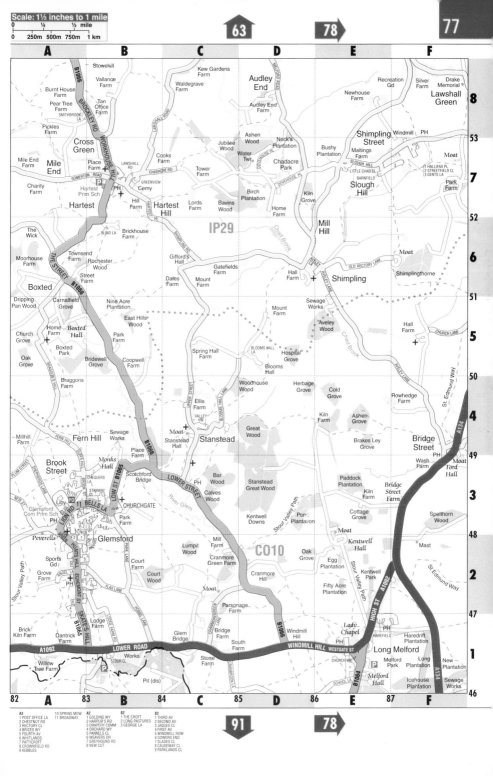

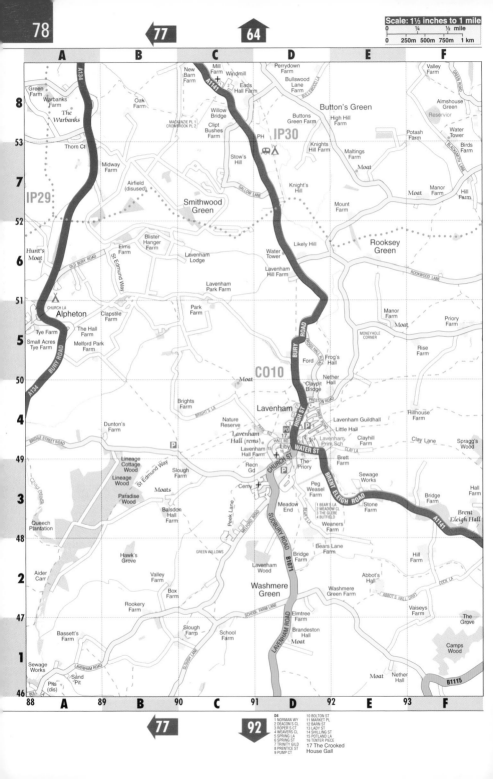

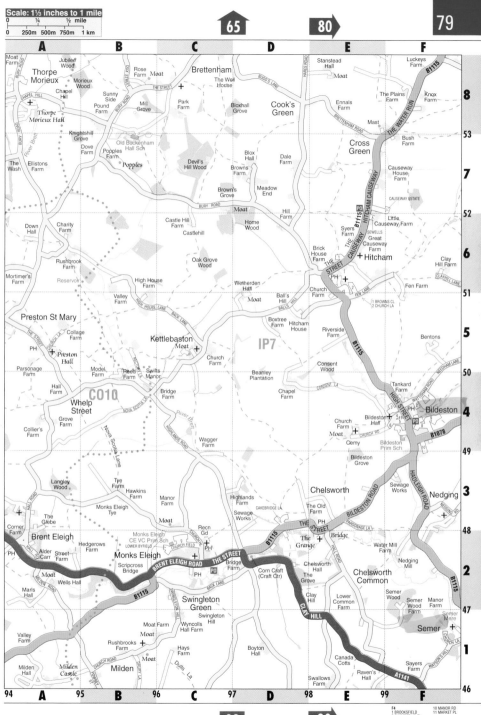

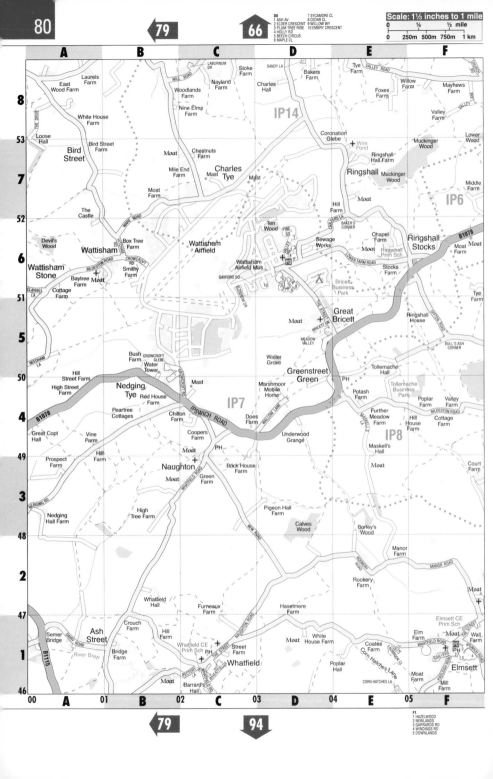

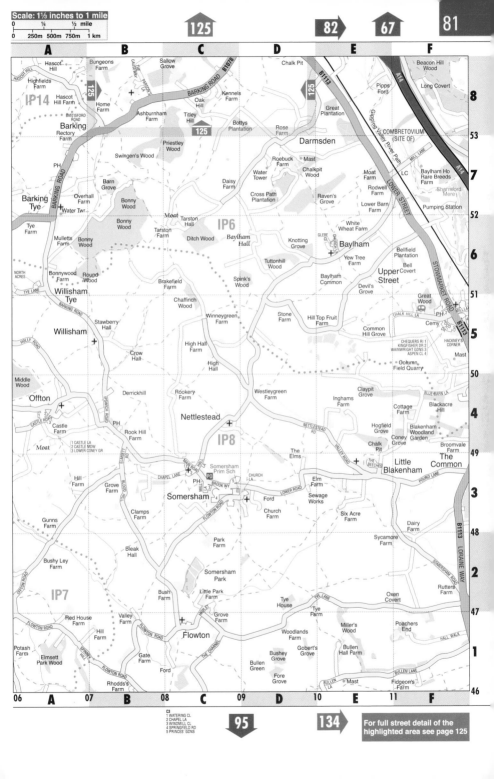

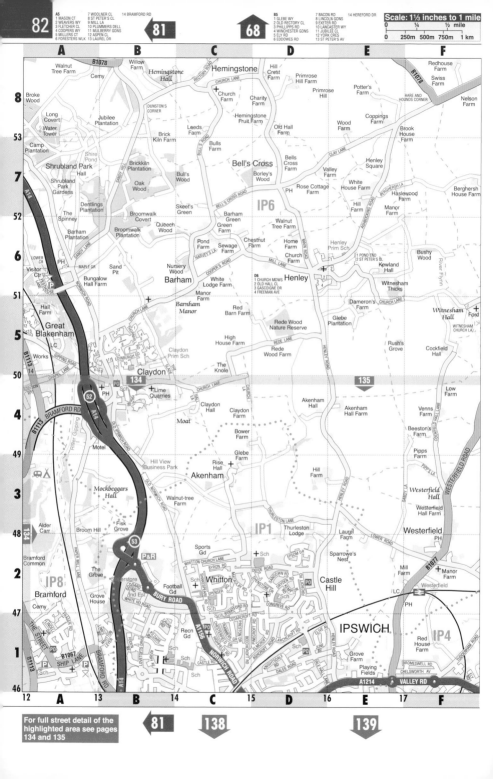

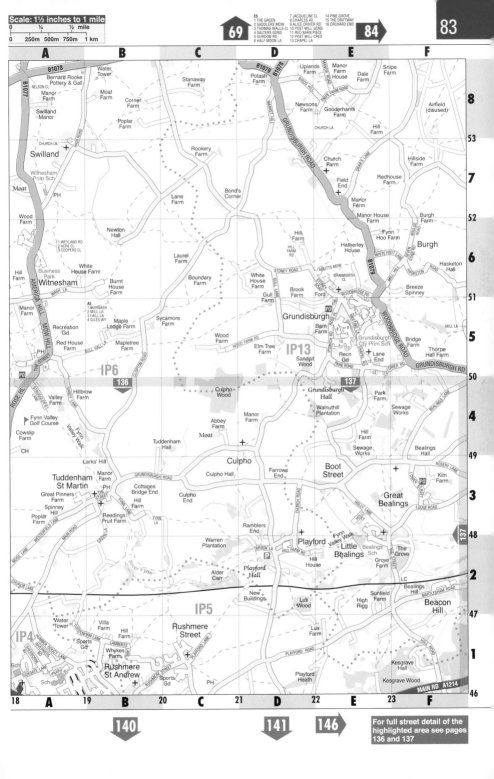

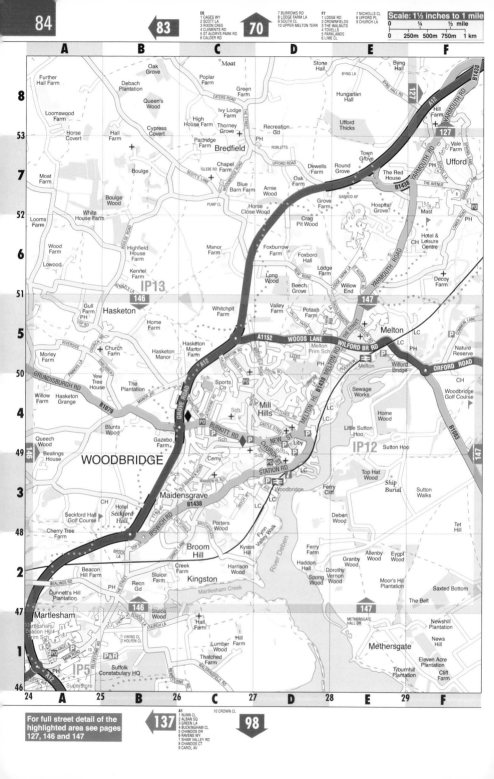

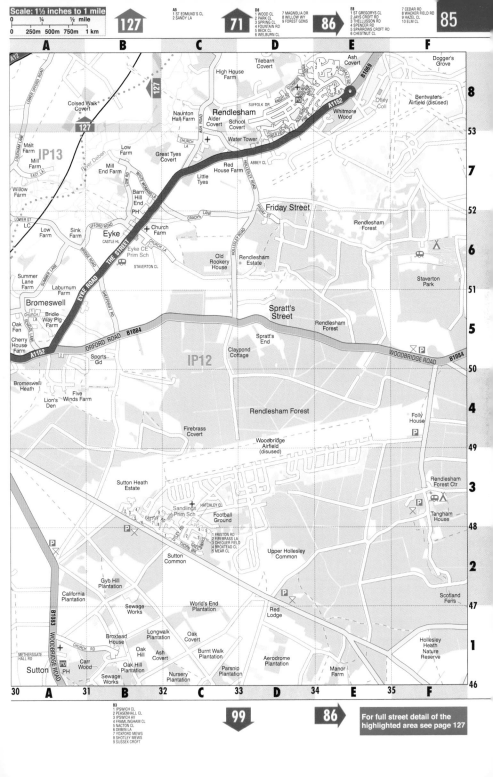

127

A5
1 ST EDMUND'S CL
2 SANDY LA

71

D8
1 WOOD CL
2 PARK CL
3 SPRING CL
4 FOUNTAIN RD
5 BECK CL
6 WELBURN CL

7 MAGNOLIA DR
8 WILLOW WY
9 FOREST GDNS

86

E8
1 ST GREGORYS CL
2 JAYS CROFT RD
3 THELLUSSON RD
4 SPENCER RD
5 SPARROWS CROFT RD
6 CHESTNUT CL

7 CEDAR RD
8 WACKER FIELD RD
9 HAZEL CL
10 ELM CL

85

B3
1 IPSWICH CL
2 PEASENHALL CL
3 IPSWICH AV
4 FRAMLINGHAM CL
5 NACTON CL
6 DEBEN LA
7 YOXFORD MEWS
8 SHOTLEY MEWS
9 SUSSEX CROFT

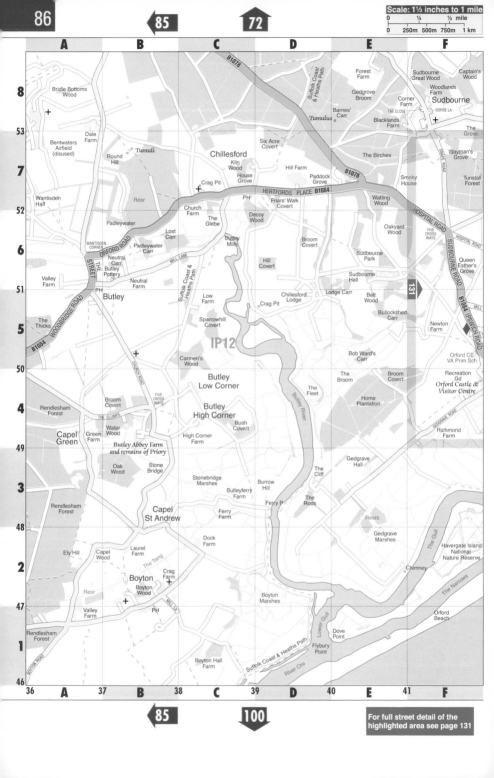

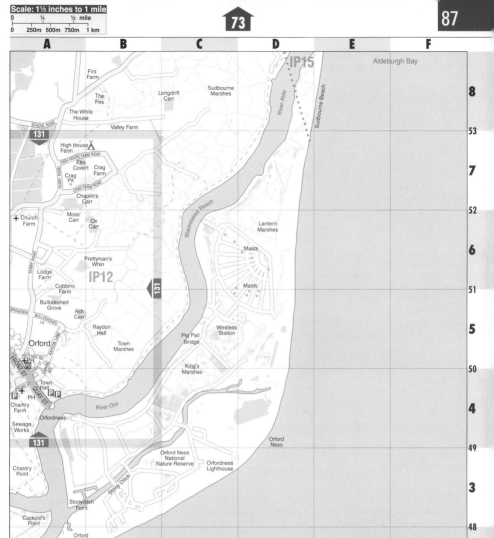

For full street detail of the highlighted area see page 131

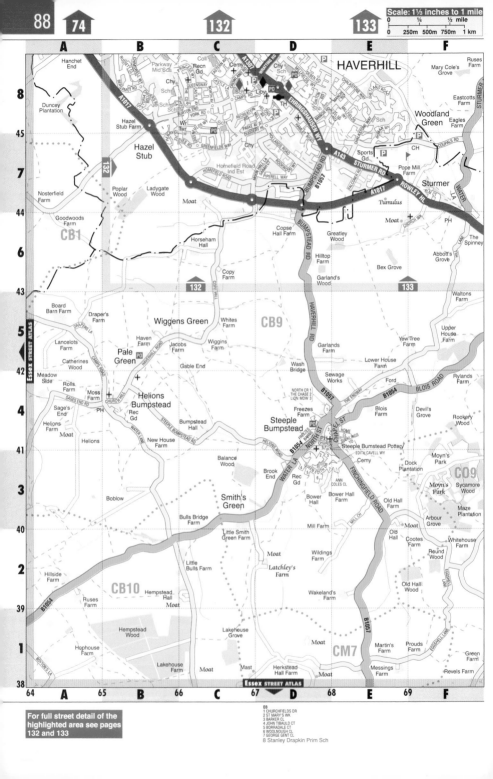

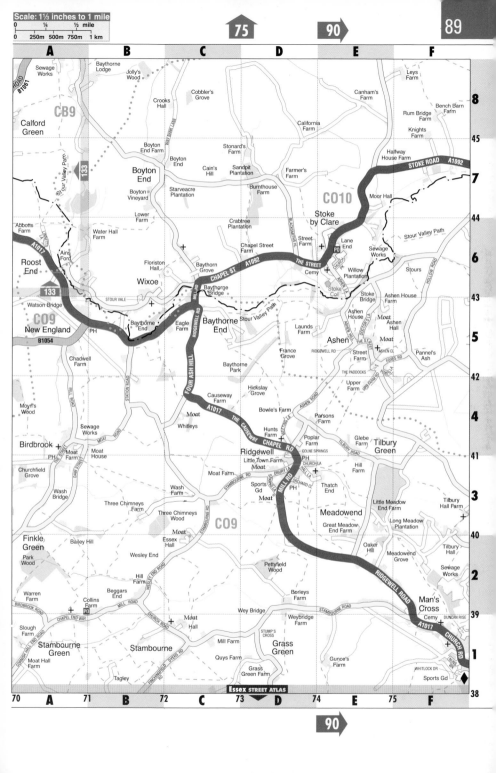

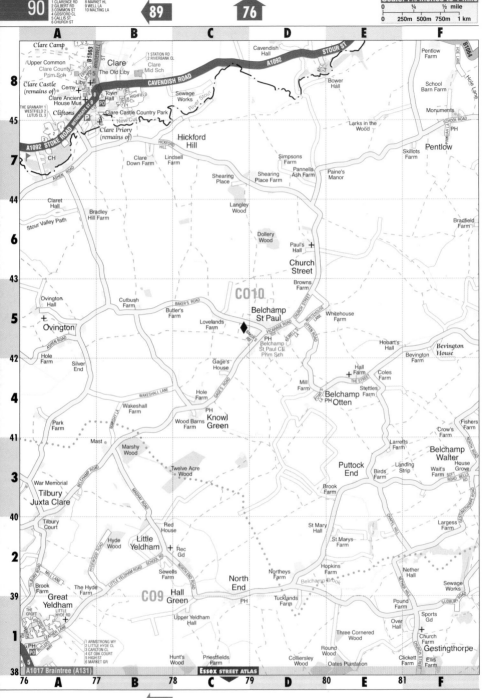

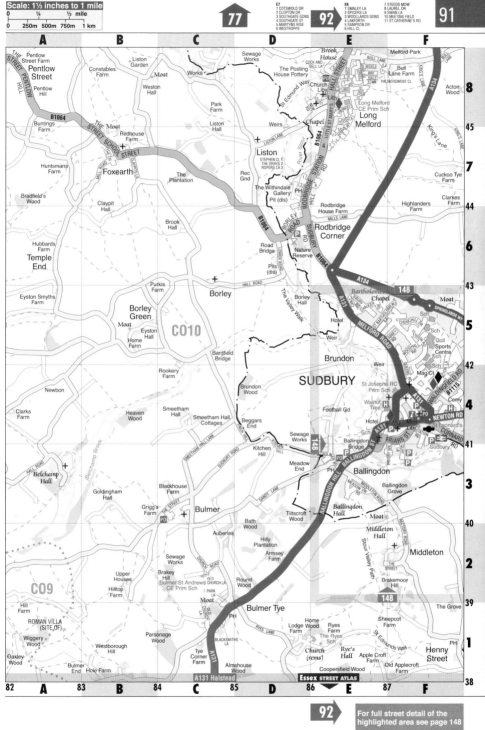

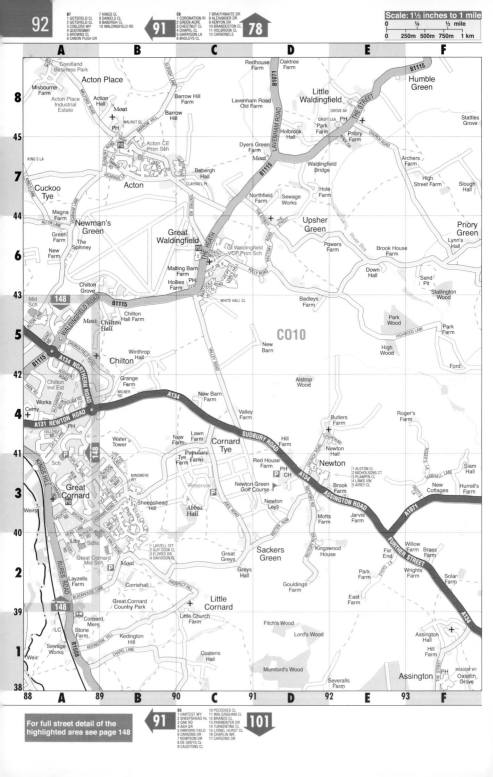

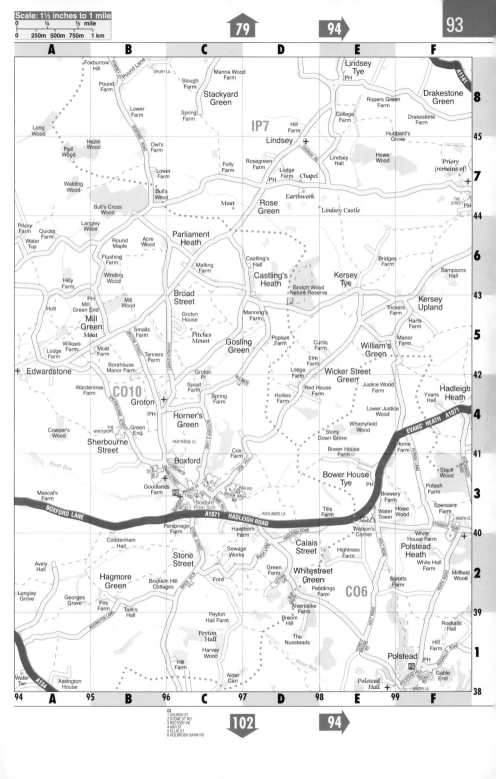

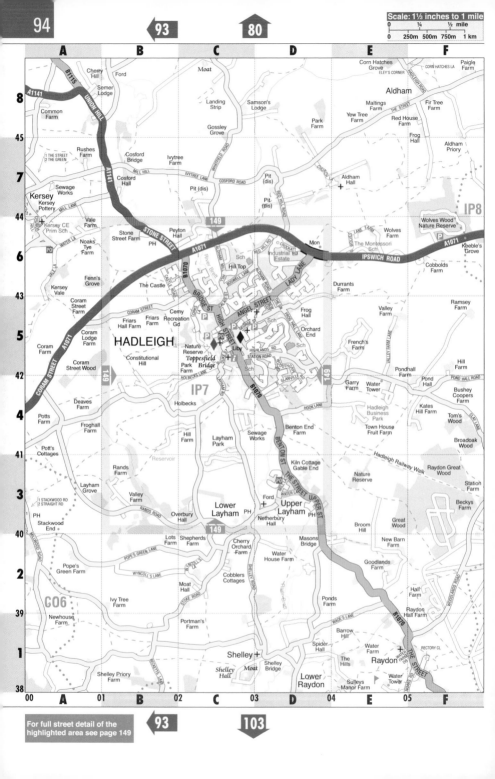

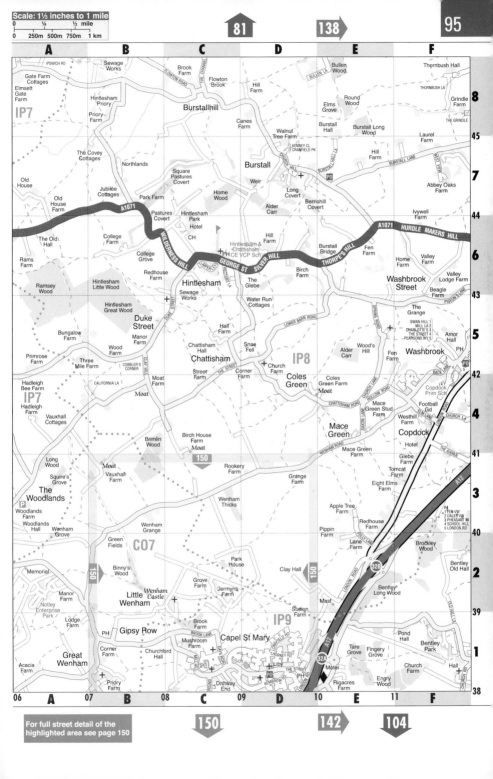

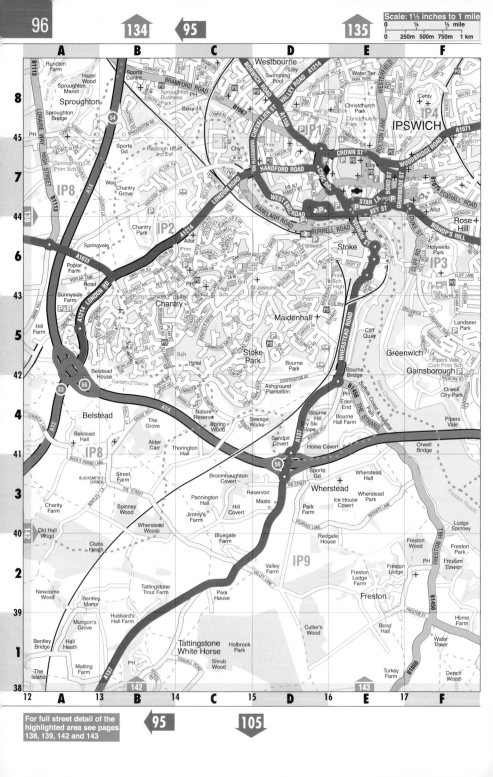

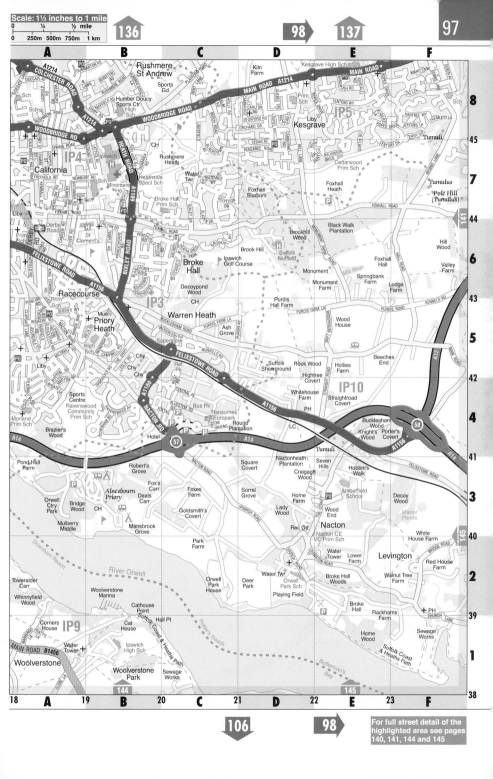

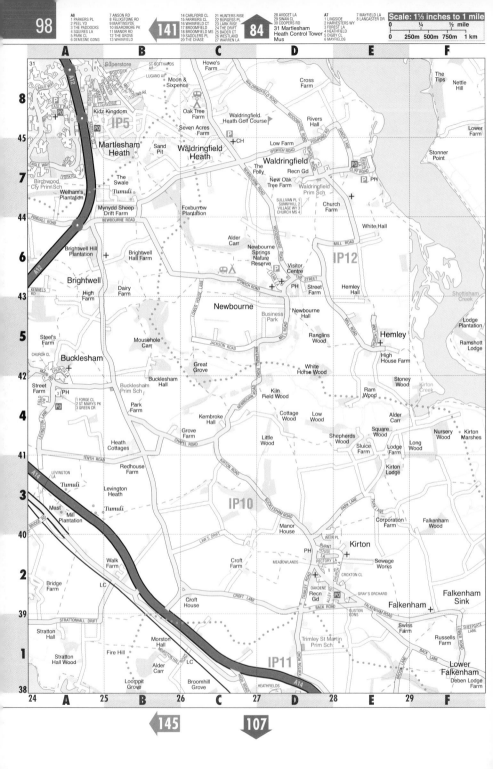

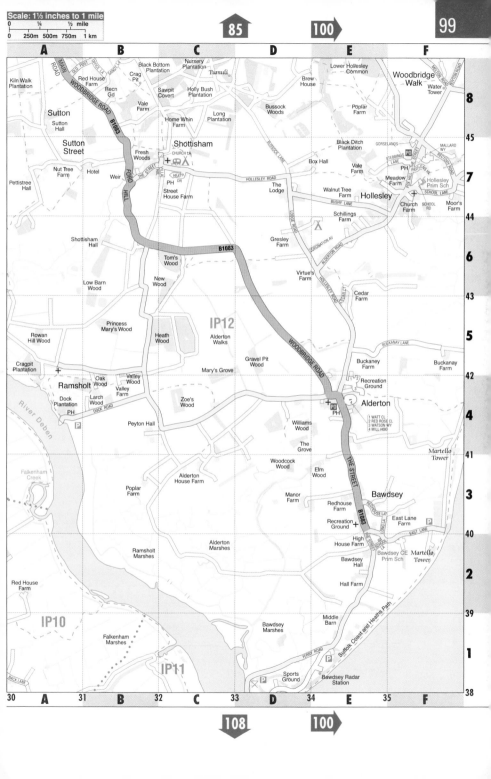

99

86

Scale: 1½ inches to 1 mile

0   ¼   ½ mile
0   250m 500m 750m 1 km

A   B   C   D   E   F

Oak
Hill

HM Prison

Sports
Ground

Grove
House

The
Grove

IP12

River Ore

8

45

+

Hollesley Bay
Colony
(HM Young Offender
Institution)

Hollesley
Bay

7

Orford
Haven

44

Sewage
Works

Oxley
Dairy

Oxley
Marshes

North Weir
Point

6

43

P

Shingle
Street

5

Martello
Tower

Suffolk Coast & Heaths
Path

42

4

41

3

40

2

39

1

38

36   A   37   B   38   C   39   D   40   E   41   F

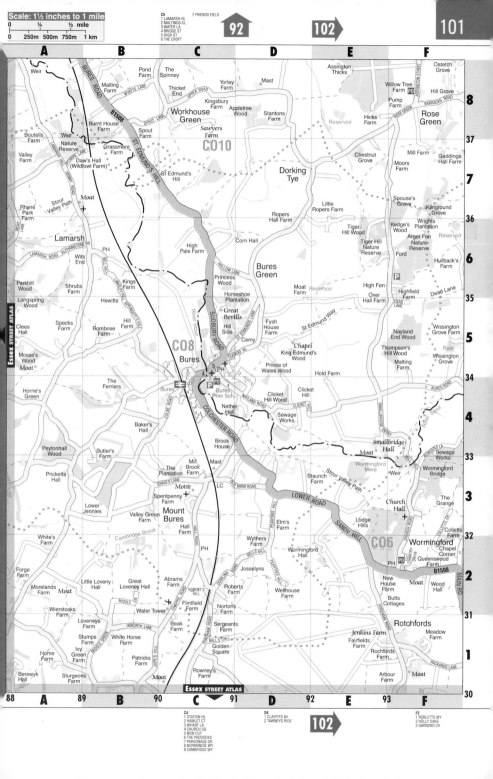

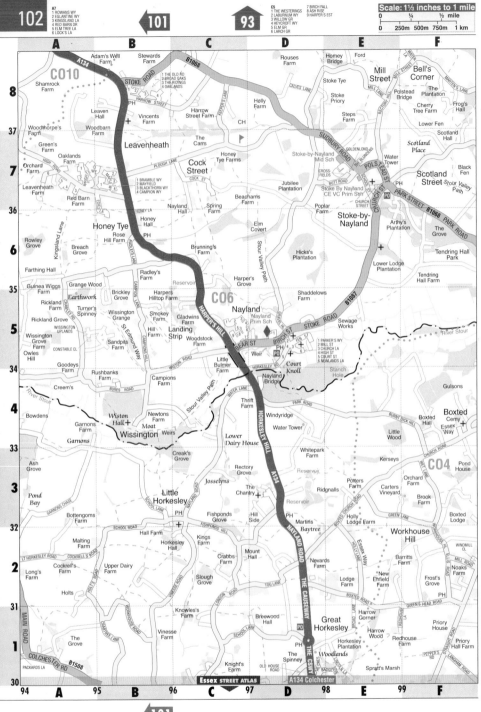

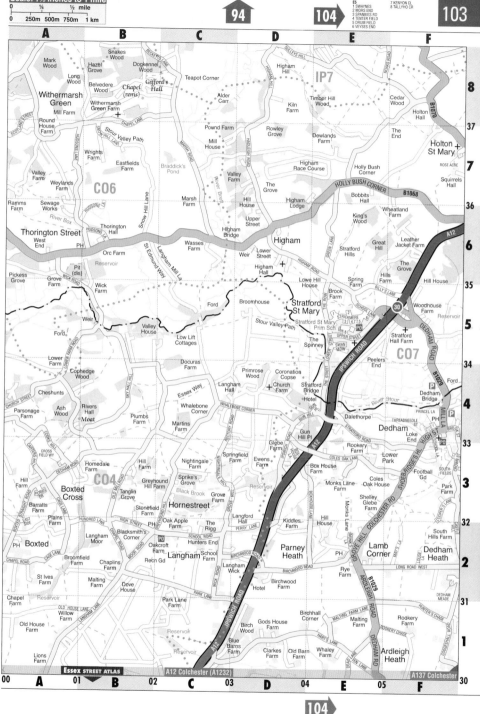

0   ¼   ½   mile
0   250m 500m 750m 1 km

White Horse Farm
Potash
Capelgrove
Springhill
Capelgrove Farm
Grove Farm
Potash Lan
Potash Farm
Falslaff Manor
A12
Great Gilberts Farm
Wenham Place
Wenham Hill
Lattinford Bridge
Boydland Farm
OLD LONDON ROAD
Boynton Hall
Windy Farm
Berry Farm
Bentley
Bentley Prim Sch

Manor House
Hill Farm
IP9
Tawneys
Station Road
LC
Lattinford Hill
Oaks Farm
Chaplain's Farm
Holly Wood
Martins Hill Farm
Willow End
Bentley Grove
1 HIGHFIELDS
2 SILVER LEYS
3 CHURCH RD
4 EAST MILL GN
5 SOUTH VIEW GN
6 WEST MILL GN

B1070
Four Sisters Farm
Hustlers Grove
Great Martin's Hill Wood
Martins Glen
Dodnash Wood
Coppey Farm
Dodnash Coppey Farm

Hughes Corner
Four Sisters
Woodgates Farm
Rookery Farm
Little Martin's Hill Wood
Dodnash Priory Farm
Little Charles New Plantation

Road Covert
East Bergholt
Sports Centre
Ford
The Grange
Augustinian Priory
Alder Carr
Keeble's Grove

Lodge Plantation
Allen's Farm
Ackworth House
Vale Farm
Swimming Pool
HEATH RD
Elm Farm
Meadow Farm
Laurel Grove
East End
Church Barn Farm
Willow Spinney
Mower's Spinney

CO7
Whistler's Wood
Sports Gd
Highlands
Home Farm
Smart's Wood
Woodlands Farm
Park Farm

Fishpond Wood
Old Hall
Willowtree Farm
Gardens
Warren Wood
Touchey's Lane
Park House
Church Farm
Brantham Glebe

Clapper Farm
Baker's End
Spooner's Wood
Braham Wood
Brookland Farm
Orchard End
Brantham

St Edmund Way
Fen Bridge
Gossnalls Farm
Sewage Works
Orvis Farm
Braham Hall
IPSWICH ROAD
A137
Sewage Works
Decoy Pond

Rare Breeds Farm
FLATFORD LANE
Lock
Flatford Mill
Valley Farm
Stour Valley Path
BERGHOLT RD
BRANTHAM HILL
Cattawade
Wks

Pound Farm
Lower Barn Farm
Weirs
White Bridge
A137
Nature Reserve
Hopping Bridge
Mistley Towers
Craft Centre

East House
St Edmund Way
CAUSEWAY END
NASH CL
MUNNINGS WY
Manningtree
LC
STATION RD
Superstore
HIGH ST
Mistley Place Park
HIGH STREET

Castle House
Stour House
Tumulus
Lawford Hall
CO11
Dale Hall
Lawford
Recreation Ground
Mistley
Long Plantation
Mistley Wood
Manningtree
Furze Hill

Keepers End
Heath Farm
Jupes Hill Farm
Mill Hill
DEDHAM ROAD
Bromley Corner
Sports Ctr
COLCHESTER RD
NEW RD
Mistley Wood
Laundry Wood
Dairy Wood

Great Hickle Farm
Bargate Farm
Birchetts Wood
WIGNALL ST
LONG RD
Recreation Ground
1 SCHOOL LA
2 CLAUDE OLIVER CL
3 MILTON CL
B1352
Mistley Hall
Beech Plantation

Cherry Tree Farm
A137
Foxash Estate
HARWICH ROAD
Glanfields
Lower Farm
Lawford House
Aldhams
DEAD LANE
Aldhams
CLACTON ROAD
Stacies Farm
Ford Farm
Brickklin Grove
B1035

Grange Farm
Lawfordhouse Farm
Essex STREET ATLAS

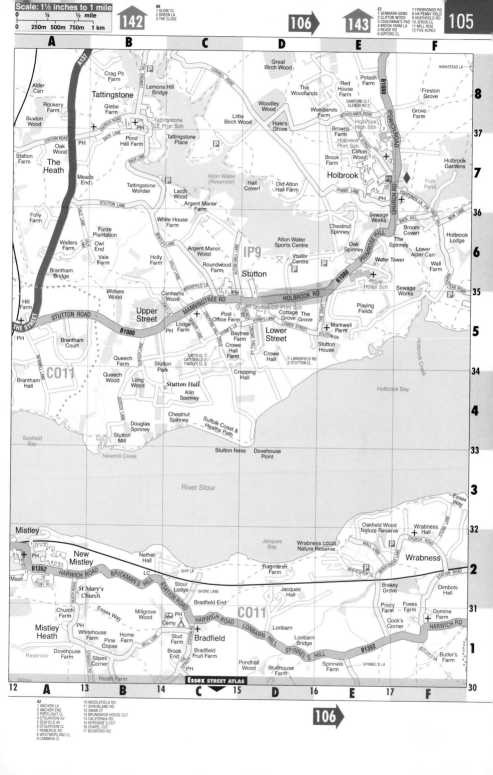

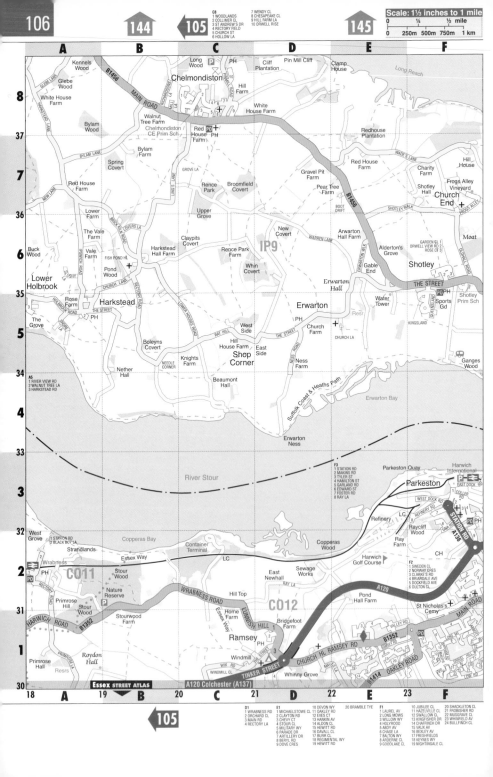

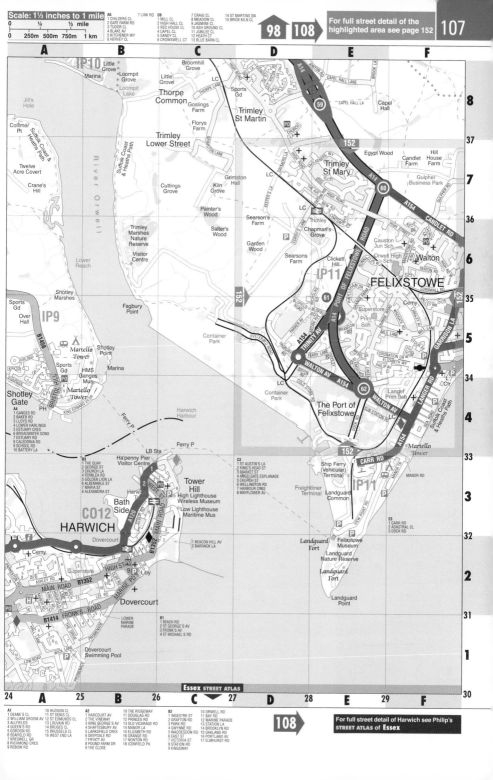

A   B   C   D   E   F

IP10

Walton
Marshes

Felixstowe
Marshes

Ferry P   Sports
Visitor   Gd
Centre   Alexanders
IP12   International Sch
Bawdsey Manor
Workshops

King's
Fleet

8

Rosier
Marshes

Felixstowe
Ferry

PH

Martello
Tower

Woodbridge Haven

37

Rue's
Farm

MARSH LA

153

Fleet
House

Felixstowe Ferry
Golf Course

Martello
Tower

Gulpher
Farm

Laurel
Farm

Marsh
End

FERRY ROAD

7   IP11

GULPHER ROAD

The
Grove

Park
Farm

Old
Felixstowe

BRINKLEY
WY

WESTMORLAND RD

Prim
Sch

CH
P

HYEM'S LANE

36

UPPERFIELD DR

WESTERN AV

LINKS AVE

Sch

COLNEIS ROAD

Sports
Gd

Felixstowe

ROSEBERY RD

ST GEORGE'S RD

ST GEORGE'S RD

DELLWOOD AV

LYNWOOD AV

HIGH RD E

CLIFF RD

6

ROMAN RD

BENTLEY RD

Sch

HAMILTON RD

ST ANDREW'S RD

PICKETT

BROOK

FOXGROVE LN

MAYBUSH LANE

P

P

35   153

A1021

PO

COBBOLD RD

UNDERCLIFF RD

Bartlet

Felixstowe

Cobbolds
Point

153

A1021

5   B1082

PO

Spa
Pavilion

34

4

153

33

3

32

2

31

1

30

30   A   31   B   32   C   33   D   34   E   35   F

For full street detail of the
highlighted area see page 153

107

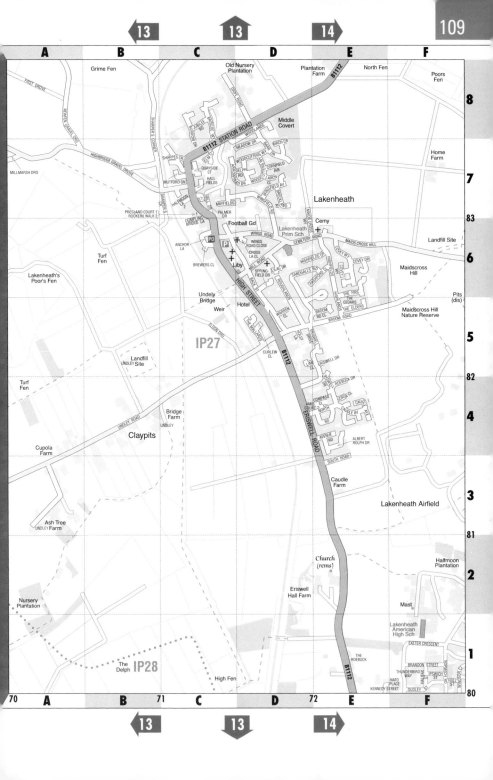

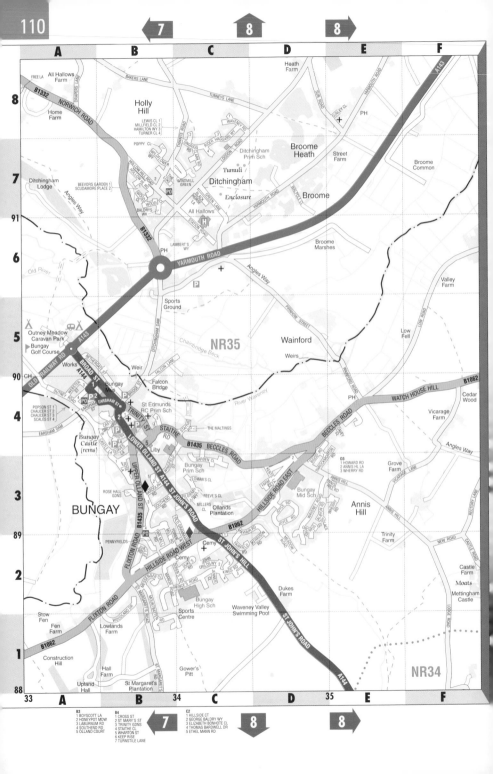

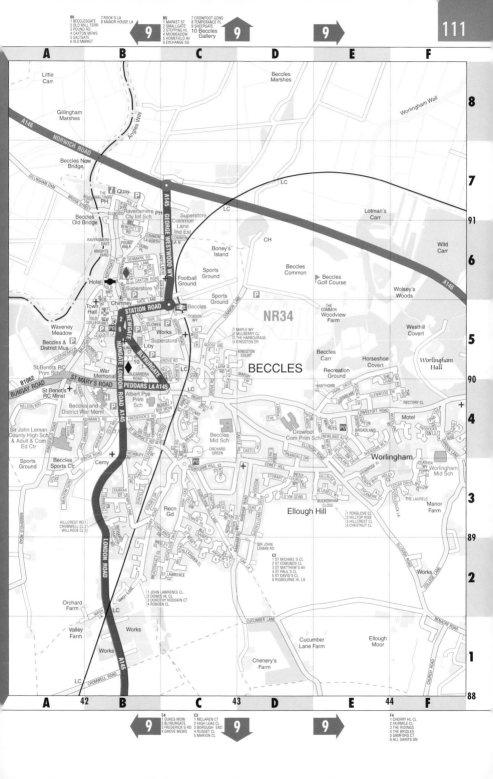

B6
1 BECCLESGATE
2 OLD MILL TERR
3 POUND RD
4 CAXTON MEWS
5 SALTGATE
6 OLD MARKET

7 ROOK'S LA
8 MANOR HOUSE LA

B5
1 MARKET ST
2 SMALLGATE
3 STEPPING HL
4 MIDMEADOW
5 HOMEFIELD AV
6 EXCHANGE SQ

7 CROWFOOT GDNS
8 TEMPERANCE PL
9 SHEEPGATE
10 Beccles Gallery

A B C D E F

8

Little Carr

Beccles Marshes

Gillingham Marshes

Worlingham Wall

A146 NORWICH ROAD

7

Beccles New Bridge

Gillingham Dam

LC

91

Lotman's Carr

The Quay
PH
The MALTINGS
BRIDGE STREET
Ravensmere PH
Beccles Old Bridge
RAVENSMERE EAST
KNIGHTS YARD
Ravensmere City Inf Sch
ELLWOOD RD
BENEDICT RD
COMMON LA NORTH
POUND WALK
DENMARK RD
PIG LANE

GEORGE WESTWOOD WY A145

Superstore
Common Lane Ind Est

Superstore
Common Lane Ind Est

LC

CH

Wild Carr

A146

6

Hotel
OLD MKT
Chimney
Superstore
Town Hall
OLD COLLEGE LA
CALE LANE
CAXTON MEWS

Boney's Island

Football Ground

Sports Ground

Beccles Common

Beccles Golf Course

Wolsey's Woods

Westhill Covert

Worlingham Hall

5

Waveney Meadow
Beccles & District Mus
St Benets RC Prim Sch

STATION ROAD
NEWGATE
FAIR CL
CLOWES
Works
Superstore
Liby
BLYBURGATE
GROVE RD

Beccles

DOBSON WY

1 MAPLE WY
2 MULBERRY CL
3 THE HARBOURAGE
4 KINGSTON DR
KINGSTON COURT
GOOSE GN

NR34

BECCLES

Beccles Carr

Recreation Ground

Beccles Common

The Woodview Farm

Horseshoe Covert

The CHASE
GLENWOOD DR

Worlingham Hall

90

B1062 BUNGAY ROAD
St Mary's RD
St Benet's RC Minst
Beccles and District War Meml
NELSON WY
WHITE LION RD
ASHMAN'S RD
Sir John Leman County High Sch & Adult & Com Ed Ctr

War Memorial
PEDDARS LA A145
Albert Pye Prim Sch
BLACK MDW

HUNGATE
LONDON ROAD A145

FREDERICK'S RD
ST GEORGE

INGATE
STUART DR

FARM
DAY'S RD
BEAR CL

MASK

HAWTHORN
RECTORY CL
LOWESTOFT ROAD
SUNBEAM
Motel
WORLINGHAM

4

Sports Ground
Beccles Sports Ctr
Cemy

FAIRFAX CT
WEMBLEY

SOUTH RD
ASHMAN'S RD

GEORGE RD

Beccles Mid Sch
ORCHARD GREEN

RIGBOURNE HILL
CONEY HILL
STOBART
PETIT CHURCH WY
HILLREST
BLUEBELL WY
SYCAMORE CL
PRIMROSE CL
CEDAR DRIVE
HOLLY
The LAURELS

Worlingham Mid Sch

Manor Farm

3

HILLCREST RD 1
CROMWELL CL 2
WILLREDE CL 3

Recn Gd

ALL SAINTS

BANHAM
DUKE RD

Ellough Hill

1 FOXGLOVE CL
2 HILLTOP RISE
3 HILLCREST CL
4 CHESTNUT CL

BUCKENHAM CLOSE
2 VW GDNS

Works

89

Orchard Farm
WASH LA
LC

Works

MARSH LANE

LONDON ROAD A145

1 JOHN LAWRENCE CL
2 DOWES HL CL
3 DOROTHY HODGKIN CT
4 RONDEN CL

SIR JOHN LEMAN RD

C5
1 ST MICHAEL'S CL
2 ST EDMUNDS CL
3 ST MATTHEW'S AV
4 ST PAUL S CL
5 ST DAVID'S CL
6 RIGBOURNE HL LA

Works

2

Valley Farm
Works

CROMWELL ROAD
A145
LC

CUCUMBER LANE

Cucumber Lane Farm

Ellough Moor

BENACRE ROAD
CHURCH ROAD

COLLEGE LA

1

Chenery's Farm

A 42 B C 43 D E 44 F

88

C4
1 DUKES MDW
2 BLYBURGATE
3 FREDERICK'S RD
4 GROVE MEWS

C3
1 MCLAREN CT
2 HIGH LEAS CL
3 BOROUGH END
4 RUSSET CL
5 MARION CL

F4
1 CHERRY HL CL
2 FAIRMILE CL
3 THE RIDINGS
4 THE BRIDLES
5 SAMFORD CT
6 ALL SAINTS GN

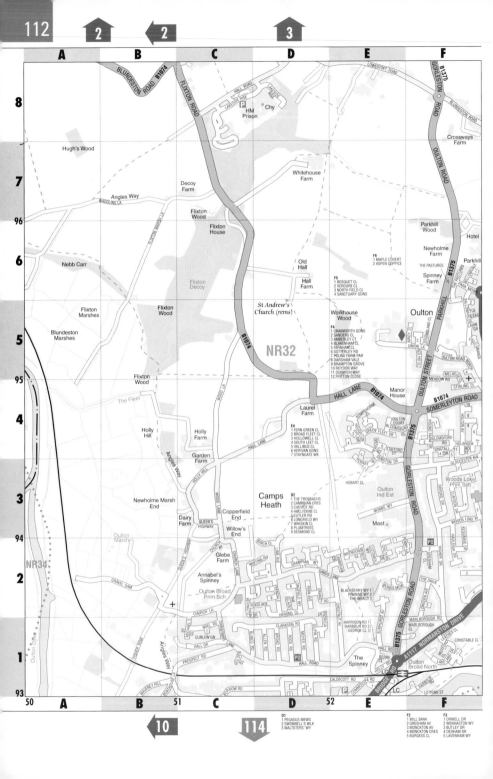

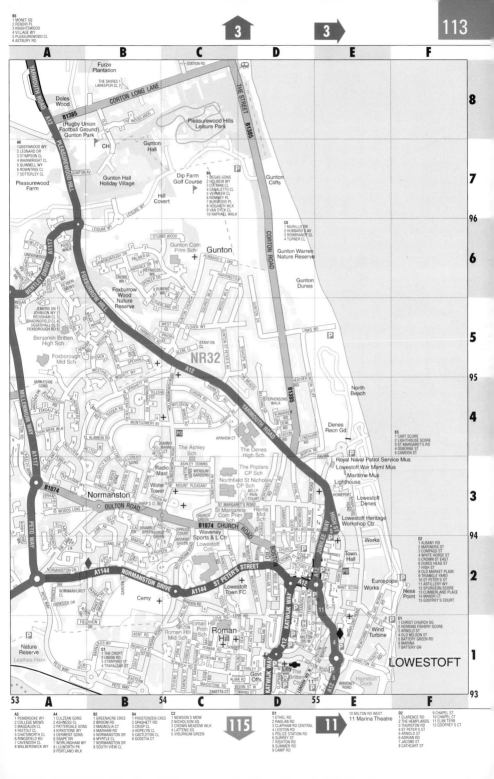

B5
1 MONET SQ
2 RENOIR PL
3 KNIGHTSWOOD
4 VILLAGE WY
5 PLEASUREWOOD CL
6 ASTBURY RD

A6
1 GREENWOOD WY
2 LEONARD DR
3 STIMPSON CL
4 WAINWRIGHT CL
5 QUINNELL WY
6 ROWNTREE CL
7 SOTTERLEY CL

B6
1 DEGAS GDNS
2 HOLBEIN WY
3 COTMAN CL
4 CANALETTO CL
5 VERMEER CL
6 ROMNEY PL
7 BURWOOD PL
8 HOGARTH WLK
9 VAN DYCK CL
10 RAPHAEL WALK

C6
1 MURILLO DR
2 HUBBARD'S AV
3 REMBRANDT CL
4 TURNER CL

E3
1 CART SCORE
2 LIGHTHOUSE SCORE
3 ST MARGARET'S RD
4 OSBORNE ST
5 CAMDEN ST

E2
1 ALBANY RD
2 MARINERS ST
3 COMPASS ST
4 WHITE HORSE ST
5 CROWN ST EAST
6 DUKES HEAD ST
7 HIGH ST
8 OLD MARKET PLAIN
9 TRIANGLE YARD
10 ST PETER'S ST
11 ARTILLERY WAY
12 SPURGEON SCORE
13 CUMBERLAND PLACE
14 MANOR CT
15 GODFREY'S COURT

E1
1 CHRIST CHURCH SQ
2 HERRING FISHERY SCORE
3 ARNOLD ST
4 OLD NELSON ST
5 BATTERY GREEN RD
6 MARINA
7 BATTERY GN

NR32

LOWESTOFT

10 MILTON RD WEST
11 Marina Theatre

A3
1 PEMBROOKE WY
2 COLLEGE MDWS
3 MAGDALEN CL
4 FASTOLF CL
5 CHATSWORTH CL
6 RINGSFIELD RD
7 CAVENDISH CL
8 WALBERSWICK WY

B2
1 GREENACRE CRES
2 BROOM RD
3 MAGNOLIA CT
4 MARHAM RD
5 KIRKSTONE WY
6 DERWENT GDNS

B4
1 FROSTENDEN CRES
2 SPASHETT RD
3 CRISP CL
4 HOPELYN CL
5 CASTLETON CL
6 GODETIA CL

C2
1 NEWSON'S MDW
2 NICHOLSON SQ
3 CROWN MEADOW WLK
4 LATTENS SQ
5 VIBURNUM GREEN

D1
1 ETHEL RD
2 RAGLAN RD
3 CLAPHAM RD CENTRAL
4 LEISTON RD
5 POLICE STATION RD
6 SURREY ST
7 RIGHTON RD
8 SUMMER RD
9 CAMP RD

D2
1 CLARENCE RD
2 THE HEMPLANDS
3 THURSTON RD
4 ST PETER'S ST
5 ARNOLD ST
6 ADRIAN RD
7 JACOBS ST
8 CATHCART ST

C3
1 CHAPEL ST
10 CHAPEL CT
11 ELIM TCE
12 GODFREY'S CT

A4
1 CULZEAN GDNS
2 ASHNESS CL
3 PATTERDALE GDNS
4 MARHAM RD
5 KIRKSTONE WY
6 DERWENT GDNS
7 WORLINGHAM WY
8 LULWORTH PK
9 PENTLAND WLK

B2
1 GREENACRE CRES
2 BROOM RD
3 MAGNOLIA CT
4 MARHAM RD
5 KIRKSTONE WY
6 DERWENT GDNS
7 NORMANSTON DR
8 SOUTH VIEW CL

C1
1 THE CROFT
2 UNION RD
3 STANFORD ST
4 TRAFALGAR ST

115 11

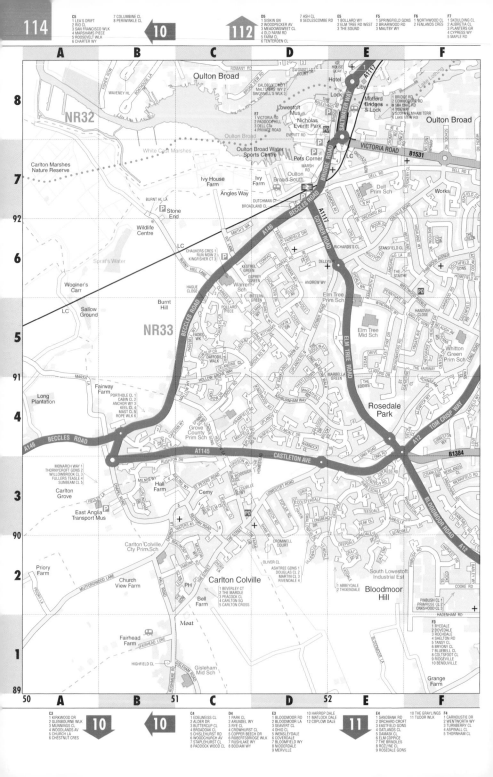

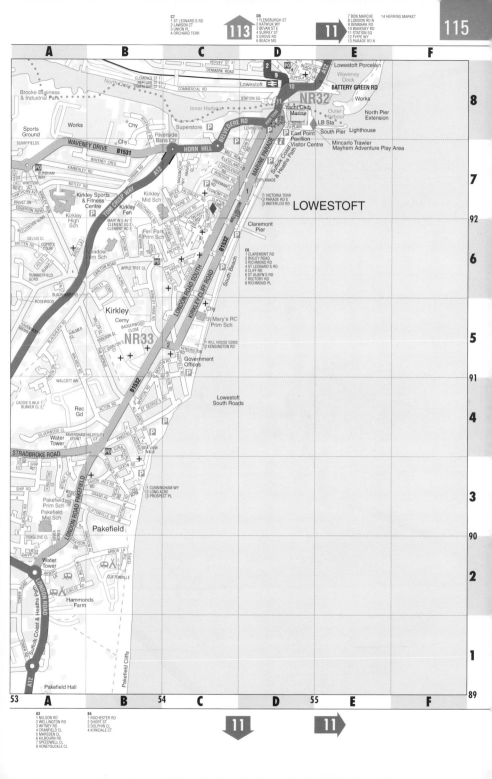

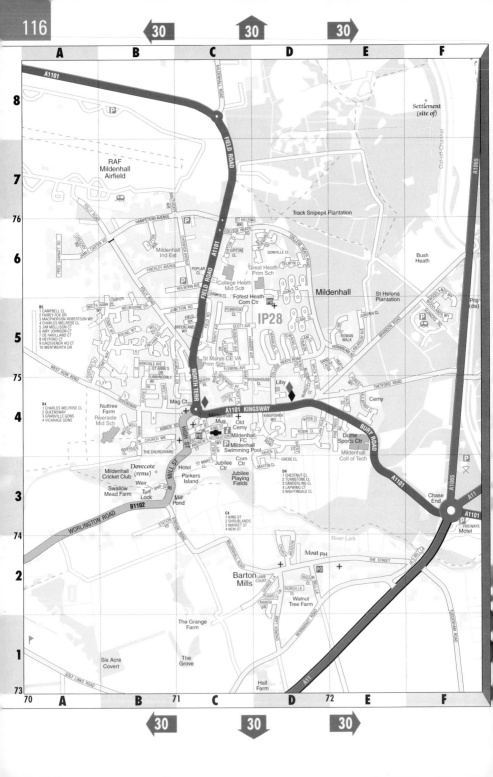

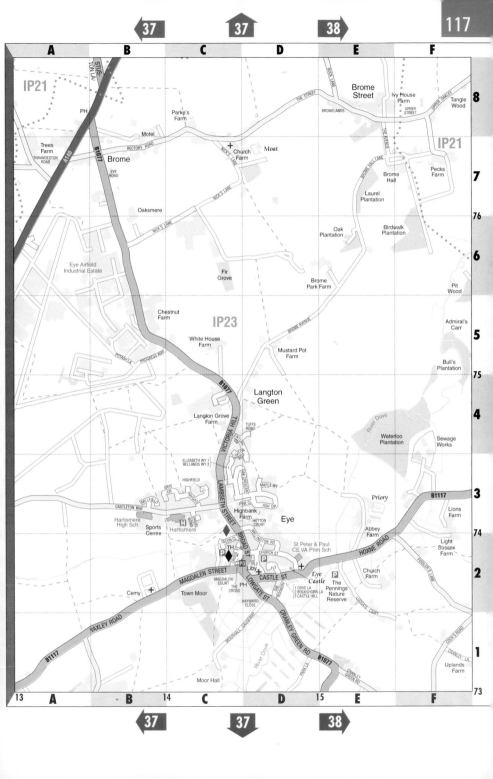

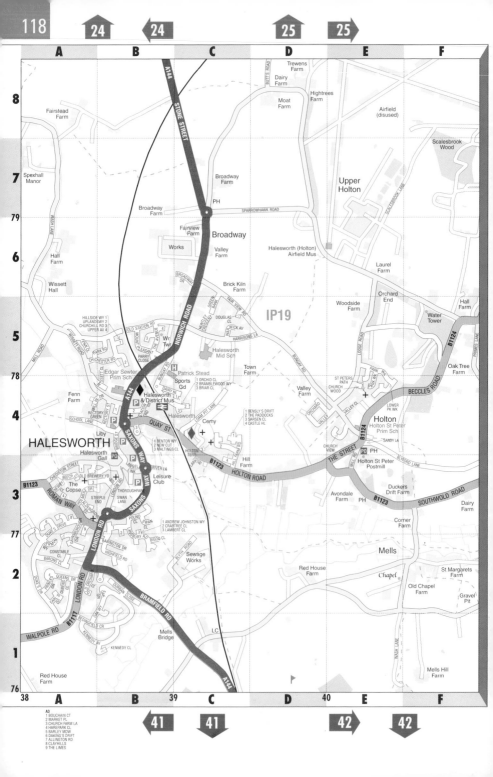

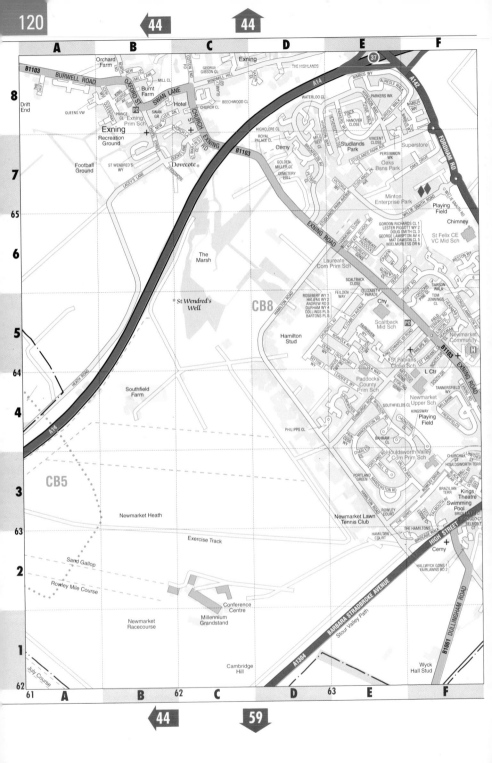

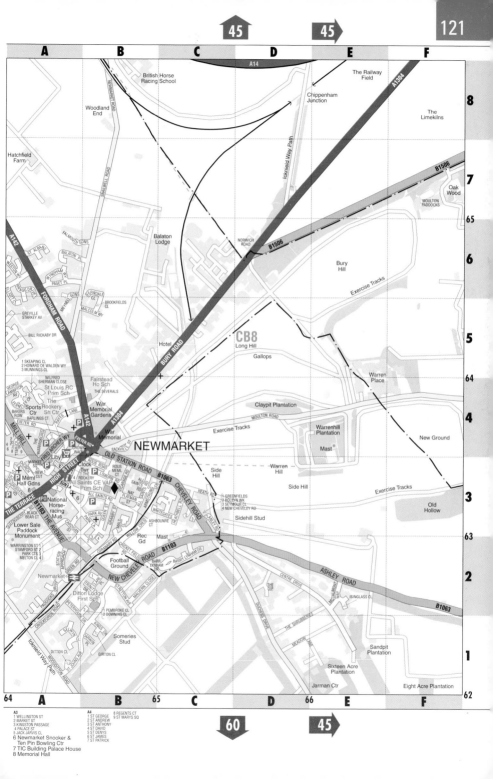

A14

British Horse Racing School

The Railway Field

Chippenham Junction

Woodland End

The Limekilns

Hatchfield Farm

B1506

Oak Wood

MOULTON PADDOCKS

FALMOUTH GDNS

Balaton Lodge

NORWICH ROAD

B1506

Bury Hill

Exercise Tracks

Hotel

Long Hill

CB8

Gallops

Warren Place

Fairstead Ho Sch

St Louis RC Prim Sch

THE SEVERALS

War Memorial Gardens

Claypit Plantation

MOULTON ROAD

Warrenhill Plantation

New Ground

War Memorial

Exercise Tracks

NEWMARKET

Mast

Old Station Road

Side Hill

Side Hill

Warren Hill

Exercise Tracks

Old Hollow

All Saints CE VAP Prim Sch

B1063

CHEVELEY ROAD

HEATH RD

1 GREENFIELDS
2 BOLEYN WK
3 SEYMOUR CL
4 NEW CHEVELEY RD

National Horse-racing Mus

Lower Sale Paddock Monument

Sidehill Stud

B1103

Rec Gd

Mast

Football Ground

NEW CHEVELEY ROAD

BARRY LYNHAM DR

THE DIP

ASHLEY ROAD

ISINGLASS CL

B1063

Newmarket

Ditton Lodge First Sch

Someries Stud

GIRTON CL

DITTON CL

Sandpit Plantation

Iknield Way Path

Sixteen Acre Plantation

Jarman Ctr

Eight Acre Plantation

A3
1 WELLINGTON ST
2 MARKET ST
3 KINGSTON PASSAGE
4 PALACE ST
5 JACK JARVIS CL
6 Newmarket Snooker &
   Ten Pin Bowling Ctr
7 TIC Building Palace House
8 Memorial Hall

A4
1 ST GEORGE
2 ST ANDREW
3 ST ANTHONY
4 ST DAVID
5 ST DENYS
6 ST JAMES
7 ST PATRICK

8 REGENTS CT
9 ST MARYS SQ

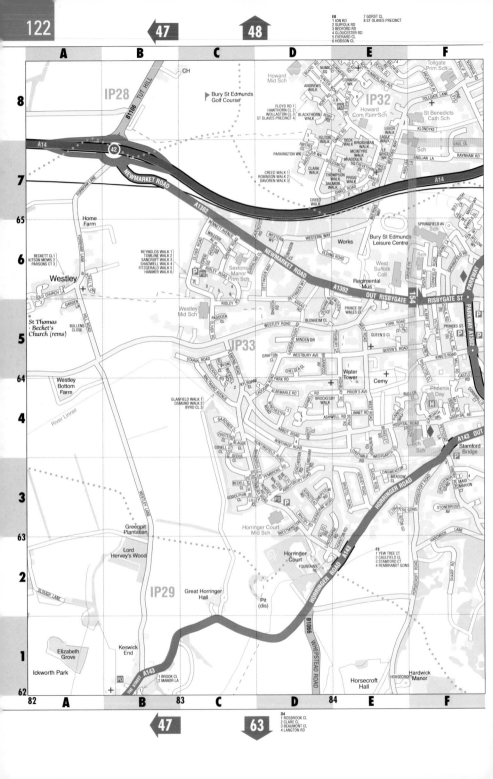

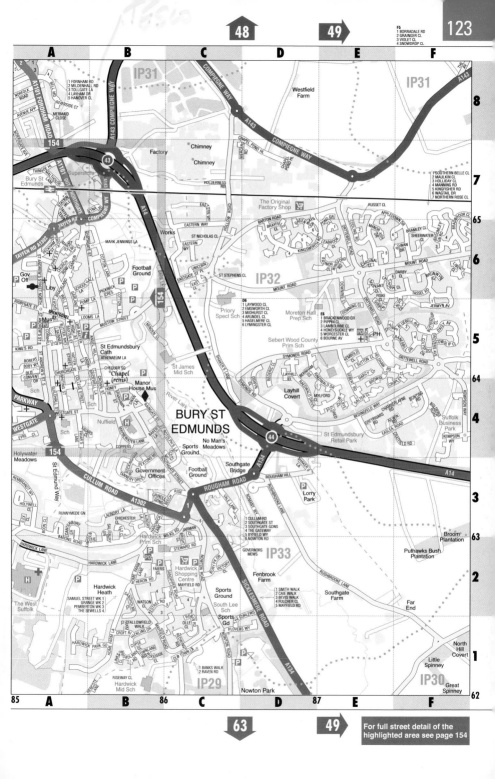

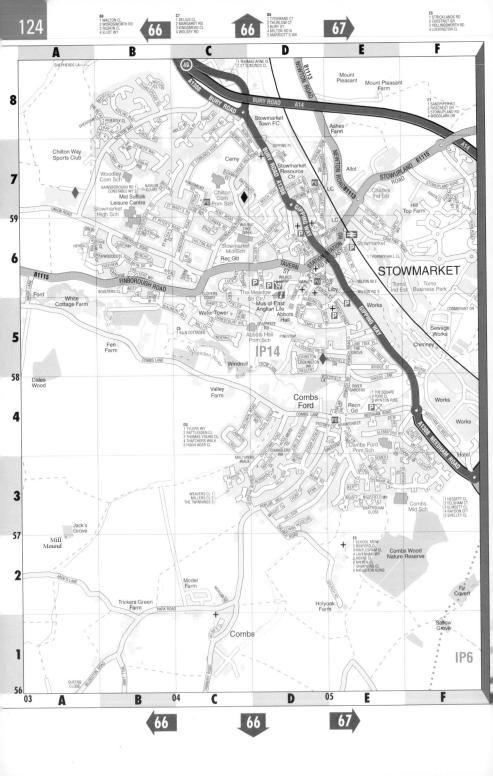

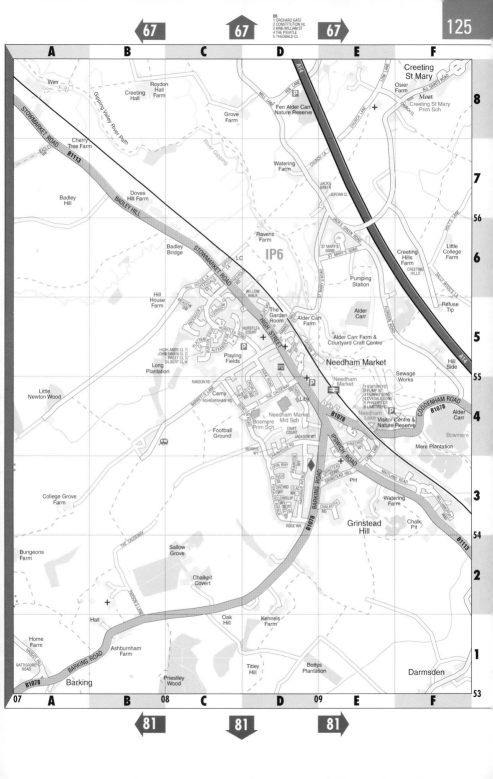

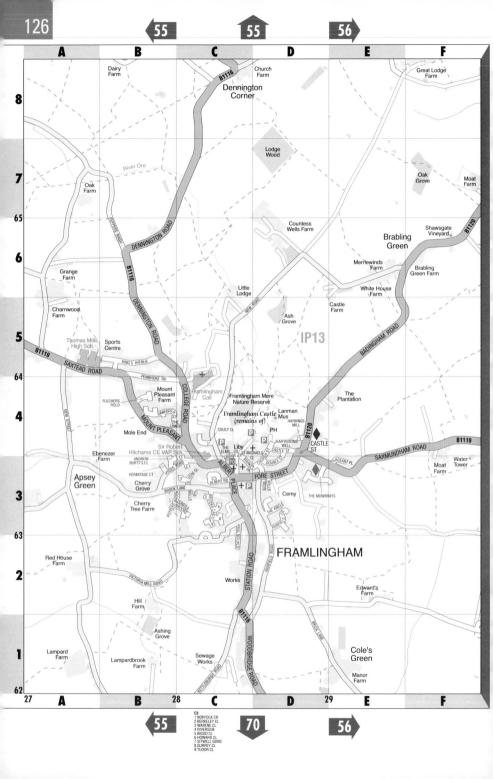

A B C D E F

8

7

65

6

5

64

4

3

63

2

1

62

27 A B 28 C D 29 E F

Dairy Farm

B1116

Church Farm

Dennington Corner

Great Lodge Farm

Lodge Wood

River Ore

Oak Farm

Oak Grove

Moat Farm

DENNINGTON ROAD

PEPER'S WAY

Countess Wells Farm

Brabling Green

Shawsgate Vineyard

B1120

Grange Farm

B1116

Merriewinds Farm

Brabling Green Farm

Charnwood Farm

Little Lodge

NEW ROAD

White House Farm

Castle Farm

Thomas Mills High Sch

Sports Centre

IP13

BADINGHAM ROAD

B1119

SAXTEAD ROAD

KING'S AVENUE

DENNINGTON ROAD

PEMBROKE RD

Ash Grove

Mount Pleasant Farm

FULCHERS FIELD

COLLEGE ROAD

Framlingham Coll

Framlingham Mere Nature Reserve

The Plantation

NEW STREET

DANFORTH

THE LIMES

Framlingham Castle (remains of)

Lanman Mus

HAYNINGS MILL

Mole End

MOUNT PLEASANT

COUCY CL

P

PH

B1120

CASTLE ST

Ebenezer Farm

Sir Robert Hitchams CE VAP Sch

JEAFFRESONS WELL

CASTLE ST

SARGEANT PL

SAXMUNDHAM ROAD

B1119

Apsey Green

ANDREW BURTT'S CL

HERMITAGE CT

The Elms

St Michaels

Liby

ALBERT PL

Water Tower

Moat Farm

Cherry Grove

BROOK LANE

ALBERT RD

BRIDGE ST

DOUBLE ST

FORE STREET

P

Cherry Tree Farm

POTTERS CASTLE BRICKS

P

Cemy

THE KING'S

THE MOWBRAYS

Red House Farm

VICTORIA MILL ROAD

STATION THR

FAIRFIELD ROAD

FRAMLINGHAM

Hill Farm

Works

STATION ROAD

Edward's Farm

Ashing Grove

B1116

BACK LANE

Lampard Farm

Lampardbrook Farm

Sewage Works

WOODBRIDGE ROAD

KETTLEBURGH ROAD

Cole's Green

Manor Farm

C3
1 NORFOLK CR
2 BERKELEY CL
3 WARENE CL
4 RIVERSIDE
5 BIGOD CL
6 HOWARD CL
7 SITWELL GDNS
8 SURREY CL
9 TUDOR CL

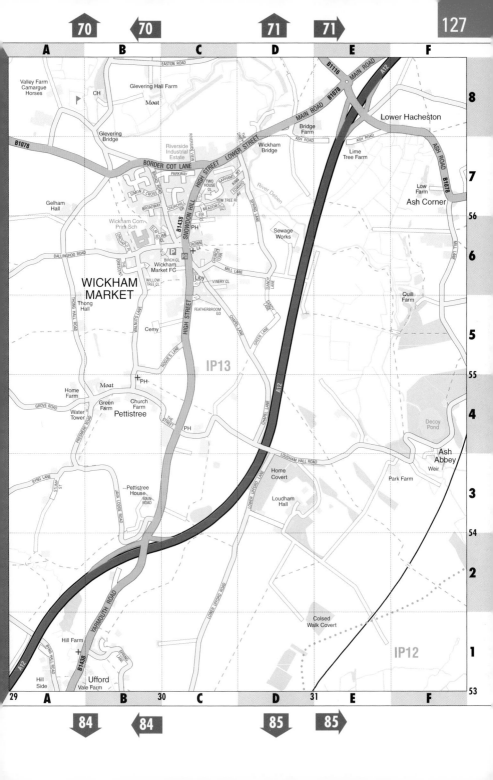

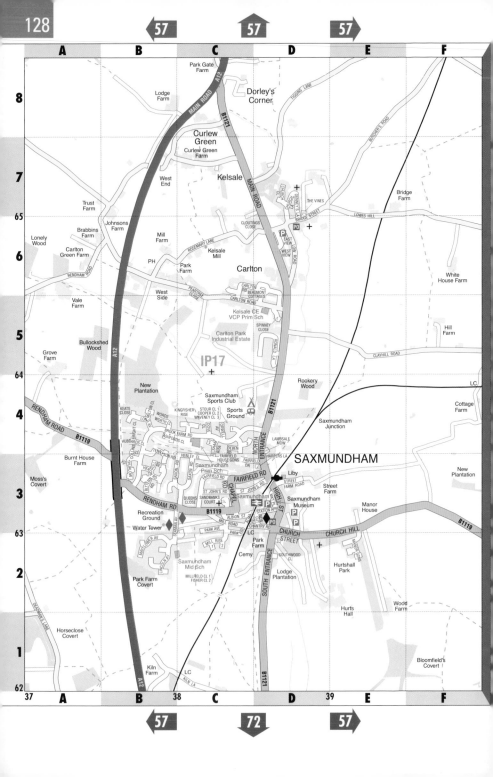

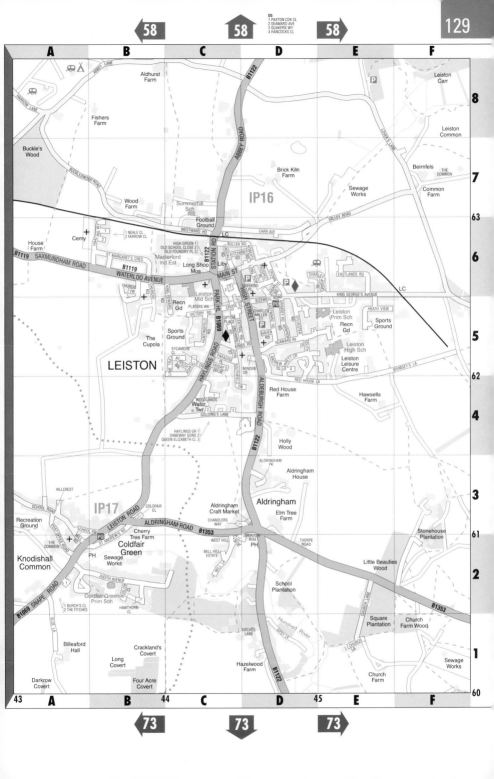

D5
1 PAXTON CDK CL
2 SEAWARD AVE
3 QUAKERS WY
4 HANCOCKS CL

◄ 58
58
58 ►

| | A | B | C | D | E | F |

Leiston
Carr

8

Aldhurst
Farm

B1122

Fishers
Farm

Leiston
Common

Buckle's
Wood

7

Brick Kiln
Farm

Beirnfels

THE
COMMON

ABBEY ROAD

Sewage
Works

Common
Farm

BUCKLESWORD ROAD

IP16

Wood
Farm

Summerhill
Sch

63

Football
Ground

VALLEY ROAD

House
Farm

B1119 SAXMUNDHAM ROAD

WESTWARD HO

LC

CARR AVE

Cemy

1 NEALE CL
2 FARROW CL

6

B1119

Masterlord
Ind Est

ST MARGARET'S CRES

WATERLOO AVENUE

HACKING WY

B1122

STATION RD

HIGH GREEN 1
OLD SCHOOL CLOSE 2
OLD FOUNDRY PL 3

BULLER RD

MAIN ST

Liby

KITCHENER

Long Shop
Mus

CHURCH VW

CHURCH

Leiston
Mid Sch

Recn
Gd

PLATERS WK

HIGH STREET

MAFEKING

CHARLES

EASTLANDS RD

KING GEORGE'S AVENUE

LC

The
Cupola

Sports
Ground

VICTORY RD

HUNTINGFIELD

PARK HL

B1069

UPTON PLACE

CROSS ST

SEWELL RD

CHARLES MILLER CT

GRIMSEY'S RD

SYLVESTER

Leiston
Prim Sch

Recn
Gd

HEATH VIEW

Sports
Ground

LEISTON

IP17

SYCAMORE CL

CRESS

PARADISE

HAYLINGS ROAD

FRIDAY'S ORCH

SOUTHFIELD

HAVEN

KINGS RD

SEAWARD AV

MINDEN DR

ANDREW BETT CR

CL 3 4

Leiston
High Sch

Leiston
Leisure
Centre

GRIMSEY'S LA

5

62

Water
Twr

WOODLANDS CL

GOLDING'S LANE

ALDEBURGH ROAD

Red House
Farm

RED HOUSE LA

Hawsells
Farm

HAYLINGS GR 1
DANEWAY GDNS 2
QUEEN ELIZABETH CL 3

Holly
Wood

4

B1122

ALDRINGHAM
PK

Aldringham
House

3

HILLCREST

LEISTON ROAD

COLDFAIR CL

Aldringham
Craft Market

CHANDLERS
WAY

Aldringham

Elm Tree
Farm

Stonehouse
Plantation

61

Recreation
Ground

SCHOOL ROAD

POST OFFICE ROAD

SCHOOL RD

BELL

ST ANDREW'S RD

Cherry
Tree Farm

ALDRINGHAM ROAD

B1353

WEST HILL

MILL HILL
ESTATE

MEADOW
RISE

PH

THORPE
ROAD

Little Beauties
Wood

THE
COMMON

PH

Coldfair
Green

Sewage
Works

JUDITH AVENUE

School
Plantation

B1353

2

Knodishall
Common

B1069 SNAPE ROAD

SLOE LA

1 BURCH'S CL
2 THE FITCHES

Coldfair Green
Prim Sch

HAWTHORN CL

CHURCH LANE

Square
Plantation

CHURCH LA

Church
Farm Wood

Billeaford
Hall

Long
Covert

Crackland's
Covert

FITCHES
LANE

BIRDS LA

Hundred River

CHURCH
LA

Church
Farm

Sewage
Works

1

Darkrow
Covert

Four Acre
Covert

Hazelwood
Farm

B1122

B1353

60

43 | A | 44 | B | C | 45 | D | E | F

◄ 73
73
73 ►

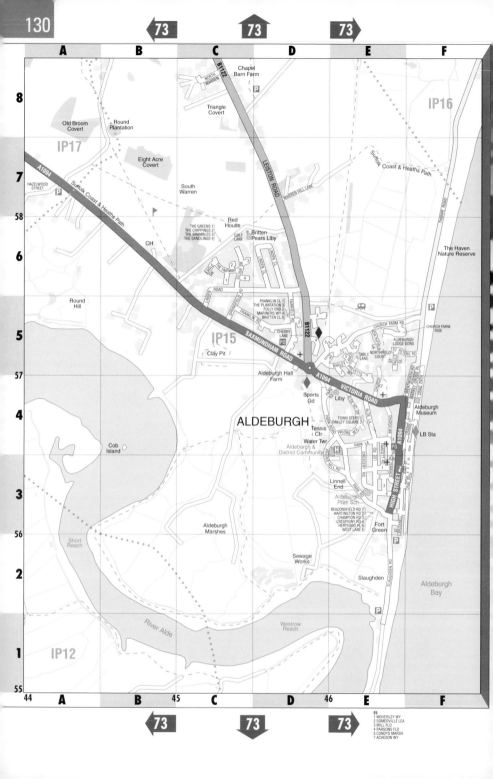

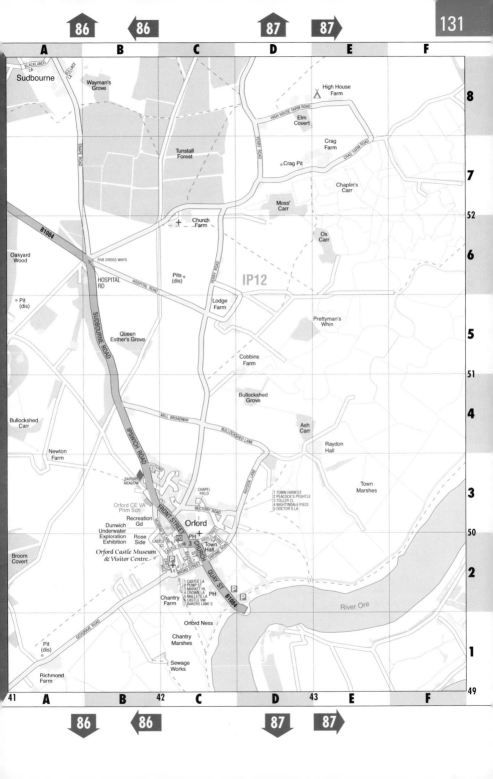

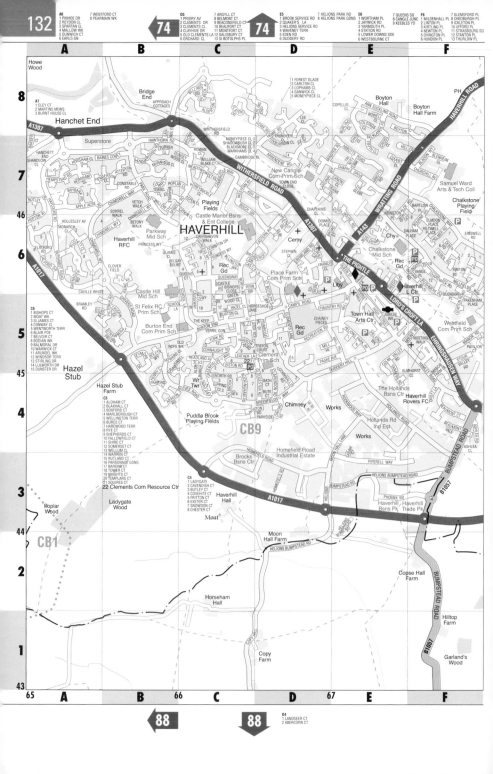

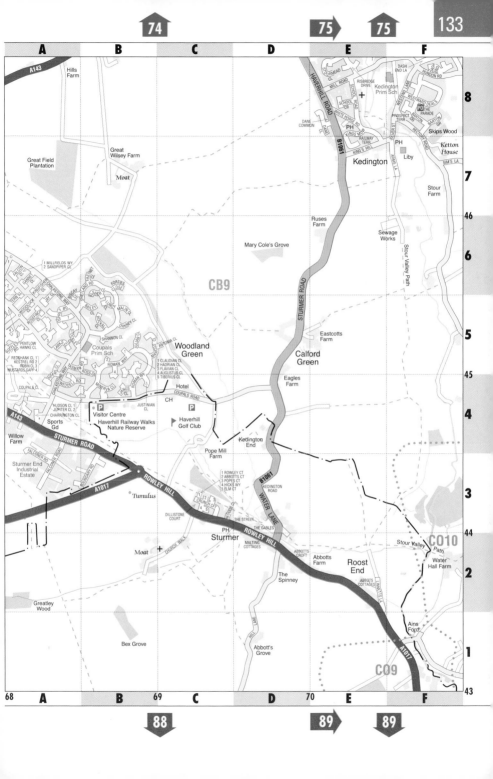

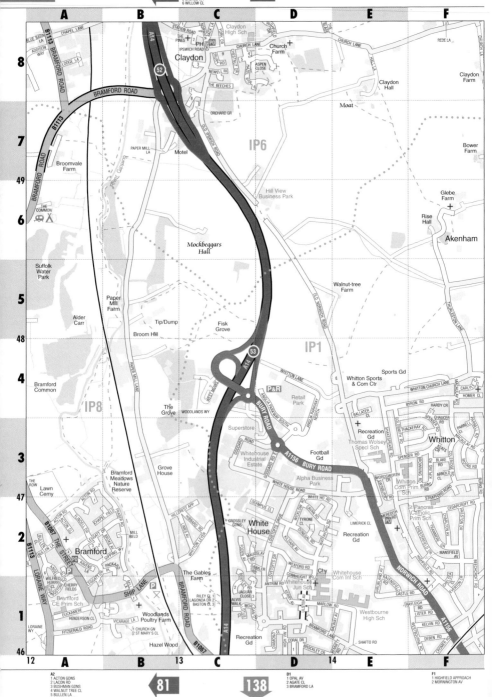

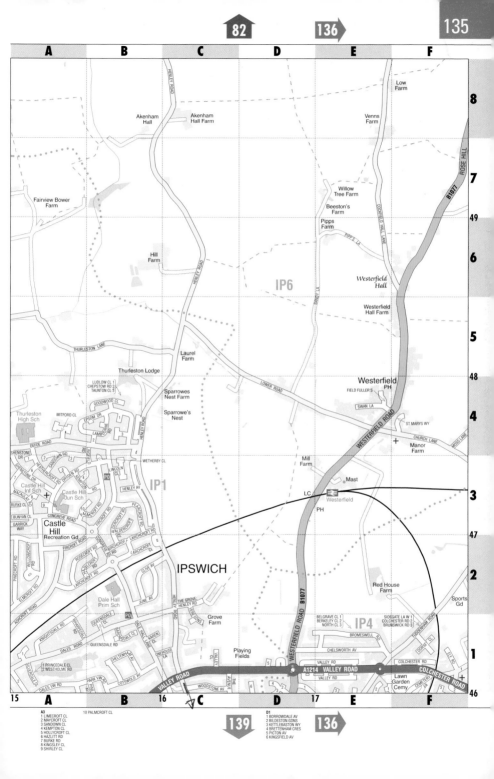

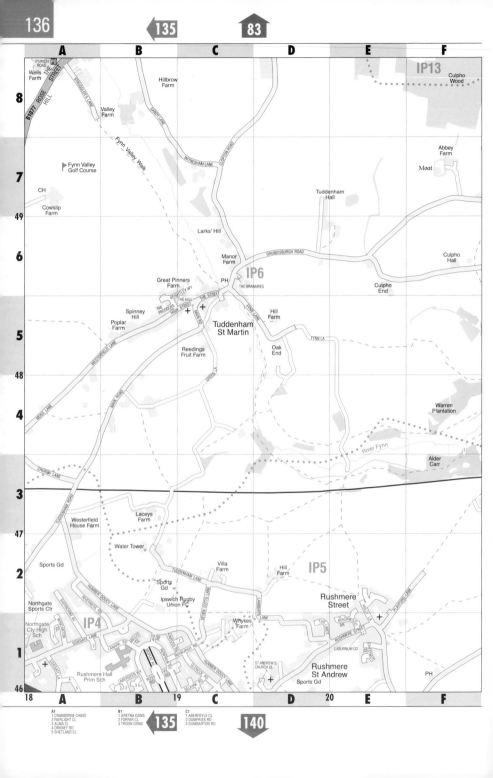

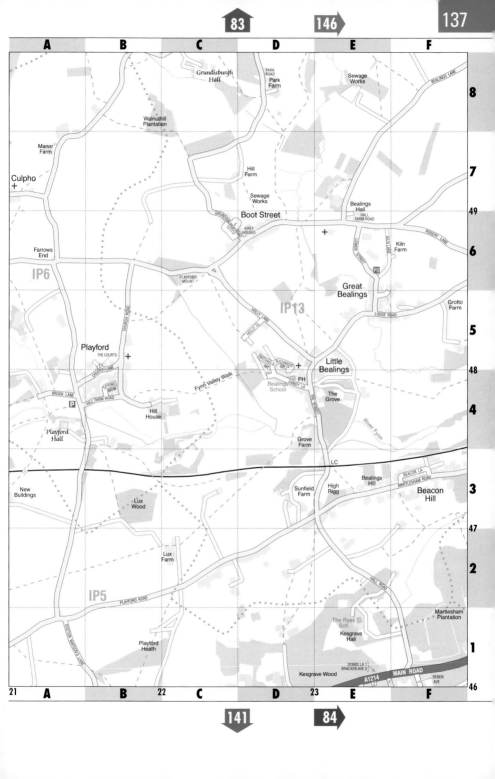

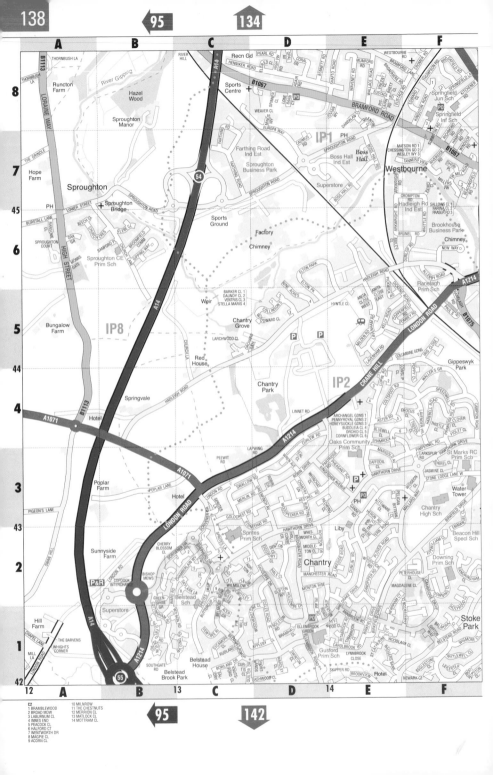

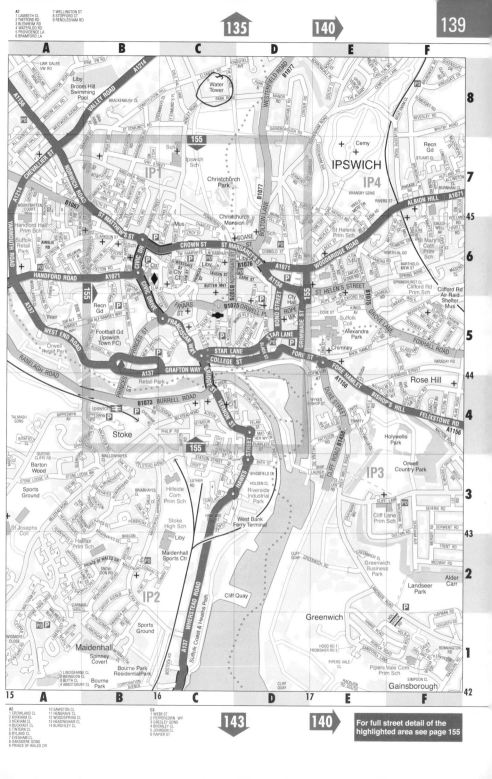

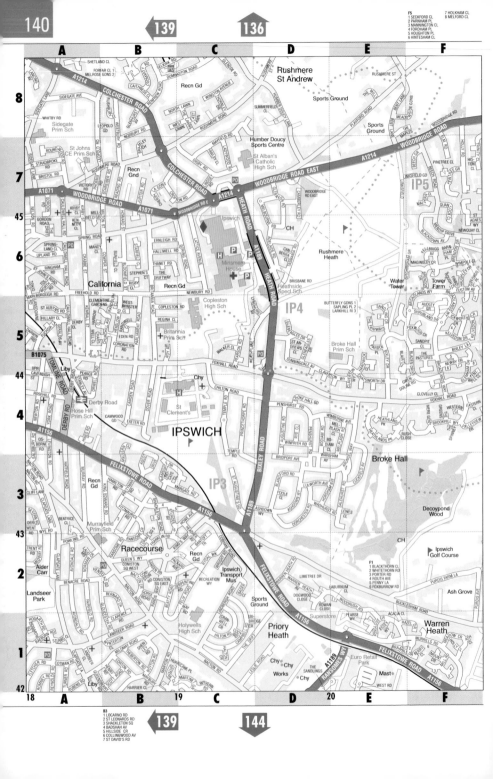

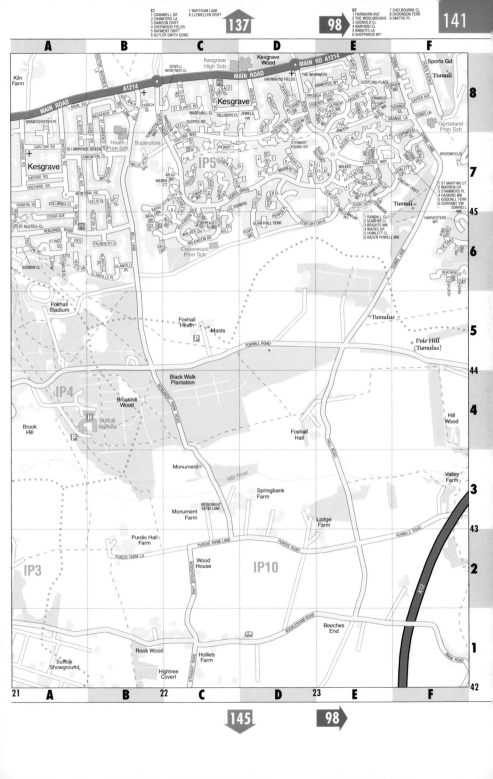

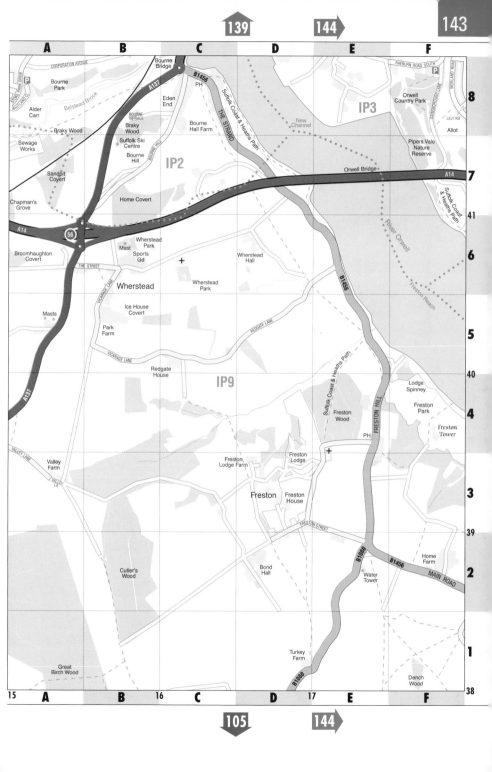

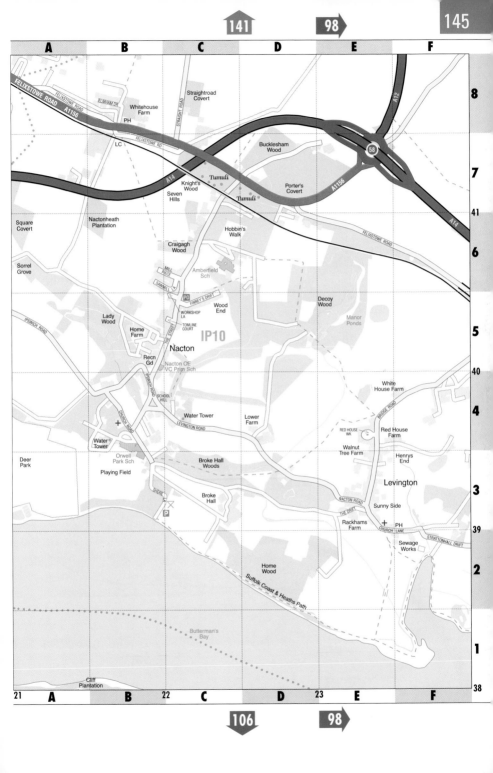

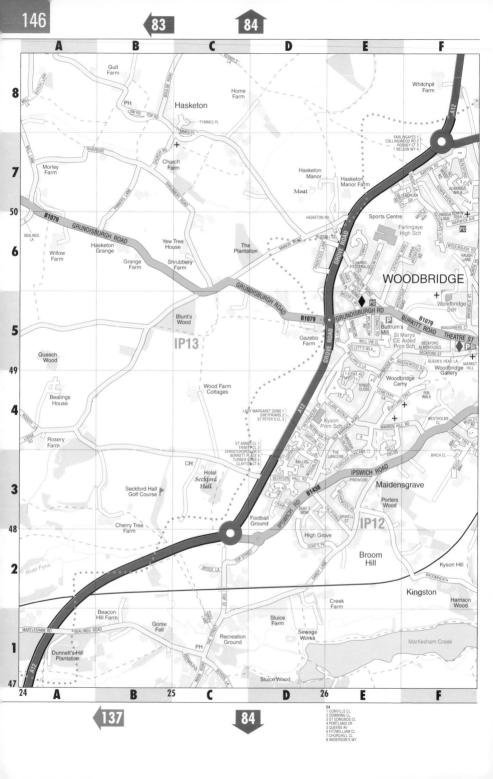

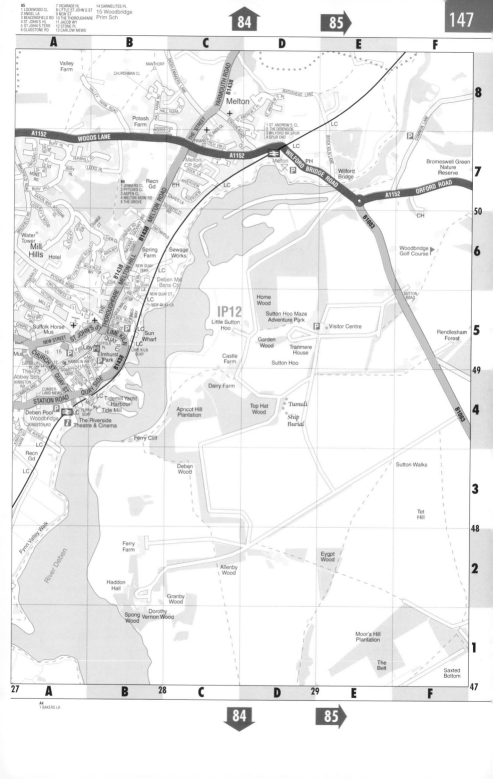

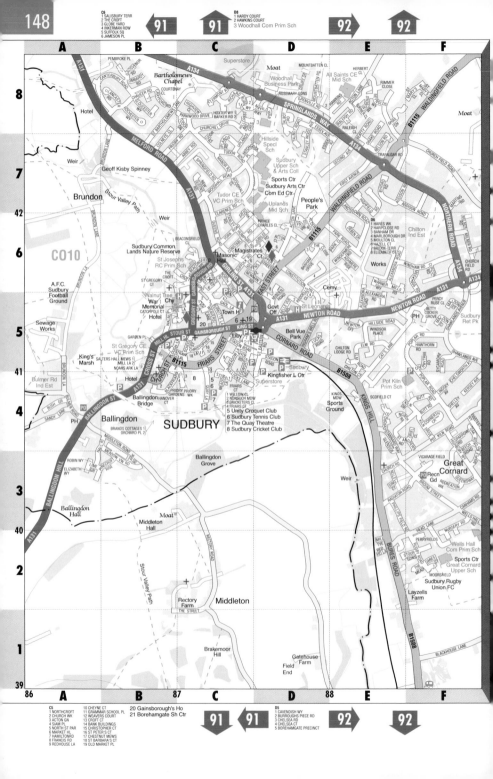

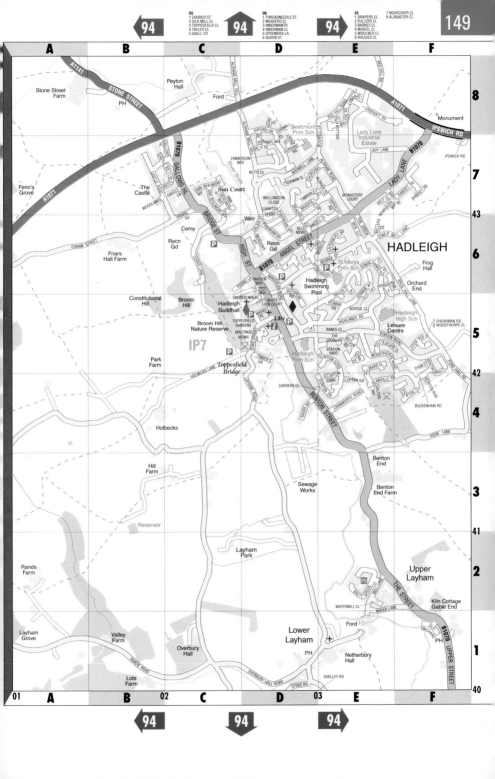

	A	B	C	D	E	F

Moat

Vauxhall Farm

Brimlin Wood

Rookery Farm

Cottage Farm

WENHAM ROAD

The Grange Farm

8

Wenham Thicks

Wenham Grange

7

40

Green Fields

IP8

6

CO7

Park House

Binny's Wood

Clay Hall

Grove Farm

5

Jermyns Farm

Lodge Farm

Little Wenham

Wenham Castle

39

Binny's Wood

Brook Farm

IP9

1 GLEBE END
2 TWO ACRES
3 ROUNDRIDGE RD
4 FARTHINGS WENT
5 THE QUEECH
6 JERMYNS CL

4

PH

Gipsy Row

Brook Lane

Churchford Farm

Churchford Hall

Mushroom Farm

HAWBRIDGE 1
RYLANDS 2
THE SQUIRRELS 3

THE PIGHTLE

PENN CL

Capel St Mary

LITTLE TUFTS

GREAT TUFTS

Corner Farm

WINDMILL HL

DAYS GN

CATE'S SART

SNOWCROFT

Liby

3

Priory Farm

MILL CL

DAYS O'EEN

OLD RECTORY WALK

Capel St Mary CE Prim Sch

PO

ELM

WHIT?

HOMEFIELD

PH

Great Wenham

THE STRING

MOWLANDS

38

Wenham Place

Driftway End

AISTHORPE 1
LITTLE GULLS 2
COOMBERS 3
RED SLEEVE 4

LONG PERRY

Capelgrove

Mast

Sewage Works

Springhill

BUSHEL?

LITTLE CL

RED LANE

2

Capelgrove Farm

POUND LANE

Bush Farm

Great Gilberts Farm

1

Wenham Hill

Dovefield Farm

Bluegate Farm

BLUEGATE LANE

Boynton Hall

37

Boydland Farm

Manor House

OLD LONDON ROAD

Bradfield Farm

A12

	A	B	C	D	E	F

07 08 09

E3
1 SCHOOL CL
2 CROTCHETS CL
3 PENNY MDW
4 PETER'S GR
5 WINDING PIECE
6 TOLL GATE RD
7 CHALKNERS CL
8 STOCKMERS END
9 SMITHERS CL

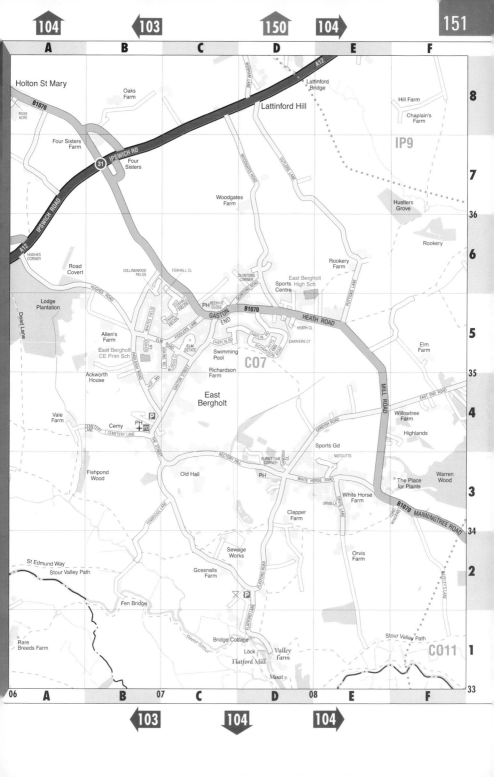

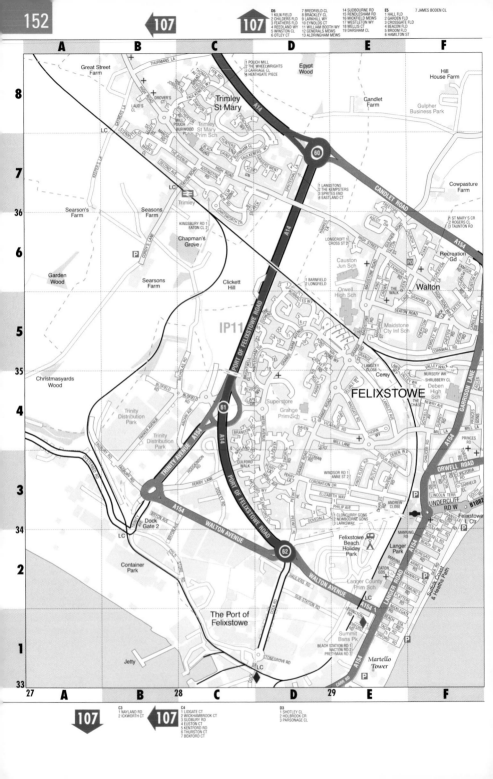

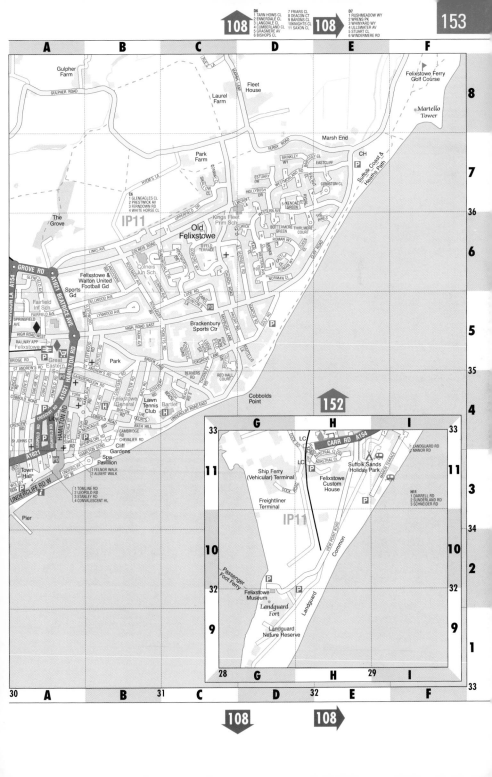

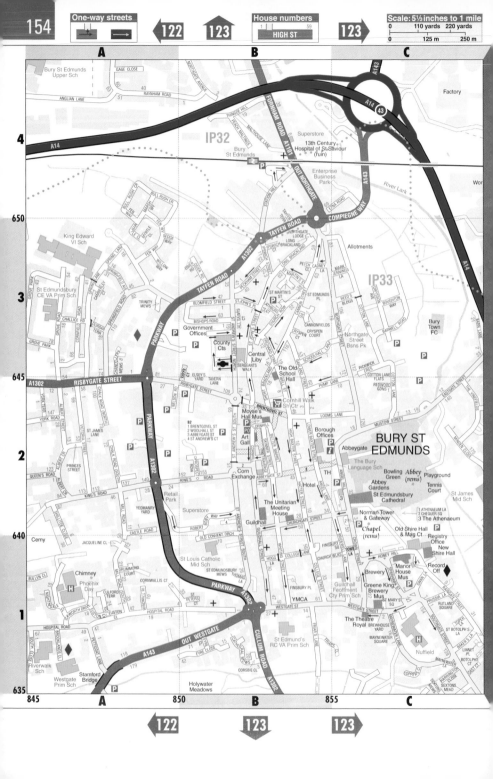

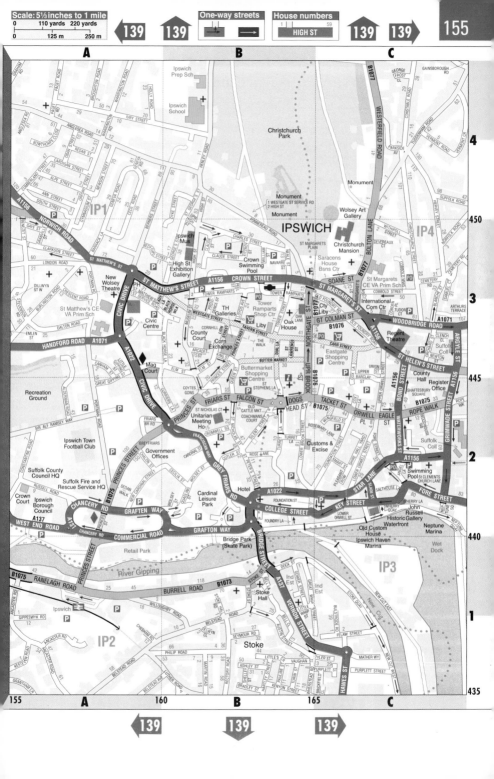

Index

Place name May be abbreviated on the map

Church Rd **6** Beckenham BR2..........**53** C6

Location number Present when a number indicates the place's position in a crowded area of mapping

Locality, town or village Shown when more than one place has the same name

Postcode district District for the indexed place

Page and grid square Page number and grid reference for the standard mapping

Public and commercial buildings are highlighted in magenta Places of interest are highlighted in blue with a star *

Abbreviations used in the index

Acad	Academy	Comm	Common	Gd	Ground	L	Leisure	Prom	Promenade
App	Approach	Cott	Cottage	Gdn	Garden	La	Lane	Rd	Road
Arc	Arcade	Cres	Crescent	Gn	Green	Liby	Library	Recn	Recreation
Ave	Avenue	Cswy	Causeway	Gr	Grove	Mdw	Meadow	Ret	Retail
Bglw	Bungalow	Ct	Court	H	Hall	Meml	Memorial	Sh	Shopping
Bldg	Building	Ctr	Centre	Ho	House	Mkt	Market	Sq	Square
Bsns, Bus	Business	Ctry	Country	Hospl	Hospital	Mus	Museum	St	Street
Bvd	Boulevard	Cty	County	HQ	Headquarters	Orch	Orchard	Sta	Station
Cath	Cathedral	Dr	Drive	Hts	Heights	Pal	Palace	Terr	Terrace
Cir	Circus	Dro	Drove	Ind	Industrial	Par	Parade	TH	Town Hall
Cl	Close	Ed	Education	Inst	Institute	Pas	Passage	Univ	University
Cnr	Corner	Emb	Embankment	Int	International	Pk	Park	Wk, Wlk	Walk
Coll	College	Est	Estate	Intc	Interchange	Pl	Place	Wr	Water
Com	Community	Ex	Exhibition	Junc	Junction	Prec	Precinct	Yd	Yard

Index of localities, towns and villages

A

Acton 92 B7
Acton Place 92 B8
Akenham 134 F6
Alburgh 7 A1
Aldeburgh 130 D4
Aldeby 9 F8
Alderton 99 E4
Aldham 94 E8
Aldringham 129 D3
All Saints South Elmham 24 B5
Allwood Green 36 A2
Alpheton 78 A5
Ampton 33 A2
Annis Hill 110 E3
Apsey Green 126 A3
Ardleigh Heath 103 F1
Ash Abbey 127 F3
Ashbocking 69 A1
Ash Corner 127 F7
Ashen 89 E5
Ashfield 54 D2
Ashfield Cum Thorpe . . 54 C1
Ashfield Green
 Stradbroke 39 D4
 Wickhambrook 62 A2
Ashley 60 F8
Ash Street 80 A1
Aspall 53 E4
Assington 92 F1
Assington Green 76 B6
Athelington 38 E2
Attleton Green 61 D1
Audley End
 Burston and Shimpling . . 20 E5
 Lawshall 77 D8

B

Babel Green 75 D3
Back Street 61 E5
Bacton 51 F5
Bacton Green 51 E4
Badingham 56 A6
Badwell Ash 50 E7
Badwell Green 51 B8
Ballingdon 148 B4
Banyard's Green 40 C4
Bardwell 34 C4
Barham 82 C6
Barking 125 A1
Barking Tye 81 A7
Barley Green 39 C5
Barnaby Green 26 C2

Barnardiston 75 B3
Barnby 10 B5
Barnham 16 C2
Barningham 34 F7
Barrow 47 A2
Barsham 9 A4
Barton Mills 116 D2
Base Green 51 B2
Bath Side 107 B3
Battisford 66 F1
Battisford Tye 66 C1
Battlesea Green 39 A6
Battles Green 49 C3
Bawdsey 99 E3
Baylham 81 E6
Baythorne End 89 C5
Beacon Hill 137 F3
Beccles 111 D5
Beck Row 30 A8
Bedfield 54 E5
Bedingfield 53 F7
Bedingham Green 7 B7
Belchamp Otten 90 A2
Belchamp St Paul 90 D5
Belchamp Walter 90 F3
Bell's Corner 102 F8
Bell's Cross 82 D7
Belstead 142 C7
Benacre 27 A7
Benhall Green 72 C8
Benhall Street 71 F8
Bentley 104 F8
Beyton 49 F1
Beyton Green 49 F2
Bigsby's Corner 72 D8
Bildeston 79 F4
Billingford 21 B1
Birdbrook 89 A4
Birds End 62 B7
Bird Street 80 A7
Blackheath 42 C5
Blacksmith's Green 53 C5
Black Street 11 A2
Blackthorpe 49 C2
Blaxhall 72 B4
Bleach Green 39 A8
Blo' Norton 18 E2
Bloodman's Corner 3 A6
Bloomoor Hill 114 E2
Blundeston 3 A4
Blyford 42 C7
Blythburgh 42 F6
Bobby Hill 35 C5
Boot Street 137 D6
Borley 91 C5
Borley Green
 Borley 91 B5

Woolpit 65 E7
Botesdale 36 B6
Bowbeck 34 C6
Bower House Tye 93 E3
Boxford 93 C3
Boxted
 Colchester 77 A6
 Glemsford 102 F4
Boxted Cross 103 A3
Boyden End 61 D2
Boyland Common 20 A7
Boyton 86 B2
Boyton End 89 B7
Brabling Green 126 E6
Bradfield 105 C1
Bradfield Combust 64 A4
Bradfield St Clare 64 C4
Bradfield St George 64 D7
Braiseworth 37 D2
Bramfield 41 F4
Bramford 134 A2
Brampton 25 E5
Brampton Street 25 E4
Brandeston 70 B7
Brandon 6 A1
Brantham 104 F4
Bredfield 84 C7
Brent Eleigh 79 F2
Bressingham 19 A2
Bressingham Common . . 19 F5
Brettenham
 Stowmarket 79 C8
 Thetford 17 B6
Brewers Green 20 B3
Bridge Green 20 F4
Bridge Street 77 F4
Brightwell 98 A6
Brinkley 59 E2
Broadgrass Green 50 C1
Broad Green
 Cheveley 60 F6
 Chevington 62 B6
 Creeting St Peter or West
  Creeting 67 C6
Broad Street 93 C5
Broadway 118 C6
Brockdish 21 F2
Brockford Green 53 A4
Brockford Street 52 F5
Brockley Corner 32 D2
Brockley Green
 Hartest 63 A1
 Hundon 75 C2
Broke Hall 140 E3
Brome 117 B7
Brome Street 117 E8
Bromeswell 85 A5

Brook Green 63 E5
Brook Street 77 A3
Broome 110 D7
Broome Heath 110 D7
Broom Hill 146 E2
Broom's Barn 46 F4
Brown Street 52 A2
Browston Green 2 E8
Bruisyard 56 C5
Brundish 55 C8
Brundish Street 39 E1
Brundon 148 A2
Bucklesham 98 A5
Bulcamp 42 D7
Bulmer 91 C3
Bulmer Tye 91 D1
Bungay 110 B3
Bures 101 C5
Bures Green 101 D6
Burgate 36 E6
Burgh 83 F6
Burgh St Peter 10 B8
Burrough End 59 E2
Burrough Green 59 F2
Burstall 95 C8
Burston 20 E6
Burthorpe 47 B3
Burwell 44 A5
Bury St Edmunds 154 C2
Bush Green 64 D4
Butley 86 B5
Butley High Corner 86 C4
Butley Low Corner 86 C4
Button Haugh Green 50 F4
Button's Green 78 E8
Buxhall 66 A6
Buxhall Fen Street 66 A6

C

Calais Street 93 D2
Calford Green 133 D5
California 140 B6
Camps Heath 112 D3
Candle Street 35 F5
Canham's Green 51 F4
Capel Green 86 A4
Capel St Andrew 86 B3
Capel St Mary 150 A4
Capon's Green 55 E6
Carlton
 Carlton 74 A8
 Kelsale cum Carlton . . . 128 C6
Carlton Colville 114 C2
Carlton Green 74 A6

Castle Hill 135 A3
Castling's Heath 93 D6
Cattawade 104 E4
Cavendish 76 D1
Cavenham 47 A8
Cay Hill 52 C2
Chantry 138 D2
Charles Tye 80 C7
Charsfield 70 B3
Chattisham 95 C5
Chedburgh 62 C4
Chediston 41 C8
Chediston Green 24 C1
Chelmondiston 106 C8
Chelsworth 79 E3
Chelsworth Common . . . 79 E2
Cheveley 60 E7
Chevington 62 C6
Chickering 38 F7
Chillesford 86 C7
Chilton 92 B5
Chilton Street 75 F1
Chimney Street 75 C3
Chippenhall Green 40 A6
Chippenham 45 C8
Church End 106 F7
Church Street 90 D6
Clare 90 B8
Clay Common 26 B4
Claydon 134 C8
Claypits 109 B4
Clay Street 35 D2
Clopton Corner 69 E1
Clopton Green
 Wickhambrook 62 A1
 Woolpit 65 D7
Cobbler's Green 7 C6
Cock & End 75 C8
Cockfield 64 C1
Cocks Green 64 A5
Cock Street 102 C7
Coddenham 68 C1
Coddenham Green 67 F2
Colchester Green 64 E2
Coldfair Green 129 B2
Coles Green 95 D4
Cole's Green 126 C1
Colton 48 F5
Combs 124 C1
Combs Ford 124 D4
Coney Weston 34 F8
Conyers Green 48 B7
Cookley 41 A6
Cookley Green 40 F6
Cook's Green 79 D8
Copdock 95 F4
Cornard Tye 92 C4

Corton ... 3 C4
Cotton ... 52 B6
Cove Bottom ... 26 E3
Covehithe ... 27 B4
Cove Green ... 51 F4
Cowlinge ... 46 C8
Cox Common ... 25 A5
Crackthorn Corner ... 19 A1
Cranley ... 37 F3
Cranmer Green ... 35 E2
Cransford ... 56 B3
Cratfield ... 40 D6
Creeting Bottoms ... 67 F5
Creeting St Mary ... 125 H8
Creeting St Peter ... 67 C5
Cretingham ... 69 F7
Cross Green
  Cockfield ... 64 B2
  Hartest ... 77 A7
  Hitcham ... 79 E7
Cross Street ... 38 C7
Crowfield ... 68 D4
Crown Corner ... 39 D1
Crownland ... 35 D1
Cuckold's Green ... 26 C5
Cuckoo Green ... 3 A6
Cuckoo Tye ... 92 A7
Culford ... 32 D1
Culfordheath ... 32 F5
Culpho ... 137 A7
Curlew Green ... 128 C7

D

Dagworth ... 66 E8
Daisy Green
  Great Ashfield ... 51 A6
  Wickham Skeith ... 52 D7
Dalham ... 46 C8
Dallinghoo ... 70 D1
Dam Green ... 19 C8
Dandy Corner ... 52 B6
Darmsden ... 125 F1
Darsham ... 42 C1
Debach ... 70 A1
Debenham ... 53 E2
Dedham ... 103 F4
Dedham Heath ... 103 F2
Denham
  Denham ... 61 F8
  Hoxne ... 38 D5
Denham End ... 46 F2
Dennington ... 55 E5
Dennington Corner ... 126 C8
Denston ... 76 A7
Denton ... 7 A3
Depden ... 62 B3
Depden Green ... 62 B4
Dickleburgh ... 21 B5
Dickleburgh Moor ... 21 D6
Diss ... 20 C4
Ditchingham ... 110 C7
Ditton Green ... 60 B4
Dockeney ... 8 F6
Dorking Tye ... 101 D7
Dorley's Corner ... 128 D8
Dovercourt ... 107 B2
Down Field ... 28 F2
Drakestone Green ... 93 F8
Drinkstone ... 65 C8
Drinkstone Green ... 65 B7
Dublin ... 53 E8
Duke Street ... 95 B5
Dullingham ... 59 F5
Dullingham Ley ... 60 A3
Dunstall Green ... 61 E7
Dunwich ... 43 B1

E

Earl's Green ... 51 D5
Earl Soham ... 54 E2
Earl Stoneham ... 67 E5
Earsham ... 7 E4
Earsham Street ... 22 C1
East Barton ... 49 C4
East Bergholt ... 151 C4
Eastbridge ... 58 D4
East End
  East Bergholt ... 104 E6
  Stonham Aspal ... 68 D6
East Green
  Great Bradley ... 74 E8
  Kelsale cum Carlton ... 57 E4
Easton ... 70 E5
Edge Green ... 19 E8
Edwardstone ... 93 A5
Ellingham ... 9 F2
Ellough ... 9 F1
Ellough High ... 111 D3
Elmsett ... 80 F1
Elmswell ... 50 E2
Elveden ... 15 D3
Eriswell ... 13 F1
Erwarton ... 106 D5
Euston ... 16 F1
Exning ... 120 B8
Eye ... 117 D3
Eyke ... 85 B6

F

Fakenham Magna ... 33 E7
Falkenham ... 98 E2
Falkenham Sink ... 98 F2

Farley Green ... 75 D8
Farnham ... 72 A7
Felixstowe ... 152 E4
Felixstowe Ferry ... 108 C8
Felsham ... 65 A3
Feltwell ... 4 D5
Fenstead End ... 76 E5
Fen Street
  Hopton ... 18 B2
  Redgrave ... 19 C2
Fern Hill ... 77 B4
Fersfield ... 19 D6
Finkle Green ... 89 A2
Finningham ... 52 B8
Flempton ... 47 F8
Flixton ... 7 D1
Flowton ... 81 C1
Foals Green ... 39 D2
Fordham ... 29 B1
Fornham All Saints ... 48 B6
Fornham St Genevieve ... 48 C6
Fornham St Martin ... 48 C6
Forward Green ... 67 B2
Four Ashes ... 35 C1
Foxash Estate ... 104 B1
Foxearth ... 91 B7
Framlingham ... 126 D2
Framsden ... 69 B6
Freckenham ... 29 F3
Frenze ... 20 F3
Fressingfield ... 39 D8
Freston ... 143 D3
Friday Street
  Benhall ... 72 B7
  Brandeston ... 70 A6
  Rendlesham ... 85 D7
Friston ... 73 C4
Fritton ... 2 B7
Frizzeler's Green ... 47 C1
Frostenden ... 26 C4
Frostenden Corner ... 26 D3

G

Gainsborough
  Ipswich ... 139 F1
  Ipswich ... 144 B8
Garboldisham ... 18 D4
Garlic Street ... 22 A6
Gasthorpe ... 18 A4
Gazeley ... 46 B3
Gedding ... 65 A5
Geldeston ... 8 F7
Genesis Green ... 61 F4
Gestingthorpe ... 90 F1
Gillingham ... 9 C6
Gipping ... 52 B2
Gipsy Row ... 150 A4
Gisleham ... 11 A3
Gislingham ... 36 D2
Gissing ... 20 F8
Glemsford ... 77 B2
Goddard's Corner ... 55 E7
Gosbeck ... 68 D2
Gosland Green ... 76 A5
Gosling Green ... 93 C1
Grass Green ... 89 D1
Great Ashfield ... 50 F6
Great Barton ... 49 A6
Great Bealings ... 137 E6
Great Blakenham ... 82 A5
Great Bradley ... 74 C7
Great Bricett ... 80 E5
Great Common ... 8 E2
Great Cornard ... 148 F3
Great Green
  Burgate ... 36 D7
  Cockfield ... 64 D2
  Denton ... 7 A4
  Thrandeston ... 37 C8
Great Horkesley ... 102 E1
Great Livermere ... 33 C2
Great Saxham ... 47 C1
Great Thurlow ... 74 E5
Great Waldingfield ... 92 C6
Great Welnetham ... 63 F6
Great Wenham ... 150 A3
Great Wratting ... 74 E3
Great Yeldham ... 90 A1
Greenstead Green ... 80 D5
Greenwich ... 139 E1
Grimstone End ... 49 F8
Grinstead Hill ... 125 E3
Gromford ... 72 C5
Groton ... 93 B4
Grundisburgh ... 83 D5
Gulling Green ... 63 A3
Gunton ... 113 C6

H

Hacheston ... 71 A6
Hadleigh ... 149 F6
Hadleigh Heath ... 93 F4
Hagmore Green ... 93 B2
Halesworth ... 118 A4
Hall Green ... 90 C2
Hanchet End ... 132 A8
Hanningfields Green ... 63 F1
Hargrave ... 62 B6
Harkstead ... 106 B5
Harleston
  Harleston ... 66 B7
  Redenhall with Harleston ... 22 E5

Harrow Green ... 63 D1
Hartest ... 77 A7
Hartest Hill ... 77 C7
Hart's Green ... 63 E2
Harwich ... 107 A3
Hasketon ... 146 C8
Haughley ... 51 C1
Haughley Green ... 51 C3
Haughley New Street ... 51 B1
Haverhill ... 132 C6
Hawkedon ... 76 D7
Hawstead ... 63 D6
Hawstead Green ... 63 E5
Hazel Stub ... 132 A5
Heckfield Green ... 38 D7
Hedenham ... 7 E8
Helions Bumpstead ... 88 B4
Helmingham ... 69 B4
Hemingstone ... 82 C8
Hemley ... 98 E5
Hemp Green ... 57 C8
Hengrave ... 48 A7
Henny Street ... 91 F1
Henstead ... 26 E8
Hepworth ... 35 A6
Herringfleet ... 2 F1
Herringswell ... 46 C8
Hessett ... 64 F8
Heveningham ... 40 F3
Hickford Hill ... 90 C7
Higham
  Bury St Edmunds ... 46 E4
  Stratford St Mary ... 103 D2
High Green ... 63 D7
High Rougham ... 49 E1
High Street
  Darsham ... 42 B1
  Iken ... 73 B2
  St Margaret, Ilketshall ... 24 D7
High Street Green ... 66 A2
Hightown Green ... 65 D3
Hinderclay ... 35 E7
Hintlesham ... 95 C6
Hitcham ... 79 E6
Hobbles Green ... 75 A8
Hockwold cum Wilton ... 5 A3
Hoggard's Green ... 64 A3
Holbrook ... 105 E7
Hollesley ... 99 D7
Hollybush Corner ... 64 D6
Holly Hill ... 110 B8
Holton ... 118 E4
Holton St Mary ... 151 A8
Holywell Row ... 30 C8
Homersfield ... 23 B8
Honey Tye ... 102 B6
Honington ... 33 C6
Hoo ... 70 B5
Hopton ... 18 C2
Hopton on Sea ... 3 C7
Horham ... 38 E3
Horner's Green ... 93 C4
Hornestreet ... 103 C3
Horringer ... 63 A8
Hoxne ... 38 B8
Hulver Street ... 10 E1
Humble Green ... 93 F5
Hundon ... 75 E3
Hunston ... 50 D7
Hunston Green ... 50 D5
Huntingfield ... 41 A5

I

Icklingham ... 31 D4
Iken ... 72 F2
Ilketshall St Andrew ... 8 E2
Ilketshall St Lawrence ... 24 F6
Ilketshall St Margaret ... 24 B8
Ingham ... 32 F1
Ipswich ... 155 B3
Isleham ... 29 B5
Ixworth ... 34 B2
Ixworth Thorpe ... 33 F4

K

Kedington ... 133 E7
Kelsale ... 128 C2
Kennett ... 45 F7
Kenninghall ... 19 B8
Kenny Hill ... 12 F2
Kentford ... 46 A5
Kenton ... 54 B5
Kenton Corner ... 54 C4
Kersey ... 94 A7
Kersey Tye ... 93 E6
Kersey Upland ... 93 E5
Kesgrave ... 141 C8
Kessingland ... 11 C2
Kessingland Beach ... 27 C8
Kettlebaston ... 79 C5
Kettleburgh ... 70 C7
Kingshall Green ... 64 D7
Kingshall Street ... 64 D8
Kingston ... 146 F2
Kirby Cane ... 8 E8
Kirby Row ... 8 E7
Kirkley ... 115 B5
Kirtling ... 60 E3
Kirtling Green ... 60 E2
Kirton ... 98 E2
Knaves Green ... 53 A5
Knettishall ... 17 F3
Knodishall ... 73 A8

Knodishall Common ... 129 A2
Knowl Green ... 90 C4

L

Lackford ... 31 F1
Lady's Green ... 61 F6
Lakenheath ... 109 E7
Lamarsh ... 101 A6
Lamb Corner ... 103 E2
Lambfair Green ... 75 A8
Lampardbrook ... 70 E8
Landwade ... 44 D6
Langham
  Bury St Edmunds ... 50 D8
  Stratford St Mary ... 103 C2
Langton Green ... 117 D4
Lattinford Hill ... 151 D8
Lavenham ... 78 D4
Lawford ... 104 E2
Lawshall ... 63 E1
Lawshall Green ... 77 F8
Laxfield ... 40 C3
Leavenheath ... 102 B7
Leiston ... 129 B5
Letheringham ... 70 C4
Levington ... 145 E3
Lidgate ... 61 C4
Lindsey ... 93 D7
Lindsey Tye ... 93 E8
Linstead Parva ... 40 E8
Liston ... 91 D7
Little Bealings ... 137 E5
Little Blakenham ... 81 F3
Little Bradley ... 74 E6
Little Cornard ... 92 C2
Little Ditton ... 60 C5
Little Finborough ... 66 B1
Little Glemham ... 71 E5
Little Green
  Burgate ... 36 D5
  Gislingham ... 36 C3
Little Horkesley ... 102 B3
Little London ... 66 E2
Little Knowles Green ... 62 B5
Little Saxham ... 47 D2
Little Stonham ... 67 F6
Little Thurlow ... 74 E5
Little Thurlow Green ... 74 E5
Little Waldingfield ... 92 D8
Little Welnetham ... 64 B6
Little Wenham ... 150 B5
Little Whittingham
  Green ... 40 A8
Little Wratting ... 74 E2
Little Yeldham ... 90 B2
Long Green ... 36 D8
Long Melford
  Long Melford ... 77 F1
  Long Melford ... 91 E8
Long Thurlow ... 51 B7
Lound ... 2 F5
Lower Common ... 25 B3
Lower Falkenham ... 98 F1
Lower Green ... 46 E4
Lower Hacheston ... 127 F8
Lower Holbrook ... 106 A6
Lower Layham ... 149 D1
Lower Raydon ... 94 D1
Lower Street
  Stansfield ... 76 C6
  Stutton ... 105 D5
Lowestoft ... 113 F1
Low Green ... 63 E7
Lynford ... 6 C5

M

Mace Green ... 95 E4
Magpie Green ... 19 E1
Maidenhall ... 139 B1
Maidensgrave ... 146 D2
Malting End ... 61 D6
Manningtree ... 104 F2
Man's Cross ... 89 F2
Market Weston ... 35 A8
Marlesford ... 71 C5
Martlesham ... 84 A1
Martlesham Heath ... 98 B7
Maypole Green
  Bradfield St George ... 64 D6
  Dennington ... 55 D6
Meadowend ... 89 E3
Mellis ... 37 A5
Mellis Green ... 36 F5
Mells ... 118 E2
Melon Green ... 63 C4
Melton ... 147 C8
Mendham ... 23 A6
Mendlesham ... 52 E4
Mendlesham Green ... 52 D2
Metfield ... 23 C3
Methersgate ... 84 E1
Mettingham ... 8 D4
Mickfield ... 68 B8
Mickley Green ... 63 B4
Middle Green ... 46 E4
Middle Harling ... 18 B8
Middleton
  Leiston ... 58 B6
  Sudbury ... 148 C2
Middleton Moor ... 58 B6
Middlewood Green ... 67 D8
Milden ... 79 B1
Mildenhall ... 116 D6
Mile End ... 77 A7

Mill Common ... 25 C4
Mill End ... 60 F3
Mill Green
  Burston and Shimpling ... 20 E7
  Buxhall ... 65 F4
  Edwardstone ... 93 B5
  Stonham Aspal ... 68 B7
Mill Hill ... 77 E6
Mill Hills ... 147 A6
Mill Street ... 102 E8
Mistley ... 105 A2
Mistley Heath ... 105 A1
Moats Tye ... 66 E2
Monewden ... 69 F5
Monks Eleigh ... 79 B2
Monk Soham ... 54 D4
Moulton ... 45 F3
Mount Bures ... 101 C3
Mount Pleasant ... 75 D2
Mundford ... 6 B8
Mutford ... 10 D2

N

Nacton ... 145 C5
Naughton ... 80 C3
Nayland ... 102 C5
Nedging ... 79 F3
Nedging Tye ... 80 B4
Needham ... 22 B4
Needham Market ... 125 E5
Needham Street ... 46 B4
Nether Street ... 64 E8
Nettlestead ... 81 C4
Newbourne ... 98 C5
New England ... 89 A5
Newman's Green ... 92 A6
Newmarket ... 121 B4
New Mistley ... 105 A2
Newton ... 92 D3
Newtown ... 54 D7
Normanston ... 113 B3
North Common ... 34 F6
North Cove ... 10 C4
North End ... 90 C2
North Green
  Cratfield ... 40 C7
  Kelsale cum Carlton ... 57 D5
  Parham ... 56 B1
North Lopham ... 19 A5
Norton ... 50 B4
Norton Little Green ... 50 D5
Nowton ... 63 E7

O

Oak Hill ... 100 A8
Oakley ... 38 A8
Occold ... 37 F1
Offton ... 81 A4
Old Felixstowe ... 153 C6
Oldhall Green ... 64 C3
Old Newton ... 51 F1
Onehouse ... 66 C6
Orford ... 131 C3
Otley ... 69 C2
Oulton ... 112 F5
Oulton Broad ... 114 C8
Ousden ... 61 E6
Ovington ... 90 A5

P

Page's Green ... 53 C4
Pakefield ... 115 B3
Pakenham ... 49 E6
Palgrave ... 20 C1
Parham ... 71 A7
Parkeston ... 106 F3
Park Gate ... 61 A8
Park Green ... 53 B3
Parliament Heath ... 93 C6
Parney Heath ... 103 D2
Peasenhall ... 56 E8
Peats Corner ... 69 B7
Pentlow
  Pentlow ... 76 E1
  Pentlow ... 90 F7
Pentlow Street ... 91 A8
Pettaugh ... 68 E6
Pettistree ... 127 B4
Pinford End ... 63 D6
Pitcher's Green ... 64 D5
Pitman's Corner ... 53 C5
Playford ... 137 B5
Polstead ... 93 F1
Polstead Heath ... 93 F2
Pooley Street ... 19 D4
Poslingford ... 76 A3
Potash ... 104 F8
Pound Green ... 61 B1
Poystreet Green ... 65 E5
Preston St Mary ... 79 A5
Priory Green ... 92 F6
Priory Heath ... 140 D1
Pulham St Mary ... 21 F8
Puttock End ... 90 E3

R

Racecourse ... 140 B2
Ramsey ... 106 C1
Ramsholt ... 99 A4

Rattlesden...........65 E6
Raydon...........94 E1
Reading Green.........38 E5
Rede.............62 E2
Redenhall..........22 E7
Redgrave..........36 A8
Redisham..........25 B7
Redlingfield........38 D2
Red Lodge.........30 B1
Rendham..........56 E3
Rendlesham........85 C8
Reydon...........119 C7
Reydon Smear.......26 F1
Rickinghall........36 A6
Ridgewell.........89 D4
Ringsfield.........9 B3
Ringsfield Corner.....9 B2
Ringshall.........80 E7
Ringshall Stocks.....80 F6
Risby............47 D5
Rishangles........53 D7
Rodbridge Corner.....91 E6
Roman Hill........113 C1
Rooksey Green......78 E6
Roost End........133 E2
Rosedale Park......114 E4
Rose Green
  Assington.......101 F8
  Lindsey........93 D7
Rose Hill........139 F4
Rotchfords........101 F1
Rougham.........64 D8
Rougham Green.....64 C8
Roydon..........20 A3
Rumburgh.........24 A6
Rushall..........21 F5
Rushbrooke........64 B8
Rushford.........17 B4
Rushmere.........10 D1
Rushmere St Andrew..136 E1
Rushmere Street.....136 E2
Russel's Green......39 C3

S
Sackers Green.......92 D2
St Cross South Elmham.23 D7
St James South Elmham.23 F4
St Margaret South
  Elmham.........23 E6
St Michael South
  Elmham.........24 A6
St Nicholas South
  Elmham.........23 E6
St Olaves.........2 A6
St Peter South Elmham.24 A7
Santon Downham.....6 C2
Sapiston..........33 F6
Saxham Street......67 C8
Saxmundham.......128 D3
Saxon Street.......60 D6
Saxstead Bottom.....55 C5
Saxtead..........55 C4
Saxtead Green......55 B3
Saxtead Little Green...55 B5
Scole...........21 A2
Scole Common......20 F3
Scotland Street.....102 F7
Semer...........79 F1
Shadingfield.......25 E7
Shadwell.........17 C6
Shelfanger........20 C6

Shelland..........66 A7
Shelley..........94 C1
Sherbourne Street....93 B4
Shimpling
  Burston and Shimpling..21 A6
  Shimpling.......77 E6
Shimpling Street.....77 E8
Shingle Street......100 A5
Shipmeadow.......8 F4
Shop Corner.......106 C5
Shotford Heath.....22 D4
Shotley..........106 F6
Shotley Gate.......107 A4
Shottisham........99 C7
Sibton...........57 A8
Sibton Green.......41 D2
Sicklesmere.......63 F7
Silverlace Green.....71 C7
Silverley's Green....40 B6
Sizewell..........58 F1
Slough Hill........77 E7
Smallwood Green.....64 F5
Smallworth........18 D3
Smith's Green......88 C3
Smithwood Green....78 C7
Snailwell.........45 A6
Snape...........72 D4
Snow Street.......20 A4
Soham..........28 D4
Soham Cotes.......28 B6
Somersham........81 C3
Somerton.........76 F8
Sotherton........25 E2
Sotherton Corner....25 E1
Sotterley.........26 A7
South Cove........26 F4
South Green
  Hoxne.........38 B5
  Pulham St Mary...21 F6
South Lopham......19 B4
Southolt.........54 B7
Southwold........119 C5
Sowley Green......75 A5
Spexhall.........24 F3
Spratt's Street......85 D5
Sproughton........138 A7
Stackyard Green.....93 C8
Stambourne.......89 B1
Stambourne Green...89 A1
Stanningfield......64 A4
Stansfield.........76 C7
Stanstead........77 C4
Stanton..........34 D4
Stanton Chare......34 D5
Stanton Street......50 B5
Stanway Green......39 C1
Starston.........22 C7
Steeple Bumpstead...88 D4
Sternfield.........72 D8
Stetchworth.......60 A5
Stock Hill........50 E8
Stoke...........155 B1
Stoke Ash........37 B1
Stoke by Clare......89 E6
Stoke-by-Nayland....102 E6
Stoke Park........138 F1
Stone Street
  Boxford........93 C2
  Spexhall.......24 F5
Stonham Aspal......68 A6
Stoven..........25 F4
Stowlangtoft.......50 C7
Stowmarket.......124 E6

Stoupland.........67 B6
Stradbroke........39 A5
Stradishall........75 F7
Stratford St Andrew...71 F7
Stratford St Mary....103 D5
Stubbing's Green.....36 C5
Sturmer..........133 C2
Stuston..........20 E1
Stutton..........105 D6
Sudbourne........86 F8
Sudbury..........148 C4
Sutton..........85 A1
Sutton Street......99 A7
Swan Green........40 B5
Swefling.........56 E2
Swilland.........83 A7
Swingleton Green....79 C2
Syleham.........22 A1

T
Tannington........55 A6
Tan Office........52 F2
Tan Office Green....62 C6
Tattingstone.......105 B8
Tattingstone White
  Horse.........142 D1
Temple End
  Foxearth.......91 A6
  Little Thurlow....74 C5
Theberton........58 B4
The Brook........36 E7
The Common.......81 F3
The Heath........105 A7
Thelnetham.......18 D1
Thelveton........21 A4
The Marsh........36 E8
The Port of Felixstowe.152 C1
Thetford.........16 D5
The Woodlands.....95 A3
Thistley Green......29 E7
Thorington........42 C4
Thorington Street...103 A6
Thorndon.........53 B8
Thorney Green......67 A7
Thornham Magna....37 A2
Thornham Parva....37 B3
Thorpe Abbotts.....21 E2
Thorpe Common.....107 C8
Thorpe Green......64 F1
Thorpe Morieux.....79 A8
Thorpeness.......73 E6
Thorpe Street......35 D8
Thrandeston.......37 B7
Thurston.........49 E3
Thurston End......76 D6
Thwaite.........52 F7
Tilbury Green......89 E4
Tilbury Juxta Clare..90 A3
Timworth.........48 D8
Timworth Green....48 D7
Toad Row........10 F1
Tostock..........50 B2
Tower Hill........107 C3
Trimley Lower Street..107 C7
Trimley St Martin....107 D8
Trimley St Mary....107 D8
Troston..........33 D3
Tuddenham.......30 F2
Tuddenham St Martin..136 C5
Tunstall.........71 F2

Wheatacre........2 B1
Whelp Street......79 B4
Whepstead........63 B5
Wherstead........143 B6
Whitestreet Green...93 D2
Whitton.........134 F3
Wicken..........28 B1
Wicker Street Green..93 E5
Wickhambrook.....61 E2
Wickham Green....52 C8
Wickham Market....127 B6
Wickham Skeith.....52 E8
Wickham Street
  Wickhambrook....61 F1
  Wickham Skeith...52 C8
Widgham Green....60 B2
Wiggens Green.....88 C5
Wilby...........39 C2
Wilde Street.......13 D2
William's Green....93 E5
Willingham........25 E7
Willisham.........81 A5
Willisham Tye......81 A6
Wilney Green......19 D4
Windsor Green.....64 B2
Winfarthing.......20 B8
Wingfield........39 B8
Wingfield Green....38 F8
Winston.........68 F6
Wissett..........24 D2
Withermarsh Green..103 A8
Withersdale Street...22 F4
Withersfield.......74 B2
Witnesham........83 A6
Wixoe...........89 B6
Woodbridge.......146 F6
Woodbridge Walk...99 F8
Woodditton.......60 C5
Woodland Green....133 C5
Woodton.........7 C8
Woolpit.........50 D1
Woolpit Green......65 D8
Woolpit Heath......65 E8
Woolverstone......144 B1
Wootten Green......39 B3
Wordwell.........32 D3
Workhouse Green...101 C8
Workhouse Hill.....102 F2
World's End.......65 F2
Worlingham.......111 F3
Worlington.......30 A4
Worlingworth......54 F8
Wormingford......101 F2
Wortham.........36 D8
Wortwell.........23 B8
Wrabness.........105 F2
Wrentham........26 E5
Wrentham West End..26 C7
Wyverstone.......51 E6
Wyverstone Green...51 E6
Wyverstone Street...51 D6

U
Ubbeston.........40 E4
Ubbeston Green....40 D3
Ufford..........84 F7
Uggeshall........25 F3
Undley..........13 C4
Upend..........60 F5
Upgate Street......7 B6
Upper Green.......46 E3
Upper Holton......118 E7
Upper Layham.....149 F2
Upper Street
  Baylham.......81 E6
  Dickleburgh and Rushall..21 C2
  Stansfield.......76 C6
  Stutton........105 B5
Upper Town.......49 E7
Upper Weybread....22 B2
Upsher Green......92 D6
Upthorpe........34 F3

W
Wainford.........110 D5
Walberswick......119 A2
Walcot Green......20 D4
Waldringfield......98 D7
Waldringfield Heath..98 C7
Wales End........76 D4
Walpole.........41 C5
Walsham le Willows..35 C2
Walton..........152 F6
Wangford........26 B2
Ward Green.......51 E3
Warren Heath......140 F1
Washbrook........95 F5
Washbrook Street...95 F6
Washmere Green....78 D2
Waterloo
  Aldeby.........9 E8
  Dickleburgh and Rushall..20 F2
Wattisfield.......35 D5
Wattisham........80 B6
Wattisham Stone....80 A6
Weeting.........5 E3
Wenhaston.......42 C6
Westbourne......138 F7
Westbrook Green...20 C4
West End........26 B6
Westerfield.......135 E4
Westhall.........25 C4
West Harling......18 A8
Westhorpe.......51 D8
Westleton........58 B7
Westley.........122 A6
Westley Waterless...59 E3
Weston.........9 D1
Weston Ditch......29 F7
West Row........29 F6
West Stow........32 B1
West Street
  Rickinghall Inferior..35 E5
  Walsham-le-willows..35 A1
West Tofts........6 E7
Wetherden.......51 B1
Wetherden Upper Town.51 B4
Wetheringsett.....53 A5
Wetherup Street....53 C3
Weybread........22 D3
Whatfield........80 C1

Y
Yaxley..........37 B5
Yoxford.........57 D7

1

13th Century Hospl of St
Saviour* IP32 ......154 B4
100th Bomb Group Meml
Mus* IP21 ....21 D4

9

95th Bomb Group Hospl
Musuem* IP21 ......38 C4

A

Abbey Cl 10 Burwell CB5 ..44 A5
10 Ixworth IP31 ....34 B1
Rendlesham IP12 .....85 D7
Abbey Farm Jun Sch 1
IP24 ....16 B6
Abbey Fields IP14 ......66 D8
Abbey Gdns IP13 ....71 C2
Abbey Hill IP21 ....38 C7
Abbey La IP16 ....129 B8
Abbey Rd Flixton NR35 ..23 F8
Leiston IP16 ....129 C7
Sudbury CO10 ....93 C8
Abbey Sch The IP12 ...147 A4
Abbeydale NR32 ......114 E2
Abbeygate St 3 IP33 ..154 B2
Abbot Cl IP33 ....122 D4
Abbot Rd IP33 ......122 D4
Abbot's Hall Drift CO10 ..78 E2
Abbot's Hall Rd IP14 ..124 D5
Abbots Cotts CB9 .....133 E2
Abbots Hall* IP14 ....124 D5
Abbots Hall Prim Sch
IP14 ....124 C5
Abbotsbury Cl IP2 ....139 A1
Abbotsbury Rd IP33 ..122 D3
Abbott Rd CO12 ......106 F1
Abbotts Croft CB9 ....133 D2
Abbotts Ct CB9 ....133 C3
Abbotts Gn Com Prim Sch
IP32 ....49 A3
Abbotts Meadow 8 NR30 ..50 D1
Abbotts Rd CB9 ......132 E7
Abbottsinch Rd 6 IP31 ..33 D5
Abdy Ave 5 CO12 .....106 F1
Abercorn Ct 2 CB9 ...132 D4
Aberdeen Way IP4 ....135 E6
Aberfoyle Cl 4 IP4 ...136 C1
Abingdon Cl IP2 ......139 A1
Abington Pl IP29 ......132 E7
Ablitts Meadow IP13 ...83 E6
Acacia Ave IP32 ....48 C5
Acacia Cl IP3 ....140 E1
Acer Gr IP8 ....138 C1
Acer Rd IP12 ....85 D8
Acheson Way 7 IP15 ..130 E5
Acorn Cl 8 IP3 ....138 C2
Acorn Way IP5 ....98 B8
Acorns The IP30 ....49 E3
Acre Cl IP6 ....83 A6
Acre Rd CB8 ....59 E5
Action France CB8 .....59 E5
Action CE Prim Sch
CO10 ....92 B7
Acton Cl Bramford IP8 ..134 A2
Sudbury CO10 ....148 D6
Acton Gdns 1 IP8 ....134 A2
Acton Gn 3 CO10 .....148 C5
Acton La Acton CO10 ..92 A6
Sudbury CO10 ....148 D6
Acton Pl Ind Est CO10 ..92 A8
Acton Rd Bramford IP8 ..134 A2
Lowestoft NR33 ......115 B4
Adair Rd IP1 ....138 D8
Adam's La IP18 ....43 C5
Adams Pl IP5 ....141 C7
Adamson Rd IP18 ....119 B8
Adastral Cl
Felixstowe IP11 .....153 H11
Newmarket CB8 .....120 E4
Addington Rd IP1 ....152 C7
Addison Cl IP26 ....4 F5
Addison Rd CO10 .....148 E4
Addison Way IP8 .....134 A8
Adeane Meadow IP26 ..6 A8
Adelaide Cl 17 CB7 ....28 D4
Adelaide Rd IP4 .....140 D6
Admiral Rd IP8 ......142 E8
Admirals Jun Sch 3
IP24 ....16 C7
Admirals Wlk IP12 ...147 B6
Adrian Rd 4 NR32 ....113 D2
Africa Alive* NR33 ....11 A1
Agate Cl 2 IP1 ......134 D1
Ailwin Rd IP32 ....123 E4
Ainslie Rd IP1 ....139 A6
Airedale NR33 ....114 E2
Airey Cl Lowestoft NR32 ..112 F1
Newton CO10 ....92 E3
Airey Houses IP3 ....137 D6
Airfield Rd IP32 ....49 A3
Airstation La IP21 ....21 E6
Aisthorpe IP9 ....150 D2
Akethorpe Way NR32 ..113 A3
Alabaster Cl IP7 .....149 E6
Alan Rd IP3 ....139 F4
Alandale Dr 2 NR33 ..11 C1
Alasdair Pl 8 IP6 ....134 C8
Alban Sq 2 IP22 ......84 A1
Albany Rd 1 NR32 ...113 E2
Albany The IP4 ....135 E6
Albemarle Rd IP33 ...122 D4

Albemarle St 6 CO12 ..107 B3
Albert Cres IP33 .....154 A2
Albert Pl IP13 ....126 C3
Albert Pye Prim Sch
NR34 ....111 B4
Albert Rd IP13 ....126 C3
Albert Rolph Dr IP27 ..109 E4
Albert St IP33 ....154 A2
Albert Wlk IP11 ......153 B3
Alberta Cl IP5 ....141 A8
Albion Hill IP4 ....139 F7
Albion Rd NR35 ....110 D3
Albion St IP17 ....128 C3
Aldburgh with Denton Prim
Sch IP20 ....7 A1
Alde House Dr IP15 ..130 E4
Alde La IP15 ....130 E4
Alde Rd CB9 ....132 E7
Aldeburgh & District Com
Hospl IP15 ....130 D4
Aldeburgh Cl CB9 ....130 E5
Aldeburgh Lodge Gdns
IP15 ....130 E5
Aldeburgh Mus* IP15 ..130 F4
Aldeburgh Prim Sch
IP15 ....130 E3
Aldeburgh Rd
Friston IP17 ....72 F7
Leiston IP16 ....129 D4
Aldecar La IP14 ....72 C7
Alder Carr Farm & Ctyd Craft
Ctr* IP6 ....125 E5
Alder Covert 6 IP24 ...16 D6
Alder Dr 2 NR33 .....114 C4
Alder Way CO10 .....148 D6
Aldercroft Cl IP1 .....135 B3
Aldercroft Rd IP1 ....135 B3
Aldergrove Cl IP9 ...118 A3
Alderlee IP2 ....142 F8
Alderman Rd IP1 ....155 A2
Alderton Cl CB9 .....132 C8
Alderton Rd IP12 ......99 E6
Aldham Ct 1 CB9 ....132 C5
Aldham Gdns IP14 ...124 E4
Aldham Mill Hill IP7 ..149 C8
Aldham Rd IP7 ......147 A5
Aldis Ave IP14 ......124 D4
Aldon Cl 14 CO12 ....106 E1
Aldous Cl IP7 ....149 E4
Aldous St 13 IP4 .....53 F2
Aldridge La 2 IP28 ....48 B6
IP16 ....129 C3
Aldringham Craft Mkt*
IP16 ....129 C3
Aldringham Mews 13
IP11 ....152 D5
Aldringham Pk IP16 ..129 D3
Aldringham Rd IP17 ..129 B3
Aldwyck Way NR33 ..114 F4
Alexander Cl NR34 ...114 A8
Alexander Dr
4 Great Waldingfield CO10 ..92 C6
Needham Market IP6 ..125 C5
Alexander Way IP28 ..47 E5
Alexanders Int Sch
IP12 ....108 D8
Alexandra Rd
Beccles NR34 ....111 B5
Felixstowe IP11 .....152 E6
Lowestoft NR32 .....113 D1
Sudbury CO10 ......148 E5
Alexandra St 8 CO12 ..107 B3
Alfred Corry Mus*
IP18 ....119 C2
Algar Dr CB8 ....59 F4
Alice Driver Rd 5 IP13 ..83 E5
Alicia Cl IP13 ....123 C3
All Hallows' Hospl
NR35 ....110 C7
All Saints CE Mid Sch
CO10 ....148 E8
All Saints CE Prim Sch
IP29 ....63 E1
All Saints CE VA Prim Sch
Laxfield IP13 ....40 A3
Newmarket CB8 .....121 B3
Winfarthing IP22 .....20 C8
All Saints Cl CB8 .....46 C3
All Saints Ct IP33 ....154 B3
All Saints Gn NR34 ..111 C3
All Saints Gn 6 NR34 ..111 F4
All Saints Rd IP6 ....125 F8
All Saints' Rd
Ipswich IP1 ....139 A7
Lowestoft NR33 ....115 B4
Sudbury CB8 ....121 B3
All Saints St CB8 ....121 B3
Allen Rd Hadleigh IP7 ..149 D7
Lowestoft NR32 .....112 D1
Allenby Rd IP2 ......138 D2
Alleyne Rd IP10 ......98 D2
Allfields 3 CO12 .....107 A1
Allington Cl IP4 .....139 F7
Allington Rd 7 IP9 ...150 E4
Allington Wlk CB9 ...132 C6
Allotment La IP6 ......69 A1
Allthorpe Rd 12 IP20 ..22 D6
Alma Cl 3 IP4 ......136 A1
Alma Pl IP27 ....109 D6
Alma Rd NR32 ....113 C1
Almond Gr IP24 ......16 A4
Almondhayes IP2 ...139 B3
Almshouse Rd IP30 ...49 C1
Alnesbourn Cres
1 Gainsborough IP2 ..144 D8
Ipswich IP3 ....144 D7

Alnesbourne Priory
IP10 ....144 C6
Alpe St 1 IP1 ....155 A4
Alpha Bsns Pk IP1 ...134 D3
Alphamstone Rd CO8 ..101 A6
Alston Cl CO10 ....92 D3
Alston Rd IP3 ....139 F4
Alton Hall La IP9 ....105 C6
Alton Wr Sports Ctr
IP9 ....105 D6
Alton Cl IP32 ....123 F5
Alvis Wlk IP1 ....134 C1
Amber Mus The*
IP18 ....119 D5
Amberfield Sch IP10 ..145 C6
Amberley Ct 3 NR32 ..112 F4
Ambleside Gdns NR32 ..113 A4
America Hill IP6 ......83 A6
Amins Ct IP28 ....16 B2
Amy Johnson Ct 6
IP28 ....28 B6
Ancaster Rd IP2 .....155 A1
Anchor End 2 CO11 ...105 A2
Anchor La Burwell CB5 ..44 A6
Dedham CO7 ....104 A2
Lakenheath IP27 ....109 C6
1 Mistley CO11 .....105 A2
Anchor St IP33 ......115 C4
Anchor Way NR33 ...114 B4
Anderson Cl IP6 ....125 C5
Anderson Wlk IP32 ..122 D7
Anderson's Way 8 IP12 ..146 E4
Andrew Burtt's Cl
IP13 ....126 B3
Andrew Cl
Felixstowe IP11 .....152 E3
Leiston IP16 ....129 C4
Andrew Johnston Way
IP8 ....118 B3
Andrew Rd CB8 .....120 E5
Andrew Way NR33 ..114 D6
Andrews Cl 9 IP4 ....53 F2
Andrews Wlk IP32 ..122 D8
Andros Cl 7 IP4 ....144 A7
Angel Hill
Bury St Edmunds IP33 ..154 C2
Stonham Earl IP14 ...68 D7
Angel La Blythburgh IP19 ..42 F6
Bury St Edmunds IP33 ..154 B2
Glemsford CO10 .....77 A2
2 Woodbridge IP12 ..147 A5
Angel Link IP19 .....118 B3
Angel Rd IP8 ....134 A2
Angela Ct 7 IP12 ....101 A8
Angel Ct IP12 ....147 A5
Angelgate Espl 4 CO12 ..107 C3
Angerstein Cl IP27 ....5 E4
Anglesea Rd IP1 ....155 A4
Anglesey Pl 6 IP31 ...49 A5
Anglia Parkway N IP1 ..134 D4
Anglia Parkway S IP1 ..134 D3
Anglian La IP32 ......73 B4
Anglian Way IP31 .....49 A4
Angus Cl IP4 ....136 B1
Animal Health Trust Visitor
Ctr* CB8 ....45 F5
Anita Cl E IP2 ......138 E5
Anita Cl W IP2 ......138 E5
Ann Beaumont Way
IP7 ....149 C7
Ann Coles Cl CB9 ....88 E3
Ann St IP1 ....155 A4
Ann Suckling Rd CB8 ..132 B8
Annandale Dr NR34 ..111 D4
Annbrook Rd IP2 ....138 B1
Anne Bartholomew Rd
IP24 ....16 C7
Anne St IP11 ....152 E3
Annesons Cnr IP17 ...58 B6
Annis Hill NR35 .....110 E3
Annis Hill La 2 NR35 ..110 D3
Annis Hill Rd NR35 ..110 D3
Annison Cl NR33 ....115 B5
Ansell Cl IP7 ....149 D6
Anselm Ave 8 IP32 ...48 C5
Anson Rd 7 IP5 ....98 A8
Anson Way NR34 .....10 A3
Antonia Cl IP3 ......133 C5
Antrim Rd IP1 ......134 D1
Anzani Ave IP11 ....152 C4
Apple Acre Rd CB9 ..132 A7
Apple Gr IP14 ....51 A2
Apple Tree Cl NR33 ..115 B6
Appleby Cl IP4 ......138 C1
Appledore Dr NR33 ..114 D4
Appledown Dr IP30 ..123 E7
Appletree Gr 2 CB5 ...44 A6
Appletree La IP30 .....20 C3
Approach Cotts IP29 ..132 B8
Aragon Rd IP32 .....123 B4
Arbor La NR33 ......115 A4
Arcade St IP1 ......155 B3
Archangel Gdns IP2 ..138 E4
Archbishop Sancroft High
Sch IP20 ....22 C6
Archers' Ave 3 IP5 ....4 D5
Arderne Cl 3 CO12 ...106 F1
Ardleigh Rd CO7 ....103 A2
Arger Fen Nature Reserve*
CO10 ....101 F6
Argyle St IP4 ....155 C3
Argyll Ct 7 IP33 ....132 D5
Ark Cl NR33 ....11 B1
Arkle Ct IP5 ....141 D7
Arkwright Rd IP2 ...138 E6
Arlington Way IP24 ...16 C5

Arms La CB9 ....133 F7
Armstrong Cl
Hundon CO10 ......75 D4
Newmarket CB8 ....121 B3
Armstrong Way CO9 ..90 A1
Arnhem Ct NR32 ....113 C4
Arnhem Rd IP16 ....129 D5
Arnold Cl IP1 ....134 A7
Arnold St 3 NR32 ..113 E1
Arnold Way IP32 ....123 F5
Arras Rd IP33 ......122 D5
Arrendene Rd CB9 ..132 D7
Arrowhead Dr IP27 ..109 C7
Arthurs Terr IP4 ....155 C3
Artillery Dr 7 CO12 ..106 E1
Artillery Way 11 NR32 ..113 E2
Arundel Cl 3 CO12 ..123 D6
Arundel Rd
Ipswich IP3 ....140 E3
2 Lowestoft NR33 ..114 D4
Arundel Wlk 11 CB9 ..132 C6
Arwela Rd IP11 ....152 F2
Ascot Dr
Felixstowe IP11 ....152 E6
Ipswich IP3 ....140 B3
Ash Ave 11 IP2 ......80 D6
Ash Cl Bacton IP14 ...51 F6
10 Lakenheath IP27 ..13 F2
7 Lowestoft NR33 ..114 D5
Thetford IP24 ....16 A4
Warren Heath IP3 ...140 F1
Woodbridge IP12 ...146 F4
Ash Dr IP23 ....117 D3
Ash Gd Cl
3 Brantham CO11 ..104 E4
10 Felixstowe IP11 ..107 D8
Ash Gr 17 Burwell CB5 ..44 A5
Capel St Mary IP9 ...150 E3
Haverhill CB9 ....132 C7
4 Sudbury CO10 ....92 B3
Ash Rd
Campsey Ash IP12 ...71 C1
Hacheston IP13 .....127 F7
Onehouse IP14 ......66 C6
Rendlesham IP12 ....85 C7
Ash Rise 8 CO6 ....102 C5
Ash St 4 CO10 ......93 C3
Ash Tree Cl
8 Beccles NR34 .....9 F4
7 Fressingfield IP21 ..39 D8
8 Occold IP23 ....37 F1
Ash Wlk CB8 ....75 C6
Ashbocking Rd IP6 ...82 E6
Ashbourne Ct CB8 ...121 B3
Ashburnham Rd IP6 ..125 C4
Ashburnham Way
NR33 ....114 D4
Ashby Rd NR32 .....113 C1
Ashcroft Rd IP1 ....135 A1
Ashdale Dr NR34 ...111 E4
Ashdale Pk IP27 .....14 E8
Ashdown Way IP3 ...140 D3
Ashe Rd IP12 ....71 F2
Ashen Cl CO10 ......89 E5
Ashen Hill CO10 ....89 E5
Ashen La CO10 .....89 E6
Ashes The IP14 .....54 D1
Ridgewell CO9 ......89 D4
Ashfield Cres NR33 ..114 F7
Ashfield Hill IP31 ....50 F6
Ashfield Rd
Elmswell IP30 ....50 F3
Norton IP31 ....50 C4
Wetherden IP14 .....51 A2
Ashford Cl NR34 .....9 B6
Ashfords Cl IP17 ...128 B4
Ashlea Ct CB9 ......132 F4
Ashlea Rd CB9 .....132 F4
Ashley Downs NR32 ..113 C3
Ashley Rd Cheveley CB8 ..60 E8
Harwich CO12 ......107 A2
Newmarket CB8 .....121 E2
Ashley St NR32 .....113 C4
Ashman's Rd NR34 ..111 A4
Ashmere Gr IP4 ....139 F6
Ashmere Rise CO10 ..148 F5
Ashness Cl 2 NR32 ..113 A4
Ashton Cl IP2 ......138 C2
Ashton Rd IP3 ......117 C3
Ashtree Gdns NR33 ..114 D3
Ashwell Rd IP33 ....122 D4
Askins Rd CO7 .....151 C5
Aspal Cl 1 IP28 ......30 B8
Aspal Close Nature Reserve*
IP28 ....30 B7
Aspal Hall Rd IP28 ...30 B8
Aspal La IP28 ....30 B8
Aspal Pk IP28 ....30 B8
Aspall Rd IP14 ....53 F3
Aspel Est IP28 ....30 B8
Aspen Cl Claydon IP6 ..134 D8
Great Barton IP31 ...49 B6
Haverhill CB9 ....132 C7
3 Woodbridge IP12 ..147 B6
Aspen Coppice 6 NR32 ..112 F5
Aspinall Cl 4 IP33 ...114 F4
Assington La CO10 ...93 A1
Assington Rd CO10 ...93 D3
Assington St CO10 ..101 F8
Astbury Rd 8 NR30 ..113 B5
Aster Rd IP2 ....138 E4
Aston Cl IP1 ....134 C1
Ataka Rd IP11 ......152 F6
Athelington Rd IP21 ..38 F2
Athenaeum La IP33 ..154 C2

Athenaeum The*
IP33 ....154 C2
Atherton Rd IP2 ....138 D2
Atterton Rd CB9 ....132 B7
Atteria Cl 2 NR33 ...114 F7
Audley End IP21 .....20 F5
Audley Gr IP4 ......140 F5
Augusta Cl IP10 ....144 E2
Augustus Cl CB9 ....133 B5
Aureole Wlk CB8 ....120 E8
Austin Cl IP31 ....50 E7
Austin St IP2 ....155 B1
Aveley La IP29 ......77 D6
Aveling Way NR33 ..114 B3
Avenue App IP27 ...123 A8
Avenue Rd IP27 ....109 E4
Avenue The
Brome & Oakley IP23 ..117 E8
3 Burwell CB5 ......44 B6
Copdock & Washbrook
IP8 ....95 F4
Felixstowe IP11 ....152 B7
Great Barton IP31 ..123 F8
Halesworth IP19 ...118 B5
Ipswich IP1 ....135 C1
4 Kessingland NR33 ..11 B1
Lowestoft NR33 ....115 B5
Newmarket CB8 ....121 A3
Risby IP28 ....47 E5
Ufford IP13 ....84 F7
Woodbridge IP12 ..147 A4
Aves Cl IP3 ....29 C5
Avocet Cl NR33 ....114 D5
Avocet Gr 2 CB7 .....28 D5
Avocet La 28 IP5 .....98 A8
Avondale Rd
Ipswich IP3 ....140 A2
Lowestoft NR32 ....113 C1
Aylmer Cl IP28 ......47 D5
Aylward Cl IP7 .....149 E4
Ayr Rd IP4 ....136 B1

B

Babb's La IP14 ......52 F2
Babergh Cl 9 CO10 ...92 B7
Babington Dr IP19 ..118 B2
Baby La IP30 ....65 D4
Back Hamlet IP3 ....139 E5
Back Hill IP6 ....105 F6
Back Hills IP22 ......36 A7
Back La
Badwell Ash IP31 ....50 F8
Burrough Green CB8 ..59 F2
Claydon IP6 ....134 C8
Copdock & Washbrook
IP8 ....95 F5
Diss IP22 ....20 D7
Falkenham IP10 .....98 F1
Felixstowe IP11 ....152 F5
Kettlebaston IP7 .....79 C5
Lound NR32 ....2 F6
Monks Eleigh IP7 ....79 C2
St Mary, South Elmham
otherwise Homersfield
IP20 ....23 C8
Scole IP21 ....21 A5
Tattingstone IP9 ...105 B7
Wicken CB7 ....28 A1
Back Rd Brockdish IP21 ..21 E4
Middleton IP17 ......58 B6
Rattlesden IP30 .....65 C2
Trimley St Martin IP10 ..98 D2
Wenhaston with Mells Hamlet
IP19 ....42 C6
Back St
Garboldisham IP22 ...18 D5
Gislingham IP23 .....36 B1
Lakenheath IP27 ...109 D6
Bacon Rd 7 IP6 .....82 B5
Bacon's Gn Rd IP19 ..25 D3
Bacton Com Prim Sch
IP14 ....51 F6
Bacton Mid Sch IP14 ..51 E6
Bacton Rd
Felixstowe IP11 ....152 F3
Haughley IP14 ......51 C2
Baden Powell Wlk
IP5 ....141 E7
Bader Cl IP3 ....140 C2
Bader Ct 25 IP5 ......98 A8
Badger's Holt 10 NR33 ..11 B1
Badgers Bank IP2 ...138 E1
Badgers Cl CO6 ....102 D1
Badgerwood Cl NR33 ..115 B4
Badingham Rd
Badingham IP13 .....56 A4
Framlingham IP13 ..126 C5
Laxfield IP13 ....40 C1
Peasenhall IP17 .....56 D7
Badley Hill IP6 ....125 B7
Badley Wlk IP6 .....125 A7
Badleys Cl 8 CO10 ...92 C6
Badlingham Rd CB7 ..29 E5
Badsham Ave 4 IP3 ..140 B3
Badwell Ash VA Prim Sch
IP31 ....50 E8
Badwell Rd
Walsham le Willows IP31 ..35 B1
Wyverstone IP14 ....51 C6
Bagsham La IP14 ....30 A8
Bahram Cl CB8 .....120 E4
Bailey Ave IP5 .....141 E7
Bailey Cl Haverhill CB9 ..133 B5

Bailey Cl continued
Ipswich IP2 ....138 E6
Bailey La CO10 ....90 B8
Baileypool La IP31 .....49 F8
Baines Coney CB9 ......132 A7
Baird Cl IP2 ....138 F7
Baker's Dr IP5 ....141 B6
Bakehouse Hill CB8 ....59 F4
Baker Dr 2 CB5 ....44 B6
Baker Rd 2 IP7 ....107 A4
Baker's Cnr IP14 ....80 B6
Baker's Hill IP16 ......58 C4
Baker's La
　Bury St Edmunds IP33 ...154 C1
　Thorpe Morieux IP30 .....53 C6
　Wrestleton IP7 ....58 C8
Baker's Rd CO10 ....90 D5
Baker's Score 1 NR32 ....3 D4
Bakers La
　Ditchingham NR35 ....110 B8
　Orford IP12 ....131 C2
　Winston IP14 ....68 E8
　1 Woodbridge IP12 ......147 A4
Bakers La S IP12 ....131 C2
Bakers Row CB8 ....121 A4
Bakers Way IP28 ....30 F2
Balaton Pl CB8 ....121 A6
Baldry Cl IP8 ....138 C1
Baldrys Wlk NR35 ....110 B7
Baldwin Av IP32 ....122 E8
Baldwin Rd IP14 ....124 C4
Ball's Chace CO6 ....101 C1
Ballater Cl IP1 ....134 E4
Ballingdon Hill CO10 ...148 A3
Ballingdon St CO10 .....148 A4
Balliol Cl IP12 ....146 D3
Balls Hill IP7 ....79 D5
Ballygate NR34 ....111 A5
Balmoral Cl IP2 ....138 F1
Balmoral Dr 2 CB9 ......132 C6
Balton Way 7 CO12 ......106 F1
Bancroft La CB7 ....28 D5
Bangor Rd IP27 ....13 F2
Banham Dr 3 CO10 ....148 D6
Banham Rd NR34 ....111 C2
Banham's La NR35 ....7 B6
Bank Alley 5 IP18 ......119 D5
Bank Bldgs 11 CO10 .....148 C4
Bank Rd IP4 ....139 E6
Banks Cl IP7 ....149 E5
Banks' La IP19 ....24 C3
Banks Wlk IP33 ....122 C5
Bannocks La IP13 ....56 B4
Banters La NR34 ....8 F2
Bantocks Rd CO10 ....92 C5
Bantoft Terr IP3 ....140 C7
Banyard Cl 4 IP5 ....141 D7
Barbara Stradbroke Ave
　CB8 ....120 D1
Barber Cl 3 NR33 ....1 D1
Barber's La NR35 ....7 B6
Barcham Rd CB7 ....28 C7
Bardolph Rd NR33 ....110 B3
Bardwell Rd IP31 ....33 F5
Bardwell VC Prim Sch
　IP31 ....34 C5
Bardwell Windmill*
　IP31 ....34 B4
Barell's Hill IP19 .....40 F4
Bargate La
　Back Row, Holywell Row
　　& Kenny Hill IP28 .....29 F5
　Dedham CO7 ....104 A2
Bargate Rd IP28 ....30 A6
Barham Picnic Site Visitor
　Ctr* IP6 ....82 A6
Barhams Way IP13 ....127 C7
Barker Cl Ipswich IP2 ..138 D5
　8 Manningtree CO11 .....104 D2
　8 Steeple Bumpstead CB9 ..88 D3
Barker Rd CO10 ....148 C8
Barking Rd
　Barking IP6 ....125 A1
　Willisham IP8 ....81 A5
Barkis Meadow NR32 .....3 A4
Barkways 9 CB5 ....44 B5
Barley Lands IP31 ......130 E5
Barley Meadow 8 IP19 ...118 A3
Barley Way NR33 ....114 F2
Barlings Ct CB8 ....121 A4
Barn Cl
　2 Hopton on Sea NR31 ....3 C7
　Lowestoft NR33 ....114 D5
　Southwold IP18 ....119 B8
Barn Field 8 IP29 ......62 C6
Barn La IP33 ....154 C3
Barn St 12 CO10 ....78 D4
Barnaby Gn IP14 ....119 C5
Barnardiston Hall Prep Sch
　CB9 ....75 A5
Barnards Way NR32 ......113 B1
Barnby & N Cove Prim Sch
　NR34 ....10 C4
Barnes Cl Brandon IP27 ..14 E8
　8 Hadleigh IP7 ....149 E6
Barnfield
　Capel St Mary IP9 ......150 F3
　Felixstowe IP11 ....152 D6
　20 Manningtree CO11 ....104 E2
Barnham CE Prim Sch
　IP24 ....16 B1
Barnham Pl IP5 ....140 F6
Barnham Rd IP24 ....16 E2
Barningham CE VC Prim Sch
　IP31 ....34 E7

Barningham Rd IP31 .....34 E5
Barons Cl
　9 Felixstowe IP11 ......153 D6
　Halesworth IP19 ....118 A2
Barons Ct 7 CB9 ....132 C5
Barons Meadow IP12 .....131 B3
Barons Rd IP33 ....123 A2
Baronsdale Cl IP1 ......135 B1
Barr Dr IP27 ....109 D7
Barrack La
　Harwich CO12 ....107 C2
　Ipswich IP1 ....155 A3
　Ufford IP13 ....84 F7
Barrack Sq IP5 ....98 A8
Barracks Rd CO10 ....101 F8
Barrell's Rd IP31 ......49 F3
Barrett's La IP6 ....125 C4
Barrow Hill Acton CO10 ..92 B8
　Barrow IP29 ....47 A3
Barrow Prim Sch IP29 ...47 A3
Barrow Rd IP29 ....46 F1
Barrow's Cnr IP24 ......32 C8
Barry Lynham Dr CB8 ....121 B2
Barsey Cl CB9 ....132 A7
Bartholomew Gn
　IP18 ....119 D5
Bartholomew St IP4 .....139 F6
Bartholomew's La IP19 ..42 B6
Bartlet Hospl IP11 .....153 C4
Bartlow Pl CB9 ....132 F7
Barton Bottom IP31 .....48 E7
Barton Dr CB9 ....133 F8
Barton Gr CB9 ....133 F8
Barton Hamlet IP31 .....49 C6
Barton Hill IP31 ....48 D5
Barton Rd
　Bury St Edmunds IP32 ...123 D6
　Felixstowe IP11 ....153 B4
　Thurston IP31 ....49 D4
　Woodbridge IP12 ....146 F7
Bartons Pl CB8 ....120 E5
Bartrum La 2 IP5 ....141 C7
Barrens The IP8 ....138 A1
Barway Rd IP7 ....28 A6
Barwell Rd IP33 ....154 C3
Basil Brown Cl 1 IP22 ..36 A6
Bates La IP22 ....189 A3
Bath Ct CB9 ....132 D4
Bath Hill IP11 ....153 B4
Bath Hills Rd NR35 ......7 F4
Bath Rd IP11 ....153 B4
Bath St IP2 ....139 D3
Battery Gn 7 NR32 ......113 C1
Battery Rd 6 NR32 ......113 C1
Battery La 10 IP9 ......107 A4
Battisford Rd IP6 ......125 A1
Battles La IP5 ....141 D7
Battlesea Hill IP21 ....39 A6
Bawdsey Cl IP11 ....153 D7
Bawdsey Manor Workshops*
　IP12 ....99 E2
Bawdsey Radar Sta*
　IP12 ....99 E1
Bayfield Dr 4 CB5 ......44 B6
Baylham House Rare Breeds
　Farm* IP6 ....81 F7
Baynard's La IP22 ......20 A3
Bays The 6 IP16 ....73 F6
Beach Mews 6 NR32 ......115 D8
Beach Rd Dunwich IP17 ..43 B1
　1 Harwich CO12 ....107 B1
　Hopton on Sea NR31 .....3 C6
　Kessingland NR33 ....27 C8
　Lowestoft NR32 ....115 D8
Beach Rd E IP11 ....153 C4
Beach Rd W IP11 ....152 F2
Beach Sta Rd IP11 ......152 E5
Beacon Field 4 IP11 ....152 E5
Beacon Hill Ave CO12 ...107 D2
Beacon Hill La IP13 ....73 F7
Beacon Hill Specl Sch
　IP2 ....138 F2
Beacon La IP13 ....137 F3
Beaconsfield Cl CO10 ...148 C6
Beaconsfield Ct 9 CB9 ..132 D5
Beaconsfield Rd
　Aldeburgh IP15 ....118 D6
　Ipswich IP1 ....138 F7
　21 Kessingland NR33 ....115 C6
　Lowestoft NR33 ....115 C6
　8 Woodbridge IP12 ......147 A5
Bealings La IP13 ....137 F8
Bealings Rd IP12 ....137 D4
Bealings Sch IP13 ......137 D4
Bear Meadow 5 IP30 .....49 F2
Bear St CO6 ....102 C5
Beard Rd IP22 ....20 B3
Beardmore Pk 10 IP5 ....98 A8
Bear's La CO10 ....78 D3
Beatrice Ave IP11 ......153 A5
Beatrice Rd IP13 ....140 A3
Beatty Rd Ipswich IP3 ..140 B2
　Sudbury CO10 ....148 E7
Beaufort Rd IP11 ....153 A4
Beaufort St IP1 ....155 A3
Beaumont Cl 3 IP33 .....122 D4
Beaumont Ct CB9 ....132 F4
Beaumont Rd NR33 ....114 B2
Beaumont Vale CB9 ......133 F7
Beaumont Way IP14 ......124 B5

Beccles & District Mus*
　NR34 ....111 A5
Beccles & District War Meml
　Hospl NR34 ....111 B4
Beccles Gall* q0 NR34 ..111 B5
Beccles Mid Sch
　NR34 ....111 C4
Beccles Rd Aldeby NR34 ..9 F8
　Aldeby/Wheatacre/Burgh
　　St Peter NR34 ....9 F8
　Blyford IP19 ....25 C1
　Bungay NR35 ....110 C4
　Carlton Colville NR33 ..114 A4
　Fritton & St Olaves NR31 ..2 C7
　Holton IP19 ....118 F4
　Lowestoft NR33 ....114 D7
　Mutford NR34 ....10 C3
Beccles Sports Ctr
　NR34 ....111 A3
Beccles Sta NR34 ....111 C5
Becclesgate 1 NR34 .....111 B6
Beck Cl 6 IP7 ....85 D8
Beck Rd CB7 ....29 D4
Beck Row Prim Sch
　IP28 ....30 B8
Beck St IP21 ....35 A7
Beck The IP26 ....4 E5
Beck View 3 IP20 ....22 D6
Beckett Cl IP23 ....122 A6
Becketts La IP7 ....94 B1
Becketts The IP14 ......124 B8
Beckford Rd 17 CO11 ....105 A2
Beckham Rd NR12 ....10 A8
Becks Gn La NR34 ....24 F8
Bedell Cl IP33 ....122 C3
Bederic Cl IP33 ....123 D4
Bedfield CE Prim Sch
　IP13 ....54 C5
Bedfield Rd IP13 ....55 A3
Bedford Rd 3 IP22 ......122 E8
Bedford St IP1 ....138 C6
Bedingfeld Way IP32 ....123 E4
Bedingfield Cres IP19 ..118 A1
Bedingfield Rd IP23 ....53 E7
Beech Circus 5 IP7 .....80 D6
Beech Cl
　Halesworth IP19 ....118 A3
　Isleham CB7 ....29 B5
　11 Lakenheath IP27 ....113 D7
　Sproughton IP8 ....138 A6
Beech Croft CB8 ....59 E1
Beech Gr Haverhill CB9 ..132 C7
　Ipswich IP3 ....139 F3
Beech La 2 IP14 ....51 A1
Beech Paddocks 4 IP30 ..64 F8
Beech Rd Ipswich IP5 ...140 F7
　Lowestoft NR33 ....114 D3
　Sudbury CO10 ....148 F4
Beech Rise IP23 ....123 C3
Beech Row IP14 ....46 C1
Beech Tree Cl NR34 .....111 B4
Beech Tree Way NR35 ....7 F4
Beech Way
　Dickleburgh IP21 ....21 C5
　Woodbridge IP12 ....146 F3
Beech Wlk IP16 ....129 C5
Beechcroft IP1 ....134 F2
Beeches Cl 11 IP31 .....34 B1
Beeches Rd IP28 ....29 F7
Beeches The
　Benhall Green IP17 .....72 C8
　Claydon IP6 ....134 C8
　Horringer IP29 ....63 A8
　Ipswich IP3 ....139 F4
　51 Lawford CO11 ....104 E2
　Little Blakenham IP8 ...81 E3
Beeching Dr NR32 ....113 D4
Beechwood Cl CB8 ....120 C8
Beechwood Gdns
　NR33 ....115 A6
Beehive Cl CO7 ....151 C5
Beeleigh Way NR35 ......7 F4
Beevors Gdn NR35 ....110 B7
Belaugh Ave NR33 ....114 F3
Belchamp Hall* CO10 ...91 A3
Belchamp Rd CO9 ....90 A6
Belchamp St Paul CE Prim
　Sch CO10 ....90 D5
Belcher Gn IP10 ....119 C8
Belfry Rd IP3 ....144 F7
Belgrave Cl IP4 ....135 E1
Bell Cl IP2 ....155 B1
Bell Gdns 13 CB7 ....29 B5
Bell Gn IP19 ....40 C6
Bell Hill CO8 ....101 B6
Bell La
　Barton Mills IP28 ......116 D2
　Ipswich IP2 ....155 B1
　Marlesford IP13 ....71 C4
Bell Meadow IP24 ....123 A8
Bell Mews IP7 ....149 D6
Bell St IP7 ....85 D8
Bellands Way IP23 ......117 C3
Bell's Cross IP14 ......67 C6
Bell's Cross Rd IP6 ....282 C7
Bell's La Hawstead IP29 ..63 E5
　Stowupland IP14 ....67 C7
Belle Vue Rd
　Ipswich IP4 ....139 F6
　Sudbury CO10 ....148 D5
Bells Cl IP30 ....50 F2
Bells Hill IP8 ....138 C8
Bells La Glemsford CO10 ..77 A3
　Hinderclay IP22 ....19 C4
Bells Rd CO10 ....90 F3

Bellwell La
　Debenham IP14 ....53 F4
　Kenton IP14 ....54 A4
Belmont Ct
　8 Haverhill CB9 ....132 D5
　Newmarket CB8 ....120 F3
Belmont Gdns NR32 ......113 B3
Belmont Rd IP8 ....138 C2
Belsay Ct CB9 ....132 B6
Belseybridge Rd NR35 ...7 F7
Belstead Ave IP2 ....155 A1
Belstead Rd IP2 ....155 A1
Belstead Sch IP8 ....138 C2
Belt The CB8 ....61 B4
Belvedere Rd 28 NR33 ...11 C1
Belvedere Rd
　Ipswich IP4 ....139 F8
　Lowestoft NR33 ....115 C7
Belvoir Ct 2 NR32 ......132 C6
Benacre National Nature
　Reserve* NR34 ....27 B6
Benacre Rd
　Ellough NR34 ....111 E2
　Henstead with Hulver Street
　　NR34 ....26 E8
Benefield Rd IP1 ....45 F3
Benezet St IP1 ....155 A3
Benhall St Marys CE Prim
　Sch IP17 ....72 C8
Benjamin Britten High Sch
　NR32 ....113 A5
Bennett Ave
　Bury St Edmunds IP33 ...122 C6
　Elmswell IP30 ....50 F2
Bennett Rd
　Ipswich IP1 ....134 E1
　5 Red Lodge IP28 ......30 C1
Benouville IP30 ....114 F3
Bensly's Drift IP19 ....118 C4
Bentley Cl 5 IP4 ....140 E8
Bentley Dr NR32 ....113 A6
Bentley La
　Belstead IP9 ....142 C5
　Stutton IP9 ....105 B6
Bentley Prim Sch IP9 ...104 F8
Bentley Rd IP1 ....134 C2
Benton La IP7 ....65 C1
Benton St IP7 ....149 D4
Benton Way IP14 ....149 D4
Benyon Gdns IP28 ....32 D1
Beresford Dr IP12 ......146 F7
Beresford Rd NR32 ......113 D2
Bergamot Rd CB9 ....132 A6
Berghersh La IP6 ....82 E7
Bergholt Rd CO11 ....104 D4
Berkeley Cl
　2 Framlingham IP13 .....126 C3
　Ipswich IP4 ....135 E1
Berkeley Gdns
　Bury St Edmunds IP33 ...122 E4
　Lowestoft NR32 ....113 A4
Bermuda Rd IP10 ....144 D7
Bernard Cres IP3 ....140 B2
Bernard Rooke Pottery &
　Gall* IP6 ....83 A8
Berners Rd IP11 ....153 C4
Berners St IP1 ....155 A3
Bernham Cl IP32 ....123 D5
Berry Cl Ipswich IP3 ...140 F1
　Lowestoft NR32 ....112 C1
Berrycroft 11 CB7 ......28 D4
Berry Rd 8 CB9 ....132 C6
Bethel Dr 2 IP13 ....11 C1
Betjeman Cl IP24 ....16 C7
Betony Wlk IP7 ....139 B6
Betts Ave IP5 ....98 A8
Betts Cl IP7 ....149 D7
Betty Cocker Gr CO10 ...148 F5
Bevan St E 3 NR32 ......115 D8
Bevan St W NR32 ....113 C1
Beverley Cl NR33 ....114 D6
Beverley Ct NR33 ....114 C2
Beverley Rd IP4 ....139 F8
Beversham Rd IP13 ......71 F5
Bevis Wlk IP33 ....123 D2
Bewicks Mead 10 CB5 ....44 B5
Bexley Ave 18 CO12 .....106 F1
Beyond the Image
　Photographers Gall*
　IP3 ....36 F2
Beyton Mid Sch IP30 ....49 F2
Beyton Rd IP30 ....49 F1
Bibb Way IP1 ....139 A5
Bickers Hill Rd IP13 ...40 B3
Bier La IP22 ....19 C1
Big Row NR34 ....8 F6
Bigod Cl
　5 Framlingham IP13 .....126 C3
　Halesworth IP19 ....118 B2
Bigod Rd NR35 ....110 D3
Bilberry Rd IP3 ....144 C7
Bildeston Gdns 2 IP1 ...135 D1
Bildeston Prim Sch IP7 ..79 E4
Bildeston Rd
　Chelsworth IP7 ....79 E3
　Combs IP14 ....124 A1
　Offton IP7 ....80 F4
Bill Rickaby Dr CB8 ....121 A5
Billy's La CO7 ....103 E5
Bilney Rd IP12 ....146 E5
Birch Ave CO10 ....107 A2
Birch Cl
　Lowestoft NR32 ....112 D2
　1 Stowupland IP14 .....67 A6
　Wickham Market IP13 ...127 C6
　Woodbridge IP12 ....146 F3
Birch Covert IP24 ......16 D6

Birch Cres IP27 ....109 D7
Birch Dr 8 CO11 ....104 E5
Birch Fall 7 CO6 ....102 C5
Birch Gr IP5 ....98 A7
Birch Rd Onehouse IP14 ..66 C6
　10 Thurstow IP31 ....49 E4
Birch St CO6 ....102 D5
Birch Wlk 24 IP27 ......13 F2
Birchcroft Rd IP1 ......135 B2
Birches The
　Kennett IP28 ....46 A8
　Soham CB7 ....28 C5
Birchgrove IP23 ....52 F7
Birchinhill Dro IP28 ...12 F2
Birchwood Cty Prim Sch
　IP5 ....98 A8
Birchwood Dr IP5 ....136 E1
Birchwood Rd CO7 ....103 D2
Bird View Sq 1 IP26 ....4 E5
Bird's Rd IP30 ....64 D2
Bird's Rd IP31 ....63 A1
Birdbrook 3 IP29 ....63 A1
Birdbrook Rd CO9 ....89 A2
Birdcage Wlk CB8 ....139 F2
Birds Ct IP31 ....65 E5
Birds Gn IP30 ....65 E5
Birds Hill IP13 ....83 D8
Birds La Framsden IP14 ..69 F5
　Lowestoft NR33 ....115 B6
Birds Meare IP6 ....69 C2
Birkdale Ave IP28 ......116 B5
Birkdale Cl 10 IP28 ....48 C6
Birkfield Cl IP2 ....139 A4
Birkfield Dr IP2 ....138 E1
Birkin Cl CB9 ....133 A5
Bishop Mews IP6 ....138 B2
Bishop's Hill IP3 ......139 F4
Bishops Cl
　6 Felixstowe IP11 ......153 D6
　Haverhill CB9 ....132 C6
Bishops Ct 1 CB9 ....132 C6
Bishops Rd IP33 ....154 B3
Bishops Way IP21 ....39 A4
Bishops Wlk
　10 Hopton on Sea NR31 ..3 B7
　Lowestoft NR32 ....113 D5
Bittern Cl IP2 ....138 E3
Bittern Gn NR33 ....114 C6
Bittern Rd IP17 ....128 B3
Bixley Dr IP4 ....140 E5
Bixley La IP4 ....140 E5
Bixley Rd Ipswich IP3 ..140 D3
　2 Lowestoft NR33 ......115 C6
Black Barns IP11 ....152 C7
Black Bear Ct CB8 ......121 A3
Black Bear La CB8 ......120 F3
Black Boy La CO11 ......106 A2
Black Boy Meadow
　NR34 ....111 B4
Black Dyke Rd IP26 .....4 E3
Black Gr La CO10 ....75 C4
Black Hill (Tumulus)*
　IP31 ....33 C5
Black Horse La
　Ditchingham NR35 ....110 C7
　Ipswich IP1 ....155 A3
Black Horse Wlk IP15 ...155 B3
Black Mill Rd IP18 .....119 C5
Black Slough IP7 ....58 B7
Black St NR33 ....10 F1
Blackberry Way
　Lowestoft 112 C2
　Red Lodge IP28 ....30 C1
Blackbird Ave IP27 .....6 A1
Blackbird Cl 16 IP31 ...49 D4
Blackbird Dr IP32 ......49 A3
Blackbird Rd 8 IP28 ....13 B1
Blackbird Way IP14 .....67 A5
Blackbourne CE VC Mid Sch
　IP31 ....34 F4
Blackbourne Rd IP30 ....50 F2
Blackbourne Dro IP26 ...4 A2
Blackdown Ave IP5 ......140 F6
Blackdyke Cl 9 IP26 ....4 D5
Blackfriars CO10 ....148 B4
Blackheath Rd
　Lowestoft NR33 ....115 A5
　Wenhaston with Mells Hamlet
　　IP19 ....42 C5
Blackhouse La CO10 .....148 F1
Blacklands La IP12 .....131 A8
Blackmore Cl CB8 ....132 D7
Blacksmith La
　Barnham IP24 ....16 B2
　Thorpe Morieux IP30 ...78 F7
Blacksmith Rd IP14 .....52 A6
Blacksmith's Cnr IP8 ...142 C6
Blacksmith's Loke NR32 ..3 D4
Blacksmiths La CO10 ....89 D6
Blacksmiths La
　Bulmer CO10 ....91 C1
　Coddenham IP6 ....68 B1
　Stonham Earl IP14 .....67 D6
Blackthorn Cl IP1 ......140 F1
Blackthorn Ct CB7 ......28 D5
Blackthorn Way CO6 .....102 B7
Blackthorn Wlk IP32 ....122 D8
Blacktiles La IP12 .....84 A1
Bladen Dr IP4 ....140 E5
Bladon Way CB9 ....132 F7
Blagge Cl IP33 ....122 C4
Blair Cl IP4 ....140 E5
Blair Par 6 CB9 ....132 C6
Blake Ave 4 IP9 ....107 A5
Blake Cl 7 CO11 ....104 E4
Blake Rd Ipswich IP1 ...134 F3
　Stowmarket IP14 ....124 B7
Blakenham Cl 4 NR32 ....112 F4

Blakenham Woodland Gdn*
IP6 ....81 F4
Blakes Cl IP12 ....147 C7
Blanche Cl IP4 ....155 C3
Blandford Rd IP3 .....140 D3
Blaxhall Church Rd
IP12 ....71 F2
Blaxhall Ct 2 CB9 ....132 C5
Blaxhall Heath Nature
Reserve* IP12 ....72 C3
Blenheim Cl
10 Brantham CO11 .....104 E5
Bury St Edmunds IP33 ..122 D5
Haverhill CB9 ....132 F7
Blenheim Dr IP7 ....80 C6
Blenheim Rd 3 IP1 ..139 A7
Blenheim Way 2 IP22 ..20 A3
Blickling Cl IP2 ....139 B2
Blinco Rd NR32 ....112 C1
Blind La IP29 ....77 B6
Blo' Norton Rd
Blo' Norton IP22 ....18 F3
South Lopham IP22 ......19 A4
Block Rd CB7 ....28 E1
Blocka Rd NR32 ....2 C6
Blockmoor Rd CB7 .....28 A6
Blofield Rd IP11 ....152 B4
Blois Rd CB9 ....88 F4
Blomfield St IP33 .....154 B3
Blood Hill IP8 ....81 B3
Bloodmoor La 2 NR33 ..114 C3
Bloodmoor Rd 1 NR33 ..114 C3
Bloomfield St IP4 .....140 B6
Bloomfield Way
Debenham IP14 ....53 E1
7 Lowestoft NR33 ....114 E3
Blooms Ct IP28 ....116 D5
Blooms Hall La CO10 ...77 D5
Bloomsbury Cl NR32 ..112 E4
Bloomsfield 8 CB5 ....48 E5
Blower's La NR33 ....10 E2
Blue Barn Cl 13 IP11 ..107 D8
Blue Barn La IP8 ......134 A8
Blue House La IP14 .....52 F3
Bluebell Ave IP32 ....123 F5
Bluebell Cl Ipswich IP2 ..138 E4
Lowestoft NR33 ....114 F3
Bluebell Gr IP6 ....125 D3
Bluebell Way NR14 ...111 E3
Bluebell Wlk 2 CB7 ....28 C4
Bluegate La IP9 ....150 F1
Bluestem Rd IP3 ......144 D8
Blundens The CO6 ....102 E7
Blundeston Rd
Corton NR32 ....112 F8
Somerleyton, Ashby &
Herringfleet NR32 ....112 B8
Blyburgate 2 NR34 ...111 C4
Blyford La Blyford IP19 ..42 B8
Holton IP19 ....118 E3
Wenhaston with Mells Hamlet
IP19 ....42 C6
Blyford Rd IP32 ....113 A5
Blyford Way IP11 .....152 C4
Blyth Cl Ipswich IP2 ..139 A1
Wenhaston IP19 ....42 C6
Blyth Rd
Halesworth IP19 ....118 C2
Southwold IP18 ....119 B5
Blythburgh Rd IP17 ...58 C8
Boathouse La
Carlton NR32 ....114 B8
Lowestoft NR32 ....112 B1
Boatman Ct 16 IP8 ...142 E8
Bobbits La
Pinewood IP9 ....142 E8
Wherstead IP9 ....143 A7
Boby Rd IP32 ....122 D8
Bockhill Rd IP33 ......142 C5
Bodiam Cl IP3 ....140 D6
Bodiam Rd IP3 ....140 D4
Bodiam Way 8 NR33 ..114 D4
Bodian Wlk 8 CB9 ....132 C6
Bodmin Cl IP5 ....141 A6
Boeing Way IP8 ....116 B5
Boldero Rd IP32 ....123 F4
Boleyn Way 6 CB9 ....132 C6
Boleyn Wlk CB9 ....121 C3
Bollard Way NR33 ....114 E5
Bolton Cl 2 CB5 ....44 A5
Bolton La IP1 ....155 C3
Bolton St 10 CO10 .....78 D4
Bon Marche 7 NR32 ..115 D8
Bond Cl IP21 ....21 F8
Bond St Ipswich IP4 ..155 C2
Stowmarket IP14 ....124 D7
Bond's Rd NR11 ....21 C8
Bonds Meadow NR32 ..112 E2
Bonnington Rd IP3 ...139 F1
Bonny Cres IP3 ....144 C8
Bonsey Gdns NR34 .....26 E5
Boon Cl IP33 ....123 A3
Boon Dr NR33 ....114 E6
Boot Drift IP9 ....106 E7
Booth La IP5 ....141 E8
Border Cot La IP13 ...127 B7
Border La NR32 ....2 E6
Borehamgate Prec 5
CO10 ....148 D5
Borehamgate Sh Ctr 2
CO10 ....148 C5
Borley Cres 2 IP30 .....50 F2
Borley Rd CO10 ....91 D6
Borough End 3 NR34 ..111 C3
Borough La IP14 ....66 A3
Borradale Ct 5 CB9 ....88 D3
Borradale Rd IP32 ....123 F5
Borrett Pl IP12 ....146 D3

Borretts Farm La IP13 ..70 D6
Borrow Cl NR33 ....114 C3
Borrow Rd NR32 ......112 C1
Borrowdale Ave 1 IP4 ..135 D1
Bosmere Prim Sch
IP6 ....125 D4
Bosquet Cl 1 NR32 ...112 F5
Boss Hall Ind Est IP1 ..138 E7
Boss Hall Rd IP1 ......138 E7
Bostock Rd IP2 ....139 C1
Boston End 6 IP24 .....16 A5
Boston Rd Ipswich IP4 ..139 F7
Lowestoft NR32 ....113 D2
Boswell La IP7 ....149 D7
Botany La IP17 ....71 E7
Botolphs Ct IP33 ......154 C1
Bouchain Ct 1 IP19 ..118 A3
Boughton Way IP33 ..154 C3
Boulevard The NR32 ..114 D8
Boulge Rd Burgh IP13 ..83 F6
Hasketon IP13 ....146 B8
Boulters Cl IP14 ....124 B6
Boulters Way IP14 ....124 B6
Boundary Cl IP26 ....4 F3
Boundary Rd
Haverhill CB9 ....133 B3
1 Hockwold cum Wilton
IP26 ....5 A3
Red Lodge IP28 ....30 C1
Bourchier Cl 7 IP7 ...149 E6
Bourne Ave CO6 ......149 E6
Bourne Hill IP2 ....143 B7
Bourne Pk Residential Site
IP2 ....139 B1
Bourne Rd
Haverhill CB9 ....132 F6
Lowestoft NR32 ....113 B3
Bourne Terr IP17 .....143 B8
Bowdens La CO6 ....101 F3
Bower's La 12 CB7 .....29 C5
Bowl Rd IP14 ....66 C1
Bowland Dr IP8 ....138 C1
Bowman's La IP17 ......42 D1
Bowthorpe Cl IP4 .....155 A4
Box Bush La IP13 ......55 D5
Boxford Cl 2 IP11 .....124 E3
Boxford Ct
6 Felixstowe IP11 .....152 C4
3 Haverhill CB9 ....132 C5
Boxford CO10 ....93 A3
Boxford Prim Sch
CO10 ....93 C3
Boxford Rd IP7 ....93 B8
Boxhouse La CO7 .....103 D3
Boxted Church Rd
CO6 ....102 E2
Boxted Rd CO6 ....102 E2
Boxted Straight Rd
CO4 ....103 A2
Boyden Cl 1 CB8 ....61 E2
Boydlands IP9 ....150 E3
Boyne Rd IP33 ....122 E4
Boyscott La 1 NR35 ..110 B3
Boyton Cl CB9 ....132 C5
Boyton Rd
Hollesley IP12 ....86 A1
Ipswich IP3 ....140 B7
Boyton Vineyard* CO9 ..89 B7
Boyton's La CB10 ......88 A1
Braces La NR35 ....8 E7
Bracken Ave IP5 ....137 D4
Bracken Rise IP26 .....6 A8
Bracken Row 6 IP31 ..49 C7
Brackenbury Cl IP1 ..139 B8
Brackenbury Sports Ctr
IP11 ....153 C5
Brackenhayes Cl IP2 ..135 C5
Brackenwood Cres 1
IP23 ....123 E6
Brackley Cl 8 IP11 ...152 D5
Bradbrook Cl IP32 ...123 F6
Braddock Sq IP12 ....122 E7
Bradfield Ave IP7 .....149 D7
Bradfield Cres IP7 ...149 D7
Bradfield Woods National
Nature Reserve*
IP30 ....64 F4
Bradley Rd Cowlinge CB8 ..60 F1
Great Bradley CB8 ......74 F8
Kirtling CB8 ....60 F2
Bradley St IP29 ....77 A5
Braggon's Hill IP29 ....77 A5
Bramble Cl CB9 ....132 B7
Bramble Dr IP3 ....140 E1
Bramble Gn NR32 ....113 B3
Bramble Tye CO12 ...106 E1
Bramble Way CO6 ....102 B7
Brambles The IP15 ...130 C6
Bramblewood 1 CB8 ..138 C2
Bramblewood Way
IP19 ....118 C4
Brambling Cl 2 IP14 ..67 A5
Brames La IP20 ....23 D3
Bramfield CE Prim Sch
IP19 ....42 A4
Bramfield House Sch
IP19 ....41 E4
Bramfield Rd
Halesworth IP19 ....118 B2
Lowestoft NR32 ....113 A3
Walpole IP19 ....41 C5
Wenhaston with Mells Hamlet
IP19 ....42 B5
Bramford CE Prim Sch
IP8 ....134 A1
Bramford Ct IP14 .....124 E4
Bramford La 6 IP11 ..139 A7

Bramford Meadows Nature
Reserve* IP1 ....134 B3
Bramford Rd
Bramford IP8 ....134 B1
Claydon IP8 ....134 A8
Great Blakenham IP6 ..134 A8
Ipswich IP1 ....138 E8
Bramhall Ct IP2 ....138 D1
Bramley Chase IP4 ...140 B7
Bramley Cl IP32 ....123 F6
Bramley Rd Diss IP22 ..20 B3
Haverhill CB9 ....132 A5
Bramley Rise NR34 ...111 C3
Brampton CE Prim Sch
NR34 ....25 E5
Brampton Gr 8 NR32 ..112 F4
Brampton Sta NR34 ...25 C6
Brand Rd IP31 ....49 C7
Brandeston Cl 10 CO10 ..92 C6
Brandeston Rd
Cretingham IP13 ....69 E7
Earl Soham IP13 ....54 F1
Brandon Ctry Pk Visitor Ctr*
IP27 ....14 F8
Brandon Her Ctr* IP27 ..14 F3
Brandon Rd
Felixstowe IP11 ....152 C4
Lakenheath IP27 ....14 C4
Methwold IP26 ....5 B8
Mildenhall IP28 ....14 B8
Thetford IP24 ....15 F6
Weeting IP27 ....5 F3
Wordwell IP28 ....32 C3
Brandon St IP27 ....109 F1
Brandon Sta IP27 ....5 F2
Brands Cl 22 CO10 .....92 B3
Brands La IP29 ....63 D3
Bransby Gdns IP4 ....155 C3
Brantham Hill CO11 ..104 E4
Brandy Rd 9 IP31 ......33 D5
Brayfield Cl IP32 .....123 D6
Braziers La IP31 ....51 B6
Brazier's Wood Rd
IP3 ....144 B8
Brazilian Terr CB8 ...120 F3
Breckland Ave IP27 ...109 D7
Breckland Mid Sch
IP27 ....14 D8
Breckland Way
Lowestoft NR32 ....113 A3
Mildenhall IP28 ....116 C5
Brecklands 5 IP26 ....6 A8
Brecon Cl IP2 ....139 B2
Bredfield Cl IP12 ......152 D5
Bredfield Rd IP13 ....147 A2
Bredfield St IP12 .....146 F5
Brendon Cl NR32 .....112 C2
Brendon Dr IP5 ....140 F6
Brent Cl IP28 ....116 B6
Brent Eleigh Rd
Lavenham CO10 ....78 D3
Monks Eleigh IP7 ......79 B2
Brentgovel St 8 IP33 ..154 B2
Bressingham Prim Sch
IP22 ....19 E4
Bressingham Rd IP22 ..19 E4
Bressingham Steam Mus &
Gdns* IP22 ....19 E3
Brett Ave IP7 ....149 E7
Brett Cl IP7 ....138 E8
Brett Gn IP7 ....149 E2
Brettenham Cres 4
IP1 ....135 D1
Brettenham Rd
Buxhall IP14 ....65 F4
Hitcham IP7 ....79 E8
Bretts The IP5 ....141 E8
Brewers Cl IP27 ......109 C6
Brewers Gn La IP22 ...20 B3
Brewhouse La 10 CB7 ..28 D4
Breydon Way
Gainsborough IP3 ....144 C7
Lowestoft NR33 ....114 F6
Briar Cl
Halesworth IP19 ....118 C4
Ipswich IP3 ....143 B5
Briar Hill IP30 ....50 D1
Briar La IP22 ....35 F5
Briar Rd 30 IP20 ....22 D6
Briardale Ave 4 CO12 ..106 F2
Briarhayes Cl IP2 ....139 B3
Briarwood Ave IP1 ...122 D5
Briarwood Rd
Lowestoft NR32 ....113 A3
Woodbridge IP12 ......146 E3
Brices Way 3 CO10 .....77 A3
Bricett Bsns Pk IP7 ...80 E6
Bricett Gn IP7 ....80 D5
Brick Kiln Ave NR34 ..111 C4
Brick Kiln Cl 15 IP11 ..107 D8
Brick Kiln Hill CO6 .....93 C2
Brick Kiln La
Huntingfield IP19 ......40 F4
Melton IP12 ....147 E7
Brick Kiln Rd
Ellingham NR35 ....8 C8
Harkstead IP9 ....106 B6
Mildenhall IP28 ....116 D5
Brick La
Framlingham IP13 .....126 D3
Parham IP13 ....71 A7
Brickfield Cl IP22 ....35 C1
Brickfields Ave CB8 ..120 D7
Brickfields The IP14 ...24 E2
Brickiln La IP22 ....19 C3
Brickman's Hill CO11 ..105 B2
Bridewell Cl IP28 .....116 B4

Bridewell La
Botesdale IP22 ....36 A6
Bury St Edmunds IP33 ..154 C2
Bridewell St CO10 ......90 B8
Bridge Cl 16 IP20 ......22 D6
Bridge Cottage* CO7 ..151 D1
Bridge End Rd IP28 .....30 B1
Bridge Foot Cnr IP28 ..119 C7
Bridge Pk (Skate Park)*
IP1 ....155 B1
Bridge Rd
Bromeswell IP12 ....85 A6
Burston & Shimpling IP22 ..20 E7
Felixstowe IP11 ....153 A5
Levington IP10 ....145 C4
Lowestoft NR32 ....112 E1
Reydon IP18 ....119 C7
8 Scole IP21 ....20 F1
Snape IP17 ....43 E8
Bridge St Beccles NR34 ..111 A7
Brandon IP27 ....5 F2
Bungay NR35 ....110 D8
4 Bures Hamlet CO8 ..101 C5
Carlton IP17 ....128 D6
Framlingham IP13 .....126 C3
Hadleigh IP7 ....149 C7
Halesworth IP19 ....118 B4
Huntingfield IP19 ....41 A4
Ipswich IP1 ....155 B2
Moulton CB8 ....45 F3
Needham Market IP6 ..125 D3
Stowmarket IP14 ....124 F5
Thetford IP24 ....16 B5
Bridge St Rd CO10 .....78 A4
Bridge Terr IP27 ......148 C6
Bridge Wood Nature
Reserve* IP3 ....144 B6
Bridgeman Wlk IP32 ..122 E7
Bridgenhall Rd IP32 ..146 C5
Bridgham La NR16 .....17 F8
Bridgwater Rd IP2 ...138 D2
Bridlemere Ct CB8 ...124 F3
Bridles The 4 NR34 ..111 F4
Bridport Ave IP3 .....140 D3
Bright Cl
Bury St Edmunds IP33 ..123 C3
Saxmundham IP17 .....128 B4
Bright's La CO10 ....78 C4
Brighton St 3 IP27 .....14 A3
Brights Wlk IP5 ....141 E7
Brightwell Cl IP11 ...152 C4
Brimstone Rd IP8 ....142 E8
Brindles The 7 NR33 ..114 E5
Brinkley Rd Brinkley CB8 ..59 C3
Carlton CB8 ....74 A8
Dullingham CB8 ....59 F4
Brinkley Way IP11 ...153 D7
Brisbane Rd IP4 ....140 D6
Briscoe Way IP27 ....109 C8
Bristol Hill IP9 ....107 A4
Bristol Rd
Bury St Edmunds IP33 ..122 E3
Ipswich IP4 ....140 A7
Bristol St 5 IP27 ......140 A7
Britannia Prim Sch
IP4 ....140 B5
Britannia Rd IP4 ......140 B6
Britten Ave IP14 ......124 C7
Britten Cl IP15 ....130 D5
Britten Ctr The NR32 ..113 C6
Britten Rd NR33 ......115 A6
Brittons Cres 8 IP29 ..47 A2
Brittons Rd 8 IP29 .....47 A2
Broad Fleet Cl 2 NR32 ..112 E4
Broad Gn Cl 4 IP29 ....62 C6
Broad La CO6 ....102 E1
Broad Meadow
2 Walsham le Willows
IP31 ....35 C2
Broad Oaks CO6 ......102 B8
Broad Piece CB7 ....28 C5
Broad Rd Cotton IP14 ..52 A6
Little Thurlow CB9 ......74 F6
Lowestoft NR33 ....112 D1
Wickham Market IP13 ..127 B7
Broad St Boxford CO10 ..93 C3
Bungay NR35 ....110 A5
Eye IP23 ....117 C2
20 Harleston IP20 ......22 D6
Haverhill CB9 ....132 D6
Orford IP12 ....131 C2
Broad View Rd NR32 ..114 C8
Broad Way IP21 ....21 A4
Broadcroft Cres CB9 ..132 C6
Broadfields Rd 5 IP23 ..36 F1
Broadland Cl
Beccles NR34 ....111 E4
Lowestoft NR33 ....114 E3
Broadland Rd IP33 ...123 B1
Broadlands Way IP4 ..140 C8
Broadmere Rd IP1 ...138 E8
Broadoak Cl 1 NR33 ..114 C4
Broadoak Rd CB5 ......44 B5
Broads Rd Bsns Pk CB5 ..44 B7
Broadwater Gdns 6
IP9 ....107 A4
Broadwaters Rd NR33 ..114 E5
Broadway
6 Fressingfield IP21 ...39 E8
8 Glemsford CO10 .....77 A3
Pakenham IP31 ....49 F8
Wickham Market IP13 ..127 B7
Broadway Dr IP19 ....118 C6
Broadway The
Badwell Ash IP31 ....50 F8
Wickham Skeith IP23 ..52 D6
Brock La IP13 ....146 C2

Brockdish Prim Sch
IP21 ....22 A1
Brockeby Wlk IP33 ...122 D4
Brockford Rd IP14 .....52 F4
Brockley Cres IP1 ....134 D1
Brockley La IP29 ....46 F2
Brockley Rd
Hartest IP29 ....77 A8
Whepstead IP29 ....63 B4
Brocks Bsns Ctr 2 IP33 ..132 C3
Broke Ave IP8 ....134 B2
Broke Hall Gdns IP3 ..140 D4
Broke Hall Prim Sch
IP4 ....140 E5
Brome Ave IP23 ......117 D5
Brome Hall La IP23 ..117 E7
Bromelands IP23 .....117 E8
Bromeswell Gn Nature
Reserve* IP12 ....147 F7
Bromeswell Rd IP4 ..135 C1
Bromley Cl 1 IP27 ...139 C3
Bromley Rd CO11 ....104 D1
Bronyon Cl IP33 ......122 C5
Brook Cl
Horringer IP29 ....122 B1
Hundon CO10 ....75 D3
Ipswich IP4 ....155 C3
Martlesham IP5 ....141 D4
Swilland IP6 ....124 B7
Brook Dam La 22 CB8 ..28 C4
Brook Dr 3 IP17 ....56 F8
Brook Farm La 4 IP9 ..105 E7
Brook Farm Rd IP7 ..128 B4
Brook Hall Rd CO10 ...93 C3
Brook House Rd IP14 ..52 B6
Brook La Burgate IP22 ..36 E7
Capel St Mary IP9 .....150 C4
Felixstowe IP11 ....153 B5
Framlingham IP13 .....126 B3
Mickfield IP14 ....53 A2
Needham IP20 ....22 B4
Playford IP6 ....137 A4
St Margaret, Ilketshall
NR35 ....24 C7
Trimley St Martin IP10 ..98 E1
Brook Rd NR14 ....10 B4
Brook Service Rd 1
CB9 ....132 E5
Brook St Dedham CO7 ..103 F4
Glemsford CO10 ....77 A3
Soham CB7 ....28 D3
Woodbridge IP12 ......147 A5
Yoxford IP17 ....57 D7
Brook Way IP8 ....81 C3
Brooke Bsns & Ind Pk
NR33 ....115 A8
Brookfield Cl IP1 .....138 F8
Brookfields Cl CB8 ..121 B5
Brookhill Way IP14 ..140 F4
Brookhouse Bsns Pk
IP2 ....138 F6
Brooklands Cl IP2 ...153 A1
Brooklands Rd CO11 ..104 E4
Brooklands Rise IP4 ..104 C4
Brooklyn Rd 14 CO12 ..107 B2
Brooks Castle IP23 ..123 C3
Brooks Hall Rd IP1 ..139 A7
Brooksfield 1 IP7 ......79 F4
Brookside Dalham CB8 ..45 D8
Moulton CB8 ....45 F3
Brookview Ipswich IP2 ..142 E8
Pinewood IP2 ....138 E1
Brookwood Cl 7 NR34 ..9 F4
Broom Cres IP3 ....139 F1
Broom Field 5 IP11 ..152 E5
Broom Hill La 2 IP4 ...44 E4
Broom Hill Nature Reserve*
IP7 ....149 C5
Broom Hill Rd IP1 ....139 A8
Broom Hill Swimming Pool
IP1 ....139 A8
Broom Knoll 1 CO11 ..104 C5
Broom Rd
Lakenheath IP27 ....109 C5
2 Lowestoft NR32 ....113 B2
Broom Rd Cl IP27 ....109 C5
Broom St CO10 ....148 F3
Broom Wlk 9 IP9 ....30 B8
Broomfield
Martlesham IP5 ....141 F7
17 Martlesham Heath IP5 ..98 A8
Broomfield Comm
IP5 ....138 B6
Broomfield Mews 18 IP5 ..98 A8
Broomhayes IP2 ......139 A2
Broomheath IP12 ....146 F2
Broomhill Cl 2 IP28 ...30 C1
Broomhill La IP30 ......50 C1
Bromley Gn Rd IP32 ..123 F6
Broomspath Rd IP14 ..124 A8
Brotherton Ave IP11 ..152 B8
Broughton Rd IP1 ....155 A4
Brown St IP14 ....52 A3
Browning Rd
10 Brantham CO11 ....104 C4
Ipswich IP1 ....134 F3
Brownlow Rd IP11 ...153 A3
Browns Cl 8 Acton CO10 ..92 B7
Hitcham IP7 ....79 E6
2 Wickhambrook CB8 ..61 E2
Browns Gr IP5 ....141 D7
Browse Cl IP32 ....123 E4
Browston La NR32 ......2 E7
Broxstead Cl IP12 ....85 C2
Bruce St NR33 ....115 C7

Brudenell St IP15 ....130 E3
Bruges Cl [14] CO12 ......107 A1
Bruisyard Rd IP13 ....56 C3
Bruisyard Vineyard*
  IP7 ....56 C5
Brundon La CO10 ....148 A5
Brunel Rd IP2 ....138 E6
Brunel Way IP24 ....16 B7
Brunswick House Cut [18]
  CO11 ....105 A2
Brunswick Rd IP1 ....135 A3
Brunwyn Cl IP32 ....123 F6
Brussels Cl [16] CO10 ....107 A1
Brybank Rd CO9 ....132 A7
Bryon Ave IP11 ....152 B2
Bryony Cl Haverhill CB9 ..132 C7
  [6] Lowestoft NR33 ......114 F3
Buccaneer Rd IP31 ....33 D5
Buck La IP23 ....42 E4
Buckanay La IP12 ....99 E5
Buckenham Ct [17] IP18 ..119 D5
Buckenham Rd IP7 ......149 F4
Buckfast Cl [4] IP2 ......139 A2
Buckingham Cl [4] IP12 ..84 A1
Buckingham Rd CO9 ....132 A7
Buckingham's Hill IP12 ....39 E8
Buckles Field [8] IP31 ....34 E4
Buckles Prim Sch
  IP10 ....98 B4
Bucklesham Rd
  Ipswich IP3 ....140 E2
  Kirton IP10 ....98 D3
Buckleswood Rd IP6 ..129 A7
Bucknam Cl [14] NR33 ....11 C1
Buck's Head La IP6 ......62 F7
Buck's Horns La IP9 ....142 B6
Bucks La [7] CO10 ....90 A8
Buckshorn La IP23 ......117 D2
Buddleia Cl IP22 ....138 E4
Bude Cl IP5 ....141 A6
Bugg's La
  Brettenham IP7 ....65 D1
  Hitcham IP7 ....79 D8
Bugg's Rd IP22 ....36 D6
Buggs Hole La IP22 ......18 D2
Bugsby Way IP5 ....141 E7
Bulcamp Drift IP19 ......43 A7
Bull Dr IP5 ....141 C6
Bull Hall La IP6 ....83 A5
Bull La Acton CO10 ......78 A1
  Hawstead IP29 ....63 C5
  Long Melford CO10 ......91 E8
  Rickinghall Superior IP22 ..36 A4
Bull Rd IP31 ....49 F6
Bull Rush Cres IP33 ....154 A4
Bullace La IP12 ....131 A8
Bullard's La IP12 ......146 E5
Bull's Ash Cnr IP7 ......80 F5
Bull's Rd IP6 ....82 C7
Bullen Cl Bramford IP8 ..134 A2
  Bury St Edmunds IP33 ..154 A1
Bullen La [5] IP8 ......134 A2
Bullens Cl IP33 ....122 A5
Buller Rd IP16 ....129 C6
Bullfinch Cl [24] CO12 ..106 F1
Bullion's La NR34 ....26 B2
Bullock Fair Cl [8] CO10 ..148 C5
Bullocksfield La IP12 ....131 C4
Bull's Wood Nature Reserve*
  IP30 ....64 E1
Bullshall Rd [6] IP33 ....37 F1
Bullswood La CO10 ......64 D1
Bulmer La CO10 ....93 C4
Bulmer Rd CO10 ....148 A4
Bulmer Rd Ind Est
  CO10 ....148 A4
Bulstrode Rd IP2 ......155 C1
Bulwer Rd IP1 ....139 A6
Bumpstead Rd CB9 ......132 A3
Bunbury Ave
  [1] Great Barton IP31 ..49 A5
  Mildenhall IP28 ......116 C5
Bunbury Rd [6] IP32 ....48 C5
Bungay Castle (rems)*
  NR35 ....110 A4
Bungay High Sch
  NR35 ....110 C2
Bungay Mid Sch NR35 ..110 C3
Bungay Mus* NR35 ..110 B4
Bungay Prim Sch
  NR35 ....110 C2
Bungay Rd Barsham NR34 ..9 B4
  Beccles NR34 ....111 A4
  Dickleburgh & Rushall
  IP21 ....21 B1
  Ellingham NR35 ....118 D4
  Halesworth IP19 ......118 B8
  Scole IP21 ....21 A1
  Stockton NR34 ....3 F8
Bunker Cl NR33 ....115 A5
Bunn's La IP20 ....22 C6
Bunters Rd [8] CB8 ......6 A2
Buntry La CO10 ....75 C2
Bunyan Cl IP1 ....135 A3
Burch's Cl IP17 ....129 A2
Burdock La IP26 ....4 C3
Buregate Rd IP11 ......152 F2

Bures Cl IP14 ....124 E4
Bures Ct [6] CB9 ....132 C5
Bures Prim Sch CO8 ....101 C4
Bures Rd
  Little Cornard CO10 ....101 A8
  Nayland-with-Wissington
  CO6 ....101 F4
  Sudbury CO10 ....148 E2
Bures Sta CO8 ....101 C4
Burgate Rd
  Gislingham IP23 ....36 D3
  Higham IP28 ....46 E3
Burgess Cl [5] NR32 ....112 F2
Burgess Pl [22] IP5 ......98 A8
Burgh Rd NR34 ....2 C1
Burghley Cl [14] IP2 ....139 A2
Burghley Rise [5] CB5 ..44 B5
Burke Cl IP1 ....135 A3
Burke Rd [7] IP1 ......135 A3
Burkitt La CO10 ....148 C5
Burkitts Rd IP12 ......146 E5
Burlingham Dr NR33 ....114 B3
Burlingham Rd IP1 ....155 A3
Burnet Cl IP8 ....142 D8
Burnham Cl
  Felixstowe IP11 ......152 C7
  Ipswich IP4 ....139 F7
Burnham Way NR33 ....115 A7
Burns Cl IP23 ....37 B5
Burns Rd IP1 ....134 E3
Burnt Dick Hill CO4 ....102 E4
Burnt Fen Turnpike
  IP28 ....12 D6
Burnt Hill La NR33 ....114 B7
Burnt Hill Way NR33 ..114 B7
Burnt House Cl [3] CB9 ..132 A7
Burnt House La IP10 ....98 D2
Burnt La IP12 ....131 C2
Burnt Oak Cnr CO7 ..151 D3
Burnthouse La
  Battisford IP14 ....66 D1
  Needham IP20 ....22 B4
Burntoak La IP20 ....22 E8
Burr Cl [17] CO12 ......106 E1
Burrell Cres IP28 ......116 D2
Burrell Rd IP2 ....155 B1
Burrell Way IP24 ......16 A5
Burrell's Orch IP33 ....122 A6
Burrough Gn CE Prim Sch
  CB8 ....59 F2
Burroughs Piece Rd [2]
  CO10 ....148 D5
Burrow Dr IP27 ....109 C8
Burrows Cl [5] CO11 ..104 D2
Button's Rd IP13 ......71 D6
Burrows Rd [7] IP12 ..84 E6
Burstall Hall La IP8 ....95 E7
Burstall La IP8 ....95 E7
Burston Com Prim Sch
  IP22 ....20 E6
Burston Rd
  Dickleburgh & Rushall
  IP21 ....20 F8
  Diss IP22 ....20 D4
  Gissing IP22 ....20 F7
Burton Cl CB9 ....132 C5
Burton Dr IP6 ....125 C5
Burton End CO9 ......132 C5
Burton End Com Prim Sch
  CB9 ....132 B5
Burton Hill CB9 ....74 B3
Burton St NR32 ......113 D2
Burwash [1] IP6 ....95 A3
Burwell Mus* CB5 ......44 B5
Burwell Rd CB8 ......120 A8
Burwood Pl
  [7] Lowestoft NR32 ....113 B6
  Trimley St Mary IP11 ..152 C8
Bury Bottom IP27 ......13 A8
Bury Drift IP31 ....48 E6
Bury Hill IP12 ....147 A7
Bury Hill Cl IP12 ......147 A7
Bury La Lidgate CB8 ......61 C4
  Moulton CB8 ....45 F3
  Stanton IP31 ....34 E3
  Wickhambrook CB8 ....61 E4
Bury Language Sch The
  IP33 ....154 C2
Bury Pk Dr IP3 ......123 C2
Bury Rd Alpheton CO10 ..78 A5
  Barrow IP29 ....47 A2
  Beyton IP30 ....49 E2
  Botesdale IP22 ....36 B7
  Bradfield St Clare IP30 ..64 C4
  Brandon IP27 ....14 B8
  Brettenham IP7 ....79 C7
  Brockley IP29 ....63 A2
  Chedburgh IP29 ....62 D4
  Felsham IP30 ....65 A2
  Flempton IP28 ....47 F8
  Great Barton IP31 ......49 A5
  Great Thurlow CB9 ......74 F5
  Great Welnetham IP30 ..63 F4
  Haughley IP14 ....46 A2
  Hengrave IP28 ....48 A7
  Hepworth IP22 ....35 A4
  Ipswich IP1 ....134 D4
  Lavenham CO10 ....78 D5
  Lawshall IP29 ....63 D2
  Market Weston IP22 ....18 B1
  Mildenhall IP28 ......116 B8
  Newmarket CB8 ......121 C5
  Rickinghall Inferior IP22 ..35 F5
  Stanton IP31 ....34 F4
  Stowmarket IP14 ....124 C8
  Thetford IP24 ....16 C5
  Thorpe Morieux IP30 ..64 E2

Bury Rd continued
  Wickhambrook CB8 ......61 F1
  Wortham IP22 ....36 E8
Bury St [3] IP14 ......124 D6
Bury St Edmunds Abbey*
  IP33 ....154 C2
Bury St Edmunds Abbey
  Gdns* IP33 ....154 C2
Bury St Edmunds Art Gall*
  IP33 ....154 B2
Bury St Edmunds Leisure Ctr
  IP33 ....122 E6
Bury St Edmunds Sta
  IP32 ....154 B4
Bury St Edmunds Upper Sch
  IP32 ....154 A4
Bush Cnr IP14 ....53 E1
Bush Gr CO10 ....148 A4
Bushel La CB7 ....28 D4
Bushey Cl IP9 ....150 E3
Bushman Gdns [3] IP18 ..134 A2
Bushy La IP17 ....99 E7
Bussock La IP12 ....99 D7
Buston Rd [3] IP22 ....20 B6
Butcher's La CO10 ......93 C4
Butcher's Rd IP17 ....128 E7
Butchers La IP9 ......150 F3
Bute Ct IP9 ....132 D4
Butfield CO10 ....78 D3
Butler Smith Gdns [2]
  IP5 ....141 C7
Butler's La CO10 ......105 F1
Butlers Way CO9 ....90 A1
Butley Cl IP2 ....142 F8
Butley Cl [3] CB9 ......132 C3
Butley Dr [3] NR32 ....112 F3
Butley Pottery* IP12 ..86 B6
Butley Rd IP11 ......152 E3
Butt Rd
  Stoke-by-Nayland CO6 ..102 E7
  Sudbury CO10 ....148 F4
Butt's Rd Holton IP19 ..118 D8
  Spexhall IP19 ....25 A4
Butter Mkt
  Bury St Edmunds IP33 ..154 B2
  Ipswich IP1 ....155 B3
Buttercup Cl
  Bury St Edmunds IP32 ..123 F5
  Ipswich IP8 ....138 C1
  [3] Lowestoft NR33 ....114 C4
Butterfly Gdns IP4 ....140 E5
Buttermarket Sh Ctr
  IP1 ....155 B3
Buttermere Gn IP11 ....153 D6
Button's Rd IP13 ....71 D6
Buttram's Mill* IP12 ..146 E5
Butts The
  Debenham IP14 ....53 E2
  Soham CB7 ....28 D3
Buxhall Musuem*
  IP14 ....66 A5
Buxlow Cl IP17 ....129 B2
Byfield Way IP3 ......123 C3
Byford Rd CO10 ......148 E7
Bylam La IP9 ....106 A7
Byland Cl [6] IP2 ......139 A2
Byng Hall Rd
  Pettistree IP13 ....84 E8
  Ufford IP13 ....127 A1
Byng La IP13 ....72 A3
Byrd Cl IP33 ....122 C4
Byron Rd IP1 ....134 E4

Cambridge Way
  [9] Bures CO8 ....101 C4
Camden Rd IP3 ....140 B4
Camden St [5] NR32 ..113 E3
Camp Cl [2] IP22 ....4 D5
Camp Rd NR32 ....113 D1
Campbell Cl [8] IP28 ..116 B5
Campbell Rd IP3 ......140 C1
Campion Cl CB7 ....28 C5
Campion Cres IP14 ....124 C4
Campion La CO6 ......102 B6
Campion Rd IP2 ......138 F4
Campion Way CO6 ....102 B7
Campions Hill CO6 ....102 B5
Camps Rd
  Haverhill CB9 ....132 D5
  Helions Bumpstead CB9 ..88 A5
Camwood Gdns IP3 ....140 B4
Canaletto Cl [4] NR32 ..113 B6
Canberra Cl
  Ipswich IP4 ....140 D6
  [2] Mildenhall IP28 ....30 A8
Canberra Rd IP31 ......33 D4
Candler's La [18] IP20 ..22 D6
Candlet Gr IP11 ......152 F5
Candlet Rd IP11 ......152 E7
Cangle Junc [8] CB9 ..132 E6
Cangles La IP30 ....49 F1
Canham St IP1 ....155 A3
Canhams Rd CO10 ....148 F3
Cannon St IP33 ......154 B3
Cannonfields IP33 ....154 B3
Canon Cl CB9 ....132 D7
Canon Pugh Dr [6] CO10 ..92 B7
Canterbury Cl
  Ipswich IP2 ....142 F8
  [7] Lakenheath IP27 ....14 A2
Canterbury Gdns IP7 ..149 E6
Canterbury Gn IP33 ..123 A3
Canterbury Inf Sch [2]
  IP24 ....16 B6
Canterbury Jun Sch IP24 ..16 B6
Canterbury Rd CO10 ..148 B8
Canterbury Way IP24 ..16 B6
Capel Cl
  [4] Felixstowe IP11 ..107 D8
  Troston IP31 ....33 D3
Capel Gn IP12 ....86 B2
Capel Hall La IP11 ....107 E8
Capel St Mary CE Prim Sch
  Capel St Mary IP9 ....150 E3
  Copdock IP7 ....95 F4
Capell Wlk [2] IP31 ....34 E4
Capps La IP19 ....23 F5
Capstan Way NR33 ....114 B4
Captain's La IP14 ......51 A2
Caraway Rd IP24 ......16 D6
Carbonels [12] CO10 ....92 C6
Carders Cl IP27 ......149 D4
Cardew Drift IP5 ......141 D8
Cardiff Ave IP2 ......139 B1
Cardigan St
  Ipswich IP1 ....155 A4
  Newmarket CB8 ......121 A3
Cardinal Cl [8] IP24 ..123 E6
Cardinal Pk IP1 ......155 B2
Cardinal St IP1 ......155 B2
Cardinal Way CO10 ....132 D7
Cardinalls Rd IP14 ....124 D7
Carford Cl [14] IP5 ....98 A8
Carlow Mews [18] IP27 ..147 A5
Carlton Cl
  Great Yeldham CO9 ....90 A1
  Haverhill CB9 ....132 C7
  Huntingfield IP19 ......40 F5
  Lowestoft NR33 ......115 B4
Carlton Colville Cty Prim Sch
  NR33 ....114 D2
Carlton Cross NR33 ..114 C2
Carlton Gn Rd CB8 ....74 A7
Carlton Marshes Nature
  Reserve* NR33 ......114 A7
Carlton Pk Ind Est
  IP17 ....128 C5
Carlton Rd Brinkley CB8 ..59 F1
  Carlton IP17 ....128 C5
  Ipswich IP5 ....115 B6
  Lowestoft NR33 ......115 B6
Carlton Sq NR33 ......115 B6
Carlton Way IP4 ......139 E8
Carlton Wlk IP7 ......149 E4
Carlyle Cl IP1 ....134 E4
Carmarthen Cl IP2 ....139 A2
Carmelite Pl [4] IP12 ..147 A5
Carnation Way [4] IP28 ..46 A8
Carnoustie Dr
  [10] Fornham St Martin IP28 ..48 C6
  [1] Lowestoft NR33 ....114 B4
Carol Ave [8] IP12 ....84 A1
Carol Cl IP11 ....153 C5
Carolbrook Rd IP2 ....138 E3
Carr Ave IP16 ....129 D6
Carr Rd IP11 ....155 C3
Carriage Cl IP11 ......152 C6
Carters Cl CO7 ......151 D5
Carrops The CB8 ......46 A7
Carrs Hill IP23 ....56 B6
Carson Wlk CB8 ......120 F6
Carsons Dr [8] CO10 ..92 B3
Cart Score NR32 ......113 E3
Carter Rd CB8 ....120 E4
Carter St CB7 ....29 B1
Carters La CO10 ......103 A3
Carters Rd IP18 ....40 E6
Carters Teapot Pottery*
  IP14 ....53 C1
Carters Vineyard*
  CO4 ....102 F3
Casburn La [18] CB5 ....44 A6

Case La IP9 ....104 E8
Castle Ave CB9 ....132 C6
Castle Brooks IP6 ....126 B3
Castle Cl
  Felixstowe IP11 ......153 D6
  Orford IP12 ....131 B2
  Weeting-with-Broomhill
  IP27 ....5 E3
Castle Hill
  Beccles NR34 ....111 C4
  Dedham CO7 ....103 F2
  Eye IP23 ....117 D2
  Eyke IP12 ....85 B6
  Halesworth IP19 ......118 C3
  Orford IP12 ....131 C2
  Thorndon IP23 ....37 E1
Castle Hill Inf Sch
  IP1 ....135 A3
Castle Hill Jun Sch
  IP1 ....135 A3
Castle Hill Mid Sch
  CB9 ....132 B6
Castle La Bungay NR35 ..110 A4
  Hadleigh IP7 ....149 C7
  Haverhill CB9 ....132 C6
  Offton IP8 ....81 A4
  Orford IP12 ....131 C2
  Thetford IP24 ....16 C5
Castle Manor Bsns &
  Enterprise Coll CB9 ..132 C6
Castle Meadow IP8 ....81 A4
Castle Orch NR35 ....110 B4
Castle Rd
  Bury St Edmunds IP33 ..154 A1
  Hadleigh IP7 ....149 B7
  Ipswich IP1 ....134 E1
  Mettingham NR35 ......110 F2
  Offton IP8 ....81 A4
Castle Rise
  Hadleigh IP7 ....149 B7
  Saxmundham IP17 ......51 C1
Castle St Eye IP23 ....117 D2
  Framlingham IP13 ....126 D4
  Thetford IP24 ....16 C5
  Woodbridge IP12 ......147 A5
Castle Terr IP12 ......131 C2
Castle View IP33 ......131 C2
Castleton Ave IP11 ....153 B4
Castles Cl [5] NR32 ..113 B4
Castleton Way
  Eye IP23 ....117 B3
  Yaxley IP23 ....37 C5
Catchpole Ct [19] NR33 ..11 B1
Catchpole Cl CO10 ....148 B5
Catchpole Way [10] IP31 ..34 E4
Catchpole Wlk IP21 ..21 C5
Caters Rd IP13 ....84 C8
Catesbrarg IP9 ....150 D3
Cathcart St [8] NR32 ..113 D3
Cathedral Meadows
  IP33 ....154 B1
Catherine Rd IP2 ......146 E6
Catkin Cl CB9 ....132 B7
Cat's La CO10 ....148 E5
Cattawade St [12] CO11 ..105 C5
Catts Cl IP9 ....105 C5
Cattsfield IP9 ....105 C5
Caudle Ave IP27 ......109 E4
Cauldwell Ave IP4 ....139 F6
Cauldwell Hall Rd IP4 ..140 A5
Caulfield Cl [2] IP32 ..123 F5
Causeway
  Haverhill CB9 ....132 C5
  Huntingfield IP19 ......40 F5
  Lowestoft NR33 ......115 B4
Causeway Cl
  Brockdish IP21 ....21 F2
  [8] Glemsford CO10 ....77 B3
Causeway End CO11 ..104 D3
Causeway Est IP27 ......79 F7
Causeway The
  Barking IP6 ....125 B2
  Boxford CO10 ....93 C3
  Burwell CB5 ....44 A5
  Earl Soham IP13 ......128 B4
  Great Horkesley CO6 ..102 D1
  Hitcham IP7 ....79 E6
  Isleham CB7 ....29 C5
  Needham Market IP6 ..125 D4
  [4] Occold IP23 ....37 F1
  Ridgewell CO9 ....89 C4
  Soham CB7 ....28 D3
  Walsham le Willows IP31 ..35 B2
  Westhall IP19 ....25 C4
  Causton Jun Sch IP11 ..152 E6
Caustons Cl [3] CO10 ..92 B3
Cautley Rd IP11 ......119 D6
Cavan Rd IP2 ....134 D2
Cavendish CE Prim Sch
  CO10 ....76 E1
Cavendish Cl
  [7] Lowestoft NR32 ..113 A3
  [2] Thurston IP31 ......49 E4
Cavendish Dr [21] CO11 ..104 D2
Cavendish La CO10 ....92 E6
Cavendish Rd
  Bury St Edmunds IP33 ..122 C6
  Clare CO10 ....90 B8
  Felixstowe IP11 ......152 F3
  Stowmarket IP14 ......124 E4
Cavendish Way [1] CO10 ..148 D5
Cavenham Heath National
  Nature Reserve*
  IP28 ....31 C3
Cavenham Rd IP28 ......31 A1

Caville White CB9 . . . . . . **132** A6
Cawley Rd CO6 . . . . **102** A5
Caxton Mews **4** NR34 . . . **111** B6
Caxton Rd NR34 . . . . **111** B6
Cecil Lodge Cl CB8 . . . . **120** F3
Cecil Rd IP1 . . . . **155** A4
Cecilia St IP1 . . . . **155** B2
Cedar Ave IP5 . . . . **141** A6
Cedar Cl Bacton IP14 . . . **51** F6
  7 Brantham CO11 . . . . . **104** E5
  8 Great Brickett IP7 . . . . **80** D6
  52 Lakenheath IP27 . . . . . **13** F2
  Occold IP23 . . . . **37** F2
  Stradbroke IP21 . . . . **39** B4
Cedar Ct
  6 Barrow IP29 . . . . **47** A2
  6 Manningtree CO11 . . . **104** E2
  10 Beck Row, Holywell
  Row & Kenny Hill IP28 . . **13** B1
Cedar Dr
  Lowestoft NR33 . . . . **114** E5
  Worlingham NR34 . . . . . **111** F3
Cedar Rd **1** Barrow IP29 . . **47** A2
  6 Bentwaters Airfield IP12 . **85** E8
Cedarcroft Rd IP1 . . . . . **134** F2
Cedars La IP9 . . . . **150** D3
Cedars The IP7 . . . . **109** E5
Cedarwood Prim Sch
  IP5 . . . . **141** C6
Celandine Cl NR33 . . . . **114** C5
Cemetery La CB8 . . . . . . **120** D7
Cemetery La
  East Bergholt CO7 . . . . . **151** A4
  Ipswich IP4 . . . . **135** F1
  Woodbridge IP12 . . . . . . **146** E4
Cemetery Rd
  Ipswich IP4 . . . . **155** C3
  Lakenheath IP27 . . . . . . **109** D6
  Wickhambrook CB8 . . . . **61** E2
Central Ave IP3 . . . . **144** D8
Central Rd IP16 . . . . **129** C5
Centre Cl NR34 . . . . **111** C3
Centre Cliff IP18 . . . . . . **119** D5
Centre Dr CB8 . . . . **121** D2
Centre Rd CB7 . . . . **28** E2
Century Dr IP5 . . . . **141** E7
Century Rd IP23 . . . . . . **117** C4
Chadacre Rd IP29 . . . . . **77** B7
Chaffinch Dr **10** CO12 . . **106** F1
Chaffinch Rd IP32 . . . . . **49** A3
Chaffinch Way IP14 . . . **124** F7
Chainey Pieces IP9 . . . . **125** D3
Chainhouse Rd IP6 . . . . **125** D3
Chalfont Dr **1** IP17 . . . . . **72** C5
Chalk Hill La IP6 . . . . . . **81** E5
Chalk La Culford IP31 . . **32** E5
  2 Ixworth IP31 . . . . **34** B1
Chalk Rd (North)
  IP33 . . . . **154** A2
Chalk Rd (South)
  IP33 . . . . **154** A2
Chalk Rd IP12 . . . . **D1**
Chalkeith Rd IP6 . . . . . . **125** E3
Chalkners Cl **1** IP1 . . . . **150** E3
Chalkstone Mid Sch
  CB9 . . . . **132** E6
Chalkstone Way CB9 . . **133** A6
Challice Rd IP33 . . . . . . **144** E4
Chalon St IP1 . . . . **155** A2
Chamberlain Way IP8 . . **138** C2
Chamberlayne Rd
  IP32 . . . . **123** E4
Chamberlin Cl **2** IP27 . . **79** F4
Champion Rd IP15 . . . . . **130** E3
Chancellery Mews
  IP33 . . . . **154** A3
Chancery La **5** IP14 . . . . **53** F2
Chancery Rd IP1 . . . . . . **153** A2
Chandlers Ct **4** CB5 . . . . **44** A6
Chandlers Way IP14 . . . **129** C3
Chandlers Wlk IP14 . . . **124** D4
Chandos Ct **8** IP12 . . . . . **84** A1
Chandos Dr **5** IP12 . . . . . **84** A1
Channel The IP8 . . . . . . **81** C1
Chantry Cl IP13 . . . . **71** C2
Chantry Dr CO6 . . . . **101** F2
Chantry Gn CO6 . . . . . . **138** D3
Chantry High Sch IP3 . . **138** F3
Chantry Rd IP17 . . . . . . **128** C3
Chapel Cl
  Capel St Mary IP9 . . . . . **150** E3
  4 Fressingfield IP21 . . . . **39** E8
  Garboldisham IP22 . . . . . **18** D4
  4 Great Waldingfield CO10 **92** C6
Chapel Ct **8** NR32 . . . . . **113** D2
Chapel Cut **8** CO11 . . . . **105** A2
Chapel End Way CO9 . . . **89** A1
Chapel Farm La IP23 . . . **37** A4
Chapel Field IP14 . . . . . **134** A2
Chapel Hill
  Belchamp Walter CO10 . . **90** E3
  Framsden IP14 . . . . **69** F8
  Thorpe Morieux IP30 . . . **79** A8
Chapel La Belstead IP8 . **142** C7
  Botesdale IP22 . . . . **36** A6
  4 Brockley IP29 . . . . **63** A1
  Claydon IP6 . . . . **134** A8
  Copdock & Washbrook
  IP8 . . . . **138** A1
  Drinkstone IP30 . . . . . . **56** D1
  15 Grundisburgh IP13 . . . **83** E5
  Horham IP21 . . . . **38** F2
  Kirby Row NR35 . . . . . . **8** E7
  Kirtling CB8 . . . . **60** E3
  Little Cornard CO10 . . . **92** B1
  2 Somersham IP8 . . . . . **81** C3

Chapel La continued
  Stoke-by-Nayland CO6 . . **103** B7
  Wenhaston with Mells Hamlet
  IP19 . . . . **42** C6
  Wicken CB7 . . . . **28** A1
  Wickham Market IP13 . . **127** C5
  Wortham IP22 . . . . **36** D7
Chapel Pond Hill IP32 . . **123** C8
Chapel Rd
  Beck Row, Holywell Row
  & Kenny Hill IP28 . . . . . . **29** F6
  Bedingham NR35 . . . . . . **7** C8
  Boxted CO4 . . . . **103** A2
  Bradfield Combust with
  Stanningfield IP29 . . . . . . **64** A3
  Bucklesham IP10 . . . . . . **98** B4
  Cockfield IP30 . . . . **64** D2
  Grundisburgh IP13 . . . . . **83** E5
  Langham CO4 . . . . **103** B2
  Lowestoft NR33 . . . . **114** B3
  Mendlesham IP14 . . . . . **52** E5
  Mutford NR14 . . . . **10** D3
  Old Newton with Dagworth
  IP14 . . . . **52** A1
  Otley IP6 . . . . **69** D3
  Rendham IP17 . . . . **56** E3
  Ridgewell CO9 . . . . **89** D4
  St Andrew, Ilketshall
  NR34 . . . . **8** F2
  Saxmundham IP17 . . . . **128** C3
  Saxtead IP13 . . . . **55** A4
  Scole IP21 . . . . **21** B5
  Stoke Ash IP23 . . . . **37** B2
  Theberton IP16 . . . . **58** C5
  Wattisfield IP22 . . . . **35** C4
  Wrentham NR34 . . . . . . **26** D5
Chapel Row **3** CB8 . . . . . **61** E2
Chapel St **5** Bildeston IP7 **79** F4
  Diss IP22 . . . . **20** C2
  Exning CB8 . . . . **120** B8
  6 Lowestoft NR32 . . . . . **113** D2
  Peasenhall IP17 . . . . **56** E4
  Steeple Bumpstead CB9 . **88** E4
  Stoke-by-Clare CO9 . . . . **89** C6
  Woodbridge IP12 . . . . . **147** A5
Chapelfield IP14 . . . . . . **131** C3
Chaplains Cl CB9 . . . . . **132** D7
Chaplin Rd IP7 . . . . **151** C5
Chaplin Wlk **16** CO10 . . . **92** B3
Chappel Rd CO10 . . . . . **101** C2
Chapple Dr CB9 . . . . . . **132** E7
Chare Rd IP31 . . . . **34** D5
Charity La IP13 . . . . **64** A4
Charles Adams Cl
  IP16 . . . . **129** D6
Charles Ave **3** IP3 . . . . . **83** E5
Charles Burrell High Sch
  IP24 . . . . **125** D3
Charles Cl CB8 . . . . **120** E3
Charles Ind Est IP32 . . . **49** A5
Charles Melrose Cl **1**
  IP28 . . . . **116** B4
Charles Miller Ct
  IP16 . . . . **129** D5
Charles Rd IP28 . . . . **152** E3
Charles St IP1 . . . . **155** B3
Charlock Rd **5** IP24 . . . . **16** D7
Charlotte's IP8 . . . . **95** F5
Charlton Ave IP1 . . . . . . **134** F2
Charrington Cl CB9 . . . . **133** A4
Charsfield CE Prim Sch
  IP13 . . . . **70** B3
Charter Cl IP7 . . . . **149** D7
Charter Way **6** NR33 . . . **114** C5
Chartres Piece NR34 . . . **25** E2
Chartwell Cl IP14 . . . . . **140** A5
Chase Cl IP13 . . . . **132** E7
Chase La **6** CO12 . . . . . **106** F1
Chase Rd IP28 . . . . **48** C5
Chase The
  Beccles NR34 . . . . **111** E5
  Brandon IP27 . . . . **6** A1
  Brantham CO11 . . . . . . **104** F5
  Dedham CO7 . . . . **104** A3
  Felixstowe IP11 . . . . **152** F4
  Foxearth CO10 . . . . **91** B7
  24 Manningtree CO11 . . . **104** E2
  20 Martlesham Heath IP5 . **98** A8
  8 Stanton IP31 . . . . **34** E4
  Steeple Bumpstead CB9 . **88** E4
Chaser Cl **8** IP3 . . . . **144** C8
Chase's La IP17 . . . . **72** C5
Chatham Rd **6** IP27 . . . . **14** A2
Chatsworth Cl **1** NR32 . . **113** A3
Chatsworth Cres
  Felixstowe IP11 . . . . **152** C7
  Ipswich IP2 . . . . **139** A2
Chatsworth Dr IP14 . . . **140** E4
Chatten Cl **1** IP14 . . . . . **26** E5
Chattisham Cl IP10 . . . . **124** E3
Chattisham Rd IP8 . . . . **95** E4
Chaucer Rd
  Felixstowe IP11 . . . . **152** F3
  Ipswich IP1 . . . . **134** F2
  Sudbury CO10 . . . . **148** B8
Chaucer St NR35 . . . . . . **110** A4
Chaukers Cres NR33 . . . **114** C5
Chauntry Rd IP28 . . . . . **116** D1
Chedburgh Pl **8** CB9 . . . **132** F6
Chedburgh Rd
  Chevington IP29 . . . . . . **62** F5
  Whepstead IP29 . . . . **62** F5
Chedgrave Rd IP33 . . . . **114** F6
Chediston Pottery*
  IP19 . . . . **24** B1
Chediston Rd IP19 . . . . . **24** B2
Chediston St
  Chediston IP19 . . . . **41** D8

Chediston St continued
  Halesworth IP19 . . . . . . **118** A3
Chelmer Rd CB9 . . . . . . **132** F6
Chelmondiston CE Prim Sch
  IP9 . . . . **106** B8
Chelsea Ct
  Bury St Edmunds IP33 . . **122** D5
  Ipswich IP1 . . . . **134** F1
Chelsea Ct **4** CO10 . . . . **148** D5
Chelsea Rd **3** CO10 . . . . **148** D5
Chelsworth Ave
  Ipswich IP4 . . . . **135** E1
  Sudbury CO10 . . . . **148** F4
Chelsworth Rd IP11 . . . **152** D3
Chelsworth Way IP14 . . **124** E3
Cheltenham Ave IP1 . . . **135** B1
Chepstow Rd
  Bury St Edmunds IP33 . . **122** D3
  Felixstowe IP11 . . . . **152** F5
  Ipswich IP1 . . . . **135** B4
Chequer Field IP12 . . . . **85** C2
Chequer Sq IP33 . . . . . . **154** C2
Chequers La
  Bressingham IP22 . . . . . . **19** F3
  Burston & Shimpling IP22 . **20** E8
  Glemsford CO10 . . . . . . **77** B3
Chequers Rd CO11 . . . . **104** E1
Cherington Rd IP3 . . . . . **140** B2
Cherry Blossom Cl
  IP8 . . . . **138** B2
Cherry Hill IP29 . . . . **30** E3
Cherry Hill Cl **1** NR34 . . **111** F4
Cherry La
  Aldeburgh IP15 . . . . **130** D5
  Belton with Browston NR31 **2** E8
  Lakenheath IP27 . . . . . . **13** F2
Cherry Tree Cl
  Mundford IP26 . . . . **6** A8
  North Lopham IP22 . . . . **19** A6
  Yaxley IP23 . . . . **37** B5
Cherry Tree La IP14 . . . . **53** F1
Cherry Tree Rd
  Stowmarket IP14 . . . . . **124** C8
  Woodbridge IP12 . . . . . **146** F4
Cherry Tree Row **8** IP31 . **35** C2
Cherry Tress Sch IP28 . . **47** D5
Cherryfields IP14 . . . . . **134** A1
Cherrytree La
  Rickinghall Inferior IP22 . . **36** A7
  Soham CB7 . . . . **28** D3
Cherrytree Rd CO10 . . . **148** F5
Cherrywood **10** IP20 . . . **22** D5
Chervil Wlk **8** IP7 . . . . . **149** D7
Chesapeake Cl **8** IP9 . . . **106** C8
Chesapeake Rd IP3 . . . . **144** A8
Chesham Rd IP2 . . . . . . **155** A1
Chessington Gdns IP1 . . **138** F8
Chester Ct **8** CB9 . . . . . **132** C4
Chester Pl **8** IP31 . . . . . **49** A5
Chester Rd
  Felixstowe IP11 . . . . **152** F5
  Ipswich IP1 . . . . **119** D5
Chester St **4** IP27 . . . . . **14** A3
Chesterfield Dr IP1 . . . . **134** F2
Chesterton Cl IP2 . . . . . **138** F1
Chestnut Ave
  Great Brickett IP7 . . . . . **80** D6
  Lowestoft NR32 . . . . . . **112** E2
Chestnut Cl
  4 Beccles NR34 . . . . . . **111** E3
  6 Bentwaters Airfield IP12 . **85** E8
  17 Fornham All Saints IP28 **48** B5
  Great Barton IP31 . . . . . **49** A3
  3 Great Waldingfield CO10 **92** C6
  Haverhill CB9 . . . . **132** D6
  1 Mildenhall IP28 . . . . . **116** D4
  Rushmere St Andrew
  IP5 . . . . **136** E1
  4 Stowupland IP14 . . . . **67** A6
Chestnut Cres
  Chedburgh IP29 . . . . **62** D4
  6 Lowestoft NR33 . . . . **114** C3
Chestnut Dr
  Claydon IP6 . . . . **134** A8
  6 Soham CB7 . . . . **28** D4
Chestnut Gr **2** IP14 . . . . **124** D6
Chestnut Mews **17**
  CO10 . . . . **148** C5
Chestnut Rd
  Dickleburgh IP21 . . . . . . **21** C5
  Glemsford CO10 . . . . . . **77** A3
  Pulham St Mary IP21 . . . **21** F8
  Stradishall CB8 . . . . **75** C6
Chestnut Rise **1** CB5 . . . **44** A6
Chestnut Way **21** IP27 . . **14** A3
Chestnuts The
  5 Great Finborough IP14 . **66** B4
  11 Ipswich IP2 . . . . . . **138** C2
  Rickinghall Superior IP22 . **36** A6
  Wrentham NR34 . . . . . . **26** E5
Chevalier Rd IP11 . . . . . **153** B4
Chevalier St IP1 . . . . **155** A3
Chevalley Prim Sch CB8 . **60** E7
Cheveley Rd
  Newmarket CB8 . . . . . . **121** C3
  Woodditton CB8 . . . . . . **60** E6
Chevington Rd
  Hargrave IP29 . . . . **62** B6
  Horringer IP29 . . . . **63** A7
Cheviot Rd **8** NR32 . . . . **112** D2
Chevy Ct **8** CO12 . . . . . **106** E1
Cheyne Ct **10** CO10 . . . . **148** C5
Chichester Cl IP33 . . . . **123** B3
Chichester Dr NR33 . . . **114** D6
Chichester Rd IP19 . . . . **118** A5
Chickering Rd IP21 . . . . **38** D6
Childer Rd IP14 . . . . **124** D6

Childers Cl **1** IP9 . . . . . **107** A5
Childers Field **2** IP11 . . **152** D5
Chiltern Cres NR32 . . . . **112** E2
Chilton Ave IP14 . . . . . . **124** C6
Chilton Com Prim Sch
  IP14 . . . . **124** C7
Chilton Ct CO10 . . . . . . **148** E5
Chilton Ind Est CO10 . . **148** F6
Chilton Lodge Rd
  CO10 . . . . **148** E5
Chilton Rd IP3 . . . . **140** C4
Chilton Way IP14 . . . . . **124** C6
Chilton Way Sports Club
  IP14 . . . . **124** A7
Chimer's La **3** IP13 . . . . **70** A4
Chimney Mill Galleries*
  IP19 . . . . **24** C1
Chimney Mills IP28 . . . . **32** C1
Chimswell Way CB9 . . . **132** A6
Chippenham Fen National
  Nature Reserve* CB7 **45** A8
Chippenham Rd
  Chippenham IP28 . . . . . **29** E2
  Fordham CB7 . . . . **29** C1
  Moulton CB8 . . . . **45** F3
Chipperfield Rd **20** NR33 **11** C1
Chippings The IP15 . . . . **130** C6
Chislehurst Rd **8** NR31 . **114** C4
Chisnall Cl IP7 . . . . **149** D8
Chiswick Ave IP28 . . . . **116** C6
Chivers Rd IP3 . . . . **132** B5
Christ Church Sch
  NR32 . . . . **113** C1
Christchurch Dr IP12 . . **146** D3
Christchurch Mansion*
  IP1 . . . . **155** C3
Christchurch St IP4 . . . . **155** C3
Christmas La
  Lowestoft NR32 . . . . . . **112** C1
  Metfield IP20 . . . . **23** D3
Christopher Ct **15** CO10 . **148** C5
Christopher La CO10 . . . **148** C5
Church Ave NR32 . . . . . **112** C2
Church Cl
  Aldeburgh IP15 . . . . **130** E4
  Bucklesham IP10 . . . . . . **98** A5
  Carlton IP17 . . . . **128** D7
  4 Cavendish CO10 . . . . **76** E1
  Creeting St Mary IP6 . . **125** F8
  Dullingham CB8 . . . . . . **59** F4
  Exning CB8 . . . . **120** C8
  Fornham St Martin IP28 . **48** D5
  Hepworth IP22 . . . . **35** A5
  Ipswich IP5 . . . . **141** B8
  Pulham St Mary IP21 . . . **22** A8
  Rede IP29 . . . . **62** E3
  Risby IP28 . . . . **47** E5
  1 Roydon IP22 . . . . **20** A3
  13 Stanton IP31 . . . . **34** E4
  Wangford NR34 . . . . . . **26** B2
  Wickham Market IP13 . . **127** F7
  Wortwell IP20 . . . . **22** F7
Church Cres IP8 . . . . . . **138** A6
Church Dr IP13 . . . . **71** E5
Church Farm Cl IP17 . . . **38** F3
Church Farm La **3**
  IP19 . . . . **118** A3
Church Farm Rd
  Aldeburgh IP15 . . . . **130** E5
  Bramfield IP19 . . . . **41** F4
Church Field
  Monks Eleigh IP7 . . . . . . **79** C2
  Walberswick IP18 . . . . . **119** A2
Church Field Rd CO10 . . **148** F7
Church Fm Rise IP5 . . . **130** F5
Church Gdns
  1 Barningham IP31 . . . . **34** E7
  8 Beck Row, Holywell
  Row & Kenny Hill IP28 . . **29** F6
Church Gn
  Bramford IP8 . . . . **134** B1
  Normanston NR32 . . . . **113** D3
Church Hill Benhall IP17 . **72** C8
  Burstall IP8 . . . . **95** D7
  Cookley IP19 . . . . **41** C3
  Helions Bumpstead CB9 . **88** B4
  Hoxne IP21 . . . . **38** C8
  Kersey IP7 . . . . **94** A6
  Lawford CO11 . . . . **104** C2
  Monks Eleigh IP7 . . . . . . **79** C2
  Pakenham IP31 . . . . **49** E6
  Ramsey & Parkeston
  CO12 . . . . **106** D1
  Saxmundham IP17 . . . . **128** D2
  Starston IP20 . . . . **22** C7
  Westhall IP19 . . . . **25** E8
  Whepstead IP29 . . . . . . **63** B5
  Wyverstone IP14 . . . . . . **51** E6
Church La
  Aldeby/Wheatacre/Burgh
  St Peter NR34 . . . . **2** B1
  Aldham IP7 . . . . **94** D7
  Aldringham cum Thorpe
  IP16 . . . . **129** E1
  Alpheton CO10 . . . . **77** F5
  Arwarton IP9 . . . . **106** E5
  Barnham IP24 . . . . **16** C2
  Barton Mills IP28 . . . . . **116** D1
  Bedingham NR35 . . . . . . **81** E6
  Beck Row, Holywell Row
  & Kenny Hill IP28 . . . . . . **29** F6
  Bedfield IP13 . . . . **54** E5
  Birds End IP29 . . . . **62** A7
  Blo' Norton IP22 . . . . . . **18** E1
  Blythburgh IP19 . . . . **42** E6
  Brantham CO11 . . . . . . **104** F5
  Bressingham IP22 . . . . . . **19** E3

Church La continued
  Brockdish IP21 . . . . **21** F2
  Bromeswell IP12 . . . . . . **85** A5
  Broome NR35 . . . . **8** B7
  Brundish IP13 . . . . **53** C8
  Bucklesham IP10 . . . . . . **98** A5
  Burrough Green CB8 . . . **59** F2
  15 Burwell CB5 . . . . **44** A5
  Carlton IP17 . . . . **128** D7
  1 Cheveley CB8 . . . . . . **60** E7
  Claydon IP6 . . . . **134** E8
  Clopton IP13 . . . . **83** E8
  Cockfield IP30 . . . . **64** C1
  Copdock & Washbrook
  IP8 . . . . **142** A7
  Corton NR32 . . . . **3** C4
  Creeting St Mary IP6 . . **125** D7
  Dalham CB8 . . . . **46** C1
  Ditchingham NR35 . . . . . **8** C7
  Dullingham CB8 . . . . . . **59** F4
  Earl Soham IP13 . . . . . . **55** A2
  Exning CB8 . . . . **120** B8
  Felixstowe IP11 . . . . **152** E6
  Finningham IP14 . . . . . . **52** A8
  Fritton & St Olaves NR31 . . **2** C7
  Frostenden NR34 . . . . . . **26** C6
  Harkstead IP9 . . . . **106** B6
  8 Harwich CO12 . . . . . **107** B3
  Hemingstone IP6 . . . . . . **82** C8
  Hemley IP12 . . . . **98** E5
  Henley IP6 . . . . **82** E5
  Hepworth IP22 . . . . **35** A5
  Hitcham IP7 . . . . **79** E6
  Hockwold cum Wilton IP26 . **5** A2
  Hoo IP13 . . . . **70** B6
  Iken IP12 . . . . **72** F3
  Kennett CB8 . . . . **45** F6
  Kenton IP14 . . . . **54** A4
  Kirton IP10 . . . . **98** D3
  Levington IP10 . . . . **145** E3
  Lowestoft NR33 . . . . . . **114** B2
  Martlesham IP12 . . . . . . **84** B1
  Mistley CO11 . . . . **104** F2
  6 Mundford IP26 . . . . **6** B8
  Nayland CO6 . . . . **102** D5
  Newmarket CB8 . . . . . . **121** A3
  Norton IP31 . . . . **50** C4
  2 Occold IP23 . . . . **37** F1
  Playford IP6 . . . . **137** B4
  Preston St Mary CO10 . . **79** A5
  Redenhall with Harleston
  IP20 . . . . **22** E7
  Rendlesham IP12 . . . . . . **85** C7
  Rickinghall Superior IP22 . **36** A5
  Ridgewell CO9 . . . . **89** D3
  St James, South Elmham
  IP19 . . . . **23** F4
  St Mary, South Elmham
  otherwise Homersfield
  IP20 . . . . **23** B8
  Semer IP7 . . . . **79** F1
  Shottisham IP12 . . . . . . **99** C7
  Somersham IP8 . . . . **81** D3
  Spexhall IP19 . . . . **24** F3
  Sproughton IP8 . . . . . . **138** B6
  Stetchworth CB8 . . . . . . **60** E5
  Stoke Ash IP23 . . . . **37** B1
  Stonham Earl IP14 . . . . . **67** E6
  Stuston IP21 . . . . **37** D8
  Swilland IP6 . . . . **83** A7
  Thelnetham IP22 . . . . . . **18** E1
  Thwaite IP23 . . . . **52** F7
  Timworth IP31 . . . . **48** E8
  Troston IP31 . . . . **33** E3
  1 Walberswick IP18 . . . . **43** C5
  Wenhaston with Mells Hamlet
  IP19 . . . . **42** C6
  Westerfield IP6 . . . . **135** F4
  Westley Waterless CB8 . . **59** D3
  Weston NR34 . . . . **9** E2
  Winfarthing IP22 . . . . . . **20** A4
  Worlington IP28 . . . . **30** B4
  Yaxley IP23 . . . . **37** C4
Church La Cl IP28 . . . . . **116** D2
Church Meadow
  Barton Mills IP28 . . . . . **116** D2
  Rickinghall Inferior IP22 . **35** F6
Church Meadows
  1 Henley IP6 . . . . **82** D6
  Waldingfield IP12 . . . . . . **98** D7
Church Pk CO10 . . . . . . **89** E6
Church Rd Alburgh IP20 . . **7** A2
  Ashbocking IP6 . . . . **68** E1
  Bacton IP14 . . . . **51** F6
  Bardwell IP31 . . . . **34** B4
  Barningham IP31 . . . . . . **34** F7
  Barrow IP29 . . . . **47** A3
  Battisford IP14 . . . . **66** E1
  Bedfield IP13 . . . . **54** E5
  Bentley IP9 . . . . **142** A1
  Beyton IP30 . . . . **49** F1
  6 Bildeston IP7 . . . . **79** F4
  Blaxhall IP12 . . . . **71** F4
  Blundeston NR32 . . . . **3** B6
  Boxted CO4 . . . . **102** F3
  Bradfield Combust with
  Stanningfield IP29 . . . . . . **63** F3
  Bradfield St George IP30 . **64** D6
  Brandon IP27 . . . . **5** E1
  Brettenham IP7 . . . . **65** C1
  Brockdish IP21 . . . . **21** F2
  Bruisyard IP17 . . . . **56** C5
  Bulmer CO10 . . . . **91** C2
  Butley IP12 . . . . **86** B5

Church Rd *continued*
Carlton CB8 ....74 A8
Chevington IP29 ....62 C6
Combs IP14 ....124 E2
Cotton IP14 ....52 B5
Cratfield IP19 ....40 D5
Crowfield IP6 ....68 C4
Dallinghoo IP13 ....70 C1
Denham IP21 ....38 C5
Dickleburgh & Rushall
IP21 ....20 F3
Earsham NR35 ....7 F3
Ellingham NR35 ....8 D7
Ellough NR34 ....111 F1
Elmswell IP30 ....50 E2
Felixstowe IP11 ....153 C6
Felsham IP30 ....65 A4
Flixton NR35 ....7 E1
Friston IP17 ....72 F7
Garboldisham IP22 ......18 D4
Gillingham NR34 ....9 C7
Gisleham NR33 ....11 A3
Great Barton IP31 ....49 A5
1 Great Finborough IP14 ..66 B4
Great Yeldham CO9 ......89 F1
Hasketon IP13 ....146 B7
Hedenham NR35 ....71 E6
Henstead with Hulver Street
NR34 ....26 E8
Heveningham IP19 ....40 E3
Holbrook IP9 ....105 F6
Honington IP31 ....33 F5
Kessingland NR33 ....11 B1
Kettleburgh IP13 ....70 C7
Kirby Cane NR35 ....8 E8
Knodishall IP17 ....58 A1
Leiston IP16 ....129 B6
Lindsey IP7 ....93 D7
Little Glemham IP13 .....71 E5
Little Thurlow CB9 ....74 D6
Little Waldingfield CO10 ..92 E8
Lowestoft NR32 ....113 C3
Market Weston IP22 .....18 C1
Marlesford IP13 ....71 C5
Mendlesham IP14 ....52 E4
Milden IP7 ....77 B1
Monewden IP13 ....69 F5
5 Moulton CB8 ....45 F3
Mutford NR34 ....10 D3
Nacton IP10 ....145 B4
Newton CO10 ....92 D3
North Lopham IP22 ......19 A5
Old Newton with Dagworth
IP14 ....51 F1
Otley IP6 ....69 C1
Pettaugh IP14 ....68 E6
Playford IP6 ....137 B5
Redlingfield IP23 ....38 C1
Rushbrooke with Rougham
IP30 ....49 C1
Shelfanger IP22 ....20 B6
Snape IP17 ....72 D5
Stambourne CO9 ....89 B1
Stowmarket IP14 ....124 D3
Stowupland IP14 ....67 B7
Stutton IP9 ....105 D5
Sudbury CO10 ....148 E3
Sutton IP12 ....85 A1
Tattingstone IP9 ....105 B7
Theberton IP16 ....58 B4
Thistley Green IP28 .....29 F6
6 Thorpeness IP16 ....73 F6
Thurston IP31 ....49 E4
Tostock IP30 ....50 B2
Uggeshall NR34 ....26 A3
Weybread IP21 ....22 D2
Wheatacre NR34 ....2 A1
Wicken CB7 ....28 B1
Wilby IP21 ....39 C3
Wingfield IP21 ....39 A7
Worlingworth IP13 ....54 E7
Wormingford CO6 ....101 F2
Wortham IP22 ....19 F1
Wrabness CO11 ....105 F2
Church Rd N IP21 ....21 F3
Church Row
Bury St Edmunds IP33 ...154 B3
Framsden IP14 ....69 C6
Church Sq 4 CO8 .....60 F8
Church St 2 Ashley CB8 ..60 F8
Belchamp Otten CO10 ..90 D5
1 Boxford CO10 ....93 C3
Boxted CO4 ....103 A4
6 Chelmondiston IP9 ...106 C8
6 Clare CO10 ....90 A8
Diss IP22 ....20 C2
Exning CB8 ....120 C8
Eye IP23 ....117 D2
Fordham CB7 ....29 B1
Framlingham IP13 ....126 D3
2 Fressingfield IP21 .....39 E8
Gestingthorpe CO9 ......90 F1
Groton CO10 ....93 C5
1 Hadleigh IP7 ....149 D5
8 Harleston IP20 ....22 D6
5 Harwich CO12 ....107 C3
Holton IP19 ....75 D3
10 Isleham CB7 ....29 C5
Lavenham CO10 ....78 D3
Orford IP12 ....131 C2
Peasenhall IP17 ....56 F8
Saxmundham IP17 ......128 D3
12 Southwold IP18 ......119 D5
Steeple Bumpstead CB9 ..88 D4
Stoke-by-Nayland CO6 ..102 E6

Church St *continued*
Stradbroke IP21 ....39 B4
Sudbury CO10 ....148 B4
Wangford NR34 ....26 B2
Wetherden IP14 ....51 A1
Wetheringsett-cum-Brockford
IP14 ....53 A6
Withersfield CB9 ....74 A2
Woodbridge IP12 ....147 A5
Worlingworth IP13 ....54 F7
Church Terr IP13 ......127 C6
Church View
Halesworth IP19 ....118 E4
1 Harleston IP20 ....22 E6
1 Haughley IP14 ....51 C1
Leiston IP16 ....129 B6
Stowlangtoft IP31 ....50 B7
Wyverstone IP14 ....51 E6
Church View Cl IP12 ..147 C7
Church Walks IP33 ....154 C1
Church Wlk
Aldeburgh IP15 ....130 E4
Hadleigh IP7 ....149 C5
3 Laxfield IP13 ....40 B3
Long Melford CO10 .....77 E1
Mildenhall IP28 ....116 B4
Shelfanger IP22 ....20 B6
Stowmarket IP14 ....124 D6
Sturmer CB9 ....133 C2
4 Sudbury CO10 ....148 C5
Church Wood IP19 ....118 E4
Churchfields Dr 1 CB9 ..88 D3
Churchgate CO10 ......77 B3
Churchgate St
Bury St Edmunds IP33 ..154 B2
15 Soham CB7 ....28 D4
Churchill Ave
Hadleigh IP7 ....149 D7
Halesworth IP19 ....132 F7
Ipswich IP4 ....140 B5
Newmarket CB8 ....120 D5
Churchill Cl
3 Lawshall IP29 ....63 D1
Lowestoft NR32 ....113 C4
7 Woodbridge IP12 .....146 E4
Ipswich IP3 ....142 B5
Churchill Cres IP13 ....127 C7
Churchill Ct CB8 ....120 F3
Churchill Dr
Mildenhall IP28 ....116 B5
Sudbury CO10 ....148 C8
Churchill Rd
Halesworth IP19 ....118 B5
5 Southwold IP18 ....119 C8
Thetford IP24 ....14 C6
Churchman Cl IP12 ....147 B8
Churchway 3 IP21 .....36 A8
Churchyard IP33 ....154 C2
Churchyard The IP28 ..116 B4
Cinnabar Ct **11** IP8 ....142 E8
Civic Dr IP1 ....155 A2
Clacton Rd CO11 ....104 E1
Clapgate La IP3 ....140 A1
Clapham Rd Central 3
NR32 ....113 D1
Clapham Rd S NR32 ...113 D1
Clare Ancient House Mus*
CO10 ....90 A8
Clare Ave IP12 ....146 E4
Clare Castle (remains of)*
CO10 ....90 A8
Clare Castle Ctry Pk*
CO10 ....90 B8
Clare Cl
2 Bury St Edmunds IP33 ..122 D4
Mildenhall IP28 ....116 D5
Stowmarket IP14 ....124 E3
Clare Cty Prim Sch
CO10 ....90 A8
Clare Mid Sch CO10 .....90 B8
Clare Pl CB8 ....121 B2
Clare Rd Hundon CO10 ..75 E2
Ipswich IP4 ....139 F8
2 Kessingland NR33 ....11 C1
Poslingford CO10 ....76 A2
Claremont Rd 1 NR33 ..115 C6
Clarence Rd
7 Clacton CO10 ....76 A1
Ipswich IP3 ....140 B1
1 Lowestoft NR32 ......113 D2
Sudbury CO10 ....148 C6
Clarendale Est CB9 ....74 C7
Clarendon Rd CB9 .....132 D5
Clark Rd NR35 ....110 C7
Clark Wlk IP32 ....122 D7
Clark's Dro CB7 ....22 B8
Clare Cl IP22 ....20 C1
Clarke's La IP14 ....8 F3
Clarke's Rd 3 CO12 ....106 F2
Clarkes La NR33 ....114 C6
Clarkson Rd NR32 ......112 D1
Clarkson St IP1 ....155 A3
Claude Oliver Cl CO11 ..104 D1
Claude St IP1 ....155 B3
Claudian Cl CB9 ....133 B5
Claverton Way IP14 ....140 D5
Clay Hill Dennington IP13 ..55 F5
Hintlesham IP8 ....95 B5
Monks Eleigh IP7 ....79 D2
Ubbeston IP19 ....40 E3
Clay La Bacton IP14 ....51 F6
Bildeston IP7 ....94 F4
Henley IP6 ....82 E7
Hepworth IP22 ....35 B5
Ixworth IP31 ....34 A2
Lavenham CO10 ....78 E4
Stoke Ash IP23 ....37 B1
Clay Rd
20 Bury St Edmunds IP32 ..48 C5

Clay Rd *continued*
Bury St Edmunds IP32 ..122 E8
Fornham All Saints IP32 ..48 B5
Clay St Soham CB7 .....28 D4
Thornham Magna IP23 ..36 F1
Claydon Dr NR32 ....112 C7
Claydon High Sch IP6 ..134 C8
Claydon Prim Sch IP6 ..82 B5
Clayhall La CO10 ....92 C7
Clayhall Pl CO10 ....92 C7
Clayhill La Hitcham IP7 ..79 F6
Wattisham IP7 ....80 A6
Clayhill Rd IP17 ....128 E5
Clayhive Dr 1 CB9 ......118 A3
Claypits Ave 1 CO8 ....101 D4
Claypits La CO10 ....91 B7
Clayton Ct IP12 ....146 D3
Clayton Rd 2 CO12 .....106 E1
Clearwing Cl 15 IP8 ....142 E8
Clematis Cl 4 IP28 .....30 B1
Clemence St NR32 .....113 C1
Clement Prim Sch
CB9 ....132 D5
Clement Rd NR33 ......115 B6
Clement Sq NR33 ......115 B6
Clement's Way 11 IP28 ..30 B8
Clementine Gdns IP4 ..140 A5
Clements Cl
3 Haverhill CB9 ....132 D5
3 Scole IP21 ....20 F1
Clements Dr 2 CB9 .....132 D5
Clements La CB9 ....132 D5
Clements Rd 4 IP12 ....84 E6
Clench Cl IP4 ....155 C3
Clench Rd IP9 ....105 E8
Clerk's Piece NR34 .....111 D3
Clermont Ave CO10 ....148 C8
Cleveland Rd NR33 .....115 C7
Cleves Rd CB9 ....132 B4
Cley Ct 1 CB9 ....132 A7
Clicket Hill CO10 ....101 D4
Cliff Farm La NR33 .....11 B2
Cliff La
Great Yarmouth NR31 ....3 B8
Ipswich IP3 ....139 E3
Cliff La Prim Sch IP3 ..139 E3
Cliff Quay IP3 ....139 D2
Cliff Rd
Felixstowe IP11 ....153 D6
Harwich CO12 ....107 B2
Ipswich IP3 ....139 E3
Lowestoft NR33 ....115 C6
Waldringfield IP12 ......98 E7
Clifford Dr NR33 ....114 E5
Clifford Rd IP4 ....139 F4
Clifford Rd Air Raid Shelter
*Mus** IP4 ....139 F5
Clifford Rd Prim Sch
IP4 ....139 F6
Cliffs The NR33 ....115 B2
Clifton Hill IP31 ....33 F6
Clifton Way IP2 ....138 D2
Clifton Wood 2 IP9 .....105 E7
Clifton Wood IP31 .....115 B2
Cliftonville Rd NR33 ....115 B3
Clink The IP19 ....41 C5
Clint Hill IP31 ....33 F6
Clint Rd IP23 ....37 D1
Clive Ave IP1 ....135 B2
Clockhall La CO10 ......76 D3
Clockhouse La IP14 ....67 F7
Cloncurry Gdns IP11 ..152 D3
Clopton Dr 2 CO10 .....91 E7
Clopton Gdns IP7 ......149 E4
Clopton Pk CB8 ....62 A1
Clopton Rd IP6 ....136 C7
Close The Corton NR32 ..3 D4
3 Harwich CO12 ....107 A2
Kennett CB8 ....45 F7
North Lopham IP22 .....19 A6
Sudbury CO10 ....148 D6
3 Tattingstone IP9 .....105 B8
Clough Dr 10 IP26 .....4 E5
Cloutings Cl IP7 ....128 C6
Clovelly Cl IP4 ....140 F4
Clovelly Rise NR32 .....113 B3
Clover Cl Ipswich IP2 ..138 F4
Needham Market IP6 ....125 D3
Clover Field CB9 ....132 B6
Clover Way
Lowestoft NR32 ....113 C5
1 Red Lodge IP28 ......30 C1
Cloverfield Dr CB7 .....28 C5
Cloverfields 2 IP7 ......79 F4
Clovers Ct IP14 ....124 C6
Clowes Ct NR34 ....111 B5
Clowes's Cnr IP14 ......54 D2
Cluanie Orch CO10 .....76 F1
Clumps The IP12 ....86 A4
Coach La CB8 ....60 F8
Coachman's Paddock 3
IP9 ....105 E7
Coachmans Ct IP1 .....155 B2
Coakers La IP13 ....70 A1
Coalpit La IP29 ....46 F4
Coast Guards The 6
IP16 ....73 F6
Coast Rd NR32 ....3 C5
Coastguard La 22 NR33 ..11 C1
Coates Dro 1 CB7 ......69 F5
Cobbler's Cnr IP6 ......95 B5
Cobbold Cl IP14 ....66 C1
Cobbold Mews IP4 .....155 C3
Cobbold Rd
Felixstowe IP11 ....153 A4
Woodbridge IP12 ....146 E7
Cobbold St Diss IP22 ..20 B2

Cobbold St *continued*
Ipswich IP4 ....155 C3
Cobden Pl IP4 ....155 C3
Cobham Rd IP3 ....140 C2
Coblers Way 1 IP31 ....92 B7
Cock & Bel La CO10 ....91 E8
Cock La CO10 ....78 F2
Cock Rd IP14 ....52 A6
Cock's Rd IP23 ....117 F1
Cockfield CE Prim Sch
IP30 ....64 C1
Cockfield Hall La IP6 ..135 E7
Cockfield Rd IP30 ......65 A3
Cockpen Rd CB7 ....28 F1
Cockrell's Rd CO6 ......102 A2
Cocks Gn La IP30 ......64 A5
Coddenham Rd IP6 .....91 E7
Coddington Way 8 IP31 ..34 B1
Codling Rd IP32 ....123 E6
Cody Rd IP3 ....140 C1
Coggeshall Rd
Dedham CO7 ....104 A2
Foxash Estate CO7 .....103 F1
Colbeck Rd CB9 ....132 C8
Colchester Cl 4 IP27 ...13 F2
Colchester Rd
Bures CO8 ....101 C4
Dedham CO7 ....103 E2
Ipswich IP4 ....135 F1
Wormingford CO6 ......102 A1
Cold Store Rd IP11 ....152 B2
Coldfair Cl IP17 ....129 B3
Coldfair Gn Prim Sch
IP17 ....129 B2
Coldham La IP23 ....36 D2
Cole Ness Rd IP3 ......144 A8
Cole St IP21 ....39 D7
Coleman Rd IP22 ......20 C1
Coleridge Rd IP1 ....134 F3
Coles Croft IP19 ....42 C6
Coles Hill IP19 ....42 C7
Coles La CB8 ....59 E1
Coles Oak La CO7 .....103 E3
Coles View IP19 ....42 C6
Colethorpe La IP29 ....46 F3
College Gn IP29 ....63 A8
College Gn IP11 ....153 C5
College Heath Mid Sch
IP28 ....116 C6
College Heath Rd
IP28 ....116 D6
College La
Bury St Edmunds IP33 ..154 B1
Worlingham NR34 ....111 F2
College Meadows 2
NR32 ....113 A3
College Rd
Framlingham IP13 ....126 C4
Hockwold cum Wilton IP26 ..4 F3
Lowestoft NR33 ....115 B5
2 Saxmundham IP17 ...28 D3
College St
Bury St Edmunds IP33 ..154 B1
Ipswich IP3 ....155 B2
Collett's Wlk IP12 .....146 E5
Colletts Chase CO6 ....101 F2
Collimer Cl 2 IP9 ......106 C8
Collin's Hill CB7 ....29 B1
Collings Pl CB8 ....120 E5
Collingwood Ave 8 IP3 ..140 B3
Collingwood Fields
CO7 ....151 B6
Collingwood Rd IP12 ..146 F7
Collins Cl IP17 ....128 B3
Collinson's IP22 ....138 D5
Colman Rd 4 NR32 .....3 D4
Colne Rd CO8 ....101 B4
Colne Springs CO9 .....89 D4
Colne Valley Rd CB9 ...132 E5
Colneis Jun Sch IP11 ..153 B6
Colneis Rd IP11 ....153 B6
Colneys Cl CO10 ....148 B7
Colsterdale NR33 ......114 D3
Coltsfoot Cl
7 Ixworth IP31 ....34 B1
3 Lowestoft NR33 .....114 F3
8 Wickhambrook CB8 ..61 E2
Coltsfoot Cnr IP32 .....123 F5
Coltsfoot Rd IP2 ....138 E4
Columbia Cl IP5 ....141 A7
Columbine Cl 3 NR33 ..114 C5
Columbine Gdns IP2 ..138 E5
Columbine Way 1 IP23 ..36 D2
Columbines The CO10 ..76 F1
Columbyne Cl IP14 ....67 A7
Colville Rd NR33 ....114 E6
Colville Way NR33 .....114 C3
Comber Cl IP21 ....21 A2
Combers The IP5 ......141 E7
Combs Ford Prim Sch
IP14 ....124 E4
Combs Gn IP14 ....66 D2
Combs La IP14 ....124 D4
Combs Mid Sch IP14 ..124 F3
Combs Wood Dr IP14 ..124 E4
Combs Wood Nature
*Reserve** IP14 ....124 E2
Comet Way IP14 ....116 B5
Comfrey Way IP24 .....16 D6
Commerce Way 3
CO11 ....104 E3
Commercial Rd
Ipswich IP1 ....155 A1
Lowestoft NR32 ....115 C8
Commister La 14 IP31 ..34 B1
Commodore Rd NR32 ..112 C1
Common Gate Dro CB7 ..29 A5

Common La
Beccles NR34 ....111 C5
Bromeswell IP12 ....147 F7
Syleham IP21 ....22 A2
Troston IP31 ....33 E3
Common La Ind Est
NR34 ....111 C6
Common La N NR34 ....111 B6
Common Rd
Aldeby NR34 ....10 B7
Botesdale IP22 ....36 B5
Bressingham IP22 ......19 F4
Hopton IP22 ....18 C2
St James, South Elmham
IP19 ....23 D4
Scole IP21 ....21 B4
Shelfanger IP22 ....19 F7
Common St 3 CO10 ....90 A8
Common The
Beccles NR34 ....111 E5
Claydon IP8 ....134 A6
1 Harleston IP20 ......22 D5
Knodishall Common
IP17 ....129 A1
Leiston IP16 ....129 F7
Southwold IP18 ....119 C5
Compass Cl IP27 ....109 D4
Compass St NR32 .....113 D2
Compiegne Way IP32 ..154 B3
Conach Rd IP22 ....146 E5
Coney Ave IP14 ....16 A6
Coney Hill NR34 ....111 D3
Coney Weston Rd
Sapiston IP31 ....34 D8
Fakenham Magna IP31 ..33 F6
Congreve Rd IP1 ....135 A3
Coniston Cl 1 IP3 ......153 E7
Coniston Rd IP3 ....140 B2
Coniston Sq E IP3 ......140 B2
Coniston Sq W IP3 .....140 B2
Connaught Rd
Haverhill CB9 ....132 C5
Ipswich IP1 ....134 D2
Conrad Cl NR33 ....114 D6
Conrad Rd NR33 ....114 C6
Consent La IP7 ....79 E4
Constable Cl
Halesworth IP19 ....118 A2
Lowestoft NR32 ....112 F1
3 Manningtree CO11 ...104 D2
Nayland-with-Wissington
CO6 ....102 A5
Constable Ct 18 IP20 ..22 D6
Constable Rd
Bury St Edmunds IP33 ..122 E4
Felixstowe IP11 ....153 B4
Haverhill CB9 ....132 E5
Ipswich IP1 ....155 C4
Sudbury CO10 ....148 C6
Constable Way IP14 ...124 B7
Constantine Rd IP1 ....155 A2
Constitution Hill
Ipswich IP1 ....139 B8
2 Needham Market IP6 ..125 D5
Southwold IP18 ....119 D4
Sudbury CO10 ....148 B5
Convalescent Hill
IP11 ....153 A3
Conway Cl
Felixstowe IP11 ....153 C7
4 Haverhill CB9 ....132 C6
Ipswich IP3 ....139 B2
Conway Rd 2 IP32 .....48 C5
Conyers Way IP31 .....49 A6
Cook's Dro IP26 ....12 D2
Cook's La
Hawkedon IP29 ....62 E1
Wortwell IP20 ....22 F6
Cooke Cl NR33 ....114 F2
Cooke Rd NR33 ....114 F2
Cookley & Walpole CE Prim
Sch IP19 ....41 B5
Cookley La IP23 ....41 B5
Cookley Rd Cookley IP19 ..41 B5
Eye IP23 ....38 A5
Cooks Hill Boxted CO4 ..103 A4
Letheringham IP13 .....70 D4
Cooks Rd IP30 ....50 D2
Coombers IP9 ....150 D3
Cooper Cl 2 IP17 ....128 C4
Cooper La IP29 ....63 E8
Cooper Rd IP6 ....68 C1
Cooper's Cl CB8 ....60 A5
Cooper's La CO7 ....103 F3
Cooper's Rd IP6 ....82 C6
Coopers Cl IP1 ....83 A6
Coopers Dr 27 NR33 ...11 C1
Coopers La IP14 ....51 B5
Coopers Rd 20 IP6 .....98 A8
Coopers Way IP6 ....82 A5
Coppersfield 1 IP14 ...124 B7
Copdock Intc IP8 ....138 B2
Copdock Prim Sch IP8 ..95 F4
Copellis Cl IP28 ....116 B6
Copeman Rd 3 IP22 ...20 A3
Copland Way NR34 ....111 E4
Copleston High Sch
IP4 ....140 C5
Copleston Rd IP4 ......140 B5
Coplow Dale 12 NR33 ..114 E3
Copper Beech Dr 5
NR33 ....114 D4
Copper Gr 4 IP32 ......48 E8
Copperfield Rd IP2 ....138 E5
Copperfield Way 11 CB5 ..44 B5
Coppers Cl IP33 ....154 C1

Copperwheat Ave
  IP18 ....119 B8
Coppice Cl IP12 ....147 A6
Coppice Ct NR33 ....115 A6
Coppice The IP31 ....49 A6
Copplestone Cl 12 NR34 ....9 F4
Coprolite St IP3 ....139 E5
Copse Cl IP33 ....123 B1
Copswood Cl IP5 ....141 F7
Copy Hill CB9 ....132 C1
Coral Dr IP1 ....134 D1
Coram St IP7 ....149 A6
Cordell Pl CO10 ....91 E8
Cordell Rd CO10 ....91 E8
Corder Rd IP4 ....139 D8
Cordwinders CO7 ....151 F3
Cordy's La IP11 ....152 B6
Coriander Dr IP24 ....16 D6
Corks La IP7 ....149 C6
Corkway Dro IP26 ....4 A4
Cormorant Dr IP14 ......124 F5
Cornhill
  Bury St Edmunds IP33 ..154 B2
  Ipswich IP1 ....155 B3
Cornhill Wlk Sh Ctr
  IP33 ....154 B2
Cornish Hall End Rd
  CO9 ....89 A1
Cornish Wlk IP32 ....122 E8
Cornmill Gn 9 IP30 ....50 D1
Cornmills Rd IP7 ....94 C3
Cornwall Cl 25 CO11 .....104 D2
Cornwall Rd IP11 ....152 F5
Cornwallis Cl IP28 ....32 C1
Cornwallis Ct IP33 ......154 A1
Cornwallis Rd CB9 ....132 D4
Cornwell Cl CB7 ....29 B4
Coronation Ave IP12 .....99 D6
Coronation Dr IP11 .....152 D3
Coronation Rd IP14 .....140 B5
Coronation Rise 11 CO10 ..92 C6
Corporation Ave IP2 ....139 B1
Corsbie Cl IP33 ....154 B1
Corsican Pine Cl CB8 ...120 F5
Corton CE VC Prim Sch
  NR32 ....3 D4
Corton Long La NR32 ....113 B8
Corton Rd Ipswich IP3 ...140 B1
  Lowestoft NR32 ....113 D6
Cosford Rd IP7 ....94 C7
Cotes The IP7 ....28 B6
Cotman Ave 8 CO11 .....104 D2
Cotman Cl 1 NR32 ......113 B4
Cotman Rd IP3 ....140 A1
Cotmer Rd NR33 ....114 D6
Cotswold Ave IP1 ....135 B1
Cotswold Dr 1 CO10 .....91 E7
Cotswold Way NR32 .....112 E2
Cottesford Cl IP7 ....149 E5
Cottingham Rd IP8 .....138 B2
Cotton End Rd CB8 ......120 C8
Cotton La
  Bury St Edmunds IP33 ..154 C3
  Cotton IP14 ....52 A6
Cotton La Flats IP33 ....154 C3
Coucy Cl IP13 ....126 C4
Coulson La 1 IP27 ....5 F1
Coupals Cl CB9 ....133 A4
Coupals Prim Sch
  CB9 ....133 B5
Courier Cl IP28 ....116 B5
Court Knoll (Earthworks)*
  CO6 ....102 D4
Court St CO6 ....102 D5
Courtenay Cl CO10 ......148 B8
Courts The
  Felixstowe IP11 ....153 B4
  Playford IP6 ....137 B5
Covehite Ct 4 CB9 ......132 C4
Covell Cl IP33 ....122 C4
Coverdale 6 NR33 ....114 E3
Covert Cl CB9 ....132 E7
Covert Rd IP18 ....119 C8
Covert Sycamore 5
  IP24 ....16 D6
Covey Dr IP27 ....109 E6
Covey Way IP27 ....109 E6
Cow and Sheep Dro
  IP28 ....29 E7
Cow Fair 7 IP30 ....50 D1
Cowell St IP27 ....139 C2
Cowle's Dro IP26 ....4 D1
Cowley Rd IP1 ....153 A4
Cowper St IP4 ....140 B6
Cowslip Cl
  Bury St Edmunds IP32 ..123 F5
  Ipswich IP2 ....138 E4
Cowslip Cres NR33 .....114 C5
Cowslip Way IP6 ....125 D3
Cox Cl IP5 ....141 B6
Cox Hill CO10 ....93 C3
Cox La Great Barton IP31 ..49 B6
Cox's Cl NR34 ....111 C3
Cox's Hill CO11 ....104 D2
Cox's La IP18 ....119 C8

Coxhall Rd IP9 ....142 E1
Coxs Cl CB9 ....132 A5
Coytes Gdns IP1 ....155 B2
Crabbe St
  Aldeburgh IP15 ......130 F4
  Ipswich IP4 ....140 A6
Crabbe's Cl 8 IP26 ......4 E5
Crabtree Cl IP19 ......118 B2
Crabtree La Aldeby NR34 ..9 F8
  Little Horkesley CO6 ...102 B1
Crabtree Meadow 6
  IP30 ....50 F2
Crabtree Rise IP21 ......21 F2
Cracks La IP12 ....85 C6
Crag Farm Rd IP12 .....131 E7
Crag Path IP15 ....130 F3
Craig Cl IP11 ....107 D8
Craig's La CO8 ....101 B3
Cramswell Cl IP3 ....140 A1
Cranberry Sq 2 IP3 ....144 C7
Cranborne Chase 1
  IP4 ....136 A1
Cranbrook La CO10 ......77 C1
Crane Cl IP12 ....146 D3
Crane Hill London Rd
  IP2 ....138 A4
Cranes Meadow 31 IP20 ..22 D6
Cranesbill Dr IP32 .....123 E5
Cranesbill Rd NR33 .....114 F3
Cranfield Cl 4 NR33 ....115 A3
Cranfield Pk IP6 ....95 D7
Cranleigh Rd IP32 ......114 F3
Cranley Gn Rd IP21 ......61 F8
Cranley La IP23 ....117 F1
Cranmoregreen La
  CO10 ....77 C1
Cranwell Cres IP3 .....140 C1
Cranwell Gr 1 IP5 .....141 C7
Cranworth Gdns 1
  NR32 ....112 F4
Cranworth Rd IP7 .....149 E4
Cratfield La IP19 ....40 C4
Cratfield Rd
  Bury St Edmunds IP32 ..123 E4
  Fressingfield IP21 ......39 F8
  Huntingfield IP19 ......40 E5
Craven Way CB8 ....120 E6
Crawford Ave IP14 ......66 D8
Crawford Cl 3 IP1 ......51 A1
Crawford La 2 IP1 .....141 C7
Crayford Rd CO10 ......148 B8
Creed Wlk IP32 ....122 D7
Creeting Hills IP14 .....125 F6
Creeting La IP14 ....67 B7
Creeting St IP14 ....124 E6
Creeting St Mary Prim Sch
  IP6 ....125 F8
Crepping Hall Dr IP9 ...105 C5
Crescent Rd
  Aldeburgh IP15 ......130 E4
  Felixstowe IP11 ......153 E4
  Ipswich IP3 ....155 A3
Crescent The
  Dullingham CB8 ....59 D5
  East Harling NR16 .....18 C8
  Great Horkesley CO6 ...102 D1
  6 Soham CB7 ....28 D3
  Stowmarket IP14 .....124 D4
  7 Thurston IP31 ....49 B6
  Wicken CB7 ....28 A1
  Wickham Market IP13 ..127 B6
Crescents The IP18 .....119 B8
Cresmeadow Way IP30 ..50 F2
Crespigny Rd IP15 ......130 E3
Cresslands La IP29 ......76 D8
Crestland Bsns Pk
  CO10 ....92 A8
Crestview Dr IP11 .....153 A4
Crick's Rd
  Back Row, Holywell Row
  & Kenny Hill IP28 .....30 A6
  Thistley Green IP28 .....29 F6
Cricket Field Rd CB8 ...121 B2
Cricket Hill Rd IP11 ....152 D5
Cricketers Cl CO10 .....148 C4
Crimbold's La NR34 ......64 D1
Crimp Cramp La NR34 ..10 B8
Crisp Cl 5 NR32 ....113 B4
Crisp Rd NR35 ....8 E7
Crispin Cl IP32 ....132 B5
Crockatt Rd IP7 ....149 E8
Crockfords Rd CB8 .....121 A1
Crocus Cl IP2 ....138 F4
Croft Cl Beccles NR34 ...111 E4
  Diss IP22 ....20 C2
  6 Harleston IP20 ....20 D6
  2 Wickhambrook CB8 ...61 E2
Croft La Diss IP22 ....20 C2
  Haverhill CB9 ....132 F4
  Trimley St Martin IP10 ..98 C2
Croft Lea CO8 ....92 E8
Croft Rd IP33 ....123 B1
Croft Rd 8 Isleham CB7 ..29 C5
  Newmarket CB8 ....120 F5
  Sudbury CO10 ....148 C6
Croft Rise IP33 ....123 B1
Croft St IP2 ....155 B1
Croft The 6 Bures CO8 ..101 C5
  1 Glemsford CO10 .....77 A2
  Great Waldingham CO6 ..90 A1
  6 Lowestoft NR32 .....113 C1
  2 Sudbury CO10 ......148 C6
Crofton Rd IP4 ....140 B7
Cromarty Rd IP4 ....140 B8
Crome Wlk NR32 ....113 B4
Cromer Rd IP1 ....134 F1

Crompton Rd
  Ipswich IP2 ....138 F7
  Lowestoft NR33 ....114 E7
Cromwell Ave NR34 ....111 B3
Cromwell Cl NR33 .....111 B3
Cromwell Ct NR33 ....114 D2
Cromwell Rd
  Ringsfield NR34 ....9 C2
  Weeting IP27 ....5 E4
  Weston NR34 ....111 B1
Cromwell Sq IP1 ......155 B2
Crooked House Gall The*
  CO10 ....78 D4
Cropley Cl IP32 ....123 E4
Cross Cl CB9 ....132 E7
Cross Field Way CO4 ...13 B5
Cross La Cl IP27 ....109 D6
Cross Rd IP20 ....22 C6
Cross St 1 Bungay NR35 ..110 B4
  Drinkstone IP30 ....65 C7
  Eye IP23 ....117 C2
  Felixstowe IP11 ....152 E6
  Hoxne IP21 ....38 C6
  Leiston IP16 ....129 C5
  Sudbury CO10 ....148 B4
Cross The IP23 ....117 C2
Cross Ways IP30 ....50 E2
Crossfields CO6 ....102 E7
Crossgate Field 3 IP11 ..152 E5
Crossgreen La IP29 .....57 F5
Crossley Gdns IP1 .....134 C2
Crotchets Cl 2 IP9 .....150 E3
Croutel Rd IP11 ....153 B5
Crow Cl IP14 ....124 D5
Crow St IP31 ....34 D8
Crowbrook Pl IP30 ......78 C8
Crowcroft Glebe IP7 .....80 B5
Crowcroft Rd IP7 ....80 B5
Crowe Hall La IP9 ......105 D5
Crowe St IP14 ....124 D6
Crowfield Rd IP14 ....68 C6
Crowfoot Com Prim Sch
  NR34 ....111 C4
Crowfoot Gdns 7 NR34 ..111 B5
Crowhurst Cl 4 NR34 ...114 D4
Crowland Cl 3 IP12 ....139 A2
Crowland Rd CB9 ....132 D4
Crowley Rd IP6 ....125 D4
Crown Cl 10 IP12 ....84 A1
Crown Cnr IP6 ....68 B1
Crown Cres 15 IP31 .....34 B1
Crown Gn IP22 ....20 C6
Crown La
  Coney Weston IP31 .....17 E1
  Ixworth IP31 ....34 B1
  Orford IP12 ....131 C2
  Wickham Market IP13 ..127 C6
Crown Meadow Wlk 3
  NR32 ....113 C2
Crown Mill 3 IP30 ......50 F2
Crown Pl IP22 ....147 A4
Crown Rd IP26 ....6 B8
Crown St Brandon IP27 ..14 E8
  Bury St Edmunds IP33 ..154 C1
  Dedham CO7 ....103 F3
  Felixstowe IP11 ......155 B3
  Ipswich IP1 ....155 B3
  Leiston IP16 ....129 D6
  Needham Market IP6 ...125 D5
  Stowmarket IP14 .....124 D6
Crown St E NR32 ......113 E2
Crown St W NR32 .....113 D2
Crown Swimming Pool
  IP1 ....155 B3
Crown Wlk IP1 ....121 A4
Crownfield Rd 8 CO10 ...77 A3
Crownfields 2 IP13 .....84 F7
Crowsheath Rd IP11 .....35 C1
Crowswell Ct 8 IP31 ...107 D8
Croxton Cl IP10 ....98 E2
Croxton Rd IP24 ....16 C7
Crunch Croft CB9 ......133 C3
Cryspen Ct IP33 ....154 B3
Cuckfield Ave IP11 .....153 C4
Cuckoo Hill (Tumulus)*
  IP23 ....47 C8
Cuckoo Hill CO8 ....101 C5
Cuckoo La IP20 ....22 C6
Cucumber La IP21 ....41 D1
Culford
  Bury St Edmunds IP28 ...48 C6
  Ingham IP31 ....32 F1
Culford Sch IP28 ....32 D1
Culford Terr IP33 ......154 A1
Culford Wlk IP11 ......152 C3
Culley Way 2 NR31 ....3 B6
Cullingham Rd IP1 .....139 A6
Cullum Rd IP33 ....154 A1
Culvers Meadow 4 IP31 ..34 E4
Culzean Gdns 1 NR32 ..113 A4
Cumberland Cl
  4 Southwold IP18 .....153 D6
  5 Southwold IP18 .....119 D5
Cumberland Mews
  IP12 ....147 A4
Cumberland Pl 18 NR32 ..113 E2
Cumberland Rd IP18 ....119 D5
Cumberland St
  Ipswich IP1 ....155 A4
  Woodbridge IP12 .....147 A5
Cundle Gn La IP17 ......72 C5
Cundys Marsh IP15 .....130 E5
Cunningham Way
  NR33 ....115 A3
Curlew Cl IP27 ....109 D5
Curlew Gn NR32 ....113 B4
Curlew Rd IP2 ....138 D4

Curlews The IP33 ......123 C1
Curriers' La IP1 ......155 A2
Curtis Cl IP11 ....138 C1
Curtis Dr 1 IP26 ....4 D5
Curtis Way IP5 ....141 D7
Curwen Rd IP14 ....124 C6
Curzon Rd CO10 ......148 F6
Cuthbert Cl 4 IP24 .....16 D6
Cutler Rd 5 NR32 .....112 D2
Cutler St IP1 ....155 B2
Cutler's La IP14 ....66 A6
Cutlers Cl CO7 ....151 D7
Cutter's La IP31 ....49 E8
Cutting's Rd IP21 ....21 E4
Cypress Way 4 NR33 ..114 F7

D

Daffodil Cl IP2 ....138 E3
Daffodil Wlk NR33 ....114 C5
Dagworth La IP14 ......66 D8
Daimler Rd IP1 ....134 D2
Dains Pl IP11 ....152 C7
Daires La IP7 ....147 C7
Dairy Dr 4 IP28 ....48 B6
Dairy Hill IP19 ....118 B4
Dairy La Ixworth IP31 ...34 A2
  Mutford NR34 ....10 C3
Dairy Rd IP7 ....80 A1
Daisy Ave IP32 ....123 F5
Daisy Gn La IP14 ....32 D4
Daisy Hill IP21 ....39 F8
Daking Ave CO10 ....93 B3
Daking's Drift 6 IP19 ..118 A3
Dakota Rd 6 IP28 ....30 A8
Dale End NR34 ....114 E2
Dale Hall La IP1 ......135 B1
Dale Hall Prim Sch
  IP1 ....135 B2
Dale Haven NR33 ......114 D3
Dale Hill IP14 ....53 A6
Dale Rd
  Fressingfield IP21 ......22 D1
  Stanton IP31 ....34 E5
Dale Tree Rd 11 IP29 ...47 A2
Dales Rd IP1 ....135 A1
Dales View IP8 ....95 F4
Dales View Rd IP1 .....135 A1
Dalham Pl CB9 ....132 F6
Dalham Rd Ashley CB8 ...61 B8
  Moulton CB8 ....45 F2
Dallinghoo Rd IP13 ....127 A6
Dalton Rd IP1 ....155 A3
Dam La Burgate IP22 ....36 F7
  Kessingland NR33 ......1 A1
Damask Cl 5 NR33 .....114 E4
Damselfly Rd IP3 .....144 C8
Dandalan Cl IP18 .....138 E8
Dane Cl CB9 ....133 E8
Dane Comm CB9 ....133 D8
Dane Hill Rd CB8 ....45 E7
Danes Cl IP11 ....144 C4
Danes Cl IP4 ....148 F2
Danescourt Ave IP1 ...124 C5
Danesgreen Gdns IP16 ..129 C4
Danforth Cl IP3 ......126 B4
Daniel Gdns IP23 .....117 C3
Daniels Cl 8 CO10 ......92 B7
Daphne Rd IP2 ....131 C2
Darby Cl IP32 ....123 F5
Darby Rd NR34 ....111 B3
Darcy Cl IP32 ....123 E4
Dark La
  Dickleburgh & Rushall
  IP21 ....20 E2
  Easton IP13 ....70 E2
Darkings La IP30 ....64 F2
Darrell Rd 1 IP11 .....153 H11
Darrow Gn Rd IP20 ......2 F4
Darrow Wood La IP20 ...20 A5
Darsham Cl IP19 5 ....152 D5
Darsham Marshes Nature
  Reserve* IP17 ....57 F8
Darsham Rd IP17 ....58 B8
Darsham Sta IP17 ......57 E8
Darsham Vale 8 NR32 ..112 F4
Darter Cl 3 IP3 ....144 C8
Darwin Cl IP29 ....116 C6
Darwin Pl CB8 ....121 B1
Darwin Rd IP14 ......139 F5
Dash End La CB9 ......133 F8
Dashwood Cl IP8 ......138 A2
Daundy Cl IP2 ....138 D5
Davall Cl IP22 ....106 E1
Davenport Rd 6 IP30 ...50 F2
Davey's La IP13 ....70 B4
Davey's La IP1 ....34 C4
Davidson Cl CO10 ....92 B2
Davoren Wlk IP32 .....122 D7
Daw St CO9 ....89 A3
Dawson Cl IP9 ....150 D4
Dawson Dr IP1 ....152 C8
Dawson Drift 3 IP5 ....141 C7
Dawson Mews NR32 ...113 A6
Day's La IP1 ....140 A3
Daysgn's La IP9 ....150 D3
Dazeley's La CO7 .....151 F2
De Burgh Pl 6 CO10 ....76 A1
De Greys Cl 8 CO10 ....76 A1
De Havilland Ct 7 IP28 ..116 B5
De Vere Cl IP31 ......153 B8
Deacon Ct 8 IP11 .....153 D6
Deacon's Cl 2 CO10 ....78 D4
Dead La Ardleigh CO7 ..103 E1

Dead La continued
  Bures St Mary CO8 ....101 F5
  Lawford CO11 ....104 E1
Deadman's La
  Benhall IP17 ....128 A2
  Combs IP14 ....66 E1
  Rendham IP17 ....57 A3
  Stoke Ash IP23 ....53 A8
  Woolpit IP30 ....50 C1
Deane's Cl 1 CO12 ....107 A3
Deans Cl IP29 ....132 E7
Debden Ave Ipswich IP5 ..141 F6
  Martlesham IP5 ....137 F1
Deben Dr CO10 ....148 E6
Deben High Sch IP11 ..152 F4
Deben La
  Waldringfield IP12 .....98 E7
  6 Woodbridge Airfield
  IP12 ....85 B3
Deben Mill Bsns Ctr
  IP12 ....147 B6
Deben Pool IP12 ......147 A4
Deben Rd Haverhill CB9 ..132 F6
  Ipswich IP1 ....134 F1
  Saxmundham IP17 .....128 C4
  Woodbridge IP12 .....147 B5
Deben Rise IP14 ....53 F1
Deben Valley Dr IP5 ...141 C7
Deben Way IP11 ....152 E3
Debenham CE High Sch
  IP14 ....53 E2
Debenham CE Prim Sch
  Crowfield IP6 ....68 E5
  Winston IP14 ....53 F1
Debenham Sports Ctr
  IP14 ....53 E2
Debenside The IP12 ...147 C7
Deck Wlk IP33 ....122 E7
Decoy Rd IP27 ....12 F8
Dedham Dr 4 NR32 ...112 F3
Dedham Meade CO7 ...103 F2
Dedham Rd
  Ardleigh CO7 ....103 E1
  Boxted CO4 ....103 A3
  Lawford CO11 ....104 C2
Deepdale NR33 ....114 E2
Deepdale Rd 6 CO12 ..107 A2
Deer Row NR35 ....8 E7
Defoe Rd IP1 ....135 A4
Degas Gdns 1 NR32 ...113 B6
Delbrig Dro IP27 ....29 A5
Delius Cl IP1 ....137 E7
Dell Cl NR33 ....115 A6
Dell Prim Sch NR33 ...114 E7
Dell Rd NR33 ....114 E7
Dell Rd E NR33 ....114 E7
Dellview NR33 ....114 D6
Dellwood Ave IP11 ....153 B5
Delph Dro IP28 ....12 D1
Delph Rd IP27 ....109 D7
Demesne Gdns 6 IP5 ...98 A8
Dene Rd NR32 ....113 D4
Denes High Sch The
  NR32 ....113 D4
Denham Cnr IP29 ....38 D3
Denham La IP29 ....47 A2
Denham Low Rd IP21 ...38 C5
Denham Rd Dalham CB8 ..61 C8
  Hoxne IP21 ....38 B6
Denmark Gdns 1 IP9 ..105 E7
Denmark Hill IP22 ......20 C2
Denmark La IP22 ....20 C2
Denmark Rd
  9 Lowestoft NR32 ....115 D8
Denmark Rise IP22 .....20 C2
Denmark St IP22 ....20 C2
Denney's La IP17 .....128 D7
Dennington CE Prim Sch
  IP13 ....55 D6
Dennington Rd
  Dennington IP13 ....55 F8
  Framlingham IP13 .....126 B5
  Laxfield IP13 ....40 B1
Denny Ave IP14 ....66 D8
Denny's Hill IP20 ......23 A4
Denton Cl IP2 ....138 D2
Denton Dr IP27 ....114 F5
Denton Rd NR33 ......114 F5
Depden La IP29 ....62 C5
Depot Rd CB8 ....120 E6
Derby Cl IP33 ....140 A5
Derby Pl 8 IP31 ....49 A5
Derby Rd IP3 ....140 A4
Derby Way CB8 ....120 E6
Dereham Ave IP3 .....139 F3
Dereham Cl 17 IP27 ...13 F2
Derry Brook La 9 IP14 ..53 F2
Derwent Gdns 5 NR32 ..113 A4
Derwent Rd
  18 Bury St Edmunds IP32 ..48 C5
  Ipswich IP3 ....139 F3
Desmond Cl 3 NR32 ...112 D2
Dettingen Way IP33 ...122 D5
Devereaux Ct IP7 .....155 C3
Devil's La IP17 ....42 C1
Devils Dyke Nature Reserve*
  CB5 ....44 A3
Devlin Rd IP32 ....138 B1
Devon Cl IP32 ....122 E8

Devon Rd
Felixstowe IP11 ....**152** F5
7 Stowupland IP14 ....**67** A6
Devon Way 10 CO12 .....**106** E1
Devonshire Rd IP3 ......**139** F5
Dewar La IP5 ....**1** C7
Dewarrene Dr IP27 ....**5** E3
Dhobi Pl IP1 ....**138** F7
Dial La IP1 ....**155** B3
Diamond Cl IP1 ....**134** D1
Dickens Ct 6 NR32 ....**3** A4
Dickens Rd IP2 ....**138** E6
Dickinson Terr 8 IP5 ....**141** D7
Dickleburgh Prim Sch
IP21 ....**21** B5
Dickleburgh Rd IP21 .....**21** A5
Dicks Mount NR34 ....**10** D7
Dicky Hill IP20 ....**22** D7
Didsbury Cl IP2 ....**138** D2
Digby Cl 8 IP5 ....**98** A7
Digby Rd IP4 ....**152** D5
Dillistone Ct CB8 ....**133** C3
Dillwyn St W IP1 ....**155** A3
Dinsdale Pl IP16 ....**129** C6
Diomed Dr IP31 ....**49** A5
Dip The CB8 ....**121** D2
Diprose Dr NR32 ....**113** A6
Dirty La IP21 ....**21** F7
Diss Church Jun Sch
IP22 ....**20** C3
Diss High Sch IP22 ....**20** D3
Diss Inf Sch IP22 ....**20** C3
Diss Mus* IP22 ....**20** C3
Diss Rd
Burston & Shimpling IP22 ..**20** E5
Garboldisham IP22 ....**18** D4
3 Scole IP21 ....**20** D1
South Lopham IP22 ....**19** C4
Wattisfield IP22 ....**35** D5
Diss Sta IP22 ....**20** D2
Ditchingham Dam
NR35 ....**110** B5
Ditchingham Gr NR14 ....**140** F6
Ditton Cl CB8 ....**121** A1
Ditton Gn CB8 ....**60** B5
Ditton Lodge Fst Sch
CB8 ....**121** B2
Dixon Cl 11 CO11 ....**104** D2
Dixon Dr IP5 ....**114** E7
Dobbs Drift IP5 ....**141** F7
Dobbs La IP5 ....**137** E1
Dobson Way NR34 ....**111** C5
Dock La IP12 ....**147** C7
Dock Rd
Felixstowe IP11 ....**152** C1
Ramsholt IP12 ....**99** B4
Dock St IP2 ....**155** B1
Dockfield Ave 5 CO6 ....**106** F2
Dockings La IP14 ....**67** C7
Doctor Watson's La
IP5 ....**137** A1
Doctor's La Ashen CO10 .**89** E5
Orford IP12 ....**131** C3
Pulham St Mary IP21 ....**22** A6
Doctors La IP21 ....**39** B4
Dodmans IP9 ....**150** E3
Dodson Vale IP5 ....**141** C7
Does Field IP14 ....**68** C6
Dog La Shelfanger IP22 ..**20** A8
Tannington IP13 ....**55** A4
Dogs Head St IP4 ....**155** B2
Dogs La NR34 ....**9** C7
Dogwood Cl IP33 ....**123** D6
Dogwood Wlk 31 IP27 ...**13** D7
Doit La IP22 ....**20** A3
Doit The IP22 ....**19** F2
Dolphin Cl 8 NR33 ......**115** B4
Dombey Rd IP2 ....**138** E5
Dome Leisure Ctr
IP28 ....**116** E4
Donegal Rd IP1 ....**134** D2
Donkey La
Bradfield Combust with
Stanningfield IP29 ....**63** F2
Friston IP17 ....**72** F7
Dooley Rd IP11 ....**152** C3
Dorchester Rd
Bury St Edmunds IP33 .....**122** D3
Ipswich IP3 ....**140** D3
Doric Pl IP22 ....**147** A4
Doris St CB8 ....**120** F3
Dorking Rd NR32 ....**3** A6
Dorley Dale NR33 ....**114** E3
Dorothy Hodgkin Ct
NR34 ....**111** B2
Dorset Cl IP4 ....**135** F1
Double St IP13 ....**126** D3
Doubleday Cl IP22 ....**20** C2
Doug Smith Cl CB8 ......**120** F6
Doughty Wylie Cres
IP6 ....**58** B4
Douglas Cl
Halesworth IP19 ....**118** C5
Lowestoft NR33 ....**114** D3
Douglas Rd CO12 ....**107** A2
Doune Way 9 IP20 ....**22** D6
Dove Cl 15 Debenham IP14 .**53** F7
9 Harleston IP20 ....**22** D6
Saxmundham IP17 ....**128** C4
Dove Cres 8 CO10 ....**106** E1
Dove Gdns 2 IP14 ....**67** A5
Dove House Rd CB8 ......**121** D2
Dove La IP23 ....**117** D2
Dove Rd IP18 ....**119** B7
Dove St Ipswich IP4 ......**139** E4

Dove St continued
Lowestoft NR32 ....**113** D2
Dovedale
Felixstowe IP11 ....**152** D3
2 Lowestoft NR33 ....**114** F3
Dovehouse Hill IP29 .....**77** D7
Dover Rd IP3 ....**140** B4
Dovercourt Sta CO12 ....**107** B2
Dovercourt Swimming Pool
CO12 ....**107** B1
Dowes Hill Cl NR34 ......**111** B2
Dowling Rd CO8 ....**101** C2
Downham Bvd IP3 ....**144** C7
Downham Way IP27 ....**6** A1
Downing Cl
Bury St Edmunds IP33 .....**123** E5
Ipswich IP2 ....**138** F2
Mildenhall IP28 ....**116** D5
Newmarket CB8 ....**121** B2
2 Woodbridge IP12 ......**146** E4
Downing Dr 4 IP31 ....**49** A6
Downing Prim Sch
IP2 ....**138** F2
Downlands 6 IP7 ....**80** F1
Downs Cres CB8 ....**132** D6
Downs Farm La IP20 .....**23** B7
Downs Pl CB9 ....**132** D6
Downs The
Felixstowe IP11 ....**152** D5
Rushbrooke with Rougham
IP30 ....**49** C2
Downside IP14 ....**124** B6
Downside Cl IP1 ....**142** F8
Downton Dr CB9 ....**132** C6
Dowson Dr 2 NR33 ......**11** B1
Drab's La IP13 ....**83** E7
Drake Cl IP14 ....**124** A6
Drake Inf Sch 3 IP24 ....**16** C7
Drake Rd CO10 ....**148** F2
Drake Sq 5 IP3 ....**140** B2
Drake's Heath NR32 .....**113** B2
Drapers Cl 1 IP7 ....**149** E6
Drapers Hill IP7 ....**39** B5
Drapers La
Ditchingham NR35 ....**8** A7
Helions Bumpstead CB9 ....**88** B8
Drapery Comm 3 CO10 ..**77** A2
Draymans Way IP3 ....**139** E3
Drays The CO10 ....**91** D7
Drift Ct IP6 ....**125** D4
Drift Rd IP27 ....**109** C8
Drift The Botesdale IP22 ..**36** A7
2 East Bergholt CO11 ....**104** E5
Exning CB8 ....**120** A8
Fornham St Martin IP31 ....**48** D5
Holbrook IP9 ....**105** E5
Ipswich IP3 ....**140** C1
Nacton IP10 ....**140** A6
Levington IP10 ....**145** E3
24 Martlesham Heath IP5 ..**98** A8
Middleton IP17 ....**58** B6
Polstead CO6 ....**93** D2
Sudbury CO10 ....**93** B7
Tostock IP30 ....**50** B2
Wickham Market IP13 .....**127** D8
Driftway The
18 Grundisburgh IP13 ....**83** E5
Ipswich IP4 ....**140** B6
Drinkstone Gn Cl IP30 ..**65** B7
Drinkstone Mills*
IP30 ....**50** C1
Drinkstone Rd
Beyton IP30 ....**49** F2
Gedding IP30 ....**65** B5
Drinkwater Cl CB8 ....**120** E4
Drive The
Harwich CO12 ....**107** A1
Heveningham IP19 ....**41** B3
Hitcham IP7 ....**62** A6
Lowestoft NR32 ....**112** F2
Martlesham Heath IP5 .....**98** B8
Rushbrooke with Rougham
IP30 ....**64** B8
Southwold IP18 ....**119** B7
Drout's La IP31 ....**34** E2
Drove La IP14 ....**58** D2
Drove The IP27 ....**14** D8
Drover's Ct IP11 ....**152** B8
Drovers Ave IP32 ....**123** F5
Druids La IP22 ....**20** B6
Druids' La IP22 ....**20** A7
Drum Field 5 CO7 ....**103** E5
Drummond Cl IP33 ....**154** A1
Drury Cl 16 NR33 ....**11** C1
Drury Dr CO10 ....**148** D8
Drury La Milden IP7 ....**79** B1
Ridgewell CO9 ....**89** D3
Wicken CB7 ....**28** B1
Drury Pk IP17 ....**72** D5
Drury Rd IP6 ....**134** C8
Drybridge Hill IP12 ......**146** E4
Dryden Rd IP1 ....**135** A3
Dublin Rd IP23 ....**53** E8
Duchess Dr
Newmarket CB8 ....**121** D2
Woodditton CB8 ....**60** C8
Duck Dro CB7 ....**12** A6
Duckamere IP8 ....**134** A1
Ducks La CB8 ....**120** C7
Ducksen Rd IP14 ....**52** A6
Duddery Hill CB9 ....**132** E5
Duddery Rd 6 CB9 ....**132** E5
Dudley St IP27 ....**109** F1
Duffs Hill CO10 ....**77** A4
Duke St Beccles NR34 ...**111** D3
4 Bildeston IP7 ....**79** F4
Hadleigh IP7 ....**149** D5
Haughley IP14 ....**51** C1

Duke St continued
Hintlesham IP8 ....**95** C5
Ipswich IP3 ....**139** E4
7 Stanton IP31 ....**34** E4
Duke's Dr IP19 ....**118** A2
Duke's Meadow IP12 ....**146** D3
Duke's Pk IP12 ....**146** D2
Duke's Rd NR35 ....**110** C2
Dukes Cl IP1 ....**153** D6
Dukes Head St 6 NR32 ..**113** E2
Dukes Meadow
1 Beccles NR34 ....**111** C4
Cockfield IP30 ....**64** D3
Dukesway 1 NR35 ....**7** F4
Dulgate Rd NR35 ....**7** B7
Dullingham Rd
Newmarket CB8 ....**120** F1
Woodditton CB8 ....**59** F7
Dullingham Sta CB8 .....**59** D5
Dumbarton Rd 3 IP4 ....**136** C1
Dumfries Rd 2 IP4 ....**136** C1
Dumplingbridge La
IP27 ....**109** C6
Dun Cow Rd NR34 ....**10** B8
Dunburgh Rd NR34 ....**9** A6
Duncan Rise CO9 ....**89** F1
Dunche's La IP6 ....**67** E4
Dunhill La IP22 ....**35** B5
Dunlin Rd IP2 ....**138** E2
Dunn Cl IP2 ....**149** E5
Dunnock Cl 18 IP14 .....**67** A5
Dunsey Wood Cl CB9 ...**132** C7
Dunstall Gn Rd CB8 .....**61** E6
Dunster Dr 15 CB9 ....**132** C6
Dunston Dr IP22 ....**112** F4
Dunston's Cnr IP6 ....**82** B8
Dunton Gr IP27 ....**149** E4
Dunwich Cl CB8 ....**132** C6
Dunwich Heath Nature
Reserve* IP17 ....**58** F7
Dunwich La IP17 ....**41** A2
Dunwich Mus* IP17 .....**43** B1
Dunwich Pl 2 IP31 ....**49** A5
Dunwich Rd
Blythburgh IP19 ....**42** F5
4 Southwold IP18 ....**119** D5
Westleton IP17 ....**58** D8
Dunwich Underwater
Exploration Ex*
IP12 ....**131** B3
Dunwich Way 11 NR32 ..**112** F4
Durban Cl IP19 ....**118** B2
Durban Rd NR32 ....**115** B7
Durbar Terr IP33 ....**154** A3
Durbidge's Hill IP22 .....**20** E5
Durham Cl 2 IP4 ....**48** C5
Durham Rd 2 IP27 ....**14** A3
Durham Way CB8 ....**120** E5
Durrant Rd IP7 ....**149** D7
Durrant View IP21 ....**141** E7
Durrant's Cl 8 NR33 ....**11** C1
Dutchman's Rd NR33 ...**114** D7
Dux St IP7 ....**65** B1
Dyer Ct IP7 ....**149** F5
Dyers Cl CO10 ....**92** E2
Dyers Rd CO9 ....**89** C1
Dyke St IP1 ....**155** B3
Dyson's Dro CB5 ....**44** A7

E

Eades Wlk NR33 ....**114** C5
Eagle Ct NR34 ....**26** E5
Eagle Dr IP15 ....**130** C6
Eagle La CB8 ....**59** E5
Eagle St IP4 ....**155** C2
Eagle Way IP5 ....**98** A8
Eagle Wlk IP2 ....**122** E8
Eagles Cl IP11 ....**152** F4
Earl Soham Prim Sch
IP13 ....**54** F2
Earl's Cl IP19 ....**118** A2
Earls Cl IP11 ....**152** F5
Earls Gn 6 CB9 ....**132** A6
Earlsbrook IP14 ....**51** E6
Earlsfield IP27 ....**13** F2
Earlsford Rd Mellis IP23 ..**36** F5
Thornham Parva IP23 ......**37** A4
Easdale NR33 ....**114** E2
Easlea Rd IP32 ....**123** D4
East Anglia Transport Mus*
NR33 ....**114** A3
East Barton Rd IP31 .....**49** B5
East Bergholt CE Prim Sch
CO7 ....**151** D6
East Bergholt High Sch
CO7 ....**151** D6
East Church St NR16 ....**19** B8
East Cl IP33 ....**123** C6
East Cliff IP18 ....**119** E5
East Dock Rd CO12 ......**106** F3
East End La CO7 ....**104** E6
East End Rd
East Bergholt CO7 ....**151** F4
Stonham Aspal IP14 ....**68** C6
East Fen Dro CB7 ....**28** F4
East Fen Rd CB7 ....**29** D5
East Gn IP18 ....**119** D5
East Harling Rd NR16 ...**18** F8
East La Bawdsey IP12 ....**99** F2

East La continued
Dedham CO7 ....**104** A2
Middleton IP17 ....**58** B6
Ufford IP13 ....**85** A7
East Lawn IP14 ....**124** C8
East Mill Gn IP9 ....**104** F7
East Point Pavilion Visitor
Ctr* NR33 ....**115** D8
East Rd CB7 ....**29** C5
East Side CO10 ....**119** D5
East St 6 Harwich CO12 ..**107** B2
Southwold IP18 ....**119** D5
Sudbury CO10 ....**148** D5
East Station Rd IP27 ....**128** D6
Freckenham IP28 ....**29** E3
Eastcliff IP11 ....**153** E7
Eastern Ave
Haverhill CB9 ....**132** D6
18 Soham CB7 ....**28** D4
Eastern Cl IP4 ....**140** F4
Eastern Way
Bury St Edmunds IP32 ....**123** C6
Elmswell IP30 ....**50** F2
Lowestoft NR32 ....**113** B1
Eastfen Dro IP26 ....**5** B2
Eastfield Gdns 3 NR33 ..**114** F4
Eastgate Sth Ctr IP4 ....**155** C3
Eastgate St IP33 ....**154** C2
Eastland Ct IP11 ....**152** D7
Eastland Rd IP27 ....**39** B4
Eastlands La IP23 ....**52** B8
Eastlands Rd IP16 ....**129** E6
Eastlow Hill (Tumulus)*
IP30 ....**64** C8
Eastlowhill Rd IP30 .....**64** C8
Easton Farm Pk* IP13 ..**70** D5
Easton La
Hacheston IP13 ....**70** F5
Reydon IP18 ....**27** A1
Easton Prim Sch IP13 .....**70** E5
Easton Rd
Hacheston IP13 ....**71** A4
Woodbridge Airfield IP12 ..**85** B3
Eastward Ho IP16 ....**129** D5
Eastward Pl IP14 ....**124** C7
Eastwood Ave NR33 .....**114** F6
Eaton Cl IP11 ....**152** C7
Eaton Gdns IP11 ....**152** E2
Eccles Rd IP2 ....**138** D2
Economy Rd NR33 ....**115** C7
Eddies The NR33 ....**114** E4
Eddowes Rd 6 IP6 ....**82** B5
Edelweiss Cl 1 NR32 ...**113** A4
Eden Rd 6 Haverhill CB9 ..**132** E5
Ipswich IP4 ....**140** B5
Edendale NR32 ....**112** D2
Edes Paddock 9 IP5 .....**49** A6
Edgar Ave IP14 ....**124** C5
Edgar Sewter Prim Sch
IP19 ....**118** B5
Edgeborough Cl IP8 .....**46** A5
Edgecomb Rd IP14 ......**124** D3
Edgefield Ave 10 CO11 ..**104** D2
Edgerton Rd NR33 ....**115** A7
Edgworth Rd CO10 ......**148** C4
Edies La CO10 ....**102** B7
Edinburgh Cl
6 Barnham IP24 ....**16** C2
Stowmarket IP14 ....**124** B6
Edinburgh Gdns IP6 .....**82** B5
Edinburgh Rd
Lowestoft NR33 ....**113** D3
Newmarket CB8 ....**120** E4
Edith Cavell Way CB8 ...**88** E3
Edmonton Cl IP1 ....**141** A7
Edmonton Rd IP1 ....**141** A7
Edmund Cl IP8 ....**138** D6
Edmund Moundford Rd 1
IP26 ....**4** E5
Edmund Rd IP27 ....**14** E5
Edmunds Rd IP14 ....**65** C7
Edward Cl IP1 ....**138** F8
Edward Fitzgerald Ct
IP12 ....**146** E6
Edwards Cl IP33 ....**88** E3
Edwards La IP19 ....**41** F5
Edwin Ave IP12 ....**146** F7
Edwin Panks Rd IP7 .....**149** E6
Edwin Terr IP21 ....**146** F6
Egglestone Cl IP2 ....**138** E1
Eggshell La CO9 ....**88** F1
Eglantine Way 2 CO6 ...**102** A7
Egremont St CO10 ....**77** A2
El Alamein Rd NR32 .....**113** A4
Elder Crescen 2 IP7 .....**80** D6
Elders The IP27 ....**109** E5
Elderstub La IP30 ....**49** B1
Eldith Ave CB7 ....**29** C7
Eldo Gdns 8 IP28 ....**29** F6
Eldo Rd IP28 ....**29** F6
Eldon La IP28 ....**30** D8
Eldred Cl
Bury St Edmunds IP32 ....**123** E4
Westbourne IP1 ....**138** D8
Eldred Dr CO10 ....**92** B2
Eleanor Pl 6 IP31 ....**49** A4
Eley's Cnr IP7 ....**94** E8
Elgar Cl NR33 ....**115** A6
Elim Terr 11 NR32 ....**113** B2
Eliot Way 4 IP14 ....**124** B8
Elizabeth Ave CB8 ......**120** E5
Elizabeth Bonhote Cl 3
NR35 ....**110** C2
Elizabeth Cl NR32 ....**113** A4
Elizabeth Ct 8 CO10 ....**148** D6
Elizabeth Dr IP29 ....**62** D5

Elizabeth Par CB8 ....**120** E5
Elizabeth Rd
Brandon IP27 ....**5** F1
18 Harwich CO12 ....**107** A3
Elizabeth Way
Burrough Green CB8 ....**59** F2
Eye IP23 ....**117** C3
Felixstowe IP11 ....**152** D3
Stowmarket IP14 ....**124** E6
Sudbury CO10 ....**148** A3
Elizabeth Wlk 27 IP20 ..**22** D6
Ellenbrook Gn IP2 ....**138** D1
Ellenbrook Rd
Ipswich IP2 ....**138** D1
Pinewood IP9 ....**142** D8
Ellingham VC Prim Sch
NR35 ....**8** D7
Ellington Rd 1 IP24 .....**16** C1
Elliott Ave IP18 ....**119** C8
Elliott Cl CB8 ....**121** A6
Elliott St IP1 ....**139** A6
Ellis Rd CO4 ....**102** F2
Ellis St CO10 ....**93** C3
Elliston Cl 4 IP30 ....**50** F2
Ellough Ind Est NR34 ...**10** A3
Ellough Rd
Beccles NR34 ....**111** D4
Worlingham NR34 ....**111** F2
Ellwood Cl NR34 ....**111** B7
Ellwoods Cl 2 CB7 ......**29** C5
Elm Cl
10 Bentwaters Airfield IP12 ..**85** E5
6 Brantham CO11 ....**104** E5
Dullingham CB8 ....**59** E5
Haverhill CB9 ....**132** D6
Lakenheath IP27 ....**109** C7
Lowestoft NR33 ....**114** C4
Elm Coppice 6 NR33 ....**114** E4
Elm Ct CB9 ....**133** C3
Elm Dr IP30 ....**49** F1
Elm Est CO7 ....**151** C5
Elm Gdns 2 IP11 ....**152** C7
Elm Gr
Garboldisham IP22 ....**18** D4
3 Nayland CO6 ....**102** C5
Elm La
Capel St Mary IP9 ....**150** E3
Copdock & Washbrook
IP8 ....**95** F4
Elm Lodge Rd 7 IP13 ...**40** B3
Elm Rd
East Bergholt CO7 ....**151** B5
Felixstowe IP11 ....**140** F7
Stowmarket IP14 ....**124** C6
Sudbury CO10 ....**148** B5
Thetford IP24 ....**16** B4
Wickham Market IP13 .....**127** B6
Elm St IP1 ....**155** B3
Elm Tree Cl 1 IP14 ......**51** E1
Elm Tree La 5 CO6 ......**102** A7
Elm Tree Mid Sch
NR33 ....**114** C5
Elm Tree Prim Sch
NR33 ....**114** C5
Elm Tree Rd NR33 ....**114** C5
Elm Tree Rd W NR33 ...**114** C5
Elm Way IP14 ....**51** F6
Elmcroft Cl 2 IP28 ......**30** A8
Elmcroft La IP11 ....**153** C7
Elmcroft Rd IP1 ....**135** A2
Elmdale Dr
Lowestoft NR33 ....**114** D4
20 Mistley CO11 ....**104** E2
Elmdon Pl CB9 ....**132** F6
Elmers La IP5 ....**141** D7
Elmham Dr IP10 ....**145** B8
Elmhurst Ave NR32 .....**112** E1
Elmhurst Cl CB9 ....**132** F5
Elmhurst Dr IP3 ....**139** F3
Elmhurst Rd 17 CO12 ...**107** B2
Elms Cl 6 Earsham NR35 ..**7** F4
Great Barton IP31 ....**49** B6
Elms La NR34 ....**26** B2
Elms Rd Cowlinge CB8 ..**75** B7
Freckenham IP28 ....**29** F2
Elms The
Framlingham IP6 ....**126** C4
4 Horringer IP29 ....**63** A8
Elmsett CE Prim Sch
IP7 ....**80** F1
Elmsett Cl IP14 ....**124** F3
Elmsett Rd IP9 ....**81** B3
Elmsley Way IP17 ....**57** C8
Elmswell Prim Sch
IP30 ....**50** F2
Elmswell Rd
Great Ashfield IP31 ....**50** F6
Wetherden IP14 ....**51** A1
Elmswell Sta IP30 ....**50** E3
Elmtree Bsns Pk IP30 ...**50** E3
Elsey's Yd IP33 ....**154** B3
Elsmere Rd IP1 ....**139** C8
Elton Pk IP2 ....**138** D6
Elveden CE Prim Sch
IP24 ....**15** F2
Elveden Rd IP24 ....**15** F2
Elveden Sta CB8 ....**120** C5
Ely Cl IP33 ....**123** B3
Ely Rd 8 Claydon IP6 ...**82** B5
Ipswich IP4 ....**135** F1
Soham CB7 ....**28** B6
Embry Cres 10 IP7 ......**80** D6
Emerald Cl IP5 ....**141** C8
Emily Frost Cl 4 CB8 ...**61** C2
Emlen St IP1 ....**155** A3
Emmanuel Cl
Ipswich IP2 ....**138** F2

Emmanuel Cl continued
Mildenhall IP28 ....116 D5
Emmerson Way IP7 ....149 D7
Emperor Circ IP3 ......144 C8
Emsworth Cl 2 IP32 ...123 D6
Endway The CB9 ....88 E4
Engine Rd CB7 ....28 B5
Ennerdale Cl 4 IP11 ...153 D6
Ensign Way IP22 ....20 E2
Enstone Rd NR33 ....115 B6
Enterprise Bsns Pk
IP33 ....154 C4
Entry The IP23 ....52 D3
Epsom Dr IP1 ....135 A4
Erbury Pl CO10 ....90 A8
Eriswell Dr IP27 ....109 D5
Eriswell Rd
  Beck Row, Holywell Row
  & Kenny Hill IP28 ......13 C1
  Haverhill CB9 ....132 F6
  Lakenheath IP27 ......109 D4
Ernleigh Rd IP4 ....140 B6
Erratts Hill CB8 ....61 B1
Errington Way IP30 .....50 E2
Erskine Rd 10 CO11 ...104 C2
Erwarton Wlk IP9 ....106 E6
Eskdale Way NR32 .....113 A4
Esplanade IP15 ....115 D7
Essex Ave CO10 ....148 A7
Essex Rd NR32 ....113 B1
Essex Way IP31 ....140 E1
Estuary Cres 6 IP9 ....107 A4
Estuary Dr IP11 ....153 A4
Estuary Rd 7 IP9 ......107 A4
Ethel Mann Rd 5 NR35 .110 C2
Ethel Rd NR32 ....113 D1
Etheldreda Dr 1 IP24 ...16 D7
Etna Rd IP23 ....154 B4
Europa Rd NR32 ......113 C4
Europa Way
  9 Harwich CO12 .....106 F2
  Ipswich IP1 ....138 D8
Euroscope* NR32 ....113 E2
Eustace Rd IP1 ....138 E8
Euston Ave IP4 ....140 F6
Euston Cl IP33 ....154 A1
Euston Ct 4 IP1 ....152 C4
Euston Hall* IP24 .....16 E1
Evans Cl IP18 ....119 C7
Evans Dr NR32 ....113 B2
Evans' Heath CO10 .....93 F4
Eve Balfour Way IP14 ..66 D8
Evelyn Cl IP21 ....38 C7
Everard Cl 8 IP32 ....122 E8
Evergreen La CB8 ......74 C8
Evergreen Rd NR32 ...113 B2
Everitt Rd NR33 ....114 C8
Everton Cres IP4 ......134 F1
Eves Ct 12 CO12 ......106 E1
Evesham Cl 7 IP22 ...139 A2
Exchange Sq 9 NR34 ..111 B5
Exchange St IP20 ......22 D6
Exeter Cres IP27 ......109 C5
Exeter Ct 6 IP8 ....134 C1
Exeter Rd 8 Claydon IP6 ..82 B5
  Felixstowe IP11 ......152 F6
  Ipswich IP3 ....140 B4
  Newmarket CB8 ....121 A4
Exeter Way IP24 ....16 A6
Exmoor Rd IP11 ....152 F6
Exning Prim Sch CB8 ..120 B8
Exning Rd CB8 ....120 D6
Eye Airfield Ind Est
IP23 ....117 A6
Eye Castle* IP23 ....117 D2
Eye Hill Dro CB7 ....28 B7
Eye Rd Brome IP23 .....37 C5
  Yaxley IP23 ....37 C5
Eyke CE Prim Sch IP12 ..85 B6
Eyke Rd IP12 ....85 A5
Eyre Rd IP33 ....154 B1

F

Factory La
  Brantham CO11 ......104 E4
  Chevington IP29 ......62 C5
  Diss IP22 ....20 B3
Factory St NR32 ......113 D2
Fagbury Rd IP11 ......152 A4
Faiers Cl IP33 ....123 B2
Fair Cl Beccles NR34 ..111 B5
  Felixstowe IP11 ....4 E5
Fair View Rd IP19 .....118 C5
Fairbairn Ave 1 IP5 ...141 D7
Fairey Fox Dr 2 IP28 ..116 A5
Fairfax St NR44 ....111 B3
Fairfax Dr IP27 ....35 E4
Fairfax Gdns IP6 ......125 E4
Fairfield Ave IP11 .....153 A5
Fairfield Cres IP13 ...126 C3
Fairfield Dr
  Lowestoft NR33 ......114 D6
  Saxmundham IP17 ....128 C3
Fairfield Hill IP14 ....124 D6
Fairfield House Gdns
IP17 ....128 C3
Fairfield Ind Sch IP11 .153 A5
Fairfield Rd
  Aldeburgh IP15 ....130 D5
  Bungay NR35 ....110 C2
  Framlingham IP13 ....126 D2
  Ipswich IP3 ....140 A2
  Lowestoft NR33 ......114 D6
  Reydon IP18 ....119 C8
  Saxmundham IP17 ....128 C3

Fairfield Way 12 IP26 ...4 E5
Fairfields IP24 ....16 C7
Fairhaven Way CB8 ...120 E5
Fairhead Loke NR33 ..114 B1
Fairlawns Rd CB8 .....120 F2
Fairlight Cl 2 IP4 .....136 A1
Fairmead IP30 ....50 F3
Fairmile Cl 3 NR34 ...111 F4
Fairstead House Sch
CB8 ....121 B4
Fairstead The IP22 ....36 A7
Fairway The
  Aldeburgh IP15 ......130 C6
  1 Great Yarmouth NR31 ..3 B8
  Lowestoft NR33 ......114 C5
Fairways The IP4 ......140 C5
Fakenham Hill IP31 ...33 F5
Falcon Ave IP22 ....20 D3
Falcon Cl CB9 ....133 A6
Falcon Dr IP27 ....6 A1
Falcon Inn Rd NR34 ...26 C7
Falcon La NR35 ....110 B5
Falcon Rd 15 IP26 .....4 E5
Falcon St
  Felixstowe IP11 ......152 E6
  Ipswich IP1 ....155 B2
Falcon Way IP28 ......13 B1
Falconer Ave 3 IP41 ...51 E1
Falconer Rd CB8 ......133 A3
Falkenham Rd IP10 ...98 E2
Falklands Dr 2 CO11 .104 E2
Falklands Rd CB9 .....132 E7
Fallowfield 2 IP30 .....49 F2
Fallowfield Ct 10 CB9 .132 C5
Fallowfield Wlk IP33 ..123 B1
Fallowfields NR32 ....112 F5
Falmouth Ave CB8 ...120 F3
Falmouth Cl IP5 ......141 B6
Falmouth Gdns CB8 ..121 A6
Falmouth St CB8 .....120 F3
Famona Rd NR33 .....114 C2
Faraday Rd IP3 ....140 F8
Farford Field 5 CO10 ..92 B3
Farina Cl IP1 ....138 A6
Farlingaye High Sch
IP12 ....146 E6
Farlingayes IP12 ......146 F7
Farm Ct 1 Bungay NR35 .110 D3
  Bury St Edmunds IP33 ..123 B1
  5 Lowestoft NR33 ...114 C5
  Wissett IP19 ....24 E2
Farm Ct St IP20 ....23 A5
Farmerie Rd CO10 ....75 D3
Farmland Cl IP18 .....119 B8
Farmland Cl 5 NR32 ..112 F4
Farnham Rd
  Blaxhall IP12 ....71 F5
  Snape IP17 ....72 D6
Farrier's Rd IP14 .....124 C3
Farriers Cl
  15 Martlesham Heath IP5 ..98 A8
  Stradbroke IP21 ......39 B4
Farriers Went IP11 ...152 D7
Farrow Cl 16 IP26 ...129 B6
Farthing Dro
  Beck Row, Holywell Row
  & Kenny Hill IP28 ....12 C6
  Lakenheath IP27 ......13 A6
Farthing Rd IP1 ......138 C7
Farthing Rd Ind Est
IP1 ....138 C7
Farthings The IP28 ....31 D3
Farthings Went IP9 ...150 F4
Fastnet Cl CB8 ....133 B6
Fastoll Cl 4 NR32 ....113 A3
Faulkeners Way IP1 ..152 C7
Faversham Ct NR33 ..115 A4
Fawcett Rd IP5 ....130 E4
Fayrefield Rd IP12 ...147 B7
Feast Cl 7 CB8 ....29 A1
Featherbroom Gdns
IP13 ....127 C5
Feathers Field 3 IP14 .152 D5
Feilden Way CB8 .....120 E5
Felaw St IP2 ....155 C1
Felix Cl IP5 ....141 B7
Felix Rd
  Felixstowe IP11 ......153 B4
  Ipswich IP3 ....140 C2
  3 Stowupland IP14 ...67 A6
Felixstowe General Hospl
IP11 ....153 B4
Felixstowe Leisure Ctr
IP11 ....152 F3
Felixstowe Mus*
IP11 ....107 E2
Felixstowe Rd
  Ipswich IP3 ....139 F4
  3 Martlesham IP5 .....98 A8
Fellbrigg Ave IP5 ....140 F6
Fellows Cl IP21 ....21 A1
Felnor Wlk IP11 ......153 B3
Felsham Chase CB5 ...44 D3
Felsham St IP14 ......124 F3
Felsham Rd
  Bradfield St Clare IP30 ..64 D4
  Rattlesden IP30 ....65 C5
Felsham Rise IP30 ....64 C7
Felton Wlk IP22 ......122 D8
Feltons CB8 ....29 A1
Feltwell Elementary Sch
IP26 ....
Feltwell Pl CB9 ....132 F6
Feltwell Prim Sch IP26 ..4 D5
Feltwell Rd IP26 ....4 F3

Fen Alder Carr Nature
Reserve* IP6 ....125 D8
Fen Bank CB7 ....29 C6
Fen Ct NR33 ....115 A6
Fen La Ardleigh CO7 ..103 E1
  Beccles NR34 ....111 B7
  8 Kenny Hill IP28 ....13 D1
  Braiseworth IP23 .....37 D3
  Creeting St Peter or
  West Creeting IP6 ...125 D8
  Ditchingham NR35 .....7 E7
  Garboldisham IP22 ....18 D3
  Hitcham IP7 ....79 E5
  Rickinghall Inferior IP22 ..36 A6
  Roydon IP22 ....19 E7
  Stonham Earl IP6 .....67 D4
  Thelnetham IP22 .....18 E1
Fen Meadow IP11 ....152 C8
Fen Pk Prim Sch
NR33 ....115 B6
Fen Rd Blo' Norton IP22 ..18 F2
  Hengrave IP31 ....49 F6
  8 Kenny Hill IP28 ....14 E5
Fen St Boxford CO10 ..93 C3
  Hinderclay IP22 ....18 D4
  Nayland CO6 ....102 D5
Fen View
  Copdock & Washbrook
  IP8 ....95 F4
  Thorndon IP23 ....53 B8
  Walsham le Willows IP31 ..35 A8
Fen Way IP12 ....146 F4
Fen Wlk IP12 ....146 E4
Fenbridge La CO7 ....151 B3
Fengate Dro IP7 ....5 E2
Fenlands Cres NR33 ..114 F6
Fenn Cl
  Halesworth IP19 .....118 A5
  Stowmarket IP14 ....124 D3
Fenn La IP12 ....98 D6
Fenstreet Rd IP17 .....58 A7
Fenton Rd CB9 ....132 F6
Fentons Way IP5 .....141 C7
Fern Ave NR32 ....112 D2
Fern Gn Cl 1 NR32 ...112 E4
Fern Gr CB9 ....132 C6
Fern Hill CO10 ....77 A4
Ferndale Ave NR32 ...113 B3
Ferndale Cl CB8 ......121 B6
Ferndown Rd 3 IP11 .153 C6
Ferneley Cres CB8 ...121 A4
Fernhayes Cl IP2 .....139 A3
Fernhill Cl IP12 ......147 A7
Fernlea Rd 4 CO12 ..107 B3
Ferry La
  Beck Row, Holywell Row
  & Kenny Hill IP28 ....29 C5
  Felixstowe IP11 ......152 C3
Ferry Quay IP12 ......147 A4
Ferry Rd Bawdsey IP12 ..99 D1
  Felixstowe IP11 ......153 D7
  Southwold IP18 ......119 C3
  Sudbourne IP12 ......146 E3
  Walberswick IP18 ....119 B2
Fersfield Rd IP22 ......19 D5
Festival Cl 4 IP17 .....72 C8
Festival Rd 14 CB7 ....29 C5
Feveryears Way 4 IP21 ..39 D8
Fiddler's La IP23 .....117 F2
Fiddlers La IP27 ......151 C5
Field Cl 5 IP30 ....49 F2
Field Fuller's IP6 .....133 E4
Field Grange NR32 ...112 F5
Field House Gdns IP22 ..20 D2
Field La NR33 ....11 B1
Field Stile Rd 2 IP18 .119 D5
Field View CB8 ....120 F5
Field View
  Buckleham IP10 ......98 A4
  8 Thurstow IP31 .....49 F7
Field View Gdns NR34 .111 D3
Field Way
  Debenham IP14 ....53 F1
  18 Stanton IP31 ......34 E4
Field Wlk IP28 ....116 C5
Fields View CO10 ....148 D6
Fieldview Cl IP18 ....119 B8
Fieldview Dr NR32 ...113 A1
Fife Rd IP4 ....136 B1
Finbars Wlk IP11 ....139 F5
Finborough Cl IP4 ...140 F6
Finborough Rd IP14 .124 B6
Finborough Sch IP14 ..66 B5
Finch Cl 1 IP14 ....67 A5
Finch Hill CO10 ....91 D4
Fincham Rd IP28 ....116 B5
Finchingfield Rd
  Stambourne CO9 .....89 B1
  Steeple Bumpstead CO9 ..88 E3
Finchley Ave IP28 ...116 B6
Finchley Rd IP4 ......139 C6
Findley Cl IP7 ....80 D8
Fingal St IP13 ....39 A1
Finney's Drift IP10 ..145 C5
Finningham Rd
  Gislingham IP23 ......36 D1
  Old Newton with Dagworth
  IP14 ....51 F2
  Rickinghall Superior IP22 ..36 B4

Fir Tree Cl IP21 ....22 D2
Fir Tree Hill IP9 ....105 F7
Fir Tree La IP14 ....51 C3
Fir Tree Rise IP28 ....138 C2
Fir Wlk 20 IP27 ....13 F2
Fircroft Rd IP1 ....135 A2
Firebrass La IP12 ......85 C2
Firebronds Rd IP9 ...105 E7
Firecrest Dr 2 IP14 ..124 F7
Firefly Way 1 IP3 ....144 B8
Firfield Cl IP14 ....111 B3
Firmin Cl IP1 ....139 A6
Firs The Beccles NR34 ..111 F4
  Lakenheath IP27 .....109 E6
  Lowestoft NR33 ......114 C3
  Southwold IP18 ......119 B8
First Ave
  4 Glemsford CO10 ....77 B3
  Sudbury CO10 ....148 E7
First Dro Burwell CB5 ..44 B8
  Lakenheath IP27 .....109 A8
Firtree Cl IP32 ....122 D7
Fir Pond Hill IP9 .....106 B6
Fishbane Cl 3 IP3 ....144 A8
Fisher Cl Haverhill CB9 ..133 B5
  2 Saxmundham IP17 ..128 C2
Fisher Rd IP22 ....20 D2
Fisher Row
  Carlton Colville NR32 .114 B8
  Lowestoft NR32 ......112 B1
Fisher's Dro IP28 .....12 D3
Fisher's La
  East Bergholt CO7 ...104 E6
  Hoxne IP21 ....38 C8
Fisherman's Way 13
NR33 ....11 C1
Fishers The IP5 ......141 C7
Fishpond Rd IP12 ....98 D7
Fishponds Hill CO6 ..102 C3
Fishponds La IP9 ....105 F7
Fishponds Way IP4 ...66 C8
Fiske Cl IP32 ....123 E6
Fison Way IP24 ....16 B7
Fitches La IP16 ....129 D1
Fitches The IP17 .....129 A2
Fitzgerald Cl 4 CO11 .104 D2
Fitzgerald Rd
  Bramford IP8 ....134 A1
  Woodbridge IP12 ....147 A6
Fitzmaurice Rd IP3 ..140 B3
Fitzroy St Ipswich IP1 .155 B3
  Newmarket CB8 ......121 A1
Fitzwilliam Cl
  6 Woodbridge IP12 .146 E4
Five Acre La NR35 .....7 E3
Five Acres 12 IP9 ...105 E7
Five Cross Ways
  Butley IP12 ....86 B4
  Sudbourne IP12 .....131 B6
Fiveways IP28 ....116 F3
Flatford Cl IP14 ......124 E3
Flatford La CO7 ......151 D1
Flatford Mill* CO7 ...151 D1
Flatford Rd
  East Bergholt CO7 ...151 D2
  Haverhill CB9 ....132 A6
Fleet Dyke Dr NR33 .114 C5
Fleetwood Ave IP11 .153 B5
Fleetwood Rd IP11 ..153 B5
Fleming Ave IP28 ....116 C5
Flempton Rd IP28 .....47 D5
Flemyng Rd IP23 ....122 D1
Fletcher Cl 5 IP5 ......82 A5
Fletcher Rd IP1 ......140 A1
Fletcher's La IP17 ....58 B6
Fletchers La IP5 .....141 E8
Flindell Dr IP8 ....134 A2
Flint Cl IP22 ....139 B2
Flixton Marsh La
NR32 ....112 B6
Flixton Rd
  Blundeston NR32 ....112 C8
  Bungay NR35 ....110 A1
  Flixton NR35 ....7 E2
  St Mary, South Elmham
  otherwise Homersfield
  IP20 ....23 B8
  Somerleyton, Ashby &
  Herringfleet NR32 ......2 F4
Flora Rd NR33 ....115 A3
Flordon Rd IP6 ....125 E5
Florence Rd NR33 ...115 B3
Florence Way NR35 ...8 D7
Flowerday Cl 4 NR31 ..3 B7
Flowton Rd Elmsett IP7 ..81 A3
  Flowton IP9 ....95 B8
Floyd Rd IP32 ....81 C3
Foal's Gn Rd IP21 .....39 D2
Fodderdike Dro
  Beck Row, Holywell Row
  & Kenny Hill IP28 .....12 C1
  Feltwell PE38 ....4 A3
Foden Ave IP1 ....134 C2
Folly End IP15 ....130 D5
Folly La
  Bressingham IP22 ....19 F4
  Copdock & Washbrook
  IP8 ....95 E2
  Lawshall IP29 ....63 C3

Folly Rd
  Great Waldingfield CO10 ..92 C6
  Hundon IP29 ....75 F3
  Mildenhall IP28 ......116 A7
Folly The Harleston IP14 ..66 C8
  Haughley IP14 ....51 C1
Fonnereau Rd IP1 ...155 B3
Forbes Dr NR34 ......111 B3
Ford Cl
  Beck Row, Holywell Row
  & Kenny Hill IP28 .....29 F7
  Stowmarket IP14 ....124 E4
Ford Hill IP12 ....99 B7
Ford Rd IP12 ....71 C5
Ford View Rd IP14 ..124 E4
Fordham Moor CB7 ...29 A3
Fordham Pl
  4 Ipswich IP4 ....140 F5
  24 Ixworth IP31 ......34 B1
Fordham Rd
  Fordham CB8 ....44 F7
  Freckenham IP28 .....29 D2
  Mount Bures CO8 ...101 C1
  Newmarket CB8 .....120 F7
  Snailwell CB8 ....45 A7
  Soham CB7 ....38 A2
  7 Soham CB7 ....30 A2
  Wormingford CO6 ...101 E2
Fordhams Cl 21 IP31 ..34 E4
Fordley Rd IP17 ......57 F6
Fordson Way NR33 ..114 C3
Fore Hamlet IP3 .....139 E5
Fore St
  Framlingham IP13 ...126 D3
  Ipswich IP4 ....155 C2
Forest End CB8 ....46 A7
Forest Gdns 8 IP12 ...85 D8
Forest Glade IP32 ...132 D8
Forest La 3 IP5 ....98 A7
Forest Mount NR31 ...2 B7
Forest Prim Sch The
IP27 ....5 F1
Forest Rd IP14 ....66 B6
Forest Ret Pk IP28 ...16 A5
Forest Way IP28 .....116 E4
Forester Cl IP8 ......142 E8
Foresters Wlk 6 IP6 ..82 A5
Forfar Cl 2 Ipswich IP4 ..136 B1
  Ipswich IP4 ....140 B8
Forge Cl 2 Benhall IP17 ..72 C8
  Buckleham IP10 ....98 A4
Forge Dr IP22 ....20 C1
Forge End IP28 ....48 B6
Forge Gr NR34 ....9 B6
Forge St CO7 ....104 A3
Forge Way IP1 ....138 D4
Fornham La IP33 .....123 A7
Fornham Rd
  Bury St Edmunds IP32 ..154 B4
  Great Barton IP31 ....49 A5
Forties Cl CB9 ....133 B6
Fortress Rd NR33 ...114 E3
Foster Cl IP18 ....119 C6
Foster Rd 7 CO12 ...106 F3
Foundation St IP4 ...155 B2
Foundry La IP1 ......155 B2
Fountain Cl 6 IP12 ...85 D8
Fountain Way IP18 .119 C8
Fountain's La NR34 ..10 C4
Fountains Rd
  Bury St Edmunds IP33 ..122 D2
  Ipswich IP2 ....139 A1
Four Elms Residential Sch
IP14 ....68 A8
Four Wheel Dr IP30 ..49 B2
Fourth Ave 6 CO10 ..77 A3
Fowe's La CO10 ......90 D4
Fowler's Cres 2 NR32 ..3 D4
Fox And Pin La IP29 ..63 E8
Fox Cl IP14 ....124 D6
Fox Gn CB8 ....74 C8
Fox Hill Holley Cl IP12 ..99 F7
  St Cross, South Elmham
  IP20 ....23 C7
Fox La IP17 ....42 B1
Fox Lea IP5 ....141 E8
Fox Wood N 7 CB7 ...28 D5
Fox Wood S 2 CB7 ...28 D5
Fox Yd IP18 ....119 D5
Foxborough Mid Sch
NR32 ....113 A5
Foxborough Rd NR32 .113 A4
Foxburrow Cl IP32 ...132 D7
Foxburrow Farm Nature
Reserve* IP12 ....84 D6
Foxburrow Hill NR32 .113 A6
Foxburrow Rd IP4 ...140 F6
Foxburrow Wood Nature
Reserve* IP13 ......113 B6
Foxes La Ashen CO10 ..89 E5
  Mendham IP20 ....23 B4
Foxes Rd CO10 ....89 E5
Foxes Wlk NR33 .....113 A6
Foxglade NR32 ....3 D4
Foxglove Ave IP6 ...125 D3
Foxglove Cl
  Lowestoft NR33 ......114 E3
  1 Worlingham NR34 .111 E3
Foxglove Cres IP3 ...140 E1
Foxglove La IP14 ....16 D6
Foxglove Gdns IP11 .153 C5
Foxgrove La IP11 ...153 C5

Foxhall Cl CO7 151 C6
Foxhall Fields CO7 151 C5
Foxhall Rd Foxhall IP10 98 A6
Ipswich IP3 139 F5
Foxhall Stadium IP4 141 A5
Foxtail Rd IP3 144 D8
Foxwood Cl CO11 104 B1
Foxwood Cres IP4 140 F5
Framfield Rd NR33 114 C4
Framlingham Cl 4 IP12 85 B3
Framlingham Coll IP13 126 C4
Framlingham Mere Nature Reserve* IP13 126 C4
Framlingham Rd
Dennington IP13 39 F2
Easton IP13 70 E5
Laxfield IP13 40 A2
Framlington Castle (remains of)* IP13 126 C4
Framlinham Coll Prep Sch IP13 70 A7
Frampton Rd IP3 144 A8
Framsden Rd IP14 69 E7
Framsden Windmill* IP14 69 B6
Francis Cl
Haverhill CB9 132 D6
Ipswich IP5 141 E8
Francis Rd
13 Kessingland NR33 11 B1
8 Sudbury CO10 148 C5
Franciscan Way IP1 155 B2
Frank Bridges Cl 4 CB7 28 D3
Franklin Cl IP15 130 D5
Franklin Rd
Aldeburgh IP15 130 C5
Ipswich IP3 140 B2
Fraser Rd
Bramford IP8 134 B2
Ipswich IP1 138 F7
Freckenham Rd
Freckenham CB7 29 E2
Worlington IP28 30 A3
Fred Archer Way CB8 121 A3
Fred Dannatt Rd IP28 116 A6
Frederick Talbot Cl 14 CB7 28 D4
Frederick's Rd 3 NR34 111 C4
Free La NR35 110 A8
Freehold Rd
Ipswich IP4 140 A6
Needham Market IP6 125 C6
Freelands IP14 52 E4
Freeman Ave 4 IP6 82 D6
Freeman Cl IP7 149 D7
Freeman Prim Sch The IP14 67 B7
Freemantle Rd NR33 115 C7
Freewood St IP30 64 D6
Freezes Barns CB9 88 D4
Frenze Hall La IP22 20 D3
Frenze Rd IP22 20 D2
Frere Cnr 7 IP22 20 A3
Frere Rd 30 IP20 22 C6
Freshfields
17 Harwich CO12 106 F1
Newmarket CB8 120 F4
Fressingfield CE Prim Sch IP21 39 D8
Fressingfield Rd IP20 23 C1
Freston Hill IP9 143 E4
Freston St IP9 143 D3
Freston Twr* IP9 143 F4
Friar Cl CB9 132 D7
Friar's La IP33 154 B1
Friars IP9 150 F2
Friars Bridge Rd IP1 155 A2
Friars Cl
Bury St Edmunds IP33 154 B1
7 Felixstowe IP11 153 D6
Friars Croft IP21 22 D3
Friars Ct Melton IP12 147 C7
Sudbury CO10 148 C4
Friars Meadow IP21 22 D3
Friars Rd IP7 149 C6
Friars St Ipswich IP1 155 B2
Sudbury CO10 148 C5
Friary Meadow IP28 48 D5
Friday St
Beck Row, Holywell Row & Kenny Hill IP28 29 F6
Rendlesham IP12 85 D7
Friday St Farm Maize Maze* IP17 72 B7
Friday's Orch IP16 129 C5
Friends Field 7 CO8 101 C5
Friends Wlk IP5 141 D8
Friston Rd IP12 85 C2
Fristonmoor La
Knodishall IP17 57 E1
Sternfield IP17 72 E8
Fritillary Cl IP8 142 E8
Fritton Cl Ipswich IP2 139 A1
12 Oulton NR32 112 F4
Fritton Ct 5 CB9 132 C4
Fritton Lake Ctry World* NR31 2 C6
Frobisher Rd
21 Harwich CO12 106 F1
Ipswich IP3 139 E1
Frog Hall La IP7 149 F6
Frogmore CB8 120 B7
Frogs Alley IP9 106 F6
Frogs Alley Vineyard* IP9 106 F7
Frogs Hall Rd CO10 78 D5
Frogs Hole NR32 2 C5
Fronk's Ave 3 CO12 107 B1
Fronk's Rd CO12 107 A1
Front Rd IP3 144 D8
Front St
Mendlesham IP14 52 E4
Orford IP12 131 B3
Ousden CB8 61 E6
Frostenden Cres 1 NR32 113 B4
Frowd Cl CB7 29 B1
Fryatt Ave 7 CO12 107 A2
Fryth Cl CB9 132 E7
Fuchsia La IP4 140 A5
Fulcher Cl IP33 123 D2
Fulchers Field IP13 126 B4
Fulford Cl 8 IP28 48 C6
Fuller Rd IP20 22 D5
Fullers Cl 2 IP7 149 E6
Fullers Teasle NR33 114 A3
Fulmar Way NR33 114 D5
Fulmerston Rd IP24 16 B5
Furness Cl IP2 142 F8
Further St CO10 92 E2
Furthest Dro IP27 4 D1
Furze Cl 4 IP31 49 D4
Furze Way IP22 36 D5
Fyffe Way 12 NR33 115 D8
Fynn La IP6 136 C5
Fynn Rd IP12 146 D3

G

Gables The CB9 133 D3
Gaell Cres 5 IP7 149 D5
Gage Cl IP32 154 A4
Gage's Rd CO10 90 C4
Gainsborough Ctr IP3 144 B8
Gainsborough Dr
Halesworth IP19 118 A2
Lowestoft NR32 113 B6
Manningtree CO11 104 D2
Gainsborough La IP3 143 F8
Gainsborough Rd
Bury St Edmunds IP33 122 D5
Felixstowe IP11 153 A4
Haverhill CB9 132 B7
Ipswich IP4 155 C4
Stowmarket IP14 124 B6
Sudbury CO10 148 C5
Gainsborough St CO10 148 C5
Gainsborough's House* w0 CO10 148 C5
Galley Cl NR33 114 B4
Galley Rd CO10 75 D3
Gallow La IP30 78 C7
Gallows Hill IP7 149 B7
Gallows La IP14 66 C7
Galway Ave IP1 134 E1
Gandish Cl CO7 151 D3
Gandish Rd CO7 151 E4
Ganges Rd 1 IP9 107 A4
Gannet Cl CB9 133 A6
Gannet Rd IP2 138 E3
Ganwick Cl CB9 132 D8
Gaol La Beccles NR34 111 B5
Sudbury CO10 148 C5
Gap The NR33 114 F6
Garboldisham Rd
Harling NR16 18 C7
Kenninghall NR16 18 F7
Garboldisham VC Prim Sch IP22 18 D4
Garden Cl
Bungay NR35 110 C3
5 Great Barton IP31 49 A6
Normanston NR32 113 B2
Shotley IP9 106 F6
Garden Ct 2 CB5 44 B6
Garden Field 2 IP11 152 E5
Garden Fields IP31 33 D3
Garden House La IP30 65 C6
Garden La
Beccles NR34 111 F4
Westley IP33 122 A5
Garden Pl CO10 148 B5
Garden Sq IP12 85 D8
Gardeners La 21 CB7 28 D4
Gardeners Rd IP14 53 F1
Gardeners Wlk IP30 50 E2
Gardenhouse La IP22 36 A6
Gardens The
4 Beyton IP30 49 F2
Lowestoft NR33 114 C2
Gardiner Cl IP33 122 C4
Gardner Rd IP18 119 D5
Garfield Cl IP11 152 F3
Garfield Rd IP11 152 F3
Garland Rd 5 CO12 106 F3
Garland St IP33 154 B3
Garlic St IP21 22 A6
Garnons Chase 3 CO6 101 F2
Garrard Pl 12 IP31 34 B1
Garrards Rd 3 IP7 80 F1
Garrett Cl IP17 72 D5
Garrett Cres IP16 129 D5
Garrick Way IP1 135 A3
Garrison La
Felixstowe IP11 152 F4
5 Great Waldingfield CO10 92 C6
Garrod App IP12 84 E7
Garrods IP9 150 F3
Garrods End IP29 62 C5
Gas Works Rd NR32 113 E2
Gascoigne Dr 3 IP6 82 D6
Gashouse Dro IP27 5 F1
Gaston End CO7 151 C5
Gaston St CO7 151 C4
Gatacre Rd IP1 139 A7
Gate Farm Rd 2 IP9 107 A5
Gatesbury's La IP29 62 C2
Gateway The IP33 123 C3
Gavell St IP19 24 D5
Gawdy Cl 2 IP20 22 D6
Gaye Cres IP23 117 B3
Gaye St IP1 155 A3
Gayfer Ave IP5 141 F8
Gayford Sq IP7 80 C6
Gaymers La IP11 152 B8
Gazeley Rd Ashley CB8 46 A1
Kentford CB8 46 A5
Gdn Room The* IP6 125 D5
Gedding Hill IP30 65 B4
Gedding Rd IP30 65 B7
Gedge Cl IP33 122 C4
Gedgrave Rd IP12 131 A1
Geldeston Hill NR34 8 F6
Geldeston Rd
Ellingham NR35 8 D6
Geldeston NR34 9 B6
General Castle Way IP30 49 B2
Generals Mews 12 IP11 152 D5
Genesta Dr 2 IP31 49 D4
Geneva Gdns 4 NR31 3 C6
Geneva Rd IP1 155 A4
Gentle Ct 3 IP27 5 F1
Gents La IP29 77 F7
George Baldry Way 2 NR35 110 C2
George Brown Way NR34 111 C3
George Cl NR32 112 E1
George Frost Cl IP4 155 C4
George Gent Cl 7 CB9 88 D3
George Gibson Cl CB8 120 C8
George Hill IP31 34 E4
George La 3 CO10 77 B2
George Lambpton Ave CB8 120 F5
George Rd 3 IP24 16 D6
George St Brandon IP27 5 F1
Hadleigh IP7 149 E6
2 Harwich CO12 107 B3
Hintlesham IP8 95 C6
George Westwood Way NR34 111 C6
Geralds Ave IP4 140 A5
Gestingthorpe Rd CO10 90 F2
Gibbon Cl IP32 123 E5
Gibraltar Cl IP33 122 C6
Gibraltar Rd IP6 69 B1
Gifford Cl 6 IP9 105 E7
Giffords Pl IP4 140 F6
Gilbert Cl IP6 125 C5
Gilbert Rd 2 CO10 90 A8
Giles Way Risby IP28 47 E5
4 Witnesham IP6 83 A5
Gillingham Rd NR34 9 A6
Gillngham Dam NR34 111 A7
Gilpin Rd NR32 112 D1
Gilray Rd IP22 20 D2
Gilstrap Rd IP31 48 D5
Gimbert Rd 7 CB7 28 D4
Gin La IP13 40 C2
Gippeswyk Ave IP2 139 A4
Gippeswyk Rd IP2 155 A1
Gipping Cl CB9 132 C4
Gipping Pl IP14 124 D7
Gipping Rd Claydon IP6 82 A5
Stowupland IP14 67 A7
Gipping Way
Bramford IP8 134 B2
Sproughton IP8 138 B6
Stowmarket IP14 124 D7
Gippingstone Rd IP8 134 A1
Gipsy La
Aldringham cum Thorpe IP16 129 D1
Frostenden NR34 26 D4
Needham Market IP6 125 C6
Girling St CO10 148 C6
Girton Cl
Mildenhall IP28 116 C6
Woodbridge IP12 146 D4
Woodditton CB8 121 B1
Girton Rd CB9 132 F5
Girton Way IP2 138 F1
Gisleham Mid Sch NR33 114 C1
Gisleham Rd NR33 114 B1
Gislingham CE Prim Sch IP23 36 C2
Gislingham Rd IP14 36 C1
Gissing Rd IP22 20 F6
Glade Prim Sch The IP27 5 F1
Glade The IP24 16 C7
Glades The NR32 112 D2
Gladstone Rd
1 Corton NR32 3 C4
Ipswich IP3 139 F5
6 Woodbridge IP12 147 A5
Glamis Cl CB9 132 B6
Glamis Ct 20 IP20 22 D6
Glamorgan Rd IP2 139 B1
Glanely Gdns CB8 120 C8
Glanfield Wlk IP33 122 C4
Glanville Pl IP5 141 B6
Glanville Rd IP7 149 E4
Glassfield Rd IP31 34 D4
Glastonbury Cl IP2 138 F1
Glastonbury Rd IP33 122 C3
Glebe Cl Bayliham IP6 81 E6
Horringer IP29 63 A7
Ingham IP31 32 F1
Lowestoft NR32 113 C5
Sproughton IP8 138 B6
1 Tattingstone IP9 105 B8
Glebe End IP9 150 F4
Glebe La IP9 144 B1
Glebe Meadow IP13 54 F2
Glebe Rd Bredfield IP13 84 C7
Gissing IP21 21 A8
Weeting IP27 5 E3
Glebe Rd E 15 NR33 11 C1
Glebe Rd W 18 NR33 11 B1
Glebe The
Haverhill CB9 132 E7
Lavenham CO10 78 D3
Glebe View NR34 111 C3
Glebe Way 1 Claydon IP6 82 B5
Mendlesham IP14 52 E4
Glebes The IP17 72 D5
Glemham Dr IP4 140 F4
Glemham Hall* IP13 71 E6
Glemham Rd IP17 56 E2
Glemsford Cl IP11 152 D3
Glemsford Com Prim Sch CO10 77 A3
Glemsford Pl 7 CB9 132 F6
Glemsford Rd
Lowestoft NR32 112 F4
Stowmarket IP14 124 E4
Glenavon Rd IP4 140 D7
Glenbourne Wlk 2 NR33 114 C3
Glencoe Rd IP4 136 C1
Gleneagles Cl
4 Bury St Edmunds IP28 48 C6
1 Felixstowe IP11 153 C6
Gleneagles Dr IP4 140 D5
Glenfield Ave IP11 153 A6
Glenhurst Ave IP4 140 B8
Glenside CO10 148 E4
Glenwood Ct CB8 120 F3
Glenwood Dr NR34 111 E4
Globe Yd 3 CO10 148 C6
Gloster Rd IP5 98 A8
Gloucester Ave NR32 112 F3
Gloucester Pl 4 CO10 76 A1
Gloucester Rd
4 Bury St Edmunds IP32 122 E8
Haverhill CB9 132 D5
Ipswich IP3 140 A2
Gloucester Way CO10 148 B8
Go Ape* IP27 15 C8
Gobbets La IP22 35 E7
Gobbett's Rd IP22 35 E8
Gobbitts Yd IP12 147 A4
Godbold Cl 3 IP5 141 D7
Goddard Pl IP14 66 B7
Goddard Rd IP1 134 C3
Goddard Rd E IP1 134 D3
Godetia Ct 6 NR32 113 B4
Godfrey's Ct 12 NR32 113 D2
Godfrey's Hill IP19 40 F8
Godfrey's Wood IP12 147 A7
Godolphin Cl IP33 122 C3
Godyll Rd IP18 119 C5
Goldcrest Rd IP2 138 C3
Golden La IP29 63 C2
Golden Lion La 5 CO12 107 B3
Golden Miller Cl CB8 120 D7
Goldenlond CO6 102 E7
Golding Way 1 CO10 77 A2
Golding's La IP16 129 C4
Goldings Cl CB9 132 E8
Goldsmith Cl IP32 122 D7
Goldsmith Rd IP1 134 E3
Goldsmith Way IP21 21 F8
Golf La IP15 130 C6
Golf Links Rd
Barton Mills IP28 30 C3
Worlington IP28 116 A1
Golf Rd IP11 153 D5
Gondree NR33 114 E3
Gonville Cl
Mildenhall IP28 116 D6
1 Woodbridge IP12 146 E4
Goodall Terr IP5 141 E8
Goodchilds Gdns 8 CB7 29 C5
Goodlake Cl 9 CO12 106 F1
Goodman Gr IP5 141 E7
Goodwood Cl IP1 135 B4
Goose Gn E NR34 111 C5
Goose Gn W NR34 111 C5
Gorams Mill La IP13 40 B3
Gordon Rd
California IP4 140 A6
5 Harwich CO12 107 A1
Ipswich IP4 140 A7
Lowestoft NR32 113 D1
Gordon Richards Cl CB8 120 F6
Goring Rd IP4 140 C6
Gorleston Rd
Blundeston NR32 112 F8
Corton NR32 3 B4
Gorse Cl
Lakenheath IP27 109 E4
6 Red Lodge IP28 30 C1
Gorse Gn NR32 113 B3
Gorse Ind Est IP24 16 A3
Gorse La IP18 119 C7
Gorse Rd Ipswich IP3 140 B2
Southwold IP18 119 C6
Gorse View IP17 58 C8
Gorsehayes IP2 139 B3
Gorseland Prim Sch IP5 141 F8
Gorselands IP12 99 F7
Gorst Cl 7 IP32 122 E8
Gosford Cl 4 CO10 90 A8
Gosford Rd NR34 111 C5
Gosford Way IP11 153 C6
Gostling Cl 2 IP22 20 B2
Gostling Pl IP5 141 E8
Gothic Cl 2 IP20 22 D5
Gotsfield Cl 1 CO10 92 B7
Gough Pl 9 IP31 34 B1
Governors Mews IP33 123 C2
Gower St IP2 155 B1
Gowers Cl IP5 141 E7
Gowers End 6 CO10 77 B3
Gowle Rd IP14 124 C8
Goyfield Ave IP11 152 F4
Gracechurch St IP14 53 E2
Graften Way IP1 155 A2
Grafton Cl IP33 122 D5
Grafton Rd 2 CO12 107 B2
Grafton Way IP1 155 B2
Graham Ave IP1 139 B8
Graham Rd
Felixstowe IP11 152 F5
Ipswich IP1 155 A4
Grainge Way 3 IP14 51 C1
Grainger Cl IP32 123 F5
Grammar Sch Pl 11 CO10 148 C5
Grampian Way NR32 112 D2
Granaries The IP6 136 C6
Granary Rd CB8 121 B2
Granary The Clare CO10 90 A7
Hadleigh IP7 149 E5
Granby St CB8 121 B3
Grand Ave NR33 115 B3
Grange Cl
Felixstowe IP11 152 E5
Ipswich IP5 141 F8
Grange Ct IP12 147 B6
Grange Farm Ave IP11 152 D5
Grange La
Barton Mills IP28 116 D2
Ipswich IP5 141 E8
Grange Mill 3 IP29 62 C6
Grange Prim Sch IP11 152 D4
Grange Rd
Beccles NR34 111 A4
Felixstowe IP11 152 D3
Flixton NR35 23 E8
16 Harwich CO12 107 A2
Ipswich IP4 139 E6
Lawford CO11 104 C1
Lowestoft NR32 112 D2
Wickham Skeith IP23 52 D7
Grange View IP17 58 B7
Grange Wlk IP33 123 A2
Grantchester Pl IP5 141 A8
Grantchester Rise CB5 44 A7
Grantham Cres IP2 155 A1
Granville Gdns 3 IP28 116 A4
Granville Rd IP11 152 F3
Granville St IP1 155 A3
Granworth Cl IP13 83 E6
Grasmere Ave 5 IP11 153 D6
Gratton Dale NR33 114 E2
Gravel Dam NR32 112 B2
Gravel Dro IP28 29 E6
Gravel Hill CO6 102 D5
Gravel Hill Way CO12 106 F1
Gravel Pit La CO11 104 F5
Gray's La IP19 24 D4
Gray's Orch IP10 98 E2
Grayling Rd IP8 142 E8
Graylings The 10 NR33 114 E4
Grays Rd NR34 10 C7
Grayson Ave NR33 115 A3
Grayson Dr NR33 115 A2
Great Back La 4 IP14 53 F2
Great Barton Prim Sch IP31 49 B6
Great Colman St IP4 155 C3
Great Comm La NR34 8 E1
Great Cornard Ctry Pk* CO10 92 B2
Great Cornard Mid Sch CO10 92 B2
Great Cornard Sports Ctr CO10 148 F2
Great Cornard Upper Sch CO10 148 F2
Great Dro CB7 28 A4
Great Eastern Rd CO10 148 D5
Great Eastern Sq IP11 153 A5
Great Fen Rd CB7 28 D8
Great Field IP11 152 C8
Great Finborough Prim Sch IP14 66 A4
Great Gipping St IP1 155 A2
Great Harlings IP9 107 A5
Great Heath Prim Sch IP28 116 D6
Great Oak Ct CO9 90 A1
Great Tufts IP9 150 F3
Great Waldingfield VCE Prim Sch CO10 92 C6
Great Whelnetham CE Prim Sch IP30 63 F6
Great Whip St IP2 155 B1
Grebe Cl Ipswich IP2 138 E2
Mildenhall IP28 116 D3

Grebe Cl *continued*
Stowmarket IP14 . . . . .124 A6
Green Acre 2 CO10 . . . . . . .92 C6
Green Cres IP10 . . . . .98 A4
Green Dr NR33 . . . . .115 A4
Green Farm La 5 IP29 . .47 A2
Green Fleet Dr NR32 . . .112 E4
Green Hill IP6 . . . . .68 B1
Green La Boxted CO4 . . .102 E3
  Burgh St Peter NR34 . . . . . .10 C8
  Cockfield IP30 . . . . .64 D2
  Creeting St Mary IP14 . . . . .67 F5
  Ditchingham NR35 . . . . . . .110 C7
  6 Feltwell IP26 . . . . .4 E5
  Frostenden NR34 . . . . .26 C4
  Great Barton IP31 . . . . .49 B5
  Hundon CO10 . . . . .75 D2
  Kessingland NR33 . . . . .11 C1
  3 Martlesham IP12 . . . . . .84 A1
  Pettistree IP13 . . . . .127 D5
  Redenhall with Harleston
    IP20 . . . . .22 E6
  Reydon IP18 . . . . .26 E1
  Shipmeadow NR34 . . . . .8 F5
  Somerleyton, Ashby &
    Herringfleet NR32 . . . . . . .1 A2
  Southwold IP18 . . . . .119 B8
  Starston IP20 . . . . .22 D8
  Stratford St Mary CO7 . . . .103 E6
  Syleham IP21 . . . . .38 E8
  2 Tattingstone IP9 . . . . .105 B8
  Thelnetham IP22 . . . . .35 C6
  Thetford IP24 . . . . .16 C6
  Thrandeston IP21 . . . . .37 B6
  Troston IP31 . . . . .33 C5
  Tuddenham St Martin
    IP6 . . . . .136 C4
  Wetheringsett-cum-Brockford
    IP14 . . . . .53 A6
Green La Cl IP18 . . . . . . .119 B8
Green Man Pl IP12 . . . . . .71 F2
Green Man Way CO10 . . .115 B4
Green Oak Glade IP8 . . .128 C8
Green Pk Brinkley CB8 . . .59 E1
  4D Knodishall IP17 . . . . .73 D8
Green Rd Brandon IP27 . . . .6 A1
  Newmarket CB8 . . . . .121 A2
  Thorpe Morieux IP30 . . . . . .64 F1
  Woolpit IP30 . . . . .50 D1
Green St IP21 . . . . .38 C8
Green The 4 Ashley CB8 . .60 F8
  Beck Row, Holywell Row
    & Kenny Hill IP28 . . . . . . .29 E7
  Chedburgh IP29 . . . . .62 C4
  8 Earsham NR35 . . . . .7 F4
  Fornham All Saints IP26 . . .48 B6
  1 Grundisburgh IP13 . . . . .83 E5
  Hadleigh IP7 . . . . .149 E6
  Hessett IP30 . . . . .64 F8
  Kersey IP7 . . . . .94 A7
  Kirtling CB8 . . . . .60 E3
  Lound NR32 . . . . .2 F6
  Lowestoft NR33 . . . . .114 F6
  Mendlesham IP14 . . . . .52 D2
  2 Mistley CO11 . . . . . . .104 F2
  North Lopham IP22 . . . . . . .19 A6
  Snailwell CB8 . . . . .45 A6
  Walberswick IP18 . . . . . . .119 B2
Green Willows CO10 . . . . .78 C2
Greenacre Cres 1
  NR32 . . . . .113 B2
Greenacres IP14 . . . . .51 F1
Greenbank IP19 . . . . .118 C5
Greene King Brewing Mus*
  IP33 . . . . .154 C1
Greene Rd IP13 . . . . .122 C6
Greenfield Rd NR33 . . . . .114 F5
Greenfields CB8 . . . . .121 C3
Greenfields Way CB9 . . . .132 C5
Greenfinch Ave IP2 . . . . . .138 D3
Greenhills CB9 . . . . .132 C5
Greens The
  Aldeburgh IP15 . . . . .130 C6
  Lowestoft NR33 . . . . .140 F4
Greensmill 2 CO11 . . . . .104 E3
Greenspire Gr IP8 . . . . . . .138 B2
Greenview IP29 . . . . .77 B7
Greenway 4 IP31 . . . . . . .49 A5
Greenway The NR34 . . . .111 B4
Greenways IP12 . . . . .85 C2
Greenways Cl IP12 . . . . . .139 B8
Greenways Cres IP12 . . . .124 D5
Greenwich Bsns Pk
  IP3 . . . . .139 E2
Greenwich Cl IP3 . . . . . . .139 E2
Greenwich Rd IP3 . . . . . .139 D2
Greenwood Cl CB9 . . . . . .132 C5
Greenwood Way 1
  NR32 . . . . .113 A6
Greenwoods The IP31 . . . .49 E6
Gregory Rd IP28 . . . . .116 A6
Gregory St CO10 . . . . . . .148 C5
Grenadier Rd CB9 . . . . . .132 A6
Grenville Rd CO10 . . . . . .148 D8
Gresham Ave NR32 . . . . . .112 F2
Gresham Cl NR32 . . . . . . .112 F2
Gresham Rd IP4 . . . . .136 C1
Gresley Gdns 8 IP2 . . . . .139 C3
Gretna Gdns 8 IP4 . . . . .136 B1
Greville Starkey Ave
  CB8 . . . . .121 A5
Grey Friars Rd IP1 . . . . . .155 B2
Greyfriars*
  Dunwich IP17 . . . . .43 B1
  Ipswich IP1 . . . . .155 A2
Greyfriars Rd IP32 . . . . . .123 E4
Greyhound Hill CO4 . . . .103 C2

Grebe Cl *continued*
Stowmarket IP14 . . . . .124 A6
Greyhound La IP22 . . . . . .18 B1
Greyhound Rd 7 CO10 . . .77 A2
Greys Cl 5 CO10 . . . . .76 E1
Greys La CB9 . . . . .75 A3
Grice Cl IP31 . . . . .11 C1
Griffith Cl 4 NR33 . . . . . .11 C1
Grime's Graves (Flint
  Mines)* IP27 . . . . .6 C4
Grimsey Rd IP16 . . . . .129 D5
Grimsey's La IP16 . . . . . .129 E5
Grimston La IP11 . . . . . . .107 C8
Grimwade Cl 9 CO11 . . .104 E4
Grimwade St IP4 . . . . . . .155 C2
Grinder's La IP21 . . . . .22 D4
Grindle Gdns IP33 . . . . . .123 B3
Grindle The IP8 . . . . .95 F8
Grinstead Gdns IP6 . . . . .125 E3
Grinstead Hill IP13 . . . . .125 E3
Gromford La IP17 . . . . .72 C5
Groomes Cl 5 NR31 . . . . . .3 B7
Grosvenor Cl IP3 . . . . . . .139 E8
Grosvenor Gdns IP33 . . . .122 F3
Grosvenor House Ct 9
  IP28 . . . . .116 B5
Grosvenor Rd
  Lowestoft NR33 . . . . .115 C7
  Sudbury CO10 . . . . .148 B8
Grosvenor Yd CB8 . . . . . .121 A3
Groton St CO10 . . . . .93 B5
Groton Wood Nature
  Reserve* CO10 . . . . .93 D6
Grove Ave CO10 . . . . .92 E8
Grove Cty Prim Sch
  NR33 . . . . .114 C4
Grove End IP21 . . . . .39 B5
Grove Gdns
  Carlton Colville NR33 . . . .114 C4
  Fordham CB7 . . . . .29 A2
  Woodbridge IP12 . . . . .146 E6
Grove Hill Belstead IP8 . .142 C7
  Dedham CO7 . . . . .103 E2
  Langham CO4 . . . . .103 C3
Grove La
  Ashfield cum Thorpe IP14 . .54 C2
  Elmswell IP30 . . . . .51 A3
  Harkstead IP9 . . . . .106 C7
  Ipswich IP4 . . . . .139 E5
  Mendham IP20 . . . . .23 A2
  Stanton IP31 . . . . .34 F4
  Thetford IP24 . . . . .16 C6
Grove Mews NR34 . . . . . .111 C4
Grove Pk
  Bury St Edmunds IP33 . . . .154 A3
  Fordham CB7 . . . . .29 A2
  8 Walsham le Willows
    IP31 . . . . .35 B1
Grove Rd Beccles NR34 . . .111 B5
  2 Brantham CO11 . . . . . .104 E4
  Brockdish IP21 . . . . .21 F3
  Bury St Edmunds IP33 . . . .154 A3
  Felixstowe IP11 . . . . .153 A6
  Gissing IP21 . . . . .21 A8
  Knodishall IP17 . . . . .72 F7
  Lowestoft NR33 . . . . .114 C4
  Pettistree IP13 . . . . .127 A4
  Starston IP20 . . . . .22 C6
  Walsham le Willows IP31 . . .35 C2
  Woodbridge IP13 . . . . .146 E6
Grove Rd N NR33 . . . . . .114 D5
Grove The
  Great Glemham IP17 . . . . . .56 F1
  12 Martlesham Heath IP5 . .98 A8
  Mildenhall IP28 . . . . .29 F8
  Stowmarket IP14 . . . . .124 E5
  5 Woodbridge IP12 . . . . .147 B6
Grove Wlk IP8 . . . . .142 D8
Grove; Henley Rd The
  IP1 . . . . .135 C2
Grub La IP19 . . . . .83 E5
Grundisburgh Cty Prim Sch
  IP13 . . . . .83 E5
Grundisburgh Rd
  Clopton IP13 . . . . .83 D8
  Great Bealings IP13 . . . . .137 C6
  Tuddenham St Martin
    IP6 . . . . .136 D6
Grundle Cl 8 IP31 . . . . . . .34 E4
Guildhall Feoffment Cty Prim
  Sch IP33 . . . . .154 C1
Guildhall La NR34 . . . . . . .26 C6
Guildhall of Corpus Christi
  The* CO10 . . . . .78 D4
Guildhall St IP33 . . . . . . .154 B2
Guineas Cl CB8 . . . . .120 E6
Gules Gn IP21 . . . . .22 F1
Gull Hill IP19 . . . . .25 C3
Gull La
  Grundisburgh IP13 . . . . . . .83 D6
  Thornham Magna IP23 . . . . .37 A2
Gull Rd IP17 . . . . .128 B2
Gull The IP13 . . . . .70 C2
Gull's La CO7 . . . . .104 A2
Gulpher Bsns Pk IP11 . . .152 F8
Gulpher Rd IP11 . . . . .152 E6
Gun Hill Dedham CO7 . . .103 D4
  Southwold IP18 . . . . .119 D4
Gun La NR32 . . . . .113 E2
Gunn Church La
  NR32 . . . . .113 C5
Gunton Cl IP33 . . . . .113 D5
Gunton Com Prim Sch
  NR32 . . . . .113 C6
Gunton Dr NR32 . . . . .113 D5
Gunton St Peter's Ave
  NR32 . . . . .113 C5
Gunton Warren Nature
  Reserve* NR32 . . . . .113 D6

Guntons Cl 12 CB7 . . . . . .28 D4
Gurdon Rd 5 IP13 . . . . . .83 E5
Gurlings Cl IP8 . . . . .132 E8
Guscot Ct NR32 . . . . .113 A6
Gusford Prim Sch IP2 . . .138 D1
Guston Gdns IP10 . . . . . . .98 E2
Guthrum Rd IP7 . . . . .149 D6
Guy Cook Cl CO10 . . . . . . .92 B2
Guyatt Ct 6 CB5 . . . . .44 A5
Gwendoline Rd IP4 . . . . . .140 E4
Gwynne Rd 4 CO12 . . . . .107 B2
Gymnasium St IP1 . . . . . .155 A3

H

Hacheston Rd IP13 . . . . . .70 F5
Hackney Rd
  Peasenhall IP17 . . . . .56 E8
  Woodbridge IP12 . . . . .147 B6
Hackney Terr IP12 . . . . . .147 B6
Hackney's Cnr IP6 . . . . . . .81 F5
Haddiscoe Rd NR31 . . . . . .2 A5
Hadenham Rd NR33 . . . . .114 F1
Hadleigh Bsns Pk IP7 . . . .94 E4
Hadleigh Dr NR32 . . . . . .112 F3
Hadleigh Guildhall*
  IP7 . . . . .149 D5
Hadleigh High Sch
  IP7 . . . . .149 F5
Hadleigh Prim Sch
  IP7 . . . . .149 D5
Hadleigh Railway Walk*
  IP7 . . . . .94 E3
Hadleigh Rd Aldham IP7 . .94 E8
  Bildeston IP7 . . . . .79 F3
  Boxford CO6 . . . . .93 D2
  East Bergholt CO7 . . . . . . .151 B4
  Elmsett IP7 . . . . .80 F1
  Higham CO7 . . . . .103 D7
  Ipswich IP2 . . . . .138 E6
Hadleigh Rd Ind Est
  IP7 . . . . .138 E7
Hadleigh Swimming Pool
  IP7 . . . . .149 D6
Hadrian Cl CB9 . . . . .133 B5
Haggars Mead IP14 . . . . .67 D7
Hague Cl NR32 . . . . .114 C6
Halcyon Cres NR32 . . . . .113 C1
Hale Cl IP12 . . . . .138 D2
Halesowen Cl IP2 . . . . . . .142 F8
Halesworth & District Mus*
  IP19 . . . . .118 B4
Halesworth (Holton) Airfield
  Mus* IP19 . . . . .118 D8
Halesworth Gall*
  IP19 . . . . .118 C5
Halesworth Mid Sch
  IP19 . . . . .118 C5
Halesworth Rd
  Brampton with Stoven
    IP19 . . . . .25 E3
  Heveningham IP19 . . . . . . .40 F3
  Linstead Parva IP19 . . . . . .40 F8
  Reydon IP18 . . . . .119 B7
  St Andrew, Ilketshall
    NR34 . . . . .25 A6
  St Lawrence, Ilketshall
    NR34 . . . . .24 E8
  Sibton IP17 . . . . .41 B1
  Uggeshall NR34 . . . . .25 F3
  Walpole IP19 . . . . .41 C5
  Wenhaston with Mells Hamlet
    IP19 . . . . .41 F6
Halesworth Sta IP19 . . . .118 B4
Half Moon La
  6 Grundisburgh IP13 . . . . .83 E5
  Redgrave IP22 . . . . .36 A8
Half Moon St IP30 . . . . . . .65 D5
Halfar Rd 2 IP31 . . . . .33 D5
Halfmoon La IP27 . . . . . . .109 C2
Halford Ct 6 IP30 . . . . . . .138 C2
Halford La IP22 . . . . .19 B8
Halifax Prim Sch IP2 . . . .139 A2
Halifax Rd Ipswich IP2 . . .139 B2
  9 Mildenhall IP28 . . . . . . .30 A8
Halifax St IP27 . . . . .109 F1
Halifax Way CB8 . . . . . . .120 E5
Haling Way 2 IP23 . . . . . .16 A6
Hall Barn Rd CB7 . . . . . . .29 B5
Hall Cl IP29 . . . . .62 B4
Hall Cl The IP28 . . . . .30 A8
Hall Dr 7 Feltwell IP26 . . . .4 E5
  Lakenheath IP27 . . . . .109 C7
  Lowestoft NR32 . . . . .112 C1
  Santon Downham IP27 . . . . .6 C2
Hall Farm Cl IP7 . . . . .147 B8
Hall Farm La NR34 . . . . . . .10 E1
Hall Farm Rd
  Boot Street IP13 . . . . .137 E6
  Woodbridge IP12 . . . . .147 B8
Hall Field 1 IP11 . . . . . . .152 E5
Hall La Blundeston NR32 . . .3 A4
  Bressingham IP22 . . . . .19 D5
  Brinkley CB8 . . . . .59 F1
  Burston & Shimpling IP21 . .21 A6
  Burwell CB5 . . . . .44 A6
  Claydon IP6 . . . . .134 E8
  Harwich CO12 . . . . .107 A1
  Hawkedon CO10 . . . . .76 C7
  Otley IP6 . . . . .69 C2
  Oulton NR32 . . . . .112 C4
  Redgrave IP22 . . . . .36 A8
  Ridgewell CO9 . . . . .89 D3
  Risby IP28 . . . . .47 A5
  Roydon IP22 . . . . .20 A3
  Scole IP21 . . . . .21 C4
  Shelfanger IP22 . . . . .20 B6

Hall La *continued*
  Somersham IP8 . . . . .81 C3
  Spexhall IP19 . . . . .24 E4
  Wetheringsett-cum-Brockford
    IP14 . . . . .53 B4
  3 Witnesham IP6 . . . . . . .81 C4
  Yaxley IP23 . . . . .37 B4
Hall Pond Way IP11 . . . . .152 D5
Hall Rd Barnardiston CB8 . .75 B5
  Barsham NR34 . . . . .8 F3
  Bedingfield IP23 . . . . .54 A7
  Belchamp Walter CO10 . . . .91 A3
  Blundeston NR32 . . . . .112 C8
  Borley CO10 . . . . .91 D5
  Brent Eleigh CO10 . . . . . . .79 A3
  Brockdish IP21 . . . . .22 A3
  Burston & Shimpling IP22 . .20 E7
  Carlton Colville NR33 . . . .114 B2
  Charsfield IP13 . . . . .69 E6
  Chelsworth IP7 . . . . .79 E2
  Cowlinge CB8 . . . . .75 A7
  Earsham NR35 . . . . .7 E4
  Ellingham NR35 . . . . .8 C7
  Foxhall IP10 . . . . .141 E4
  7 Hopton on Sea NR31 . . . .3 B7
  Hundon CO10 . . . . .75 C3
  8 Kessingland NR33 . . . . .11 C1
  Lavenham CO10 . . . . .78 D4
  Little Bealings IP5 . . . . . . .137 E2
  Lowestoft NR32 . . . . .112 D1
  Marlesford IP13 . . . . .71 C5
  Mount Bures CO8 . . . . . . .101 C3
  Parham IP13 . . . . .71 B7
  Pulham St Mary IP21 . . . . .22 E8
  Stowmarket IP14 . . . . .124 B8
  Thorndon IP23 . . . . .53 C7
  Wenhaston with Mells Hamlet
    IP19 . . . . .42 D5
Hall Rise CO10 . . . . .148 A3
Hall St
  Long Melford CO10 . . . . . . .91 E8
  Soham CB7 . . . . .28 D8
Hall Wlk IP8 . . . . .81 F1
Hall's La IP21 . . . . .50 B5
Hallfields IP27 . . . . .109 C7
Halifax Pl IP29 . . . . .77 F7
Halliwell Rd IP4 . . . . .140 B6
Halls Drift IP5 . . . . .141 B6
Hallwong La IP20 . . . . . . .22 D7
Hallwyck Gdns CB8 . . . . .120 E7
Halton Cres IP3 . . . . .140 C1
Hamblin Rd IP12 . . . . . . .147 A5
Hamblin Wlk IP12 . . . . . .147 A5
Hambling's Piece NR16 . .18 C8
Hambrook Cl IP30 . . . . . . .63 F7
Hambros The 3 IP9 . . . . . .99 D4
Hamilton Ct CB8 . . . . . . .120 E7
Hamilton Gdns IP12 . . . . .153 A3
Hamilton Rd
  Felixstowe IP11 . . . . .153 A4
  Ipswich IP3 . . . . .140 B3
  Lowestoft NR32 . . . . .120 D5
  7 Sudbury CO10 . . . . . . .148 D5
Hamilton St
  8 Felixstowe IP11 . . . . . .152 E5
  4 Harwich CO12 . . . . . . .106 F3
Hamilton Way
  Ditchingham NR35 . . . . . . .110 C8
  Stowmarket IP14 . . . . .124 D7
Hamiltons The CB8 . . . . . .120 D7
Hamlet Ct 2 CO8 . . . . . . .101 C4
Hamlet Rd CB9 . . . . .132 F5
Hammond Cl CB8 . . . . . . .120 E6
Hammond's Cnr IP14 . . . . .67 C6
Hammonds Wlk IP12 . . . . .42 C6
Hampstead Ave IP28 . . . .116 B6
Hampton Rd IP1 . . . . .138 F7
Hanchet End CB9 . . . . .74 A1
Hancocks Cl 4 IP16 . . . . .129 D5
Handford Cut IP1 . . . . . . .155 A2
Handford Hall Prim Sch
  IP1 . . . . .139 A6
Handford Rd IP1 . . . . .155 A3
Hankin Ave 18 CO12 . . . .106 C1
Hanmer Ave IP28 . . . . . . .116 C6
Hanmer Wlk IP33 . . . . . . .122 B6
Hanover Cl
  8 Bury St Edmunds IP32 . .123 A8
  Leiston CB8 . . . . .120 E8
  Oulton Broad NR32 . . . . . .113 A1
Hanover Ct CO10 . . . . . . .148 B4
Ha'penny Field 8 IP9 . . . .105 E7
Ha'penny Pier Visitor Ctr*
  CO12 . . . . .107 B3
Harbour Cres 7 CO12 . . . .107 C3
Harbour La IP21 . . . . .23 B6
Harbour Rd IP32 . . . . .112 E1
Harbourage The NR34 . . .111 C5
Harcourt Ave 1 CO12 . . . .107 A2
Harding's La 1 IP31 . . . . . .50 E4
Hardwick Cl IP4 . . . . .140 E5
Hardwick La IP33 . . . . . . .122 F2
Hardwick Mid Sch
  IP33 . . . . .123 B3
Hardwick Pk Gdns
  IP33 . . . . .123 A1
Hardwick Prim Sch
  IP33 . . . . .123 B2
Hardwick Rd
  Haverhill CB9 . . . . .132 F6
  Starston IP20 . . . . .22 C7
Hardy Cl
  2 Brantham CO11 . . . . . .104 E4
  Lowestoft NR33 . . . . .115 A7
Hardy Cres IP1 . . . . .134 F4

Hardy Ct 1 CO10 . . . . . . .148 D8
Hare & Hounds Cnr
  IP6 . . . . .82 F8
Harebell Rd
  Ipswich IP2 . . . . .138 F4
  Red Lodge IP28 . . . . .30 C1
Harebell Way NR33 . . . . .114 C1
Harefield CO10 . . . . .77 E1
Harefield Rd 9 IP19 . . . . . .25 B4
Hares Rd IP7 . . . . .65 D1
Hares Wlk 1 CO10 . . . . . .148 D6
Harewood Terr 7 CB9 . . .132 C5
Hargrave Rd IP29 . . . . . . .125 D3
Hargrave Rd IP29 . . . . . . .62 B6
Harkstead La
  Freston IP9 . . . . .105 F8
  Woolverstone IP9 . . . . . . .144 A1
Harkstead Rd 3 IP9 . . . . .106 A5
Harland St IP2 . . . . .139 C3
Harleston Hill IP21 . . . . . .39 E8
Harleston Mus* IP20 . .22 D6
Harleston Prim Sch
  IP20 . . . . .22 D6
Harleston Rd
  Metfield IP20 . . . . .23 B3
  Pulham Market IP21 . . . . . .21 E8
  Scole IP21 . . . . .21 D5
  Weybread IP21 . . . . .22 D4
Harling Dro IP27 . . . . .6 D3
Harling Rd
  Garboldisham IP22 . . . . . . .18 C6
  North Lopham IP22 . . . . . . .19 A6
  Roydon IP22 . . . . .20 B4
  Thetford IP24 . . . . .16 C6
Harman's La IP20 . . . . .22 C5
Harold Rd NR33 . . . . .115 C6
Harp's Cl Rd NR32 . . . . . .113 B3
Harpclose Rd 2 CO10 . . .148 D6
Harper's Est 9 CO6 . . . . .102 C5
Harper's Hill CO6 . . . . . . .102 C5
Harpers La IP17 . . . . .128 D3
Harrier Rd IP14 . . . . .67 A2
Harrier Cl IP3 . . . . .140 B1
Harrier Way IP14 . . . . .67 A5
Harriers Wlk IP3 . . . . .70 E5
Harrington Ave NR32 . . . .113 C6
Harrington Cl IP33 . . . . . .154 C1
Harris Ave NR32 . . . . .113 C4
Harris Mid Sch NR32 . . . .113 D3
Harrison Gn 3 IP18 . . . . .119 C8
Harrison Gr IP5 . . . . .141 C8
Harrison Rd NR32 . . . . . .112 E1
Harrison Way IP26 . . . . . . .4 F3
Harrisons La IP19 . . . . . . .118 C5
Harrod Cl NR33 . . . . .114 C3
Harrop Dale 10 NR33 . . . .114 E3
Harrow Cl IP14 . . . . .140 A5
Harrow Gn IP29 . . . . .63 D1
Harrow La 2 Benhall IP17 . .72 A7
  Theberton IP16 . . . . .129 A8
Harrow Rd
  Haverhill CB9 . . . . .132 C5
  Troston IP31 . . . . .33 D4
Harry Palmer Cl 1 CB7 . . .29 A4
Hart Cl CB9 . . . . .132 D8
Hart's La CO7 . . . . .103 E1
Hartest Hill IP29 . . . . .77 C6
Hartest La IP29 . . . . .63 C1
Hartest Prim Sch IP29 . . . .77 A7
Hartest Rd IP29 . . . . .63 A1
Hartest Way
  Stowmarket IP14 . . . . .124 F3
  Sudbury CO10 . . . . .148 F4
Hartfield Rd CB8 . . . . .59 F2
Hartington Rd IP15 . . . . .130 A4
Hartismere High Sch
  IP23 . . . . .117 B3
Hartismere Hospl
  IP23 . . . . .117 C3
Hartley St IP2 . . . . .155 B1
Hartree Way IP5 . . . . .141 E7
Harvard Rd 6 IP26 . . . . . . .4 D5
Harvest Cl IP14 . . . . .51 D1
Harvest Dr NR33 . . . . .114 C2
Harvesters Way
  Martlesham IP5 . . . . .141 F6
  2 Martlesham Heath IP5 . .98 A7
Harvey Cl 7 CO11 . . . . . .104 E2
Harvey La IP21 . . . . .21 C5
Harvey's La IP6 . . . . .82 C6
Harwich Int Port CO12 . . .106 F3
Harwich Rd
  Foxash Estate CO11 . . . . .104 A1
  Mistley CO11 . . . . .105 A2
  Ramsey & Parkeston
    CO11 . . . . .105 F1
  Wrabness CO11 . . . . .105 F1
Harwich Town Sta
  CO12 . . . . .107 B3
Harwood Ave IP24 . . . . . . .16 C7
Hascot Hill Barking IP6 . . .125 A1
  Battisford IP14 . . . . .81 A8
Haselmere Cl 3 IP32 . . . .123 D6
Hasketon Rd Burgh IP13 . .83 F6
  Woodbridge IP13 . . . . .146 E6
Haslemere Dr IP4 . . . . . . .139 E7
Haskins Wlk IP5 . . . . .141 E7
Hasse Rd CB7 . . . . .28 E8
Hasted Cl IP33 . . . . .122 C4
Hatchley Cl IP12 . . . . .125 C3
Hatfield Rd IP3 . . . . .140 A3
Hatley Dr CB5 . . . . .44 A6
Hatter St IP33 . . . . .154 B2

Haugh La
Great Ashfield IP31 .....50 F5
Haughley IP14 .....51 D1
Woodbridge IP12 .....146 F6
Haughgate Cl IP12 .....146 F6
Haughley Crawfords CE Prim Sch IP14 .....51 C1
Haughley Dr IP4 .....140 F6
Haughley Pk* IP14 .....51 A1
Haughley Rd IP14 .....66 B7
Hauliers Rd IP11 .....152 D2
Haven Ave NR32 .....113 B3
Haven Cl IP11 .....152 D4
Haven Nature Reserve The* IP16 .....130 F6
Haven Rd IP16 .....129 D5
Haven The IP16 .....73 F6
Havens The IP10 .....144 E7
Havergate Island National Nature Reserve* IP12 .....86 F2
Havergate Rd 3 IP3 .....144 D8
Haverhill & District Local History Ctr* CB9 .....132 E5
Haverhill Arts Ctr* CB9 .....132 E5
Haverhill Bsns Pk CB9 .....132 F3
Haverhill Leisure Ctr CB9 .....132 F6
Haverhill Railway Walks Nature Reserve* CB9 .....133 B4
Haverhill Rd
Haverhill CB9 .....132 F8
Helions Bumpstead CB9 .....88 B5
Kedington CB9 .....133 E8
Steeple Bumpstead CB9 .....88 D5
Haverhill Trade Pk CB9 .....132 F3
Haward St NR32 .....113 C1
Hawbridge IP9 .....150 E4
Hawe's La Norton IP31 .....50 B4
Wicken CB7 .....28 A2
Hawes St IP2 .....155 C1
Hawk End La IP30 .....50 E2
Hawk's La IP29 .....63 A2
Hawke Rd IP3 .....139 E1
Hawker Dr IP5 .....98 A8
Hawkes La IP11 .....152 D6
Hawkins Ct 2 CO10 .....148 D8
Hawkins Rd CO10 .....148 E8
Hawks Mill St IP6 .....125 D5
Hawstead La IP29 .....63 E6
Hawthorn Ave NR33 .....115 A7
Hawthorn Cl
Beccles NR34 .....111 E4
Bury St Edmunds IP32 .....122 D8
Knodishall IP17 .....129 B2
8 Stowupland IP14 .....67 A6
Hawthorn Dr
9 Horringer IP29 .....63 A8
Ipswich IP2 .....138 D2
Hawthorn La 25 IP27 .....13 F2
Hawthorn Pl IP12 .....146 E6
Hawthorn Rd
Haverhill CB9 .....132 B7
Middleton IP17 .....58 A5
Sudbury CO10 .....148 F5
Theberton IP16 .....57 F4
Hawthorn Way CB5 .....44 B6
Hawthorn Wlk 10 IP28 .....30 B8
Hawthorns The 8 IP31 .....49 D4
Hay Barn Meadow 2 IP30 .....50 D1
Haycocks Rd CB9 .....132 A7
Haygate IP23 .....117 C3
Hayhill Rd IP4 .....139 E7
Hayland Dro IP28 .....29 D7
Haylings Gr IP16 .....129 C4
Haylings Rd IP16 .....129 C4
Hayman Rd IP3 .....139 F1
Haynings Mill IP13 .....126 D4
Haysborder Rd IP29 .....46 F3
Haythill La IP26 .....4 D6
Hayward Cl IP23 .....117 D2
Haywards Fields IP5 .....141 D8
Hazel Cl
9 Bentwaters Airfield IP12 .....85 E8
Haverhill CB9 .....132 C5
Mildenhall IP28 .....116 E4
Hazel Covert 4 IP24 .....16 D6
Hazel Ct 6 CO10 .....148 D6
Hazel Dr
10 Horringer IP29 .....63 A8
Ipswich IP3 .....140 E1
Hazel Rise IP6 .....134 C8
Hazelcroft Rd IP1 .....135 B2
Hazels La IP17 .....42 D5
Hazelville Cl 11 CO12 .....106 F1
Hazelwood 1 IP7 .....80 F1
Hazelwood Cl 10 IP31 .....49 D4
Hazelwood Marshes Nature Reserve* IP15 .....73 B4
Hazelwood St IP17 .....130 A7
Hazlitt Rd 6 IP1 .....135 A3
Head La CO10 .....148 F2
Headingham Cl 13 IP2 .....139 A2
Headland Ave CB9 .....132 C5
Headland Dro IP26 .....4 A1
Healey Cl NR32 .....113 A5
Heasman Cl CB8 .....120 F5
Heath Cl
East Bergholt CO7 .....151 D5
Hessett IP30 .....64 F8
Polstead CO6 .....93 F3
Heath Ct 12 IP11 .....107 D8
Heath Dr IP12 .....99 C7
Heath Farm Rd IP28 .....30 B1
Heath La Blundeston NR32 .....3 A4
Ipswich IP4 .....140 C5
Pakenham IP31 .....49 D8
Heath Prim Sch IP5 .....141 B7
Heath Rd Burwell CB5 .....44 C2
East Bergholt CO7 .....151 D5
Exning CB8 .....120 A4
Fritton & St Olaves NR31 .....2 B5
Geldeston NR34 .....9 A7
Hessett IP30 .....64 F8
Ipswich IP4 .....140 C7
Ixworth IP31 .....33 E2
Kenninghall NR16 .....19 A7
Lowestoft NR33 .....114 F8
Mildenhall IP28 .....116 E5
Mistley CO11 .....105 A2
Newmarket CB8 .....121 C3
Norton IP31 .....50 B4
Polstead CO6 .....93 F2
Sapiston IP31 .....34 B7
Swaffham Prior CB5 .....44 A1
Thurston IP31 .....49 D4
Troston IP31 .....33 D4
Wenhaston with Mells Hamlet IP19 .....42 B7
Woolpit IP30 .....50 D1
Heath The
Dedham CO7 .....104 A2
Great Waldingfield CO10 .....92 C6
Woolpit IP30 .....65 F8
Heath View
Ipswich IP5 .....141 A6
Leiston IP16 .....129 E5
Heath Way CO10 .....92 C6
Heath Wlk IP12 .....72 A4
Heathbell Rd CB8 .....121 C3
Heather Ave IP3 .....140 C2
Heather Cl
1 Great Barton IP31 .....49 D4
Martlesham Heath IP5 .....141 F6
Heather Rd NR32 .....113 D4
Heather Way
Brandon IP27 .....6 A1
Worlingham NR34 .....111 F3
Heathercroft Rd IP1 .....135 A3
Heatherhayes IP2 .....139 A3
Heatherset Way IP28 .....30 C1
Heathfield IP5 .....141 F6
Heathfield Mews IP5 .....141 F6
Heathfield Rd 9 IP9 .....105 E7
Heathfields IP11 .....98 D1
Heathgate Piece IP11 .....152 C8
Heathlands Pk IP4 .....140 E4
Heathside Specl Sch IP4 .....140 D6
Hedley La NR33 .....114 A3
Heigham Dr NR33 .....114 F5
Heights The NR34 .....111 C4
Heldhaw Rd IP32 .....123 E5
Helena Rd IP3 .....139 E4
Helens Cl 2 IP22 .....36 A8
Helions Bumpstead Rd CB9 .....132 D3
Helions Pk Ave CB9 .....132 E5
Helions Pk Gdns 8 CB9 .....132 E5
Helions Pk Rd 7 CB9 .....132 E5
Helions Rd CB9 .....88 D4
Helions Service Rd 3 CB9 .....132 E5
Helions Wlk CB9 .....132 E5
Helmingham Hall & Gdns* IP14 .....69 A4
Helmingham Prim Sch IP14 .....69 B6
Helmingham Rd IP6 .....69 C2
Helston Cl IP5 .....141 B7
Hemmant Way NR34 .....9 B7
Hemplands The 2 NR32 .....113 D2
Hempnall Rd NR35 .....7 A8
Hempstead Rd CB9 .....132 A7
Hen Reed Bed Nature Reserve* IP18 .....43 B8
Hencote La
Horringer IP29 .....63 C8
Nowton IP33 .....123 B1
Henderson Cl
Bramford IP8 .....134 A1
Haverhill CB9 .....132 A7
Hengrave Cl 11 IP2 .....139 A2
Hengrave Hall* IP28 .....48 A7
Hengrave Rd IP28 .....48 B6
Henham Rd NR32 .....113 A5
Henley Ave IP1 .....135 B3
Henley Cl IP17 .....128 C3
Henley Prim Sch IP6 .....82 E6
Henley Rd Henley IP6 .....82 D5
Ipswich IP1 .....155 B4
Henniker Rd
3 Debenham IP14 .....53 F2
Ipswich IP1 .....138 C8
Henny Rd CO8 .....101 A7
Henry Cl CB9 .....132 B4
Henry Rd IP3 .....140 B1
Henry St IP14 .....53 E2
Henry Ward Rd 1 IP20 .....22 D6
Henry Watson's Potteries* IP22 .....35 D5
Henslow Rd IP4 .....140 B5
Henstead Gdns IP3 .....140 A2
Hepworth Ave IP33 .....122 D5
Hepworth Rd
Barningham IP31 .....34 F7
Hepworth IP22 .....35 A7
Stanton IP31 .....34 E4
Hepworth Rd *continued*
Thelnetham IP22 .....35 B7
Herbert Cl CO10 .....148 E8
Herbert Human Cl 3 CB7 .....28 D4
Herbert Rd IP5 .....141 E8
Hereford Dr 14 IP6 .....82 B5
Hereward Ave IP28 .....116 C5
Hereward Way
5 Feltwell IP26 .....4 D5
Littleport CB7 .....12 B7
Weeting-with-Broomhill IP27 .....5 E3
Heritage Gn 6 NR33 .....11 B1
Heritage Workshop Ctr* NR32 .....113 E3
Herivan Cl NR32 .....112 E4
Herivan Gdns 6 NR32 .....112 E4
Hermitage Ct IP13 .....126 B3
Hermitage Meadows CO10 .....76 B1
Herolf Way 11 IP20 .....22 D6
Heron Cl
5 Mildenhall IP28 .....13 B1
Stowmarket IP14 .....124 A6
Heron Ct CB7 .....28 C5
Heron Hill IP14 .....66 C6
Heron Rd
Bury St Edmunds IP33 .....123 B2
Ipswich IP2 .....138 E3
Saxmundham IP17 .....128 B3
Herons Cl NR32 .....112 D2
Herring Fishery Score 2 NR32 .....113 E1
Herring Mkt 14 NR32 .....115 D8
Herringfleet Drainage Mill* NR32 .....2 B4
Herringfleet Rd NR31 .....2 B5
Herringswell Rd
Herringswell IP28 .....30 D2
Kentford CB8 .....46 A6
Hertford Cl 19 IP32 .....48 C5
Hertford Pl IP15 .....130 E3
Hertford Rd 5 CO10 .....76 A1
Hertfords Pl IP12 .....86 D7
Hervey Cl 6 IP9 .....107 A5
Hervey Rd IP33 .....122 E3
Hervey St Ipswich IP4 .....155 C4
Lowestoft NR32 .....115 C8
Hessett Cl IP14 .....124 F3
Hethersett Cl CB8 .....120 E8
Heveningham Long La IP17 .....41 A1
Heveningham Rd IP19 .....40 C5
Hewitt Rd
15 Harwich CO12 .....106 E1
19 Ramsey CO12 .....106 E1
Hexham Cl 3 IP2 .....139 A2
Heycroft Way 4 CO6 .....102 C5
Heyford Ct 8 IP28 .....116 B5
Heyford Rd 12 IP31 .....33 D5
Heywood Ave IP22 .....20 C3
Heywood Cl IP2 .....138 D1
Heywood Rd IP22 .....20 C4
Hibbard Rd IP8 .....134 C2
Hickford Hill CO10 .....90 B7
Hickling Dr IP33 .....123 B1
Hicks Way CB9 .....133 C3
High Baxter St IP33 .....154 B2
High Beach IP11 .....153 C4
High Beech NR32 .....113 B2
High Comm Rd IP22 .....18 F5
High Ct IP20 .....22 E6
High Gn IP16 .....129 C6
High Hall Cl 2 IP11 .....107 D8
High House Farm Rd IP12 .....131 D8
High House La IP7 .....79 B5
High La IP14 .....53 B6
High Leas NR34 .....111 C3
High Leas Cl 2 NR34 .....111 C3
High Lighthouse Wireless Mus* CO12 .....107 C3
High Lodge Visitor Ctr Thetford Forest Pk* IP27 .....15 C7
High London La IP22 .....20 A8
High Rd Badingham IP13 .....56 C6
Bressingham IP22 .....19 F4
Felixstowe IP11 .....152 B8
Great Finborough IP14 .....66 A2
Kettleburgh IP13 .....55 B2
Leavenheath CO6 .....102 A7
Needham IP20 .....22 B3
Roydon IP22 .....20 A3
Swilland IP6 .....83 A7
Trimley St Martin IP11 .....98 C1
Wortwell IP20 .....23 A7
High Rd E IP11 .....153 B5
High Rd W IP11 .....152 F5
High Row Field IP11 .....153 C5
High St Acton CO10 .....92 B7
Aldeburgh IP15 .....130 E3
Ashley CB8 .....60 F8
Brandon IP27 .....5 F1
Brinkley CB8 .....59 F1
5 Bures CO8 .....101 C5
Burwell CB5 .....44 A5
Cavendish CO10 .....76 E1
Cheveley CB8 .....60 E8
Chippenham CB7 .....45 C8
Clare CO10 .....90 A8
Debenham IP14 .....53 F2
Dedham CO7 .....103 F3
Dunwich IP17 .....43 B1
Felixstowe IP11 .....152 E6
Feltwell IP26 .....4 E5
Flowton IP8 .....81 C1
High St *continued*
Gislingham IP23 .....36 D2
Great Yeldham CO9 .....90 A1
Hadleigh IP7 .....149 D6
Harwich CO12 .....107 B2
Haverhill CB9 .....132 E5
Hemingstone IP6 .....68 C1
Hitcham IP7 .....79 F4
Hopton IP22 .....18 C2
Ipswich IP1 .....155 B3
Ixworth IP31 .....34 B1
Kessingland NR33 .....11 B1
Lakenheath IP27 .....109 C6
Langham CO4 .....103 B2
Lavenham CO10 .....78 D4
Laxfield IP13 .....40 B3
Leiston IP16 .....129 C6
Long Melford CO10 .....77 E1
7 Lowestoft NR32 .....113 E2
Manningtree CO11 .....104 E2
Mildenhall IP28 .....116 C4
Nayland CO6 .....102 D5
Needham Market IP6 .....125 D5
Newmarket CB8 .....120 F2
Orford IP12 .....131 C2
Pettistree IP13 .....127 C5
Rattlesden IP30 .....65 D6
St Margaret, Ilketshall NR35 .....24 D7
Saxmundham IP17 .....128 D3
Soham CB7 .....28 D4
Southwold IP18 .....119 D5
Sproughton IP8 .....138 A6
Stansfield CO10 .....76 C6
Stetchworth CB8 .....60 A5
Thelnetham IP22 .....18 E1
Thorndon IP23 .....53 C8
Tuddenham IP28 .....30 F2
Tuddenham St Martin IP6 .....136 B5
Wangford with Henham NR34 .....26 B2
Wicken CB7 .....28 A1
Wickham Market IP13 .....127 C7
Wrentham NR34 .....26 E5
Yoxford IP17 .....57 D8
High St Ex Gall* IP1 .....155 B3
High View Rd IP1 .....134 D1
Higham Hill IP7 .....103 D8
Higham Race Course CO7 .....103 D7
Higham Rd
Higham CO7 .....103 D6
Tuddenham IP28 .....31 A1
Highbridge Gravel Dro IP27 .....109 B7
Highbury Cres IP33 .....122 E5
Highbury Rd IP33 .....122 E5
Highbury Way CO10 .....148 F4
Highclere Cl CB8 .....120 D8
Higher Dr NR32 .....112 F2
Highfield
Blythburgh IP19 .....42 F6
Clare CO10 .....90 B8
Eye IP23 .....117 C3
Highfield App 1 IP1 .....134 F1
Highfield Ave CO12 .....107 A2
Highfield Cl NR33 .....114 B1
Highfield Dr IP6 .....134 D8
Highfield Rd
Felixstowe IP11 .....153 A4
Halesworth IP19 .....118 B2
Ipswich IP1 .....134 F2
6 Stowupland IP14 .....67 A6
Sudbury CO10 .....148 E7
Highfields Bentley IP9 .....104 F7
Great Yeldham CO9 .....90 A1
Lakenheath IP27 .....109 E6
Highfields Dr IP27 .....109 D6
Highgate La IP13 .....70 B2
Highgrove Cl NR32 .....113 A3
Highland Dr NR34 .....111 E4
Highland Way NR33 .....114 F6
Highlands IP27 .....109 E6
Highlands Cl IP6 .....125 C5
Highlands Rd
Hadleigh IP7 .....149 E5
Monks Eleigh IP7 .....79 C4
Highlands The CB8 .....120 D8
Highview Cl CO10 .....148 C8
Highwood Cres CB8 .....46 B2
Highwood La CO10 .....92 E5
Highwood Rd CB8 .....46 B2
Hildesley Ct NR33 .....115 B4
Hill Cl
6 Long Melford CO10 .....91 E8
Newmarket CB8 .....120 E3
Hill Cres CB9 .....132 E7
Hill Farm La 9 IP9 .....106 C8
Hill Farm Rd
Grundisburgh IP13 .....83 D6
Halesworth IP19 .....118 C3
Playford IP6 .....137 B4
Rendham IP17 .....56 E4
Hill House Gdns NR33 .....115 C5
Hill House La IP6 .....125 C6
Hill House Rd IP4 .....139 E5
Hill La CB9 .....133 D1
Hill of Health (Tumulus)* IP28 .....32 D2
Hill Rd Lowestoft NR32 .....113 C1
Southwold IP18 .....119 C6
Wangford with Henham NR34 .....26 B1
Westley IP33 .....122 A5
Hill Rise IP14 .....124 D3
Hill St 20 IP26 .....4 E5
Hill The North Cove NR34 .....10 C4
Hill The *continued*
Shipmeadow NR34 .....8 F4
Tuddenham St Martin IP6 .....136 C5
Westleton IP17 .....58 C8
Hill Top IP31 .....34 E5
Hill View CB8 .....61 C4
Hill View Bsns Pk IP6 .....134 D6
Hillary Cl IP4 .....140 A5
Hillcrest IP17 .....129 A3
Hillcrest App IP8 .....134 B2
Hillcrest Cl 3 NR34 .....111 E3
Hillcrest Dr NR32 .....113 B4
Hillcrest Gdns NR32 .....113 B3
Hillcrest Rd
Beccles NR34 .....111 B3
Sudbury CO10 .....148 C8
Hillcroft Prep Sch IP14 .....51 D2
Hillrise Cl NR34 .....111 E3
Hillside Brandon IP27 .....14 D8
Stowmarket IP14 .....124 D3
Hillside Ave NR34 .....111 E4
Hillside Com Prim Sch IP2 .....139 C3
Hillside Cres 5 IP3 .....140 B3
Hillside Ct 1 NR35 .....110 C2
Hillside Meadow CB7 .....29 B1
Hillside Rd
Southwold IP18 .....119 C7
Sudbury CO10 .....148 E5
Hillside Rd E NR35 .....110 D3
Hillside Rd W NR35 .....110 B2
Hillside Specl Sch CO10 .....148 D7
Hillside Way IP19 .....118 B5
Hilltop Gn NR32 .....113 A4
Hilltop Rise 2 NR34 .....111 E3
Hilltop Way IP31 .....34 E5
Hilly Cl IP31 .....33 F5
Hilly Fields IP12 .....146 E4
Hilton Cl 15 CO11 .....104 E2
Hilton Rd Ipswich IP3 .....140 C1
Martlesham Heath IP5 .....98 A8
Hinderclay La IP22 .....18 E1
Hinderclay Rd
Redgrave IP22 .....19 A1
Rickinghall Inferior IP22 .....35 F6
Hines Rd IP3 .....140 A4
Hintesham Cl 6 IP4 .....140 F5
Hintlesham & Chattisham CE VCP Sch IP8 .....95 C6
Hintlesham Cl 3 IP14 .....124 E3
Hintlesham Dr IP11 .....152 D4
Histon Cl IP5 .....140 F7
Hitcham Cswy IP7 .....79 E6
Hitcham Rd
2 Debenham IP14 .....53 F2
Wattisham IP7 .....80 B6
Hitcham's La NR34 .....26 E4
Hitchcock Pl CO10 .....148 C7
HMS Ganges Mus* IP9 .....107 B4
Hobart Cl NR32 .....112 E3
Hobart Way NR32 .....112 E3
Hobbies La IP14 .....52 D4
Hobbs Dr CO4 .....103 A3
Hobbs La CO10 .....77 B2
Hobland Rd
Belton with Browston NR31 .....2 F8
Bradwell NR31 .....3 A8
Hocket Cres IP12 .....71 F2
Hockey Hill IP14 .....53 A5
Hockney Gdns IP3 .....144 A8
Hockwold Prim Sch IP26 .....5 A2
Hodgkinson Rd IP11 .....152 C3
Hodson Cl 6 IP32 .....122 E8
Hoe La CO10 .....90 F8
Hog La
St Lawrence, Ilketshall NR34 .....24 F6
Wenhaston with Mells Hamlet IP19 .....42 C5
Westhall NR34 .....25 A6
Hogarth Rd IP3 .....139 F1
Hogarth Sq IP3 .....140 A1
Hogarth Wlk NR32 .....113 B6
Hogg La
Bury St Edmunds IP33 .....154 B1
Earsham NR35 .....7 C5
Hoggars Rd IP14 .....52 C4
Hogsty La IP21 .....22 A5
Holbecks La IP7 .....149 C4
Holbein Way 2 NR32 .....113 B6
Holborn Ave IP28 .....116 B6
Holbrook Barn Rd 6 CO10 .....93 C3
Holbrook Cl 11 CO10 .....92 C6
Holbrook Cres IP11 .....152 D4
Holbrook High Sch IP9 .....105 E8
Holbrook Prim Sch IP9 .....105 E7
Holbrook Rd
Haverhill CB9 .....132 C4
Holbrook IP9 .....106 A5
Ipswich IP3 .....139 F1
Lowestoft NR32 .....112 F4
Stutton IP9 .....105 D5
Holcombe Cres IP2 .....138 D2
Holdans La IP17 .....56 D2
Holdans Meadow IP17 .....56 E2
Holden Cl Ipswich IP2 .....139 D3
Lowestoft NR32 .....112 C1
Holden Rd IP28 .....31 F1
Holderness Rd IP32 .....123 C7
Holeywall La IP31 .....35 A1
Holfen Cl IP12 .....84 B1

Holkham Cl 7 IP4 ....140 F5
Holkham Mead 1 CB5 ...34 B5
Holland Pk CB8 ....60 E8
Holland Rd
  Felixstowe IP11 ....152 F3
  Ipswich IP4 ....139 F6
Holland Rise IP19 ....41 A4
Holland's La NR35 ....7 C7
Hollands Bsns Ctr The
  CB9 ....132 E4
Hollands Rd CB9 ....132 E4
Hollands Rd Ind Est
  CB9 ....132 E4
Hollesley Ave CB9 .....132 A6
Hollesley Prim Sch
  IP12 ....99 F7
Hollesley Rd
  Hollesley IP12 ....99 D7
  Rendlesham IP12 ....85 D7
Holliday Cl IP32 ....123 F7
Hollingsworth Rd
  Lowestoft NR32 ....113 C3
  3 Stowmarket IP14 ....124 E5
Hollow Gr Way NR33 ...114 C4
Hollow Hill IP6 ....74 A2
Hollow Hill Rd NR35 ...110 B7
Hollow La
  Badingham IP13 ....56 C6
  Barningham IP31 ....34 F8
  Bures St Mary CO8 ....101 C6
  Carlton Colville NR33 ..114 C4
  6 Chelmondiston IP9 ..106 C8
  Coney Weston IP31 ......18 A1
  Earl Soham IP13 ....54 F3
  Mendham IP20 ....23 C4
  Thurston IP31 ....49 F3
  Tostock IP30 ....50 A2
Hollow Rd Ashen CO10 ..89 F6
  Bury St Edmunds IP32 ..154 B1
  Copdock & Washbrook
  IP8 ....95 E4
Hollow Way Hill NR34 ....9 D8
Hollowell Cl 3 NR32 ...112 E4
Hollows The IP6 ....64 F7
Holly Blue Cl IP14 .....142 E8
Holly Bush Cnr CO7 ...103 E7
Holly Cl Beccles NR34 ..111 E3
  5 Haughley IP29 ....63 A8
  6 Red Lodge IP28 ......30 B1
  Warren Heath IP3 .....140 E1
Holly Ct 34 IP20 ....22 D6
Holly End IP5 ....141 F6
Holly Gr NR34 ....111 C4
Holly La NR32 ....112 C3
Holly La Belstead IP8 ..142 C7
  Great Horkesley CO6 ...102 E2
  Lakenheath IP27 ....109 D5
  Little Bealings IP13 ...137 D5
  Rushmere St Andrew
  IP5 ....136 E2
  Stutton IP9 ....105 C6
Holly Oaks 2 CO6 .....101 F2
Holly Rd
  4 Great Bricett IP7 ...80 D6
  Ipswich IP1 ....155 A4
  Lowestoft NR32 ....112 E1
  Willisham IP8 ....81 A5
Holly Wlk 8 IP28 ....30 B8
Hollybush Pl IP13 .....153 D7
Hollybush La IP30 ......64 D6
Hollycroft Cl 5 IP1 ...135 A3
Hollydene Cl IP22 .....112 D2
Holm Cl 4 NR34 ....9 F4
Holme Cl IP22 ....18 C2
Holme's Hill IP17 ......41 A1
Holmere Dr IP19 ....118 A3
Holmes La 5 CB7 ....28 D5
Holmsey Gn
  Beck Row, Holywell Row
  & Kenny Hill IP28 ......13 C1
  Mildenhall IP28 ....30 B8
Holmsey Gn Gdns 7
  IP28 ....30 B8
Holst Cl NR33 ....115 A6
Holst Mead IP14 ....124 C8
Holt Rd CO6 ....93 E2
Holt's La IP6 ....125 F6
Holt's Rd CO6 ....102 A2
Holton Ave NR32 ....112 C4
Holton Rd IP19 ....118 C3
Holton St Peter Postmill*
  IP19 ....118 E4
Holton St Peter Prim Sch
  IP19 ....118 E4
Holton Terr IP19 ......118 C4
Holy Wells Rd IP3 .....139 E3
Holyhouse Drift 1 IP9 ..49 A6
Holyrood Cl IP12 ......106 F1
Holyrood IP7 ....138 T1
Holywell Cl IP33 ......123 A3
Holywell Dro IP28 .....123 A7
Holywells High Sch
  IP3 ....140 C1
Home Cl CB9 ....88 E4
Home Farm La IP33 ....123 A1
Home Farm Rd NR35 .....8 C7
Home Meadow 4 IP13 ...40 B3
Home Piece IP22 ....35 A8
Homefield Boxford CO10 .93 C3
  Capel St Mary IP9 ....150 F3
Homefield Ave
  8 Beccles NR34 ....111 B5
  Lowestoft NR33 ....114 F6
Homefield Paddock
  NR34 ....111 B5

Homefield Rd CB9 .....132 C4
Homefield Rd Ind Est
  CB9 ....132 C4
Homeport NR32 ....113 E3
Homer Cl IP1 ....134 F4
Homestall Cres CB9 .....74 A2
Homestead Dr 2 IP29 ...28 D8
Homestead The NR33 ...114 D3
Homey Bridge Rd CO6 ..93 E1
Honey Hill IP33 ....154 C1
Honey La CO6 ....102 B6
Honeymeade Cl 25 IP21 .34 E4
Honeypot La
  Kelsale cum Carlton IP17 .57 E4
  Mendham IP20 ....23 C4
  Monewden IP13 ....69 F4
  Wattisfield IP22 ....35 D4
Honeypot Meadow 2
  NR35 ....110 B3
Honeysuckle Cl
  Haverhill CB9 ....132 C7
  8 Lowestoft NR33 .....115 A3
  4 Red Lodge IP28 .....46 A8
  5 Soham CB7 ....28 D4
Honeysuckle Gdns
  IP2 ....138 E4
Honeysuckle Way 4
  IP32 ....123 E6
Honington CE VC Prim Sch
  IP31 ....33 F5
Honington Rise IP31 ...33 E5
Hoo La IP13 ....71 E4
Hood Dr IP6 ....81 F5
Hood Rd IP3 ....139 E1
Hood's La NR34 ....25 F7
Hook La IP7 ....149 F4
Hooper Sq IP33 ....122 C6
Hop Meadow CO7 ....151 B4
Hope Cres IP12 ....147 A6
Hopelyn Cl 4 NR32 ....113 B4
Hopper Way IP22 ....20 E2
Hopton CE VC Prim Sch
  IP22 ....18 C1
Hopton Fst Sch NR31 ....3 C6
Hopton Gdns IP22 ....18 C1
Hopton Rd
  Barningham IP31 ....34 F8
  Thelnetham IP22 ....18 D1
Hopton Rise CB9 ......132 A6
Horham Rd IP21 ....38 E1
Horkesley Hill CO6 ...102 D4
Horkesley Rd CO6 .....115 C7
Horn Hill NR33 ....115 C7
Horn La CB8 ....60 D3
Hornbeam Cl
  Beccles NR34 ....111 E4
  Rosedale Park NR33 ..114 F4
Hornbeam Dr IP29 ......63 A8
Hornbeam Rd
  Mildenhall IP28 ....116 E5
  2 Stowupland IP14 .....67 A6
Horringer Ct Mid Sch
  IP33 ....122 D3
Horringer Rd IP29 ....122 D2
Horsecroft IP29 ......122 E1
Horsecroft Rd
  Bury St Edmunds IP33 .122 F2
  Horringer IP29 ....63 C8
Horsefair IP30 ....50 D1
Horsefair Cl IP14 ......52 E4
Horseheath Rd CB9 ....74 A2
Horseshoe Dr IP28 .....30 C1
Horseshoe Cl CB9 .....132 C5
Horsham Ave IP3 ......140 D3
Horsham Cl IP3 ....132 A7
Hospital Rd
  Bury St Edmunds IP33 .154 A1
  Orford IP12 ....131 B6
Hossack Rd IP3 ....144 A8
Hotson Rd IP19 ....119 D6
Houghton Dr
  Hopton on Sea NR31 ....3 B6
  Oulton NR32 ....112 E4
Houghton Pl 1 IP4 ...140 F5
Houghtons La IP7 ......29 D5
Houldsworth Terr CB8 .120 F3
Houldsworth Valley Prim Sch
  CB8 ....120 F3
How Hill (Tumulus)*
  IP27 ....31 B7
Howard 2
  8 Framlingham IP13 ..126 C3
  Harleston IP20 ....22 E6
  Haverhill CB9 ....132 B5
Howard Com Prim Sch
  IP32 ....122 E6
Howard de Walden Way
  CB8 ....121 A4
Howard Mid Sch
  Bury St Edmunds IP32 ..48 B5
  Fornham All Saints IP28 .122 D8
Howard Rd 1 NR35 ....110 D3
Howard St IP4 ....140 B7
Howards Way IP5 .....141 D8
Howe Ave IP3 ....140 C3
Howe La Cockfield IP30 .64 C1
  Thornham Parva IP23 ...37 A3
Howe Rd CB9 ....132 D7
Howes Ave IP3 ....140 D4
Howlett Cl IP5 ....141 E7
Howlett Way IP24 ......16 B7
Howley Gdns NR32 ....113 A6
Hoxne Cl 5 IP14 ......124 E3
Hoxne Rd Eye IP23 ....117 E2
  Hoxne IP23 ....38 D3
  Syleham IP21 ....38 A4
  Upper Weybread IP12 ..22 B2
Hoxter Way CO10 .....148 C8

Hoylake Cl 6 IP28 .....48 C6
Hubbard's Ave 2 NR32 .113 C6
Hubbard's Hill IP17 ....41 B1
Hubbard's La IP17 .....80 B1
Hubbard's Loke NR32 ..113 C6
Hubbards Cl IP17 .....128 B4
Hudson Cl
  10 Harwich CO12 ......107 A1
  Haverhill CB9 ....133 A4
Hudson Way 6 IP29 ....47 A2
Huggins Cl IP28 ....30 C1
Huggins La IP23 ....37 B1
Hugh Ager Cl 5 IP14 ..124 D3
Hughes Cnr CO7 ......151 A6
Hughes La CO7 ....151 B6
Hull St IP27 ....109 F1
Hulver La IP17 ....72 C6
Hulver Rd NR34 ....9 F2
Humber Doucy La IP4 .136 A2
Humber Doucy Sports Ctr
  IP4 ....140 D7
Hummingbird Cl IP32 ...49 A3
Humphry Rd CO10 .....148 C6
Hundon Cl CB8 ....75 B6
Hundon Pl 6 IP29 .....132 F6
Hundon Prim Sch
  CO10 ....75 D3
Hundon Rd
  Hundon CO10 ....75 B1
  Kedington CB9 ....133 F8
Hundred La
  Boxted CO4 ....103 B2
  Old Newton with Dagworth
  IP14 ....51 F3
Hungate NR34 ....111 B5
Hungate Cl NR34 .....111 B5
Hungate La NR34 .....111 B5
Hungerdown La CO11 ..104 B1
Hunston Rd IP31 ....50 E7
Hunt Cl
  5 Redenhall with Harleston
  IP20 ....22 D6
  Stowmarket IP14 .....124 D3
Hunter Dr
  10 Manningtree CO11 ..104 D2
  8 Thurstow IP31 ....49 D4
Hunter Rd
  Bury St Edmunds IP32 .122 D8
  Honington IP31 ....33 D5
  2 Ipswich IP3 ....144 C8
Hunter's Chase CO7 ...63 A7
Hunter's La IP20 ....23 A3
Hunters End IP11 .....152 C7
Hunters La IP20 ....23 B2
Hunters Ride 21 IP5 ...98 A8
Huntingdon Cl 9 NR33 .115 A3
Huntingfield Rd
  Bury St Edmunds IP33 .122 C4
  Cratfield IP19 ....40 D5
  Leiston IP16 ....129 C5
Huntley Cres IP10 ....118 C5
Hunts Hill CO10 ....77 A2
Hurdle Dro IP28 ....29 F8
Hurdle Makers Hill IP8 .95 F6
Hurn Crag Rd IP18 ...119 C7
Hurricane Pl IP3 .....140 B1
Hurstlea Ct IP6 ....125 D5
Hurstlea Rd IP6 ......125 D5
Hurth Way IP24 ....16 C6
Hurts Croft 3 IP12 ....29 A1
Hut Hill (Tumulus)*
  IP31 ....17 E3
Hutland Rd IP4 ....140 C3
Hutton Ct IP23 ....117 D3
Hyam's La IP7 ....105 E7
Hyams La IP7 ....105 E7
Hyde Rd CO10 ....148 C5
Hydewood Rd CO9 .....90 A2
Hyem's La IP11 ....153 B7
Hyntle Cl IP7 ....141 D3
Hyperion Way CB8 ....120 D8
Hythe Cl 9 CB5 ....44 A6
Hythe La CB5 ....44 A6
Hythe IP26 ....4 C7

Ice House Quay NR32 .114 E8
Iceni Way CB8 ....120 B8
Icepits Cl IP31 ....49 C6
Icewell Hill CB8 .....121 A4
Ickleton Pl IP32 ....82 B2
Icklingham Rd IP28 ....32 B2
Icknield Cl 3 CB8 .....60 E7
Icknield Way IP26 ....16 B5
Ickworth Cres IP14 ..140 F5
Ickworth Cl 2 IP11 ...153 A5
Ickworth Dr IP33 ....154 A1
Ickworth House Pk & Gdn*
  IP29 ....62 F8
Ickworth Pk Prim Sch
  IP29 ....63 A8
Ickworth Vineyard*
  IP29 ....62 E6
Ilex Cl IP33 ....123 A3
Iliffe Way IP14 ....124 D3
Imperial Mews NR31 ....3 B6
Impson Way IP26 ......6 A8
Ingate NR34 ....111 C4
Ingestre St 1 CO12 ..107 B2
Ingham Rd
  Haverhill CB9 ....132 E6
  West Stow IP28 ....32 C1
Ingram's Rd IP21 .....21 F3
Ingram's Well Rd
  CO10 ....148 D5
Inkerman Cl 4 IP7 ...149 D6

Inkerman Row 4 CO10 .148 C6
Inkerman Terr 3 IP7 ..149 D6
Innes End IP32 ....138 C2
Inverness Rd IP4 .....136 A2
Inverness Way NR34 ...26 A8
Inworth La CO6 ....101 B1
Ion Rd 1 IP32 ....122 E8
Ipswich Ave 3 IP12 ....85 B3
Ipswich Cl 1 IP12 .....85 B3
Ipswich Ct IP33 ......154 B3
Ipswich High Sch IP9 .144 C2
Ipswich Hospl IP4 ....140 C7
Ipswich Mus* IP1 ....155 B3
Ipswich Pre Prep Sch
  IP14 ....68 B6
Ipswich Prep Sch IP1 .155 B3
Ipswich Rd
  Brantham CO11 ....104 E5
  Charsfield IP13 ....70 B2
  Claydon IP6 ....134 C8
  Dedham CO4 ....103 D3
  East Bergholt CO7 ....151 A6
  Elmsett IP7 ....95 A8
  Grundisburgh IP13 .....83 E5
  Hadleigh IP7 ....149 F7
  Harkstead IP9 ....106 A6
  Holbrook IP9 ....105 E8
  Lowestoft NR32 ....113 D3
  Nacton IP10 ....145 A5
  Needing-with-Naughton
  IP7 ....80 C4
  Needham Market IP6 ..125 E4
  Newbourne IP12 ....98 C6
  Orford IP12 ....131 B4
  Otley IP6 ....69 B2
  2 Scole IP21 ....20 F1
  Scole NR15 ....21 C7
  Stowmarket IP14 .....124 E4
  Stratford St Mary CO7 .103 E4
  Tattingstone White House
  IP9 ....142 D1
  Waldringfield IP12 ....98 D7
  Willisham IP8 ....81 B4
  Winston IP14 ....53 F1
  Witnesham IP6 ....136 A8
  Woodbridge IP12 .....146 E3
  Yaxley IP23 ....37 B4
Ipswich Sch IP1 ......155 B4
Ipswich St
  Bury St Edmunds IP33 .154 B3
  Lakenheath IP27 ......109 F1
  Stowmarket IP14 .....124 D6
Ipswich Transport Mus*
  IP3 ....140 C2
Ipswich Way IP14 ......68 E6
Ireland Rd IP3 ....139 F1
Irex Rd NR33 ....115 B3
Iris Cl IP2 ....138 F5
Irlam Rd IP2 ....138 D2
Isaacson Rd CB8 ....44 B4
Isinglass Cl CB8 .....124 E2
Isleham Rd CB7 ....29 E8
Ivry St IP1 ....155 A4
Ivy Cl IP33 ....114 C7
Ivy La NR33 ....114 C7
Ivy Lodge Rd IP12 .....71 D1
Ivytree La IP7 ....94 C7
Ixer La IP30 ....64 E3
Ixworth Abbey IP31 ....34 A1
Ixworth CE Prim Sch
  IP31 ....34 B1
Ixworth Mid Sch IP31 ..34 B1
Ixworth Rd
  Haverhill CB9 ....132 C4
  Honington IP31 ....33 F5
  Stowlangtoft IP31 .....50 B6
  Troston IP31 ....33 D3
  Walsham le Willows IP31 .35 A1

J

Jack Jarvis Cl 5 CB8 ..121 A3
Jack's Gn Rd IP5 .....125 E6
Jack's La IP14 ....124 A2
Jacks Gn IP6 ....125 E7
Jackson Cl IP5 ....141 F7
Jackson Rd IP2 ....98 C5
Jackson Way IP5 .....125 D4
Jacob Way 11 IP12 ...147 A5
Jacobs Cl IP33 ....34 E4
Jacobs Meadow IP30 ...65 D5
Jacobs St 7 NR32 ....113 C6
Jacqueline Cl
  Bury St Edmunds IP33 .154 A1
  7 Grundisburgh IP13 ..83 E5
James Boden Cl 7
  IP11 ....152 E5
James Carter Rd IP30 .116 A6
Jameson Pl 8 CO10 ..148 A6
Janet Hadenham Cl 11
  NR34 ....9 F4
Janus Cl IP1 ....133 B4
Jaques Cl 3 CO10 .....77 B3
Jarman Cl IP33 ......123 C3
Jarman's La IP28 .....29 F7
Jarrold Cl 1 IP31 ....34 F7
Jarvis Way IP18 .....120 C5
Jasmine Cl
  9 Felixstowe IP11 ....107 D8
  Ipswich IP2 ....138 F3
Jasmine Gn NR32 .....113 A5
Java Lodge Rd IP12 ..127 B3
Jay Cl CB9 ....133 A5
Jay La NR32 ....3 A6
Jay's Gn IP20 ....22 E6
Jay's Hill Rd
  Ellough NR34 ....10 B2

Jay's Hill Rd continued
  Willingham St Mary NR34 .26 A8
Jays Croft Rd 2 IP12 ...85 E8
Jaywick Rd 2 CB9 .....132 E6
Jeaffresons Well IP6 ..126 D4
Jeannie Mann Ct
  NR32 ....113 B3
Jeavons La IP5 ....141 E8
Jefferies Rd IP4 .....139 E6
Jellicoe Ave NR33 ....114 D6
Jenkins Gn NR32 ......113 A5
Jenkinsons Pightle
  NR35 ....7 B8
Jenner Cl NR35 ....110 C2
Jenners Cl 1 IP22 ....147 B6
Jennings Way IP22 .....23 C3
Jermyn Ave IP32 ......123 F5
Jermyn Way IP19 .....118 A2
Jermyns Cl IP9 ....150 F4
Jermyns Rd IP18 .....119 B8
Jervis Cl 10 IP19 .....105 E7
Jewell View IP5 ......141 D8
Jim Mollison Cl 8 IP28 .106 B5
Jimmy's Farm* IP9 ...142 E5
Jimmy's La CO11 .....104 F5
Jocelyn Cl 18 IP22 ....48 C5
Jockey's La Combs IP14 ..66 C2
  Framsden IP14 ....69 B7
Joes Rd CO10 ....92 C3
John Childs Way
  NR35 ....110 C2
John Lawrence Cl
  NR34 ....111 B2
John Russell Gall*
  IP3 ....155 C2
John Shepherd Rd 1
  IP21 ....39 D8
John St Leiston IP16 .129 C5
  Lowestoft NR33 ....115 C7
  Rose Hill IP3 ....139 C4
John Swain Cl IP6 ....125 E6
John Tibauld Ct 4 CB9 .88 D3
Johnson Cl 5 IP2 .....139 C3
Johnson Rd 7 IP29 ....47 A2
Johnson Way NR32 ....113 A5
Jolly's Way IP1 ....35 C1
Jones Rd CO10 ....76 C3
Jordan Cl IP29 ....125 E7
Jordan Rise IP7 ....149 F6
Joshua Ct 5 IP11 .....153 B8
Josselyns The IP11 ...152 B8
Jovian Way IP1 ....138 E8
Joyce Rd NR35 ....110 D3
Jubilee Ave IP14 .....124 D4
Jubilee Cl IP12 ....128 C5
Jubilee Cl 11 Claydon IP6 .82 B5
  10 Harwich CO12 .....106 F1
  25 Isleham CB7 ....29 E8
  2 Laxfield IP13 ....40 B3
  4 Thetford IP24 ....16 B5
  Weeting IP27 ....25 E7
Jubilee Cres IP14 ......67 A7
Jubilee Ct CB8 ....60 A5
Jubilee Ctr IP28 .....116 C3
Jubilee End 8 CO11 ..104 E3
Jubilee Rd
  Bungay NR35 ....110 B2
  Lakenheath IP27 ......109 C8
  Lowestoft NR33 ....115 A2
  Sudbury CO10 ....148 D6
Jubilee Terr 17 IP30 ...50 F2
Jubilee Way
  Lowestoft NR32 ....113 E2
  Mildenhall IP28 ....116 C4
Judas La IP13 ....37 B5
Judith Ave IP17 ......129 B2
Julian Cl CB9 ....133 B5
Julian Way 12 NR31 ....3 B7
Julius Martin La CB7 ..28 E4
Junction Rd IP28 .....116 B5
June Ave Ipswich IP1 .135 B2
  Lowestoft NR32 ....113 B2
Juniper Cl IP28 ....116 E5
Juniper Rd IP28 ....30 C1
Jupe's Hill CO6 ....101 B1
Jupes Hill CO7 ....104 B3
Jupiter Cl CB9 ....133 B4
Jupiter Rd IP4 ....140 B7
Justinian Cl IP1 .....133 B4

K

Karen Cl Ipswich IP1 .135 B1
  4 Scole IP21 ....20 F1
Kate's La IP14 ....51 A1
Katwijk Way 2 NR32 ..115 D8
Keating Cl 2 CO11 ...104 D2
Keats Cl IP17 ....128 B4
Keats Cres IP1 ....134 F3
Kebbles 3 CO10 ....77 A3
Kedington Hill CO10 ...92 A1
Kedington Prim Sch
  CB9 ....133 E8
Kedington Rd CB9 ....133 D3
Keebles Yd 5 CB9 ....132 C6
Keel Cl NR33 ....114 B4
Keeling La IP13 ....56 C5
Keep Rise NR33 ......110 B4
Keeper's La
  Marlesford IP13 ....71 D5
  Stoke-by-Nayland CO6 .102 C8
  Trimley St Mary IP11 .152 A7
Keightley Way IP6 ...136 B5

Kell's Acres NR34 .... 8 F7
Kell's Way NR34 .... 8 F6
Kelly Rd IP2 .... 138 E5
Kelly-Pain Ct NR32 ..... 113 D3
Kelsale CE VCP Sch
IP17 .... 128 C5
Kelso Rd IP33 .... 122 D2
Kelvedon Dr IP4 .... 140 F5
Kelvin Pl IP4 .... 16 A4
Kelvin Rd IP1 .... 134 F1
Kemball St IP4 .... 140 A5
Kembold Cl IP32 .... 123 E5
Kemps La NR34 .... 111 B3
Kempshorne Cl NR32 ... 112 C4
Kempson Dr 2 CO10 .... 92 B3
Kempson Way IP30 ..... 123 F4
Kempsters The IP11 .... 152 D7
Kempton Cl 4 IP1 ...... 135 A3
Kempton Cross NR34 ... 111 C4
Kempton Rd IP1 .... 135 A3
Kemsley Rd IP11 .... 152 F5
Kendal Gn IP11 .... 153 D7
Kendal Rd NR33 .... 115 B5
Kennedy Ave IP19 ...... 118 A1
Kennedy Cl
Halesworth IP19 .... 118 B1
Ipswich IP4 .... 140 A6
Kennedy Rd 9 CB7 ...... 29 C5
Kennedy St IP27 .... 109 E1
Kennel Loke NR31 .... 3 B8
Kennels La IP13 .... 146 C8
Kennels Rd
Brightwell IP10 .... 98 A6
Foxhall IP10 .... 141 F2
Kennetside 61 B1
Kennett Prim Sch CB8 ... 45 F6
Kennett Rd or Moulton
CB8 .... 45 F3
Kennett Sta CB8 .... 45 F6
Kenney Cl IP8 .... 95 D7
Kenninghall Prim Sch
NR16 .... 19 A8
Kenninghall Rd NR16 .... 19 A7
Kennyhill Dro IP28 ...... 13 A3
Kensington Rd
Ipswich IP1 .... 139 A8
Lowestoft NR33 .... 115 C5
Stowmarket IP14 ...... 124 D5
Kent Rd Lackford IP28 ... 31 F1
Lowestoft NR32 .... 113 B1
Stowmarket IP14 ...... 124 C7
Kentford Rd 5 IP11 .... 152 C4
Kenton Rd IP1 .... 53 F2
Kents La Bungay NR35 ... 110 D3
Soham CB7 .... 28 D4
Kentwell Cl IP4 .... 140 F4
Kentwell Hall* CO10 ... 77 E2
Kentwell Pl 3 CB5 ...... 44 B5
Kenyon Cl 7 CO7 .... 103 E5
Kenyon Dr 9 CO10 ...... 92 C6
Kenyon Row NR34 .... 9 B6
Kenyon St IP2 .... 17 A2
Keppie Way 12 IP20 ..... 22 D6
Kerridge's Cut 16 CO11 . 105 A2
Kerridges NR16 .... 18 C8
Kerrison Con Ctr IP23 ... 37 D1
Kerrison Rd NR35 ...... 110 D2
Kerry Ave IP1 .... 134 D1
Kerrys Farm La IP14 .... 51 F4
Kersey CE Prim Sch
IP7 .... 94 A6
Kersey Cl IP4 .... 124 E3
Kersey Rd IP11 .... 152 D4
Kersey Hall La IP31 ..... 39 A3
Kesgrave Dr NR32 ..... 112 F2
Kesgrave High Sch
IP5 .... 141 C8
Kessingland CE VCP Sch
NR33 .... 11 C2
Kesteven Rd IP2 .... 155 A1
Kestrel Cl
1 Beck Row, Holywell
Row & Kenny Hill IP28 ... 13 B1
Thetford IP24 .... 16 C4
Kestrel Dr IP14 .... 67 A5
Kestrel Gn NR33 .... 114 C6
Kestrel Rd
Bury St Edmunds IP33 ... 123 B2
Haverhill CB9 .... 133 A5
Ipswich IP2 .... 138 D3
Keswick Cl IP11 ...... 153 C6
Kettle La IP6 .... 67 E1
Kettlebaston Way 3
IP1 .... 135 A1
Kettleborrow Cl 21 IP31 . 34 B1
Kettleburgh Rd IP13 ... 126 C1
Kettlefields CP Sch
CB8 .... 59 F5
Kevington Dr NR32 .... 112 C2
Key St IP3 .... 155 C2
Keynes Way 18 CO12 ... 106 F1
Khartoum Rd IP4 ...... 139 F7
Kidz Kingdom* IP5 ..... 98 A8
Kilbourn Rd 3 NR33 .... 115 A3
Kilbrack NR34 .... 111 C5
Kilbrack Gdns NR34 ... 111 C5
Kildare Ave IP11 ...... 152 D4
Kilmaine Rd 22 CO12 .. 106 F1
Kiln Bottom IP7 ...... 149 E8
Kiln Cotts IP4 .... 124 C5
Kiln Dr CO10 .... 148 E4
Kiln Farm La IP14 ..... 35 F5

Kiln Field 1 IP11 .... 152 D5
Kiln La Benhall IP17 ... 128 C1
Boot Street IP13 ...... 137 E6
Buxhall IP14 .... 65 F3
Dickleburgh & Rushall
IP21 .... 21 C2
Elmswell IP30 .... 50 E1
Friston IP17 .... 72 D7
1 Mistley CO11 .... 104 F2
Needham IP20 .... 22 D6
Rede IP29 .... 62 E4
Stowlangtoft IP31 ...... 34 E1
Kiln Rd NR34 .... 26 C3
Kilverstone Rd IP24 .... 17 A6
Kimberley Rd NR33 .... 115 A4
Kimms Belt IP24 .... 16 B5
King Edward Ave
IP13 .... 127 C7
King Edward Rd
Ipswich IP3 .... 140 B3
Leiston IP16 .... 129 C6
King Edward VI Sch
IP33 .... 154 A3
King Edward VII Dr
IP9 .... 107 A4
King Edward VII Rd
CB8 .... 120 E5
King George Ave CB8 ... 120 B8
King George's Ave
3 Halesworth CO12 ... 107 A2
Leiston IP16 .... 129 E6
King St Aldeburgh IP15 . 130 E3
Felixstowe IP11 .... 152 E6
Ipswich IP1 .... 155 B3
1 Mildenhall IP28 ..... 116 C4
Sudbury CO10 .... 148 C5
Weybread IP21 .... 22 D3
King William St 3 IP6 .. 125 D5
King's Ave IP13 .... 126 B5
King's Dam NR34 ...... 9 B6
King's Head St 2 CO12 . 107 C3
King's Hill CB8 .... 133 E7
King's La Blyford IP19 .. 42 C8
Gosbeck IP6 .... 68 D3
Long Melford CO10 .... 92 A7
Sotherton NR34 .... 25 D2
Tannington IP13 .... 55 B7
Walsham le Willows IP31 . 35 C3
Weston NR34 .... 9 D1
King's Rd
Bury St Edmunds IP33 . 154 A2
Harwich CO12 .... 107 A2
Topcroft NR35 .... 7 A8
King's Theatre CB8 .... 120 F3
King's Way IP4 .... 140 D2
Kingfisher Ave IP2 .... 138 D3
Kingfisher Cl CB9 ..... 133 A6
Kingfisher Cres IP18 .. 119 A7
Kingfisher Dr
6 Burwell CB5 .... 44 A6
Claydon IP6 .... 81 F5
13 Harwich CO12 ..... 106 F1
Kingfisher Leisure Ctr
CO10 .... 148 D4
Kingfisher Rd 3 IP2 ... 123 F7
Kingfisher Rise IP17 .. 128 C4
Kingfisher Way
Mildenhall IP28 .... 116 D4
6 Stowmarket IP14 .... 67 A5
Kings Ave IP4 .... 139 E5
Kings Cl 7 Acton CO10 . 92 B7
1 Manningtree CO11 .. 104 F2
Mildenhall IP28 .... 116 D5
Woodbridge IP12 ..... 146 E4
Kings Dr CB8 .... 121 B1
Kings Fleet Prim Sch
IP11 .... 153 C6
Kings Fleet Rd IP11 ... 152 E3
Kings Head La IP22 .... 19 A6
Kings Hill CO10 .... 148 E4
Kings Mead CB8 .... 60 E8
Kings Meadow
Great Cornard CO10 ... 148 E4
Kedington CB9 .... 133 E7
Kings Parade CB7 ...... 28 D3
Kings Pk IP29 .... 62 D5
Kings Rd Bungay NR35 . 110 C2
Glemsford CO10 .... 77 A3
Leiston IP16 .... 129 C5
Kingsbury Rd IP11 .... 152 C7
Kingsfield Ave IP1 .... 139 D8
Kingsgate Dr IP4 ..... 139 F8
Kingshall St IP30 ...... 64 D8
Kingsland IP9 .... 106 F5
Kingsland La 3 CO6 ... 102 A7
Kingsley Cl 8 IP7 ..... 135 A3
Kingsmead Cl 3 IP4 .. 124 C2
Kingsmead Rd IP14 ... 124 C7
Kingston Cl NR33 ..... 115 A3
Kingston Dr NR34 .... 111 C5
Kingston Farm Rd
IP12 .... 147 A4
Kingston Pas 5 CB8 .. 121 A3
Kingston Rd
Ipswich IP1 .... 138 F8
Woodbridge IP12 ..... 147 A4
Kingsway 4 Earsham NR35 . 7 F4
Mildenhall IP28 .... 116 B2
Newmarket CB8 .... 120 D6
Woodbridge IP12 ..... 147 A4
Kingswood Ave NR33 . 114 D4
Kingsworth Rd CO10 . 148 A2
Kinross Rd IP4 .... 136 B1
Kipling Cl 5 NR33 ..... 11 C1
Kipling Rd IP1 .... 134 F3

Kipling Way IP14 ...... 124 B8
Kirby Cane Wlk NR32 .. 113 A3
Kirby Cl IP4 .... 140 A7
Kirby St IP4 .... 140 A7
Kirkdale Ct 4 NR33 ... 115 B4
Kirkham Cl 2 IP22 .... 139 A2
Kirkley Cliff Rd NR33 . 115 C5
Kirkley Gdns NR33 ... 115 B6
Kirkley High Sch
NR33 .... 115 A6
Kirkley Mid Sch NR33 . 115 B7
Kirkley Pk Rd NR33 ... 115 B6
Kirkley Run NR33 ..... 115 A7
Kirkley Sports & Fitness Ctr
NR33 .... 115 B7
Kirkley St NR33 .... 115 C5
Kirton Rd IP33 .... 122 D3
Kirkstone Way 4 NR32 . 113 A4
Kirkton Cl IP7 .... 107 A5
Kirkwood Dr 1 NR33 .. 114 C3
Kirtling Pl 3 CB9 ..... 132 F6
Kirtling Rd CB8 .... 60 E5
Kirton Rd IP11 .... 107 D8
Kitchen Hill CO10 ..... 91 D4
Kitchener Rd
Ipswich IP1 .... 138 F8
Leiston IP16 .... 129 C6
Kitchener Way 5 IP7 .. 107 A5
Kitson Meadows IP33 . 122 A5
Kittiwake Cl
Ipswich IP2 .... 138 E3
Lowestoft NR33 ...... 114 D5
Klondyke IP32 .... 123 A6
Knaves Acre Dro CB7 ... 29 B6
Knettishall Heath Ctry Pk*
IP31 .... 17 C3
Knight Rd IP12 .... 85 D8
Knights Cl
7 Debenham IP14 ..... 53 F2
10 Felixstowe IP11 ... 153 D6
6 Manningtree CO11 . 104 E2
15 Old Newton with Dagworth
IP14 .... 51 E1
Knights Ct
10 Haverhill CB9 ..... 132 C5
Roman Hill NR33 ..... 113 C1
Knights La 5 IP5 ...... 141 D7
Knights Yd NR34 ...... 26 C3
Knightsdale Rd IP1 ... 135 A1
Knightswood 8 IP30 .. 64 D8
Knoll The IP13 .... 126 D3
Knowle The 17 NR34 .. 34 E4
Knox La IP31 .... 34 C4
Knutsford Cl IP2 ...... 138 C1
Kreswell Gr 7 CO12 ... 107 A1
Kylborne Cl IP7 .... 122 C4
Kyson Hill* IP12 ...... 146 F2
Kyson Prim Sch IP12 .. 146 D4

L

La Salle Cl IP2 .... 139 B3
Laburnum Ave IP28 ... 116 E5
Laburnum Cl
Ipswich IP8 .... 138 C2
5 Red Lodge IP28 ..... 30 B1
Worlingworth IP13 ..... 54 E7
Laburnum Dr IP3 ..... 140 C8
Laburnum Gdns IP5 .. 141 C5
Laburnum La 11 CB5 . 44 A6
Laburnum Rd 3 IP15 . 110 B3
Laburnum Way 1 CO6 . 102 C5
Lacewing Cl 15 IP8 ... 142 E8
Lacey St IP4 .... 139 E6
Lacey's La CB8 .... 120 B7
Lachlan Gn IP12 ...... 146 F7
Lackford La IP28 ...... 47 D6
Lackford Pl 7 IP1 .... 134 F4
Lackford Wildfowl Nature
Reserve* IP28 .... 31 F1
Lacon Rd 2 IP6 .... 134 A2
Ladbrook Cl IP7 ...... 80 E1
Lady La Hadleigh IP7 . 149 E7
Ipswich IP1 .... 155 A3
Lady La Ind Est IP7 ... 149 E6
Lady Margaret Gdns
IP13 .... 146 D4
Lady St 18 CO10 ...... 78 D4
Lady's La IP22 .... 19 F5
Lady's Meadow NR34 . 111 B6
Ladyfield IP14 .... 66 D8
Ladygate 1 CB9 ...... 132 C4
Ladywell Rd IP14 ..... 51 F7
Ladywood Rd IP4 .... 140 C7
Lagonda Dr IP1 .... 134 C1
Lake Ave IP32 .... 48 C5
Lake Side IP14 .... 124 C6
Lake View Rd IP14 ... 114 E8
Lakeland 3 IP26 ...... 5 A3
Lakeland Dr NR32 .... 112 F1
Lakeside Rise 112 C6

Lakforth 4 CO10 ...... 91 E8
Lamarsh Hill 1 CO8 ... 101 C5
Lamarsh Rd CO8 ..... 101 A6
Lamb Ct IP28 .... 116 D2
Lambert Cl
Halesworth IP19 ..... 118 B3
Weeting IP27 .... 5 E4
Lambert Dr CO10 ..... 92 B7
Lambert's La
Mendlesham IP14 ..... 52 C3
Sudbourne IP12 .... 73 B1
Lambert's Way NR35 .. 110 C6
Lamberts Cl 21 IP26 .. 4 E5
Lamberts La IP5 ...... 136 D2
Lambeth Cl IP7 .... 139 A7
Lambeth Way IP11 ... 67 F7
Lamble Ct IP28 ...... 30 B8
Lambourne Cl 3 IP32 . 123 E6
Lambourne Rd IP1 ... 135 B4
Lambs La IP29 .... 63 D1
Lambsale Meadow
IP17 .... 128 D4
Lambseth St IP23 ... 117 C3
Lamdin Rd IP32 ...... 48 C5
Lamdon Cl IP31 ...... 34 A4
Lanark Rd IP4 .... 136 B1
Lancaster Ave IP32 .. 122 F8
Lancaster Cl IP29 .... 62 C4
Lancaster Dr 8 IP5 .. 98 A7
Lancaster Rd
5 Feltwell IP26 .... 4 E5
Ipswich IP4 .... 139 E6
7 Mildenhall IP28 .... 30 A8
Sudbury CO10 .... 148 B8
Lancaster Way
10 Claydon IP6 .... 82 B5
Stradishall CB8 ...... 75 C7
Lancers The IP12 .... 146 E3
Lancewood Wlk 7 IP27 . 13 F7
Lancing Ave IP4 ..... 140 A8
Landguard Fort*
IP11 .... 107 E2
Landguard Nature Reserve*
IP11 .... 107 E2
Landguard Rd IP11 .. 153 I11
Landsdown Rd CO10 . 148 E7
Landseer Cl IP3 ..... 140 A1
Landseer Ct 1 CB9 .. 132 D4
Landseer Rd IP3 .... 139 E2
Landspring La NR33 . 114 C6
Landwade Rd CB8 ... 44 D6
Lane The
Creeting St Peter or West
Creeting IP6 .... 67 B5
3 Mistley CO11 ...... 104 F2
Wrentham NR34 ...... 26 E5
Yoxford IP17 .... 57 C8
Lanercost Way IP2 .. 139 A1
Langdale Cl 3 IP11 .. 153 D6
Langdale Pk NR32 ... 113 A4
Langer Prim Sch IP11 . 152 E2
Langer Rd IP11 ...... 152 E2
Langford Cl IP14 .... 124 B8
Langham La CO4 .... 103 B1
Langham Rd
Blaxhall IP12 .... 72 B4
Boxted CO4 .... 102 F1
Langham Way CB9 ... 74 A1
Langley Ave IP11 .... 152 E4
Langley Cl IP11 ...... 152 C6
Langley Gdns NR33 . 114 F5
Langmere Rd IP21 .. 21 C4
Langridge The IP11 .. 34 B2
Langstons IP11 ...... 152 D7
Langton Rd 4 IP33 .. 122 D4
Lanman Mus* IP13 .. 126 C4
Lansbury Rd IP19 .. 118 B3
Lansdowne Rd
Ipswich IP4 .... 153 B6
Lowestoft NR33 ..... 140 A5
Lanwades Bsns Pk CB8 . 46 A5
Lapwing Cl 17 IP31 . 49 D4
Lapwing Ct 1 IP28 .. 116 D4
Lapwing Rd IP2 ..... 138 D3
Lapwing Way CB7 ... 28 C5
Larch Cl IP14 .... 124 B8
Larch Gr 13 CO6 .... 102 C5
Larch Rd NR33 ..... 113 B3
Larchcroft Cl IP1 ... 135 B2
Larchcroft Rd IP1 .. 135 A2
Larches The NR34 .. 25 E6
Larchwood Cl IP8 .. 138 C6
Largent Gr IP5 ..... 141 E8
Lark Cl
4 Stowmarket IP14 .. 67 A5
Worlington IP28 ...... 30 B4
Lark Hill CB8 .... 45 F3
Lark Rise
28 Martlesham Heath IP5 . 98 A8
Sudbury CO10 .... 148 B3
Lark Valley Dr 6 IP28 . 48 C6
Larkhall Rd IP4 ..... 140 D8
Larkhill Rise IP4 .... 140 D8
Larkhill Way 9 IP11 . 152 D5
Larks Cl CB9 .... 133 A5
Larks Gate IP19 .... 118 C3
Larks Rise IP19 .... 118 C3
Larksfield Cres 5 CO12 . 107 A1
Larkspur Cl
Corton NR32 .... 113 B8
1 Red Lodge IP28 ... 30 B1
Larkspur Rd IP2 .... 138 D3
Larksway IP11 ...... 152 D3

Larters La IP14 ...... 67 D8
Lathbury Ct IP33 ... 154 B3
Lattens Sq 4 NR32 . 113 C2
Lattice Ave IP4 ..... 140 C6
Laud Mews IP3 ..... 140 A2
Laud's Cl IP11 ...... 152 B8
Laundry La
Bury St Edmunds IP33 . 123 B3
Huntingfield IP19 .... 41 A4
Laureate Com Prim Sch
CB8 .... 120 E6
Laureate Gdns CB8 . 120 E6
Laureate Paddocks
CB8 .... 120 E6
Laureate Sch Rd CB8 . 120 E6
Laurel Ave
1 Harwich CO12 ..... 106 F1
Ipswich IP5 .... 141 A7
Laurel Cl Haverhill CB9 . 132 B7
7 Red Lodge IP28 ... 30 C1
8 Thurstow IP31 .... 49 D4
Laurel Ct 9 IP30 .... 50 F2
Laurel Dr 7 IP13 ... 126 C7
Laurel Rd 4 CO10 .. 82 A5
Laurel Way 8 IP6 .. 134 C8
Laurel Way 5 IP6 .. 134 C8
Laurelhayes IP2 .... 139 A3
Laurels The
8 Hopton on Sea NR31 . 3 B7
Worlingham NR34 ... 111 F3
Lavender Cl 3 IP28 . 30 B1
Lavender Hill IP22 . 138 F4
Lavenham Guildhall of
Corpus Christi* CO10 . 78 E4
Lavenham Prim Sch
CO10 .... 78 D4
Lavenham Rd
Great Waldingfield CO10 . 78 D1
Ipswich IP2 .... 138 E5
Lavenham Way
6 Lowestoft NR32 ... 112 F3
4 Stowmarket IP14 . 124 E3
Law's Drift IP14 .... 98 C2
Lawn Gr NR12 ..... 112 F5
Lawn Way IP11 ..... 152 E5
Lawns The IP4 ..... 140 C8
Lawrence Dr NR32 . 113 B6
Lawrence Rd 2 IP24 . 16 D7
Lawshall Rd
Hartest IP29 .... 77 B8
Hawstead IP29 ..... 63 D4
Lawshall Row IP29 . 63 D2
Lawson Cl 2 NR33 . 115 C7
Lawson Pl IP33 .... 123 E5
Lawson Rd NR33 .. 115 C7
Laxfield & District Mus*
IP13 .... 40 B3
Laxfield Rd
Badingham IP13 .... 56 B8
Dennington IP13 ... 55 E6
Fressingfield IP21 .. 39 F7
Laxfield IP13 .... 40 C1
Stradbroke IP21 .... 39 E4
Laxfield Way NR33 . 114 F4
Layer Rd CB9 ...... 132 C5
Layham Dr 3 IP32 . 123 A8
Layham Gdns IP7 . 124 F3
Layham Rd IP7 .... 149 D4
Layhill Cl IP32 .... 123 D5
Laywood Cl 1 IP32 . 123 D6
Layzell Croft CO10 . 92 B2
Le Grice Wlk IP32 . 122 E7
Lea The IP8 .... 138 F1
Lea's Drift 8 NR33 . 114 C5
Leabrook Cl IP32 .. 123 B6
Leader's Way CB8 . 120 E4
Leas The IP11 ..... 152 F5
Leather La
Great Yeldham CO9 . 90 A1
Haverhill CB9 .... 132 C5
Leathes Cl NR32 .. 112 F1
Leathes Ham Nature
Reserve* NR32 .... 113 A1
Lee Cl IP28 .... 132 D8
Lee Rd Aldeburgh IP15 . 130 E3
Harwich CO12 ...... 107 B2
Ipswich IP3 .... 139 F3
Leech Wlk IP32 ... 122 E8
Leeks Cl IP7 .... 80 D2
Leeks Hill IP12 .... 147 A7
Leggatt Dr IP8 .... 134 A2
Leicester Cl IP2 ... 138 F1
Leighton Rd IP3 ... 144 A8
Leighton Sq 8 IP3 . 144 A8
Leiston Abbey* IP16 . 58 C3
Leiston High Sch IP16 . 129 E5
Leiston Leisure Ctr
IP16 .... 129 E5
Leiston Mid Sch IP16 . 129 C6
Leiston Prim Sch
IP16 .... 129 C6
Leiston Rd
Aldeburgh IP15 ..... 130 D7
Coldfair Green IP17 . 129 A3
4 Lowestoft NR33 . 113 D1
Theberton IP16 .... 58 B5
Leisure Way NR32 . 113 B7
Lely Rd IP3 .... 143 F8
Lemons Hill IP9 ... 105 B8
Lentins The IP14 . 68 E6
Leona Cres NR33 . 114 C2
Leonard Dr 7 IP32 . 123 B6
Leonard's La IP26 . 4 D5
Leopold Gdns IP4 . 140 B8
Leopold Rd
Felixstowe IP11 ... 153 A3
Ipswich IP4 .... 140 B7

Leslie Rd IP3 ....140 C1
Lester Piggott Way
 CB8 ....120 F6
Letton Cl IP9 ....150 E3
Leverett's La IP18 ....119 B2
Levington Ct NR33 ....115 D8
Levington La IP10 ......98 A3
Levington Rd
 Felixstowe IP11 ......152 E1
 Ipswich IP3 ....140 A4
 Nacton IP10 ....145 C4
Lewes Cl IP3 ....140 E3
Lewis Cl
 Ditchingham NR35 ....110 C8
 Hopton IP22 ....140 A4
Leys La IP23 ....37 B5
Ley Rd Barrow IP29 ....47 A2
 Stetchworth CB8 ......60 A5
Leys La IP23 ....37 B5
Leys Rd IP30 ....50 B2
Leyton Ave IP28 ......116 B6
Liberty Cl IP32 ....123 F6
Liberty Intermediate Sch
 IP27 ....14 A3
Lidgate Ct [1] IP11 ....152 C4
Lidgate Rd CB8 ....61 C8
Lighthouse Score [2]
 NR32 ....113 E3
Lilac Cl IP27 ....14 D8
Lilac Dr
 Lakenheath IP27 ......109 D6
 Lowestoft NR32 ......113 C3
Lilac Wlk IP6 ....125 D3
Lilley Cl IP33 ....122 C3
Lily La NR34 ....9 D4
Lily Way NR33 ....114 C5
Lime Ave
 Harwich CO12 ....107 A2
 Lowestoft NR32 ......113 C3
Lime Cl Burwell CB5 ....44 B5
 [6] Harleston IP20 ....22 D5
 Lakenheath IP27 ......109 D5
 Mildenhall IP28 ......116 E5
 [6] Ufford IP13 ....84 F7
 Wickham Market IP13 ..127 B6
Lime Gr CO10 ....148 A3
Lime Kiln Quay IP12 ..147 B5
Lime Kiln Quay Rd
 IP12 ....147 B5
Lime Tree Ave IP16 ....129 C5
Lime Tree Cl [3] IP30 ..64 F8
Lime Tree Pl IP14 ......124 E5
Lime Wlk IP30 ....65 A3
Limecroft Cl [1] IP11 ..135 A3
Limekiln Cl [7] IP6 ....134 C8
Limerick Cl IP3 ....134 E2
Limes Ave IP6 ....133 E5
Limes The
 Framlingham IP6 ......126 B4
 Halesworth IP19 ......118 A3
 [6] Horringer IP29 ....63 A8
 Long Melford CO10 ....91 E8
 Rushmere St Andrew
 IP5 ....136 D1
Limestone Cl [2] CB7 ..29 C5
Limetree Cl IP6 ....125 E4
Limetree Dr IP3 ....140 D2
Limmer Ave IP21 ......21 C5
Lincoln Ave IP17 ......128 B2
Lincoln Cl IP1 ....135 B3
Lincoln Ct [1] NR31 ....3 B7
Lincoln Gdns [5] IP6 ..82 B5
Lincoln Gn IP33 ......123 B2
Lincoln La CO6 ....102 E1
Lincoln Rd [10] IP28 ..30 A8
Lincoln Terr IP11 ......152 F3
Linda Cl IP32 ....3 D4
Lindbergh Rd IP3 ......146 C1
Linden Cl
 Aldeburgh IP15 ......130 D6
 [20] Manningtree CO11 ..104 D2
Linden Rd IP15 ....130 C5
Linden Wlk IP28 ....13 B1
Lindisfarne Cl IP2 ....139 A1
Lindisfarne Rd IP33 ..122 D2
Lindsey Ave CO10 ......148 F4
Lindsey Rd IP4 ....134 E4
Lindsey Way IP14 ......124 E3
Ling Rd Palgrave IP22 ..20 B2
 Wortham IP22 ....19 F2
Ling's La IP9 ....106 B7
Lingfield Rd IP1 ......135 B4
Lingheath Rd IP27 ......6 A1
Lings Field IP13 ....70 C7
Lingside [1] IP5 ....98 A7
Link La IP9 ....104 E7
Link Rd
 Capel St Mary IP9 ....150 E3
 [7] Shotley Gate IP9 ..107 A5
Link The IP9 ....104 E7
Links Ave IP11 ....153 B6
Links Cl
 Bury St Edmunds IP33 ..123 B1
 Lowestoft NR33 ......114 F5
 Worlington IP28 ......30 B4
Links Rd
 Great Yarmouth NR31 ..3 B8
 Lowestoft NR32 ......113 D5
Links The Flempton IP28 ..32 B1
 Woodditton CB8 ......59 E8
Links View CO10 ....92 D3
Linksfield IP4 ....134 F3
Linksfield Gdns IP5 ..140 E7
Linkwood Rd IP30 ......64 B7
Linnet Dr [14] IP14 ....67 A5
Linnet La IP33 ....154 C1
Linnet Rd
 Bury St Edmunds IP33 ..123 E4

Linnet Rd continued
 Ipswich IP2 ....138 D4
Linnetts La CO10 ......133 E2
Linstead Rd IP19 ......40 F5
Linton Cl CB8 ....120 F5
Linton Gdns IP33 ......122 E3
Linton Pl [2] CB9 ......132 F6
Linx The [6] IP13 ......40 B3
Lion La IP6 ....125 E3
Lion Meadow CB9 ......133 D8
Lion Rd Glemsford CO10 ..77 A3
 Palgrave IP22 ....20 B1
 Wortham IP22 ....36 F8
Lion St IP1 ....155 B3
Lionel Hurst Cl [15] CO10 ..92 B3
Lisburn Rd CB8 ....121 B3
Lister Rd Hadleigh IP7 ..149 F5
 Ipswich IP1 ....134 F1
Liston La CO10 ....147 A5
Lithgo Paddock [8] IP31 ..49 A6
Little Back La [8] IP14 ..53 F2
Little Fen Dro CB5 ......44 A7
Little Gipping St IP1 ..155 A3
Little Gn Cheveley CB8 ..60 E6
 Earl Soham IP13 ......54 F1
 Elmswell IP30 ....50 E2
Little Gn Cl IP23 ......36 C3
Little Gr IP23 ....150 E2
Little Gulls IP9 ....150 D3
Little Hall* CO10 ......78 E4
Little Hasse Dro IP14 ..28 E6
Little Horkesley Rd
 CO6 ....102 A2
Little Hyde Cl CO9 ....90 A1
Little Hyde Rd CO9 ....90 A1
Little London Hill IP14 ..53 E3
Little London La IP7 ..29 B5
Little Lumpkid IP7 ....149 E8
Little Meadows Dr IP6 ..69 C2
Little Mill La IP29 ....47 A3
Little Oulsham Dro IP26 ..4 B6
Little St IP17 ....57 C8
Little St John's St [8]
 IP12 ....147 A5
Little St Mary's CO10 ..91 E7
Little Tufts IP9 ....150 F3
Little Whip St IP2 ....155 B1
Little Yeldham Rd CO10 ..90 B2
Little's Cres IP2 ......155 B1
Littlemoor Rd IP7 ......57 E6
Livermere Drift IP31 ..48 E6
Livermere Rd
 Great Barton IP31 ....49 A6
 Troston IP31 ....33 D2
Llewellyn Drift [5] IP15 ..141 C7
Lloyd Cl [3] IP9 ......107 A4
Lloyds Ave Ipswich IP1 ..155 B3
 [15] Kessingland NR33 ..11 B1
Lloyds The IP5 ....141 C7
Loam Pit La IP9 ......118 C4
Locarno Rd [1] IP3 ....140 B3
Loch Rannoch Cl IP30 ..50 E2
Lock Cl [14] IP14 ......53 F2
Lock's La
 [8] Leavenheath CO6 ..102 A7
 Shipmeadow NR34 ....8 F5
 Wrentham NR34 ....26 C5
Lock's Rd NR34 ....9 D5
Lockhart Rd NR35 ......8 D7
Lockington Cl [4] IP14 ..124 E5
Lockington Cres IP14 ..124 D5
Lockington Rd IP14 ....124 D5
Lockington Wlk IP14 ..124 D5
Lockwood Cl [1] IP12 ..147 A5
Loddon Rd
 Ditchingham NR35 ....110 C7
 Gillingham NR34 ......9 B6
 Kirby Cane NR35 ......8 A8
Lode Cl [1] CB7 ....28 D3
Lode La CB7 ....28 A1
Lodge Cl IP14 ....51 E1
Lodge Farm Dr IP12 ..153 C5
Lodge Farm La
 Barsham NR34 ....9 B4
 [8] Melton IP12 ......84 E6
Lodge Farm Rd CO10 ..77 B1
Lodge La Claydon IP6 ..81 A4
 Riddlesworth IP22 ....18 A3
 Shelfanger IP22 ......20 B5
Lodge Rd Feltwell IP26 ..4 F6
 Great Bealings IP13 ..137 E5
 Hollesley IP12 ....99 D7
 Holton IP19 ....118 E5
 St John, Ilketshall
 NR35 ....110 F2
 [3] Ufford IP13 ......84 F7
 Walberswick IP18 ....119 A2
Lodge Way IP24 ......116 B7
Lofft Cl [1] IP31 ......34 E4
Loftus Ave IP1 ....119 C7
Loganberry Rd [4] IP3 ..144 C7
Loggers La IP13 ....18 E1
Loke The
 Blundeston NR32 ......3 A4
 Ditchingham NR35 ....110 B7
Lombardy Rd IP24 ....148 B8
Lonbarn Hill CO11 ....105 D1
London City Rd IP21 ..39 C3
London La
 Harleston IP20 ....66 C7
 [4] Mundford IP26 ....6 B8
London Rd
 Beccles NR34 ....111 B2
 Blythburgh IP19 ......42 E5
 Brampton with Stoven
 NR34 ....25 E6
 Brandon IP27 ....14 E8
 Capel St Mary IP9 ....150 F2

London Rd continued
 Copdock & Washbrook
 IP8 ....138 A1
 Elveden IP24 ....15 C2
 Great Horkesley CO6 ..102 C1
 Halesworth IP18 ......118 A2
 Harleston IP20 ....22 D5
 Icklingham IP27 ......31 E8
 Ipswich IP1 ....155 A3
 Kessingland NR33 ......11 B2
 Lowestoft NR33 ......115 A2
 Pinewood IP8 ....138 B2
 Thetford IP24 ....16 A5
 Westley Waterless CB8 ..59 A4
 Weston NR34 ....9 D2
 Wrentham NR34 ....26 C5
London Rd N NR32 ....113 D1
London Rd Pakefield
 NR33 ....115 A2
London Rd S NR33 ....115 C5
Lone Barn Ct IP1 ......138 D8
Lonely Rd IP21 ....21 C6
Long Acre
 Lowestoft NR33 ......115 B3
 Southwold IP18 ......119 B7
Long Ave IP17 ....128 B4
Long Bessels IP7 ......149 D6
Long Brackland IP33 ..154 A3
Long Dolver Dro CB7 ..28 D6
Long Field IP11 ......152 D6
Long La Bawdsey IP12 ..99 E3
 Burston & Shimpling IP22 ..24 B6
 Feltwell IP26 ....4 D5
Long Marsh Cl IP18 ..119 C7
Long Meadow Wlk
 NR33 ....114 D5
Long Meadows [2] CO10 ..106 F1
Long Melford CE Prim Sch
 CO10 ....91 E8
Long Pastures [2] CO10 ..77 B2
Long Perry IP9 ....150 F3
Long Rd
 Lowestoft NR33 ......114 E3
 Manningtree CO11 ....104 D1
Long Rd E CO7 ....104 A2
Long Rd W CO7 ....103 F2
Long Row IP6 ....129 D6
Long Shop Mus*
 IP16 ....129 C6
Long St IP13 ....139 E5
Long Thurlow Rd IP31 ..51 A7
Longacre Gdns IP13 ..122 E3
Longbeach Dr NR33 ..114 D3
Longcroft IP11 ....152 E6
Longfield CO10 ....148 A2
Longfield Rd IP9 ......106 C6
Longfield Way [6] NR32 ..112 D2
Longfulans La NR31 ....3 B6
Longmeadow IP33 ......122 E3
Longmere La CB9 ......28 C5
Longrigg Rd NR35 ....110 C7
Lonsdale Cl IP4 ......139 F7
Looe Rd IP11 ....153 D3
Lopham Rd NR16 ......18 D8
Lophams Cl IP14 ......132 D8
Loraine Way IP8 ......134 A1
Lord Rd IP22 ....20 D2
Lord's Croft La CB9 ..132 E5
Lord's Highway The
 IP14 ....67 E5
Lord's La CB8 ....61 E5
Lord's Wlk IP27 ....13 F2
Lorne Pk Rd NR33 ....115 C6
Lorne Rd
 Lowestoft NR33 ......115 D5
 Southwold IP18 ......119 D5
Lothing St NR32 ......112 F1
Lothingland Cl NR32 ..112 F5
Lothingland Mid Sch
 NR32 ....3 A5
Lotus Cl IP1 ....134 C1
Loudham Hall Rd
 IP13 ....127 D3
Loudham La IP13 ......85 A7
Louie's La IP22 ....20 C3
Lound Dam NR34 ......2 A3
Lound Rd
 Belton with Browston NR31 ..2 E8
 Blundeston NR32 ......3 A4
Louse La Dedham CO7 ..103 F2
 Rattlesden IP30 ......65 C3
Louvain Rd [13] CO12 ..107 A1
Lovat Cl IP7 ....149 C8
Love La Lowestoft NR33 ..114 F4
 Thorndon IP23 ....53 B8
 Westleton IP17 ......58 C7
Love Rd NR32 ....113 C1
Lover's La IP16 ......129 C6
Lovers La IP29 ....106 B6
Lovetofts Dr IP1 ......134 D1
Lovewell Rd NR33 ....115 C6
Low Comm La CO10 ....10 E8
Low Comm La NR34 ....2 A1
Low Comm Rd IP22 ....19 B3
Low Farm Dr NR32 ....113 A3
Low La Brandeston IP13 ..70 A7
 Creeting St Mary IP6 ..125 D8
Low Lighthouse Maritime
 Mus* CO10 ....107 C3
Low Rd Alburgh IP20 ....7 A1
 Bramfield IP19 ....42 A5
 Brampton with Stoven
 NR34 ....25 D5
 Burwell CB5 ....44 A5
 Carlton IP17 ....128 D6
 Cransford IP17 ....56 C4
 Darsham IP17 ....57 F8

Low Rd continued
 Debenham IP14 ....53 E1
 Denham IP21 ....38 C2
 Denton IP20 ....7 B1
 [1] Dickleburgh & Rushall
 IP21 ....20 F2
 [1] Fressingfield IP21 ..39 E8
 Friston IP17 ....72 F6
 Great Glemham IP17 ..56 C1
 Harwich CO12 ....106 F1
 Hasketon IP13 ....146 B8
 Hedenham NR35 ....7 D8
 Marlesford IP13 ......71 C5
 Mettingham NR35 ....110 F5
 Monk Soham IP13 ......54 D3
 Redenhall with Harleston
 IP20 ....22 F5
 St John, Ilketshall NR34 ..8 D2
 Starston IP20 ....22 C7
 Stratford St Andrew IP17 ..71 F7
 Swefling IP17 ....56 A3
 Ubbeston IP19 ....40 D3
 Wenhaston with Mells Hamlet
 IP19 ....42 C7
 Wortham IP22 ....19 E2
 Wortwell IP20 ....23 A7
Low St Badingham IP13 ..56 A7
 Bardwell IP31 ....34 C3
 Glemsford CO10 ......77 B2
 Hoxne IP21 ....38 B8
 Kettleburgh IP13 ......70 B7
 St Margaret, Ilketshall
 NR35 ....24 B8
Low Wr La IP20 ....20 A1
Low's La IP22 ....20 C1
Lower Barn Rd IP8 ....95 D5
Lower Baxter St IP33 ..154 B2
Lower Brook St IP4 ..155 B2
Lower Broom Rd IP30 ..50 C1
Lower Byfield IP7 ......79 C2
Lower Coney Gr IP8 ..81 A4
Lower Cres IP8 ....82 A6
Lower Dales View Rd
 IP1 ....139 A8
Lower Downs Slade [8]
 CB9 ....132 E6
Lower Drag Way IP22 ..19 A4
Lower Farm Rd
 Boxted CO4 ....103 A4
 Ringshall IP7 ....80 E6
Lower Harlings [4] IP27 ..107 A4
Lower House La IP12 ..98 C5
Lower Houses Rd IP6 ..106 B5
Lower Marine Par
 CO12 ....107 B1
Lower N St CO10 ......75 D3
Lower Oakley IP17 ....37 F8
Lower Olland St NR35 ..110 B4
Lower Orwell St IP4 ..155 C2
Lower Pk Wlk IP19 ..118 E4
Lower Rd Borley CO10 ..91 D6
 Coddenham IP6 ......68 C1
 Falkenham IP10 ......98 F1
 Glemsford CO10 ......77 B1
 Grundisburgh IP13 ..83 E5
 Hemingstone IP6 ......68 C1
 Hundon CO10 ....75 D3
 Lavenham CO10 ......78 D4
 Little Blakenham IP8 ..81 D3
 Melton IP13 ....84 F6
 Mount Bures CO8 ......101 D3
 Onehouse IP14 ....66 B5
 Westerfield IP6 ......135 D4
 Wicken CB7 ....28 A2
Lower Rose La IP21 ....20 D1
Lower St Bayham IP6 ..81 E7
 Cavendish CO10 ......76 E1
 Great Bealings IP13 ..137 E6
 Rattlesden IP30 ......65 D6
 Sproughton IP8 ......138 A6
 Stansfield CO10 ......76 C6
 Stansted CO10 ....77 C3
 Stratford St Mary CO7 ..103 E5
 Stutton IP9 ....105 D5
 Ufford IP13 ....85 A6
 Wickham Market IP13 ..127 C7
Lower Ufford La IP13 ..127 D3
Lower Ufford Rd IP13 ..127 C1
Lowes Hill IP7 ....128 E7
Lowestoft & E Suffolk
 Maritime Mus*
 NR32 ....113 E3
Lowestoft Coll NR32 ..113 C2
Lowestoft Hospl NR33 ..113 D5
Lowestoft Mus*
 NR33 ....114 D8
Lowestoft Porcelain*
 NR33 ....113 E8
Lowestoft Rd
 Beccles NR34 ....111 E4
 Blundeston NR32 ......112 E8
 Hopton on Sea NR33 ..3 B6
 Lowestoft NR33 ......114 D3
 Reydon IP18 ....119 C8
 Worlingham NR34 ....10 A4
Lowestoft War Meml
 Musuem* NR32 ......113 E3
Lowgate St IP23 ......117 D2
Lowry Cl NR33 ....11 C1
Lowry Ct CB9 ....132 B7
Lowry Gdns [6] IP3 ..144 A8
Lowry Way
 Lowestoft NR33 ......113 C5
 Stowmarket IP14 ....124 B7
Lowther St CB8 ....120 F3

Loxley Rd NR33 ....114 E6
Lucas Rd CO10 ....148 D5
Lucena Ct IP14 ....124 C6
Lucerne Cl
 Lowestoft NR33 ......114 C5
 [5] Red Lodge IP28 ....30 B1
Ludbrook Cl IP6 ......125 C5
Ludgate Cswy IP23 ..117 E2
Ludlow Cl IP1 ....135 B4
Luff Meadow IP6 ......125 D5
Lugano Ave IP8 ....98 B8
Lulworth Ave IP3 ....140 D3
Lulworth Dr [2] CB9 ..132 C6
Lulworth Pk [8] NR32 ..113 A4
Lummis Vale IP1 ......141 C7
Lundy Cl IP8 ....133 B5
Lunnish Hill CO12 ....106 C2
Lupin Cl IP18 ....119 B7
Lupin Rd IP2 ....138 E4
Lupin Way IP28 ......125 D3
Lushington Rd [5] CO10 ..104 E2
Luther Rd IP3 ....155 B1
Lutus Cl CO10 ....90 A7
Lydgate Cl
 [11] Bury St Edmunds IP32 ..48 C5
 [4] Lawford CO11 ....104 D2
Lydgate Rd IP14 ......124 C6
Lyle Cl IP5 ....141 E7
Lymingster Cl [6] IP32 ..123 D6
Lymm Rd NR32 ....113 B5
Lyncroft Rd NR32 ....113 B5
Lyndhurst Ave IP4 ....140 C5
Lyndhurst Rd NR32 ..113 D4
Lyng La IP22 ....18 F5
Lyngate Ave NR33 ....114 F5
Lynn's Baxter St CO10 ..92 C6
Lynnbrook Cl IP2 ....138 E1
Lynton Gdns NR32 ....113 C3
Lynwood Ave IP1 ....153 B5
Lynx Bsns Pk CB8 ......44 F7
Lyon Cl IP23 ....37 C4
Lysander Dr [3] IP3 ..144 C8

M

MacAulay Rd IP1 ......134 F3
MacKenzie Dr IP5 ....141 B8
MacKenzie Pl IP30 ....78 C8
MacKenzie Rd IP24 ....16 A5
Maconochie Way
 NR33 ....115 C7
MacPherson Robertson Way
 [3] IP28 ....116 B5
Mafeking Rd IP16 ....129 D6
Magdalen Cl [3] NR32 ..113 A3
Magdalen Ct IP23 ....117 C2
Magdalen Dr IP12 ....146 D3
Magdalen Rd IP12 ....146 D3
Magdalen St IP23 ....117 C2
Magdalen Cl IP2 ......138 F2
Maginglex Cres IP4 ..140 F6
Magnolia Cl
 [3] Beck Row, Holywell
 Row & Kenny Hill IP28 ..13 B1
 [2] Red Lodge IP28 ....30 B1
Magnolia Ct [3] NR32 ..113 B2
Magnolia Way [7] IP12 ..85 D8
Magpie Cl
 [8] Ipswich IP2 ......138 C2
 Ramsey CO12 ....106 F1
Magpie Hill IP12 ......19 E1
Maid Marion Ct IP33 ..122 F3
Maiden Way IP7 ......149 D6
Maidenhall App IP2 ..139 B2
Maidenhall Sports Ctr
 IP2 ....139 C2
Maids Cross Hill IP27 ..109 E6
Maids Cross Way
 IP27 ....109 D6
Maidscross Hill Nature
 Reserve* IP27 ......109 F5
Maidstone City Inf Sch
 IP11 ....152 E5
Maidstone Rd
 Felixstowe IP11 ......152 E5
 Lowestoft NR32 ......113 C1
Main Rd Benhall IP17 ..72 C8
 Bucklesham IP10 ....141 F1
 Chelmondiston IP9 ..106 B7
 Darsham IP17 ....42 A1
 Hacheston IP13 ......127 D8
 Harwich CO12 ....106 F1
 Henley IP6 ....82 B6
 Ipswich IP5 ....141 A8
 Kelsale cum Carlton
 IP17 ....128 C8
 Marlesford IP13 ......71 D4
 Martlesham IP12 ....146 C1
 Parham IP13 ....70 F8
 Pettistree IP13 ......127 B3
 [3] Ramsey & Parkeston
 CO12 ....106 D1
 Somersham IP8 ....81 C3
 Tuddenham St Martin
 IP6 ....136 B4
 Wooverstone IP9 ....143 F2
 Wormingford CO6 ....101 F2
Main St
 Hockwold cum Wilton IP26 ..4 F3
 Leiston IP16 ....129 C6
Maine Cl [4] IP24 ......16 A5
Maisie's Meadow IP13 ..54 D7
Maitland Rd IP6 ......125 E3

Major La IP23 ....37 A2
Major's Cl IP29 ....62 C5
Makins Rd **2** CO12 ....106 F3
Malcolm Way CB8 ......121 A5
Maldon Ct CO10 ....148 C7
Malin Cl CB9 ....133 B5
Mallard Rd IP18 ....119 B7
Mallard Way
  Brandon IP27 ....6 A1
  Hollesley IP12 ....99 F7
  Ipswich IP2 ....138 F3
  Stowmarket IP14 ....144 A2
  Sudbury CO10 ....92 B3
Mallards The IP27 ......109 D5
Mallets La IP12 ....131 C2
Mallow Rd **1** IP24 .....16 D6
Mallow Way NR33 .....114 C4
Mallow Wlk **4** CO9 ...132 A6
Mallowhayes Cl IP12 ..139 B3
Malmesbury Cl IP12 ...139 A2
Malt Cl **6** Laxfield IP13 ..40 B3
  Newmarket CB8 ....121 B3
Malt Office Ave IP19 ...24 B4
Malt Office La IP19 .....24 A4
Malt's La IP26 ....47 F2
Malthouse Ct **21** IP20 ...22 D6
Malthouse La
  Bury St Edmunds IP32 ..154 A4
  Gissing IP22 ....20 F8
Malthouse Rd **22** CO11 ..104 E2
Malting Cotts CB9 .....133 D2
Malting End CB8 ....62 C5
Malting Farm La CO7 ..103 E1
Malting La **10** Clare CO10 ..90 A8
  Isleham CB7 ....29 C5
Malting Row IP31 ....33 F5
Maltings IP14 ....52 D3
Maltings Cl
  2 Bures Hamlet CO8 ..101 C5
  1 Chevington IP29 ......62 C6
  Halesworth IP19 ....118 B4
  Moulton CB8 ....45 F3
Maltings Dr **5** IP20 ...22 D6
Maltings Garth **9** IP31 ..49 D4
Maltings La IP31 ....32 F1
Maltings Mews IP7 ....149 D5
Maltings The
  Beccles NR34 ....111 B7
  Bungay NR35 ....110 C4
Maltsters' Way NR32 ..114 D8
Maltsters Wlk IP14 ....124 C3
Maltward Ave IP33 .....122 C5
Malvern Cl Ipswich IP3 ..140 B3
  Newmarket CB8 ....121 B2
Malvern Rd IP33 ....122 D3
Malvern Rise IP13 ......113 B3
Malyon Rd IP7 ....149 E8
Manchester Rd IP12 ..138 C2
Manderston Rd CB8 ..120 E3
Mandeville Rd IP33 ...122 C4
Mandeville **10** CB5 ....44 A5
Mandy Cl IP4 ....140 A6
Mannall Wlk IP5 ....141 E8
Manners Rd IP31 ....48 D5
Manning Rd
  Bury St Edmunds IP32 ..123 F7
  Felixstowe IP11 ....152 E2
Manning's La IP22 ....35 D5
Mannings La IP9 ....144 A2
Mannington Cl **8** IP4 ..140 C4
Manningtree High Sch
  CO11 ....104 D2
Manningtree Mus*
  CO11 ....104 E2
Manningtree Rd
  Dedham CO7 ....104 A3
  East Bergholt CO7 ......151 F3
  Stutton IP9 ....105 C5
Manningtree Sports Ctr
  CO11 ....104 D2
Manningtree Sta
  CO11 ....104 D3
Manor Ash Dr IP32 ....123 E6
Manor Cl **9** Beccles NR34 ..9 F4
  3 Cavendish CO10 .....70 F1
  Walberswick IP18 ....119 A2
  Worlingham NR34 ....9 F4
Manor Farm Cl
  Haverhill CB9 ....132 F5
  11 Southwold IP18 ....119 D5
Manor Farm Rd
  St John, Ilketshall NR34 ..8 D7
  8 Thistley Green IP28 ..29 F6
Manor Garth IP31 ....49 E6
Manor Gdns
  8 Hopton on Sea NR31 ..3 C6
  Saxmundham IP17 ......128 E2
Manor House Mus*
  IP33 ....154 C1
Manor La Gosbeck IP6 ..68 D2
  10 Harwich CO12 ......107 A2
  Horringer IP29 ....122 B1
  Stutton IP9 ....105 C5
Manor Pk Rd
  Corton NR32 ....3 C4
  9 Southwold IP18 ....119 D5
Manor Rd **10** Bildeston IP7 ..79 F4
  Brandon IP27 ....5 E1
  Bungay NR35 ....110 B2
  Clopton IP13 ....69 E1
  Elmsett IP7 ....80 F2
  Felixstowe IP11 ....107 A2
  Harwich CO12 ....107 A2
  Haskelon IP13 ....146 D6
  Haverhill CB9 ....132 F5

Manor Rd continued
  Hessett IP30 ....64 F7
  Hopton on Sea NR31 ......3 B6
  Ipswich IP4 ....139 D8
  11 Martlesham Heath IP5 ..98 A8
  Mildenhall IP28 ....116 B4
  Roydon IP22 ....20 B3
  Sudbury CO10 ....148 C7
  Trimley St Martin IP11 ..153 I11
Manor Terr IP11 ....107 F3
Manor View IP11 ....116 D2
Manor Wlk **20** NR33 ...11 B1
Manorhouse La **8**
  NR34 ....111 B6
Mansbrook Byd **5** IP3 ..144 C7
Manse La IP19 ....40 C6
Mansfield Ave IP1 ......134 F2
Manthorp Cl IP12 ......147 B8
Manwick Rd IP11 ....152 E2
Maple Cl
  6 Great Bricett IP7 ...80 D6
  Ipswich IP7 ....139 A3
  12 Lakenheath IP27 ..113 F2
  Rendlesham IP12 ....85 D8
  Yaxley IP23 ....37 B5
Maple Covert **5** NR32 ..112 F5
Maple Gn **8** IP31 ....49 A6
Maple Gr **6** IP6 ....82 A6
Maple Hill CO10 ....75 E1
Maple Rd
  5 Lowestoft NR33 ....114 F7
  Newmarket CB8 ....67 A6
  Sudbury CO10 ....148 F3
Maple Way
  Beccles NR34 ....111 C5
  Eye IP23 ....117 D3
  Leavenheath CO6 ....102 B7
Maples The IP5 ....140 E8
Marbella Gn IP13 ....139 A4
Marbled White Dr IP9 ..142 E8
March Pl **2** CO10 ......76 A1
Marcus Cl CB9 ....133 B5
Marcus Rd IP11 ....153 D5
Mardle Rd Reydon NR34 ..43 B8
  Wangford with Henham
  NR34 ....26 C1
Mardle The NR33 ....114 C2
Mare Hill CO10 ....75 D3
Margaret Rd IP4 ....124 C7
Margaret St IP11 ....152 E5
Margate Rd IP3 ....140 B3
Marham Rd **4** NR32 ..113 B2
Maria St **7** CO12 ....107 B3
Marigold Ave IP2 ......138 E3
Marigold Dr **8** IP28 ...46 A6
Marina Rd **3** NR33 ....113 E1
Marina Gdns IP12 ......152 E2
Marina Theatre **11**
  NR32 ....113 D1
Marine Cl **3** NR31 ......3 B8
Marine Par
  12 Harwich CO12 ......107 B2
  Lowestoft NR33 ....115 D7
Mariner's Cl **2** NR31 ...3 B8
Mariners Pk Cl **11** NR31 ..3 B7
Mariners Rd NR32 ......113 E2
Mariners Way IP15 ....130 D5
Marion Cl **5** NR34 ....111 C3
Mark Jennings La
  IP33 ....154 C3
Mark's La IP27 ....47 F2
Markant Cl IP32 ....123 E6
Market Cross Pl IP15 ..130 F4
Market Gr CO9 ....90 A1
Market Hill **8** Clare CO10 ..90 A8
  Clopton IP13 ....83 D8
  Framlingham IP13 ......126 C3
  Haverhill CB9 ....132 E6
  Orford IP12 ....131 C2
  2 Sudbury CO10 ......148 C5
Market La
  Blundeston NR32 ....3 B4
  Burston & Shimpling IP22 ..20 E5
  Somerleyton, Ashby &
  Herringfleet NR32 ....2 D6
Market Pl **11** Bildeston IP7 ..79 F4
  Hadleigh IP7 ....148 C5
  2 Halesworth IP19 ...118 A3
  2 Harleston IP20 ......22 D6
  8 Kessingland NR33 ...11 B1
  11 Lavenham CO10 ....78 D4
  Saxmundham IP17 ......128 D3
  Southwold IP18 ....119 D5
  Stowmarket IP14 ....124 D6
Market Row NR34 ......111 B5
Market Sq CB8 ....121 A3
Market St
  1 Beccles NR34 ......111 B5
  Fordham CB7 ....29 A1
  8 Harwich CO12 ......107 C3
  Laxfield IP13 ....40 B3
  3 Mildenhall IP28 ....116 C4
  2 Newmarket CB8 ....121 A3
  5 Soham CB7 ....28 D4
Market Thoroughfare
  IP33 ....154 B2
Market Weston Rd
  IP22 ....35 A7
Markhams Cl CB9 ......132 D7
Marlborough Ct
  4 Haverhill CB9 ....132 C5
  Newmarket CB8 ....112 F1
Marlborough Dr **4**
  CO10 ....148 D6
Marlborough Rd
  Ipswich IP4 ....140 A5
  Lowestoft NR32 ....112 F1
  Saxtead IP13 ....55 A4

Marlborough Rd continued
  Southwold IP18 ....119 D6
Marlesford Rd IP13 .....71 B5
Marlow Rd IP14 ....134 D1
Marriott's Wlk **5** IP14 ..124 D5
Marsden Cl **5** NR33 ...115 A3
Marsh La Aldeby NR34 ..2 A2
  Carlton Colville NR33 ..114 A4
  8 Earsham NR35 ....7 F4
  Felixstowe IP11 ....153 C8
  26 Kessingland NR33 ..11 C1
  Kessingland NR33 ....27 C8
  North Cove NR34 ....10 B5
  Reydon IP18 ....26 D2
  Somerleyton, Ashby &
  Herringfleet NR32 ....2 C4
  Worlingham NR34 ....9 D5
  Wortham IP22 ....20 A1
Marsh Rd Boxford CO10 ..93 C3
  Fritton & St Olaves NR31 ..2 B7
  Lowestoft NR33 ....114 F2
  Stoke-by-Nayland CO6 ..103 C7
Marsh View NR34 ......111 D5
Marsh Way IP14 ....12 A4
Marshall Cl IP5 ....141 C8
Marshalls Meadow **3**
  IP14 ....67 A6
Marshams Piece **4**
  NR33 ....114 C5
Marsho La CO10 ....90 B4
Martello La IP11 ....153 D5
Martello Rd NR32 ......113 B4
Marten's La CO6 ....102 F8
Martin Cl Brandon IP27 ..6 A1
  Lowestoft NR33 ....114 D3
  Mildenhall IP28 ....116 D3
  8 Soham CB7 ....28 D5
Martin Rd **8** Burwell CB5 ..44 A6
  Ipswich IP3 ....140 E1
  Ipswich IP2 ....155 B1
Martin's Ave NR33 .....115 B6
Martin's Meadow Nature
  Reserve* IP13 ....69 E4
Martinet Gn IP3 ....140 C1
Martins La IP13 ....69 F2
Martins Mead **8** IP29 ..36 C5
Martins Mews **2** IP29 ..132 A7
Martins Rd CO10 ....148 F7
Martinsyde **3** IP5 ......98 A8
Maryday Cl IP6 ....68 B1
Maryon Rd IP3 ....140 B1
Masefield Rd Diss IP22 ..20 D2
  Stowmarket IP14 ....124 B8
Mashay Rd CO10 ....90 B3
Maskell's La IP7 ....149 F7
Mason Cl **1** IP6 ....82 A5
Mason Gdns **2** IP28 ...29 F6
Mason Rd CB5 ....44 A7
Mason's La **8** IP30 ....50 D1
Masons Cl IP4 ....139 F6
Mast Cl NR33 ....114 B4
Masterland Ind Est
  IP16 ....129 B6
Masterson Gr IP5 ....141 C6
Mat Dawson Cl CB8 ...120 F6
Mather La IP20 ....22 B8
Mather Way IP2 ....155 C1
Matlock Cl **18** IP8 ......138 C2
Matlock Dale **18** NR33 ..114 E3
Matson Rd IP3 ....140 F8
Matthews La CB8 ....74 C7
Maude St IP3 ....139 F4
Maudslay Rd IP1 ....134 C2
Maulkin Cl IP32 ....123 F7
Mautby Way NR33 .....114 F5
May Rd Ipswich IP3 ....140 C2
May's La CO7 ....103 B2
Maybush La IP11 ....140 B1
Maybush La IP11 ....153 C5
Maycroft Cl **2** IP1 ....135 A3
Mayes La CO12 ....106 D1
Mayfair Rd NR35 ....110 C3
Mayfield CO6 ....102 B7
Mayfield Ave **12** NR33 ..11 C1
Mayfield La **7** IP15 ...95 A7
Mayfield Rd
  Bury St Edmunds IP33 ..123 B1
  Ipswich IP4 ....140 C7
  Lowestoft NR33 ....114 C4
Mayfield Way IP14 ......52 E5
Mayfields
  Lakenheath IP27 ....109 C7
  6 Martlesham Heath IP5 ..98 A7
Mayflower Ave
  4 Harwich CO12 ....107 C3
  Saxmundham IP17 ......128 B2
Mayflower Way
  14 Harleston IP20 ......22 D5
  Sudbury CO10 ....148 D8
Mayfly Cl **13** IP8 ....142 E8
Mayhem Adventure Play
  Area* IP11 ....115 E8
Maynewater La IP33 ..154 C1
Maynewater Sq IP33 ..154 C1
Maypole Cl CB8 ....60 C6
McCalmont Way CB8 ..121 E2
McIntyre Wlk IP32 .....122 E7
McLaren Cl **5** NR34 ...111 C3
McLean Dr **10** NR33 ....11 B1

Mead Dr IP5 ....141 C7
Mead The CO10 ....148 F2
Mead Way IP14 ....52 E5
Meadow Barn IP14 ......66 C2
Meadow Cl
  Bury St Edmunds IP33 ..122 E3
  8 Felixstowe IP11 ....107 D8
  Felsham IP30 ....65 A4
  Lavenham CO10 ....78 D3
  8 Soham CB7 ....28 D4
  Westhall IP19 ....25 B4
Meadow Cres IP3 ......140 F1
Meadow Ct
  4 Great Yarmouth NR31 ..3 B8
  4 Stanton IP31 ....34 E4
Meadow Dr
  Horringer IP29 ....63 A8
  Lakenheath IP27 ....109 D7
Meadow Gdns NR34 ...111 A3
Meadow La
  Newmarket CB8 ....121 D1
  9 Soham CB7 ....148 C4
  Thurston IP31 ....49 B7
Meadow Prim Sch
  NR33 ....115 B6
Meadow Rd
  8 Barrow IP29 ....47 A2
  Bungay NR35 ....110 D2
  Lowestoft NR32 ....112 F4
Meadow Rise IP15 .....130 F3
Meadow Sh Ctr The
  IP14 ....124 D6
Meadow Valley IP7 .....80 D5
Meadow View
  Needham Market IP6 ..125 C5
  Woolpit IP30 ....65 E8
Meadow View Rd
  CO10 ....148 B4
Meadow Way
  Assington CO10 ....92 F1
  Lowestoft NR33 ....114 C2
Meadow Wlk **3** IP17 ...72 C8
Meadowlands
  11 Blundeston NR32 ....3 A4
  1 Burwell CB5 ....44 A6
  Kirton IP10 ....98 D2
  Woolpit IP30 ....50 D1
Meadowlands Cl IP17 ..57 C8
Meadows The
  Drinkstone IP30 ....65 B7
  Worlington IP28 ....30 B4
Meadows Way IP7 .....149 D6
Meadowside
  Blo' Norton IP22 ....18 E2
  Wickham Market IP13 ..127 C7
Meadowside Gdns
  IP4 ....140 E8
Meadowsweet Cl
  Haverhill CB9 ....132 C7
  8 Lowestoft NR33 ....114 D5
Meadowvale Cl
  Beccles NR34 ....111 B2
  Ipswich IP4 ....139 F8
Meadway **22** CO11 ...104 E2
Mear Cl IP17 ....85 C2
Mechanical Music Mus &
  Bygones* IP14 ....52 A6
Medway Rd IP3 ....139 F2
Meikings Rd CO10 ......148 F6
Meeting Field **11** CO10 ..91 E8
Meeting La
  Grundisburgh IP13 ......83 E5
  Ridgewell CO9 ....89 D4
Meeting Wlk CB9 ....132 F5
Melbourne Dr IP28 ....116 B5
Melbourne Rd
  Ipswich IP4 ....140 D7
  Newmarket CB8 ....113 D3
Melford Cl **2** Burwell CB5 ..44 B5
  8 Ipswich IP4 ....140 C4
Melford Hall* CO10 .....77 E1
Melford Rd Acton CO10 ..92 A8
  Cavendish CO10 ....76 F1
  Lavenham CO10 ....78 C3
  Lawshall IP29 ....63 D1
  Stowmarket IP14 ....124 D4
  Sudbury CO10 ....148 B7
Melford Way IP11 ......152 C3
Mellis Cl IP2 ....142 A5
Mellis Ct **18** IP11 .....152 D5
Mellis Rd
  Gislingham IP23 ....36 D3
  Thrandeston IP21 ....37 B6
  Wortham IP22 ....36 E7
  Yaxley IP23 ....37 B5
Mellisash Rd IP3 ....136 F5
Melplash Cl IP3 ....140 E4
Melplash Rd IP3 ....140 E4
Melrose Cl NR32 ....112 F5
Melrose Gdns
  Ipswich IP4 ....140 B8
  Lowestoft NR32 ....112 F5
Melton Cl CB8 ....120 E4
Melton CP Sch IP12 ...147 C7
Melton Grange Rd
  IP12 ....147 A6
Melton Hill IP12 ....147 B6
Melton Meadow Rd **4**
  IP12 ....147 B6
Melton Rd
  Hollesley IP12 ....99 F8
  Woodbridge IP12 ....147 B7
Melton Sta IP12 ....147 D7
Melville Rd IP4 ....139 F5
Mendham Cl **36** IP20 ..22 D6
Mendham La

Mendham La continued
  St Cross, South Elmham
  IP20 ....23 C6
Mendham Prim Sch
  IP20 ....23 A6
Mendham Rd IP20 ......23 A4
Mendip Dr IP5 ....140 F6
Mendip Rd NR32 ....112 E2
Mendlesham Prim Sch
  IP14 ....52 D4
Mendlesham Rd IP14 ..52 B5
Mercers Rd IP32 ....123 D7
Mere Cl IP31 ....49 C8
Mere Gdns IP4 ....140 F4
Mere Rd IP28 ....48 A6
Mere Manor Ct IP22 ...20 C2
Mere Side CB7 ....28 C4
Meredith Rd IP1 ....134 C2
Meriton Rise IP7 ....149 F4
Merivale Rd **17** CO11 ..104 D2
Merlewood IP21 ....21 C5
Merlin Rd IP2 ....138 C3
Mermaid Cl IP32 ....123 A8
Merriam Cl **5** CO11 ...104 E4
Merrifield Rd NR33 ...114 F3
Merrion Cl **12** IP28 ...138 C2
Merrylees NR34 ....111 C4
Mersey Rd IP3 ....139 F2
Merville Rd **8** NR33 ...11 B1
Messenger Cl NR35 ...110 B2
Metfield Rd IP20 ....23 D3
Metfield St IP20 ....23 D3
Methersgate Hall Dr
  IP12 ....84 E1
Meynell Gdns CB8 ....121 A5
Micawber Mews **4** NR32 ..3 A4
Michaelhouse Way IP32
  IP31 ....34 E4
Michaels Mount **1** IP3 ..137 D5
Michaelstowe Cl **1**
  CO12 ....106 C1
Michigan Cl IP5 ....141 B7
Mickfield Mews **18**
  IP11 ....152 D5
Micklegate Rd IP11 ...152 E2
Micklesmere Dr **26** IP31 ..34 B1
Mid Suffolk Leisure Ctr
  IP14 ....124 B7
Middle Dro CB7 ....28 B4
Middle Gn CO6 ....101 B1
Middle La NR34 ....10 D8
Middle Rd
  Blo' Norton IP22 ....18 F2
  Earsham IP20 ....7 C4
Middle Way CO10 ....91 E8
Middle Wlk NR32 ....3 A4
Middlefield Dr **3** IP14 ..66 B4
Middlefield Rd **10** CO11 ..105 A2
Middleton Cl IP7 ....138 D2
Middleton Prim Sch
  IP17 ....58 B6
Middleton Rd
  Sudbury CO10 ....148 B4
  Yoxford IP17 ....57 E7
Midhurst Cl IP32 ....123 D6
Midmeadow **4** NR34 ..111 B5
Mid-Suffolk Light Rly Mus
  The* IP14 ....53 B4
Mighten's Rd IP18 ....119 C6
Milano Ave IP27 ....90 B8
Milburn Dro CB8 ....45 F3
Milden Cl **6** IP14 .....124 E3
Milden Rd
  Brent Eleigh CO10 ......79 A2
  Ipswich IP2 ....138 E5
Mildenhall Airfield
  IP28 ....30 B7
Mildenhall Coll of Tech
  IP28 ....116 F4
Mildenhall Dro IP28 ...12 F3
Mildenhall Ind Est
  IP28 ....116 B6
Mildenhall Mus*
  IP28 ....116 C4
Mildenhall Rd
  Barton Mills IP28 ....116 C2
  Beck Row, Holywell
  Row & Kenny Hill IP28 ..116 C8
  2 Bury St Edmunds IP32 ..123 A8
  Fordham CB7 ....29 C1
  Icklingham IP28 ....31 A5
  Littleport CB7 ....12 A8
Mildenhall Stadium
  IP28 ....29 D8
Mildmay Rd IP3 ....140 B1
Mile End IP27 ....21 C5
Mile End Rd CB7 ....12 A7
Miles Hawk Way IP28 ..116 A6
Miles Paddock IP14 .....52 A6
Milford Rd IP4 ....138 C2
Military Way **8** CO12 ..106 C1
Mill Bank **8** NR32 ....112 F2
Mill Broadway IP12 ...131 C4
Mill Chase CB9 ....88 E3
Mill Cl **6** Haverhill CB9 ..44 B5
  Capel St Mary IP9 ......150 C3
  Exning CB8 ....120 B8
  Felixstowe IP11 ....152 D4
  Kirby Row NR35 ....9 B1
  1 Walsham le Willows
  IP31 ....35 C2
  Woolpit IP30 ....50 D1
Mill Cnr CB7 ....28 C3
Mill Drift IP28 ....5 A3
Mill Dro CB7 ....28 C3
Mill End La IP14 ....67 C2

Mill Field
3 Aldeburgh IP15 ......130 E5
Bramford IP8 ....134 B2
Pettaugh IP14 ....68 E6
Mill Fields IP14 ......51 D1
Mill Gdns
Bedingham NR35 ....7 B8
Elmswell IP30 ....50 C2
Mill Hill (Tumulus)*
NR31 ....2 C8
Mill Hill Bungh IP13 ....83 F6
Capel St Mary IP9 ....150 C3
Cotton IP14 ....52 A6
Earl Soham IP13 ......54 E1
Hadleigh IP7 ....94 B7
Haverhill CB9 ....132 D5
Lawford CO11 ....104 B2
Leiston IP16 ....129 C2
Manningtree CO11 ...124 E2
Mettingham NR35 ......8 D5
Newmarket CB8 ......121 A4
Peasenhall IP17 ......56 F8
Rattlesden IP30 ....65 D6
Sudbury CO10 ....148 B5
Wormingford CO6 ...101 F3
Mill Hill Dr IP19 ....108 B8
Mill Hill Est IP16 ...129 C2
Mill Hoo IP12 ....99 E4
Mill La
All Saints & St Nicholas,
South Elmham IP20 ...23 E5
Barnham IP24 ....16 B2
Barrow IP29 ....47 A2
Baylham IP6 ....81 F7
Benhall IP17 ....72 C8
Boyton IP12 ....86 B2
Bradfield CO11 ......105 B1
Bramford IP8 ....134 B1
Brandeston IP13 ......70 A7
Bruisyard IP17 ....56 C5
7 Burwell CB5 ....44 B5
Butley IP12 ....86 B6
Campsey Ash IP13 ...127 F6
Cavendish CO10 ....90 D8
Chelmondiston IP9 ...106 B8
Coddenham IP6 ....68 B1
Combs IP14 ....124 B1
Copdock & Washbrook
IP8 ....138 A1
Corton NR32 ....3 D4
Cowlinge CB8 ....75 B8
Creeting St Peter or
West Creeting IP6 ...125 D8
Dedham CO7 ....103 F4
Dennington IP13 ......55 D5
Ellingham NR35 ....8 E7
Exning CB8 ....120 B8
Felixstowe IP11 .....152 F4
Fordham CB7 ....29 B1
Garboldisham IP22 ....18 D3
9 Great Blakenham IP6 ..82 A5
Great Yeldham CO9 ...90 A2
Haskelton IP13 ......146 A7
Henley IP6 ....82 D6
Hockwold cum Wilton IP26 ..5 A3
Hoo IP13 ....70 C6
Hopton IP22 ....18 C3
Hundon CO10 ....75 D3
Kersey IP7 ....94 A7
Layham IP7 ....149 E2
Leiston IP16 ....129 C2
18 Manningtree CO11 ...124 E2
Marlesford IP13 ......71 C5
Metfield IP20 ....23 C3
North Cove NR34 ......10 C4
Polstead CO6 ....102 E8
Pulham St Mary IP21 ..21 F8
4 Redgrave IP22 ......36 A8
St John, Ilketshall NR34 ..8 E2
Shadingfield NR34 ....25 D7
Somersham IP8 ....81 C3
Southwold IP18 ......119 D5
Stetchworth CB8 ......59 F5
Stoke Ash IP23 ....52 F8
Stonham Earl IP14 ....67 D5
Stradbroke IP21 ....39 C5
Sudbury CO10 ......148 B5
Thetford IP24 ....9 A8
Thurston IP31 ....49 D5
Tunstall IP12 ....72 B1
Weybread IP21 ....22 C3
Wickham Market IP13 ..127 C6
2 Witnesham IP6 .....83 A5
Woodbridge IP12 ....147 A5
Woolpit IP30 ....50 D1
Wrentham NR34 ....26 F5
Mill Piece IP15 ....80 B8
Mill Pool La NR35 .....3 D6
Mill Pouch IP11 .....152 C6
Mill Rd (South) IP33 ..154 A1
Mill Rd
Aldeby/Wheatacre/Burgh
St Peter NR34 ....10 B8
Ashley CB8 ....45 F1
Badingham IP13 ....56 A7
Barningham IP31 ......34 B2
Battisford IP14 ....80 E8
Beccles NR34 ....111 C2
Birdbrook CO9 ....89 C5
Botesdale IP22 ....36 B6
Boxted CO4 ....102 F2
Brockish IP21 ....21 E3
Bures St Mary/Assington
CO8 ....63 A1
Burston & Shimpling IP22 ..24 D6
Bury St Edmunds IP33 ..154 A2
Buxhall IP14 ....65 F4
Chevington IP29 ......62 C6
Clare CO10 ....90 B8

Mill Rd continued
Coldfair Green IP17 ...129 A2
Cotton IP14 ....52 A6
East Bergholt CO7 ...151 E4
Ellingham NR35 ....8 D7
Foxearth CO10 ....91 B7
Friston IP17 ....72 E6
Gazeley CB8 ....46 B3
Great Barton IP31 ....49 A6
Halesworth IP19 .....118 E3
Haverhill CB9 ....132 E5
Hemley IP12 ....98 E5
Hengrave IP28 ....48 A7
Honington IP31 ....33 F5
Hundon CO10 ....75 D4
Ipswich IP3 ....140 F1
Kedington CB9 ......133 E8
Kirtling CB8 ....60 F3
Lakenheath IP27 ....109 D6
Laxfield IP13 ....40 B2
Lowestoft NR33 .....115 C7
Mendlesham IP14 .....52 D4
Moulton CB8 ....46 A1
Mutford NR34 ....2 C5
Newbourne IP12 ......98 D5
Occold IP23 ....37 F1
Peasenhall IP17 ......56 E8
Redlingfield IP23 .....40 B1
Ridgewell CO9 ....89 D3
Rumburgh IP19 ....24 B4
Saxmundham IP17 ...128 E7
Stambourne CO9 ......89 B2
Swefling IP17 ....56 E3
Thelnetham IP22 .....35 B4
Westleton IP17 ....58 C7
Weybread IP21 ....22 C4
Winfarthing IP22 .....20 B8
Wissett IP19 ....118 A5
Worlingworth IP13 ...54 D7
Wyverstone IP14 .....51 D6
Mill Rd S IP22 ....36 B6
Mill Reef CI CB8 ....120 D7
Mill Rise 11 Holbrook IP9 ..105 E7
Saxmundham IP17 ...128 E7
Mill St Gislingham IP23 ..36 B2
Isleham CB7 ....29 C5
Middleton IP17 ....58 A6
Mildenhall IP28 .....116 B3
Nayland CO6 ....102 D5
Stowupland IP14 ......67 A6
Westleton IP17 ....58 A7
Mill Tye CO10 ......148 E2
Mill View CB8 ....46 B3
Mill View CI IP12 ...146 E5
Millbank CB8 ....120 F4
Millennium Grandstand
CB8 ....120 C1
Millennium Way
Kesgrave IP5 ....141 E7
Lowestoft NR32 .....113 A4
Miller CI Elmswell IP30 ..50 F2
Lowestoft NR32 .....115 D5
Millers CI Bungay NR35 ..110 C3
Hadleigh IP7 ....149 E6
Stowmarket IP14 ...124 C3
Millers Ct 5 IP6 ......82 A5
Millers Dr IP21 ....21 B5
Millers Gn 4 IP20 ....22 C5
Millers View IP11 ...138 F7
Millfield IP23 ....117 B3
Millfield Ave IP14 ...124 C5
Millfield CI
1 Saxmundham IP17 ..128 C2
Millfield Dr IP14 .....65 F4
Millfield Gdns IP14 ..140 A7
Millfield Rd
2 Barningham IP31 ...34 F7
Walberswick IP18 ...119 A2

Minden Dr continued
Leiston IP16 ....129 D5
Minden Rd
Lowestoft NR32 .....113 C2
Sudbury CO10 ....148 D5
Minerva CI IP9 ......133 B4
Minos Rd NR32 ......113 C4
Minos Way IP1 ......108 D8
Minsmere House Hospl
IP4 ....140 C6
Minsmere Nature Reserve*
IP17 ....58 E6
Minsmere Rd IP4 .....58 F8
Minsmere Rise IP17 ..58 A6
Minsmere Way CO10 ..92 B3
Minster Rd CB9 .....132 D7
Minton Ent Pk CB8 ..120 E7
Mirbeck's CI 6 NR34 ..9 F4
Misburgh Way NR31 ...3 C4
Mission La CO7 .....104 D6
Mission Rd IP22 ......20 D2
Mistley Sta CO11 ...104 F2
Mistley Way IP12 ...146 F6
Mitchell Ave IP32 ....48 C5
Mitchery La IP14 .....65 E4
Mitford CI IP1 ....135 A4
Mitford Rd IP17 ......72 B8
Mitre CI 6 NR34 ......50 D1
Mitre Way IP1 ......139 E4
Moat Farm CI IP4 ...139 F8
Moat La
Alphamstone CO8 ...101 A6
Rushbrooke with Rougham
IP30 ....49 D1
Theberton IP16 ....57 F6
Moat Wlk 2 CB9 ....132 C6
Mobbs Way NR32 ...112 E3
Mockbeggars Hall*
IP5 ....134 C6
Moffat Ave IP4 .....136 B1
Moles La NR34 ....8 A3
Moll's La NR34 ....25 D5
Monarch CI CB9 ......46 B3
Monarch Way
Carlton Colville NR33 ..114 A3
Pinewood IP8 ....142 D8
Monastery Ct IP7 ...149 E7
Monastery Hill IP7 ...149 E7
Monckton Ave NR32 ..112 F2
Monckton Cres NR32 ..112 F2
Monet St 1 NR32 ...113 B5
Monewden Rd IP13 ...70 A3
Moneyhole Cnr CO10 ..78 E7
Moneypiece CI IP14 ..132 D7
Moneypot La IP22 ...19 F6
Monk's La CO7 .....103 E2
Monks CI IP11 ......152 A4
Monks Eleigh CE VC Prim
Sch IP7 ....79 B2
Monks Gate IP4 ....138 A6
Monksgate IP24 ......16 B6
Monkshood CI NR33 ..114 F2
Monmouth CI IP2 ...139 B1
Montagu Dr IP27 .....5 E1
Montague Rd IP11 ...153 A4
Montague St IP1 ....155 A4
Montana Rd IP5 .....141 A7
Montessori Sch The
IP7 ....94 E6
Montford CI CB5 ......44 C6
Montfort CI 11 CB9 ..132 D5
Montgomery Ave
NR32 ....113 B4
Montgomery Rd IP2 .139 B1
Monton Rise IP2 ....138 D2
Montpelier Dr 1 IP24 ..16 A5
Monument Farm La
IP10 ....141 C3
Monument Farm Rd
IP10 ....141 B4
Moo Play Farm* NR34 ..25 C5
Moon Hall La CB9 ...132 E3
Moor Rd
Burston & Shimpling IP21 ..21 B6
Langham CO4 ....103 B2
Middleton IP17 ....57 F6
Moor's Way IP12 ...146 E5
Moorbridge La IP14 ..66 B8
Moore Rd Ipswich IP1 ..134 F3
Rushbrooke with Rougham
IP30 ....49 A1
Moore's CI 17 IP14 ...53 F2
Mooreland Dr IP31 ...49 C6
Moorfield Rd IP12 ..146 E5
Moorhall Cswy IP23 ..117 C1
Moorsfield CO10 ...148 F2
Moreton Hall Prep Sch
IP32 ....123 D5
Morgan CI 3 IP31 ....34 F7
Morgan Dr IP11 .....134 C1
Morgan Meadow IP14 ..124 C2
Morland Prim Sch
IP3 ....144 A4
Morland Rd 1 IP3 ...144 A4
Morley Ave IP12 ...146 F4
Morley CI 3 IP28 ....30 B8
Morley La IP23 ....26 D6
Mormor La IP21 .....21 E4
Mornington Ave IP1 ..134 F1
Morris Way IP6 ....125 D4
Mors End 2 CO7 ...103 E5
Morston Hall Rd IP1 ..98 B1
Mortimer La IP28 ....29 E3
Mortimer PI 2 CO10 ..76 A1
Morton Peto CI NR32 ..113 B4
Morton Rd NR33 ....115 B4
Moss La IP7 ....135 F4
Mother Quy's IP24 ...15 C5

Mottram CI 14 IP8 ...138 C2
Moulton Ave CB8 .....46 A5
Moulton CE Prim Sch
Moulton CI 5 CO10 ..148 D6
Moulton CB8 ....45 F1
Moulton Packhorse Bridge*
CB8 ....45 F3
Moulton Paddocks
CB8 ....121 F7
Moulton Rd
Cheveley CB8 ....121 D6
Gazeley CB8 ....46 B3
Kentford CB8 ....46 B3
Moulton CB8 ....45 F1
Mount CI 5 IP30 .....64 F8
Mount Dr IP3 ....140 F1
Mount Pleasant
Framlingham IP13 ...126 B4
Halesworth IP19 ....118 B5
Lowestoft NR32 .....113 C3
1 Peasenhall IP17 ...56 F8
Southwold IP18 .....119 C8
Mount Rd
Bury St Edmunds IP32 ..123 D6
Haverhill CB9 ....132 E5
Rushbrooke with Rougham
IP30 ....49 A3
Mountbatten CI CO10 ..148 D8
Mountbatten Ct IP1 ..139 A7
Mountbatten Rd
Bungay NR35 ....110 B2
Lowestoft NR32 .....113 B4
Sudbury CO10 ....148 D5
Mounts The IP17 .....56 F8
Mouse La IP30 ....49 A3
Moverley Way IP5 ...130 E5
Mow Hill IP6 ....83 A5
Mowbrays The IP13 ..126 D3
Mowlands IP9 ......150 F3
Mowness Hall La IP14 ..68 A6
Moyes Rd NR32 .....112 D1
Moyse Ave CB9 .....119 C8
Moyse's Hall Mus*
IP3 ....154 B2
Mulberry CI
Beccles NR34 ....111 C5
18 Feltwell IP26 ......4 E5
Mildenhall IP28 ....116 E4
Mulberry Gdns 11 IP6 ..82 A5
Mulberry Rd 3 IP3 ..144 C7
Mumford Rd IP1 ....138 E8
Munday's La IP12 ...131 B3
Mundford Prim Sch
IP26 ....6 A8
Mundford Rd
Brandon IP27 ....5 F2
Thetford IP24 ....9 A6
Weeting-with-Broomhill
IP27 ....6 A4
Mundy's Rd IP20 ....23 A5
Munnings CI
Haverhill CB9 ....132 B7
3 Lowestoft NR33 ..114 C3
Newmarket CB8 ....121 A5
Munnings Way CO11 ..104 D3
Munson's La IP24 ....16 B4
Munson's PI IP26 ....16 B4
Murfitt's La CB7 .....29 A2
Muriel CI IP17 ......149 E6
Murillo Dr 1 NR32 ..113 C6
Murray Rd IP3 ......140 E1
Murrayfield Prim Sch
NR32 ....113 B4
Murrills Rd IP3 .....140 E1
Murton CI 10 CB5 ...44 C6
Museum of East Anglian Life*
IP14 ....124 D5
Museum St IP1 .....155 B3
Musgrave CI IP4 ...106 F1
Mustards Gapp CB9 ..133 A5
Mustow St IP3 .....154 C2
Mutford CI NR32 ...112 F1
Mutford Gn IP27 ...109 C2
Mutford Wood NR33 ..10 D4
Mutfordwood La
NR33 ....114 A2
Mutton La IP13 ....70 A8
Mylford CI IP32 ....123 D4
Mylodon Rd NR32 ..113 C4
Myrtle CI
Bury St Edmunds IP33 ..154 A3
2 Eriswell IP27 .....13 F2
Lowestoft NR32 .....113 B2
Myrtle Rd IP3 ......139 E4

N

Nacton CE VC Prim Sch
IP3 ....145 C5
Nacton CI 5 IP3 .....85 B3
Nacton Cres IP3 ...140 B2
Nacton La 2 IP31 ...49 A6
Nacton Rd
Felixstowe IP11 ....152 E1
Ipswich IP3 ....144 D7
Levington IP10 .....145 E3
Nan Hazle's La IP22 ..36 B4
Nansen Rd IP3 ....140 B2
Napier PI IP22 ....16 B5
Naples CI 5 NR31 ....3 C4
Narrow Way IP19 ....42 C6
Nash CI CO11 ......104 D3
Nash Gdns 3 IP5 ...141 B8
Nat Flatman St CB8 ..121 B3
National Horseracing Mus*
CB8 ....121 A3

National Stud* CB8 ...59 B8
Nato PI IP2 ....109 F1
Naughton Gdns 8 IP14 ..124 E3
Naughton Rd IP7 ....80 C1
Naunton Rd IP12 ...146 E5
Navarre St IP1 .....155 B3
Naverne Meadow
IP12 ....147 A5
Nayland Prim Sch
CO6 ....102 D5
Nayland Rd
Bures St Mary CO8 ..101 D4
1 Felixstowe IP11 ..152 C3
Great Horkesley CO6 ..102 D2
Haverhill CB9 ....132 C4
Little Horkesley CO6 ..102 C3
Naylor CI IP14 .....124 B7
Neale CI IP16 ......129 B6
Neale St IP1 ....155 B3
Neath Dr IP2 ....139 A1
Neaves La IP21 ......39 B4
Nedging Rd IP7 ......79 F3
Needham La IP7 .....79 F4
Needham Lake Nature
Reserve & Visitor Ctr*
IP6 ....125 E4
Needham Mkt Mid Sch
IP6 ....125 D4
Needham Mkt Sta IP6 ..125 E4
Needham Rd
Coddenham IP6 ......67 F1
Needham IP20 ....22 C5
Stowmarket IP14 ...124 E4
Needham Rd W IP14 ..124 E4
Needle Cnr IP9 .....106 B5
Nelson CI IP6 ....83 A8
Nelson Cres 2 IP24 ..16 B5
Nelson Rd
Bury St Edmunds IP33 ..154 A2
Ipswich IP4 ....140 A7
1 Lowestoft NR33 ..115 A3
Sudbury CO10 ....148 E2
Nelson Way
Beccles NR34 ....111 A4
Woodbridge IP12 ...146 F7
Nelson Wharf NR33 ..114 F7
Nene Dr IP3 ....144 D7
Neptune Quay IP4 ..155 C2
Neptune Sq IP3 ....155 C2
Neptune St IP4 ....155 C2
Ness Rd Arwarton IP9 ..106 D5
Burwell CB5 ....44 B7
Nether Hall Mus & Gall*
CO10 ....76 E2
Nether Hill CO10 ....90 E2
Nether Rd 2 CO10 ...76 E1
Nethergate St
Bungay NR35 ....110 A5
Clare CO10 ....90 A7
Hopton IP22 ....18 B2
Netherhall CI IP14 ...52 A1
Netley CI IP2 ....142 F8
Netley Rd IP33 ....122 D3
Nettlestead Rd IP8 ..81 D4
New Gdns IP28 ......30 A6
New Cangle Com Prim Sch
CB9 ....132 D2
New Cardinal St IP1 ..155 A2
New Cheveley Rd CB8 ..121 C3
New Comm Rd IP22 ..35 B8
New Cut 5 Bures CO8 ..101 C4
8 Glemsford CO10 ...77 A2
Hadleigh IP7 ....149 E6
Halesworth IP19 ...118 B4
Newmarket CB8 ....121 A3
Saxmundham IP17 ..128 D3
New Cut E IP3 ......155 C1
New Cut W IP2 .....155 C1
New Dro
Beck Row, Holywell Row
& Kenny Hill IP28 ...12 E1
Soham CB7 ....28 A4
New England Way 2
IP24 ....16 A5
New Gn Gn Ave 15 IP31 ..49 E4
New Hampshire Way 5
IP24 ....16 A5
New House La CO10 ..76 B3
New Mkt IP14 ......111 B5
New Mkt The
New Path 4 CB7 .....29 A1
New Quay Ct IP12 ..147 B5
New Quay La IP12 ..147 B6
New Quay Terr IP12 ..147 B5
New Queens Rd CO10 ..148 C7
New Rd Ampton IP31 ..33 A1
Aspall IP14 ....54 A5
Badingham IP13 .....56 B8
Barnby NR34 ....10 C4
Barrow IP29 ....47 B3
Beccles NR34 ....111 B7
Brettenham IP24 ....17 B6
5 Burwell CB5 ....44 A6
Chevington IP29 .....62 C7
Dickleburgh & Rushall
IP21 ....21 A4
Elmswell IP30 ....50 E2
Exning CB8 ....120 B8
Felixstowe IP11 ....152 C7
Framlingham IP13 ..126 C5
Fritton & St Olaves NR31 ..2 B7
Gissing IP22 ....20 E8
Great Glemham IP17 ..57 F8
Helmingham IP14 ....69 A5
19 Ixworth IP31 ......34 B1

New Rd *continued*
Little Livermere IP31 . . . . . . .33 A2
Long Melford CO10 . . . . .91 D8
Manningtree CO11 . . . . .104 E2
Marlesford IP13 . . . . .71 C6
Melton IP12 . . . . .84 D6
Mettingham NR35 . . . . .110 F2
Nedging-with-Naughton
IP7 . . . . .80 C3
Rumburgh IP19 . . . . .24 C4
Rushbrooke with Rougham
IP30 . . . . .49 D1
St Cross, South Elmham
IP20 . . . . .23 D5
Sibton IP17 . . . . .41 D1
Thelnetham IP22 . . . . .35 B7
Thrandeston IP21 . . . . .37 C8
Timworth IP31 . . . . .48 E8
Tivetshall St Mary NR15 . . . .21 B8
Tostock IP30 . . . . .50 B2
Troston IP31 . . . . .33 D4
Worlingworth IP13 . . . . .54 F8
New River Gn CB8 . . . . . . .120 E8
New St Chippenham CB7 . . .29 E1
Framlingham IP13 . . . . .126 A4
Fressingfield IP21 . . . . .39 D8
Glemsford CO10 . . . . .77 A3
4 Mildenhall IP28 . . . . . . .116 C4
Stradbroke IP21 . . . . .39 A4
Sudbury CO10 . . . . .148 C6
9 Woodbridge IP12 . . . . . .147 A5
New St Cl IP21 . . . . .39 A4
New Way IP2 . . . . .138 F6
New Wolsey Theatre★
IP1 . . . . .155 A3
Newall Rd 2 IP24 . . . . .12 E5
Newark Cl IP2 . . . . .138 F1
Newark Rd
3 Lakenheath IP27 . . . . . . .13 F2
Lowestoft NR33 . . . . .115 B6
Newberry Rd 7 IP7 . . . . .79 F4
Newburn Rd IP10 . . . . .98 C4
Newbourne Gdns
IP11 . . . . .152 D3
Newbourne Rd
Brightwell IP10 . . . . .98 A6
Martlesham IP12 . . . . .84 B1
Waldringfield IP12 . . . . .98 C7
Newbourne Springs Nature
Reserve★ IP12 . . . . .98 D6
Newbury Rd IP4 . . . . .140 C6
Newby Cl IP3 . . . . .118 A3
Newby Dr IP4 . . . . .140 F5
Newcastle Cl 6 IP27 . . . . . . .13 F2
Newcombe Dr 16 IP26 . . . . . .4 E5
Newcombe Rd NR32 . . . . . .113 E1
Newdelight Rd IP22 . . . . . . .35 F2
Newell Rise IP6 . . . . .134 C8
Newton Gravel Dro
IP7 . . . . .109 A8
Newgate Beccles NR34 . . . .111 B5
Kirby Row NR35 . . . . .8 E7
Newgate La NR35 . . . . .8 E7
Newhaven Way IP7 . . . . . . .149 E7
Newland Ave NR34 . . . . . . .111 E4
Newlands 2 Elmsett IP7 . . .80 F1
Otley IP6 . . . . .69 D2
Newlands Cl
40 Harleston IP20 . . . . .22 D6
Lowestoft NR33 . . . . .114 F3
Newlands La IP5 . . . . .102 D5
Newman's Rd CO10 . . . . . . .148 C6
Newmarket Coll CB8 . . . . . .120 F4
Newmarket Com Hospl
CB8 . . . . .120 F5
Newmarket Lawn Tennis
Club CB8 . . . . .120 E3
Newmarket Leisure Ctr
CB8 . . . . .120 F4
Newmarket Racecourse
CB8 . . . . .120 B1
Newmarket Rd
4 Ashley CB8 . . . . .60 F8
Barton Mills IP28 . . . . .116 D1
Burwell CB5 . . . . .44 B5
Bury St Edmunds IP33 . . . . .122 D6
Cowlinge CB8 . . . . .61 B2
Fordham CB7 . . . . .44 E8
Moulton CB8 . . . . .45 F3
Newmarket CB8 . . . . .121 B8
Red Lodge IP28 . . . . .30 C2
Risby IP28 . . . . .47 C5
Snailwell CB8 . . . . .45 A5
Newmarket Sports Ctr
CB8 . . . . .121 A4
Newmarket Sta CB8 . . . . . .121 A4
Newmarket Swimming Pool
CB8 . . . . .120 F3
Newmarket Upper Sch
CB8 . . . . .120 F4
Newmill La CO11 . . . . .105 A5
Newnham Ave IP12 . . . . . .146 D4
Newnham Ct IP28 . . . . .116 D5
Newnham Ct IP2 . . . . .138 E1
Newnham Dro CB5 . . . . .44 A6
Newnham La 4 CB8 . . . . . . .121 A6
Newport Ave CB7 . . . . .29 C1
Newport Cl 7 IP27 . . . . .13 F2
Newquay Cl IP5 . . . . .140 F6
Newry Ave IP11 . . . . .152 F4
Newson Ave NR34 . . . . .10 C3
Newson St IP1 . . . . .155 A4
Newson's Meadow 1
NR32 . . . . .113 C2
Newthorpe IP30 . . . . .49 D8

Newton Croft CO10 . . . . . .148 E5
Newton Pl 4 CB9 . . . . .132 F6
Newton Rd
17 Harwich CO12 . . . . . . .107 A2
Ipswich IP3 . . . . .140 A4
Stowupland IP14 . . . . .124 D8
Sudbury CO10 . . . . .148 D5
Newton St IP4 . . . . .155 C3
Nicholas Dr IP18 . . . . .119 C7
Nicholas Everitt Pk
NR33 . . . . .114 D8
Nicholas Rd IP11 . . . . .152 C4
Nicholas's St IP22 . . . . .20 C3
Nicholls Cl 7 IP21 . . . . .84 F7
Nicholls Cl 2 CO11 . . . . . . .104 D2
Nicholson Dr NR34 . . . . . . .111 C2
Nicholson Sq 2 NR32 . . . . .113 C2
Nicholsons Ct CO10 . . . . . . .92 D3
Nick's La IP23 . . . . .117 B6
Nidderdale 8 NR33 . . . . . .114 E3
Nightall Rd 5 CB7 . . . . .28 D4
Nightingale Ave IP18 . . . . .119 B7
Nightingale Cl
Bury St Edmunds IP33 . . . . .154 A1
13 Harwich CO12 . . . . . . .106 F1
5 Mildenhall IP28 . . . . . . .116 D4
6 Stowmarket IP14 . . . . . . .67 A5
Nightingale Hill CO4 . . . . .103 C3
Nightingale La IP26 . . . . . . .4 E5
Nightingale Piece
IP12 . . . . .131 C3
Nightingale Rd
Ipswich IP3 . . . . .144 A8
Lowestoft NR33 . . . . .115 B3
Nightingale Sq 6 IP3 . . . . .144 A8
Nimbus Way CB8 . . . . .120 E8
Nine Acres IP2 . . . . .138 D6
Ninfield Cl NR33 . . . . .114 D4
No Man's Meadow★
IP33 . . . . .123 C4
Noahs Ark Pl CO10 . . . . . . .148 B5
Noahs Dr 5 NR33 . . . . .11 B1
Noaks Rd IP7 . . . . .94 F1
Nock Gdns IP5 . . . . .141 C6
Noel Cl NR31 . . . . .3 B7
Noel Murless Dr CB8 . . . . .120 F6
Noel Rd NR32 . . . . .112 C1
Noel's Wlk NR34 . . . . .111 B6
Noller's La IP19 . . . . .24 F4
Nonsuch Meadow 2
CO10 . . . . .148 C4
Norbury Rd IP4 . . . . .140 B7
Nordalls The 16 NR33 . . . . .11 C3
Norfolk & Suffolk Aviation
Mus★ NR35 . . . . .7 D2
Norfolk Ave CB8 . . . . .120 E5
Norfolk Cres 1 NR35 . . . . .126 C3
Norfolk Rd
Bury St Edmunds IP32 . . . . .123 A8
9 Honington IP31 . . . . .33 D5
Ipswich IP4 . . . . .155 C3
Norfolk St NR32 . . . . .113 B1
Norgate La IP21 . . . . .21 B2
Norman Cl
Felixstowe IP11 . . . . .153 D6
Woodbridge IP12 . . . . .147 A7
Norman Cres IP21 . . . . .140 A2
Norman Rd
6 Bury St Edmunds IP32 . . .48 C5
Bury St Edmunds IP32 . . . . .122 F8
2 Manningtree CO11 . . . . .104 E2
Norman Way 1 CO10 . . . . . .78 D8
Normandie Way 8 CO8 . . . .101 C4
Normandy Cl IP14 . . . . . . .124 D3
Normandy Rd NR31 . . . . .3 B7
Normanhurst Cl NR32 . . . .113 A2
Normanston Dr 5 NR32 . . .113 A2
Nornea La CB7 . . . . .28 A8
Norse Ave CB9 . . . . .64 A3
North Acres IP8 . . . . .81 A6
North Ave CB9 . . . . .132 C6
North Cl Bacton NR14 . . . . . .51 F6
Ipswich IP4 . . . . .135 E1
2 Stanton IP31 . . . . .34 E4
North Cres CB9 . . . . .88 D4
North Dr
Newmarket CB8 . . . . .120 F5
1 Soham CB7 . . . . .28 D5
North End CB8 . . . . .120 B8
North End Ave IP16 . . . . . . .73 F6
North End Rd CO10 . . . . . . .90 C2
North Entrance IP17 . . . . . .128 D2
North Field Cl 4 NR32 . . . .112 F5
North Gn IP18 . . . . .119 D6
North Gn Rd
Cratfield IP19 . . . . .40 C7
Pulham St Mary IP21 . . . . . . .22 A8
North Hill IP12 . . . . .146 F6
North Hill Gdns IP4 . . . . . .139 E5
North Hill Rd IP4 . . . . .139 E6
North Lawn IP4 . . . . .135 E1
North Lopham Rd
NR16 . . . . .19 A7
North Par Gdns IP18 . . . . .119 E6
North Parade
Lowestoft NR32 . . . . .113 D4
Southwold IP18 . . . . .119 E5
North Pl IP28 . . . . .116 C4
North Rd
Great Yeldham CO9 . . . . .90 A1
Lakenheath IP27 . . . . .109 E4
Southwold IP18 . . . . .119 D6
North Rise CO10 . . . . .148 D4
North St Burwell CB5 . . . . . .44 A6
Freckenham IP28 . . . . .29 E4
Hundon CO10 . . . . .75 D4

North St *continued*
11 Manningtree CO11 . . . .104 E2
Steeple Bumpstead CB9 . . . .88 D4
Sudbury CO10 . . . . .148 C6
Wicken CB7 . . . . .28 A1
North St Parade 5
CO10 . . . . .148 C5
North Terr NR33 . . . . .116 C5
North Warren IP15 . . . . . . .130 C8
North Warren Nature
Reserve★ IP15 . . . . .73 D6
Northacre 12 NR33 . . . . . . .11 B1
Northcroft 1 CO10 . . . . . . .148 C5
Northern Rd CO10 . . . . . . .148 F7
Northern Rose Cl
IP32 . . . . .123 F7
Northern Way NR32 . . . . . . .48 C5
Northfield 1 IP15 . . . . .130 E5
Northfield La IP15 . . . . . . .130 E5
Northfield Pk CB7 . . . . .28 C5
Northfield Rd
Onehouse IP14 . . . . .66 C6
Soham CB7 . . . . .28 C5
Northfield St Nicholas CP
Prim Sch NR32 . . . . . . .113 C3
Northgate
Beccles NR34 . . . . .111 B6
11 Harleston IP20 . . . . .22 D5
Lowestoft NR32 . . . . .113 B2
Northgate Ave IP32 . . . . . .154 B4
Northgate City High Sch
IP4 . . . . .136 A1
Northgate Lodge IP33 . . . .154 B3
Northgate Sports Ctr
IP4 . . . . .136 A2
Northgate St
Bury St Edmunds IP33 . . . . .154 C3
Ipswich IP1 . . . . .155 B3
Northgate St Bsns Pk
IP33 . . . . .154 C3
Northumberland Ave
IP32 . . . . .122 E8
Northwood Cl NR33 . . . . . .114 F6
Norton CE Prim Sch
IP31 . . . . .50 B5
Norton Rd
Haverhill CB9 . . . . .132 C4
Hunston IP31 . . . . .50 E5
1 Thurstow IP31 . . . . .49 D4
Tostock IP30 . . . . .50 B2
Norway Cres 2 CO12 . . . . .106 F2
Norwich La
Bardwell IP31 . . . . .34 C8
Coney Weston IP31 . . . . .17 E2
Norwich Rd Barham IP6 . . .82 A6
Claydon IP6 . . . . .134 C8
Denton IP20 . . . . .7 B3
5 Dickleburgh & Rushall
IP21 . . . . .20 F1
Ditchingham NR35 . . . . .110 A8
Earsham NR35 . . . . .7 E5
Gillingham NR34 . . . . .111 A4
Halesworth IP19 . . . . .118 C5
Ipswich IP1 . . . . .155 A3
5 Lakenheath IP27 . . . . . . .13 F2
Lakenheath IP27 . . . . .109 F1
Lowestoft NR32 . . . . .113 C1
Newmarket CB8 . . . . .121 D6
Pulham St Mary IP21 . . . . . . .21 F8
Scole IP21 . . . . .20 F6
Stockton NR34 . . . . .9 A8
Thetford IP24 . . . . .16 C6
Norwich Rd Sch IP24 . . . . . .16 C6
Norwood Rd IP27 . . . . .14 E8
Notcutts CO7 . . . . .151 E3
Notley Dr CB9 . . . . .132 A7
Notley Ent Pk CO7 . . . . . . .151 D3
Nottage Rd IP1 . . . . .139 F6
Nova Scotia La IP7 . . . . . . .79 B4
Nowton Ctry Pk★ IP29 . . . .63 E8
Nowton Rd IP29 . . . . .123 D1
Nowton Rd
Bury St Edmunds IP33 . . . . .123 C1
Nowton IP29 . . . . .63 E8
Noyes Ave IP12 . . . . .40 B3
Nuffield Hospl (Private)
IP33 . . . . .154 C1
Nunn Cl 1 IP12 . . . . .84 A1
Nunn Sq IP32 . . . . .122 D8
Nunn's Hill IP19 . . . . .24 C3
Nunn's La IP19 . . . . .23 E1
Nunnery Gn 3 CB8 . . . . . . .61 E2
Nuns' Bridges Rd IP24 . . . .16 B5
Nuns Wlk CO7 . . . . .89 F1
Nursery Cl Isleham CB7 . . . .29 B4
Mildenhall IP28 . . . . .116 D4
Nursery La IP26 . . . . .5 A2
Nursery Rd CO10 . . . . .148 F2
Nursery Wlk IP11 . . . . .152 F4
Nursey Cl NR35 . . . . .8 D7
Nuttery Vale IP23 . . . . .38 B6

O

Oak Ave NR34 . . . . .111 F5
Oak Cl
Bury St Edmunds IP28 . . . . . .48 C6
Felixstowe IP11 . . . . .152 E4
4 Great Finborough IP14 . . .66 B4
Oak Cres IP23 . . . . .117 C3
Oak Dr Diss IP22 . . . . .20 E4
6 Mildenhall IP28 . . . . . . .30 B8
Oak Eggar Chase IP8 . . . . .142 D8
Oak Farm La IP14 . . . . .52 D6
Oak Gn IP19 . . . . .118 B2

Oak Gr
Fornham St Martin IP31 . . . . .48 D5
Sproughton IP8 . . . . .138 A6
Oak Hill Cl NR34 . . . . .26 E5
Oak Hill La IP7 . . . . .139 B3
Oak La Beccles NR34 . . . . . .111 D2
Cheveley CB8 . . . . .60 E6
Elmswell IP30 . . . . .50 F3
Ipswich IP3 . . . . .155 B3
Lakenheath IP27 . . . . .13 F2
Rushbrooke with Rougham
IP30 . . . . .64 D8
Woolpit IP30 . . . . .65 E8
Oak Meadow Cl IP19 . . . . . .42 C6
Oak Rd 3 Sudbury CO10 . . .92 B3
Sudbury CO10 . . . . .148 F4
Oak St IP26 . . . . .4 E5
Oak Tree Way 8 IP20 . . . . . .22 D5
Oak Way IP19 . . . . .118 A1
Oakdene IP12 . . . . .98 D2
Oakes Rd IP32 . . . . .122 E7
Oakey Field Rd 6 IP21 . . . . .49 E4
Oakey Ley IP30 . . . . .64 D6
Oakfield Rd Bacton IP14 . . .52 A6
Copdock & Washbrook
IP8 . . . . .142 A6
Oakfield Wood Nature
Reserve★ CO11 . . . . . . .105 E3
Oakland Rd 2 CO12 . . . . . .107 B2
Oaklands CO6 . . . . .102 B8
Oaklands Dr IP27 . . . . .14 D8
Oakley Church La IP21 . . . . .37 F8
Oakley Rd IP21 . . . . .106 E1
Oakley Sq IP15 . . . . .130 E4
Oaks Bsns Pk CB8 . . . . . . .120 E7
Oaks Com Prim Sch
Chantry IP2 . . . . .138 E4
Ipswich IP2 . . . . .138 E3
Oaks Dr CB8 . . . . .120 F7
Oaks La NR34 . . . . .2 B1
Oaks The
7 Horringer IP29 . . . . .63 A8
Martlesham Heath IP5 . . . . .141 F6
Soham CB7 . . . . .28 D3
Wattisfield IP22 . . . . .35 C5
Woolpit IP30 . . . . .65 F8
Oaksmere Gdns 8 IP27 . . .139 A2
Oakwood Pk IP17 . . . . .57 D7
Oakwood Rd NR33 . . . . . . .114 F5
Oasis Camelid Ctr★
IP19 . . . . .40 C8
Oban St IP1 . . . . .155 A4
Occold Prim Sch IP23 . . . . .37 F1
Occold Rd IP23 . . . . .38 B2
O'feld Terr IP11 . . . . .153 C6
Off Sea View Rd IP18 . . . . .119 C7
Offton Rd Elmsett IP7 . . . . .81 A2
Great Bricett IP7 . . . . .80 F5
Ohio Cl 4 NR33 . . . . .114 E3
Old Barn Rd CB8 . . . . .101 C3
Old Barningham Rd 1
IP31 . . . . .34 E4
Old Barrack Rd IP12 . . . . . .146 E4
Old Brandon Rd IP26 . . . . . .4 F5
Old Brewery Yd IP19 . . . . . .118 A5
Old Buckenham Hall Sch
IP7 . . . . .79 B7
Old Bungay Rd NR35 . . . . . .8 D8
Old Bury Rd
Alpheton CO10 . . . . .78 A6
Lackford IP28 . . . . .31 F1
Palgrave IP22 . . . . .37 A8
Stanton IP31 . . . . .34 E4
Stuston IP21 . . . . .20 D1
Wortham IP22 . . . . .36 F8
Old Cattle Mkt IP1 . . . . . . .155 B2
Old Church La
Bulmer CO10 . . . . .91 C1
Westley IP33 . . . . .122 A6
Old Church Rd 1 NR31 . . . . .3 B6
Old Clements La 5
CB9 . . . . .132 D5
Old Coll Cl NR34 . . . . .111 B5
Old Convent Orch
IP33 . . . . .154 B1
Old Dairy Bsns Pk IP31 . . . .49 B5
Old Farm Rd
Beccles NR34 . . . . .111 A4
4 Lowestoft NR33 . . . . . . .114 D5
Old Forge Cl IP22 . . . . .36 D8
Old Forge Ct IP21 . . . . .22 A2
Old Foundry Pl IP16 . . . . . .129 C6
Old Foundry Rd IP4 . . . . . .155 C3
Old Gram La NR35 . . . . . . .110 B3
Old Hall Cl IP26 . . . . .82 D6
Old Hall La Bentley IP9 . . . .95 F2
Pulham St Mary IP21 . . . . . . .22 A8
Westleton IP17 . . . . .58 B8
Old Hall Meadow CO10 . . . .65 D6
Old Hall Rd IP13 . . . . .56 C8
Old Harleston Rd NR35 . . . .7 F3
Old Haverhill Rd CB9 . . . . . .74 F2
Old High Rd
Boxted IP22 . . . . .20 B3
Yoxford IP17 . . . . .57 D7
Old Homes Rd 7 IP16 . . . . .73 F6
Old House La CO4 . . . . .103 A1
Old House Rd CO6 . . . . . . .102 D1
Old Ipswich Rd IP6 . . . . . .134 C7
Old Kirton Rd IP11 . . . . . . .107 D8
Old La
Bradfield Combust with
Stanningfield IP29 . . . . . . .63 F3

Old La *continued*
Corton NR32 . . . . .113 B8
Thelnetham IP22 . . . . .35 C6
Old London Rd IP9 . . . . . . .150 D1
Old Maids' La IP13 . . . . . . .70 A7
Old Maltings App
IP12 . . . . .147 B6
Old Maltings Ct IP12 . . . . .147 B5
Old Methwold Rd IP26 . . . . .4 E6
Old Mill Dr IP21 . . . . .21 F8
Old Mill La
Barton Mills IP28 . . . . .116 F2
Beccles NR34 . . . . .111 B4
Old Mill Rd CO4 . . . . .103 B3
Old Mill Terr 2 NR34 . . . . .111 B6
Old Mkt NR34 . . . . .111 B6
Old Mkt Pl
11 Harleston IP20 . . . . .22 D6
10 Mildenhall IP28 . . . . . . .116 C5
Old Mkt Plain 8 NR32 . . . .113 C2
Old Mkt St IP14 . . . . .52 E4
Old Nelson St 4 NR32 . . . .113 C2
Old Newton CE Prim Sch
IP14 . . . . .52 A1
Old Norwich Rd
Whitton IP1 . . . . .134 D5
Yaxley IP23 . . . . .37 C5
Old Orch IP27 . . . . .149 F1
Old Orch Cl IP19 . . . . .118 A2
Old Paper Mill La 8
IP6 . . . . .134 C8
Old Post Office La
Blaxhall IP12 . . . . .72 A4
Kirby Row NR35 . . . . .8 E7
Sutton IP12 . . . . .99 A8
Old Post Office Rd
IP29 . . . . .62 C6
Old Priory Gdns NR34 . . . . .26 B2
Old Rd The CO6 . . . . .102 B8
Old Rectory Cl
2 Claydon IP6 . . . . .82 B5
2 Roydon IP22 . . . . .20 A3
Old Rectory Gdns 3
IP23 . . . . .37 F1
Old Rectory La IP29 . . . . . . .77 E6
Old Rectory Rd IP13 . . . . . .56 A6
Old Rectory Sch The
IP7 . . . . .65 C1
Old Rectory Wlk IP7 . . . . . .150 D3
Old Rly Rd Alburgh IP20 . . . .7 B1
Bungay NR35 . . . . .110 A4
Old Rope Wlk CB9 . . . . . . .132 C5
Old Sch Cl
Brampton with Stoven
NR34 . . . . .25 E5
5 Burwell CB5 . . . . .44 B6
Leiston IP16 . . . . .129 C6
4 Soham CB7 . . . . .28 D5
Old Sch Dr IP28 . . . . .26 E1
Old Sch Hall The★
IP23 . . . . .154 B3
Old Sch La CB8 . . . . .59 F1
Old Sch Rd IP29 . . . . .63 A5
Old Sch The NR34 . . . . .10 E1
Old Schools Ct IP30 . . . . . . .50 F1
Old Sta Rd
Ellingham NR35 . . . . .8 D6
Halesworth IP19 . . . . .118 B5
Mendlesham IP14 . . . . .52 E3
Newmarket CB8 . . . . .121 B4
Old Stores Cl IP13 . . . . .54 E7
Old Stowmarket Rd
IP30 . . . . .50 D1
Old Town La IP33 . . . . .123 C1
Old Vicarage Dr IP31 . . . . . .50 E7
Old Vicarage Rd
CO12 . . . . .107 A2
Oldfield Rd IP8 . . . . .138 B1
Oldhall Rd IP19 . . . . .106 F6
Olding Rd IP33 . . . . .122 D6
Olive Cl 2 IP22 . . . . .13 F2
Olive Ct NR32 . . . . .113 B3
Olive La NR34 . . . . .114 D2
Oliver Cl IP27 . . . . .5 E4
Oliver Rd IP33 . . . . .122 C6
Olivers Cl CO10 . . . . .91 E8
Olland Ct 5 NR35 . . . . .110 B3
Olle Cl IP33 . . . . .122 D6
Olympus Cl IP1 . . . . .134 C2
One Eyed La IP21 . . . . .22 B8
Onehouse La IP14 . . . . .135 C1
Onehouse Rd IP14 . . . . . . .124 B6
Onner's La IP16 . . . . .58 C4
Ontario Rd NR33 . . . . .115 C3
Opal Ave 1 Ipswich IP1 . . .134 D1
Ipswich IP1 . . . . .138 D8
Orchard Ave NR33 . . . . . . .116 C5
Orchard Cl Beyton IP30 . . . .49 F1
Bildeston IP7 . . . . .3 A4
Elmswell IP30 . . . . .50 F3
Great Livermere IP31 . . . . . .33 C2
6 Haverhill CB9 . . . . .132 D5
Lidgate CB8 . . . . .61 C4
2 Ramsey & Parkeston
CO12 . . . . .106 D1
Ridgewell CO9 . . . . .89 D3
Risby IP28 . . . . .47 D5
Rushbrooke with Rougham
IP30 . . . . .64 D8
Woodbridge IP12 . . . . .147 A4
Orchard Croft 2 NR33 . . . .114 E4
Orchard Dr IP14 . . . . .65 F4
Orchard End 1 IP13 . . . . . . .83 E5
Orchard Farm Barns 2
IP29 . . . . .47 A2

Orc - Pip 177

Orchard Farm Bsns Pk
CB7 ....28 C7
Orchard Gate
Ipswich IP2 ....138 C5
1 Needham Market IP6 ..125 D5
Orchard Gdn NR33 ....114 E7
Orchard Gn NR34 ....111 C4
Orchard Gr
Claydon IP6 ....134 C7
Ipswich IP5 ....141 A7
Orchard La
3 Blundeston NR32 ....3 A4
Thurston IP31 ....49 E5
Orchard Pl
Sudbury CO10 ....148 B4
Wickham Market IP13 ....127 B6
Orchard Rd
6 Bramford IP8 ....134 A2
Leiston IP16 ....129 C5
Orchard Rise
Badingham IP13 ....56 A7
Beccles NR34 ....111 F4
Orchard Row CB7 ....28 E2
Orchard St
Bury St Edmunds IP33 ....154 B3
Ipswich IP4 ....155 C3
Orchard Terr 4 NR33 ..115 C7
Orchard The
5 Ashley CB8 ....60 F8
Felsham IP30 ....65 A4
Redisham NR34 ....25 B7
Orchard Valley IP19 ....118 D4
Orchard Way
Badwell Ash IP31 ....50 F7
12 Barrow IP29 ....47 A2
4 Burwell CB5 ....44 A6
4 Glemsford CO10 ....77 A2
Scole IP21 ....21 A2
Orchard Way The 2
IP29 ....63 A8
Orchards The 1 IP13 ....40 B3
Orchid Cl
Halesworth IP19 ....118 C4
Ipswich IP2 ....138 E4
Orchid Way IP6 ....125 D3
Orchids Cl NR35 ....110 D3
Oregon Rd IP5 ....141 A6
Orford Castle Mus & Visitor
Ctr* IP12 ....131 B2
Orford CE VA Prim Sch
IP12 ....131 B3
Orford Dr NR32 ....112 F3
Orford Ness* IP12 ..131 C1
Orford Ness National Nature
Reserve* IP12 ....87 C3
Orford Rd
Bromeswell IP12 ....147 F7
Butley IP12 ....86 A6
Felixstowe IP11 ....152 E1
Haverhill CB9 ....132 D4
Tunstall IP12 ....71 F2
Orford St IP1 ....155 A4
Oriel Cl CO10 ....148 F4
Original Factory Shop The
IP32 ....123 D7
Orkney Cl CB9 ....133 B5
Orkney Rd 4 IP4 ....136 A1
Orttewell Rd IP32 ....123 E6
Orvis La CO7 ....151 E3
Orwell Ave IP17 ....128 C4
Orwell Ct IP12 ....146 E3
Orwell Ctry Pk* IP3 ..139 F3
Orwell Dr 1 NR32 ....112 F3
Orwell High Sch IP11 ..152 E5
Orwell Pk Sch IP10 ....145 B3
Orwell Pl IP4 ....155 C2
Orwell Rd
Felixstowe IP11 ....152 F3
10 Harwich CO12 ....107 B2
Ipswich IP3 ....140 A4
Stowmarket IP14 ....124 D4
Orwell Ret Pk IP2 ....139 A5
Orwell Rise 10 IP9 ....106 C8
Orwell View Rd IP9 ....106 F6
Osborne Rd IP3 ....140 A4
Osborne St 4 NR32 ....113 E3
Osier Cl IP12 ....147 B6
Osier Rd IP33 ....154 B3
Osiers The IP14 ....124 D7
Osmund Wlk IP33 ....122 C4
Osprey Gn NR33 ....114 C6
Osprey Rd CB9 ....133 A5
Oswyn Cl IP32 ....123 D4
Otley Coll Otley IP6 ....69 C1
Rendlesham IP12 ....85 E8
Otley Ct 6 IP11 ....152 D5
Otley Hall* IP6 ....69 C3
Otley Prim Sch IP6 ....69 C2
Otley Rd IP12 ....85 C2
Otten Rd CO10 ....90 D5
Otter Trust The* NR35 ..7 E3
Oulton Broad N Sta
NR32 ....112 F1
Oulton Broad Prim Sch
NR32 ....112 C2
Oulton Broad S Sta
NR33 ....114 D7
Oulton Broad Wr Sports Ctr
NR33 ....114 D7
Oulton Cl 6 CO12 ....106 F2
Oulton Ct NR32 ....112 E4
Oulton Ind Est NR32 ....112 E3
Oulton Rd Flixton NR32 ..112 F7
Ipswich IP3 ....139 F2
Lowestoft NR32 ....113 A4
Oulton Rd N NR32 ....112 F5
Oulton St NR32 ....112 F4
Ound Farm Nature Reserve*
IP17 ....56 C1
Ousden Rd IP29 ....62 A6
Out Northgate IP33 ....154 B4
Out Risbygate IP33 ....122 E6
Out Westgate IP33 ....154 B1
Outney Meadow Cvn Pk
NR35 ....110 A5
Outney Rd NR35 ....110 A4
Overbury Hall Rd IP7 ..149 D1
Ovington Pl 5 CB9 ....132 F6
Owell The IP31 ....49 E6
Oxer Cl IP30 ....50 F2
Oxford Cl
Mildenhall IP28 ....116 A4
Sudbury CO10 ....148 E4
Oxford Dr Hadleigh IP7 ..149 D8
Woodbridge IP12 ....146 D3
Oxford Rd 2 Feltwell IP26 ..4 E5
Ipswich IP4 ....139 E5
Lowestoft NR32 ....113 D3
25 Manningtree CO11 ....104 E2
Oxford St CB8 ....120 B8

P

Packard Ave IP3 ....140 B2
Packard Pl IP8 ....134 B2
Packards La
Fordham CO6 ....102 A1
Wormingford CO6 ....101 F1
Packway La IP31 ....50 A5
Packway The IP20 ....23 A7
Paddock Cl IP33 ....122 C5
Paddock Farm IP31 ....34 D8
Paddock Hill 2 NR33 ....114 E7
Paddock Rd 13 IP20 ....22 D6
Paddock St CB7 ....28 D4
Paddock The 16 IP31 ....34 B1
Paddock Way
Chedburgh IP29 ....62 C4
Troston IP31 ....33 D3
Paddock Wood Cl 8
NR33 ....114 C4
Paddocks Cty Prim Sch
CB8 ....120 E4
Paddocks Dr CB8 ....121 A2
Paddocks Gn NR34 ....111 F4
Paddocks The
Ashen CO10 ....89 E5
Badwell Ash IP31 ....50 F7
6 Bures CO8 ....101 C4
12 Burwell CB5 ....44 A5
Halesworth IP19 ....118 C4
3 Martlesham Heath IP5 ..98 A8
Tuddenham St Martin
IP6 ....136 B5
Worlington IP28 ....30 B4
Padstow Rd IP5 ....141 A6
Page Gdns IP5 ....141 E8
Pageant Pl IP13 ....126 E3
Page's Cl IP14 ....124 C6
Pages Hill Rd IP29 ....63 B6
Paget Cl IP6 ....125 C5
Paget Pl CB8 ....121 A6
Paget Rd IP1 ....155 A4
Pains Cl 2 NR34 ....9 F4
Pains Hill IP14 ....67 F6
Pakefield Mid Sch
NR33 ....115 A3
Pakefield Prim Sch
NR33 ....115 A3
Pakefield Rd NR33 ....115 C5
Pakefield St NR33 ....115 B4
Pakenham Pl CB9 ....132 F5
Pakenham Rd IP31 ....49 D6
Pakenham Watermill*
IP31 ....49 F8
Pakenham Windmill*
IP31 ....49 F8
Palace La CB7 ....45 B8
Palace St 4 CB8 ....121 A3
Palfrey Height CO11 ....104 E4
Palgrave VC Prim Sch
IP22 ....20 C1
Palmcroft Cl 10 IP1 ....135 A3
Palmcroft Rd IP1 ....135 A3
Palmer Cl NR32 ....113 B6
Palmer Dr IP27 ....109 C7
Palmer St IP31 ....35 C1
Palmer's La IP18 ....119 A2
Palmerston Rd IP4 ....139 E6
Palmerswent Cl CO10 ....91 F8
Pamment's La 5 IP28 ....29 F6
Pannels Cl 5 CO10 ....77 A2
Pantile La 12 CB5 ....44 A6
Papeley Meadow IP29 ..47 B2
Paper Mill La IP8 ....134 B4
Parade Dr 6 CO12 ....106 E1
Parade Rd IP4 ....139 F7
Parade Rd N 13 NR33 ....115 D8
Parade Rd S NR33 ....115 D7
Parade The CB9 ....133 F8
Paradise Pl IP16 ....129 C5
Pardoe Pl IP4 ....140 E5
Parham Airfield Mus*
IP13 ....71 C7
Parish Bush Dro CB7 ....12 A1
Park Ave
Felixstowe IP11 ....153 B5
3 Fornham St Martin IP28 .48 C6
Newmarket CB8 ....121 B3
Saxmundham IP17 ....128 C3
Park Cl
2 Bentwaters Airfield
IP12 ....85 D8
1 Lowestoft NR33 ....114 D4
Park Cl *continued*
5 Martlesham Heath IP5 ..98 A8
4 Moulton CB8 ....45 F3
Sudbury CO10 ....148 E6
Park Cotts CB8 ....121 B2
Park Dr NR34 ....111 E4
Park End IP17 ....128 C2
Park Farm Dr
Barton Mills IP28 ....30 C2
Stanton IP31 ....34 E3
Park Farm La
Euston IP24 ....33 E8
Hoxne IP21 ....38 E6
Park Hill IP16 ....129 C6
Park La Aldeburgh IP15 ..130 E4
Bulmer CO10 ....91 C2
Charsfield IP13 ....70 C3
Eye IP23 ....117 D1
Glemsford CO10 ....77 B2
Hawstead IP29 ....63 D7
Kirton IP10 ....98 E3
Langham CO4 ....103 C2
Newmarket CB8 ....121 B3
Southwold IP18 ....119 D4
Thornham Parva IP23 ....37 A3
Park Meadows NR32 ..112 F6
Park N IP1 ....139 D8
Park Pl IP17 ....57 D7
Park Rd
Aldeburgh IP15 ....130 D4
Benhall IP17 ....72 A7
Boot Street IP13 ....137 D8
Burwell CB5 ....44 A5
Bury St Edmunds IP33 ....122 D4
Cheveley CB8 ....60 D7
Combs IP14 ....124 B2
Diss IP22 ....20 C2
Drinkstone IP30 ....50 B1
East Bergholt CO7 ....104 D5
Great Horkesley CO6 ....102 D4
Grundisburgh IP13 ....83 E5
Halesworth IP19 ....118 A5
3 Harwich CO12 ....107 B2
Haverhill CB9 ....132 B7
Ipswich IP1 ....139 C8
Lavenham CO10 ....78 D4
Letheringham IP13 ....70 D4
Lowestoft NR32 ....113 D3
Needham Market IP6 ....125 D4
St Cross, South Elmham
IP20 ....23 C7
Southolt IP23 ....54 A8
Stoke-by-Nayland CO6 ....102 F6
Sudbury CO10 ....148 E6
Wetherden IP14 ....51 A1
Park St CO6 ....102 E7
Park The
3 Great Barton IP31 ....49 A5
Tanningtree CO11 ....104 E2
Park View
Botesdale IP22 ....36 B7
Weeting IP27 ....5 E3
Wetherden IP14 ....51 A1
Park View Rd IP1 ....135 B1
Park Wlk IP19 ....118 E5
Parker Ave IP11 ....152 B4
Parker's Dro 3 IP28 ....29 F6
Parker's Rd IP14 ....52 A5
Parker's Way CO6 ....102 D5
Parkers Pl 1 IP5 ....98 A8
Parkers Wlk CB8 ....120 E8
Parkeston Rd
Felixstowe IP11 ....152 D4
Harwich CO12 ....107 A2
Parkhill NR32 ....112 F5
Parkington Wlk IP32 ..122 D7
Parklands 5 IP13 ....84 F7
Parklands Cl 9 CO10 ....77 B3
Parklands Gn 2 IP28 ....48 C6
Parklands The NR33 ....114 D4
Parklands Way 41 IP20 ....22 D6
Parkside
Chippenham CB7 ....45 C8
Haverhill CB9 ....132 D4
Mildenhall IP28 ....30 C8
3 Stanton IP31 ....34 E4
Parkside Ave IP4 ....155 C4
Parkside Dr NR32 ....113 A2
Parkway
Bury St Edmunds IP33 ....154 A2
Wickham Market IP13 ....127 C7
Parkway Mid Sch CB9 ..132 B6
Parkwood Dr CO10 ....148 C8
Parliament Rd IP4 ....140 B5
Parmenter Dr 13 CO10 ....92 B3
Parnell Cl IP1 ....134 F3
Parnell La IP30 ....50 D3
Parnell Rd IP1 ....134 F3
Parnham Pl 2 IP4 ....140 F5
Parr Rd CB9 ....132 B4
Parrington Way 26
CO11 ....104 D2
Parry Cl IP19 ....118 B5
Parsonage Cl
5 Burwell CB5 ....44 A5
Felixstowe IP11 ....152 D4
Parsonage Farm La
CB8 ....60 C5
Parsonage Gdns 16 CB9 .132 C5
Parsonage Gr 7 CO8 ....101 C4
Parsonage La
Burwell CB5 ....44 A5
Chelsworth IP7 ....79 E3
Parson's Field CO7 ....104 A3
Parson's La IP6 ....125 B2
Parsons Ct IP33 ....122 A6
Parsons Field 4 IP15 ..130 E5
Parsons Hill IP12 ....99 F7
Parsons Yd 24 CO11 ....104 E2
Partridge Cl
Boxford CO10 ....93 C4
15 Thurston IP31 ....49 D4
Partridge Rd IP2 ....138 D3
Pashford Cl IP27 ....109 D6
Pashford Pl 6 IP3 ....144 C8
Paske Ave CB9 ....132 D5
Pastures The
Ipswich IP4 ....140 F5
Oulton NR32 ....112 F6
Patricia Cl NR32 ....112 D2
Patrick Stead Hospl
IP19 ....118 C5
Patten La NR15 ....21 B7
Patterdale Gdns 3
NR32 ....113 A4
Pattern Bush Cl 4
CO11 ....104 E4
Patteson Rd IP3 ....139 E4
Patticroft 7 CO10 ....77 A3
Paul's Rd IP2 ....138 F5
Pauline St IP2 ....155 B1
Pavilion Ct CB9 ....132 F5
Paxton Chadwick Cl 1
IP16 ....129 D5
Payne St NR33 ....115 C7
Payne's La IP26 ....4 E5
Peach Maltings IP33 ..154 B4
Peacock Cl
Hockwold cum Wilton IP26 ..4 F3
5 Ipswich IP8 ....138 C2
Lowestoft NR33 ....114 C2
Peacock Rise 18 IP31 ....34 B1
Peacock St IP5 ....141 E7
Peacock's Pyghtle
IP12 ....131 C3
Peacocks Cl 1 CO10 ....76 E1
Peacocks Rd CO10 ....76 E2
Peak Dale NR33 ....114 E3
Pear Cl 2 IP23 ....36 D2
Pearce Rd IP3 ....140 A4
Pearce's Cl 2 IP26 ....5 A3
Pearcroft Rd IP1 ....135 B3
Pearl Cl IP6 ....69 C2
Pearl Rd IP1 ....138 D8
Pearmain Wlk 8 CB9 ....132 A6
Pearse Way IP3 ....140 E1
Pearson Rd IP4 ....140 C5
Pearsons Way IP8 ....95 F5
Peart Gr IP5 ....141 D6
Peartree Cl IP17 ....128 C6
Peartree Hill CO8 ....101 D2
Peasecroft Rd 3 IP31 ....34 B1
Peasenhall Cl 2 IP12 ....85 B3
Peasenhall Prim Sch
IP17 ....56 E8
Peasenhall Rd IP19 ....41 C3
Peasey Gdns IP5 ....141 C6
Peasey La IP5 ....141 C6
Pebble Cl NR32 ....113 A3
Pebble View Wlk 8 NR31 ..3 C6
Peckham St IP33 ....154 B3
Pecockes Cl 10 CO10 ....92 B3
Peddars Cl 1 IP31 ....34 B1
Peddars La NR34 ....111 B4
Peddars Way NR32 ....113 B4
Peel St IP1 ....155 B3
Peel Yd 2 IP5 ....98 A8
Peewit Hill IP11 ....152 D3
Peewit Rd IP2 ....138 C3
Pegasus Mews 1 NR32 .112 D1
Pegg's Hill IP20 ....22 F2
Pelham Cl 21 CO12 ....106 F1
Pelican Cl IP2 ....138 E3
Pemberton Rd 6 IP20 ....22 D5
Pemberton Wlk IP33 ....123 A2
Pembroke Ave IP12 ....146 E4
Pembroke Cl
Ipswich IP2 ....139 B3
Mildenhall IP28 ....116 C5
Newmarket CB8 ....121 B2
Pembroke Pl CO10 ....148 B8
Pembroke Rd
Bury St Edmunds IP33 ....122 D3
Framlingham IP13 ....126 B4
Pembrooke Way 1
NR32 ....113 A3
Pendleton Rd IP2 ....138 D1
Penfold Rd IP11 ....153 A4
Penn Cl IP9 ....150 F4
Pennine Way NR32 ....112 E2
Pennings Nature Reserve
The* IP23 ....117 E2
Penny La 5 Ipswich IP3 ..140 F1
Lowestoft NR32 ....112 E3
Penny Meadow 3 IP9 ..150 E3
Pennycress Dr 4 IP24 ..16 D7
Pennyfields NR35 ....110 B2
Pennygate Dr NR33 ....114 E6
Pennyroyal Gdns IP2 ..138 E4
Penryn Rd IP5 ....141 A7
Penshurst Rd IP3 ....140 D4
Pentland Wlk 9 NR32 ..113 A4
Pentlow Dr CO10 ....76 F1
Pentlow Hawke Cl
CB9 ....133 A5
Pentlow Hill CO10 ....91 A8
Penzance Rd IP5 ....141 A6
Pepper La IP31 ....49 E3
Pepper Pl IP5 ....141 D6
Pepper's Rd CO4 ....102 F1
Peppercorn Way 2 IP2 .139 C3
Peppers Cl IP27 ....5 E3
Peppers Wash IP13 ....126 B6
Pepys Ave 1 NR34 ....9 F4
Percy Ruse Cl CO10 ....148 F5
Peregrine Way 18 NR33 ..11 C1
Periwinkle Cl 8 NR33 ..114 C5
Perkins Rd IP30 ....49 B2
Perkins Way
Ipswich IP3 ....139 F1
Tostock IP30 ....50 B3
Perry La CO4 ....103 D2
Perrydown La IP30 ....64 C1
Perryfields CO10 ....148 F2
Persimmon Wlk CB8 ..120 E7
Pesthouse La IP6 ....82 A6
Petch Cl IP33 ....154 B3
Peter Dr 3 IP24 ....16 D7
Peter's Gr 4 IP9 ....150 E3
Peterhouse Cl
Ipswich IP2 ....138 F2
Mildenhall IP28 ....116 D4
Peterhouse Cres IP12 ..146 D4
Peterhouse Dr CB8 ....121 A2
Petingo Cl CB8 ....120 D7
Petit Couronne Way
NR34 ....111 D3
Peto Way NR32 ....113 A1
Pets Cnr NR33 ....114 D7
Pettaugh La IP6 ....68 E2
Petticoat La
9 Barrow IP29 ....47 A2
Bury St Edmunds IP33 ....154 A1
Pettits La IP21 ....20 F3
Petunia Way IP27 ....14 E8
Pheasant Cl 14 IP31 ....49 D4
Pheasant Rd IP2 ....138 E3
Pheasant Rise IP8 ....95 F4
Pheasant Way IP27 ....6 A1
Pheasants Wlk NR35 ....7 E4
Philip Ave IP11 ....152 E3
Philip Rd
Bury St Edmunds IP32 ....122 F8
Ipswich IP2 ....155 B1
Philipps Cl CB8 ....120 D4
Phillipps Rd 3 IP6 ....82 B5
Phillips Cres IP6 ....125 E4
Phillips Field Rd CO10 ..148 E3
Phoenix Day Hospl
IP33 ....154 A1
Phoenix Rd IP4 ....140 A7
Phoenix Way IP14 ....124 F7
Phoenix Yd CB9 ....132 E3
Picketts Rd IP11 ....153 C5
Pickwick Cres IP33 ....154 C3
Pickwick Dr 5 NR32 ....3 A4
Pickwick Rd IP2 ....138 E6
Picton Ave 5 IP1 ....135 D1
Pier Ave IP18 ....119 D6
Pier Terr NR33 ....115 D8
Pig La NR34 ....111 B6
Pigeon La IP28 ....48 B6
Pigeon's La IP8 ....138 A3
Pightle Cl IP30 ....50 E2
Pightle The
Capel St Mary IP9 ....150 F4
Haverhill CB9 ....132 E6
4 Needham Market IP6 ..125 D5
North Cove NR34 ....10 B4
Pilgrim's Way 7 IP20 ....22 D6
Pilgrims Way
Bungay NR35 ....110 C3
6 Great Finborough IP14 ..66 B4
1 Thorpeness IP16 ....73 F6
Pimpernel Rd IP2 ....138 F3
Pin Mill Cl IP8 ....138 C1
Pin Mill Cliff* IP9 ....106 D8
Pinbush Cl NR33 ....114 F2
Pinbush Rd NR33 ....114 F2
Pine Ave IP1 ....135 B1
Pine Bank IP5 ....141 F6
Pine Cl
1 Brantham CO11 ....104 E4
Eye IP23 ....117 D3
4 Harleston IP20 ....22 D5
9 Lakenheath IP27 ....13 F2
Rendlesham IP12 ....85 D8
Pine Gr 14 IP13 ....83 E5
Pine Leys IP32 ....122 F8
Pine Sq IP7 ....80 D6
Pine Tree Cl NR34 ....111 F4
Pine Tree Ct IP22 ....18 C2
Pine Trees Ave IP28 ....116 E4
Pine View IP14 ....52 A6
Pine View Rd IP1 ....139 B8
Pinecroft Rd IP1 ....135 A2
Pinecroft Rise CO10 ....148 B3
Pinecroft Way IP6 ....125 E4
Pines Ind Est The CB8 ....44 F6
Pines The Claydon IP6 ..134 C8
Felixstowe IP11 ....153 E6
Pinetree Cl IP5 ....140 F7
Pinetrees NR31 ....2 B7
Pineview Cl IP14 ....124 D5
Pineway Cl 1 IP29 ....63 A1
Pinewood IP12 ....146 E3
Pinewood Ave NR33 ....114 F6
Pinewood Dr IP27 ....14 F8
Pinewood Gdns NR34 ....10 B4
Pinhoe Dr 1 CB9 ....132 A6
Pinkney's La 19 IP18 ....119 D5
Pinkuah La CO10 ....90 F7
Pinmill Rd IP9 ....106 C8
Pinners La IP13 ....146 B7
Pinners Way IP33 ....122 E4
Pintail Cl IP2 ....138 E3
Pintail Rd IP14 ....67 A5
Pinza Cl CB8 ....120 E8
Piperell Way CB9 ....132 E3
Pipers Cl CB9 ....133 A4
Pipers Meadow IP13 ....54 E7

Pipers Vale Cl IP3 ....**139** E1
Pipers Vale Com Prim Sch
  Gainsborough IP3 ....**139** F1
  Ipswich IP3 ....**139** F1
Pipers Vale Nature Reserve*
  IP3 ....**143** F7
Pipney Hill IP17 ....**56** F4
Pipp's La IP6 ....**135** E6
Pippin Cl IP22 ....**123** E6
Pippin Post Cl CO10 .....**76** C6
Pippins The
  Blundeston NR32 ....**3** A4
  Glemsford CO10 ....**77** B2
Pirnhow St NR35 ....**110** D5
Pit Rd NR34 ....**10** B8
Pitcairn Rd IP1 ....**138** E8
Pitman's Gr IP19 ....**42** A4
Pitmire La CO8 ....**101** A7
Pitts The CB7 ....**29** C4
Pitts End CO17 ....**151** D5
Place Farm Com Prim Sch
  CB9 ....**132** D6
Place for Plants The*
  CO7 ....**151** F3
Plampin Cl CO10 ....**92** D3
Plantation The IP15 ....**130** D5
Plantation Way IP14 ....**66** C1
Planters Gr ⬛ NK33 ....**114** F7
Plash Rd IP3 ....**53** F7
Plashwood Rd IP14 ......**51** B1
Platers Wlk IP16 ....**129** C5
Platten Cl IP6 ....**125** C5
Platters Cl IP3 ....**144** A7
Platters Rd IP11 ....**152** E2
Playfield Rd IP9 ......**150** F3
Playford La IP6 ....**136** E2
Playford Mount IP13 ...**137** C6
Playford Rd
  Ipswich IP4 ....**140** E8
  Playford IP5 ....**137** B2
Pleasant Pl NR34 ......**111** B3
Pleasant Row IP4 ......**155** C2
Pleasurewood Cl ⬛
  NR32 ....**113** B5
Pleasurewood Hill
  NR32 ....**113** A7
Pleasurewood Hills Leisure
  Pk* NR32 ....**113** C8
Plough Hill CO10 ....**76** C7
Plough La
  Leavenheath CO6 ......**102** B7
  Sudbury CO10 ....**148** B5
Plough Rd
  Capel St Mary IP9 ....**150** D3
  Woolpit IP30 ....**50** D3
Plough St IP3 ....**139** E4
Ploughman's Dro IP26 ...**4** B5
Plover Cl
  ⬛ Mildenhall IP28 .....**13** B1
  ⬛ Stowmarket IP14 ....**67** A5
Plover Rd IP2 ....**138** E2
Plovers Way
  Bury St Edmunds IP33 ..**123** C1
  Hockwold cum Wilton IP26 ..**4** F3
  Lowestoft NR33 ....**114** D5
Plum St CO10 ....**77** A3
Plum Tree Rise ⬛ IP7 ...**80** D6
Plummer Cl ⬛ IP21 .....**34** B1
Plummers Dell ⬛ IP6 ...**82** A5
Plumpton Ave IP28 .....**116** C5
Plumtrees ⬛ NR32 .....**112** D2
Plymouth Rd
  Felixstowe IP11 ......**152** F6
  ⬛ Troston IP31 ....**33** D5
Pole Hill (Tumulus)*
  IP10 ....**141** F5
Police Sta Rd ⬛ NR32 ..**113** D1
Pollard Piece NR33 ....**114** C5
Pollards La IP28 ....**29** F7
Polls La NR34 ....**9** C2
Polstead Cl IP14 ......**124** F4
Polstead Hill CO6 .....**93** F1
Polstead St CO6 ......**102** E7
Pond Cl IP11 ....**152** D5
Pond End IP6 ....**82** E6
Pond Gn CB7 ....**28** A1
Pond Gr Cl IP32 ......**123** E6
Pond Hall Rd IP7 .....**149** F5
Pond Piece IP13 ....**70** A7
Ponds End La IP22 ....**35** A8
Poole Cl IP3 ....**140** D3
Poole St CO10 ....**76** E1
Pooley St IP22 ....**19** C3
Pope's Gn La IP7 .....**94** B2
Popes Cl CB9 ....**133** C3
Poplar Cl ⬛ Barrow IP29 ..**47** A2
  ⬛ Claydon IP6 ....**134** C8
  Haverhill CB9 ......**132** D6
  Mildenhall IP28 ....**116** C6
Poplar Farm La IP31 ...**49** E5
Poplar Farm Rd IP12 ...**73** A2
Poplar Hill IP14 .....**124** E4
Poplar La IP9 ....**138** B3
Poplar Rd
  Lowestoft NR33 ......**114** D3
  Sudbury CO10 ......**148** F5
Poplars Gr ⬛ CB5 ....**44** A5
Poplars CP Sch The
  NR32 ....**113** D3
Poplars The
  Beck Row, Holywell Row
  & Kenny Hill IP28 ....**13** D1
  ⬛ Brantham CO11 ...**104** E5
  Spexhall IP19 ......**24** F5

Poppy Cl
  Bury St Edmunds IP32 ..**123** E5
  Ditchingham NR35 ....**110** B7
  Ipswich IP2 ....**138** F5
  Worlingham NR34 ....**111** F3
Poppy Fields ⬛ CB7 ....**28** D5
Popson St NR35 ......**110** A4
Port La IP23 ....**37** C3
Port of Felixstowe Rd
  IP11 ....**152** C3
Portal Ave IP5 ......**84** A1
Portal Cl ⬛ Barnham IP24 ..**16** C2
  ⬛ Feltwell IP26 .....**4** D5
Porter Rd ⬛ IP1 ....**140** F1
Porthole Cl NR33 ....**114** B4
Portland Ave ⬛ CO12 ..**107** B2
Portland Cl ⬛ IP11 ...**13** F2
Portland Cres ⬛ IP12 ..**146** E4
Portland Gn CB8 .....**120** E3
Portland Pl ⬛ IP14 ...**16** A5
Portland Rd CB8 .....**120** E3
Portlight Cl ⬛ CO11 ..**105** A2
Portman Rd IP1 ......**155** A2
Portman's Wlk IP1 ...**139** A5
Portsch Rd NR33 ....**114** E3
Portsmouth Cl ⬛ IP27 ..**5** D8
Portsmouth Rd ⬛ IP31 ..**33** D5
Post Mill Cl IP4 ....**139** F6
Post Mill Cres ⬛ IP13 ..**83** E5
Post Mill Gdns ⬛ IP13 ..**83** E5
Post Office La
  Glemsford CO10 ......**77** A3
  Martlesham IP12 ....**146** C1
Post Office Rd IP17 ..**129** A3
Posters La IP31 ......**34** A2
Posting House Pottery The*
  CO10 ....**91** D8
Pot Kiln Chase CO9 ...**90** F1
Pot Kiln Prim Sch
  CO10 ....**148** E4
Pot Kiln Rd CO10 ....**148** F4
Pot Kilns The CO10 ...**92** B3
Potash La Bentley IP9 .**104** F8
  Eye IP23 ....**117** B5
  Polstead CO6 ....**93** F4
  Wyverstone IP14 ....**51** D7
Potkins La IP12 .....**131** B3
Potland La ⬛ CO10 ....**78** D4
Pott Hall Rd IP28 ....**30** A6
Potter's La
  Rickinghall Superior IP22 ..**36** B5
  Stanton IP31 ....**34** E4
Potter's St IP16 ....**58** C4
Potters Brook IP26 ...**126** B3
Potters Dr NR31 .....**3** B7
Potters Vale IP22 ....**35** E7
Pouch Mill IP11 .....**152** B8
Poulter's La IP29 ....**62** F6
Poultry Rd IP27 .....**13** A7
Pound Cl ⬛ Burwell CB5 ..**44** A4
  Halesworth IP19 ....**118** B3
  ⬛ Harleston IP20 ...**22** D6
  ⬛ Walsham le Willows
  IP31 ....**35** C2
Pound Farm Dr
  ⬛ Harwich CO12 ....**107** A2
  Lowestoft NR32 ....**114** A8
Pound Farm Parade ⬛
  NR32 ....**112** F4
Pound Fm Nature Reserve*
  IP7 ....**56** C1
Pound Gn Rd IP13 ...**56** C7
Pound Hill Bacton IP14 ..**51** F6
  Dallinghoo IP13 ....**70** C1
Pound Hill Cl IP14 ...**51** F6
Pound La
  Blundeston NR32 ....**3** A4
  Bramford IP8 ....**83** F3
  Capel St Mary IP9 ..**150** D1
  Dallinghoo IP13 ....**70** C1
  Ditchingham NR35 ...**7** E6
  Hadleigh IP7 ......**149** C6
  Isleham CB7 ....**29** C5
  Stowmarket IP14 ...**124** D7
Pound Meadow ⬛ IP28 ..**48** B6
Pound Rd
  ⬛ Beccles NR34 ....**111** B6
  Creeting St Peter or West
  Creeting IP6 ....**67** B4
  Sotterley NR34 ....**26** A7
Pound Wlk NR34 ....**111** B6
Pouy St IP17 ....**41** B1
Powderham Alley IP3 ..**155** A2
Powney St IP7 ......**93** B8
Pratt St CB7 ....**28** D4
Pratt's La IP9 .....**144** A2
Prentice Rd IP14 ...**124** E6
Prentice St ⬛ CO10 ..**78** B4
Prentices La IP13 ...**146** D6
Prescott Dr IP30 ....**50** F2
Presland Ct IP27 ...**109** B7
Presmere Rd IP13 ...**84** F8
Preston Dr IP1 .....**134** F2
Preston Rd CO10 ....**78** D4
Prestwick Ave ⬛ IP11 ..**153** C6
Pretty Dr IP21 .....**21** A2
Pretty Rd IP16 .....**58** A4
Pretyman Ave IP14 ...**51** F6
Pretyman Rd
  Felixstowe IP11 ....**152** E1
  Ipswich IP3 ....**140** B3
Prevetts Way IP19 ..**118** E5
Prickwillow Rd CB7 ..**12** A2
Priestly Cl IP14 ...**124** E8
Priestly Rd IP6 ....**125** C4
Prigg Wlk IP32 ....**122** E7
Primes La Blyford IP19 ..**42** B8

Primes La continued
  Holton IP19 ....**118** F5
Primrose Alley IP18 .**119** D4
Primrose La NR33 ...**114** F2
Primrose Hill
  Haverhill CB9 .....**132** D5
  Ipswich IP2 ....**138** F4
  Royal Hospital School
  IP9 ....**105** G6
Primrose La
  Frostenden NR34 ....**26** B4
  Ramsey & Parkeston
  CO11 ....**106** A1
  ⬛ Soham CB7 ......**28** D5
Primrose Rise NR34 .**111** E3
Primrose Way IP6 ...**125** D3
Prince Charles Ave ⬛
  IP32 ....**48** C5
Prince Charles Cl
  CO10 ....**148** D6
Prince Cl CB8 .....**120** B8
Prince of Wales Cl
  IP33 ....**122** E5
Prince of Wales Dr ⬛
  IP2 ....**139** A2
Prince St CO10 ....**148** C6
Prince's Rd NR35 ..**110** B2
Princedale Cl IP1 ..**135** A1
Princel La CO7 ....**103** F4
Princes Gdns ⬛ IP11 ..**152** F4
Princes' Gdns ⬛ IP6 ..**81** C3
Princes Gn IP19 ...**118** A2
Princes Rd
  Felixstowe IP11 ...**152** F4
  ⬛ Harwich CO12 ..**107** A2
  Lowestoft NR32 ...**113** C2
Princes St
  Bury St Edmunds IP33 ..**154** A2
  Ipswich IP1 ....**155** A1
Princes Wlk NR32 ..**113** A2
Princess Rd ⬛ IP18 ..**119** C8
Princess Way
  ⬛ Earsham NR35 ....**7** F4
  Haverhill CB9 ......**132** B6
  Newmarket CB8 ....**120** E4
Princethorpe Rd IP3 .**140** C4
Prior Stephen Way
  IP24 ....**16** B5
Prior's Ave IP33 ...**122** E4
Priors Cl
  Lowestoft NR32 ...**113** C5
  Rushbrooke with Rougham
  IP30 ....**64** D8
Priors' Hill Rd IP15 ..**130** D3
Priors Way IP15 ...**130** E4
Priory Ave ⬛ IP1 ..**135** A3
Priory Cl ⬛ Burwell CB5 ..**44** A5
  Ingham IP31 ......**32** F1
  Palgrave IP22 ....**20** C1
  St Olaves NR31 ...**2** A6
  Stradbroke IP21 ..**39** B4
Priory Cres IP21 ..**39** D8
Priory Gdns
  Isleham CB7 ......**29** C5
  St Olaves NR31 ...**2** A6
Priory La Bungay NR35 ..**110** B4
  Carlton Colville NR33 ..**114** A2
  Darsham IP17 ....**42** B1
  Needham IP20 ....**53** F2
Priory Pk IP10 ....**144** D6
Priory Rd Beccles NR34 ..**111** B4
  Blythburgh IP19 ..**42** F6
  Fressingfield IP21 ..**39** D7
  Fritton & St Olaves NR31 ..**2** A4
  Palgrave IP22 ....**20** C1
  Snape IP17 ....**72** E5
  ⬛ Wrentham NR34 ..**26** E5
Priory Specl Sch IP22 ..**123** C5
Priory Stadium CO10 ..**148** C4
Priory Wlk CO10 ...**148** C4
Prittlewell Cl IP2 ..**138** F1
Private Rd Earsham NR35 ..**7** D4
  Mutford NR34 .....**10** B2
  ⬛ Oulton Broad NR33 ..**114** B7
Privet Gn IP33 ....**115** A7
Progress Way IP23 ..**117** B5
Promenade
  Harwich CO12 ....**107** A1
  Southwold IP18 ...**119** D4
Prospect Hill CO10 ..**92** B2
Prospect Pl
  Leiston IP16 .....**129** D6
  Lowestoft NR33 ...**115** B3
Prospect Rd
  Ipswich IP1 ......**139** A6
  Lowestoft NR32 ...**112** C1
  Norton IP31 ......**50** C4
Prospect Row IP33 ..**154** B2
Prospect Terr CB9 ..**133** F8
Providence La ⬛ IP1 ..**139** A7
Providence Stroc IP1 ..**155** B3
Provost Rd IP26 ....**4** D5
Prussia La IP33 ...**154** C1
Puddingmoor NR34 ..**111** A5
Puddleduck La NR34 ..**111** F3
Pug St IP21 ....**21** A6
Pump Cl IP13 .....**72** E5
Pump Ct ⬛ CO10 ..**78** D4
Pump House La IP7 ..**57** A8
Pump La IP33 .....**154** B2
Pump St
  Needham Market IP6 ..**125** E4
  Orford IP12 ....**131** C2
Punchard Way IP11 ..**152** C8
Purcell Rd IP14 ...**124** B8

Purdis Ave IP3 .....**140** F2
Purdis Farm La
  Foxhall IP10 ......**141** C2
  Ipswich IP3 ....**140** F2
  Purdis Farm IP10 ..**141** B2
Purdis Rd IP10 ....**141** D2
Purplett St IP2 ...**155** C1
Putney Cl IP4 .....**14** E8
Putticks La CO7 ..**151** E5
Pyes Meadow IP30 ..**50** F2
Pykenham Way IP7 ..**149** D6
Pytches Cl IP12 ...**147** B6
Pytches Rd IP12 ...**147** A6

Q

Quadling St IP1 ....**155** B2
Quail Cl IP32 ......**123** E5
Quaker La Bardwell IP31 ..**34** C4
  Beyton IP30 ......**49** F1
Quaker's La ⬛ CB9 ..**132** E5
Quakers Rd CB9 ...**132** D6
Quakers Way ⬛ IP30 ..**129** D5
Quantock Cl IP5 ..**140** F7
Quantrill Terr IP5 ..**141** D6
Quarries Cross IP14 ..**66** C8
Quaves La NR35 ...**110** B4
Quay La Reydon IP18 ..**26** D1
  Southwold IP18 ...**148** C4
Quay Side IP12 ...**147** A4
Quay St
  Halesworth IP19 ..**118** B4
  ⬛ Manningtree CO11 ..**104** E2
  Orford IP12 ......**131** C2
  Woodbridge IP12 ..**147** A4
Quay The ⬛ CO12 ..**107** B3
Quay Theatre The*
  CO10 ....**148** C4
Quay View NR32 ...**113** A1
Quay's Rd IP28 ...**47** E5
Quayside Ct IP27 ..**109** C2
Quebec Dr IP5 ...**141** B8
Queech La IP9 ...**105** B4
Queech The IP9 ..**150** F4
Queen Edith Dr CB9 ..**88** D3
Queen Elizabeth Cl
  IP16 ....**129** C4
Queen Elizabeth Dr
  NR34 ....**111** D3
Queen St Cowlinge CB8 ..**61** B1
  ⬛ Hadleigh IP7 ...**149** D6
  Haverhill CB9 ....**132** D5
  Ipswich IP1 .....**155** B2
  Lowestoft NR32 ..**121** B3
  Southwold IP18 ..**119** D4
Queen's Cl IP3 ...**122** E5
Queen's Dr IP28 ..**116** B4
Queen's Head La IP12 ..**146** F5
Queen's Head Rd CO4 ..**102** F1
Queen's Highway
  NR32 ....**112** C2
Queen's Rd
  Beccles NR34 ....**111** B6
  Bungay NR35 .....**110** B2
  Bury St Edmunds IP33 ..**154** A2
  Felixstowe IP11 ..**153** A3
  ⬛ Harwich CO12 ..**107** A1
  Lowestoft NR32 ..**113** D3
  Southwold IP18 ..**119** D4
Queens Ave IP27 ..**109** B8
Queens Cl Combs IP14 ..**124** A1
  Halesworth IP19 ..**118** A2
  Saxmundham IP17 ..**128** C3
  Sudbury CO10 ....**148** C6
Queens Ct CB9 ...**132** C6
Queens Dr IP19 ...**118** A2
Queens La IP29 ...**62** D5
Queens Rd Brandon IP27 ..**14** E8
  ⬛ Southwold IP18 ..**119** C8
  Sudbury CO10 ....**148** C6
Queens Sq ⬛ CB9 ..**132** E6
Queens View CB8 ..**74** B2
Queens Way IP3 ..**120** A8
Queensberry Rd
  ⬛ Ipswich IP1 ...**144** B8
  Newmarket CB8 ..**121** A3
Queenscliffe Rd IP2 ..**139** A3
Queensdale Cl IP1 ..**135** B1
Queensdale Rd IP1 ..**135** B1
Queensgate Dr IP4 ..**139** F8
Queensland IP9 ...**106** F5
Queensway ⬛ Acton CO10 ..**92** B7
  ⬛ Earsham NR35 ..**7** F4
  Exning CB8 ......**120** B8
  Haverhill CB9 ...**132** C6
  ⬛ Manningtree CO11 ..**104** E2
  ⬛ Mildenhall IP28 ..**116** B4
  ⬛ Soham CB7 ....**28** D4
  Sudbury CO10 ...**148** F3
  Thetford IP24 ...**16** B5
Queensway Com Jun Sch ⬛
  IP3 ....**140** B3
Queensway Inf Sch
  IP3 ....**140** B3
Quendon Pl CB9 ..**132** F6
Quendon Rd IP3 ..**140** C4
Quilter Cl IP28 ..**138** C1
Quilter Dr Ipswich IP8 ..**138** C1
  Pinewood IP8 ...**142** C8
Quilter Rd IP11 ..**153** B4
Quince Cl ⬛ CO11 ..**104** E5
Quinnell Way ⬛ NR32 ..**113** A6
Quinton Rd IP6 ..**125** C4
Quinton's La IP11 ..**153** C5
Quintons Cnr CO7 ..**151** D6

Quintons Rd CO7 ....**151** C5
Quoits Field ⬛ IP6 ..**134** C8
Quoits Meadow IP14 ..**68** B6

R

Rackham Cl ⬛ NR31 ..**3** B7
Radcliffe Dr IP2 ...**138** D2
Radcliffe Rd ⬛ IP27 ..**14** A2
Radiator Rd CO10 ...**148** E3
Radleys La CO10 ...**102** B6
Radnor Cl IP32 ....**123** E6
Raeburn Rd IP3 ...**139** E1
Raeburn Rd S IP3 ..**139** E1
Raedwald Dr IP32 ..**123** D5
Raedwald Way IP14 ..**53** F1
Rag's La IP30 .....**50** D1
Raglan Rd ⬛ NR32 ..**113** D1
Raglan St NR32 ...**113** D1
Raile Wlk CO10 ...**91** E8
Railway App IP11 ..**153** A5
Railway Cl CB5 ...**44** A4
Railway Hill IP20 ..**22** C6
Railway St ⬛ CO11 ..**104** E2
Railway Terr CB9 ..**133** E7
Raine Ave CB9 ....**132** B6
Rainey Ct ⬛ IP20 ..**22** D6
Raingate St IP33 ..**154** C1
Raleigh Cl IP1 ...**134** E8
Raleigh Inf Sch ⬛ IP24 ..**16** C7
Raleigh Rd CO10 ..**148** E8
Ram La NR15 .....**21** C8
Rampart Way IP24 ..**16** C5
Rampling Cl IP7 ..**149** D4
Ramsey Cl IP2 ...**139** A1
Ramsey Rd
  Hadleigh IP7 ....**149** F7
  Harwich CO12 ...**106** D1
Ramsgate Dr IP3 ..**140** B3
Randall Cl
  ⬛ Hopton on Sea NR31 ..**3** B7
  Ipswich IP5 .....**141** E7
Randolph Cl IP4 ..**140** B8
Rands Rd IP7 ....**149** B1
Rands Way IP3 ...**140** B2
Randwell Cl IP4 ..**140** B8
Ranelagh Prim Sch
  IP2 ....**138** F5
Ranelagh Rd
  Felixstowe IP11 ..**153** A4
  Ipswich IP2 ....**155** A1
Ransom Rd IP12 ..**146** E6
Ransome Ave IP21 ..**21** A2
Ransome Cl IP9 ..**138** A6
Ransome Cres IP3 ..**140** B2
Ransome Rd IP3 ..**140** B2
Ransomes Europark
  IP10 ....**144** F7
Ransomes Way IP3 ..**140** D1
Ranson Rd IP6 ...**125** C4
Rant Score NR32 ..**114** E3
Ranville NR33 ...**114** E3
Ranworth Ave NR33 ..**114** E5
Raphael Wlk ⬛ NR32 ..**113** B5
Rapier St ⬛ IP2 ..**139** C3
Rare Breeds Farm*
  CO7 ....**151** A1
Rat Hill IP9 ....**106** C5
Rattla Cnr IP16 ..**58** C5
Rattler's Rd IP27 ..**5** F1
Rattlerow Hill IP21 ..**39** B6
Rattlesden CE Prim Sch
  IP30 ....**65** D6
Rattlesden Cl ⬛ IP14 ..**124** D3
Rattlesden Rd IP30 ..**65** C6
Raven Cl
  Mildenhall IP28 ..**116** D3
  Stowmarket IP14 ..**124** F7
Raven Rd IP23 ...**123** C1
Raven Way IP7 ...**149** D4
Raveningham Rd NR34 ..**9** C8
Ravens La IP28 ...**134** A2
Ravens Way ⬛ IP12 ..**84** A1
Ravensfield Rd IP4 ..**135** D6
Ravensmere NR34 ..**111** B6
Ravensmere Cty Inf Sch
  NR34 ....**111** B7
Ravensmere E NR34 ..**111** B6
Ravenswood Ave IP3 ..**144** B8
Ravenswood Com Prim Sch
  IP3 ....**144** B8
Ravenwood Mews
  NR33 ....**115** A5
Ravine NR32 ....**113** E3
Rawlings Way ⬛ IP26 ..**4** E5
Ray Ave CO12 ...**107** A2
Ray La ⬛ CO12 ..**106** F3
Raydon Croft IP14 ..**124** F3
Raydon La IP12 ..**131** D3
Raydon Rd CO7 ..**92** B3
Raydon Way CO10 ..**92** B3
Rayes La CB8 ...**121** A4
Rayleigh Rd IP1 ..**134** F2
Rayment Drift ⬛ IP5 ..**141** C7
Rayner's La IP35 ..**8** D8
Raynham Rd IP32 ..**154** A4
Raynsford Rd IP30 ..**63** C7
Reach Rd CB5 ...**44** A5
Reade Rd ⬛ IP9 ..**105** E7
Reading Cl IP21 ..**38** D4
Reading Rd IP4 ..**140** B7
Reading's La IP21 ..**38** B3
Rebow Rd ⬛ CO12 ..**107** A1
Reckford Rd IP17 ..**58** B6
Recreation La IP11 ..**152** F6
Recreation Rd
  Haverhill CB9 ....**132** D5

Recreation Rd continued
Stowmarket IP14 124 C6
Recreation Way
Ipswich IP3 140 C2
Mildenhall IP28 116 C4
Recreation Wlk CO10 148 F3
Rectory Cl
Beccles NR34 111 F4
3 Glemsford CO10 77 A3
Ousden CB8 61 E6
Raydon IP7 94 F1
Rectory Field 4 IP9 106 C8
Rectory Gdns IP30 49 F1
Rectory Gn IP19 118 A4
Rectory Gr IP29 63 B5
Rectory Hill
Botesdale IP22 35 F6
East Bergholt CO7 151 C3
Polstead CO6 102 E8
Rickinghall Superior IP22 36 A5
Rectory La Beccles NR34 9 F4
Brantham CO11 104 F5
Hedenham NR35 7 D8
Hintlesham IP8 95 C6
Kettlebaston IP7 79 B5
Kirton IP10 98 D2
Mettingham NR35 110 F3
4 Ramsey & Parkeston CO12 106 D1
Scole IP21 21 C5
Stuston IP21 37 D8
Whatfield IP7 80 C1
3 Woolpit IP30 50 D1
Rectory Meadow 5 IP28 48 B6
Rectory Pk 3 CO10 93 C3
Rectory Pl IP29 47 A1
Rectory Rd
Aldeby/Wheatacre/Burgh St Peter NR34 10 A8
Bacton IP14 51 E5
Blaxhall IP12 71 F4
Brome & Oakley IP23 117 B7
Broome NR35 8 B7
Burston & Shimpling IP22 20 E6
Dickleburgh IP21 21 B5
Gillingham NR34 9 B7
Gissing IP22 20 F8
Great Waldingfield CO10 92 D6
Harkstead IP9 106 B6
Hemingstone IP6 68 C1
Hollesley IP12 99 F7
Ipswich IP2 155 B1
Kedington CB9 133 F8
Langham CO4 103 C3
7 Lowestoft NR33 115 C6
Mellis IP23 36 F5
Middleton CO10 148 C2
Newton CO10 92 D2
Orford IP12 131 C3
Shelfanger IP22 20 B6
Sotterley NR34 26 A7
Tivetshall St Mary NR15 21 C8
Whepstead IP29 63 B4
Wortham IP22 19 F1
Wrabness CO11 106 A2
Wyverstone IP14 51 D6
Rectory St IP19 118 B4
Red Barn Dr 4 CO6 102 A7
Red Barn Piece 11 IP13 83 E5
Red Dock La CB8 61 C1
Red Hall Ct IP11 153 C4
Red Hill IP7 94 D7
Red Hill Rd IP7 149 E8
Red House* IP15 130 C6
Red House Cl
3 Felixstowe IP11 107 D8
Lowestoft NR32 112 F5
Red House La
Leiston IP16 129 D4
Sudbury CO10 148 E2
Red House Wlk IP10 145 E4
Red La
Capel St Mary IP9 150 E2
Sternfield IP17 72 D8
Red Lion Cl IP21 38 C7
Red Rose Cl IP12 99 E4
Red Sleeve IP9 150 D3
Redan St IP1 155 A4
Redbarn La IP17 72 D7
Redcastle Furze Prim Sch 6 IP24 16 B5
Reddells Cl CO10 148 D5
Rede La IP6 134 F8
Rede Rd IP29 62 F4
Rede Way CO10 92 B3
Rede Wood Nature Reserve* IP6 82 D5
Redenhall Rd IP20 22 D6
Redgate IP24 16 C6
Redgate La IP9 143 D5
Redgrave & Lopham Fen National Nature Reserve* IP22 19 C2
Redgrave & Lopham Fen Visitor Ctr* IP22 19 C3
Redgrave Rd IP22 19 B3
Redhouse Gdns 5 CB7 28 D3
Redhouse La
Bawdsey IP12 99 E3
Boxted CO4 102 E1
9 Sudbury CO10 148 C5
Redhouse Rd IP13 56 B8
Redisham Cl NR32 113 A5
Redisham Rd
Redisham NR34 25 B6
Weston NR34 9 C1
Redlingfield Rd
Horham IP21 38 D2
Redlingfield Rd continued
Occold IP23 37 F2
Redshank Cl CB9 133 A5
Redwald Rd IP12 85 E8
Redwing Cl IP2 138 D3
Redwing Rd IP33 123 C1
Redwings Horse Sanctuary (Caldecott)* NR31 2 C8
Redwings Horse Sanctuary (Stonham)* IP14 68 C6
Redwold Cl IP12 146 C1
Redwood Gdns IP33 154 C2
Redwood La 23 IP27 13 F2
Reed's Bldgs IP33 154 C3
Reedland Way 4 IP11 152 D5
Reeds La CB9 132 E6
Reeds Way IP14 67 A7
Reet 1 NR32 115 D8
Reeve Cl
12 Bury St Edmunds IP32 48 C5
Scole IP21 21 A2
Reeve Gdns IP5 141 C8
Reeve St NR32 113 D2
Reeve's Cl NR35 110 C3
Reeves La IP26 5 A3
Refinery Rd CO12 106 F3
Regal Dr CB7 28 E3
Regal La CB7 28 E3
Regan Cl NR32 113 A5
Regent Pl 3 CB7 28 D3
Regent Rd NR32 113 D1
Regent St
20 Manningtree CO11 104 E2
Stowmarket IP14 124 D7
Regent Theatre* IP4 155 C3
Regents Ct 8 CB8 121 A4
Regimental Mus* IP33 122 E6
Regimental Way
18 Harwich CO12 106 E1
18 Ramsey CO12 106 E1
Regina Cl IP4 140 B5
Reigate Cl IP3 140 B3
Rembrandt Cl 3 NR32 113 C6
Rembrandt Gdns 4 IP33 122 F3
Rembrandt Way IP33 123 A3
Rembrow Rd IP9 150 E3
Rememberance Rd IP16 73 F6
Remercie Rd 7 CO11 105 A2
Rendall La IP14 67 A8
Rendham Hill IP17 56 F7
Rendham Rd
Bruisyard IP17 56 D4
Kelsale cum Carlton IP17 128 A6
Peasenhall IP17 56 F7
Rendlesham Est* IP12 85 D6
Rendlesham Forest Ctr* IP12 85 F3
Rendlesham Rd
15 Felixstowe IP11 152 D5
9 Ipswich IP1 139 A7
Renfrew Rd IP4 136 B1
Renoir Pl 2 NR32 113 B5
Renson Cl 6 IP30 64 F8
Reydon Bsns Pk IP18 119 D8
Reydon Cl 2 CB9 132 A6
Reydon La IP18 26 D1
Reydon Mews NR32 113 A6
Reydon Prim Sch IP18 119 C8
Reydon Wood Nature Reserve* IP34 26 C2
Reynolds Ave 2 IP3 144 A8
Reynolds Ct 10 IP11 152 D5
Reynolds Rd IP3 140 A1
Reynolds Way CO10 148 E8
Reynolds Wlk
Bury St Edmunds IP33 122 B6
Gunton NR32 113 B6
Ribblesdale NR33 114 E3
Riby Rd IP11 152 F3
Richard Burn Way CO10 148 C8
Richard Crampton Rd NR34 111 B3
Richard Easter Rd IP24 16 C7
Richards Dr IP13 137 D5
Richards's Cl NR33 114 E6
Richardson Rd CO7 151 D5
Richardsons La IP9 106 B8
Richer Cl IP31 50 E7
Richer Rd IP31 50 F7
Richmond Cres 8 CO12 107 A1
Richmond Pl 8 NR33 115 C6
Richmond Rd
Brandon IP27 14 E8
Ipswich IP1 138 F7
Lowestoft NR33 115 C6
Riddlesworth Hall Sch IP22 17 F4
Rider Haggard La 7 NR33 11 C1
Rider Haggard Way NR35 110 C7
Ridgeville 9 NR33 114 F3
Ridgeway IP14 124 B6
Ridgeway The 10 CO12 107 A2
Ridgeways The NR33 114 D5
Ridgewell Rd CO10 89 D5
Ridings The
3 Beccles NR34 111 F4
Leavenheath CO6 102 B8
Ridley Rd IP33 122 C6
Rigbourne Hill NR34 111 C3
Rigbourne Hill La 6 NR34 111 C2
Rigby Ave CO11 105 A2
Riley Cl IP1 134 C1
Rimmer Cl CO10 148 E8
Ringham Rd IP4 140 A6
Ringsfield CE VCP Sch NR34 9 B2
Ringsfield Rd
Beccles NR34 111 A4
6 Lowestoft NR32 113 A3
Ringsfield NR34 9 A1
Ringshall Prim Sch IP14 80 E6
Rio Cl 2 NR33 114 C5
Risbridge Dr CB9 133 E8
Risby Barn Antique & Craft Ctr* IP28 47 D5
Risby CE VC Prim Sch IP28 47 D5
Risby Cl IP4 140 B6
Risbygate St IP33 154 B2
Riseway Cl IP33 123 B1
Rishton Rd 7 NR32 113 D1
Rising Sun Hill IP30 65 D5
Rissemere La E IP18 119 C8
Ritabrook Rd IP2 138 E1
Rivendale 4 NR33 114 D3
River Gdns IP14 124 E4
River Hill IP8 138 C8
River La Fordham CB7 29 A1
Halesworth IP19 118 B3
River View NR34 111 B7
River View Rd 1 IP9 106 A5
Riverbank Cl CO10 90 B8
Rivers St IP4 139 F7
Riverside
4 Framlingham IP13 126 C3
Hasketon IP13 146 A7
Palgrave IP22 20 B2
Riverside Ave E 6 CO11 104 E3
Riverside Ave W 4 CO11 104 E3
Riverside Bsns Ctr NR33 115 C8
Riverside Cl IP28 116 B4
Riverside Ct IP32 123 A8
Riverside Ind Est IP13 127 C7
Riverside Ind Pk IP2 139 D3
Riverside Mid Sch IP28 116 B4
Riverside Rd
Ipswich IP1 138 F7
Lowestoft NR33 115 B8
Riverside Theatre The* IP12 147 A4
Riverside View IP13 127 C8
Riverside Way IP27 5 F2
Riverview IP12 147 C7
Riverwalk Sch IP33 154 A1
Rivish La CO10 91 E8
Rixon Cres 3 IP12 84 E6
Roamwood Gn La IP14 53 E3
Robeck Rd IP3 139 E1
Robert Boby Way IP33 154 B2
Robert's Hill CO8 101 C2
Roberts Rd IP16 129 D6
Robertsbridge Wlk 6 NR33 114 D4
Robin Cl Haverhill CB9 133 A5
Mildenhall IP28 116 D4
15 Stowmarket IP14 67 A5
12 Thurstow IP31 49 D4
Robin Dr IP2 138 D3
Robin Hill NR32 113 A2
Robin Rd IP33 123 C1
Robin Way CO10 148 A3
Robins Cl 16 CB7 29 C5
Robinson Cl IP33 122 D6
Robinson Rd 7 IP21 20 F1
Robinson Wlk IP32 122 D7
Robletts IP13 84 D7
Robletts Way 1 CO6 101 F2
Rochdale 3 NR33 114 F3
Rochester Rd 1 NR33 115 B4
Rochester Way CO10 148 B8
Rochfort Ave CB8 120 E5
Rock Rd NR32 112 D1
Rockall CB8 61 E6
Rockall Cl CB9 133 B5
Rockalls Rd CO6 93 F1
Rockingham Rd IP33 123 B3
Rockstone La IP19 41 C7
Rodber Way NR32 113 A6
Rodbridge Hill CO10 91 D6
Rodney Ct IP12 146 F7
Roebuck Dr IP27 109 E4
Roebuck The IP27 109 E1
Roger's Cl NR31 3 B7
Roger's La CO10 92 F4
Rogeron Cl CO10 75 D3
Rogers Cl IP11 152 F6
Rogue's La IP13 127 C5
Rokewood Pl IP29 64 A3
Roman Cl 3 CB5 44 A5
Roman Hill Mid Sch NR32 113 C1
Roman Hill Prim Sch NR32 113 C1
Roman Rd NR32 113 C1
Roman Way
Felixstowe IP11 153 D6
Halesworth IP19 118 A3
Haverhill CB9 133 B4
Long Melford CO10 91 E7
Romany La NR33 11 B3
Romany Rd NR32 114 C8
Romany Way IP33 123 D3
Romney Pl 6 NR32 113 B6
Romney Rd IP3 140 A1
Romsey Rd IP33 122 D3
Ronald La IP17 128 D5
Ronden Cl NR34 111 B2
Rook's La 7 NR34 111 B5
Rookery Chase CO7 103 F1
Rookery Cl NR33 114 F7
Rookery Dro 2 IP28 13 B1
Rookery La IP19 23 F4
Rookery Rd Elmsett IP7 80 E2
Monewden IP13 69 F5
Rookery Sh Ctr CB8 121 A4
Rookery The
Brandon IP27 5 D1
Eye IP23 117 D2
4 Manningtree CO11 104 E2
Newmarket CB8 121 B3
Rookery Way IP14 51 F1
Rookery Wlk IP27 109 B7
Rookwood La CO10 78 F6
Rookwood Way CB9 132 E4
Roosevelt Wlk 5 NR33 114 C5
Rope Wlk
Carlton Colville NR33 114 B4
Ipswich IP4 155 C2
Roper's Ct 3 CO10 78 D4
Ropers La CO10 91 D7
Ropes Dr IP5 141 B8
Rosbrook Cl 1 IP33 122 D4
Rose Acre CO7 103 F7
Rose Ave IP22 20 A3
Rose Ct Lowestoft NR32 113 B2
Shotley IP9 106 F6
Rose Gn CO10 101 F8
Rose Gn La 4 IP28 30 B8
Rose Hall Gdns NR35 110 B3
Rose Hill
Grundisburgh IP13 83 E5
Withersfield CB9 74 B3
Witnesham IP6 135 F7
Rose Hill Prim Sch IP3 140 A4
Rose La Botesdale IP22 36 A7
Bungay NR35 110 B3
Diss IP22 20 D1
Elmswell IP30 50 E2
Ipswich IP4 155 B2
Wickham Skeith IP23 52 D8
Rose La Cl IP22 20 C1
Rose Wlk IP6 125 D3
Rosebay Gdns 1 CB7 28 D4
Rosebery Rd
Felixstowe IP11 153 B4
Ipswich IP4 139 F5
Rosebery Way CB8 120 E5
Rosecroft Rd IP1 135 A2
Rosecroft Way IP24 16 D6
Rosedale Gdns 9 NR33 114 E4
Rosefinch Cl CB9 133 A5
Rosehill Cres IP3 139 F4
Rosehill Rd IP3 139 F4
Rosemary Ave IP11 153 B5
Rosemary Cl 4 IP28 30 C1
Rosemary Gdns CO10 148 D8
Rosemary La
Ipswich IP4 155 B2
Kelsale cum Carlton IP17 128 C6
Rosemary Musker Cty High Sch IP24 16 C7
Rosemary Rd 5 IP32 48 C5
Rosery La IP13 137 F6
Rosewood NR33 115 A5
Rosewood Cl 22 IP27 13 F2
Ross Cl CB9 133 B5
Ross Peers Sports Ctr The CB7 28 D3
Ross Rd IP4 136 B1
Rosyth Rd 5 IP31 33 D5
Rotherham Rd 9 IP7 79 F4
Rotten Row CO10 92 D2
Rotterdam Rd NR32 113 B1
Rougham CE Prim Sch IP30 49 D1
Rougham Control Twr Musuem* IP30 49 B3
Rougham Hill IP33 123 D3
Rougham Ind Est IP30 49 B2
Rougham Rd
Bradfield St George IP30 64 D7
Bury St Edmunds IP33 123 C3
Roughlands IP27 109 D6
Roundridge Rd IP9 150 F4
Roundwood Rd IP4 140 A7
Rous Meml Ct CB8 121 B3
Rous Rd CB8 121 B3
Rousies Cl 6 IP7 149 E6
Routh Ave 4 IP3 140 F1
Row The Bramford IP8 134 A2
Gipsy Row CO7 150 A4
Stratford St Mary CO7 103 E5
Rowan Cl Haverhill CB9 132 C7
Priory Heath IP3 140 D2
Rowan Dr Brandon IP27 14 F8
Bury St Edmunds IP32 123 F6
Rowan Gn 7 IP30 50 F2
Rowan Way
Beccles NR34 111 E3
Lowestoft NR33 114 D6
5 Thurstow IP31 49 D4
Rowan Wlk IP28 116 E5
Rowanhayes Cl IP2 139 B3
Rowans Way 1 CO6 102 A7
Rowarth Ave IP5 141 C7
Rowe's Hill IP13 40 C2
Rowell Cl CB9 132 E8
Rowell's La IP14 51 D4
Rowley Cl 7 CO11 104 E4
Rowley Ct
Newmarket CB8 120 E3
Sturmer CB9 133 C3
Rowley Dr CB8 120 F3
Rowley Hill CB9 133 B3
Rowntree Cl 6 NR32 113 A6
Rows The CB8 120 E3
Roxburgh Rd IP4 136 B1
Roy Ave IP4 140 B5
Roy Cl IP5 141 B7
Royal Ave NR32 113 D3
Royal Hospl Sch IP9 105 E6
Royal Naval Patrol Service Mus* NR32 113 E3
Royal Pal Cl CB8 120 D7
Royal Plain NR33 115 D8
Royal Terr NR33 115 D7
Roydon Fen IP22 20 B2
Roydon Prim Sch IP22 20 B3
Roydon Rd IP22 20 C3
Roydon Way 10 NR32 112 F4
Roylands La CO10 93 D3
Royston Dr IP2 138 D2
Rozlyne Cl 8 NR33 114 E4
Rubens Rd IP3 140 A1
Rubens Wlk
Gunton NR32 113 B6
Sudbury CO10 148 E8
Ruby Cl 9 NR32 3 D4
Rudlands IP8 138 C1
Rudlands Cl 6 CB7 29 C5
Rue's La IP11 153 C8
Ruffles Rd CB9 133 A5
Rugby Rd CO10 148 F2
Rumburgh La NR35 24 D6
Rumburgh Rd
Lowestoft NR32 113 B5
Rumburgh IP19 24 B3
Run Meadow NR33 114 C6
Run The NR34 26 A7
Runce's La NR33 114 C3
Runnacles Way IP11 152 D5
Runnymede Gn IP33 123 A3
Rush Cl IP4 140 E4
Rushall Rd IP20 22 B6
Rushbrooke La IP33 123 D3
Rushbury Cl IP4 140 B8
Rushford Rd
Coney Weston IP31 17 E1
Euston IP24 16 E2
Rushlake Way 7 NR33 114 D4
Rushmeadow Way 1 IP11 153 D7
Rushmere Hall Prim Sch IP4 136 A1
Rushmere Pl CB9 132 F6
Rushmere Rd
Gisleham NR33 114 B1
Ipswich IP4 140 A7
Rushmere NR33 10 F3
Rushmere St IP5 136 E1
Rushton Dr NR33 114 B3
Ruskin Cl 3 IP14 124 B8
Ruskin Rd IP4 139 F5
Russell Baron Rd IP31 48 D5
Russell Cl IP12 146 E6
Russell Rd
Felixstowe IP11 152 F2
Ipswich IP1 155 A2
Russell's Gn NR34 9 C2
Russet Cl
4 Beccles NR34 111 C3
Great Barton IP32 123 E7
Russett Cl CB9 132 A6
Rutland Ct 15 CB9 132 C5
Rutland Sq IP33 154 C1
Rydal Ave IP11 153 D7
Rydal Cl IP14 124 B6
Rydal Wlk IP3 140 C2
Ryders Way 2 IP22 36 A6
Rye Cl Ipswich IP3 140 D4
3 Lowestoft NR33 114 D4
Rye Ct 8 CB9 132 C5
Ryeburn Cl 1 NR33 11 B1
Ryedale 1 NR33 114 F3
Ryefields 9 IP31 49 E4
Ryes La CO10 91 D1
Ryes Sch The
Bulmer Tye CO10 91 E1
Kesgrave IP5 137 E1
Rylands IP9 150 E4
Rylands Cl 1 IP31 49 E4

S

Sackville St CB8 121 B4
Sackvylle St IP14 53 E1
Saddlemakers La IP12 147 C8
Saddlers Meadow 2 IP13 83 E5
Saddlers Pl 19 IP5 98 A8
Saddlers Yd 17 IP31 34 B1
Saffron Sq NR33 115 A2
Saffrons Cl IP30 50 D1
Sagehayes Cl IP2 139 B3
Sages End Rd CB9 88 A4
St Agnes Way IP5 140 F6
St Alban's Cath High Sch IP4 140 D7
St Albans CB8 121 A6

St Andrew 2 CB8 ...121 A4
St Andrew Cl 1 NR31 ...3 C7
St Andrew's Church Cl
IP5 ...136 D1
St Andrew's Cl IP12 ...147 D7
St Andrew's Ct 4 IP33 ...154 B2
St Andrew's Dr 3 IP9 ...106 C8
St Andrew's Pl IP12 ...147 D8
St Andrew's Rd
Beccles NR34 ...111 C2
Coldfair Green IP17 ...129 B2
Felixstowe IP11 ...153 A5
St Andrew's St IP28 ...116 C4
St Andrew's St N IP33 ...154 B3
St Andrew's St S IP33 ...154 B2
St Andrews CE VA Prim Sch
IP22 ...19 A5
St Andrews Cl
2 Barningham IP31 ...34 E7
2 Great Finborough IP14 ...66 B4
Ipswich IP4 ...140 D5
3 Isleham CB7 ...29 C5
St Andrews Dr 7 IP28 ...48 C6
St Andrews Mead IP14 ...68 B8
St Andrews Rd
Scole IP21 ...21 A1
Sudbury CO10 ...148 E4
St Anne's Cl NR34 ...111 C4
St Anne's Dr IP28 ...116 B4
St Anne's Rd NR34 ...111 C4
St Annes Cl IP12 ...146 D3
St Anthony 3 CB8 ...121 A4
St Anthonys Cres IP4 ...139 F6
St Aubyn's Rd 6 NR33 ...115 C6
St Aubyns Rd IP4 ...140 A5
St Audrys Pk Rd 5 IP12 ...84 E6
St Audrys Rd IP12 ...84 E6
St Augustine Rd IP3 ...140 D4
St Augustine's Gdns
IP3 ...140 C3
St Austell Cl IP5 ...141 A6
St Austin's La 1 CO12 ...107 C3
St Barbara's Ct 18 CO10 ...148 C5
St Bartholomews La
CO10 ...148 B7
St Benedict's Rd NR34 ...111 B6
St Benedicts Cath Sch
IP32 ...122 F8
St Benedicts Rd IP27 ...6 A1
St Benet's Dr NR34 ...111 C3
St Benet's RC Minst
NR34 ...111 A4
St Benets RC Prim Sch
NR34 ...111 A5
St Botolph's La IP33 ...154 C1
St Botolph's Way CB9 ...132 D6
St Botolphs CE VC Prim Sch
IP22 ...36 B7
St Botolphs Pl 13 CB9 ...132 D5
St Catherine's Cl
NR33 ...114 E4
St Catherine's Ct IP2 ...138 E1
St Catherine's Rd 11
CO10 ...91 E8
St Catherines Cl IP28 ...116 D6
St Clare Ct 15 NR31 ...3 B7
St Clement Mews 13 NR31 ...3 B7
St Clement's Hospl
IP3 ...140 C4
St Clements Church La
IP4 ...155 C2
St Cross Rd IP20 ...23 B8
St David 4 CB8 ...121 A4
St David's Cl 5 NR34 ...111 C2
St David's Rd 7 IP3 ...140 B3
St Denis Cl 11 CO12 ...107 A1
St Denys 5 CB8 ...121 A4
St Domonic's Dr IP27 ...6 A1
St Edmund Cl 5 IP31 ...34 B1
St Edmund Rd IP27 ...5 E4
St Edmund's Cl 1 IP12 ...85 A5
St Edmund's Dr IP30 ...50 F3
St Edmund's Hill CO10 ...101 B7
St Edmund's Pl IP1 ...139 C8
St Edmund's Rd
Felixstowe IP11 ...152 E2
Ipswich IP1 ...139 B8
Southwold IP18 ...119 D6
St Edmunds Cl
2 Beccles NR34 ...111 C2
12 Harwich CO12 ...107 A1
Stowmarket IP14 ...124 C8
3 Woodbridge IP12 ...146 E4
St Edmunds Cres 1
NR33 ...11 C1
St Edmunds Gate 11
IP31 ...33 D5
St Edmunds La CO8 ...101 D5
St Edmunds Pl IP33 ...154 B3
St Edmunds Prim Sch
IP21 ...38 C6
St Edmunds RC Prim Sch
NR35 ...110 B4
St Edmunds RC VA Prim Sch
IP33 ...154 B1
St Edmunds Rd IP14 ...124 C7
St Edmunds Sq 10 IP31 ...33 D5
St Edmundsbury Cath*
IP33 ...154 C2
St Edmundsbury CE VA Prim
Sch IP33 ...154 A3
St Edmundsbury Mews
IP33 ...154 B1
St Edmundsbury Ret Pk
IP32 ...123 E4
St Etienne IP14 ...69 B6
St Fabians Cl CB8 ...120 F5
St Fabians Cl Sch CB8 ...120 E5
St Felix CE VE Mid Sch
CB8 ...120 F6
St Felix Cl 2 CB7 ...28 D5
St Felix RC Prim Sch
CB9 ...132 B5
St Felix Sch IP18 ...119 A6
St George 1 CB8 ...121 A4
St George's Ave 2
CO12 ...107 B1
St George's Rd
Beccles NR34 ...111 B4
Felixstowe IP11 ...153 C6
Lowestoft NR33 ...115 B4
Stowlangtoft IP31 ...50 B7
St George's St IP1 ...155 B3
St Georges Sch IP18 ...119 A7
St Gotthards Ave IP12 ...98 B8
St Gregory Ct CO10 ...148 B6
St Gregorys CE VC Prim Sch
CO10 ...148 B5
St Gregorys Cl 1 IP12 ...85 E8
St Helena Wlk IP28 ...116 C6
St Helen's St IP4 ...155 C3
St Helens Prim Sch
IP4 ...139 E6
St Helens Way IP24 ...16 B7
St Isidores IP5 ...141 E7
St Ives Cl IP5 ...141 A6
St James 6 CB8 ...121 A4
St James Ct 3 CB9 ...132 C6
St James' Gn 7 IP18 ...119 D5
St James La IP33 ...154 A2
St James' La
Chediston IP19 ...24 A3
St James, South Elmham
IP19 ...23 F4
St James Mid Sch
IP33 ...123 C5
St James Rd
All Saints & St Nicholas,
South Elmham IP19 ...24 A5
St James, South Elmham
IP19 ...23 F4
St James's St IP17 ...43 B1
St John's Cl IP28 ...116 D6
St John's Hill
Bungay NR35 ...110 C2
4 Woodbridge IP12 ...147 A5
St John's Pl IP33 ...154 B3
St John's Rd
Bungay NR35 ...110 B3
Ipswich IP4 ...140 A6
Lowestoft NR33 ...115 D7
Saxmundham IP17 ...128 C3
St John's St
Beck Row, Holywell Row
& Kenny Hill IP28 ...30 C8
Bury St Edmunds IP33 ...154 B3
Woodbridge IP12 ...147 A5
St John's Terr 5 IP12 ...147 A5
St John's Way
13 Feltwell IP26 ...4 E5
Thetford IP24 ...16 A5
St Johns Ave CB8 ...121 A1
St Johns CE Prim Sch
IP4 ...140 A7
St Johns Ct IP11 ...153 A4
St Johns Meadow IP20 ...23 C3
St Josephs Coll IP2 ...139 A3
St Josephs RC Prim Sch
CO10 ...148 B6
St Lawrence Cl NR34 ...111 C2
St Lawrence Gn IP5 ...141 A7
St Lawrence Prim Sch
NR34 ...24 F6
St Lawrence St IP1 ...155 B3
St Lawrence Way IP5 ...141 B8
St Leonard's Rd 1
NR33 ...115 C7
St Leonards Cl IP21 ...21 A1
St Leonards Hospl
CO10 ...148 D5
St Leonards Rd 2 IP3 ...140 B3
St Leonards St IP26 ...6 B8
St Louis Cath Mid Sch
IP33 ...154 B1
St Louis RC Prim Sch
CB8 ...121 A4
St Margaret's Cres
Leiston IP16 ...129 B6
3 Thetford IP24 ...16 B5
St Margaret's Gn IP4 ...155 C3
St Margaret's Pl CB8 ...75 E7
St Margaret's Rd
Bungay NR35 ...110 B1
3 Lowestoft NR32 ...113 E3
St Margaret's St IP4 ...155 C3
St Margaret's Way 3
NR31 ...3 B7
St Margarets CE VA Prim Sch
IP4 ...155 C3
St Margarets Com Prim Sch
NR32 ...113 C3
St Margarets Plain
IP4 ...155 B3
St Marks RC Prim Sch
IP2 ...138 F3
St Martin's Cl CB8 ...120 C7
St Martin's La IP24 ...16 B2
St Martin's St IP33 ...154 B3
St Martin's Way IP24 ...16 B5
St Martins Ct IP5 ...141 E7
St Martins Gn 14 IP11 ...107 D8
St Mary's Ave 5 IP14 ...51 C1
St Mary's Cl Bacton IP14 ...51 F6
St Mary's Cl *continued*
Bramford IP8 ...134 B1
Felixstowe IP11 ...152 B7
Flixton NR35 ...7 E1
Harleston IP20 ...22 E6
Horham IP21 ...38 F3
Mildenhall IP28 ...116 C3
Sudbury CO10 ...148 F8
St Mary's Cres
Badwell Ash IP31 ...50 E7
Felixstowe IP11 ...152 F6
St Mary's Gdns IP6 ...125 E6
St Mary's Rd
Aldeby NR34 ...10 A7
Beccles NR34 ...111 A5
Creeting St Mary IP6 ...125 E5
Stowmarket IP14 ...124 B7
St Mary's Sq IP33 ...154 C1
St Mary's St 2 NR35 ...110 B4
St Mary's Wlk 2 CB9 ...88 D3
St Marys Cath Prim Sch
IP4 ...139 F6
St Marys CE Aided Prim Sch
IP12 ...146 E5
St Marys CE VA Prim Sch
IP28 ...116 C5
St Marys Cl 1 IP23 ...36 D2
St Marys Pk IP10 ...98 A4
St Marys Prim Sch
IP7 ...149 E6
St Marys RC Prim Sch
NR33 ...115 C5
St Marys Rd IP4 ...139 F6
St Marys Sq 9 CB8 ...121 A4
St Marys View IP31 ...49 E6
St Marys Way IP6 ...135 F4
St Mathew's St Service Rd
IP1 ...155 A3
St Matthew's Ave 3
NR34 ...111 C2
St Matthew's CE VA Prim Sch
IP1 ...155 A3
St Matthew's St IP1 ...155 A3
St Michael's Cl
1 Beccles NR34 ...111 C2
Ipswich IP5 ...141 A6
Lowestoft NR32 ...112 C1
St Michael's Rd 4 CO12 ...107 B1
St Michael's Way IP19 ...42 C6
St Michaels CE VA Prim Sch
NR34 ...9 B6
St Michaels Cl IP6 ...126 C4
St Michaels Ct 16 CO11 ...104 E2
St Nicholas Cl
Bury St Edmunds IP32 ...123 C6
Rattlesden IP30 ...65 D5
St Nicholas Ct IP1 ...155 B2
St Nicholas Dr 23 IP26 ...4 E5
St Nicholas St IP1 ...155 B2
St Olaves Prec IP32 ...122 D8
St Olaves Precinct
IP32 ...122 E8
St Olaves Rd
Bury St Edmunds IP32 ...122 E8
Herring Fleet NR32 ...2 D4
Ipswich IP5 ...141 C8
St Osyth Cl IP2 ...142 F8
St Pancras Cath Prim Sch
IP1 ...134 F2
St Patrick 7 CB8 ...121 A4
St Paul's Cl
4 Beccles NR34 ...111 C2
Brockdish IP21 ...21 F2
St Pauls Cl IP15 ...130 E5
St Peter & Paul CE VA Prim
Sch IP23 ...117 D2
St Peter's Ave 1 IP6 ...134 C8
St Peter's Brewery & Visitor
Ctr* NR35 ...24 A8
St Peter's Cl
Brockdish IP21 ...21 F2
8 Claydon IP6 ...82 A5
Stowmarket IP14 ...124 B6
Woodbridge IP12 ...146 D4
St Peter's Ct 16 CO10 ...148 C5
St Peter's Hall* NR35 ...24 A8
St Peter's Rd
Lowestoft NR33 ...115 C6
Stowmarket IP14 ...124 B6
St Peter's St
Ipswich IP4 ...155 B2
4 Lowestoft NR32 ...113 D2
St Peter's Wlk IP26 ...4 F3
St Peters Ave CB8 ...45 F2
St Peters Cl
Charsfield IP13 ...70 B3
6 Moulton CB8 ...45 F3
St Peters Ct IP33 ...154 B1
St Peters Path IP19 ...118 E4
St Peters Pl CB7 ...29 B1
St Peters Rd
Aldeburgh IP15 ...130 E5
Lowestoft NR33 ...114 C3
St Peters Way 11 IP31 ...49 E4
St Philips Rd CB8 ...120 F5
St Quinton's Ct NR33 ...115 B5
St Stephens Cl IP33 ...123 C6
St Stephens La IP1 ...155 B2
St Vincent Wlk 14 NR31 ...3 B7
St Wendred's Way
CB8 ...120 B7
Salehurst Rd IP3 ...140 E3
Salisbury Ct 12 CB9 ...132 D5
Salisbury Gn IP33 ...123 B3
Salisbury Rd
Ipswich IP3 ...140 A3
Lowestoft NR33 ...115 C7
1 Southwold IP18 ...119 D5
Salisbury Terr 1 CO10 ...148 C6
Sallows Cl IP1 ...138 F7
Sally Wood's La IP6 ...125 F6
Salmet Cl IP2 ...139 A3
Salmon Wlk IP32 ...122 D7
Salmond Dr 5 IP24 ...16 C2
Salter Cl IP32 ...123 E4
Salters Gdns 4 IP13 ...83 E5
Salters Hall Mews
CO10 ...148 B5
Saltgate 5 NR34 ...111 B6
Salthouse La IP4 ...155 C2
Saltwater Way NR33 ...114 E8
Samford Cl IP9 ...105 E8
Samford Ct 5 NR34 ...111 F4
Samford Pl IP8 ...138 B6
Sampson Dr 6 CO10 ...91 E8
Samson Cl 14 IP32 ...48 C5
Samson's La IP22 ...19 F4
Samuel Ct IP4 ...155 C3
Samuel St Wlk IP33 ...123 A2
Samuel Vince Rd 2
IP21 ...39 D8
Samuel Ward Arts & Tech
Coll CB9 ...132 F7
San Francisco Wlk 3
NR33 ...114 C5
Sancroft Way
5 Fressingfield IP21 ...39 D8
Wortwell IP20 ...23 A7
Sancroft Wlk IP33 ...122 B6
Sanctuary Gdns 4
NR32 ...112 F5
Sanctuary The IP16 ...73 F6
Sanctuary Way 9 NR33 ...11 B1
Sand Acre Cl IP28 ...116 D5
Sand Hill CO10 ...93 C3
Sand St CB7 ...28 D3
Sandbank Rd 1 NR33 ...114 E4
Sandbanks Ct IP17 ...128 C3
Sanderling Cl 3 IP28 ...116 D4
Sanders Cl 2 NR32 ...112 F4
Sandford Rd IP14 ...52 A1
Sandgalls Rd IP27 ...109 D6
Sandholme Cl IP33 ...123 B2
Sandhurst Ave IP3 ...139 F4
Sandling Cres IP4 ...140 E5
Sandlings Prim Sch
IP12 ...85 C3
Sandlings The
Aldeburgh IP15 ...130 C6
Ipswich IP3 ...140 D1
Sandown Cl 3 IP1 ...135 A3
Sandown Rd IP1 ...135 A3
Sandpath 5 IP21 ...39 E8
Sandpiper Cl CB9 ...133 A6
Sandpiper Rd
Bury St Edmunds IP33 ...123 C2
Ipswich IP2 ...138 E2
1 Stowmarket IP14 ...124 F7
Sandpit Cl IP4 ...140 F5
Sandpit Dr 3 IP31 ...49 E4
Sandpit Hill IP20 ...23 B3
Sandpit La
Thurstow IP31 ...49 E4
Worlingham NR34 ...9 F4
Sandringham Cl IP2 ...138 F2
Sandringham Rd
NR32 ...113 C1
Sands Cl 9 NR31 ...3 C6
Sands La NR32 ...112 D2
Sandy Cl 5 IP11 ...107 D8
Sandy Dro IP28 ...30 F3
Sandy Hill Barham IP6 ...82 B7
Wormingford CO6 ...101 E3
Sandy La Barham IP6 ...82 A6
Barningham IP31 ...34 E8
Barsham NR34 ...9 A4
2 Bromeswell IP12 ...85 A5
Bulmer CO10 ...91 D3
Diss IP22 ...20 D2
Gisleham NR33 ...11 A1
Holton IP19 ...118 E4
Hoo IP13 ...70 B4
Iken IP12 ...72 F2
Little Bealings IP13 ...137 D4
Marlesford IP13 ...71 C5
Rendham IP17 ...56 F3
Ringshall IP14 ...80 D8
St Mary, South Elmham
otherwise Homersfield
IP20 ...23 B7
Sternfield IP17 ...72 C8
Stowlangtoft IP31 ...50 A7
Sudbury CO10 ...148 A4
Sutton IP12 ...99 B8
Waldringfield IP12 ...98 E8
Westerfield IP6 ...135 E5
Wickham Market IP13 ...127 D5
Witnesham IP6 ...136 B8
Woodbridge IP12 ...146 D2
Sandyhill La IP3 ...139 E1
Sapiston Rd IP31 ...33 F5
Sapling Pl IP4 ...140 E5
Saracens House Bsns Ctr
IP4 ...155 C3
Sarah Ct CB9 ...132 E3
Sarsen Cl IP19 ...118 C4
Sascombe Vineyard*
CB8 ...60 F2
Saturn Cl NR32 ...113 D4
Sawmill La IP10 ...145 B6
Sawmills Rd IP22 ...20 E2
Sawston Cl 10 IP2 ...139 A2
Sawyers IP7 ...80 F1
Sawyers Cl IP9 ...150 E2
Saxham Bsns Pk IP29 ...47 E4
Saxmundham Mid Sch
IP17 ...128 C2
Saxmundham Mus*
IP17 ...128 D3
Saxmundham Prim Sch
IP17 ...128 C3
Saxmundham Rd
Aldeburgh IP15 ...130 C5
Framlingham IP13 ...126 E3
Friston IP17 ...72 E7
Knodishall IP17 ...57 F1
Theberton IP16 ...58 A2
Saxmundham Sports Club
IP17 ...128 C4
Saxmundham Sta
IP17 ...128 C3
Saxon Cl Exning CB8 ...120 D8
11 Felixstowe IP11 ...153 D6
Saxon Cres 7 IP31 ...33 D5
Saxon Dr 9 CB5 ...44 A5
Saxon La IP8 ...95 E4
Saxon Pl 1 Thetford IP24 ...16 B5
Weeting IP27 ...5 E3
Saxon Rd
Lowestoft NR33 ...115 B3
Saxmundham IP17 ...128 B3
Saxon Rise IP33 ...122 E3
Saxon St Rd CB8 ...60 E6
Saxon Way IP12 ...147 A7
Saxon Wlk IP26 ...6 A8
Saxonfields IP17 ...72 D5
Saxons Way IP19 ...118 B4
Saxstead Gn Postmill*
IP13 ...55 B3
Saxtead Rd
Dennington IP13 ...55 D5
Framlingham IP13 ...126 A5
Scales St NR35 ...110 A4
Scalesbrook La IP19 ...118 E7
Scaltback Cl CB8 ...120 E6
Scaltback Mid Sch
CB8 ...120 E5
Scama La IP22 ...36 C6
Scarlin Rd IP33 ...122 C3
Schneider Rd 3 IP11 ...153 H11
Scholars Wlk IP22 ...20 C3
School Ave IP30 ...50 E2
School Cl
1 Capel St Mary IP9 ...150 E3
Cheveley CB8 ...60 E8
Hadleigh IP7 ...149 E5
Kenninghall NR16 ...19 A8
North Cove NR34 ...10 C4
Norton IP31 ...50 B4
20 Stanton IP31 ...34 E4
School Cres CB9 ...133 E8
School Farm La CO10 ...78 C2
School Hill
Boxford CO10 ...93 C3
Copdock & Washbrook
IP8 ...95 F4
Kettleburgh IP13 ...70 C7
Nacton IP10 ...145 B4
School La Bardwell IP31 ...34 C4
Bawdsey IP12 ...99 E2
Benhall IP17 ...72 C8
5 Brantham CO11 ...104 E5
16 Burwell CB5 ...44 A5
Dedham CO7 ...103 F4
East Bergholt CO7 ...151 B5
Easton IP13 ...70 E5
Fornham St Martin IP31 ...48 D6
Great Barton IP31 ...49 B6
Great Horkesley CO6 ...102 C1
Halesworth IP19 ...118 A4
17 Harleston IP20 ...22 D6
Haverhill CB9 ...132 B5
Hollesley IP12 ...99 F7
Little Horkesley CO6 ...102 B3
Long Melford CO10 ...77 E1
Manningtree CO11 ...104 D1
Martlesham IP12 ...146 C1
Metfield IP20 ...23 C3
4 Mistley CO11 ...104 F2
Reydon IP18 ...26 E1
Stratford St Mary CO7 ...103 E5
Thelnetham IP22 ...18 E1
7 Thurstow IP31 ...49 E4
Ufford IP13 ...84 F7
School Meadow
1 Stowmarket IP14 ...124 E3
4 Wetherden IP14 ...51 A1
School Rd Alburgh IP20 ...7 A1
Bedingham NR35 ...7 B7
Blaxhall IP12 ...72 A3
Bressingham IP22 ...19 E4
Coddenham IP6 ...68 B1
Coldfair Green IP17 ...129 A3
Earsham NR35 ...7 F4
Elmswell IP30 ...50 E2
Great Ashfield IP31 ...50 F6
Great Barton IP31 ...49 B6
Great Wratting CB9 ...74 F3
Hinderclay IP22 ...35 E7
Hollesley IP12 ...99 F7
Kedington CB9 ...133 E8
Kirby Cane NR35 ...8 E8
Knodishall IP17 ...73 A8
Langham CO4 ...103 C2
Little Horkesley CO6 ...102 B2
Little Yeldham CO9 ...90 B2
Lowestoft NR33 ...114 F8
Monk Soham IP13 ...54 D4
Pentlow CO10 ...90 F7
Ringsfield NR34 ...9 B1
Risby IP28 ...47 E5
St Andrew, Ilketshall
NR34 ...8 E2

School Rd continued
9 Shotley Gate IP9 ....107 A4
Sudbourne IP12 ....87 A8
Tattingstone IP9 ....142 D1
Thurston IP31 ....49 C6
Tunstall IP12 ....71 F2
Waldringfield IP12 ....98 D7
Woodditton CB8 ....60 D6
School St Foxearth CO10 ...91 B7
Needham Market IP6 .....125 D4
Stoke-by-Nayland CO6 ...102 E7
Sudbury CO10 ....148 C5
School View NR34 ......24 C5
Schoolhall La IP33 .....154 B3
Schreiber Rd IP4 ....140 B7
Scofield Ct CO10 ....148 E4
Scole Comm IP21 ....20 F3
Scole Comm Rd IP21 ...21 A2
Scole Prim Sch IP21 ...21 A2
Scole Rd IP21 ....21 F2
Sconch Beck Rd IP20 ..23 A6
Scopes Rd IP5 ....141 C8
Scotland End CB7 ....29 F1
Scotland St CO6 ....103 A7
Scotred Cl CB5 ....44 A4
Scott Ave IP28 ....116 C5
Scott La 2 IP17 ....62 C4
Scott Rd Ipswich IP3 ...140 B1
16 Ixworth IP31 ....34 B1
Scott's Hill IP14 ....68 B6
Scott's La IP13 ....84 C7
Scotts Cl 14 NR33 .....11 B1
Scrivener Dr IP8 ....138 B2
Scudamore Pl NR35 ....110 B7
Scuffin's La IP14 ......52 A6
Sea Lake Rd NR32 .....114 E8
Sea Rd IP11 ....152 F2
Sea View NR33 ....11 C1
Sea View Rise NR31 .....3 C6
Sea View Wlk NR33 ....115 B4
Seabreeze Rd IP24 ....124 D5
Seafield Ave 5 CO11 ..105 A2
Seafield Dr 6 CO12 ...107 A1
Seafields Dr 3 NR31 ....3 B6
Seago St NR32 ....113 D1
Sealodes Rd CB7 ....28 A5
Seaman Ave IP17 ......128 B2
Seaton Cl 18 CO11 ....104 D2
Seaton Rd IP11 ....152 E5
Seavert Cl 3 NR33 .....114 E3
Seaview Rd IP18 ......119 C7
Seaward Ave 2 IP16 ...129 D5
Sebert Rd IP22 ....19 A1
Sebert Wood Cty Prim Sch
IP32 ....123 D5
Seckford Almshouses
IP12 ....146 F5
Seckford Cl 1 IP4 .....140 F5
Seckford Hall Rd
IP12 ....146 D3
Seckford St IP12 ....146 F5
Second Ave
Felixstowe IP11 ....152 B7
2 Sudbury CO10 ....77 B3
Sudbury CO10 ....148 E4
Second Dro IP27 ....13 C7
Sedan Wlk IP1 ....134 E3
Sedge Way IP33 ....154 A4
Sedgefen Rd IP27 ......12 F7
Sedlescombe Rd 8
NR33 ....114 D5
Sefton Way CB8 ....120 D5
Selby St NR32 ....113 C1
Self's La IP22 ....18 F3
Selkirk Rd IP4 ....136 C1
Selvale Way IP11 ......152 E4
Selwyn Cl Ipswich IP2 .155 B1
Mildenhall IP28 ....116 D6
Newmarket CB8 ....121 A1
Semer Cl IP14 ....124 E3
Semere Gn La IP21 ....21 D6
Semere La IP21 ....21 D6
Sergeants Wlk IP33 ....153 B3
Serpentine Rd IP9 .....140 B2
Seven Acres NR33 .....115 A3
Seven Cotts La IP5 ....136 C1
Seven Gdns Rd IP13 ....83 F6
Seven Hills (Barrow
Cemetery)*
Brettenham IP24 ....16 F4
Little Livermere IP31 .....33 A4
Sevenhills La IP31 .....33 A4
Several Rd IP13 ....55 B3
Severalls La IP13 ....55 D6
Severals The CB8 .....121 B4
Severn Rd
Bury St Edmunds IP32 ...48 C5
Ipswich IP3 ....139 F3
Sewell Wontner Cl
IP5 ....141 C8
Sewell's La CO10 ....90 D5
Sewells IP7 ....79 E6
Sewells The IP33 ......123 A2
Sexton Rd NR35 ....7 D6
Sextons Manor Prim Sch
IP33 ....122 C6
Sextons Mdw IP33 .....154 C1
Sextons Meadow IP33 ..123 B3
Sextons Mews IP33 ....154 C1
Seymour Dr CB9 ....132 B5
Seymour Ave IP14 .....24 D8
Seymour Cl IP33 ....154 A3
Seymour Rd IP2 ....155 B1
Shackleton Cl 20 CO12 .106 F1
Shackleton Rd IP3 .....140 B3
Shackleton Sq 8 IP13 ..140 B3
Shaddick Rd IP18 ......119 B8
Shade The CB7 ....28 C5

Shadingfield Cl NR32 ...113 A5
Shadowbush Cl IP9 ....132 D7
Shadwell Cl IP27 ....5 E3
Shadwell Wlk IP33 ....122 B6
Shaftesbury Ave 4
CO12 ....107 A2
Shaftesbury Sq IP4 ....155 C2
Shafto Rd IP1 ....134 E1
Shaker's La IP33 ......123 C5
Shaker's Rd IP29 ....47 B4
Shakers' Rd
Brandon IP27 ....15 A5
Wangford IP27 ....14 E4
Shakespeare Rd
Ipswich IP1 ....134 E3
Stowmarket IP14 ....124 B8
Shamrock Ave IP2 .....138 E4
Shannon Cl CB9 ......133 B5
Shannon Rd 4 IP3 ....144 A8
Shardlow Cl CB9 ....132 A7
Sharman's Rd IP4 ......29 A1
Sharon Dr NR32 ......113 B3
Sharon Rd IP33 ....122 D5
Sharp Rd IP33 ....122 F2
Sharp's Gn IP19 ....63 A8
Sharp's Hill IP29 ....47 B2
Sharp's La IP29 ....63 A7
Sharpe's Row IP30 .....65 E8
Sharper's Cnr IP27 ....109 B8
Sharpes Cnr IP27 .....109 C7
Shaw Ave NR33 ......114 D3
Shaw Rd CO10 ....135 E4
Shaw Valley Rd 7 IP12 ..84 A1
Shawlands Ave CO10 ...148 C4
Shawsgate Vineyard*
IP13 ....126 F6
Shearman Rd IP4 ......149 F5
Sheepdrift Rd IP12 .....85 B5
Sheepgate NR34 ......111 B5
Sheepgate La
Badwell Ash IP31 ....51 B7
Falkenham IP10 ....98 F1
Sheepshead Hill 2 CO10 .92 B3
Sheepwash La IP17 ....63 D3
Sheerwater 9 IP14 ....67 A5
Sheerwater Cl IP30 ....123 F6
Shelbourne Cl IP5 .....141 D7
Sheldrake Dr IP2 ......138 E1
Sheldrick's Rd CB7 .....29 D5
Shelley Ave CO10 .....148 F4
Shelley Cl IP14 ....124 F3
Shelley Rd
3 Bury St Edmunds IP32 .48 C5
Layham IP7 ....149 E1
Shelley St IP2 ....155 B1
Shelley Way
Bacton IP14 ....51 E5
Thetford IP24 ....16 C7
Shelterhouse Cnr IP24 ..32 C8
Shelton Hill IP21 ....39 B5
Shelton Rd 4 NR33 ...114 F3
Shenley Rd IP3 ....140 B1
Shenstone Dr IP14 ....135 A3
Shepherd Dr IP8 ......138 C2
Shepherds Ct 9 CB9 ...132 C5
Shepherds Dr 8 IP7 ...63 D3
Shepherds Gr Ind Est
IP22 ....35 B4
Shepherds La
Burgate IP22 ....36 D7
Glemsford CO10 ....77 A3
Onehouse IP14 ....124 A8
Sheppards Way 6 IP5 ..141 D7
Sherborne Ave IP4 ....136 A2
Sherborne Rd IP33 ....122 D5
Sherbourne St CO10 ...93 B4
Sheridan Cl IP14 ......124 A8
Sheridan Wlk NR34 ...111 E4
Sheriffs Ct CB8 ....59 F2
Sherrington Rd IP1 ....134 D1
Sherwood Fields 4 IP5 ..141 C7
Shetland Cl
3 Ipswich IP4 ....136 A1
5 Ipswich IP4 ....140 A8
Shetland Rd CB9 ......133 B5
Shetlands 19 IP31 .....34 E4
Shickle Pl IP2 ....18 C2
Shilling St 14 CO10 ....78 D4
Shillitoe Cl IP33 ......154 A2
Shimpling Cl 7 IP14 ...124 E3
Shimpling Rd IP29 .....77 E7
Shingle Hill IP21 ....21 B5
Ship Gdns IP28 ....116 B3
Ship La Bradfield CO11 ..105 C2
Bramford IP8 ....134 B1
Ship Launch Rd IP2 ...155 A3
Shippea Hill Sta CB7 ....12 C7
Shire Hall Yd IP4 ......155 C2
Shires The NR32 ......113 B8
Shirley Cl 9 IP1 ....135 A3
Shoals Wlk IP33 ....154 C2
Shoe Devil La NR35 ....24 C8
Shoebridge's Hill CO7 ..143 F3
Shop Hill CB8 ....61 E1
Shop La IP13 ....71 E5
Shop Rd IP13 ....69 E1
Shop St IP13 ....130 C6
Shore La
Bradfield CO11 ....105 C2
Harkstead IP9 ....106 A5
Nacton IP10 ....145 B3
Shores Cl IP28 ....6 C2
Short Beck IP26 ....4 B8
Short Brackland IP33 ..154 B2
Short La Feltwell IP26 ....4 D5
Lowestoft NR33 ....114 C2

Short La continued
Walberswick IP18 ....43 C5
Short Rd
Belton with Browston NR31 ..2 D8
Blundeston NR32 ....3 A4
Snailwell CB8 ....45 A5
Short St 2 NR33 ......115 B4
Shortlands IP21 ....138 D1
Shotford Rd IP20 ......22 D5
Shotley Cl
Felixstowe IP11 ....152 D4
Ipswich IP8 ....138 C2
Shotley Mews 8 IP12 ...85 B3
Shotley Prim Sch IP9 ...106 F5
Shotley Wlk IP9 ......106 E7
Shrimpling Rd IP29 ....77 D4
Shrub House Cl 1 IP28 ..30 B8
Shrubberies The CB8 ...131 C5
Shrubbery Cl IP11 .....152 F4
Shrubbery Rd IP13 ....146 B7
Shrubland Cl IP4 ......134 E1
Shrubland Dr IP4 .....140 F5
Shrubland Pk Gdns*
IP6 ....82 A6
Shrubland Rd 11 CO11 ..105 A2
Shrublands IP28 ......116 C4
Siam Pl 4 CO10 ....148 C5
Siamhall La CO10 ......92 F3
Sicklesmere Rd
Bury St Edmunds IP33 ..123 D2
Nowton IP30 ....63 E8
Sidegate Ave IP4 .....140 A8
Sidegate Ave E IP4 ....136 A1
Sidegate La W IP4 ....135 F1
Sidegate Prim Sch
IP4 ....140 A8
Sidegate Rd NR31 ......3 A8
Siding Rd NR34 ....10 C5
Silent St IP4 ....155 B2
Silhalls Cl 7 CB8 ......60 F8
Silk Mill Cl 2 IP7 .....149 D5
Silver Dr IP33 ....130 C6
Silver Hill IP8 ....95 D6
Silver Leys IP9 ....104 F7
Silver St Burwell CB5 ...44 A6
Kedington CB9 ....133 F7
Old Newton with Dagworth
IP14 ....51 E2
South Lopham IP22 ......19 C3
Withersdale Cmn IP20 ...22 E8
Silverdale Ave IP14 ....135 A1
Silverdale Cl IP4 ......135 A1
Silverley Way 6 CB8 ....60 F8
Silverwood Cl NR33 ....115 A4
Sim's La CB9 ....133 F7
Simon's Cross IP13 ....127 B7
Simons Rd IP12 ....147 A7
Simpers Drift IP17 ......56 D1
Simpson Cir IP23 .....138 D8
Sinclair Dr IP2 ....139 C3
Singleton Ct CO10 ....148 E3
Sir Alf Ramsey Way
IP4 ....155 A2
Sir John Leman High Sch
NR34 ....111 A4
Sir John Leman Rd
NR34 ....111 D2
Sir Robert Hitcham CE VA
Prim Sch IP14 ....126 B4
Sir Robert Hitchams CE VAP
Sch IP13 ....53 E2
Sirdar St IP1 ....139 A6
Siskin Gn 1 NR33 .....114 D5
Sitwell Cl 13 CO11 ....104 D2
Sitwell Gdns 8 IP13 ...126 C3
Sizewell Belts Nature
Reserve* IP16 ....58 E2
Sizewell Gap IP16 ......58 F1
Sizewell Power Sta
IP16 ....58 F2
Sizewell Rd IP16 ......129 D5
Sizewell Visitor Ctr*
IP16 ....58 F2
Skamacre Cres NR32 ..113 B2
Skate's Hill CO10 ......77 A2
Skeaping Cl CB8 ......121 A5
Skelton Cl 9 CO11 ....104 E2
Skelton Rd IP22 ....20 D2
Skelton's Dro IP28 ....13 A2
Skilman Hill IP18 ......119 D4
Skinner St IP33 ....154 B2
Skinner's La
Metfield IP20 ....23 C3
Starston IP20 ....22 B8
Skipper Cl IP3 ....142 E8
Skipper Rd IP22 ......138 D1
Skipper's La CB9 ....74 A3
Sky Hall Hill CO4 ......143 B7
Skylark Cl IP32 ....49 A4
Skylark La IP9 ....138 C2
Slade La IP22 ....19 E2
Slade St IP4 ....155 C2
Slade The IP6 ....134 D8
Slades Cl 7 CO10 ......77 B3
Slaters Dr IP25 ....132 C8
Slaughden Rd IP15 ....130 E2
Sleaford Cl IP2 ....139 A3
Sloe La IP17 ....129 A2
Slough Hill IP29 ....77 E7
Slough La Acton CO10 ...78 C1
Horringer IP29 ....122 A2
Slough Rd
Botesdale IP22 ....36 C5
Brantham CO11 ....104 E5
Slugs La NR32 ....2 C4
Sluice Dro IP26 ....4 E3
Slushy La IP9 ....106 A6

Smaley La 1 CO10 .....91 E8
Smallbridge Entry
CO8 ....101 E4
Smallbridge Hall*
CO8 ....101 E4
Smallworth La IP22 .....18 E3
Smart St IP4 ....155 C2
Smear La IP18 ....26 D2
Smear La E IP18 ....26 F1
Smeetham Hall La
CO10 ....91 C3
Smith Cres 17 NR33 ....11 B1
Smith Wlk IP33 ....123 D2
Smith's Wlk NR33 ....114 C6
Smithbrook La IP29 ....77 A8
Smithers Cl 9 IP9 .....155 C3
Smithfield IP22 ....147 B6
Smiths Cl IP14 ....54 E7
Smiths Dr IP21 ....21 B5
Smiths Pl 8 IP25 .....141 D7
Smithy Cl
Bradfield Combust with
Stanningfield IP29 .....64 A3
Rushbrooke with Rougham
IP30 ....64 D8
Smock Meadow 8 IP7 ...79 F4
Snab Hill NR33 ....11 A1
Snailwell Rd
Fordham CB8 ....44 F7
Newmarket CB8 ....121 B7
Snailwell Short Rd CB8 ..44 F5
Snake's La Lound NR32 ..2 F6
Topcroft NR35 ....7 A8
Snape Com Prim Sch
IP17 ....72 D5
Snape Dr NR32 ....113 A4
Snape Hill IP22 ....35 F6
Snape Maltings IP17 ...72 D4
Snape Rd Friston IP17 ..129 A2
Sudbourne IP12 ....131 A7
Tunstall IP12 ....72 A2
Snare Dro IP28 ....12 B3
Snipe Farm Rd IP13 ....69 E1
Snow Hill CO10 ....76 A1
Snow Hill La CO6 ......103 B7
Snowberry Way 6 CB2 ..28 D5
Snowcroft IP7 ....150 E3
Snowdens Yd 14 IP18 ..119 D5
Snowdon Cl 7 CB9 ....132 C4
Snowdon Hill IP13 .....132 A7
Snowdon Rd IP2 ......139 B2
Snowdrop Cl IP30 .....123 F5
Soames Cl IP14 ....124 C7
Soane St IP4 ....155 C3
Soft Rd CO10 ....90 F3
Soham Rd CB7 ....28 A8
Soham Town Cnr IP31 ..64 E7
Solace Cl NR33 ....110 D3
Solomon Rd 8 NR33 ...11 C1
Somerleyton Hall & Gdns*
NR32 ....2 E4
Somerleyton Prim Sch
NR32 ....2 D4
Somerleyton Sta NR32 ..2 C3
Somerset Cl 12 CB9 ...132 C5
Somerset Rd IP4 .....139 F8
Somersham Prim Sch
IP8 ....81 C3
Somersham Rd IP8 .....81 F2
Somerton Ave NR32 ...113 C3
Somerton Rd IP29 .....77 A7
Somerville Lea 2 IP15 ..130 E5
Sorrel Cl IP30 ....137 B6
Sorrel Wlk CB9 ....132 B7
Sorrell Gn IP14 ....51 D6
Sorrell Wlk IP5 ....141 F7
Sotterley Cl 17 NR32 ..113 A6
Sotterley Rd
6 Lowestoft NR32 .....112 F4
Sotterley NR34 ....10 C1
Willingham St Mary NR34 ..25 F7
Sound The NR33 ......114 E5
South Cl Beccles NR34 ..111 A3
Bury St Edmunds IP33 ..154 A1
Ipswich IP4 ....139 E8
Leiston IP16 ....129 D5
9 Melton IP12 ....84 E6
South Coast National Nature
Reserve* IP17 ....43 B4
South Elham Hall*
IP20 ....23 D6
South Elmham Terr
NR33 ....114 E8
South Entrance IP17 ...128 D2
South Gn IP19 ....119 D4
South Hill IP11 ....152 D3
South Lee IP33 ....123 C2
South Lee Ct 4 NR32 ..112 E4
South Lodge Dr 1 IP28 ..48 C6
South Lowestoft Ind Est
NR33 ....114 E2
South Pk IP27 ....5 E3
South Rd Beccles NR34 .111 A3
Lakenheath IP27 ....109 E3
South St
Hockwold cum Wilton IP26 ..4 A7
Ipswich IP1 ....155 A4
12 Manningtree CO11 ..104 E2
Risby IP28 ....47 D4
South Strand 1 IP27 ....5 D2
South View 18 NR32 ...113 B2
South View Rd IP9 ....104 F7
Southend Rd 4 NR35 ..110 B3
Southern Belle Cl
IP32 ....123 F7
Southern La IP22 ....19 A1

Southery Rd IP26 ....4 B6
Southfield Dr IP16 ....129 C5
Southfield Gdns IP33 ..114 F6
Southfields CO7 ....103 F3
Southfields Cl CB8 ....120 E4
Southgate 12 IP20 .....22 D5
Southgate Ave IP28 ...116 B7
Southgate Gdns
Bury St Edmunds IP33 ..123 C3
3 Long Melford CO10 ...91 E7
Southgate Rd IP38 ....138 B1
Southgate St
Bury St Edmunds IP33 ..154 C1
4 Long Melford CO10 ...91 E7
South Rd
Athelington IP21 ....38 F1
Bedfield IP13 ....54 D6
Southwell La NR34 .....26 A6
Southwell Rd NR33 ...115 B7
Southwold & District Hospl
IP18 ....119 D6
Southwold Lighthouse*
IP18 ....119 D5
Southwold Maze*
IP18 ....43 C7
Southwold Mus*
IP18 ....119 D5
Southwold Pier*
IP18 ....119 E6
Southwold Prim Sch
IP18 ....119 D5
Southwold Rd
Blyford IP19 ....42 B8
Brampton with Stoven
NR34 ....25 E5
Holton IP19 ....118 C5
Wrentham NR34 ....26 E5
Southwold Sailors Reading
Rm* IP18 ....119 D5
Southwood Cl IP27 ....128 D2
Spalding's Chair Hill
IP24 ....17 B3
Spanbies Rd 3 CO7 ...103 E5
Sparhawk St IP33 ....154 C1
Sparkes Cl 5 CB7 ......29 C5
Sparks La CO9 ....89 D3
Sparrow Cl 3 IP14 ....152 F4
Sparrow Rd CO10 .....148 F4
Sparrowhawk Rd
IP19 ....118 C7
Sparrows Croft Rd 5
IP12 ....85 C3
Spartan Cl 3 CB9 .....132 A6
Spashett Rd 2 NR32 ...113 E4
Speckled Wood Cl
IP9 ....142 D8
Speed La CB7 ....28 C8
Speedwell Cl 7 NR33 ..115 A3
Speedwell Rd IP2 .....138 F4
Speedwell Way 15 IP20 ..22 D5
Spencer Dr NR32 ......113 B6
Spencer Dro CB7 ......28 E8
Spencer Rd 4 IP12 ....85 E8
Spencer Way IP14 ....124 B7
Spenser Rd IP1 ....134 E3
Sperling Dr CB9 ......132 C4
Spexhall Way NR32 ...113 B5
Spicers La 2 CO10 .....91 E8
Spiers Way IP20 ....20 B2
Spike's La IP14 ....66 E7
Spindle Rd CB9 ....132 B7
Spindler Cl IP5 ....141 D7
Spinks' La NR15 ....7 D6
Spinnel's Hill CO11 ....105 D1
Spinnel's La CO11 ....105 E1
Spinner Cl IP21 ....138 D8
Spinners La 3 IP18 ...119 D5
Spinney Cl IP14 ....154 A4
Spinney Gdns NR33 ...114 E4
Spinney Hill IP7 ....81 A1
Spinney Rd NR31 ......33 B3
Spinney The
Beccles NR34 ....111 D4
Ipswich IP4 ....140 F4
Spinning Cl IP17 ......128 D5
Spire Chase CO10 ....148 F6
Spirkett's La CO10 ....22 D5
Spitfire Cl IP3 ....140 B1
Spong La IP20 ....50 E2
Spong The IP20 ....23 C3
Spooner's La NR34 ....26 E2
Spooners Cl CB8 ......59 E4
Spout La CO10 ....101 B8
Spring Cl
8 Bentwaters Airfield
IP12 ....85 D8
Burwell CO10 ....44 A5
Spring La
Bury St Edmunds IP33 ..154 A3
Crowfield IP6 ....68 B3
Dennington IP13 ....55 B5
8 Lavenham CO10 ......78 D4
Polstead CO6 ....93 D2
Ufford IP13 ....127 B1
Wickham Market IP13 ..146 D7
Spring Meadow
10 Glemsford CO10 ....77 A3
Playford IP6 ....137 F4
Spring Pk IP27 ....69 C2
Spring Rd Bardwell IP31 ..34 C5
Copdock & Washbrook
IP8 ....95 E5
Ipswich IP4 ....139 F6
Spring Row IP24 ......124 D7

Spring St 6 CO10 ....78 D4
Spring Wood Nature
Reserve* IP9 ....142 E7
Springbank Ave 16
CO11 ....104 D2
Springett's Hill CO8 ....101 B5
Springfield IP18 ....119 A7
Springfield Ave
Bury St Edmunds IP33 ...154 A3
Felixstowe IP11 ....153 A5
Springfield Dr IP27 .....109 D6
Springfield Gdns
NR33 ....114 F5
Springfield Inf Sch
IP1 ....138 F8
Springfield Jun Sch
IP1 ....138 F8
Springfield La IP1 .....138 F8
Springfield Rd
Aldeburgh IP15 ....130 C5
Bury St Edmunds IP33 ...154 A3
4 Somersham IP8 ....81 C3
Sudbury CO10 ....148 C7
Springhurst CI IP4 .....139 C6
Springland CI IP4 ......140 A6
Springlands Way
CO10 ....148 D8
Springtail Rd IP8 ......142 E8
Sprites End IP11 ....152 D7
Sprites La IP8 ....138 C1
Sprites Prim Sch IP2 ...138 C2
Spriteshall La IP11 ....152 D7
Sproughton Bsns Pk
IP1 ....138 D7
Sproughton CE Prim Sch
IP8 ....138 B6
Sproughton Ct IP8 .....138 A6
Sproughton Rd IP1 .....138 D7
Spruce CI 14 IP27 ......13 F2
Spruce Ct NR32 ....113 C3
Spruce Dr IP27 ....5 F1
Spur End IP12 ....147 C7
Spurgeon Score 12
NR32 ....113 C2
Spurling CI 2 CB8 ......60 E7
Square The IP4 ....124 E4
Squires Ct 21 CB9 .....132 C5
Squires La 4 IP5 ......98 A8
Squires Wlk NR32 ......113 C5
Squirrells Mill Rd 3 IP7 ..79 F4
Squirrels The IP9 ......150 E4
Stackwood Rd CO6 ......93 F3
Stafford Ct NR32 ....112 E4
Staithe CI 4 NR35 .....110 B4
Staithe Rd
Bungay NR35 ....110 B4
Burgh St Peter NR34 ....10 C7
Staithe The NR33 ....114 E6
Stambourne Rd CO9 .....89 E2
Stamford CI IP2 ....142 F8
Stamford Ct 3 IP33 ...122 F3
Stamford St CB8 ....121 B2
Stammers PI IP5 ....141 E8
Stanford St 3 NR32 ...113 C1
Stanhope CI IP4 ....72 D5
Stanley Ave IP3 ....140 A4
Stanley Drapkin Prim Sch 8
CB9 ....88 D3
Stanley Rd Diss IP22 ..20 B2
Felixstowe IP11 ....153 A3
Lowestoft NR33 ....114 E7
Sudbury CO10 ....148 C6
Stanley St NR32 ....113 D1
Stanley Wood Ave
CO10 ....148 D7
Stannard Way CO10 .....148 E4
Stanningfield Rd IP30 ...63 F5
Stansfield CI NR33 .....114 E6
Stanton CI
Beccles NR34 ....111 C3
Lowestoft NR32 ....113 C5
Stanton Com Prim Sch
IP31 ....34 E4
Stanton Hughes Way 10
CO11 ....104 D2
Stanton PI 12 CB9 .....132 F6
Stanton Postmill*
IP31 ....88 D3
Stanton Rd IP31 ....34 C4
Stanway CI CO10 ....77 B3
Staple CI IP31 ....35 C1
Staplehurst CI 7 NR33 ...114 C4
Staples La CB7 ....28 D3
Star And Garter La CB8 ..60 E8
Star La IP4 ....155 C2
Starfield CI IP4 ....140 B6
Starhouse La IP14 ......66 C5
Starre Rd IP33 ....122 C5
Starston La IP20 ....22 C5
Station App
Newmarket CB8 ....121 A4
Saxmundham IP17 ....128 D3
Station Gate CB5 ....44 A4
Station Hill
1 Bures CO8 ....101 C4
Bury St Edmunds IP33 ...154 B4
Harleston IP20 ....22 D6
Little Whelnetham IP30 ...64 B6
Thurston IP31 ....49 D4
Station La 18 CO12 ....107 B2
Station Rd Alburgh IP20 ..7 A1
Bacton IP14 ....6 C4
Barnham IP24 ....16 B2
Beccles NR34 ....111 B5

Station Rd continued
Bentley IP9 ....104 E7
Birdbrook CO9 ....89 B4
Blaxhall IP12 ....71 E3
Bradfield CO11 ....105 B2
Brampton with Stoven
NR34 ....25 C5
Burston & Shimpling IP21 ..20 F6
Clare CO10 ....90 B8
Claydon IP6 ....134 B8
8 Corton NR32 ....3 D4
Corton NR32 ....113 C8
Diss IP22 ....20 D2
Ditchingham NR35 ......110 C6
Dullingham CB8 ....59 E5
2 Earsham NR35 ....7 F4
Ellingham NR35 ....8 D7
Elmswell IP30 ....50 F2
Felixstowe IP11 ....152 C7
Fordham CB7 ....29 A1
Framlingham IP13 ......126 C2
Geldeston NR34 ....8 F6
Haddiscoe NR31 ....2 A2
Hadleigh IP7 ....149 E5
Halesworth IP19 ....118 B4
Harleston IP20 ....22 D6
1 Harwich CO12 ....106 F3
Haughley IP14 ....51 D1
Hoo IP13 ....132 E6
Hopton on Sea NR31 ....3 B6
Isleham CB7 ....29 C4
Kennett CB8 ....45 F7
Lakenheath IP27 ....109 C7
Laxfield IP13 ....39 F4
Leiston IP16 ....129 C6
Long Melford CO10 .....91 E7
Lowestoft NR32 ....113 D4
Manningtree CO11 ......104 E3
Mildenhall IP28 ....116 B3
Pulham Market IP21 ....21 E8
Pulham St Mary IP21 ....22 A8
Ramsey & Parkeston
CO12 ....106 F3
Soham CB7 ....28 C4
Somerleyton, Ashby &
Herringfleet NR32 ......2 C3
Southwold IP18 ....119 C6
Sudbury CO10 ....148 C5
Tattingstone IP9 ....105 A7
Thetford IP24 ....16 B6
Washbrook IP8 ....95 B4
Wetheringsett-cum-Brockford
IP14 ....53 B4
Woodbridge IP12 ....147 A4
Wrabness CO11 ....105 F2
Station Rd E IP14 .....124 E6
Station Rd W IP14 .....124 D6
Station Sq 11 NR32 ...115 D8
Station St IP13 ....139 C3
Station Terr IP13 .....126 C2
Station Yd
Hadleigh IP7 ....149 E5
Mildenhall IP28 ....116 B3
Needham Market IP6 ...125 E4
Staverton CI IP14 .....53 B4
Staygate Wlk 7 NR32 ...112 E4
Stearn Dr IP14 ....66 C6
Stearn's La IP14 ......67 D6
Stebbings La IP12 .....99 E7
Stedman Terr IP18 .....119 C8
Steeds Meadow 7 CO10 ..91 E8
Steeles Rd IP30 ....50 D1
Steeple Bumpstead Pottery*
CB9 ....88 D3
Steeple Bumpstead Rd
CB9 ....88 B4
Steeple End IP19 ......118 B3
Steeplechase CO10 ......75 C4
Steggall CI IP6 ....125 C6
Stella Maris IP22 .....138 D5
Stennetts CI IP11 .....152 B8
Stephen CI
Haverhill CB9 ....132 D6
Long Melford CO10 .....91 D7
Stephen Rd IP5 ....141 E8
Stephen's Ct IP4 ......140 B6
Stephenson Way IP24 ...16 A6
Stephensons Wlk
NR32 ....113 D4
Stepping Hill 3 NR34 ..111 B5
Stetchworth Rd
Dullingham CB8 ....59 F4
Stetchworth CB8 ....60 B4
Stevens St NR32 ....113 C1
Stevenson Rd IP1 .....155 A3
Steward Rd IP33 ......123 C2
Stewards Field CB7 ....29 A1
Stewart Young Gr
IP5 ....141 D7
Stimpson CI 3 NR32 ...113 A6
Stirling CI
Lowestoft NR32 ....112 F4
7 Thistley Green IP28 ..29 F6
Stirling Gdns CB8 .....120 E4
Stirling Rd 3 IP26 ....4 E5
Stirrups La NR32 ......3 C5
Stockley CI CB9 ....133 A5
Stockmers End 8 IP9 ..150 E3
Stocks La IP30 ....119 A2
Stockton CI IP7 ....149 F4
Stockton Rd NR34 ......9 A7
Stoke Ash Prim Sch
IP23 ....52 F8
Stoke Coll CO10 ....89 E6
Stoke Hall* IP7 ....155 B1
Stoke Hall Rd IP2 ....155 B1
Stoke High Sch IP2 ...139 C3

Stoke Pk Dr IP2 ....139 A1
Stoke Quay IP2 ....155 C1
Stoke St Clare CO10 ....90 A7
Layham IP7 ....149 D1
Leavenheath CO6 ......102 B8
Nayland-with-Wissington
CO6 ....102 D5
Stoke Ash IP23 ....37 D1
Stoke-by-Clare CO10 ...89 F7
Stoke St IP2 ....155 B1
Stoke-by-Nayland CE VC
Prim Sch CO6 ....102 C7
Stoke-by-Nayland Mid Sch
CO6 ....102 D5
Stollery CI IP5 ....141 B7
Stonalls IP30 ....50 C1
Stone Hall Rd IP3 .....36 A2
Stone La
Bressingham IP22 ......19 F6
Wrabness CO11 ....105 F2
Stone Lodge La IP2 ...139 A3
Stone Lodge La W
IP2 ....139 A3
Stone Lodge Wlk IP2 ..139 B3
Stone PI 12 IP12 .....147 A5
Stone St Boxford CO6 ..93 C3
Crowfield IP6 ....68 C3
Hadleigh IP7 ....149 B8
Spexhall IP19 ....118 C8
Stone St Rd 2 CO10 ...93 C4
Stonebridge Ave IP33 ..122 F3
Stonebridge La IP14 ...67 A8
Stonechat Rd IP2 .....138 C3
Stonegrove Rd IP11 ...152 D1
Stonehouse Rd IP7 ....149 D6
Stonewell Hill IP6 ...68 D1
Stoney La Barrow IP29 ..47 B2
Thurston IP31 ....49 F4
Stoney Rd IP13 ....83 D6
Stonham Aspal CE Prim Sch
IP14 ....68 B6
Stonham Barns Leisure
Complex* IP14 ....68 C6
Stonham Rd IP14 ......52 B4
Stony La
2 Aldringham cum Thorpe
IP16 ....73 F6
Debenham IP14 ....53 D2
Wortwell IP20 ....22 F8
Stopford Ct 8 IP1 ....139 A7
Store St IP20 ....20 C3
Stour Ave IP11 ....152 C3
Stour CI Glemsford CO10 ..77 B1
4 Harwich CO12 ....106 E1
Saxmundham IP17 ......128 C4
Stour Gdns CO10 ......148 E2
Stour St Cavendish CO10 ..90 D8
17 Manningtree CO11 ...104 E2
Sudbury CO10 ....148 B5
Stour Vale CO9 ....89 B5
Stour Valley Rd CB9 ..132 F5
Stour Wood Nature
Reserve* CO12 ....106 B2
Stourdale CI 2 IP14 ..104 D2
Stourmead CI CB9 .....133 E8
Stourside IP9 ....107 A4
Stourview Ave 4 CO11 ..105 A2
Stourview CI 3 CO11 ..105 A2
Stoven CI NR32 ....113 B5
Stoven Rd NR34 ....25 F3
Stow La IP31 ....50 A8
Stow Rd IP31 ....34 A6
Stowmarket High Sch
IP14 ....124 B7
Stowmarket Mid Sch
IP14 ....124 C6
Stowmarket Rd
Badley IP6 ....125 A8
Great Blakenham IP6 ...81 F6
Old Newton with Dagworth
IP14 ....51 E1
Rattlesden IP30 ....65 E6
Stonham Aspal IP14 ...68 A8
Wetherden IP14 ....51 A1
Stowmarket Sta IP14 ..124 C6
Stowupland High Sch
IP14 ....67 A7
Stowupland Rd IP14 ...124 F7
Stowupland St IP14 ...124 D6
Stradbroke CE Prim Sch
IP21 ....39 A5
Stradbroke High Sch
IP21 ....39 B4
Stradbroke Rd
Fressingfield IP21 ......39 D7
Ipswich IP4 ....140 A7
Lowestoft NR33 ....115 A4
Southwold IP18 ....119 D5
Stradishall Rd CO10 ...75 E5
Straight La IP30 ....22 D6
Straight Rd
Battisford IP14 ....66 D1
Boxted CO4 ....102 F1
Bradfield CO11 ....105 B1
Foxhall IP10 ....141 C1
Polstead CO6 ....93 F3
Thrandeston IP21 .....37 A5
Strand The IP2 ....143 C8
Strasbourg Sq 11 CB9 ..132 F6
Stratford Rd
Dedham CO7 ....103 E4
Ipswich IP1 ....134 F2
Stratford St Mary Prim Sch
CO7 ....103 E5
Strathmail Drift
IP10 ....145 F2
Straw La CO10 ....148 B5

Strawberry Fields
CB9 ....132 B5
Strawberry La IP19 ....25 D3
Street Farm La 4 IP31 ..34 B1
Street Farm Rd IP17 ..128 D3
Street The Aldeby NR34 ..9 F8
Alderton IP12 ....99 E3
Aldham IP7 ....94 E8
Ashen CO10 ....89 C5
Ashfield cum Thorpe IP14 ..54 C1
Assington CO10 ....92 F1
Bacton IP14 ....51 C5
Badwell Ash IP31 .....50 E7
Barnham IP24 ....16 B2
Barrow IP29 ....47 A2
Barton Mills IP28 .....116 E2
Bawdsey IP12 ....99 E3
Beck Row, Holywell Row
& Kenny Hill IP28 .....30 C8
Belchamp Otten CO10 ...90 E4
Belstead IP8 ....142 C6
Benacre NR34 ....27 A7
Birdbrook CO9 ....89 A3
Blo' Norton IP22 .....18 E2
Blundeston NR32 ......3 A4
Botesdale IP22 ....36 A6
Boxted IP29 ....77 A6
Bradfield CO11 ....105 C1
Bradfield Combust with
Stanningfield IP30 .....64 B4
Bramfield IP19 ....41 F5
Bramford IP8 ....134 A2
Brampton with Stoven
NR34 ....25 C4
Brandon IP27 ....5 E1
Brantham CO11 ....105 A5
Bredfield IP13 ....84 C8
Bressingham IP22 ......19 D6
Brettenham IP7 ....65 C1
Bridgham NR16 ....17 E8
Brockdish IP21 ....21 E2
Brome & Oakley IP23 ..117 D8
Bruisyard IP17 ....56 D4
Brundish IP13 ....39 D1
Bulmer CO10 ....91 C3
Burrough Green CB8 ...59 E3
12 Bury St Edmunds IP28 ..48 C6
Butley IP12 ....86 A6
Capel St Mary IP9 ....150 D3
Cavenham IP28 ....47 A8
Charsfield IP13 ....70 B3
Chattisham IP8 ....94 C5
Chedburgh IP29 ....62 C4
Chelsworth IP7 ....79 D3
Coney Weston IP31 .....17 E1
Copdock & Washbrook
IP8 ....95 F5
Corton NR32 ....3 D4
Cratfield IP19 ....40 D5
Cretingham IP13 ......69 D8
Culford IP28 ....48 B8
Dalham CB8 ....61 B8
Darsham IP17 ....42 B1
Dennington IP13 ......55 E6
Dickleburgh IP21 ......21 B5
Drinkstone IP30 ......65 B8
Earl Soham IP13 ......54 F2
Earsham NR35 ....7 F4
East Bergholt CO7 ....151 B4
Easton IP13 ....70 E5
Elmsett IP7 ....80 F1
Eriswell IP27 ....13 F1
Eye IP21 ....38 B4
Eyke IP12 ....85 B6
Farnham IP17 ....72 A7
Flixton NR35 ....7 C2
Foxearth CO10 ....91 B7
Framsden IP14 ....69 B6
Freckenham IP28 ......29 E3
Gazeley CB8 ....46 B3
Geldeston NR34 ....9 A7
Great Barton IP31 .....49 B5
Great Bricett IP7 .....80 D5
Great Finborough IP14 ..33 C2
Great Waldingfield CO10 ..92 D8
Great Wratting CB9 ...74 F3
Grundisburgh IP13 ....83 E5
Hacheston IP13 ....71 A6
Halesworth IP19 ......118 E3
Harkstead IP9 ....106 A5
48 Harleston IP20 ....22 D6
Hessett IP30 ....64 F8
Hinderclay IP22 ......35 E7
Holbrook IP9 ....105 E7
Hollesley IP12 ....99 F7
Horham IP21 ....38 E3
Horringer IP29 ....122 B1
Huntingfield IP19 ....41 A4
Icklingham IP28 ......31 D4
Kersey IP7 ....94 D5
Kettleburgh IP13 .....70 C7
Kirtling CB8 ....60 E3
Lawshall IP29 ....63 E1
Layham IP7 ....149 E2
Letheringham IP13 ...70 D4
Lidgate CB8 ....61 B4
Little Bealings IP13 ..137 D4
Little Thurlow CB9 ...74 D5
Little Waldingfield CO10 ..92 B7
Lound NR32 ....2 F6
Lowestoft NR33 ......114 C2
Market Weston IP22 ...35 A8
Martlesham IP12 .....146 C1
Middleton CO10 ....148 C1
Mildenhall IP28 ....30 B8
Monks Eleigh IP7 .....79 C2
Moulton CB8 ....45 F3
Nacton IP10 ....145 C5

Street The continued
Newbourne IP12 ....98 D6
North Cove NR34 ....10 B4
North Lopham IP22 ....18 B4
Norton IP31 ....50 B4
Occold IP23 ....37 F1
Pakenham IP31 ....49 E6
Parham IP13 ....71 A7
Peasenhall IP17 ......56 F8
Pettistree IP13 ......127 C4
Poslingford CO10 ......76 A3
Preston St Mary CO10 ..79 A5
Ramsey & Parkeston
CO12 ....106 D1
Raydon IP7 ....94 E1
Redenhall with Harleston
IP20 ....22 F5
1 Redgrave IP22 ....36 A8
Riddlesworth IP22 ....18 A3
Rumburgh IP19 ....24 C4
Rushmere NR33 ....10 E1
St James, South Elmham
IP19 ....23 F4
Shotley IP9 ....106 F6
Shottisham IP12 ......99 B7
Snailwell CB8 ....45 A6
Somerleyton, Ashby &
Herringfleet NR32 ......2 D4
South Lopham IP22 ....19 B4
Southolt IP23 ....54 B7
Stanton IP31 ....34 E4
Starston IP20 ....22 C7
Sternfield IP17 ....72 D8
Stoke Ash IP23 ....52 F8
Stoke-by-Clare CO10 ...89 D6
Stonham Aspal IP14 ...68 B6
Stowlangtoft IP31 ....50 B6
Stradishall CB8 ....75 E6
Stratford St Mary CO7 ..103 D3
Sturmer CB9 ....133 D3
Thornton IP23 ....53 B8
Thornham Magna IP23 ..37 A2
Troston IP31 ....33 D3
Tuddenham St Martin
IP6 ....136 C5
Ubbeston IP19 ....40 F3
Walberswick IP18 .....119 A2
Wattisfield IP22 ......35 C4
Wenhaston IP19 ....42 C6
Westleton IP17 ....58 C7
Wetheringsett-cum-Brockford
IP14 ....52 F6
Weybread IP21 ....22 D2
Whatfield IP7 ....80 C1
Wherstead IP9 ....143 A6
Winfarthing IP22 .....20 B8
Wissett IP19 ....24 A5
Witnesham IP6 ....136 A8
Woodbridge IP12 .....147 C7
Wooditton CB8 ....60 B6
Woolpit IP30 ....50 D1
Worlington IP28 ......30 B4
Streetfield CI IP29 ....77 F7
Stretham Rd CB7 ......28 A2
Stretton Ave CB8 .....121 B2
Strickland Manor Hill
IP17 ....57 C8
Strickland Pl 1 IP4 ..57 C8
Stricklands Rd 1 IP14 ..124 E5
Strickmere CO7 ....103 E5
Strollers Way CB8 ....60 A5
Strowger's Way 6 NR33 ..11 C1
Struggler's La IP6 ...136 A8
Stuart CI
5 Felixstowe IP11 ....153 D7
Ipswich IP4 ....139 F7
Stuart Dr NR34 ....111 C4
Stubbin's La CB8 .....46 B3
Stubbing's La IP21 ...22 E3
Stubbs CI Ipswich IP3 ..140 A1
9 Manningtree CO11 ...104 D2
Stubbs Wood NR32 ...113 B6
Studio CI IP17 ....58 C8
Studlands Pk Ave
CB8 ....120 E6
Stump St IP13 ....127 A3
Stump's Cross CO9 ...89 D1
Sturdee Ave IP3 .....140 B3
Sturgeon Way 22 IP21 ..34 E4
Sturmer End Ind Est
CB9 ....133 A3
Sturmer Rd CB9 ......133 D3
Sturston CI IP24 ......16 C7
Sturton La IP21 .....117 B8
Stuston Rd IP21 ......20 E1
Stutton CE Prim Sch
IP9 ....105 D5
Stutton CI IP3 ....105 D5
Stutton Gn IP9 ......105 E5
Stutton La IP9 ....105 D5
Stutton Rd CO11 .....105 A5
Sub-station Rd IP11 ..152 D2
Sucklings Yd CB9 .....88 E4
Sudbourne Rd
14 Felixstowe IP11 ...153 D7
Orford IP12 ....131 B5
Sudbury Arts Ctr
CO10 ....148 D7
Sudbury Common Lands
Nature Reserve*
CO10 ....148 B6
Sudbury Rd Acton CO10 ..92 B7
Bulmer CO10 ....91 C3
Bures St Mary CO8 ...101 C5
3 Felixstowe IP11 ....152 C4
Gestingthorpe CO9 ....90 F1
Great Whelnetham IP30 ..64 A6
Lavenham CO10 ....78 D3

Sudbury Rd *continued*
Long Melford CO10 ....**91** D6
Newton CO10 ....**92** C4
Stoke-by-Nayland CO6 ...**102** D7
Sudbury Ret Pk CO10 ..**148** F6
Sudbury Sports Ctr
CO10 ....**148** D7
Sudbury Sta CO10 .....**148** D5
Sudbury Upper Sch & Arts
Ctr CO10 ....**148** D7
Sue Ryder Foundation Mus★
CO10 ....**76** E1
Suffolk Ave IP31 ....**33** D5
Suffolk Bsns Pk IP30 ..**123** F4
Suffolk Coast National
Nature Reserve★
.......................**43** A5
Suffolk Coll IP4 ....**139** E5
Suffolk Ct IP27 ....**5** F1
Suffolk Dr IP12 ....**85** D8
Suffolk Horse Mus★
IP12 ....**147** A5
Suffolk Nuffield Hospl The
IP10 ....**141** B4
Suffolk Odyssey Llamas★
IP19 ....**41** D5
Suffolk Owl Sanctuary★
IP14 ....**68** C6
Suffolk Pl IP12 ....**147** B5
Suffolk Rd
⬛ Bury St Edmunds IP32 ..**122** E8
Ipswich IP4 ....**155** C4
Lowestoft NR32 ....**115** D8
Sudbury CO10 ....**148** C6
Suffolk Ret Pk IP1 .....**139** A6
Suffolk Sci Ctr★ IP2 ..**143** B7
Suffolk Sq ⑤ CO10 ....**148** C6
Suffolk Way CB8 ....**120** E5
Suffolk Wildlife Pk★
.......................**11** B1
Suffolk Wr Pk★ IP5 ...**134** A5
Sulleys Hill IP7 ....**103** D8
Sullivan Pl IP12 ....**98** D7
Summer La IP12 ....**85** A6
Summer Rd ⑧ NR32 ...**113** D1
Summerfield Ct IP4 ....**140** D8
Summerfield Gdns
NR33 ....**115** A6
Summerhill Sch IP16 ...**129** C7
Summers Rd IP32 ......**122** E8
Summit Bsns Pk IP11 ..**152** E1
Sumner Rd IP2 ....**35** B4
Sun La Newmarket CB8 ..**121** A3
Woodbridge IP12 ....**147** A5
Sun Rd NR35 ....**110** D8
Sun St ④ CB7 ....**29** C5
Sunbeam Cl NR33 ......**114** A3
Sunderland Rd ⑧
IP11 ....**153** H11
Sunfield Cl IP4 ....**140** B6
Sunley Cl NR35 ....**110** E8
Sunningdale Ave
Ipswich IP4 ....**140** D5
Mildenhall IP28 ....**116** B4
Sunningdale Dr IP11 ...**153** B6
Sunnyfields NR33 ......**115** A7
Sunnyhill IP12 ....**98** D7
Sunnyside
Bedingham NR35 ....**7** C8
Diss IP22 ....**20** C3
Sunray Ave IP11 ....**153** B6
Surbiton Rd IP1 ....**138** F7
Surrey Cl ⑧ IP13 ......**126** C3
Surrey Rd
Felixstowe IP11 ....**152** F4
Ipswich IP1 ....**139** A6
Surrey St
⑥ Lowestoft NR32 ......**113** D1
④ Lowestoft NR32 ......**115** D8
Sussex Crof ⑨ IP12 ...**85** B3
Sussex Rd IP1 ....**113** D3
Sutherland Dr NR32 ...**113** B5
Sutton Cl
Bury St Edmunds IP32 ...**123** E6
Woodbridge IP12 ....**147** B5
Sutton Hoo★ IP12 ...**147** D5
Sutton Hoo Maze Adventure
Pk★ IP11 ....**146** D5
Sutton Rd IP12 ....**147** E5
Suttons Rd ⑩ NR34 ...**9** F4
Swaffham Heath Rd
CB8 ....**59** A7
Swaffham Rd
Burwell CB5 ....**44** A3
Mundford IP26 ....**6** B8
Swainston Way IP13 ...**55** D5
Swallow Cl
Felixstowe IP11 ....**153** C7
⑫ Harwich CO12 ....**106** F1
⑬ Stowmarket IP14 .....**67** A5
Swallow Rd IP2 ....**138** C3
Swallowfields NR33 ...**114** D3
Swallowtail Cl IP8 .....**142** E8
Swamp La IP22 ....**20** A3
Swan Cl
Halesworth IP19 ....**118** B3
29 Martlesham Heath IP5 ..**98** A8
Stowmarket IP14 ....**124** A6
Swan Ct ⑫ CO11 ......**105** A2
Swan Gn La IP19 ......**40** C5
Swan Gr CB8 ....**120** B8
Swan Hill IP18 ....**119** E5
Swan La
Bury St Edmunds IP33 ..**154** C1
Coney Weston IP31 .....**34** D8
Cretingham IP13 ....**69** E8

Swan La *continued*
Exning CB8 ....**120** B8
Halesworth IP19 ....**118** B3
Haverhill CB9 ....**132** E6
⑨ Long Melford CO10 ..**91** E8
North Cove NR34 ....**10** C4
Redenhall with Harleston
IP20 ....**22** D6
Swan Meadow CO7 ...**103** E5
Swan Rd IP13 ....**54** E7
Swan St CO10 ....**93** B3
Swanfield CO10 ....**91** E8
Swansea Ave IP22 .....**139** B1
Swatchway Cl ⑧ IP3 ..**144** B8
Swaynes ⑪ CO7 ......**103** E5
Sweden Cl ⑯ IP12 ....**106** F2
Swift Cl NR33 ....**114** D3
Swift Dr IP14 ....**67** A5
Swilltub La IP14 ......**52** A4
Swinburne Rd IP3 .....**144** B7
Swine's Gn NR34 ......**111** C4
Swingleton Hill IP7 ....**79** C2
Swinton Cl IP2 ....**138** D1
Swonnell's Wlk ② NR32 ..**112** D1
Swonnells Ct NR32 ....**114** D8
Sycamore Ave NR33 ...**114** D7
Sycamore Cl
Beccles NR34 ....**111** E3
⑦ Great Bricett IP7 ....**80** D6
Ipswich IP8 ....**138** C1
Leiston IP16 ....**129** C5
Sycamore Dr
⑧ Beck Row, Holywell
Row & Kenny Hill IP28 ...**13** B1
⑤ Mildenhall IP28 .....**30** A8
Rendlesham IP12 ....**85** D8
Sycamore Rd
Stowupland IP14 ....**67** A6
Sudbury CO10 ....**148** F4
Sycamore Way
Brantham CO11 ....**104** E5
Diss IP22 ....**20** D3
Sycamore Wlk ⑳ IP27 ..**13** F2
Syleham Hall La IP21 ..**22** C1
Syleham Rd
Brockdish IP21 ....**22** A2
Syleham IP21 ....**38** D8
Sylvester Rd IP16 .....**129** D5
Symonds Rd IP33 .....**123** C4

T

Tacket St IP4 ....**155** C2
Tacon Cl IP23 ....**117** C2
Tacon Rd IP11 ....**152** E1
Takers La IP14 ....**124** E6
Talbot Rd CO10 ....**148** D7
Tallboys Cl IP1 ....**141** C8
Tallyho Cnr ⑧ CO7 ...**103** E5
Talmash Gdns IP2 ....**139** A4
Tamage Rd CO10 .....**92** B7
Tan House La CB5 .....**44** A4
Tan Office La
Chevington IP29 ....**62** C5
Mendlesham IP14 ......**52** E1
Tanners La CB7 ....**28** D3
Tanners View IP1 .....**138** F7
Tannersfield Way CB8 ..**120** F4
Tannery Bsns Ctr The
IP14 ....**66** E2
Tannery Dr IP13 ......**123** B3
Tannery Rd IP14 .....**124** C1
Tannington Long Rd
IP13 ....**71** B2
Tanns La IP22 ....**19** A6
Tansy Cl ⑤ NR34 .....**9** B6
Tansy Meadow ⑧ IP21 ..**39** D8
Target Hill IP20 ....**23** B6
Tarn Hows Cl ⑪ IP11 ..**153** C6
Tasman Rd IP4 ....**133** A5
Tasmania Rd IP4 .....**140** D6
Tassel Rd IP32 ....**123** F6
Tattingstone CE Prim Sch
IP9 ....**105** B8
Taunton Cl IP4 ....**135** B4
Taunton Rd IP11 ......**152** F5
Tavern Cl IP4 ....**154** B2
Tavern St Ipswich IP1 ..**155** B3
Stowmarket IP14 ....**124** D6
Tawneys Ride ② CO8 ..**101** A2
Tayberry Pl IP3 ....**144** C7
Tayfen Rd IP33 ....**154** B4
Tayfen Terr IP33 ......**154** B4
Tayler Cl ④ IP7 ......**149** D5
Taylor Dr IP13 ....**127** A7
Taylor Rd ⑧ CO11 ...**104** E2
Taylor Rd ⑧ IP22 ....**20** C6
Taylors Farm IP14 ....**66** C1
Taylors Farm Rd CB9 ..**75** A2
Taylors Field CB8 .....**59** F4
Tea Kettle La CB8 .....**59** E5
Teal Ave CB7 ....**28** C5
Teal Cl IP2 ....**138** D3
Teal Wlk IP27 ....**6** A1
Teasel Cl CB9 ....**133** F6
Tedder Cl ⑧ IP11 .....**64** C3
Tedder Rd NR32 ......**113** B4
Teesdale NR13 ....**114** A3
Telesia Ct NR32 ......**113** B4
Temperance Rd ⑧ NR34 ..**111** B5
Templars Ct ⑳ CB9 ...**132** C6
Temple Cl IP9 ....**31** C4
Temple End CB9 ......**74** C5
Temple Pattle ⑪ CO11 ..**104** E4
Temple Rd Ipswich IP3 ..**140** C4
Isleham CB7 ....**29** B4

Temple Rd *continued*
Stowmarket IP14 ....**124** D5
Ten Bell La ⑩ CB7 ....**28** D4
Tenby Rd IP2 ....**139** B1
Tennyson Cl IP14 .....**146** E6
Tennyson Rd
⑬ Bury St Edmunds IP32 ..**48** C5
Lowestoft NR32 ....**113** D2
Saxmundham IP17 ......**128** B4
Tennyson Way IP24 ...**16** C2
Tenter Field ④ CO7 ...**103** E5
Tenter Piece ⑱ CO10 ..**78** D4
Tenterden Cl ⑥ NR33 ..**114** D5
Tenth Rd IP10 ....**98** A3
Tentree Rd CO10 .....**92** C7
Terence Airey Ct ② IP20 ..**22** D6
Tern Cl CB9 ....**133** A5
Tern Rd Ipswich IP2 ..**138** E2
Stowmarket IP14 ....**124** F6
Terr The
Aldeburgh IP15 ....**130** E4
Newmarket CB8 ....**121** A3
Snape IP17 ....**72** D5
Terry Gdns IP5 ....**141** E7
Tewkesbury Pl ⑦ IP31 ..**49** A5
Thackeray Gr IP14 ....**124** B7
Thackeray Rd IP1 .....**134** E3
Thanet Rd IP4 ....**140** B6
Tharp Way CB7 ....**29** E1
Thatchers Wlk ④ IP4 ..**140** F4
Theatre Royal★ IP33 ..**154** C1
Theatre St IP12 ......**146** F5
Theberton Rd IP3 .....**140** B1
Thedwastre Cl ⑧ IP30 ..**50** F2
Thedwastre Rd IP31 ..**49** E3
Theinetham Fen Nature
Reserve★ IP22 ....**18** E1
Thellusson Rd ⑧ IP21 ..**85** E8
Thelnetham Rd IP22 ..**18** E2
Thelnetham Windmill★
IP22 ....**18** E1
Theobald Cl ⑥ IP6 ...**125** D4
Thetford Adult Ed Ctr ⑤
IP24 ....**16** B5
Thetford Cl ⑯ IP27 ...**13** F2
Thetford Cottage Hospl
.......................**16** C6
Thetford Gram Sch
.......................**16** B6
Thetford Heath National
Nature Reserve★
IP24 ....**16** A2
Thetford Mus★ IP24 ..**16** C6
Thetford Rd Brandon IP27 ..**5** F1
Coney Weston IP31 .....**34** D8
Euston IP24 ....**16** E2
Fakenham Magna IP24 ..**33** E8
Fornham St Martin IP31 ..**48** D5
Garboldisham IP22 .....**18** C4
② Ipswich IP1 ....**139** A7
Ixworth IP31 ....**34** A2
Ixworth Thorpe IP31 ...**33** F3
Mildenhall IP28 ....**116** E4
Santon Downham IP27 ..**6** B1
South Lopham IP22 ....**19** A4
Thingoe Hill IP1 ....**154** B4
Third Ave CO10 ......**77** B3
Thirlmere Cl IP11 .....**153** D6
Thirlmere Dr IP14 ....**124** B6
Thirlmere Wlk NR32 ..**113** A4
Thirlwall Dr CB7 ......**29** C1
Thistle Cl IP2 ....**138** D3
Thistledown NR33 ....**114** D4
Thistledown Dr IP31 ..**34** B2
Thixendale NR33 .....**114** C2
Thomas Arne Cl IP14 ..**124** B7
Thomas Ave IP11 .....**152** C8
Thomas Bardwell Dr ④
IP31 ....**53** C8
Thomas Bole Cl IP22 ..**18** D4
Thomas Cl IP20 ....**34** B1
Thomas La IP33 ......**154** B1
Thomas Mills High Sch
IP13 ....**126** A5
Thomas Wolsey Specl Sch
IP1 ....**134** E3
Thomas Young Cl ⑧
IP14 ....**124** D3
Thompson Cl IP14 ....**51** D1
Thompson Rd IP11 ...**138** F8
Thompson Wlk IP22 ..**22** A2
Thomsons La IP6 .....**69** A2
Thong Hall Rd IP13 ...**127** A5
Thorington Rd IP19 ..**42** A5
Thorn Cl CB7 ....**28** D5
Thorn Way IP11 ......**152** E4
Thorn Wlk IP2 ....**85** C2
Thornbush La IP8 .....**138** A8
Thorndon CE Prim Sch
IP23 ....**53** B8
Thorney Gn Rd IP14 ..**67** A6
Thorney Hall Cl IP14 ..**124** A6
Thorney Rd IP9 ....**150** E4
Thornham Cl ⑤ NR33 ..**114** D4
Thornham Rd IP23 ....**36** D2
Thornham Walled Gdn★
IP23 ....**37** A2
Thornhayes Cl IP2 ....**139** A3
Thornhill Rd IP6 ......**82** B5
Thorney Dr IP4 ....**140** D8
Thornley Rd IP11 .....**153** C4
Thorns Cl ⑧ CB8 .....**61** E2
Thornton Cl ⑮ IP27 ..**13** F2
Thornton Rd IP33 ....**122** F2

Thornycroft Gdns
NR33 ....**114** A3
Thoroughfare IP19 ...**118** B3
Thoroughfare The
Brundish IP13 ....**55** C8
Harleston IP20 ....**22** D6
Wilby IP21 ....**39** D1
⑩ Woodbridge IP12 ...**147** A5
Thorpe Abbots Rd
IP21 ....**21** D4
Thorpe Hall Rd IP11 ..**38** F4
Thorpe La
Ashfield cum Thorpe IP14 ..**69** C8
Debenham IP14 ....**53** F1
Trimley St Martin IP11 ..**107** C8
Thorpe Rd
Aldeburgh IP16 ....**130** F6
Aldringham IP16 ....**129** D2
Thorpe's Hill IP9 .....**95** E6
Thorpeness Windmill★
IP16 ....**73** E6
Thrandeston Rd IP23 ..**117** F7
Threadneedle St
Dedham CO7 ....**103** F4
⑧ Hadleigh IP7 ....**149** D6
Three Marsh La IP18 ..**119** B6
Throckmorton Rd
NR35 ....**110** D3
Through Duncans
IP12 ....**146** E3
Through Jollys IP5 ....**141** D8
Thunderbird Way
IP27 ....**109** F1
Thurleston High Sch
IP1 ....**135** A4
Thurleston La IP11 ...**134** F5
Thurlow CE Prim Sch
CB9 ....**74** D6
Thurlow Cl IP17 ......**128** B3
Thurlow Ct ② IP14 ...**124** D6
Thurlow Pl ⑧ IP20 ...**132** F6
Thurlow Rd CB9 ......**74** C8
Thurmans La IP11 ....**152** B8
Thurne Rd NR33 .....**114** F5
Thurston CE Prim Sch
.......................**49** E4
Thurston Com Coll
.......................**49** D4
Thurston Cl ⑧ IP11 ...**152** C4
Thurston La CO10 ....**76** C7
Thurston Rd
Ipswich IP1 ....**139** A7
Lowestoft NR32 ....**113** D2
Thurston IP31 ....**49** E3
Thurston Sta IP31 .....**49** D3
Thwaite Rd
Ditchingham NR35 .....**110** C7
Thorndon IP23 ....**53** B8
Wickham Skeith IP23 ..**52** E7
Tibbenham's Score ⑥
NR32 ....**52** D7
Tiberius Cl CB9 ......**133** A6
Tide Mill★ IP12 ......**147** B4
Tide Mill Way IP12 ...**147** A4
Tideway NR32 ....**114** E8
Tidys Cl IP33 ....**154** B3
Tiger Hill Nature Reserve★
CO8 ....**101** E6
Tiggins La IP17 ....**128** D8
Tilbury Rd
Great Yeldham CO9 .....**90** A2
Ridgewell CO9 ....**89** E4
Tile Barn La CO11 ....**104** B1
Tillbrooks Hill CO8 ...**81** B6
Timperley Cl IP27 ....**149** D7
Timperley Rd IP27 ...**149** E7
Timperleys IP8 ....**95** C3
Tinabrook Cl IP2 .....**138** E1
Tinker Brook IP13 ...**71** F5
Tinker St CO12 ......**106** C1
Tinker's La
Hadleigh IP7 ....**149** D5
Tivetshall St Mary NR15 ..**21** C8
Tinkers La IP30 ......**10** D1
Tintern Cl ⑤ IP2 .....**139** A2
Tippet Ave IP14 .....**124** C8
Titchwell Dr ② IP3 ...**144** D8
Tithe Ave IP28 ....**30** B8
Tithe Cl CB8 ....**46** C3
Title Rd IP17 ....**42** D3
Titlow Rd ⑳ IP20 ....**22** D6
Toad Row NR34 .....**10** F1
Todhunter Ave NR34 ..**9** B6
Tog La CO6 ....**102** D2
Tokio Rd IP4 ....**140** A6
Toll Gate Rd IP9 .....**150** E3
Tollemache Bsns Pk
IP7 ....**80** E4
Toller Cl IP12 ....**131** C3
Toller Rd IP3 ....**139** E3
Tolley Cobbold St ⑧
IP28 ....**30** A8
Tollgate La ⑧ IP32 ..**123** A8
Tollgate Prim Sch
IP32 ....**122** F8
Tolworth Rd IP4 .....**140** A6
Tom Jennings Cl IP8 ..**120** F5
Tomline Ct IP10 .....**145** C5
Tomline Rd
Felixstowe IP11 ....**153** A3
Ipswich IP3 ....**140** A5
Tomline Wlk IP33 ....**122** B6
Tommy Flowers Dr
IP5 ....**141** E7
Tomo Bsns Pk IP14 ..**124** F6
Tomo Ind Est IP14 ...**124** E6
Tomtit's La IP14 .....**51** B2
Tonning St NR32 ....**113** C1

Sud - Tud 183

Tooks Comm La NR34 ..**8** F1
Top Rd Hasketon IP13 ..**146** B8
Rattlesden IP30 ....**65** D5
St Andrew, Ilketshall
NR34 ....**8** E1
Wingfield IP21 ....**39** A7
Top St IP12 ....**146** C2
Toper La IP33 ....**154** C1
Toppesfield Cl ⑧ IP7 ..**149** D5
Toppesfield Gdns IP7 ..**149** D5
Tortoiseshell Cl IP9 ...**142** E8
Tostock Rd IP30 ......**49** F2
Tot Hill IP14 ....**66** C8
Tottington La IP22 ...**20** B2
Tovell's Rd IP4 ....**139** F6
Tovells ④ IP13 ....**84** F7
Tower Ct ⑱ CB8 .....**132** C5
Tower Field Rd IP12 ..**85** D7
Tower Mews IP14 ....**111** C3
Tower Mall La IP7 ....**149** E6
Tower Mill Rd
Bungay NR35 ....**110** B3
Ipswich IP1 ....**138** F7
Tower Ramparts IP1 ..**155** B3
Tower Ramparts Sh Ctr
IP1 ....**155** B3
Tower Rd
Felixstowe IP11 ....**152** F4
Lowestoft NR33 ....**115** A2
Tower St IP1 ....**155** B3
Town End Cl CB9 .....**74** C7
Town Farm Cl IP10 ...**23** C3
Town Farm Est IP12 ..**131** B3
Town Gn IP14 ....**124** C6
Town Hall Galleries★
IP1 ....**155** B3
Town House Cnr IP14 ..**68** F7
Town House La IP22 ..**35** D6
Town Rd CB8 ....**59** F5
Town Stps IP15 ......**130** E4
Townhouse Rd IP31 ..**35** C1
Townlands Dr NR34 ..**111** B3
Townlane Rd IP33 ...**123** B1
Townsend CB7 ....**28** C5
Townsend Way NR32 ..**113** A6
Toyse Cl ⑧ CB5 ......**44** B6
Toyse La CB5 ....**44** B6
Trafalgar Cl IP4 ......**139** F6
Trafalgar Rd CO10 ...**148** E7
Trafalgar St
④ Lowestoft NR32 ....**113** C1
③ Lowestoft NR32 ....**115** C8
Trafford Cl ② IP14 ...**51** E1
Tranmere Gr IP1 .....**134** F2
Traveller's Hill (Tumuli)★
IP28 ....**32** E5
Travellers Rd IP13 ....**69** E5
Traverse The IP33 ....**154** B2
Treetops IP11 ....**152** F7
Treeview IP14 ....**124** B6
Trefoil Cl IP2 ....**138** F4
Tremlett La IP5 ......**141** F7
Trenchard Sq ⑧ IP26 ..**4** D5
Trent Rd
⬛ Bury St Edmunds IP32 ..**48** C5
Ipswich IP3 ....**139** F2
Trevethan Cl IP32 ....**122** E7
Triangle Yd ⑧ NR32 ..**113** E2
Trimley Marshes Nature
Reserve★ IP11 ....**107** B6
Trimley Rd IP10 ......**98** D2
Trimley St Martin Prim Sch
IP11 ....**98** D1
Trimley St Mary Prim Sch
IP11 ....**152** C8
Trimley Sta IP11 .....**152** C7
Trinity Ave
Felixstowe IP11 ....**152** B3
Mildenhall IP28 ....**116** C5
Trinity Cl Fordham CB7 ..**29** B1
Ipswich IP5 ....**140** F7
28 Manningtree CO11 ..**104** E2
⑩ Southwold IP18 ....**119** D5
Woodbridge IP12 ......**146** D3
Trinity Distribution Pk
IP3 ....**140** F1
Trinity Gdns ⑧ NR35 ..**110** B4
Trinity Gild ⑦ CO10 ..**78** D4
Trinity Link CB9 .....**132** E7
Trinity Mews IP33 ....**154** A3
Trinity Rd
Lowestoft NR32 ....**113** C1
Manningtree CO11 .....**104** D4
Trinity St Bungay NR35 ..**110** B4
Rose Hill IP3 ....**139** E4
⑯ Southwold IP18 ....**119** D5
Trinity Wlk IP14 .....**67** A7
Triple Plea La NR35 ...**7** B8
Triple Plea Rd NR35 ..**7** B8
Troon Ct ⑤ IP28 .....**48** C6
Troon Gdns ⑧ IP4 ...**136** B1
Trossachs The ⑤ NR32 ..**113** B2
Troston Mount (Tumulus)★
IP31 ....**33** C5
Troston Rd IP31 ......**33** E5
Trott's La CO10 ......**92** F3
Trotting Horse La CB8 ..**75** A8
Trunch Hill IP20 .....**7** A3
Trunch Rd IP20 ......**7** A3
Trundley Cl CB9 .....**132** D7
Tuddenham Ave IP4 ..**139** E7
Tuddenham CE Prim Sch
IP28 ....**30** F2
Tuddenham Cnr IP28 ..**46** E6

Tuddenham La IP5 ....136 B2
Tuddenham Rd
  Barton Mills IP28 ......116 F2
  Ipswich IP4 ....155 C4
  Westerfield IP4 ....136 A3
Tudor Ave IP22 ......20 B3
Tudor CE VC Prim Sch
  CO10 ....148 C7
Tudor Cl
  Chedburgh IP29 ......62 D5
  5 Framlingham IP13 ...126 C3
  5 Shotley Gate IP9 ...107 A5
  Sudbury CO10 ....148 C7
Tudor Ct Ipswich IP4 ...155 C3
  6 Occold IP23 ....37 F1
  Westhorpe IP14 ....30 D1
Tudor Gn CO10 ......148 C8
Tudor Rd CO10 ....148 C7
Tudor Wlk
  8 Honington IP31 .....33 D5
  11 Lowestoft NR33 ...114 E4
Tuffen La IP22 ....35 D8
Tuffields Rd IP29 ....63 B3
Tuffs Rd IP23 ....117 D4
Tumbril La IP21 ......22 A3
Tunbeck Cl IP20 .....23 A7
Tunbeck Rd IP20 ....23 A7
Tunbridge Cl 4 CB5 ...44 A5
Tunneys La NR35 ....110 C8
Tuns La IP33 ....154 C1
Tunstall Dr NR32 ....112 F4
Tunstall Gn IP12 .....71 F2
Turin St IP2 ....155 B1
Turin Way 2 NR31 ....3 C6
Turino Ave IP12 .....98 B8
Turkentine Cl 14 CO10 ...92 B3
Turkeyhall La IP14 ...51 F6
Turn La IP12 ....147 A4
Turnberry Ct 8 NR33 ...114 F4
Turnberry Dr IP28 ...48 C6
Turnbull Cl IP5 ......141 E7
Turner Ave 1 CO11 ...104 D2
Turner Cl
  Ditchingham NR35 ....110 C7
  Haverhill CB9 ....132 B7
  4 Lowestoft NR32 ...113 C6
  Sudbury CO10 ....148 E8
Turner Gdns IP12 ...146 D3
Turner Gr IP5 ....141 D8
Turner La 4 IP14 ....51 C1
Turner Rd Ipswich IP3 ...144 A8
  Stowmarket IP14 ....124 B7
Turnpike Hill CB9 ...74 B2
Turnpike Rd
  Chippenham CB8 ....45 F8
  Red Lodge IP28 .....30 B1
  Woodbridge IP12 ...147 B6
Turnstile La 7 NR35 ...110 B4
Turnstone Cl 2 IP28 ...116 D4
Turnstone Dr IP32 ...49 A3
Turret La IP4 ....155 B2
Tutelina Rd IP30 ....44 B5
Tutt Hill IP28 ....48 B5
Tutt Hill (Tumulus)*
  IP24 ....16 D4
Tuyar Wlk CB8 .....120 E8
Tweed Cl CB8 ......45 F3
Twelve Acre App IP5 ...141 B7
Twin Oak Dr IP13 ...56 B7
Twinnings The IP14 ...124 C3
Twiss Cl 5 IP22 .....20 A3
Two Acres IP9 ......150 F4
Two House Cl IP13 ...127 C7
Two Pole Dro CB7 ...28 A7
Tydemans Ct 1 IP14 ...124 D6
Tye Gn CO10 ....77 A3
Tye La IP8 ....96 A3
Tyler St 3 Harwich CO12 ...106 F3
  Ipswich IP2 ....155 B1
Tylers Gn IP11 .....152 C7
Tylers Way 8 IP14 ...124 D3
Tymmes Pl IP13 ....146 C8
Tyrone Cl IP1 ....134 D2

U

Ubbeston Way NR33 ...114 F4
Ufford Pl
  16 Haverhill CB9 ....132 F6
  8 Ufford IP13 ......84 F7
Ufford Rd Bredfield IP13 ...84 D7
  Eyke IP12 ....85 B6
Uggeshall Cl NR32 ...113 A5
Ullswater IP3 ......134 C3
Ullswater Ave 4 IP11 ...153 D7
Ullswater Rd IP2 ...71 C2
Ulster Ave IP1 .....134 D1
Una Rd CO12 ......106 F2
Uncle's La IP29 ....24 B6
Undercliff Rd E IP11 ...153 C4
Undercliff Rd W IP11 ...153 A3
Underhill IP14 .....124 C5
Underwood Cl NR32 ...113 A6
Undley IP27 ....109 B5
Undley Rd IP27 ....109 B4
Unicorn Pl IP33 ...123 C6
Union Hill IP7 .....94 A8
Union La
  Lowestoft NR32 ....112 F5
  Wortham IP22 .....20 A1
Union Pl 8 NR33 ...115 C7
Union Rd
  Lowestoft NR32 ....113 C1
  Onehouse IP14 ....66 C6

Union Rd continued
  Stowmarket IP14 ....124 A7
Union St IP4 ....155 C3
Union St E IP14 ...124 D6
Union St W IP14 ...124 D6
Unitarian Meeting House*
  IP1 ....155 B2
Unitarian Meeting House
  The* IP33 ....154 B2
Unity Rd IP14 .....124 D5
Unity St IP1 ....155 E4
Up St IP31 ....34 C4
Upland Rd IP4 ....140 A6
Uplands Cl NR33 ...114 D4
Uplands Cres CO10 ...148 C7
Uplands Mid Sch
  CO10 ....148 D7
Uplands Rd
  Aldringham cum Thorpe
  IP16 ....73 F6
  Sudbury CO10 .....148 C7
Uplands Rd N NR33 ...114 D5
Uplands Rd S NR33 ...114 C3
Uplands The
  Aldringham cum Thorpe
  IP16 ....73 E6
  Beccles NR34 .....111 D4
Uplands Way Diss IP22 ...20 C3
  Halesworth IP19 ...118 B5
Upper Ave IP19 ....118 B5
Upper Barclay St IP4 ...155 C2
Upper Brook La IP20 ...22 B4
Upper Brook St IP4 ...155 B3
Upper Burnthouse La
  IP20 ....22 A5
Upper Cavendish St
  IP3 ....140 A5
Upper E St CO10 ...148 D6
Upper Farm Rd CO10 ...89 E4
Upper Grange Rd
  NR34 ....111 A4
Upper Harmans La
  IP20 ....22 B5
Upper High St IP1 ...155 B4
Upper Melton Terr 10
  IP12 ....84 E6
Upper Moorfield Rd
  IP12 ....146 F6
Upper Oakley IP23 ...117 F8
Upper Olland St NR35 ...110 B3
Upper Orwell St IP4 ...155 C2
Upper Rd CO10 ...101 C8
Upper Rose La IP22 ...20 C1
Upper St
  Brome Street IP23 ...117 F8
  Gissing IP22 ....20 E8
  Layham IP7 ....149 F1
  Stansfield CO10 ...76 C6
  Stanstead CO10 ...77 C4
  Stratford St Mary CO7 ...103 E5
Upper Tumbril La IP20 ...22 A4
Upperfield Dr IP11 ...153 C6
Upsons Way IP5 ...141 E8
Upthorpe Rd IP31 ...34 F4
Upton Cl IP4 ......139 E6
Upton Rd IP4 .....129 C5
Urban Rd IP16 ....73 C6
Uvedale Gdns IP6 ...125 E4
Uxbridge Cres IP3 ...140 C1

V

Vale Ct IP27 ....5 E4
Vale La
  Bury St Edmunds IP33 ...123 C3
  Kersey IP7 ....94 A6
  Stutton IP9 ....105 A6
Valentine Way IP30 ...64 F7
Valerian Rise 7 IP24 ...16 D6
Valiant Cl IP31 ....33 D4
Valiant Rd 8 IP28 ...13 B1
Valley Cl
  4 Brantham CO11 ...104 E5
  Halesworth IP19 ...118 E4
  Ipswich IP1 ....135 C1
Valley Farm Camargue
  Horses* IP13 .....127 A8
Valley Farm La IP7 ...94 E5
Valley Farm Rd IP14 ...80 F8
  Buxhall IP14 ......65 F3
  Wherstead IP9 ....143 A3
Valley Rd Battisford IP14 ...66 E1
  Chilton CO10 ......92 C5
  Great Bricett IP7 ...80 D6
  Harwich CO12 ....106 E1
  Ipswich IP1 ....135 B1
  Leiston IP16 ......73 E8
  Little Blakenham IP8 ...81 E4
Valley View CO10 ...77 C4
Valley Way CB8 ...120 E3
Valley Wlk IP11 ...152 F5
Valleyview Dr IP4 ...140 F4
Vallibus Cl 8 NR32 ...112 D2
Van Dyck Cl 9 IP3 ...143 B6
Vandyck Rd 7 IP3 ...144 A8
Vanners Rd CB9 ...132 E5
Vaughan St IP2 ...155 B1
Vaunce's La IP21 ...21 E4
Vaunce's La IP21 ...21 E4
Vaux Ave 15 CO12 ...106 F1
Ventris Cl IP2 .....138 C3
Verdons La IP21 ...39 E4
Verdure Cl 2 NR32 ...112 F5
Vere Gdns IP1 ....135 C2

Vermeer Cl 5 NR32 ...113 B6
Vermont Cres IP4 ...155 C4
Vermont Rd IP4 ...155 C4
Verneuil Ave IP14 ...124 D3
Vernon St IP2 .....155 B1
Vetch Wlk CB9 ...132 B7
Veyses End 6 CO7 ...103 E5
Viburnum Gn NR32 ...113 C2
Vicarage Cl CB8 ...59 E5
Vicarage Field CO10 ...148 F3
Vicarage Gdns
  10 Debenham IP14 ...53 F2
  4 Mildenhall IP28 ...116 B4
Vicarage Hill 7 IP12 ...147 A5
Vicarage La Acton CO10 ...92 A6
  Bramford IP8 .....134 B1
  Bungay NR35 .....110 E3
  Wherstead IP9 ....143 B5
  Woodditton CB8 ...60 B6
Vicarage Rd
  Belchamp St Paul CO10 ...90 D5
  Felixstowe IP11 ...152 D4
  Laxfield IP13 .....40 B3
  Newmarket CB8 ...121 B3
  Thetford IP24 ....116 B4
  Wingfield IP21 ....39 A8
  Winston IP14 .....54 A1
Victor Charles Cl IP7 ...5 E3
Victor Rd IP31 ....33 D4
Victoria Cl 5 IP31 ...49 E4
Victoria Cres 2 CO11 ...104 E2
Victoria Hill IP23 ...117 C4
Victoria Mill Rd IP13 ...126 B2
Victoria Rd
  Aldeburgh IP15 ...130 E4
  Diss IP22 ....20 D2
  Felixstowe IP11 ...152 F3
  Haverhill CB9 ....132 B5
  1 Lowestoft NR33 ...114 E7
  Stowmarket IP14 ...124 E7
  Woodbridge IP12 ...147 A5
Victoria St
  Bury St Edmunds IP33 ...154 A2
  Felixstowe IP11 ...153 A4
  7 Harwich CO12 ...107 B2
  Ipswich IP1 ......139 A6
  16 Southwold IP18 ...119 D5
Victoria Terr
  9 Fressingfield IP21 ...39 E8
  Lowestoft NR33 ...115 D7
Victoria Way CB8 ...120 E7
Victory Cl IP33 ...123 C2
Victory Ct IP14 ...124 D4
Victory Rd Ipswich IP4 ...140 A7
  Leiston IP16 .....73 E8
View Point Rd IP11 ...153 H10
Viking Cl IP12 ....84 B1
Viking Hts IP22 ...84 B1
Viking Rd IP14 ...124 C5
Villa Hill IP12 ....99 B7
Village Way
  Lowestoft NR32 ...113 B5
  Waldringfield IP12 ...98 D7
Vince's Rd IP22 ...20 D2
Vincent Cl Exning CB8 ...120 F7
  8 Feltwell IP26 ...4 E5
  Ipswich IP1 ......138 E8
Vincent Drift IP5 ...141 F7
Vine Cl IP31 ......17 E1
Vine Rd IP6 ......69 C2
Vine Wlk IP9 .....150 E3
Vinefields The IP33 ...154 C2
Vinery Cl IP13 ...127 C6
Vinery Rd IP33 ...122 F3
Vines The IP17 ...128 D7
Vinesse Rd CO6 ...102 B2
Vineway The 2 IP12 ...107 A2
Violet Cl
  Bury St Edmunds IP32 ...123 F5
  Ipswich IP2 ......138 F4
Violet Hill Rd IP14 ...124 C7
Virginia Rd 11 IP28 ...30 A8
Viscount Cl IP32 ...20 E2
Vyces Rd IP13 ...126 B3

W

Wacker Field Rd 8 IP12 ...85 E8
Wadd La IP17 ....72 C6
Waddesdon Rd 6 CO12 ...107 B2
Waddlegoose La IP14 ...54 D2
Waddling La IP14 ...112 A7
Wade Cres CO10 ...92 E8
Wade's La Raydon IP7 ...94 E1
  Shotley IP9 ......106 C7
Wadehall La NR34 ...109 C7
Wades La IP5 ....141 E7
Wades Wood 11 IP30 ...50 D1
Wadgate Rd IP11 ...152 E4
Wadhurst Rd IP3 ...140 D3
Waggoners Ct IP12 ...146 F5
Wagtail Dr IP32 ...123 F7
Wainford Cl 5 NR34 ...9 F4
Wainford Rd NR35 ...110 E5
Wainwright Cl 4 IP30 ...113 A6
Wainwright Gdns IP6 ...51 C1
Wainwright Way IP5 ...141 D8
Wake Ave IP28 ...116 C5
Wakeshall La CO10 ...90 B4
Walberswick Visitor Ctr*
  IP18 ....119 B2
Walberswick Way 8
  NR32 ....113 A3
Walcot Rd IP22 ...20 D3
Walcot Rise IP22 ...20 D3
Walcott Wlk NR33 ...115 B5
Waldegrave Cl 28 CO11 ...104 D2

Waldegrave Rd CO11 ...104 D2
Waldingfield Rd
  10 Acton CO10 .....92 B7
  Chilton IP14 ......148 F8
Waldringfield Prim Sch
  IP12 ....98 D7
Waldringfield Rd IP12 ...84 C1
Walk The Bacton IP14 ...51 D5
  Beccles NR34 ....111 B6
  Ipswich IP1 ......152 E6
  Walton IP11 .....152 E6
Walker Chase IP5 ...141 C6
Walker Cl IP4 ....140 C5
Walker Gdns NR34 ...26 E5
Walks The NR34 ...10 A8
Wall La CO11 ....105 E2
Wallace Rd IP1 ...138 E8
Walled Gdn The* IP17 ...72 E3
Waller's Gr IP2 ...138 F4
Wallow La IP7 ...80 D4
Walls The CO11 ...104 E2
Walmer Cl NR33 ...115 A5
Walmer Rd NR33 ...115 A5
Walnut Cl Acton CO10 ...92 B8
  Felixstowe IP11 ...153 D7
  Hopton IP22 .....18 C1
  16 Lakenheath IP27 ...13 F2
Walnut Gr IP28 ...30 A4
Walnut Tree Ave IP12 ...85 D8
Walnut Tree Cl 4 IP8 ...134 A2
Walnut Tree La
  2 Harkstead IP9 ...106 A5
  Sudbury CO10 ...148 B5
Walnut Tree Meadow
  IP14 ....68 B6
Walnut Tree Wlk IP14 ...124 C6
Walnuts La IP13 ...127 B5
Walnuts The
  Beccles NR34 ....111 E4
  8 Ufford IP13 ....84 F7
Walnuttree Hospl
  CO10 ....148 B5
Walpole Cl NR35 ...110 D7
Walpole La IP19 ...41 D5
Walpole Rd
  Bramfield IP19 ...41 E3
  Halesworth IP19 ...118 A1
Walsham Le Willows CE VC
  Prim Sch IP31 ...35 C2
Walsham Rd
  Finningham IP14 ...36 A1
  6 Ixworth IP31 ...34 B1
  Wattisfield IP22 ...35 C3
Walsingham Cl 11 CO10 ...92 B3
Walsingham Rd IP33 ...122 D3
Walters Cl 8 NR31 ...3 B7
Waltham Cl IP2 ...138 C3
Walton Ave IP11 ...152 C3
Walton Cl 8 Fordham CB7 ...29 A1
  1 Stowmarket IP14 ...124 B8
Walton Rd NR32 ...113 D1
Wamil Rd IP28 ...30 B5
Wamil Way IP28 ...116 B4
Wangford Rd
  Lakenheath IP27 ...13 F7
  Reydon IP18 .....26 D1
  Southwold IP18 ...119 B8
  Uggeshall NR34 ...26 A3
  Westhall IP19 ....25 B4
Wannock Cl NR33 ...114 D4
Wantisden Cnr IP12 ...86 A6
Ward Cl IP7 ......149 D8
Ward Rd 6 NR32 ...113 B7
Ward's View IP5 ...141 E8
Wardlaw Ct 10 IP14 ...53 F2
Wardley Cl IP22 ...138 D1
Wardley Hill Rd NR35 ...8 D8
Ware Rd IP7 .....80 B6
Wareham Ave IP3 ...140 D3
Warene Cl 8 IP13 ...126 C3
Warham Rd CO12 ...106 F1
Warner Way CO10 ...148 E6
Warren Chase IP5 ...141 E7
Warren Cl Elmswell IP30 ...50 E2
  Lakenheath IP27 ...109 D5
Warren Ct 14 CB9 ...132 C5
Warren Heath Ave
  IP3 ....140 D2
Warren Heath Rd IP3 ...140 D2
Warren Hill La IP15 ...130 D7
Warren Hill Rd IP12 ...86 C2
Warren La
  Arwarton IP9 .....106 D6
  Elmswell IP30 ...50 E2
  27 Martlesham Heath IP5 ...98 A8
  Woolpit IP30 .....50 F1
Warren Loke IP31 ...2 B7
Warren Rd
  Great Yarmouth NR31 ...3 B8
  Herringswell CB8 ...46 A8
  Hopton on Sea NR31 ...3 C7
  Lowestoft NR32 ...113 D4
  Red Lodge IP28 ...30 C1
  Warren Rd NR33 ...114 C6
Warren The IP18 ...119 B6
Warren's La NR34 ...10 A2
Warrington Rd IP1 ...155 A4
Warrington St CB8 ...121 A4
Warwick Ave
  Halesworth IP19 ...118 C5
  Woodbridge IP12 ...146 F6
Warwick Ct 10 CB9 ...132 C6
Warwick Rd IP4 ...139 E6
Wash La Beccles NR34 ...111 E4
  Boxford CO6 .....93 D2
  Burgh St Peter NR34 ...10 C8
  Dennington IP13 ...55 E6
  Frostenden NR34 ...26 C3

Wash La continued
  Great Finborough IP14 ...124 A5
  Hinderclay IP22 ...35 E8
  Kessingland NR33 ...11 C1
  Mendlesham IP14 ...52 E3
  Redgrave IP22 ....19 D1
  Reydon IP18 .....26 D2
  St Peter, South Elmham
  NR35 ....23 F7
  Sheffanger IP22 ...20 B6
  Spexhall IP19 ....118 A7
  Stanton IP31 .....34 F3
  Topcroft NR35 ...7 A8
  Wenhaston with Mells Hamlet
  IP19 ....118 E1
  Westleton IP17 ...58 B8
  Witnesham IP6 ...83 A6
Washington St 4 IP28 ...30 A8
Wassicks La IP14 ...51 E3
Watch House Hill
  NR35 ....110 E4
Water Farm Dr IP7 ...94 E1
Water La
  Athelington IP21 ...38 F1
  Barnardiston CB9 ...75 B4
  Barnham IP24 ....16 C2
  Botesdale IP22 ...35 F5
  3 Bures CO8 ......101 C5
  Cavendish CO10 ...76 E1
  Debenham IP14 ...53 F2
  Denston CB8 .....75 F7
  Garboldisham IP22 ...18 D4
  Great Ashfield IP31 ...35 A8
  Great Horkesley CO6 ...102 C4
  Great Whelnetham IP30 ...64 A6
  Helions Bumpstead CB9 ...88 B4
  Kersey IP7 ....94 A6
  Layham IP7 ......149 E1
  Lowestoft NR32 ...113 C2
  Polstead CO6 ....102 F8
  Steeple Bumpstead CB9 ...88 D3
  Sturmer CB9 .....133 D3
  Thelnetham IP22 ...18 E1
  Thornham Magna IP23 ...37 A1
  Weybread IP21 ...22 D4
  Worlingworth IP13 ...54 D8
Water Mill La IP21 ...38 C8
Water Run The IP7 ...93 F4
Water Stcet CO10 ...78 D4
Watercourse The CB8 ...121 A4
Waterford Rd IP1 ...134 D2
Waterhead La IP12 ...147 D8
Watering Cl 1 IP8 ...81 C3
Watering La IP11 ...72 C7
Watering Rd IP21 ...38 D5
Waterloo Ave
  Leiston IP16 .....129 B6
  8 Roydon IP22 ...20 A3
Waterloo Cl CB8 ...120 D8
Waterloo Rd
  4 Ipswich IP1 ....139 A7
  Lowestoft NR33 ...115 D7
  Sotterley NR34 ...26 A7
Watermill Ct IP7 ...149 E2
Watermill Rd IP12 ...98 C5
Waters Ave NR33 ...114 C3
Waterside IP7 ....29 C5
Waterworks Rd 12 IP28 ...30 A8
Waterworks St IP4 ...155 C2
Watery La IP14 ...146 A8
Watson Cl IP33 ...123 B2
Watson Way IP14 ...99 E4
Watson's Hill IP7 ...79 F1
Watsons Cl 8 NR31 ...3 C7
Watt Cl IP12 .....99 E4
Wattisfield Rd IP31 ...35 C2
Wattisham Airfield IP7 ...80 C6
Wattisham Airfield Mus*
  IP7 ....80 C6
Wattisham Rd IP7 ...79 F4
Waveney Cl 8 IP17 ...128 C4
Waveney Cres NR33 ...115 B7
Waveney Dr NR33 ...115 A7
Waveney Hill
  Carlton Colville NR33 ...114 B8
  Lowestoft NR32 ...112 B1
Waveney Hts IP21 ...21 F2
Waveney Sports & Leisure
  Ctr IP19 ....118 C4
Waveney Terr 8 CB9 ...132 E5
Waveney Valley Swimming
  Pool NR35 ....110 D2
Way Bank La CO9 ...29 C7
Wayne Cl NR32 ...113 B5
Wayside Cl IP14 ...124 D3
Weald The NR32 ...112 E2
Weatherells Cl 9 CB7 ...28 D4
Weaver Cl IP11 ...138 D8
Weavers Cl
  2 Hadleigh IP7 ...149 D6
  4 Lavenham CO10 ...78 D4
  Stowmarket IP14 ...124 C3
Weavers Croft 8 IP20 ...22 D6
Weavers Ct 8 CO10 ...148 C5
Weavers Dr 6 CO10 ...77 A2
Weavers La CO10 ...78 D4
Weavers Marsh La
  IP17 ....41 E2
Weavers Way 2 IP6 ...82 A5
Webb Rd IP14 ...124 D3

Webb St **1** IP2 ....139 C3
Webb's Cl IP11 ....124 C1
Webbs Ct IP5 ....141 C7
Webster St NR35 ....110 A4
Weddell Rd CB9 ....133 A4
Weeting Castle* IP27 ....5 E4
Weeting Heath Nature
Reserve* IP27 ....5 C3
Weeting Heath Visitor Ctr* IP27 ...5 C3
Weeting Prim Sch IP27 ....5 E3
Weir Pl IP10 ....98 D2
Weirs Dro CB5 ....44 A6
Welbeck Cl
  Felixstowe IP11 ....152 C7
  North Grove NR34 ....10 C4
Welbourne Way NR34 ....10 C4
Welch Cl NR34 ....10 D3
Welham La IP28 ....47 D5
Well Bottom CB8 ....45 D4
Well La **9** CO10 ....90 A8
Well St IP33 ....154 B2
Wellesley Rd
  Ipswich IP1 ....139 F5
  Troston IP31 ....33 D4
Wellington Cl
  Hadleigh IP7 ....149 D7
  Thistley Green IP28 ......30 A6
Wellington Espl NR33 ......115 C6
Wellington Rd
  Eye IP23 ....117 D3
  4 Feltwell IP26 ....4 E5
  6 Harwich CO12 ......107 C3
  2 Lowestoft NR33 ....115 A4
  8 Mildenhall IP28 .....30 A8
  16 Troston IP31 ....33 D5
Wellington St
  7 Ipswich IP1 ....139 A7
  1 Newmarket CB8 .....121 A3
Wellington Terr **5** CB9 ..132 C5
Wells Cl IP14 ....139 E6
Wells Cnr IP28 ....39 F2
Wells Ct IP28 ....116 D5
Wells Hall Com Prim Sch
CO10 ....148 F2
Wells La IP20 ....22 D5
Wells Rd IP20 ....22 C5
Wells Way IP14 ....53 F1
Wellum Cl **13** CB9 .....132 C5
Wembley Ave NR34 ....111 B4
Wendy Cl **7** IP20 ......106 C8
Wenham La
  East Bergholt CO7 ......151 D8
  Wenham Magna CO7 ....150 A2
Wenham Rd IP8 ....150 E8
Wenhaston La IP19 ....42 D5
Wenhaston Prim Sch
IP19 ....42 C6
Wenhaston Rd IP19 ....42 B5
Wenhaston Way **2**
NR32 ....112 F3
Wensleydale **8** NR33 ...114 E3
Wensum Gdns NR32 ....113 C3
Wentford Ct **7** CB9 ....132 A6
Wentford View IP14 ....76 A1
Wentworth Cl **7**
  14 Fornham All Saints IP28 ..48 C6
  Hadleigh IP7 ....149 F5
  Weeting IP27 ....5 E4
Wentworth Dr
  Felixstowe IP11 ....153 C6
  7 Ipswich IP8 ......138 C2
  6 Mildenhall IP28 ..116 B5
Wentworth Rd IP15 ....130 F4
Wentworth Terr **5** CB9 ..132 C6
Wentworth Way **2**
NR33 ....114 F4
Wesel Ave IP11 ....152 D3
Wesley Cl NR34 ....111 B2
Wesley End Rd CO9 ....89 B2
Wesley Way IP1 ....138 F8
West Dock Rd CO12 ....106 F3
West Dr
  Mildenhall IP28 ....116 B4
  Soham CB7 ....28 C4
West Dr Cres CB7 ....28 C4
West Dr Gdns CB7 ....28 C4
West End CB8 ....60 B5
West End La
  Great Thurlow CB9 ....74 B4
  10 Haverhill CO12 ...107 A1
West End Rd IP1 ....155 A2
West Ger NR33 ....115 A3
West Hall Dr IP26 ....6 A8
West Hall Rd
  1 Mundford IP26 ......6 B8
  Walsham le Willows IP22 ..35 F3
West Harling Rd NR16 ......18 B8
West Herne La IP22 ....19 A1
West Hill IP16 ....129 C2
West La IP15 ....130 E3
West Lawn IP14 ....140 C8
West Meadows IP1 ....134 C4
West Mill Gn IP9 ....104 F7
West Rd
  Bury St Edmunds IP33 ...122 E4
  Ipswich IP3 ....140 E1
West Row Prim Sch
IP28 ....29 E2
West Row Rd IP28 ....116 A5
West Side Cl NR32 ....113 C5
West St Harwich CO12 ....107 B3
  Icklingham IP28 ....31 C4
  Isleham CB7 ....29 B5
  Rickinghall Inferior IP22 ..35 E3
West Stow Anglo-Saxon
Village* IP28 ....31 F2

West Stow Ctry Pk* IP28 ...31 F2
West Stow Rd IP28 ....32 B1
West Suffolk Coll
IP33 ....122 E6
West Suffolk Hospl The
IP33 ....123 A2
West Tofts IP26 ....6 D7
West View Burstall IP8 ....95 F7
  Carlton IP17 ....128 D6
  Stowmarket IP14 ....124 B6
West View Gdns **4** IP23 ..36 D2
West Wood **3** IP21 ......49 A5
Westbourne Ct **6** CB9 ..132 E6
Westbourne High Sch
IP1 ....134 E1
Westbourne Rd IP1 ....134 F1
Westbury Ave IP33 ....122 D5
Westbury Rd IP4 ....138 F1
Westend La CB9 ....133 F8
Westerfield **6** CB9 ....136 A5
Westerfield Rd
  Ipswich IP1 ....155 C4
  Westerfield IP6 ....135 E4
Westerfield Sta IP6 .....135 D5
Westerings The **1** CO6 ..102 C5
Western Ave
  Felixstowe IP11 ....153 D6
  Haverhill IP3 ....132 C3
Western Cl **4** Feltwell IP26 ..4 D5
  Ipswich IP4 ....140 F4
Western Way IP33 ....122 D6
Western's End **6** CO11 ..104 E4
Westfield CO10 ....90 A7
Westfield Com Prim Sch
CB9 ....132 C3
Westgate Gdns IP33 ......122 E3
Westgate Prim Sch
IP33 ....154 A1
Westgate St
  Bury St Edmunds IP33 ...154 C1
  Ipswich IP1 ....155 B3
  Long Melford CO10 ....77 C1
Westgate St Service Rd
IP1 ....155 B3
Westhall IP21 ....39 B5
Westhall Rd IP32 ....113 B5
Westholme Cl IP12 ....146 F4
Westhorpe CB5 ....44 A6
Westhorpe **8** CB5 ......44 A6
Westhorpe Rd
  Finningham IP14 ....52 A8
  Wyverstone IP14 ....51 E6
Westland **26** IP5 ......98 A8
Westland Rd IP14 ....114 E6
Westleton Heath National
Nature Reserve*
IP17 ....58 E8
Westleton Rd IP17 ....57 E8
Westleton Way **17** IP11 ..152 D5
Westley Bottom Rd
CB8 ....59 A4
Westley La IP29 ....122 B3
Westley Mid Sch IP33 ....122 D5
Westley Way IP33 ....122 D5
Westley Way IP31 ....50 E7
Westminster Cl IP4 ......140 B5
Westminster Dr IP33 .....122 D3
Westmorland Cl **8**
CO11 ....157 D7
Westmorland Rd IP11 .....153 D7
Weston Colville Rd
CB8 ....59 E1
Weston Rd NR32 ....113 B5
Weston Way CB8 ....120 F6
Westropps **6** CO10 .....91 E7
Westward Deals CB9 ......133 E8
Westward Ho IP16 ....129 C6
Westwood Ave
  Ipswich IP1 ....139 A8
  Lowestoft NR33 ....114 E3
Wet La CO10 ....102 F3
Wetherby Cl IP1 ....135 B3
Wetherden Rd
  Elmswell IP30 ....50 F2
  Great Ashfield IP31 .....51 B6
Wetheringsett CE Prim Sch
IP14 ....53 A5
Wexford Rd IP1 ....134 D2
Weyland Rd IP6 ....83 A6
Weylands Cl IP14 ....67 D7
Whalebone Cnr CO4 ......103 C4
Whapload Rd NR32 ....113 E1
Wharf La **3** CO8 ......101 C4
Wharfedale NR33 ....114 F3
Wharfedale Rd IP1 ......135 A1
Whatfield CE Prim Sch
IP7 ....80 C1
Whatfield Rd
  Aldham IP7 ....94 C7
  Elmsett IP7 ....80 F1
Whatfield Way IP14 ......124 E3
Wheatacre Dr **8** NR32 ...3 C4
Wheatacre Rd NR33 ......114 D4
Wheatfields
  3 Botesdale IP22 ....36 A6
  4 Thurston IP31 .....49 E6
  Whatfield IP7 ....80 C1
Wheatsheaf Cl CO11 .....105 E2
Wheatsheaf La CO11 .....105 E2
Wheelbarrow La IP20 ......23 F5
Wheeler's La IP31 ....51 B2
Wheelwright Cl IP30 .....49 C2
Wheelwrights The
IP11 ....152 D8

Whepstead Rd
  Hawstead IP29 ....63 B7
  Horringer IP29 ....122 D1
Wherry La IP4 ....155 C2
Wherry Quay IP4 ....155 C2
Wherry Rd
  3 Bungay NR35 .....110 D3
  3 Dunnis Hill NR35 .110 D3
Wherstead Rd IP2 ....155 B1
Wights Cnr IP8 ....138 A1
Wish Marsh IP5 ....130 E5
Winchat Cl IP2 ....138 D3
Winfield **18** IP5 ......98 A8
Winfield Ave **23** CO12 .106 F1
Winfield Ct **16** IP5 ...98 A8
Whinneys The IP5 ....141 D8
Whinyard Way **3** IP11 ..153 D7
Whistle Binkie NR32 ....112 C2
Whistle Dro IP28 ....12 D5
Whitby Rd
  Bury St Edmunds IP33 ...122 D3
  Ipswich IP4 ....139 F8
White Elm Rd IP30 ....50 C1
White Elm St IP3 ....139 E4
White Foot La IP13 ......83 E6
White Hart Cl IP30 ......92 C5
White Hart La **20** CB7 ..28 C4
White Horse Cl **4** IP15 .130 E5
White Horse Hill IP9 ....142 D1
White Horse La IP30 .....64 D7
White Horse Rd
  Capel St Mary IP9 .....150 F3
  East Bergholt CO7 .....151 D3
White Horse St IP13 ....127 C7
White Horse St **2** IP13 .113 E2
White Horse Farm La
IP21 ....22 B6
White House Gdns
NR34 ....111 A4
White House Rd IP14 ....134 D2
White Lion Cl IP27 .....149 D5
White Lion Rd NR34 ......10 B8
White Meadow **3** IP14 ..51 A1
White Womans La IP12 ....85 B7
White's La NR33 ....11 B1
Whitedike Dro IP26 ....4 A4
Whitegates CB8 ....121 B3
Whitehall Rd IP14 ....51 F1
Whitehouse Com Inf Sch
IP1 ....134 C3
Whitehouse Ind Est
IP1 ....134 C3
Whitehouse Jun Sch
IP1 ....134 D3
Whitehouse La
  Belchamp Otten CO10 ....90 D5
  Earsham NR35 ....7 C3
  Stansfield IP14 ....78 D8
Whitepost Cnr IP14 ......54 C1
Whites Cl IP21 ....39 B4
Whites Field CO7 ....151 B5
Whitethorn Rd IP3 ......140 F1
Whitewood Wlk **8** IP7 ..13 F2
Whithersfield Rd CB9 ....132 C4
Whiting Rd NR32 ....113 D1
Whitland Cl IP2 ....138 C1
Whitlands **6** CO10 .....77 A3
Whitlock Dr CO9 ....89 F1
Whittle Rd IP2 ....138 F6
Whitton Church La
IP1 ....134 F4
Whitton Cl NR33 ....115 A3
Whitton Com Prim Sch
IP1 ....134 D3
Whitton St NR33 ....115 A3
Whitton Gn Prim Sch
NR33 ....114 D4
Whitton La IP1 ....134 D4
Whitton Leyer IP8 ......134 C2
Whitton Sports Ctr
IP1 ....134 E4
Whitworth Cl IP2 ....138 D2
Whyteway IP19 ....24 B4
Wick La CO12 ....107 A1
Wick Rd Langham CO4 ....103 C2
  Stoke-by-Nayland CO6 ..103 A2
Wicken Rd CB7 ....28 D1
Wickham Com Prim Sch
IP27 ....158 B6
Wickham La IP4 ....52 A6
Wickham Mkt Sta IP12 ....71 C2
Wickham Rd IP23 ....52 F7
Wickhambrook Ct **2**
IP11 ....152 C4
Wickhambrook Prim Sch
CB8 ....61 E2
Wicklow Rd IP1 ....134 D2
Wicks La IP17 ....44 F7
Widgeon Cl IP2 ....138 F3
Wigg's Way **3** IP31 ....49 B2
Wiggin Cl IP28 ....116 D2
Wiggs Acre NR34 ....10 C4
Wigmore Cl
  Ipswich IP2 ....138 F1
  Stoke Park IP2 ....139 A1
Wignall St CO11 ....104 C2
Wigston Rd IP33 ....122 C3
Wigwam Hill IP22 ....19 F1
Wilberforce St IP1 .....139 A6
Wilby CE Prim Sch
IP21 ....39 B2
Wilby La IP13 ....134 C8
Wilby Rd IP21 ....39 A4
Wilbye Cl IP32 ....123 E4
Wild Acres **13** CB5 ....44 A5

Wild Tracks Offroad Activity
Pk* CB7 ....45 E7
Wilde St Est IP28 ....13 C1
Wilderness Cl **3** IP20 ..22 C5
Wilderness Hill IP8 ......95 B6
Wilderness La
  Harleston IP20 ....22 D6
  Woodbridge IP12 ....147 A6
Wildflower Way NR35 ....110 B7
Wilding Dr IP5 ....141 D7
Wilding Rd IP8 ....138 C1
Wildmere La IP28 ....13 D1
Wilford Bridge Rd
IP12 ....147 D7
Wilford Bridge Spur
IP12 ....147 D7
Wilkes Ct IP15 ....141 E7
Wilkes Way IP14 ....124 C6
Wilkinson Dr IP5 ....141 C6
Wilkinson Way IP12 .....147 A6
Wilks Rd IP23 ....123 B2
Willby Ave IP22 ....20 D3
Wilks Ave IP22 ....20 D3
William Armstrong Cl **6**
IP30 ....50 F2
William Blake Ct CB9 ...132 C7
William Booth Way **11**
IP11 ....152 D5
William Groom Ave **2**
CO12 ....107 A1
William St IP1 ....155 B3
William's Way **4** IP28 ..29 F6
Williamsport Way IP25 ..125 F3
Willie Snaith Rd CB8 ...120 F6
Willoughby Cl IP13 ......71 A7
Willoughby Rd IP2 ......155 A1
Willow Cl
  Badwell Ash IP31 ....50 F8
  6 Claydon IP6 .....134 C8
  Haverhill CB9 ....132 B7
  Stradbroke IP21 ....39 B5
  1 Sudbury CO10 ....148 C4
Willow Cres CB8 ....121 B2
Willow Gn IP31 ....49 B2
Willow Gr **3** CO6 .....102 C5
Willow La
  Bedingham NR35 ....7 B7
  Broome NR35 ....8 C7
  Cotton NR14 ....52 B6
Willow Marsh La
  Darsham IP17 ....42 A1
  Yoxford IP17 ....41 F2
Willow Rd NR33 ....115 A2
Willow Tree Cl IP13 ....127 B6
Willow Way
  Bury St Edmunds IP33 ...154 A3
  8 Great Bricett IP7 ..80 D6
  2 Harwich CO12 ....106 F1
  2 Rendlesham IP12 ...85 D8
Willow Wlk
  6 Harleston IP20 ....22 D5
  Needham Market IP6 ....125 D6
Willowbrook Cl NR33 ....114 A3
Willowcroft Rd IP1 .....135 A2
Willowvale NR32 ....112 F6
Willrede Cl NR34 ....111 B3
Willsmore Ave IP12 .....146 D4
Willmslow Dr IP8 ....138 C2
Wilson Rd Hadleigh IP7 ..149 E5
  Ipswich IP3 ....138 B1
  Lowestoft NR33 ....115 C5
Wilton Rd IP26 ....4 E5
Wimbledon Ave IP27 ......14 E8
Wimborne Ave IP3 ....140 D4
Wimpole Cl IP5 ....140 F6
Wincanton Cl IP4 ....136 A1
Winchester Cl IP4 ......124 B6
Winchester Gdns **4** IP6 ..82 B5
Winchester Way IP2 .....142 F8
Windermere Cl IP3 ......144 B8
Windermere Pk NR32 ....113 A4
Windermere Rd
  6 Felixstowe IP11 ...153 D7
  Stowmarket IP14 ....124 C6
  Sudbury CO10 ....148 E6
Windgap La IP14 ....51 D1
Windham Rd CO10 ....148 C6
Winding Piece **5** IP9 ..150 E3
Windings Rd **4** IP7 ....80 F1
Windmill Ave IP30 ....50 C1
Windmill Cl
  Boxted CO4 ....102 F2
  Ramsey & Parkeston CO12 ..106 C1
  Soham CB7 ....28 E2
  3 Somersham IP8 ....81 C3
Windmill Gn
  Ditchingham NR35 ......110 C7
  10 Ditchingham IP31 ..34 E4
Windmill Hill
  Capel St Mary IP9 .....150 C3
  Exning CB8 ....120 C8
  Long Melford CO10 ......77 D1
Windmill La IP21 ....38 F8
Windmill Rd IP30 ....50 C1
Windmill Rise
  Bury St Edmunds IP33 ...154 A1
  Hundon CO10 ....75 D4
  1 Wetherden IP14 ....51 A1
Windmill Row **5** CO10 ..77 B3
Windrush Rd IP5 ....141 D8

Windsor Circ
  1 Lakenheath IP27 ....14 A3
  Lakenheath IP27 ....109 F1
Windsor Cl
  7 Barnham IP24 ......16 C2
  Lawshall IP29 ....63 D2
Windsor Pl CO10 ....148 E5
Windsor Rd
  Felixstowe IP11 ....152 E3
  Ipswich IP1 ....138 F7
  Lowestoft NR33 ....115 C7
  Newmarket CB8 ....120 E4
  Southwold IP18 ....119 B8
Windsor Terr **8** CB9 ...132 C5
Windward Wlk NR33 ......114 E5
Windyridge Rd IP10 ......65 D5
Winfarthing Rd IP22 .....20 B6
Winfrith Rd IP3 ....140 D4
Wingfield Ave IP27 .....109 D7
Wingfield Meadows
IP14 ....68 B6
Wingfield Old Coll & Gdns*
IP21 ....39 A7
Wingfield Rd
  Lakenheath IP27 ....109 D7
  Syleham IP21 ....21 F1
  Weybread IP21 ....22 C2
Wingfield St
  Bungay NR35 ....110 B3
  Ipswich IP4 ....155 C2
Wings Rd IP27 ....109 D6
Wings Rd Cl IP27 ....109 D6
Winnipeg Rd NR32 ....113 D2
Winsford Rd IP32 ....123 E6
Winston Ave
  Ipswich IP4 ....140 C8
  Lowestoft NR33 ....114 E7
Winston Cl
  5 Felixstowe IP11 ...152 D5
  8 Kessingland NR33 ..11 C1
Winston Rd
  Southwold IP18 ....119 C7
  Winston IP14 ....53 F1
Winthrop Rd IP33 ....122 D4
Winthrops The CO10 ......93 B4
Wissett Cl IP19 ....118 B4
Wissett Rd
  Chediston IP19 ....41 B8
  Halesworth IP19 ....118 A5
  Wissett IP19 ....24 D1
Wissett Way IP32 ....113 B4
Wissey View **2** IP26 ....6 B8
Wissington Uplands
CO6 ....102 A5
Wiston Rd CO6 ....102 A4
Withers Pl **2** CB5 .....29 A1
Withersdale Rd
  Mendham IP20 ....23 A5
  Weybread IP21 ....22 D4
Withersfield Rd
  Haverhill CB9 ....132 C7
  Withersfield CB9 ....74 C4
Withersfield Gall The*
CO10 ....91 D7
Withipoll Sl IP4 ....155 C3
Witnesham Church La
IP6 ....82 F5
Witnesham La IP6 ....136 C7
Witnesham Prim Sch
IP6 ....83 A7
Witney Gn NR33 ....115 A3
Witney Rd **3** NR33 ....115 A3
Wittons La IP21 ....38 C7
Wix Rd CO12 ....106 C1
Wollaston Cl IP32 ......122 D8
Wollaston Rd NR32 ......113 D1
Wolsey Art Gall* IP1 ...155 C4
Wolsey Gdns IP11 ....153 A3
Wolsey Rd **4** NR33 ....115 A3
Wolsey St IP1 ....155 B2
Wolton Rd IP5 ....141 C7
Wolves Farm La IP7 ......94 E6
Wolves Wood Nature
Reserve* IP7 ....94 F6
Wood Cl
  3 Bentwaters Airfield
  IP12 ....85 D8
  Kenninghall NR16 ....19 A8
  Tostock IP30 ....50 B3
Wood Farm La IP18 ....26 C2
Wood Farm Rd IP13 ......83 C5
Wood Hall La IP23 ....37 B1
Wood La Beddingham NR35 ..7 C6
  Bressingham IP22 ....19 E6
  Dallinghoo IP13 ....70 B1
  Dickleburgh & Rushall
  IP21 ....21 C2
  Fressingfield IP21 .....40 A8
  Henstead with Hulver Street
  NR34 ....26 E7
  Hepworth IP22 ....35 A6
  Oulton NR32 ....112 C2
  Reydon IP18 ....26 C1
  Scole IP21 ....21 C4
  Thelnetham IP22 ....35 C6
Wood Rd
  Badingham IP13 ....56 B6
  Woolpit IP30 ....65 F8
Wood Side IP14 ....124 B5
Wood View **4** IP18 .....56 F8
Woodbridge Gall*
IP12 ....146 F5
Woodbridge Mus The*
IP12 ....147 A5

Woodbridge Prim Sch 15
IP12 . . . . .147 A5
Woodbridge Rd
Alderton IP12 . . . . .99 D5
Bredfield IP13 . . . . .84 C7
Butley IP12 . . . . .86 A5
Framlingham IP13 . . . . . .126 C1
Grundisburgh IP13 . . . . . .83 E6
Ipswich IP4 . . . . .155 C3
Sutton IP12 . . . . .85 A1
Tunstall IP12 . . . . .71 E1
Waldringfield IP12 . . . . . .98 D6
Wantisden IP12 . . . . .85 E5
Woodbridge Rd E IP4 . .140 C7
Woodbridge Sch IP12 . .146 F5
Woodbridge Sta 147 B4
NR33 . . . . .114 C4
Woodcock Cl CB9 . . . . .133 A5
Woodcock Rd IP2 . . . . .138 E2
Woodcock Rise IP26 . . . . .6 A1
Woodcote IP14 . . . . . . .124 B6
Woodcrofts Cl 2 IP29 . . .63 A1
Woodcutters Way
IP27 . . . . .109 D7
Woodditton Rd
Kirtling CB8 . . . . .60 D3
Newmarket CB8 . . . . . . .121 A1
Woodditton CB8 . . . . .60 B6
Woodfield Cl NR34 . . . . .25 E7
Woodfield Dr IP14 . . . . .124 E5
Woodfield La
Stowmarket IP14 . . . . . .124 D4
Stutton IP9 . . . . .105 C5
Woodfields IP21 . . . . . . .39 A4
Woodgates Rd CO7 . . . .151 D7
Woodhall Bsns Pk
CO10 . . . . .148 D8
Woodhall Cl CO10 . . . . .148 C7
Woodhall Com Prim Sch 3
CO10 . . . . .148 D8
Woodhall Rd CO10 . . . . .148 C7
Woodhouse La IP10 . . . .141 C2
Woodhouse Sq IP4 . . . .155 C2
Woodland Ave NR34 . . .111 F4
Woodland Cl
Onehouse IP14 . . . . .66 C6
Risby IP28 . . . . .47 D5
Thurston IP31 . . . . .49 E3
Woodland Dr
Bungay NR35 . . . . .110 B1
Ellingham NR35 . . . . .8 E7
Woodland Pl 7 IP31 . . . .49 A6

Woodlands
1 Chelmondiston IP9 . . . .106 C8
Hadleigh IP7 . . . . .149 B7
32 Harleston IP20 . . . . . . .22 D6
Lakenheath IP27 . . . . . . .109 D8
Leiston IP16 . . . . .129 C4
Woodlands Ave 4
NR33 . . . . .114 C3
Woodlands Bsns Pk
IP30 . . . . .49 B3
Woodlands Dr IP24 . . . . .16 C7
Woodlands Rd
Holbrook IP9 . . . . .105 E8
Raydon IP7 . . . . .94 F2
Rushbrooke with Rougham
IP30 . . . . .49 B3
Woodlands Rise IP27 . . .14 D8
Woodlands The NR32 . . .113 B8
Woodlands Way
Bramford IP8 . . . . .134 C4
Mildenhall IP28 . . . . . . .116 F5
Woodlane Rd IP23 . . . . . .38 C1
Woodlark Cl IP2 . . . . . .138 E1
Woodlark Dr 4 IP14 . . . .124 F7
Woodley Com Sch
IP14 . . . . .124 B7
Woodleys Yd IP18 . . . . .119 D5
Woodpecker Ave 2
NR33 . . . . .114 C5
Woodpecker Cl 16 IP14 . .67 A5
Woodpecker Rd IP2 . . . .138 D3
Woodrush Rd IP3 . . . . . .140 E2
Woods Cl
Ditchingham NR35 . . . . .110 B7
Sturmer CB9 . . . . .133 C3
Woods La IP12 . . . . . . .147 B7
Woods Loke E NR32 . . .113 A3
Woods Loke Prim Sch
NR32 . . . . .112 F3
Woods Loke W NR32 . . .112 F3
Woodside
Beccles NR34 . . . . .111 D3
Brampton with Stoven
NR34 . . . . .25 E5
Martlesham Heath IP5 . . . .98 B8
Woodside Bsns Pk
IP31 . . . . .32 F2
Woodside Cl
Bury St Edmunds IP33 . . .123 B1
Lowestoft NR33 . . . . . . .114 C3
Woodspring Cl 12 IP22 . .139 A2
Woodstone Ave IP1 . . . .135 C1
Woodthorpe Cl IP7 . . . .149 F5
Woodthorpe Rd IP7 . . . .149 E5
Woodville Rd IP4 . . . . . .139 F5
Woodward Ave IP14 . . . .51 F6

Woodward Cl IP2 . . . . . .138 D5
Woolhall St 2 IP33 . . . .154 B2
Woollards Cl IP1 . . . . . .139 A6
Woollards Gdns 3 CO10 . .91 E8
Woolmers Cl IP14 . . . . .124 D4
Woolner Cl
7 Claydon IP6 . . . . .82 A5
5 Hadleigh IP7 . . . . .149 E6
Woolnough Cl 6 CB9 . . . .88 D3
Woolnough Rd IP12 . . . .146 F6
Woolnoughs The 2
IP5 . . . . .141 D7
Woolpit & District Musuem*
IP30 . . . . .50 D1
Woolpit Prim Sch IP30 . .50 D1
Woolpit Rd IP31 . . . . . . .34 C2
Woolverstone Cl IP2 . . .138 D1
Worcester Cl 5 IP32 . . .123 E6
Worcester Rd IP3 . . . . .144 A8
Wordsworth Cl IP17 . . .128 B4
Wordsworth Cres IP1 . . .134 E3
Wordsworth Rd
4 Bury St Edmunds IP32 . .48 C5
2 Stowmarket IP14 . . . . .124 B8
Worell Dr NR34 . . . . . . .111 E4
Workhouse Hill
Boxted CO4 . . . . .102 F3
Hartest IP29 . . . . .77 B8
Workhouse La IP17 . . . . .57 E2
Workhouse Rd
Little Horkesley CO6 . . . .102 B2
Thornham Magna IP23 . . . .37 A1
Workshop La IP10 . . . . .145 C5
World's End La IP14 . . . .65 F2
World's End Rd IP13 . . . .55 B4
Worlingham Mid Sch
NR34 . . . . .111 F3
Worlingham Prim Sch
NR34 . . . . .9 F5
Worlingham Way
NR32 . . . . .113 A4
Worlington Rd
Barton Mills IP28 . . . . . . .30 E3
Worlington IP28 . . . . . . .116 A3
Worlingworth CE Prim Sch
IP13 . . . . .54 D7
Worlingworth Rd IP21 . . .38 F3
Wortham Ling Nature
Reserve* IP22 . . . . .19 F2
Wortham Pl 1 CB9 . . . .132 E6
Wortham Prim Sch
IP22 . . . . .36 E7
Worthing Rd NR32 . . . . .113 D3
Wrabness Local Nature
Reserve* IP9 . . . . .105 E2
Wrabness Rd 1 CO12 . .106 D1

Wrabness Sta CO11 . . .106 A2
Wragg Dr CB8 . . . . .121 A6
Wratting Rd
Great Thurlow CB9 . . . . . .74 D5
Haverhill CB9 . . . . .132 E7
Wren Ave IP2 . . . . .138 D3
Wren Cl
Bury St Edmunds IP32 . . . .49 A4
Mildenhall IP28 . . . . . . .116 D4
1 Stowmarket IP14 . . . . .67 A5
18 Thurstow IP31 . . . . . . .49 D4
Wrens Pk 2 IP11 . . . . . .153 D7
Wriggle St IP13 . . . . . . .70 A7
Wright Cl IP14 . . . . .124 D3
Wright La IP5 . . . . .141 D8
Wright Rd IP3 . . . . .140 C2
Wrights Way
Leavenheath CO6 . . . . . .102 A7
Woolpit IP30 . . . . .50 C1
Wroxham Rd IP3 . . . . . .139 F3
Wyatt Cl IP30 . . . . .50 F3
Wyatt Way IP24 . . . . . . .16 B7
Wyatts La CO10 . . . . . . .101 B8
Wye Rd IP3 . . . . .140 A2
Wyken Rd IP31 . . . . .34 D3
Wyken Vineyard & Gdns*
IP31 . . . . .34 E2
Wykes Bishop St IP3 . . .139 E4
Wymering Rd 10 IP18 . . .119 D5
Wyncoll's La IP7 . . . . . . .94 B2
Wyndham Way CB8 . . . .121 A6
Wynterton Cl IP3 . . . . . .140 B1
Wynton Rise IP14 . . . . .124 E4
Wytchwoods The IP14 . . .68 E6
Wyvern Rd IP3 . . . . .140 C1
Wyverstone Rd
Badwell Ash IP31 . . . . . . .51 B7
Wyverstone Green IP14 . . .51 E6

Y

Yale Bsns Pk IP3 . . . . . .144 F8
Yarmouth Pl 3 CB9 . . . .132 E6
Yarmouth Rd
Corton NR32 . . . . .113 A8
Ditchingham NR35 . . . . .110 D7
Geldeston NR34 . . . . .9 A7
Ipswich IP1 . . . . .139 A6
Kirby Cane NR35 . . . . .8 E7
Lound NR32 . . . . .2 F7
Lowestoft NR32 . . . . . . .113 B5
Melton IP12 . . . . .84 E6
Ufford IP13 . . . . .127 B1
Woodbridge IP12 . . . . . .147 C8
Yarrow Dr NR33 . . . . . . .114 C4

Yaxley Hall La IP23 . . . . .37 C4
Yaxley Rd IP23 . . . . .37 C3
Yeldham Pl CB9 . . . . . .132 E6
Yeoman Cres IP7 . . . . . .149 E5
Yeoman Rd IP11 . . . . . .152 D3
Yeoman Way IP7 . . . . . .149 E5
Yeoman's Cl NR35 . . . . .110 C3
Yeomanry Yd IP33 . . . . .154 A2
Yeovil Rd NR32 . . . . . . .113 C2
Yerril Gdn CB9 . . . . . . .132 C5
Yew Cl 1 IP27 . . . . .13 F2
Yew Ct IP2 . . . . .139 A3
Yew Tree Cl 1 IP33 . . . .122 F3
Yew Tree Rise IP13 . . . .127 C7
Yewdale NR33 . . . . .114 D2
Yewlands Gr IP30 . . . . . .65 A4
Yewtree Gr IP5 . . . . . . .140 F7
Yewtree Rise IP8 . . . . . .138 C1
York Cl
Bury St Edmunds IP33 . . .122 E5
1 Mildenhall IP28 . . . . . . .30 A8
Sudbury CO10 . . . . .148 C7
York Cres 12 Claydon IP6 . .82 B5
Claydon IP6 . . . . .134 C8
York Rd
Bury St Edmunds IP33 . . .154 A4
Felixstowe IP11 . . . . . . .153 A4
Foxhall IP5 . . . . .98 A4
Haverhill CB9 . . . . .132 C5
Ipswich IP3 . . . . .140 A4
Lowestoft NR32 . . . . . . .113 C1
Southwold IP18 . . . . . . .119 B5
Sudbury CO10 . . . . .148 C6
York Terr IP33 . . . . .154 A2
Yoxford Gdns* IP17 . . . .57 C8
Yoxford Mews 7 IP12 . . .85 B3
Yoxford Prim Sch IP17 . .57 D8
Yoxford Rd
Middleton IP17 . . . . .57 F6
Sibton IP17 . . . . .57 A8

Z

Zanetta Ct NR32 . . . . . .113 C1
Zurich Cl 3 NR31 . . . . . . .3 C6

Name and Address	Telephone	Page	Grid reference

Addresses

Name and Address	Telephone	Page	Grid reference

NG	NH	NJ	NK
NM	NN	NO	NP
NR	NS	NT	NU
	NX	NY	NZ
SC	SD	SE	TA
SH	SJ	SK	TF	TG
SM	SN	SO	SP	TL	TM
SR	SS	ST	SU	TQ	TR
SW	SX	SY	SZ	TV

Any feature in this atlas can be given a unique reference to help you find the same feature on other Ordnance Survey maps of the area, or to help someone else locate you if they do not have a Street Atlas.

The grid squares in this atlas match the Ordnance Survey National Grid and are at 500 metre intervals. The small figures at the bottom and sides of every other grid line are the National Grid kilometre values (**00**°to°**99** km) and are repeated across the country every 100°km (see left).

To give a unique National Grid reference you need to locate where in the country you are. The country is divided into 100 km squares with each square given a unique two-letter reference. Use the administrative map to determine in which 100 km square a particular page of this atlas falls.

The bold letters and numbers between each grid line (**A**°to°**F**,°**1**°to°**8**) are for use within a specific Street Atlas only, and when used with the page number, are a convenient way of referencing these grid squares.

Example   *The railway bridge over DARLEY GREEN RD in grid square B1*

Step 1: Identify the two-letter reference, in this example the page is in **SP**

Step 2: Identify the 1 km square in which the railway bridge falls. Use the figures in the southwest corner of this square: Eastings **17**, Northings **74**. This gives a unique reference: **SP 17 74**, accurate to 1°km.

Step 3: To give a more precise reference accurate to 100 m you need to estimate how many tenths along and how many tenths up this 1 km square the feature is (to help with this the 1 km square is divided into four 500 m squares). This makes the bridge about **8** tenths along and about **1** tenth up from the southwest corner.

This gives a unique reference: **SP 178 741**, accurate to 100°m.

Eastings (read from left to right along the bottom) come before Northings (read from bottom to top). If you have trouble remembering say to yourself Along the hall, THEN up the stairs !

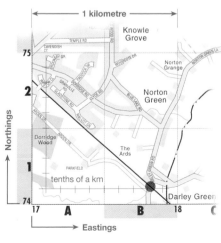

PHILIP'S MAPS

the Gold Standard for drivers

◆ **Philip's street atlases cover every county in England, Wales, Northern Ireland and much of Scotland**

◆ Every named street is shown, including alleys, lanes and walkways

◆ Thousands of additional features marked: stations, public buildings, car parks, places of interest

◆ Route-planning maps to get you close to your destination

◆ Postcodes on the maps and in the index

◆ Widely used by the emergency services, transport companies and local authorities

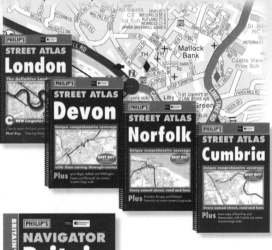

For national mapping, choose **Philip's Navigator Britain** the most detailed road atlas available of England, Wales and Scotland. Hailed by Auto Express as 'the ultimate road atlas', this is the only one-volume atlas to show every road and lane in Britain.

Street atlases currently available

England

Bedfordshire
Berkshire
Birmingham and West Midlands
Bristol and Bath
Buckinghamshire
Cambridgeshire
Cheshire
Cornwall
Cumbria
Derbyshire
Devon
Dorset
County Durham and Teesside
Essex
North Essex
South Essex
Gloucestershire
Hampshire
North Hampshire
South Hampshire
Herefordshire Monmouthshire
Hertfordshire
Isle of Wight
Kent
East Kent
West Kent
Lancashire
Leicestershire and Rutland
Lincolnshire
London
Greater Manchester
Merseyside
Norfolk
Northamptonshire
Northumberland
Nottinghamshire
Oxfordshire
Shropshire
Somerset
Staffordshire
Suffolk
Surrey

East Sussex
West Sussex
Tyne and Wear
Warwickshire
Birmingham and West Midlands
Wiltshire and Swindon
Worcestershire
East Yorkshire Northern Lincolnshire
North Yorkshire
South Yorkshire
West Yorkshire

Wales

Anglesey, Conwy and Gwynedd
Cardiff, Swansea and The Valleys
Carmarthenshire, Pembrokeshire and Swansea
Ceredigion and South Gwynedd
Denbighshire, Flintshire, Wrexham
Herefordshire Monmouthshire
Powys

Scotland

Aberdeenshire
Ayrshire
Dumfries and Galloway
Edinburgh and East Central Scotland
Fife and Tayside
Glasgow and West Central Scotland
Inverness and Moray
Lanarkshire
Scottish Borders

Northern Ireland

County Antrim and County Londonderry
County Armagh and County Down
Belfast
County Tyrone and County Fermanagh

How to order Philip's maps and atlases are available from bookshops, motorway services and petrol stations. You can order direct from the publisher by phoning **01903 828503** or online at **www.philips-maps.co.uk** For bulk orders only, phone 020 7644 6940